CREATING
AMERICA

CREATING AMERICA

READING AND

WRITING ARGUMENTS

EDITED BY
Joyce Moser and Ann Watters
Stanford University

A BLAIR PRESS BOOK

Prentice Hall, Englewood Cliffs, New Jersey 07632

Library of Congress Cataloging-in-Publication Data
Creating America: reading and writing arguments /
    edited by Joyce Moser and Ann Watters.
"A Blair Press book."
Includes index.
ISBN 0-13-061557-9
I. Moser, Joyce, 1946– . II. Watters, Ann.
PE1429.C74   1995
808'.0427—dc20

94-23916
CIP

For Tom Moser and Tom Watters

Cover design: John Klotnia
Interior design: Sally Steele
Photo Editor: Lorinda Morris-Nantz
Photo researcher: Elsa Peterson
Buyer: Robert Anderson
Editorial, production, and design supervision: John Svatek

The acknowledgments appear on pages 609–612,
which constitute a continuation of the copyright page.

A BLAIR PRESS BOOK

 © 1995 by Prentice-Hall, Inc.
A Simon & Schuster Company
Englewood Cliffs, New Jersey 07632

Printed in the United States of America
10 9 8 7 6 5 4 3 2 1

ISBN 0-13-061557-9

Prentice-Hall International (UK) Limited, *London*
Prentice-Hall of Australia Pty. Limited, *Sydney*
Prentice-Hall Canada Inc., *Toronto*
Prentice-Hall Hispanoamericana, S.A., *Mexico*
Prentice-Hall of India Private Limited, *New Delhi*
Prentice-Hall of Japan, Inc., *Tokyo*
Simon & Schuster Asia Pte. Ltd., *Singapore*
Editora Prentice-Hall do Brasil, Ltda., *Rio de Janeiro*

Preface

Creating America is a reader-rhetoric focusing on argument and persuasion in American cultures. Spanning centuries, traditions, and genres, the selections demonstrate the core debates and discussions that have always interested and engaged Americans. The selections—eighteenth-century woodcuts, nineteenth-century essays and political cartoons, and twentieth-century speeches, narratives, photographs, advertisements, and legal cases—all help students learn to analyze and criticize the arguments they encounter in academic discourse and in popular culture.

We developed *Creating America* because we saw a need for a book that focuses on arguments in context: that is, a book that brings together diverse materials revolving around certain issues that have always concerned Americans and demonstrating ways in which to argue about these issues. The issues themselves engender certain strategies of argument; arguing about who is really an American, for example, understandably focuses on strategies of definition. Arguing about what creates an American family naturally taps into values and assumptions about family and gender roles.

A unique aspect of *Creating America* is the way in which it blends thematic readings with rhetorical lessons in analyzing and writing arguments. The overall focus on theme and argument is established by Part One, "Contexts for Reading and Writing Arguments." Chapter 1,

"Reading and Analyzing Arguments," includes explanations of the ways in which different media—whether written or visual or both—can be persuasive. The chapter also introduces students to the general theme of the book, provides an overview of the chapter themes, and connects the themes to strategies of reading and writing arguments. Chapter 2, "Writing and Research," focuses on writing essays, including researched essays, and provides references for researching specifically American topics.

Part Two, "Arguments in the American Tradition," offers textual and visual arguments for analysis and discussion. While Chapters 3 through 9 are organized around thematic issues, each chapter focuses on a specific element of argument and includes a rhetorical discussion at the end of the chapter. Chapter 3, "Identities," teaches students to critique and write definitions; Chapter 4, "American Dreams," focuses on the evidence of examples and the ways in which writers support their points with examples, whether from research or their own experience. Chapter 5, "Family Values," examines assumptions and the function they serve within arguments—in some cases, as a principle on which to base other assertions, in other cases, as a part of a deductive argument that must be questioned and perhaps refined or refuted. Chapter 6, "Work and Success," considers the process of making and supporting assertions. Chapter 7, "Justice and Civil Liberties," focuses on refutation. Chapter 8, "War and the Enemy," examines the ways in which language develops and sustains arguments, particularly the ways in which language can create enemies. Chapter 9, "Frontiers," focuses on revision—of views, of expectations, of written texts.

Each chapter includes an introduction to the core issue and rhetorical focus. Selections follow, accompanied by headnotes for context and background information; journal prompts for guided journal writing; and questions for discussion and writing, with a focus on analysis. Rounding out the Chapter are a list of films related to the chapter theme, the end-of-chapter rhetorical discussion, and a list of suggested argumentative and expository writing assignments, including some assignments requiring various kinds of research. The student essay included in every chapter is an actual student's response to one of the end-of-chapter writing suggestions; these student essays demonstrate too that student writing can serve as appropriate material for analysis and discussion.

Creating America is designed for use in a first-year course in composition, particularly one emphasizing argumentative writing. The underlying pedagogy is based on an Aristotelian model, but it is informed by the theories of Kenneth Burke, Carl Rogers, and feminist critics. Our approach stresses that people use, to quote Aristotle, "all of the available means of persuasion" to argue a point; therefore, we do not treat argument and persuasion separately. Rather, we focus on the appeals to ethos, pathos, and logos, introducing induction and deduction under logos as the basic principles by which to evaluate and through which to develop arguments. The selections we chose represent a range of arguments, from combative debate-style presentations to more dialogic, narrative, explorations of difficult questions and complex issues.

For instructors who prefer to use their own pedagogical materials in teaching argumentation, the flexible organization of this text supports individual approaches. Instructors emphasizing the Toulmin model, for example, can draw upon the wide range of selections to teach students about claims and warrants using that particular vocabulary. We worked hard to ensure that the arguments included in *Creating America* provide material for thoughtful exploration and analysis regardless of the specific approach to teaching argumentation.

Because it includes a chapter on research as well as several documented student examples, *Creating America* is ideal for a second-term composition course focusing on writing research papers. In addition to offering suggestions for developing essays, Chapter 2 discusses strategies for conducting research and for integrating that research into documented expository and argumentative essays. The chapter includes samples of MLA and APA documentation styles, and it lists specialized references, sources for exploring specifically American themes. We do not view the research paper as a kind of writing divorced and distinct from other kinds of essays; *Creating America* therefore encourages students to include outside research whenever they need it to support their views, within the parameters of their course assignments.

Creating America can also be used in expository writing courses as a thematic reader focusing on American cultures. The selections are organized around the themes of "Identities," "American Dreams," "Family Values," "Work and Success," "Justice and Civil Liberties," "War and the Enemy," and "Frontiers." Instructors who create their own pedagogical material or who ask students to buy a handbook can use the diverse written and visual selections included here as a rich source of texts for critical reading and analysis and of ideas for writing.

Acknowledgments

We gratefully acknowledge the colleagues and friends who supported our efforts throughout this project. We thank our students, who worked through all of the materials with us in class; their insights, comments, and responses helped to shape *Creating America*. In our department, we thank especially Tom Moser, Jay Fliegelman. Susan

Wyle, Joan and John L'Heureux, Barbara and Al Gelpi for consistently excellent advice and unwavering support. We thank Kathy Kerns and Rose Adams of Green Library Reference at Stanford University for assistance and advice, and we acknowledge the Ellis Island Museum and Library, the Bishop Museum, the Hoover Archives, and David Gray and Tom Goodrich of Libraries and Information Resources at Stanford. Allison Bailin provided helpful research assistance, while Susan Cohn, Laurene Spencer, Jennifer Raiser, Charlotte Moser, and Caroline Cohn offered creative suggestions, intellectual support, and strong coffee, as did Virginia Bassi and Jane Marcus. Dennis Matthies and Michael Day generously shared their views and materials on argumentation and Don Bacon offered suggestions for readings. We acknowledge as well the influences of Nancy Packer, Michael Tratner, Victor Luftig, Gail Perez, and Rich Holeton and their views on teaching writing. At Blair Press, we are indebted to Nancy Perry, publisher, for her vision of and faith in the project from the beginning and for her unfailing support, advice, and encouragement. Denise Wydra was a superb development editor whose relentless energy, keen intelligence, and purple pen kept the project on track and helped shape it into the book it is today. Lynn Walterick provided excellent editing and advice as the manuscript developed, and John Svatek saw the mauscript and us through the final stages of editing and production with intelligence, wit, and fortitude. We appreciate being able to work with such talented and supportive people. We acknowledge the helpful critiques from our reviewers, Beth E. Kolko, University of Texas, Austin; Dennis A. Lynch, Michigan Technological University; Michael G. Moran, University of Georgia; Elizabeth Roberts, Lousiana State University; Marjorie Roemer, Rhode Island College; Melita Schaum, University of Michigan, Dearborn; Nancy S. Shapiro, University of Maryland; Elizabeth Webb, State University of New York, Brockport; and Donna Haisty Winchell, Clemson University. Finally, and with abiding affection, we thank our friends and our family circles, especially Thomas Moser, Tom Jr., and Frederika, and Tom, Andy, and Mike Watters.

JOYCE MOSER
ANN WATTERS

Contents

PART TWO
Argument in the American Tradition

CHAPTER 5   FAMILY VALUES   211

NB
wrong century

"The truth is that the last decade has seen a powerful counter-assault on women's rights, a backlash, an attempt to retract the handful of small and hard-won victories that the feminist movement did manage to win for women."

"The legacies that parents and church and teachers left to my generation of Black children were priceless but not material: a living faith reflected in daily service, the discipline of hard work and stick-to-it-ness, and a capacity to struggle in the face of adversity."

"The model-minority myth precludes the possibility that some Asian Americans may not be upwardly mobile and successful. Yet our parents expect us to become upwardly mobile and successful. Our parents' expectations personalize the society's model minority expectations for us."

"As I knew, or thought I knew, what was right and wrong, I did not see why I might not always do the one and avoid the other. But I soon found I had undertaken a Task of more Difficulty than I had imagined. While my Care was employ'd in guarding against one Fault, I was often surpriz'd by another."

"Each woman born, re-humanized by the current of race activity carried on by her father and re-womanized by her traditional position, has had to live over again in her own person the same process of restriction, repression, denial; the smothering 'no' which crushed down all her human desires to create, to discover, to learn, to express, to advance."

"Private investigators Sharon McCone, Kinsey Millhone, and V. I. Warshawski are intelligent, liberated detectives, as capable in all aspects as the men who preceded them. By incorporating their own femininity in their work, they are forming a new breed of detective fiction."

$\mathcal{P}_{\text{ART}}$ $\mathcal{O}_{\text{NE}}$

Contexts for Reading and Writing Arguments

1

READING AND ANALYZING ARGUMENTS

*W*hen the founding fathers were about to publish the Declaration of Independence and set themselves on a course that would put them in direct conflict with the British government, Benjamin Franklin is reported to have said, "Gentlemen, we must all hang together—or else we will all hang separately."

In a sense, this book takes Franklin's observation and applies it more generally to thinking and writing about the nation Franklin and his co-Revolutionists were in the process of establishing. The pieces of American life—people who come from many countries, cultures, and religions; states that differ from one another in topography, industry, and demographics; huge variations in urban and suburban life-styles, in income and interests—are so heterogeneous that they could have hardly been expected to coexist as they have for more than two-hundred years, but they have. *Creating America* offers a way of examining and writing about what it is that has caused them to hang together.

Reading American Cultures

The selections assembed in this book are not limited to any one time period; there are eighteenth-century cartoons, nineteenth- and twentieth-century advertisements, and contemporary films; great political speeches from the 1770s to the present; essays on relations between men and women and between parents and children; paintings of the pre–Civil War South and photographs of Yosemite in the 1870s; propaganda posters from World War I, and Thoreau on civil disobedience; Frederick Douglass on the horrors of slavery, Paul Fussell on the horrors of war, and Gloria Steinem on the pleasure and pain of a good day's work.

Our central premise is that there are ideas that run back to the earliest days of America as a political and social entity and continue to do so today, and those threads can be read across centuries and across genres. Every generation of Americans reinterprets and reargues these ideas in the light of its own experience. This book provides a wide array of materials that vary in kind and across time—fiction, essays, cartoons, posters, journals, paintings, poetry, legal proceedings, advertisements, movies—and thus form a core sample of American culture.

The ability to analyze these materials can work both ways. An eighteenth-century etching about what constitutes appropriate behavior for a young woman instructs us about earlier norms and helps us to understand more recent conflicts about feminism, freedom, and self-expression. And a contemporary advertisement that sells sex in order to sell clothing also helps us to understand the limits against which earlier generations of women defined themselves.

In the same way, excerpts from F. Scott Fitzgerald's novel *The Great Gatsby* are highly informative on the American romance with money, which Fitzgerald understood so well; but so is advertising on MTV, and so is the career of Buffalo Bill, who made a fortune by writing books about himself and selling a sanitized idea of the Old West to anyone who would buy it. Reading Susan B. Anthony on the First Amendment and freedom of speech may give you insight into the argument about whether controversial rap music lyrics should be censored, and reading Martin Luther King, Jr., on nonviolent resistance may help you understand why his intellectual ancestor, Henry Thoreau, refused to pay taxes and insisted, with some relish, on going to jail to protest a war he could not support.

Each chapter is organized around a particular theme that has deep roots in American history and culture and contains a thematic introduction, readings, illustrations, and questions; suggestions for journal entries, starting discussion, or finding a related writing topic; a starter list of movies; a section on a rhetorical skill or practice related to the selections—from definition of terms in Chapter 3 to revising myths in the last chapter; and a longer list of writing possibilities that includes thematic and rhetorical concerns and gives suggestions for creative projects.

The first two chapters set the stage. After presenting brief outlines of the chapters, Chapter 1 deals with critical reading and the analysis of themes and persuasive strategies. It explains what arguments mean in an American context and considers the tools, media, and genres for argument that Americans have incorporated into their rhetoric.

Chapter 2 concerns itself with writing analytically and persuasively, as well as integrating research into writing. It identifies techniques for developing essays and thesis statements, for structuring arguments, and for handling opposing viewpoints. It also examines overall patterns, like chronological order, and questions of effective organization. Finally, it sets out the entire process of how to go about research, from selecting a topic and setting a schedule to researching expository versus argumentative essays to gathering information from a variety of sources. The chapter also contains a list of specialized source materials for doing research on American themes.

The second part of *Creating America,* Chapters 3 through 9, contains the selections themselves—essays, stories, illustrations, advertisements, and other material—that express the richness and variety characteristic of American cultural patterns.

Chapter 3, "Identities," begins with questions of qualification and inclusion: Who is an American? What do Americans have in common besides their citizenship? How many varieties of Americans are there? Is there such a thing as mainstream American culture? What do Americans identify with: their religion, their work, their family, their neighborhood, their friends? What does it mean for someone who comes from another country to be Americanized, and what is the cost?

Alexis de Tocqueville, a Frenchman who came here to study Americans when the United States was still young, wrote a book about America as an interested outsider, fascinated by his subject. His observations, set out in *Democracy in America,* are so acute that even today they are still uncannily perceptive.

More recently, Studs Terkel, a Chicago writer and interviewer, has become famous for his ability to get Americans to talk honestly about their lives. He has put together several books of interviews and oral histories with all kinds of Americans on all kinds of formative experiences, from the traumas of living through and surviving the Great Depression or fighting in World War II, to the everyday drama of working in America. In this chapter's selection, Terkel interviews Frank Chin on being a Chinese American and thus touches on one of the most common issues in American identity: having a dual heritage.

Adrienne Rich, one of the foremost poets and essayists in the country, examines her own background in an essay whose title, "Split at the Root," is a perfect metaphor for the multiple religious, sexual, and political identities she lives with: white southerner, transplanted northerner and then Californian, child of Christian and Jewish parents, wife, mother, grandmother, lesbian activist, and writer. Other Americans, in and out of the establishment, inquire into public and private aspects of American identity. In his "Inaugural Address," John F. Kennedy defines America's identity as an international power in the latter part of the twentieth century, while African American novelist Ralph Ellison, in his Prologue to his novel *Invisible Man*, defines black identity by its invisibility to white American consciousness.

In Chapter 4, "American Dreams," the question of what it means to be an American advances another step. That there is an American dream is an accepted idea, but what exactly is the dream? Is it about money? Only money? Is money the element that mathematicians call necessary but not sufficient—the first requirement for the American dream but not the only one? If it isn't just money, what else is involved?

The selections that explore these ideas come from Americans with varying experiences of the American dream and different, if overlapping, ambitions. Benjamin Franklin, a genius with charm who was the first conspicuously successful American to record his own accomplishments, is the mold for the American dream that subsequent generations try to fit or to change. His ironic but thoughtful account of the good life he made for himself is remarkable not only for his talent at just about everything he tried but also for his ability to laugh at himself.

Raised in slavery before the Civil War, Frederick Douglass learned to read and write when it was a crime for slaves to learn to do either and became an abolitionist and a hero; his autobiography, *The Life and Times of Frederick Douglass,* written after his hair-raising escape from slavery, both echoes Franklin's and breaks new ground. His is still the story of a man who believes in and is able to achieve an American dream, but he struggled against odds that most people would have found insurmountable.

A somewhat later believer in the American dream, Mary Antin, a turn-of-the-century writer who came to Boston as an immigrant child from Russia, fell in love with America and wrote a best-selling autobiography, *The Promised Land,* to celebrate it and to defend the contributions of immigrants. Meanwhile, an anonymous artist painted a poster about a magical California of the imagination, hoping to convince the immigrants Mary Antin defended, and other Americans, to move to the enormous but underpopulated state and find their own dreams waiting there. As California turned into the best and worst of the American dream, Dolores Hayden, an urban studies scholar who examines how Americans live when the dream has supposedly come true, examines what three of its main domestic components—home, mom, and apple pie—are really like.

Chapter 5, "Family Values," takes up where Dolores Hayden leaves off and looks at the American family in a broad context. The first selection, *Keep within Compass,* is an eighteenth-century etching depicting the limits of proper female behavior. It does so by confining a drawing of a woman neatly and firmly between the borders of a compass.

Pulitzer Prize–winning journalist Susan Faludi would certainly recognize the sentiments in *Keep within Compass.* She writes in a surprisingly similar but contemporary vein in the essay "Blame It on Feminism" from her recent book, *Backlash: The Undeclared War on Feminism.* In the essay, she says that hostility to the modern women's movement has led the media to blame the movement for everything from bag ladies to bad complexions to meager savings accounts to mental depression. An honest examination of family values today requires recognition of the realities of one-parent families, divorces, remarriages, latchkey children, and nontraditional couples. So this chapter also includes: two argumentative essays by Thomas Stoddard and Bruce Fein about marriage, heterosexuality, homosexuality, and fundamental rights; an ad that embodies stereotypes of masculinity; and an essay that challenges traditional definitions of family.

Chapter 6, "Work and Success," focuses on the delicate relationship between money and happiness in American culture. To that end, it deals with several issues, including the Protestant work ethic. Here too Benjamin Franklin is the benchmark; an excerpt from his *Autobiography* clarifies the interconnection of economic freedom and personal self-worth. As in the chapter on the American dream, Franklin is simultaneously the model and the exception: his other projects—particularly in science—set him apart from traditional images of the successful entrepreneur.

Another exception, but for very different reasons, is Charlotte Perkins Gilman, author of *Women and Economics.* The first major American woman economist, she writes out of her own experience as an upper-class Victorian woman unwillingly dependent on her husband for financial support as well as social status. More recently, Gloria Steinem writes about what work means to women and men, while Alfred Lubano addresses work and class.

In other selections, F. Scott Fitzgerald's Jay Gatsby tries to find out if money really can buy happiness, while Tom Wolfe experiences Las Vegas—and convinces us to experience it—as though its excesses were a cross between a hallucinogenic joyride and a visit to Disneyland. And Phyllis Rose, a serious literary scholar, here indulges in a semiserious account of the benefits of malls, where shopping becomes the modern American equivalent of a religious experience.

Chapter Seven, "Social Justice and Civil Liberties," deals with equality and justice, prejudice, and the power of the individual. The writers are extremely aware of their effect on the audience. All of them express strong emotions—anger, outrage—but do so without losing control of their arguments. The most effective writings of this kind express the significance social justice and liberty in our political life and have become part of the American consciousness.

The first selection, the Declaration of Independence, frames and justifies the American Revolution in a mixture of legal reasoning, classical logic, intense feeling, and elegant prose. Frederick Douglass's "Independence Day Speech at Rochester" is a descendant of the Declaration, because of its eloquence and passion and because of Douglass's ability to argue against slavery by using the promise of equality in the Declaration. In a more recent example of an argument for justice, during the modern civil rights movement, Martin Luther King, Jr.'s "Letter from Birmingham Jail," argues for action instead of caution when the apathy of good people allows evil to flourish.

The central documents of this chapter, aside from the Declaration, are opinions from two Supreme Court cases, *Plessy* v. *Ferguson* (1896) and *Brown* v. *Board of Education* (1954), the two most important civil rights cases of the last hundred years. Between *Plessy,* which justifies and institutionalizes segregation, and *Brown,* which refuses to approve either the reasoning or the consequences of *Plessy,* lies a gulf between slavery and freedom that is still in the painful process of being bridged.

The selections that deal specifically with civil liberties look at the other side of the self-expression in a democracy: What happens when Americans hold unpopular, eccentric, or off-center opinions on issues of great public importance? Here are the voices of Henry Thoreau in *On Civil Disobedience,* serenely opposing slavery and a popular war— the Mexican-American War—and happy to be a man who marches to a different drummer, even if that means going to jail; and of Susan B. Anthony, intellectual heir of Jefferson and the other founding fathers, barred from voting because she was a woman, and using the language of the Declaration of Independence, as Frederick Douglass did, to advance social justice for women in future generations.

Chapter 8, "War and the Enemy," touches on both patriotism and xenophobia. In a country with as many ethnic and economic groups as this one, war has the effect of unifyng a diverse population against an identifiable other; issues of American identity tend to be resolved in favor of us versus them. Paul Fussell's essay, "Type-casting," uses American attitudes toward the Japanese in World War II as an example of this mentality. In a more savage vein, Mark Twain's parody of patriotic prayers for victory, "The War Prayer," written thirty-five years before World War II, is at least as critical of the bloodthirstiness that civilians at home feel toward their distant foes as it is of war itself.

The war in which Americans suffered the most casualties was the Civil War, but there the act of identifying the other as the enemy was problematic because the "other" were also Americans, and the conflict was that of a country fighting within itself. Abraham Lincoln recognized the intractable nature of this struggle—and its enormous cost— in "The Gettysburg Address," the shortest (about two minutes) great speech in American history, which is as notable for its compassion as for its extraordinarily compressed language.

The attempt to dehumanize the other side may be more characteristic of wartime attitudes than Lincoln's forgiveness, but sometimes the issues of the morality of war itself fragment allegiances. During the Vietnam War, Americans disagreed so bitterly with each other about whether patriotism demanded that they be for the war or against it that the antiwar movement became a major issue itself. Jacqueline Navarra Rhoads's memoir, "Nurses in Vietnam," recalls the conflict in highly personal terms and from the unusual angle of the experiences of women who served as army nurses. This memoir and two of the famous photographs of the war—of a child on fire from napalm and a prisoner being shot in the head—made it difficult for Americans to characterize the Vietnam conflict easily, if at all. George Lakoff's "Metaphor and the Gulf War" shows how even the supposedly objective language of war reporters can be used and abused to distort the reality of military action and thereby the beliefs of people at home about what happened and why.

The final chapter, "Frontiers," returns to American dreams in general and one dream in particular—what Huckleberry Finn calls "lighting out for the territory": moving west, finding open spaces and land unspoiled by the presence of other human beings, knowing that somewhere out there the wilderness and its promise still beckon. And if there isn't any more wilderness to discover, frontiers still abound, in outer space, computers, cybernetics, or inner space.

As a young historian in Chicago during the 1893 Exposition (the equivalent of a world's fair), Frederick Jackson Turner articulated the most important problem in American historical studies when he announced that the frontier had closed and the greatest epoch in American history was at an end. Ever since, historians have been disagreeing with, refining, upholding, or raging against Turner's ideas, but they have never been able to ignore them. It remained for a later scholar of American intellectual history, Richard Hofstadter, to formulate the most significant and reasoned opposition to Turner's insistence on the absolute primacy of the American frontier as the shaper of the American character.

Jane Gould Tortillot is not famous, but as a woman who crossed the plains to California with her family in 1862, she knew the frontier first-hand. Her diary is an unvarnished adventure: friendly Indians who wanted to trade, hostile Indians who attacked wagon trains, bad weather, illness, enormous and beautiful landscapes, and death from illness and accident. Mark Twain, on the other hand, goes west riding on top of a stagecoach and gives us, in *Roughing It,* a reason to envy him for having such a wonderful time. Looking back from a very different viewpoint, American Indian poet Louise Erdrich writes a poem about what it is like to be an American Indian watching a John Wayne movie in which one Indian after another is shot by heroic white men.

As you learn to evaluate different kinds of texts, both written and visual, contemporary and historical, and their effect on you, their audience, we hope you will also develop a greater appreciation for the richness and texture of American culture and the sources from which it comes.

Persuasion

As you study the selections in this book, you will find that most of the authors are engaged in arguments of one kind or another about a particular political stance, a contemporary ethical problem, or the status quo. Frequently the fight is not so much about an individual opponent as about an idea or a belief. However varied the subject matter or the historical events surrounding it, this kind of argument is characteristically a manifestation of disagreement in a democracy. It is argument that encourages rather than stifles disagreement and allows the expression of different, even completely opposing points of view, and it protects the right of individual Americans to say and express ideas that other Americans find highly offensive. It is argument designed not to bludgeon opposition into submission but rather to persuade.

The target of such persuasive argument is often the American public at large or a particular group of citizens within a larger political unit. Americans take for granted their right to argue publicly and privately and to criticize their government, their elected officials, their school boards, their neighbors. This chapter provides suggestions for analyzing and using persuasion as a basis for your own experiments in reading and writing about American materials critically.

Persuasion is a process in which a *rhetor*—a speaker, writer, or artist—tries to elicit a desired response from an *audience* by identifying commonalities in the interests of both parties. It is a process that deals not in certainties but in probabilities—in arguing from evidence or reasons and assumptions to a conclusion. This textbook is designed to enable you to develop your ability to understand and analyze the strategies of persuasion in what you read and to develop your own ability to write persuasively. Studying persuasive texts can help you to become a more critical reader and listener and to communicate more clearly and effectively. By focusing on diverse kinds of arguments in American culture, by looking at context and purpose, by looking beneath the surface at strategies and appeals, you will see persuasion all around you in daily life—in books you read but also in advertising, flyers, posters, news magazines, newspapers, and so forth. A persuasive text is one that asserts a point of view and seeks a desired response; it attempts to induce the readers to agree with whatever is being expounded on. A description of orderly governance in an American Indian tribe, for example, implicitly argues for respect for that culture. Sometimes the desired response is self-sacrifice; a poster advertising war bonds appeals to the interests of the audience—whether self-interest or desire to belong—to garner financial support for the war effort. Ultimately, persuasion can change beliefs, behavior, or even government policy; in *Brown* v. *Board of Education*, a legal argument citing inequities in segregated education changed the law of the land and the future of millions of Americans.

Persuasion and American Cultures

American cultures have common threads that are woven in tremendous diversity. Persuasive appeals in public discourse must take this into account in order to succeed, tapping into the assumptions and common values and beliefs while acknowledging divergent views. More so than the speakers and writers in more homogeneous cultures, Americans wishing to persuade their fellow Americans must understand something about their audience: who they are, what they believe and assume, how they communicate, and what they value. Some assumptions and values remain constant over time, but each age brings with it a different view anchored in that particular time and culture. Examining persuasive texts from different time periods in American history and from different cultural perspectives may help us to understand our own age and culture better while considering them in a larger historical context.

As the preceding discussion suggests, the themes in this text represent some of the core debates in American history: Who are Americans? What are their dreams? What makes an American family? What are Americans' values about work and success? What are their concepts of justice and liberty? Why do they construct an "other" or enemy and how do they take action against them? What is their image of the frontier and how, having reached the geographical limits of the continent, do they search for new frontiers? Each type of question or problem lends itself to a particular aspect of argumentation.

Rhetor and Audience

Understanding the arts of persuasion entails understanding how others persuade you and how you can persuade others through your own arguments. Although some scholars have argued that argument relies on logic and persuasion on emotion, Aristotelian rhetoric makes no such clear-cut distinction. Aristotle's *Rhetoric* suggests that reason, beliefs and values, and emotion—*logos, ethos,* and *pathos*—work together to engage the whole person and guide him or her toward appropriate judgment of the issue at hand. A traditional view suggests that argument entails an adversarial relationship between two sides—generally writer or speaker and audience. In debate, for example, the two opposing sides each offer arguments that the other side then refutes; in propaganda, the audience is inundated with generally one-sided, unsupported assertions. Such persuasion is rhetoric "to gain advantage, of one sort or another," as critic Kenneth Burke notes, and to some degree, it reflects Aristotle's primary definition of rhetoric as "understanding all of the available means of persuasion."

Recently some scholars have argued for different approaches to argumentation. Drawing on the work of psychologists such as Carl Rogers, they outline a model that suggests that both rhetor, or communicator, and audience are participants in the argument and should work together, much like a client and therapist, to pursue knowledge and truth. Some feminist critics suggest that our traditional views of argumentation are male-centered, adversarial, and combative; they suggest a more collaborative approach to argumentation, with negotiation rather than debate as the dominant mode. In such an approach, both sides identify their common interests and attempt to close the distance between their respective positions.

Another view suggests rereading Aristotle to understand the connection between rhetor and audience. (The term *rhetor* will in this textbook refer to an individual attempting to persuade orally or in written text or image.) In this view, the rhetor and audience work together to pursue and develop a solution to a problem, a difference of opinion, or an issue. Audience and rhetor are dynamically involved in argument, and no argument can begin from scratch; the rhetor relies on and presumes a certain background on the part of the audience, including certain assumptions, beliefs, values, and reservoir of knowledge.

Audiences and Cultures

Scholars of rhetoric have shown that persuasion in homogeneous cultures tends to leave many reasons and assumptions unexpressed; a shared heritage tends to include a fair number of shared assumptions and values. In a heterogeneous society such as the United States, arguments rely on some common ground, but they tend to be more forcefully and clearly articulated, with premises and steps in the logic more often stated than assumed. The argumentative style and organization tend to be more indirect in countries where a direct approach could be considered offensive and where the rhetor might instead broach a subject, move away from it, then return to supporting points later. The point, again, is to analyze audiences carefully, to visualize them and consider their beliefs, values, attitudes, and style of interaction, rather than concentrating only on one's own point of view. Understanding audience assumptions and expectations is crucial in developing persuasive argumentative strategies.

Audiences from Other Times

Analyzing arguments written for readers from other time periods brings with it its own complexity. Although the basic strategies of argument remain much the same through the ages, the role of public debate and the particular concerns and issues vary with each age and culture. The early America of European colonial culture was largely agricultural, with people living on farms and in towns isolated from each other; it took days for information to reach New York City from Philadelphia. Today Americans and the rest of the world are connected by a global media. Colonial culture was more homogeneous, but space and time separated its communications; American society today is more diverse, but most Americans are exposed to the same news and popular culture. Superficially, then, we have more in common, but the increased variety in cultures means that we come to the discussion with different cultural perspectives. People who seek to persuade others in American cultures and media cannot count on the kinds of shared assumptions held by the audiences of Benjamin Franklin or Thomas Jefferson. Understanding persuasive texts from other times, then, will require not only analyzing the texts themselves but considering the assumptions, values, beliefs, and needs of the audiences for whom they were intended.

Audience and Appeals: Ethos, Logos, and Pathos

In order to induce others to identify with them or their point of view, rhetors use a number of strategies. Aristotle outlined three modes of persuasion that relate to the connection between writer and audience: appeals to ethos, pathos, and logos.

Appeals to Ethos   Rhetors commonly attempt to establish credibility, authority, and a common identity with the audience by using appeals to ethos, which invoke the values and beliefs that the rhetor and audience have in common in order to establish credibility and authority. According to Aristotle, ethos appeals establish the "personal character of the speaker." A politician who presents himself as the product of an economically poor background is appealing to common beliefs about success as a product of hard work and drive. John F. Kennedy appealed to an ethos of service to others in his "Inaugural Address." Franklin Delano Roosevelt appealed to Americans' beliefs and values about fair play when he vilified the Japanese during World War II. Martin Luther King, Jr., appealed to values of fairness in arguing for civil rights on behalf of all Americans. Academic writers appeal to the ethos of rigorous inquiry and well-supported assertions by presenting themselves as being reasonable and well-informed, using credible sources, and paying attention to the conventions of academia and of various disciplines. Writers who include unsupported assertions, use inflammatory or biased language, or fail to consider opposing views violate an ethos of reasoned discourse expected in academic writing; they also undermine their credibility as scholars and writers.

Appeals to Pathos   The good rhetorician, said Aristotle, seeks to understand the emotions and then to put the audience in the right frame of mind to hear an argument. Appeals to pathos, like appeals to ethos, relate to identification. If one can emphathize, one can identify with another, put oneself in the other's position, and understand the other's feelings and point of view. Critics have argued that emotional appeals are less appropriate than logos or ethos appeals, perhaps over concern about manipulating audience emotions or relying on emotional appeals to cover up a lack of logic and evidence. Yet persuasion engages the whole individual, and pathos appeals can create a more balanced argument or a more ethical decision. Cost-benefit analyses may argue against any intervention in postcommunist Eastern Europe, but showing the human costs and suffering, in text or images, may provide a kind of evidence that eludes the rigorous economical and political analyses. By the same token, logically staking out political benefits for U.S. oil shipments may not present the whole picture unless one includes the human costs on both sides of a war in the Middle East.

The rhetor cannot generally invoke emotions directly by asking the readers to feel a certain way or to empathize with someone. He or she must use language, examples, and details that clearly convey situations with which the audiences can identify. Appeals to pathos are frequently made through specific detail or connotative language—language that evokes feelings or emotional responses. In the Prologue to *Invisible Man*, for example, Ralph Ellison invites the reader to identify with a man who is invisible in his society; Ellison persuades readers to see another point of view by invoking their empathy for the narrator's situation. (For more on language and persuasion, see the end-of-chapter discussion for Chapter 8.)

Appeals to Logos Appeals to logos refer to the logic and shape of the argument. Nearly every argument at least pretends to possess some logic in the form of reasons why the audience should change their views. Aristotle cites two basic methods of developing logos appeals: induction, arguing from evidence; and deduction, arguing from general principles.

In *induction*, the rhetor generalizes from a number of observations, specific cases, or examples and draws inferences or conclusions based on data. Induction deals not with certainties but with probabilities; the rhetor cannot test every single case or provide an infinite number of examples, so he or she uses the examples and evidence at hand or ~~can obtain~~ obtainable to draw conclusions about another case or a larger population.

When the rhetor reasons from examples to conclusion, she asks the audiences to make an inductive leap—a leap of faith from the known and verifiable specific cases presented in the argument, across an unknown and unknowable stretch, to a probable conclusion. The relevance, breadth, and number of examples reduce the leap audiences must make and therefore strengthen the credibility of the argument. Since rhetors have a limited amount of time and space to devote to their examples, they must select those most persuasive and most suited to the audience and purpose. When Martin Luther King, Jr., describes driving all night because he can't find a motel that will accept his business, or having to explain to his child why she can't play in a playground that is for whites only, or seeing that his people's wives, mothers, and sisters are denied the respected title of "Mrs." and that grown men are called "boy," his vivid, specific examples make a strong case for the conclusion that Americans of African descent endure relentless and pervasive racism. In academic writing as well, each author must include relevant, sufficient, and representative examples to build a persuasive case for the conclusion. Scientists carefully record data about sampling, methods, and observations to substantiate credibly the conclusions they draw from their data.

Inductive arguments can go wrong in one of two ways: either the evidence is inadequate for the conclusion drawn, or the reasoning from evidence to conclusion is faulty. Readers of academic prose as well as other kinds of arguments must be critical of the kinds of examples offered and mindful of biased or inadequate sampling. They should also examine critically the "leap" they are asked to make from evidence to conclusion.

Say, for example, a friend of yours works in a hospital transcribing medical notes written by physicians. On his first day of work, he sees six patient charts, and all six contain doctors' notes in handwriting that is almost illegible. He might conclude that doctors have terrible handwriting. If he tells you, "All doctors have terrible handwriting," he would be guilty of overgeneralizing. In fact, he hasn't seen all doctors' handwriting. If he said, "All of the doctors whose handwriting I have seen write illegibly," he would be making a statement that is accurate (assuming others share his standards) but is limited to the sample he describes. Induction, like other forms of argumentation, is open to question; if it weren't, there would be no reason for debate. But reasonable people will be likely to accept the conclusions one draws if they are based on sufficient evidence and if the conclusion logically follows from the evidence. What we most want induction to do is to enable us to generalize from a sample to larger populations and other cases; we want to be able to say, with some degree of certainty, that the conclusion is true based on our evidence.

Deduction, the other primary method of organizing arguments, takes a general principle (also called a premise or an assumption) and draws a conclusion or makes an assertion based on it. The *syllogism* is a classic outline of deduction used to test the logic of the argument. It entails a statement of a general premise, a specific case, and a conclusion derived from the general premise and specific case. For example, consider the following statements:

> All physicians have terrible handwriting.
> Dr. Weller is a physician.
> Therefore, Dr. Weller has terrible handwriting.

Clearly the generalization forming the conclusion of the argument is highly questionable. Sketching out an argument in this form frequently enables readers to examine both the premises being made and the conclusions being drawn. Generally, though, arguments don't occur in this explicit form. More often, writers persuade through collapsed arguments, with generalizations and assumptions left out or buried within the argument.

Such a compact deductive argument, known as an *enthymeme*, unites the author's statement and conclusion with a part of the argument that is understood or assumed by the audience. The syllogism generally spells out the general principle, the specific case, and the conclusion. The enthymeme leaves out one of the premises, often the generalization or underlying assumption. Drawing from the example, the argument would appear something like this:

Dr. Weller, being a physician, has terrible handwriting.

or

Of course Dr. Weller has terrible handwriting—she's a physician.

Both statements have buried within them the outlined argument in the syllogism, but rather than sketching out all the steps, the rhetor relies on assumptions shared with the audience. The rhetor's task is to analyze the audience and to know how much background information to supply, what definitions to include or exclude, what the audience already accepts or believes, what points must be argued and supported with evidence. In the compact argument of the enthymeme, the rhetor assumes that the audience will supply certain links in the chain of argument.

A number of selections in this book provide examples of deductive arguments. The Declaration of Independence (Chapter 7) argues extensively from principle, explicitly stating premises and assumptions, testing those premises against a specific case (the British government of the colonies) and then drawing the conclusion that the break with Britain is justified. If one accepts the premises—governments derive their authority from the consent of the governed; governments exist to protect the rights of life, liberty, and the pursuit of happiness—then one must accept the validity of the conclusion—that governments that do not protect these rights no longer deserve their authority and should be abolished.

Often one can identify enthymemes by examining assertions connected to subordinate clauses beginning with conjunctions such as *since* and *because.* In the selection from *Backlash* included in Chapter 5, Susan Faludi identifies and then questions the logic in an enthymeme commonly cited by detractors of feminism: Women are unhappy because of their newfound equality. Faludi refutes the argument by questioning the assumption that women are equal and by claiming that women are unhappy, in fact, because they are blocked from full equality.

Errors in Logic

Arguments can go wrong in a number of ways. Critical readers and careful writers need to question the arguments in what they read and take care with the evidence, assumptions, and reasons they offer and the conclusions they draw. In a deductive argument, a critical reader can argue with the reasons and assumptions, sometimes called premises, on which the conclusion is based or question the reasoning process from premises to conclusions. In inductive reasoning, one can question the evidence offered or the conclusion drawn about that evidence. Both methods can lead to a number of errors in logical argumentation, or fallacies. Below are some of the most common fallacies.

1. **Hasty generalization.** Leaping in logic from a very few cases to a broad conclusion can be considered hasty generalization. If, for example, we find that two senators have financial assets worth millions of dollars and we conclude that all public officials are wealthy, we have made a leap that is unsupported by the evidence. We have leaped too hastily from examples to a conclusion.

2. **Inadequate or biased sampling.** This fallacy is related to hasty generalizaiton. If a writer's conclusions are based on too few samples or a skewed or biased collection of samples, the conclusions are not necessarily generalizable to the larger issue or population. If we sampled only the senators included in a list of the fifty wealthiest Americans to draw conclusions about all senators, we would be using a biased sample. We need to cast our net wider and draw from a more representative sampling. Drawing at random a sample of ten or twenty from the list of one hundred senators and examining their financial statements would give us more representative and complete data and enable us to generalize to the larger population of senators.

3. **Straw man.** A straw man in argumentation is a false target: the writer sets up a misstatement of the opponent's view and then attacks that misstatement instead of the real argument. An argument attacking someone who does not support specific pro-choice legislation might sugggest that the opponent wants "all women barefoot and pregnant" instead of discussing the specific legislation in question.

4. **Ad hominem.** In the ad hominem argument, literally "against the man," the writer attacks an individual holding the position rather than the position. If a writer says, "Governor Jones is in favor of nationalized health insurance, so it must be a bad idea," that writer

is attacking the governor but not addressing the merits of his specific arguments.

5. **False analogy.** Argument by analogy is one of the weakest strategies and highly vulnerable to attack. A false analogy entails erroneously suggesting that two people, situations, or issues are analogous or comparable in certain ways. In recent years, any number of potential military conflicts have been argued against because they might represent "another Vietnam," whether or not there are, in fact, any similarities between the two situations.

6. **Post hoc ergo propter hoc.** Literally, this expression translates into "after this therefore because of this." The mistake in logic lies in suggesting that because A happened before B, A caused B. The watchword in statistics and many social sciences, however, is that correlation does not equal causation. Because the divorce rate increased after the advent of widespread television viewing, there is no reason to conclude that television viewing causes divorce.

7. **False dilemma.** A false dilemma is an either-or situation in which the writer implies that we have only two choices: "Either we get rid of television once and for all, or we resign ourselves to being a nation with the leading divorce rate in the civilized world."

8. **Slippery slope.** In this lapse in logic, the writer argues that one first step will inevitably lead to disastrous consequences. For example, someone opposed to genetic engineering might argue, "Once we allow scientists to map human chromosomes, we will see people murdering their children because they don't have blond hair and blue eyes."

9. **Begging the question.** Begging the question is essentially assuming something as a given that has not been proved. A related strategy, circular reasoning, restates the proposition as a conclusion: "Students who have bad grades and don't study should not be allowed to watch television because viewing might be detrimental to their school work."

10. **Non sequitur.** Literally, this term means, "It does not follow." Advertisements are full of fallacious reasoning but make something of a specialty of non sequiturs: "Crock Cola tastes great: America's fastest growing cola company!" Taste and relative corporate growth are juxtaposed as if one leads to the other; such, regrettably for consumers, is not necessarily the case. Sometimes the term *non sequitur* is used more generally to indicate any lapse in logic.

Understanding Persuasion in Practice

In addition to evaluating the appeals to ethos, pathos, and logos in an argument, taking arguments apart on a structural, sentence-by-sentence level to see how they work can be instructive. Understanding both general principles of persuasion and specific, sentence-level strategies enables us to evaluate the arguments that confront us daily, in college studies and in our communities.

Examples of persuasion surround us in academic texts, mass media, personal conversations—even as we walk down the street. Let's examine a specific piece of persuasion encountered on a college campus recently. A flyer posted on the wall of a campus building has the following message spray-painted on it, in red letters on a white background, as if through a stencil:

> Oil in Kuwait
> Oil in Panama
> No Oil in Bosnia
> Get it?

Unpacking the argument takes a bit of thought and involves reader response and input to make the argument work. First, we observe that this is not an impromptu message, since it was created through a stencil, which presumes multiple applications of the message in various locations. The somewhat diffuse red spray-paint draws attention to the message and suggests blood; the rhetor, through the parallel structure of the phrases, argues that the situations are analogous: that the United States intervened militarily in other countries when doing so was in its own best interests; that it has not intervened in Bosnia because there is no economic motive to do so. In a rather taunting manner, the rhetorical question of the last line invites audience engagement in the discussion.

As it happens, some audience members—people of the academic community who passed by the notice—did engage in the argument. Written in ball point pen ink between lines two and three are, "No oil in Vietnam" and "No oil in Grenada," a reference to other U.S. military involvement without apparent economic benefit.

Except for the rhetorical question, each of the other elements in the argument is a phrase, which the audience has to fill in to complete a statement. Those statements might look something like this:

> The United States intervenes militarily in other countries only to protect its interests, such as access to suppliers of oil.
> Bosnia is not a supplier of oil.
> Therefore the United States will not intervene militarily to protect its interests in Bosnia.

For the conclusion to be true, the premises leading to the conclusion must be true. If they are not, the argument breaks down. When critiquing an argument, the audience can question the premises or the reasoning process that lead to the conclusion or claim. The scrawled messages in ballpoint pen refute the argument by attacking the premise that the United States intervenes militarily only when oil is at stake.

Examining the style of the message, we see that the rhetor made use of an excellent stylistic tactic, parallelism. The grammatical structures of the first three lines are equivalent: noun, preposition, noun, with a negative added to the last line. Parallel structures can help to clarify and emphasize connections and equivalence between ideas, as the rhetor was trying to suggest.

Let's examine another use of helpful grammatical structure, a balanced sentence:

When guns are outlawed, only outlaws will have guns.

What is your immediate reaction to this slogan? Imagine you saw it on a bumper sticker of a car. Does it seem sensible or logical? Now read it aloud and take it apart:

When guns are outlawed
Only outlaws will have guns.

First, examine the rhythm. Which words are stressed? How do the stresses contribute to the rhythm? What words are then destressed and deemphasized? How does the sense of balance, of equivalence, contribute to the sense of logic or that the slogan "makes sense"?

Now look critically at the diction, or word choice. First look at the ambiguous term, *guns*. Does it refer to handguns? Shotguns? Rifles? Semiautuomatics? Uzis? What does *outlawed* mean? Does it mean people must register for a gun? That they must wait ten days before purchasing one so that the seller can check for a criminal record? Does it mean children can't buy guns? Then examine that unstressed word, *only*. Is it true that only outlaws or criminals will have guns? What about police officers? Forest rangers? Brinks guards? The assumptions and assertions of the slogan do not bear up under close examination. In a fleeting statement as on a bumper sticker or in a cartoon, such arguments can sometimes make an impression, or erode the position of the opposition just a bit.

Though you need to avoid falling into fallacious arguments, or those in which the logic breaks down, as in the example of the bumper sticker, you can use structures such as parallelism and balance to show relationships between things and ideas. You can choose whether to use *denotative* language, which is explicit language that attempts to convey objectivity, or *connotative* language, which is an emotion-laden language that attempts to evoke an image or idea. By the same token, you can understand when you are being hornswoggled or fooled by eloquent language disguising a weak argument.

Let's look at the way another rhetorical strategy, antithesis, which is a balanced structure with opposing elements, can reinforce the effects of language:

> We observe today
> not a victory of party
> but a celebration of freedom

These opening lines to John F. Kennedy's "Inaugural Address" stress the orderly changing of administrations, emphasizing not the rancorous 1960 presidential race against and defeat of Richard Nixon, not the onset of Democratic rule, but the sense that the inauguration itself is a link of history, part of the ritual of democratic government. A few lines later, Kennedy makes use of highly connotative language to evoke a sense of tradition, grandeur, and solemnity:

> For I have sworn before you and Almighty God the same, solemn oath our forebears prescribed nearly a century and three quarters ago.

Why would a modern president—one who used the relatively new medium of television to his advantage, one who represented youth and change, one who frightened some citizens simply by virtue of being Catholic—speak in archaic, formal diction? How do you think you would have reacted to such a speech? What tone, approach, and mood does this rhetor evoke? And how do these strategies support his goals?

Sometimes simple repetition of a key phrase can drive a point home forcefully and eloquently. You may have been told in the past to avoid being repetitious; now is a good time to examine the difference between needless, annoying repetition that occurs when you have not taken care with your essay or paragraph organization, and repetition that reinforces points and ideas, suggests connections between ideas, clarifies meaning, and delivers pleasing balance and rhythm to the audience. As we saw with the bumper sticker, rhythm and balance are no substitute for logic and evidence; nevertheless, well-crafted prose is itself more persuasive than plodding, hard-to-follow prose. And unless you are deliberately trying to obfuscate or muddy up the issues, clarity too is a virtue. Let's look at an eloquent example of anaphora, or a repeated sentence opener, from Martin Luther King, Jr.'s "I Have A Dream" speech:

> So let freedom ring from the prodigious hilltops of New Hampshire.
> Let Freedom ring from the mighty mountains of New York.
> Let freedom ring from the heightening Alleghenies of Pennsylvania!
> Let freedom ring from the snowcapped Rockies of Colorado!
> Let freedom ring from the curvaceous peaks of California!
> But not only that;
> Let freedom ring from Stone Mountain of Georgia!
> Let freedom ring from Lookout Mountain of Tennessee!
> Let freedom ring from every hill and molehill of Mississippi.
> From every mountainside, let freedom ring!

This section follows King's recitation of the lyrics to "My Country 'Tis of Thee" and picks up the thread of the last line of that song in the repeated "let freedom ring," and the image of "from every mountainside" in the second to last line of the song. Examine the progression of the first set in the above lines. What geographical regions are included? Then examine the break, midway, and the change in direction. In what ways does this repetition, attached to the diverse regions, reinforce a theme?

You can read the full text of this speech in Chapter 4. As you review this and other selections, remember to analyze not only themes and overall structure but patterns of sentences, words, and images; all contribute to and underscore the persuasive message of the rhetor.

Persuasion works on many levels: to engage the audience, to get them to identify with the point of view of the rhetor, and, if possible, to move them in belief or in action to the position suggested by the rhetor. Since argument relies on moving beyond the supporting materials to draw conclusions, whether that support is based on examples or derived from a general proposition, the strength and effectiveness of appeals to ethos, pathos, and logos are crucial in persuading audiences. Such appeals operate at the level of the main point of a text, the supporting points, and the words and sentences themselves that convey those points. In Chapter 2 we focus the discussion of appeals and logical arrangement on the writing process; in every chapter that follows, we urge you to analyze texts critically, and when you write, to reason carefully and to provide solid support for your arguments.

Elements of Persuasion in Chapter Selections

Underlying all of the rhetorical strategies discussed are appeals to ethos, logos, and pathos. These concepts form the framework of critical reading and persuasive writing. This textbook is designed to build on these basic strategies of persuasion and to provide additional guidance for analyzing and implementing them in Part Two, through the chapter introductions, the end-of-selection questions, and the end-of-chapter discussions. The additional elements of argumentation we will discuss are definition, examples, assumptions, assertions, refutation, language, and revision.

Definition

Definition is both a building block of argument and an argument in itself. Definition is the core strategy explored in Chapter 3, "Identities." In asking who is an American, we immediately encounter the process of definition: of defining terms, setting out categories, establishing common ground for discussion. Effective argumentation entails successfully identifying with the audience and identifying common ground and common interests. Definition of terms can help to develop that connection between oneself and one's audience. The end-of-chapter discussion surveys the types and uses of definitions.

Examples

In Chapter 4, "American Dreams," we look at *examples,* including personal experience and observation, as the evidence from which we often draw conclusions. All of the authors in this chapter rely, to varying degrees, on providing examples to convey a general impression. Sometimes the examples are narratives or anecdotes, sometimes lists of specifics, sometimes the experience of the individual or a group. Critical readers need to examine the credibility and sufficiency of such examples and analyze the conclusions that the authors want us to draw from them. The end-of-chapter discussion offers guidelines on both analyzing arguments and using examples in the arguments you write, including examples derived from personal experiences and observation, field research, and library research.

Assumptions

As we consider and evaluate examples and data, we call upon our own *assumptions* and previously held beliefs as we draw conclusions. In the case of a deductive argument or enthymeme, the rhetor draws a conclusion about a specific case based on assumptions held by the audience. In induction, the rhetor relies on the audience to accept the kind and amount of examples and evidence offered. Since arguments about the family nearly always rest on deeply held beliefs about gender, marriage, family, and the role of families in the community,

Chapter 5, "Family Values," examines assumptions about what has historically constituted a family in American cultures and appropriate roles within that family. The end-of-chapter discussion and assignments focus on analyzing assumptions in the arguments of others and in your own writing.

Assertions

From definitions, examples, and assumptions, we turn to making and supporting *assertions.* In Chapter 6, "Work and Success," we examine the assertions writers make and the kinds of evidence they use to support those assertions. The end-of-chapter discussion focuses on ways to develop and support assertions in your own arguments. Keep in mind the strategies for developing a core assertion or thesis statement, described in Chapter 2, and the strategies of logical organization described in Chapter 1. You may also find it helpful to review the logical fallacies defined in this chapter as you begin to draft your own arguments.

Refutation

As you practice crafting and developing assertions, you will need to be mindful of those who disagree with you so that you can maintain your credibility as a reasonable, careful writer. In any argument, the assertion is arguable by definition, implying an opposing view. Chapter 7, "Justice and Civil Liberties," focuses on *refutation* as the core rhetorical method in the selections and the end-of-chapter discussion. The court cases in particular demonstrate the struggle of proponents of different views and different sides of an argument to refute opposing views and offer solid arguments to support their own side. The models in this chapter demonstrate a wide range of strategies for refutation, many of which can be modified and used in both academic and personal writing; the selections can also draw your attention to ways of critiquing and analyzing the arguments of others.

Language and Imagery

Chapter 8, "War and the Enemy," takes the other side of the identity question of Chapter 3 and looks at the ways in which we create through language, not our own identity, but that of an "other." Using highly connotative language (language that evokes imaginative or emotional associations) can be effective, but it can also erode the audience's trust in the author. A task for critical readers is to examine coolly and critically the language of persuasion and to evaluate it: Is it being used to cover up a lack of evidence or to appeal to the worst prejudices and emotions of audiences? Or does it clarify an issue or appeal to the emotions in conjunction with appeals to the audience's intellect and values? A difficult task for student writers is learning to judge the effective use of language and to use concrete, specific language appropriate to the situation.

Revision

The definitions, evidence, assumptions and values, assertions, and language we use to develop a point of view and refute opposing views help us to devise sound arguments, but sometimes we need to reassess our own views, review our thinking, and revise our beliefs or position in view of new information or persuasive arguments made by others. Chapter 9 takes on this process with an end-of-chapter discussion of *revision*. Revision works at the theoretical level, when we take into account new information to revise our views. It is also crucial on a practical level, as we learn to clarify and revise our assertions and reasoning to develop coherent arguments of our own.

Persuasion in Diverse Genres

There are any number of genres in which a writer or artist can be persuasive; some of them are obviously argumentative, like a pro-and-con debate, a legal case, or a series of political cartoons; some of them less obviously so, like fiction, poetry, or film. But all of them can be enormously successful at conveying a point of view and swaying an audience. In this book we include a variety of genres with strong persuasive elements. The brief explanations that follow are designed to help you read these materials, regardless of medium, for content, theme, and argumentative and persuasive content, as well as for the pleasure of encountering American writers and artists on their home ground.

Essays

Essays generally come in two varieties: reflective and argumentative—that is, expository. The reflective essay was invented by the Renaissance writer Michel de Montaigne. He used it as a way of getting to know himself better. Informal, ironic, funny, full of anecdotes and charm, Montaigne's essays started as quotations on which he made comments and ended as an exploration of his psychological makeup and view of the world. He tested out his thoughts, pains, prejudices, and pleasures against the measure of his own intelligence. Great reflective essays demand a high level of honesty from the writer, but they also provide a kind of immediacy and intimacy, a one-on-one exchange between reader and writer that is very satisfying. The essay persuades through a form of verbal seduction—by enabling the reader to look with the writer's eyes and the writer's own viewpoint. Reflective essays also present the personality of the writer distinctively; when you get to know a great essayist, invariably you will recognize his or her voice.

In an expository essay, you give information in order to explain a point of view on a topic. This kind of essay presents you, as the writer, with an opportunity to work out your ideas in a broad context—on the environment, for example, or privacy, or relations between men and women. Your research, reflections, and interpretations all contribute to the assertions you make and how you make them, but the goal of an expository essay is to express or explain your ideas clearly and to persuade the reader to accept the merit of your thesis or main point, rather than to change the reader's opinion or behavior.

An argumentative essay is just that—one side of an argument. It presupposes an opposing point of view, and it is geared directly to anticipating and refuting that point of view. Like the expository essay, it clearly puts ideas in the public arena, but with the goal of stimulating debate, eliciting criticism, or persuading readers to change the way they think or what they do or to persuade them to take action in a particular direction. The best argumentative essays, however, are not divorced from the writer; they engage readers most thoroughly when the author is passionate about the subject matter.

Occasionally an author is able to write an essay that is simultaneously reflective and argumentative, for example, Thoreau's *On Civil Disobedience* in Chapter 7. Thoreau tells us about himself—his political beliefs, how he expresses them, why he believes civil disobedience to unjust laws is the most accurate expression of his individuality and personality. He is so eloquent on the importance of the lone conscience in a democracy, the trouble with Congress, and the moral obligation to stand up and be counted at any cost that his personal creed also becomes a persuasive argument for nonviolent resistance as a general political tool. Few essayists can manage to combine both forms of the essay in one, but Thoreau will give you some idea of how many forms of self-expression and powerful persuasion a good essay can present.

Fiction and Poetry

Students don't usually think of fiction or poetry as persuasive writing because the arguments they make are more subtly stated, enveloped in character and language and plot. They are *about* someone or something. In fact, a great story or poem can move people profoundly and change their ideas, or enlighten them, in ways that more direct forms of address cannot. For example, Fitzgerald's *The Great Gatsby* is a novel about a mysterious man who makes millions of dollars illegally to get close to the woman he loves. Nowhere in the text does Fitzgerald give a lecture on the power of money in American society or the corrupting influence of power, or the tragic loss of the American dream. But his characters, the voice of the narrator, and the story are so lucid and so affecting that the theme argues more profoundly than any explicit statement could.

Poetry is characterized by a kind of compression that makes its point through concentrated images and language. In her poem, "Dear John Wayne," Louise Erdrich makes a forceful argument against the treatment American Indians have received in the media, in popular culture, and in the way other Americans perceive them. Rather than assemble statistics about life on the reservation, she sets out an illustration whose point is vividly clear: the experience of Indian teenagers at at drive-in watching John Wayne, the all-American hero, shoot apparently endless numbers of their ancestors in a movie battle. The oversimplification of the movie's portrait of good guys and bad guys, combined with the ordinariness of the situation, urge us to rethink our perspective and reevaluate our ideas—the goal of every well-written argument.

Legal Cases

Legal cases are a good way to clarify the elements of persuasive argument because that's exactly what they are: two opponents in a court of law, arguing against each other in order to persuade a judge or jury to decide in their favor, knowing that only one side can win, and using every psychological and intellectual strategy they can think of to get the decision to go their way.

Trials are adversarial by definition; there have to be two sides and a neutral third party—a judge or a jury guided by a judge. Once the verdict has been reached, based on the evidence—once the third party has been persuaded by one side or the other—the trial is over. If the losing side is dissatisfied with the verdict, it can write an appeal, a piece of purely persuasive writing that goes to a panel of judges who then decide if they want to overrule the trial court decision or have the case tried again.

The U.S. Supreme Court is the court of last resort for appeals, but certain threshold conditions must be met for an appeal to be submitted to it; for example, the Court can decide to rule on a case involving the interpretation or application of the Constitution of the United States to a particular situation. Both of the cases in this book (see Chapter 7) are Supreme Court cases. As you read the decisions the Court made in *Plessy* v. *Ferguson* and *Brown* v. *Board of Education,* keep four points in mind.

First, the Court often relies on the accumulated body of law already decided in related cases—called *precedent*—to explain why it is not overturning the verdict in the case before it. Occasionally—and *Brown* is the most famous example in American law—the Court rejects all precedent and makes new law or takes the law, and the country, in a new direction.

Second, every year the Court receives many requests to hear cases on appeal and accepts only a fraction—usually those involving issues of substantial national importance. When it refuses a case, whatever the previous state or federal court decided remains unchanged.

Third, once the Supreme Court makes a decision, it is the law. There is no higher court to appeal. It is a remarkable feature of our political life that Americans accept the Court's authority, though many of them may disagree with individual decisions.

Finally, Supreme Court decisions are rarely unanimous. With nine justices, the vote on a given case can be anything from 9-to-0 to 5-to-4. When you turn to *Plessy,* you will first read the majority decision, which prevailed. Then you will see Justice Harlan's minority dissent— an opinion written by a justice who disagrees with the majority or is not persuaded by its reasoning and wants to set the reasons down clearly. *Brown,* in contrast, was decided unanimously.

Sometimes a dissenting opinion in one case forms the basis for a majority decision in another case years later. That is what happened between the *Plessy* decision and the *Brown* case almost fifty years afterward; Justice Harlan's argument against racial segregation was rejected in his lifetime, but in 1954 the Supreme Court found his language persuasive and used it in reversing the *Plessy* decision.

Images and Pictures

Every chapter in this book contains images or pictures—paintings, advertisements, posters, cartoons, or etchings. Images are persuasive. Advertisements, for example, convince us to buy certain food, drink, or clothing or to cultivate a certain appearance; movie and television images attract us by creating heroes, reinforcing our ideas, or catering to our fantasies or our need to escape. Posters and cartoons communicate social and political ideas to vast audiences.

Your experience as a viewer will serve you well in analyzing how the persuasiveness of images works, even when the images are previously unfamiliar to you. For example, you've seen automobile advertisements all your life; you don't have to have lived in the 1950s to get the point of an advertisement for a 1958 car complete with enormous fins and a huge front grill. And when you see an eighteenth-century etching showing a woman confined within the outlines of a compass, you will probably have little difficulty in figuring out that it illustrates the limits of what women are allowed to do. Although pictures from different times are directed to different audiences and your own reaction to those from the past may be different from those of the original viewers, keep in mind that the skill involved in "reading" images is one you practice every time you look at the advertisements in a magazine, on television, or in a movie theater.

Following is a brief rundown of some of the kinds of visual images in this book, as well as some strategies for analyzing and enjoying them.

Photographs, Paintings, and Cartoons   Photographs punctuate news coverage of any number of events. Whether still photos in a newspaper or "live-action video" on a television news program, photographs bring the story to life and capture the event in ways that complement the textual material and sometimes supplant it entirely. They appear to be objective records, yet the photographer selectively "edits" by choosing what is left out of the picture. Photographs are taken from a certain perspective, from a specific point of view; they record, but they also edit; they capture the event, but at the same time they leave out part of the picture and often, the larger context. Photos taken to report the news can move viewers to change their point of view and, in some cases, to change policy; the Pulitzer Prize–winning photographs in Chapter 8 are examples of the persuasive power of photography.

Perhaps it is more common to think of paintings as persuasive even when they capture specific events or appear to be recording a simple moment in time. Like fiction or poetry, students don't often think of paintings as being persuasive. *The Power of Music*, for example (Chapter 7), ostensibly paints a musician with appreciative audiences inside a building and just outside the doorway. But the placement of the figures—the man of African descent outside the door, the white people inside the room; the symmetrical nature of the photo with a clear dividing line between the whites and the black individual, make a poignant observation about insiders and outsiders, about division between the races, and about the power of music to cross that dividing line.

Editorial cartoons make no pretense of objectivity. Often a visual image with a brief text citation, they must capture attention and make a point in only a second or two; to do so, they must evoke immediate recognition and tap into common associations and assumptions. Franklin's woodcut evoking a myth about snakes and the *U.S. Hotel* cartoon, both in Chapter 3, and most of the editorial cartoons in contemporary newspapers tap into cultural references common to rhetor and audience as a kind of short hand for longer arguments. In a sense, they are visual enthymemes, since the audience supplies the missing links in the argument in order to get the point.

Broadsides and Posters   Broadsides and posters are records of events and issues of their times. A broadside, a single sheet printed on one side and meant to be circulated, can inform about current events, argue a point, comment on an issue, or entertain with humorous verse. For example, in the eighteenth century, the hangings of convicted criminals were carried out in public and attracted large audiences. These events were frequently accompanied by broadsides with melodramatic or lurid descriptions of the crime and were sold at the scene of the execution. Their tone was not altogether dissimilar from some of the tabloid newspapers that are so successful today.

Posters developed out of nineteenth-century technology and the need to communicate with a larger audience. They advertised performances and goods, appealed for labor and military recruits, and in time of war and national distress sought to maintain morale and denounce the enemy. Posters were a dominant communication device from the late nineteenth century until the rise of newsreel, radio, and later television. They were still useful, as a quickly and cheaply produced mass medium, but their impact declined as the other media appeared. For posters to persuade (and that was generally their purpose), they had to be able to attract attention and to inform. The audience generally would have been passers-by, so, rather like the political cartoons of today, they had to make their point quickly. Effective posters generally convey a strong impression in a matter of seconds, and a single strong element and strategic use of color, such as a single bold color accent on a muted background, can draw the eye to the core issue or theme in a second. Other elements can be more subtle; in one poster in the Hoover Archives collection, for example, a German poster stressing soldiers' efforts to save women and children of the fatherland includes a small cross hanging around a woman's neck, tapping into the "Christian" identity of the woman and, presumably, her soldier-savior.

In evaluating posters as persuasive discourse, we look to some of the same criteria we use in judging other works of art. While we can't always know the artist's personal beliefs or the extent to which the poster represents mass opinion, we can examine the rhetorical strategies employed by the artist and the themes implicit in the poster. We can assume that the posters were meant to inform or persuade and that the appeals employed by the artist were designed to evoke audience response. We can then make inferences about the intended audience, remembering that we are generalizing from the data the posters provide. We can look to color, placement of objects in the poster, designs, motifs, and themes to analyze their effectiveness.

Advertisements   Like posters, advertisements reveal much about the cultures in which they appear, or at least the dominant culture of the society. Often shortchanging logic in favor of associations and emotional appeals, ads can appear in print or on video, radio, or film; they can be text or image or both; and their arguments can be expected and explicit or unexpected and implicit. Purveyors of products go to great effort to have their products featured in films. Ads have moved to a more explicit form in home videos, where product advertisement often precedes the featured film. And an enormous battle is being waged as schools and school boards have debated whether to accept offers of free television equipment in exchange for a certain amount of advertising included in the television "curriculum." Even a historically advertising-free medium, public television, is offering longer and longer "thanks" to corporate sponsors of their programs.

As in writing about art, posters, and texts, writing about advertisements entails evaluating purpose, appeals, and aesthetics. The purpose is generally evident: the purchase of a product. Much fruitful analysis of advertising focuses on the assumptions, the flaws in logic, and the ethos, pathos, and logos appeals in the ads. Many of the points made earlier about these appeals pertain to advertising. Logical fallacies are rampant. Emotional appeals are often evident but are also often hidden beneath ostensibly logical claims. For example, an advertisement for soup might claim that soups will warm a child up before she runs outside on a cold day; such an ad relies on emotional appeals (warmth, nurturing, home and hearth) more than physiological fact.

Critically assessing the layout, color, and image of advertisements can yield rich information about the persuasive tactics. Often products are strategically placed on the page, or near certain parts of the anatomy of a model; other times, a product (lipstick, beverage) is deliberately presented in a sexually suggestive position. Sometimes the advertiser wants part of the ad to recede into the background. For example, look at some magazine advertisements for cigarettes and try to find the surgeon general's warning. A good way to see where the eye falls in magazine ads is to flip through a magazine and notice which position on the page you see first; then assess what key feature of the product is made prominent and which pushed to the side.

The language of advertising is highly connotative, associative, and image-laden; writers have to convey maximum impact in the fewest words possible. Student writers could indeed learn a lot about conciseness by examining well-written advertisements. The structure of textual arguments in advertising, though, is something to avoid in academic arguments; it is commonly designed to shortchange logic and to get consumers to draw a particular inference (they should buy a certain product) from the limited "data" presented.

There is no getting away from advertising in mainstream American culture. There are different ways of approaching the issue—from economic, sociological, psychological, political, and aesthetic pespectives, to name a few. You may wish to investigate some of these perspectives as you develop longer, documented essays for college courses. Professor Jean Kilbourne, for example, examines damaging attitudes toward and treatment of women in advertisements in the lecture/film *Still Killing Us Softly* that may be available through your college library. For the purposes of this text, we focus on the rhetorical strategies used to persuade the ads' audiences.

Films

We have included a list of movies at the end of each chapter. Film critic Robin Wood says that movies express not only the dreams of the people who make them but the dreams of the audience watching them. No other art form is more wholly or characteristically American. Hollywood became known long ago as the "Dream Factory," and there is no aspect of American life that is not refracted sooner or later through the lens of a camera. Sometimes the result is realistic; sometimes it is more an expression of wish fulfillment or escapism. Sometimes it is insulting; minorities watched movies for generations, looking for images of themselves and seeing nothing or seeing themselves portrayed in stereotypical or debased characterizations. But it would be impossible to imagine American culture in the twentieth century without movies. And every theme in this book has provided and continues to provide material for the vast film audience. Movies are so embedded in our lives that many of the most profound notions Americans have about themselves are as much a result of what they see on the screen as of what they read or learn from experience.

* * *

We can look for common themes among the posters, political cartoons, films, fiction, public essays, and arguments to find the common denominators in the way different media treat particular themes. You can pursue research by looking up particular themes or issues (women in the work force, support on the home front, vilification of the enemy) that interest you and then analyzing treatment of them in the different media. Maybe your library has access to back issues of *Life* magazine, for example. One student researched issues of *Time* magazine from the 1940s, found an article entitled, "How to Tell Your Friends from the Japs," and was able to trace racial stereotypes from posters and cartoons as well as the popular general interest magazines of the times. Other sources for this kind of research include Sam Keen's book, *Faces of the Enemy*, and the film of the same name for a thoughtful look at the ways in which we create an enemy through various media, including posters and cartoons. Another excellent source for propaganda and war-era posters is *Persuasive Images*, by Peter Paret et al. Included in Chapter 8 is an excerpt from Paul Fussell's *Wartime*, "Type-casting," which discusses the stereotypes used in wartime propaganda and advertising. Fussell's essay provides a useful context for an analysis of political posters, cartoons, and advertisements.

Critical Reading and Persuasive Writing

We hope that these suggestions for analyzing persuasive strategies, audiences, cultures, and genres will help you to learn to read diverse arguments critically and to become better thinkers, learners, and writers. While this chapter focuses on critical and analytical skills for reading arguments, Chapter 2 offers suggestions for developing written essays and for integrating research into your arguments. In order to integrate critical reading and persuasive writing, the chapters in Part Two, "Persuasion in the American Tradition," combine critical readings with suggestions for analytical and persuasive writing. Each chapter develops a core thematic issue and links that issue to an important aspect of argumentation, through an introduction that frames the issues, diverse persuasive materials, an end-of-chapter discussion, and assignments that develop your ability to construct your own effective arguments. We hope that the arguments you find included in this book, as well as the suggestions for good writing, will stimulate your imagination, your critical thinking, and your understanding of persuasion in what you read and what you write. Debate in American culture rages on, and we hope you will jump in and become part of our ongoing discussion and debate—part of the American tradition.

WRITING AND
RESEARCH

Developing Essays

Writing an essay is a recursive process: you start with an idea or
something you've wondered about, or you get an idea, maybe from
reading or discussion. You read, review, discuss, perhaps take notes—
and in the process integrate what you are learning with what you already know. Writing is a way of learning; we write to elicit what we
already know and to develop and clarify thoughts and ideas. Writing
essays and other prose forces us to develop, organize, and transmit
clearly our ideas, evidence, and interpretations. Writing is also a way
to record information and demonstrate knowledge. It remains the primary means of disseminating knowledge and information in the academic world, and despite the pervasiveness of visual and audio media,
it remains a crucial means of communication in the rest of society as
well.

There are several different kinds of persuasive writing: reports, exposition, and argumentation. The writing situation—the audience,
purpose, and subject—dictates the form that is needed. This book focuses on argumentation, but we suggest considering persuasion in
communication not as a discrete, separate genre but as a continuum
with varying degrees of argumentative edge.

Along the continuum of persuasion in written discourse, *reports* tend to be the least overtly persuasive. A report writer presents information accurately in a relatively unbiased manner; indeed, the writer's thoroughness and accuracy may in themselves be persuasive of a certain conclusion, but the report itself does not necessarily suggest that conclusion. A lab report is an example of the kind of report writing commonly used in college. In business, people other than the report writer often make decisions based on the report, although some reports also include recommendations.

An *expository essay* is more persuasive; it asserts a point of view and is persuasive insofar as the writer wants to convince readers of the merits of his or her case. The expository or analytical essays most college students write often work in conjunction with other texts and materials; that is, the writer is responding to a text, an idea, a concept, or a situation. Such essays often entail developing a point of view or an assertion about a subject and then supporting that point of view with evidence from personal observation, a literary text, or a prominent theory in the field. Essays analyzing a literary work or a historical event are good examples of the kinds of expository writing commonly practiced in college courses.

An *argumentative essay* clearly attempts to persuade its readers: to identify with the writer, to change their minds, to change their behavior, to adopt or abandon a policy or course of action. The argument rests on assumptions, reasoning, and assertions that one infers or derives from the evidence.

All three kinds of essays can integrate research. We suggest that you consider research a process you undertake whenever the response to a question or the testing of a hypothesis requires that you look beyond your own knowledge and experience for supporting evidence. John Wu, for example, whose essay "Making and Unmaking the 'Model Minority'" appears in Chapter 5, could have written a piece based solely on his own experience. It might have persuaded the reader of the truth of Wu's experience but wouldn't necessarily suggest that the myth is pervasive in American society. Instead, drawing from outside experts and evidence, Wu presents a far more persuasive case. In the sections that follow, we first discuss developing essays that may not require outside research and then outline suggestions for intergrating research.

Techniques for Developing Essays

All forms of writing involve a process of prewriting, writing, and revising. During this process, it may be helpful to use some of the following prompts and questions to help you think about, focus, structure, and develop your paper.

1. **Freewrite.** Start with a focused freewrite, that is, writing without attention to grammar, style, or spelling. Keep pen to page, or fingers to keyboard, and write for five or ten minutes to get started. Do you have some general topic area to think about? Jot down everything you can think of about your topic. Then review your notes and try again with a more focused view of some aspect of the topic that came up in the freewrite. If you don't have an assignment or a specific topic in mind, freewriting can help you figure out what you might find interesting to write about.

2. **Brainstorm.** Write down ideas, images, possible directions—anything that comes to mind about your potential topic—in a line down the page, rather than in the continuous flow of the freewrite. Review your list and try again, focusing on something interesting that came up in the brainstorming.

3. **Do invisible writing.** If you have access to a computer, this exercise may be useful. Turn off the monitor or screen brightness and write continuously without viewing what you are writing. This technique is useful for people who tend to get writer's block or censor their writing and ideas even before they can get the words out.

4. **Review what you have written.** Do you see possibilities to focus on? Do you see connections or angles you didn't think of before? If so, select one of the exercises above—freewriting, brainstorming, or invisible writing—that seemed the most productive for you, and do another session of writing on the focused area you discovered in the exercises. Review the topic and see if it looks promising for further development.

5. **Consider your own biases.** After you have developed a tentative focus, the next couple of exercises may be useful. First, write out all of your biases or preconceived notions about the topic. This is particularly important if you are developing an argumentative researched essay. It is crucial that you conduct your research in an open-minded manner, one that enables you to seek out material and data on both sides of the question. An argument implies an opposition, so take care to look at both sides in your research as well as in your structuring of your argument.

6. **Construct a dialogue between the two sides.** Personify each side of the argument and have the two sides debate the issue. That is, assign a position or a personality to each side, and let them argue for a while, with you writing the script.

7. **Refine your topic and focus.** In a sentence, try to write what the focus and approach of your paper will be. If you can't write it now,

at least narrow your topic to something that seems manageable for the length and depth of the paper assigned.

8. **Try the journalistic method.** After generating some material about your topic, it might be useful to adopt a systematic approach based on the journalistic method, which asks and responds to the following questions: What, who, when, where, why, and how.

   - *What* is happening, or what has happened, in terms of your topic?
   - *Who* (or perhaps *what*) was or is involved in your topic? Who or what does something, or to whom or to what does something happen?
   - *When* did it happen?
   - *Where* did it happen? What is the background of the situation?
   - *Why* did it happen? Why did the agent (Who) cause it to happen? What are the implications of this purpose?
   - *How* was the action or event brought about? What were the means, methods, resources involved?

9. **Break your topic into parts.** After generating yet more information, through prewriting and through research and note taking, think about how you might break down or analyze the parts of your topic. Draft out the major divisions or aspects of your topic on paper or on screen. Don't worry about the form of the outline; just get the major divisions on paper so you can see where your project is going and so that you have a sense of the magnitude and direction of the topic at this stage.

10. **Go back to the question of focus.** Have you determined a tentative, working thesis statement? If not, review your notes, your preliminary thoughts and ideas, and the materials you have developed. Try to understand where they are taking you. What connections can you make? What inferences can you make from your findings? Draft several thesis statements; one or two probably will come close to representing the direction your research is taking you. Also, review the guidelines below on thesis statement.

11. **Consider coherence.** Having listed the major division of your subject area, consider whether all of the parts you have set forth still belong in your paper. Are all parts closely related to the key question of your preliminary focus? If not, will you adapt your thesis or throw out the irrelevant material?

12. **Review your main topic divisions.** Does an order suggest itself? Does there seem to be a best way to present your points to the reader?

13. **Pay attention to contradictions and opposing views.** At what point do they suggest themselves? If you are writing a persuasive essay, opposing views may come up at any time in the process; if they don't come to mind, you'll need to seek them out. Ask yourself questions. Why isn't what I propose already in place? Why wouldn't people want what I am advocating? If you don't consider and deal with opposing views, the reader will certainly be thinking of them, and you will undercut your credibility if you don't concede or refute opposing arguments.

14. **Focus your thesis statement.** Try to write a more focused thesis statement to state the argument or point you want to make (review notes on thesis statements in the introduction).

15. **Write out a plan.** If at this point you see the overall pattern of your paper emerging, take the time now to write a prospectus—a plan that summarizes the purpose, organization, and main points of your paper. If you are not yet ready to do so, answer some of the following questions:

   - Why is the subject important to you or to potential readers? Why have you chosen to write about it, and what do you plan to transmit to others?

   - How much additional reading will you need to do, and where will you go to find the information you need?

   - How much background information do your readers need to understand the significance of your topic or the issues involved?

   - What points will you be making about your topic, and what kinds of evidence will you include?

16. **Consider methods and sources of research.** For researched essays, review the rest of the chapter for advice about taking notes, integrating sources, and documenting sources.

Developing a Core Assertion: The Thesis Statement

Critical readers learn to detect and analyze the main idea in a text. Persuasive writers develop a thesis statement to focus and guide the development of their essays. By *thesis statement,* we mean the core assertion, the main point being argued for and supported. In an expository or informative essay, the thesis statement indicates your limited topic and your approach to that topic; it still asserts a point of view or perspective, but it tends not to have an argumentative edge to it. A thesis statement in a persuasive piece of discourse seeks to argue for a certain position or point of view, not merely informing but pushing for some change in viewpoint or attitude on the part of the audience. An expository thesis statement does not necessarily provoke a response or an argument; a persuasive thesis statement generally does. While readers of informative or explanatory information will want to see the evidence or support that led to the thesis statement, the persuasive essay will also need to respond to counterarguments; the thesis itself will generally be a stronger assertion of a position than the expository thesis statement. Clearly there is overlap between expository and argumentative thesis statements, but the edge of an opinion, statement of belief, or more forceful assertion generally signals to the reader that an argument follows. For example, an essay might include one of the following core assertions.

- "Martin Luther King, Jr.'s 'I Have a Dream' speech was the turning point of the March on Washington."
- "Martin Luther King, Jr.'s 'I Have a Dream' speech confronted white America with its own sorry record on civil rights for black Americans."
- "If America is to support the ideals for which Martin Luther King, Jr., fought, it must do more than pay lip-service to civil rights rulings—it must enforce them."

The first statement could serve as the thesis for an expository essay; it selects and limits a topic and conveys an approach and an attitude toward that topic. The writer may try to convince the reader as to the merits of his case but does not invite counterarguments or try to change attitudes. The second statement also focuses the topic and indicates an approach; in addition, it addresses beliefs and values and engages the reader through value-laden terms (*confronted, sorry*), though it could soften them (i.e., *poor record*) and still argue a point. This sentence invites debate, if not dialogue. The third sentence doesn't argue a point of view or value judgment, as in the second sentence, but it proposes a course of action: enforcing civil rights legislation. Buried within the third statement is the assumption or principle that all Americans should support the values for which King fought.

Many expository thesis statements look something like the first sentence; some arguments about values, beliefs, and principles look like the second; proposals or attempts to move the reader to a specific course of action often look like the third. There are many different variations and types of sentences, and we will examine them throughout this book. Essentially, though, a thesis is an assertion that focuses the topic; it indicates an approach to be followed in the essay or other discourse, and in the case of persuasive and argumentative works, it argues for a position, a belief or value, or a course of action.

A thesis is not a statement of acknowledged fact, or there would be little point in discussion. It is not an effusion of emotion or a matter of taste; those too defy reasoned debate. It is an element that reflects and guides the essay. An essay exists to amplify or prove the thesis; the thesis is an encapsulation of the essay. The two must echo and reinforce each other if the essay is to be coherent, to be linked throughout.

Not all pieces of writing explicitly state a thesis. Some use implication, meaning the audience has to infer, or figure out, from the essay what the point or assertion is. Generally, argumentative essays clearly state a position, but pieces that are less explicitly persuasive often do not. The selection from *The Great Gatsby* in Chapter 6 conveys beliefs and values about work, money, and success in America without overt statement. The etching *Keep Within Compass* in Chapter 5 states its point, though the values and beliefs supporting that point are implied through other text and the artwork.

As you practice writing, you will generally need to develop a clear statement of purpose, focus, approach, or proposal. Not every piece of writing you will ever do will need a clear, explicit thesis statement, but generally college writing (and much out-of-college writing) will require you to state your position or point clearly and then support it with appropriate evidence. When do you devise a thesis statement? That depends. If you have an idea of what you want to assert, even if it is not fully formed or is tentative, write it down, perhaps trying several variations. Often freewriting a bit after you have jotted down several possibilities will help you to discern what it is you are trying to say. If you are exploring a topic—say, an analysis of an argumentative piece—read, discuss, and take notes until you feel ready to develop a working thesis statement. Some students find that a simple outline for a thesis statement can help them focus. While writing down a topic or a phrase is a good start, it is more difficult to get off the fence and state an assertion or proposal. Two outlines that students have found useful are the following:

1. I shall argue that _____ .

This reminds you that you need to assert something, not just throw out a topic, even a narrowed topic, although that is a useful stage in the process before you develop a thesis.

2. Although _____ , I believe/I shall argue that _____
   because _____ .

This outline can guide you by making sure you are looking at potential objections to your argument, that you assert something, and that you have lined up some evidence to support your view.

These are working outlines and need not appear in your essay. In fact, the second outline could produce an exceedingly cumbersome thesis, or at least an inelegant one. But you will be able to decide how explicit to make your thesis statement as you revise, and you will be able to refine the language in revision as well. The Hofstadter selection in Chapter 9 is a superb example of an explicitly stated thesis.

Structuring Arguments

In Chapter 1 we discussed the basic logical approaches of induction and deduction. Reasoning from evidence to conclusion, from examples or specific cases to a conclusion based on those examples, is called *induction* (or, sometimes, *scientific method*). Many of your processes of research and writing entail induction; you generally begin with a question or hypothesis and then investigate it, through reading or other research methods, to confirm or refute it. But in presenting your findings, you will often find it useful to reverse this order, stating your conclusion or thesis and *then* presenting the evidence that led you to draw that conclusion.

Handling Opposing Views   In argumentative essays, you need to deal with your readers' assumptions, views, and expectations. Argument implies another view. Do you meet such alternative or opposing views early on in an argument, to refute or concede? Or do you develop your own case, offering evidence to support your view, before responding to objections and counterarguments? The answer depends on your audience, purpose, and topic. Will your readers want to have certain immediate objections cleared away before they will listen to your case? Or is it more important to establish your main point and supporting arguments first? Will certain alternative views or objections surface only after the readers have considered some of your views or proposals? Will your argument be clearer and more convincing if you end on several strong points?

This last question brings us to the topic of conclusions. In traditional argumentation, the conclusion is the time for a ringing reiteration of your core point or argument—sometimes as a summary, sometimes with an example or a look to the future, sometimes with a reference to the theme or tone established in the introduction. Recent critics have suggested a more collaborative, cooperative approach to argumentation, with the goal not simply a hammering away at the writer's position but a search for common ground and a joint pursuit of knowledge. Such an approach calls for a conclusion that reflects and recognizes the audience's position, reiterates common ground agreed upon or established in the essay, and perhaps acknowledges issues that remain to be resolved.

Choosing a Pattern   A direct pattern calls for the writer to assert and then support. It is often a preferred pattern in academic essays and in writing in the workplace. You assert and then prove, and your reader knows the destination and makes the trip with you. An indirect pattern entails setting out evidence and reasoning first and then deriving a thesis, presented later in the essay, from that evidence. An indirect organization can be preferable when dealing with controversial topics; you want your readers to listen to your evidence and reasons before you assert your main point; if they know where you are headed they may hop off the train at the next stop. Within these overall patterns there are a number of ways to arrange the materials in the body of the essay. Several possible methods are sketched out below.

1. **Chronological order.** This pattern refers to presenting material over time, in a linear manner. It is more common in expository writing, especially in narratives and case histories, than in argumentation, but sometimes within a persuasive essay, such an organization is useful—for example, in presenting a series of events that preceded a current condition or proposal.

2. **Spatial order.** This method uses a physical description—organizing details by the physical layout of a place—in supporting and working with other argumentative strategies. A reformer's description of a tenement, for example, could persuade others to deal with the problems of slums. With such methods of development, the reader must decide whether to lead with such information, or to assert a point and then support with the information.

3. **Increasing order of importance.** This method starts with less-strong assertions and builds up to the strongest ones in order to establish a sense of momentum and emphasize the most important points.

4. **Cause and effect.** This strategy begins with an issue or entity and points to potential effects in the future. The writer needs to take care not to overstate potential effects in order to avoid fallacious reasoning.

5. **Effect and underlying causes.** The writer starts by describing an event or effect and examines underlying causes—why things happened, for example, or what caused particular effects. As with a cause-and-effect strategy, the writer must take care to avoid post

hoc fallacies (after this, therefore because of this) and not to confuse correlation (two things being associated with each other) with causation (one thing causing the other).

6. **Proposal.** In a proposal the writer outlines a problem and proposes a solution. The writer can cite a problem; mention a number of previously proposed solutions, showing why each will not work; and then propose one that, the writer argues, will work. The writer can also outline a proposed course of action, argue why it will work, then sketch out alternative methods that won't work and reiterate the original plan. Other proposals can argue for a specific course of action, arguing why action is needed and then outlining the steps to be taken in chronological order. Objections can be responded to at each stage as they are likely to come up in the reader's mind, or they can be answered all at once after the proposal is sketched out.

Using Organization for Effective Style

Effective organization at the paragraph and sentence level can add to the persuasiveness of your writing. Whether you are dealing with essays, paragraphs, or sentences, first and last elements get the most attention. Thesis statements tend to appear early on or near the end in an essay; bad news in business memos tends to get delayed to the middle paragraph. Topic ideas tend to be stated early on or near the end of paragraphs; the subjects of clauses tend to appear near the beginning of clauses, with important nouns or verbs ending sentences more often than prepositions, articles, or other less important parts of the sentence. Emphasis deals not with correctness but with style; it is not a grammatical rule that writers avoid ending sentences with prepositions but a stylistic one—why waste that important end-of-sentence emphasis on a word that serves to connect rather than denote an object or an action?

Most of the authors in this book make excellent use of the organization and placement of words, sentences, and ideas to emphasize their messages. As you craft your essays in response to the writing suggestions, consider what you have learned from writers whose style you admire, and practice using placement of sentences and words within sentences to achieve the emphasis you desire. For more discussion of language and persuasion, see Chapter 1 and the end of chapter discussion for Chapter 8.

Integrating Research into Writing

College is a community of scholars. The academic community develops and transmits scholarly opinion, research findings, and reports in papers, books, lectures, and, in some cases, computer programs. Being part of that community entails pursuing the ongoing and exciting enterprise known as research. As you begin to research, you take part in worldwide conversations and construction of knowledge. As you see how to integrate research into your writing and writing into your research, you learn to set other ideas and evidence next to your own and to draw connections between them.

A writer who invites other voices into the text must strive to represent their views fairly, to credit them appropriately, and to manage these multiple voices in such a way that she remains the author of this particular paper and the dominant voice in it. The experts can support her, but she must make the core proposal and maintain control of the flow of conversation. She must also take responsibility for everything in the paper and must stand behind her core assertion, her key supporting points, and the evidence she includes.

Researched essays sometimes get a poor reputation for being long, dry exercises in library treasure hunts or fussy documentation styles. To maintain this view is to miss one of the most exciting aspects of the academic community: learning to think, read, write, and contribute as a scholar. As you learn to conduct and carry out research, to use the library, to communicate with other scholars, you claim membership in the community and also equip yourself to become a thoughtful, contributing member of society.

Research activities are complex and recursive processes. As in writing an essay, you start with an idea—maybe from reading or discussion. You discuss, read, review, perhaps take notes, and in the process integrate what you are learning with what you already know. You determine what you know enough about and what you need to learn more about—and that "learning more about" is one of the main reasons you do research. During the process of research, it may be useful to use some of the prompts and questions included in the above "Techniques for Developing Essays" to help you think about, focus, structure, and develop your paper. Generally your process of writing researched essays will entail the steps of prewriting, close reading, note taking, organizing ideas, drafting, and revising.

Before proceeding, it may be useful to look at the role of research in expository and argumentative essays. Remember that they are different parts of a continuum, with exposition developing an assertion that is not highly controversial and argument developing an assertion with an argumentative edge.

Expository essays can be based on your own experience, observations, reflections, interpretations of readings, and the like. They are used to explain, and although they convey a point of view and develop an assertion, their goal is not necessarily to change beliefs or behavior. Sometimes you will research a subject to add credibility to the assertions you make in your expository essay; you will analyze a development, a historical process, the causes of a situation, the potential effects of some event. You might research the history of jazz or different drafts of a novel, or convey the history or the background of some event or issue. Expository essays in the humanities might include materials from the text to support an interpretation; essays in the sciences and social sciences generally incorporate evidence acceptable in their disciplines to support their assertions, whether that evidence is statistics or observations. The point of the evidence is generally to suggest how the assertion or conclusion was obtained and to support the writer's interpretations.

In an *argumentative essay,* you need to be concerned with the skeptical reader who asks, "Who says so?" and "Why should I believe it?" To answer the first question, you bring in reinforcements in the form of expert opinion and testimony to back up any claims. While your voice needs to remain dominant in the essay, the authority of the experts you quote adds their support to your argument. To answer the second question, you turn to evidence—examples, observations, statistics, or whatever other data are respected in the discipline.

An argumentative essay that integrates outside research is still similar to one that does not in that its goal is to persuade people to change their minds—about the ramifications of European settlement of the American continent, or the behavior of an ethnic group toward other Americans, or support of educational or public policy. For example, Susan Faludi's essay in Chapter 5 offers substantial evidence to support her argumentative thesis that there is a backlash against the modest gains American women have made. In deciding the landmark case *Brown* v. *Board of Education,* the Supreme Court used a sociologist's report to help decide the case.

Research has an important place in both expository and argumentative essays, but special caution must be exercised in argumentative essay research. As you browse through potential sources, it may be tempting to fall prey to "selective attention," a situation in which you look for evidence that supports your view and avoid materials that contradict it. Remember that you must consider opposing views; similarly, in researching controversial or argumentative topics, you need to consider material that contradicts your hypothesis or your belief. Such open-mindedness will help you to develop sound scholarly research methods and ultimately will strengthen your paper by demonstrating that you have researched alternatives to your belief or proposal. Dealing with contradictory evidence in your essay will appeal to ethos by ensuring readers that you have a broad background in the topic, that you are not trying to slant the evidence in your favor, and that your argument is strong and well supported enough to withstand contrary evidence. In any case, your readers will already be considering opposing views; your willingness to acknowledge them will only strengthen your case.

Beginning the Process

Begin by selecting the topic and developing a research question. If you have been assigned a topic, determine some aspect of it that interests you and that you can develop fully in the time and space allowed. If you choose your own topic, be guided by your interests but also by the limits of time and paper length; having the freedom to choose a topic often entails a more careful assessment of what you can manage. Additional concerns about topic selection for a documented essay include selecting a subject about which you can find enough materials with the resources available to you; also, since you will likely spend considerable time with your topic, you should find a subject that genuinely engages your interest. Finally, remember your role as a contributing member of the academic community; don't bother researching something that is obvious or a foregone conclusion. And consider researching subjects about which you can truly contribute: legislative research that serves the public interest, for example, or environmental research that can help your community or school make informed decisions about policy.

An underappreciated aspect of research papers, especially in first-year courses, is developing a research question. When you identify a question to which you truly want to find some answers, you are more likely to be interested in your topic and to keep an open mind as you research. For example, "Was the Civil War truly about economic issues?" or "What stereotypes have remained constant through different stages in American history?" are both much more likely to help you focus and develop a topic than if you say to yourself, "Maybe I can write about the Civil War or about prejudice." A research question can guide your research, help you to develop a working thesis, and prevent you from floundering around in a sea of readings, papers, notes, and miscellaneous unfocused ideas.

The next step is to set the schedule. Determine the due dates for your paper and any intermediate due dates for parts of the paper during the research process. Often instructors establish checkpoints by which time you will have established a research question, tentative thesis, preliminary research, a working bibliography, an annotated bibliography, a working outline and revised thesis statement, a draft, peer reviews, a revision. If you have not received such guidelines, make your own, and stick to the schedule. It is too easy to let big projects slide in the face of daily competing demands for your time and interest. The results of waiting too long to start include finding that most of the best sources have been checked out, that you don't have time to do careful research, and that you are fresh out of ideas late in the night before the draft is due.

Finally, consider the audience. With any piece of writing, the audience is crucial in making decisions about the subject and focus of the research essay. If you are writing about literature in a composition class, you are in the position of being a generalist writing to an expert in the field. Your audience knows more about the topic than you do, but you bring with you new insights on the topic and unique responses to the texts you are interpreting. You may also uncover unique connections between sources and new insights in recent critical interpretations. In that same composition class, when you research particular topics of interest that are not literary topics, you will probably become the expert on the topic at hand. You will then have to be particularly aware of your readers' backgrounds and assumptions about your topic.

When you write as an expert to other experts, as you do when you are advancing in your chosen major or discipline, you have the advantage of a common language and a common understanding of the core concepts of the discipline. If you are writing papers for your courses, you will still be writing to specialists who know more than you do in the discipline, but you will have less explaining of terminology to do and can draw on shared assumptions and background knowledge.

Let us say that you are interested in physics or astronomy—in string theory or dark matter in the universe or nanotechnology. Your interest in the topic may carry you through the extensive technical research that will be needed, but if you are writing the essay in response to an open assignment in your writing class, the additional task remains of translating concepts and technical jargon for an audience of writing class peers and instructor. Such a writing situation is not restricted to writing courses; scientists and scholars frequently must translate the concepts of their work either to publish in general periodicals or to write grant proposals to outside funding sources who may be highly educated but unfamiliar with the particulars of the scientist's work.

Gathering Information

In addition to thinking about the functions of research and researched essays in college, you should consider expanding your sense of sources. Probably in high school, you used books and articles as main sources for papers, and these remain excellent choices, but in the

academic community other sources now become necessary and helpful. For example, your college faculty includes experts in various fields
and disciplines; plan to visit these faculty to obtain their expert opinion
on issues related to your research. Faculty are away from time to time,
so plan ahead; call the department and find out who in the field is
knowledgeable about the issue in question. Then ask for that professor's office hours and call to schedule an appointment. Try to read this
person's articles or books before your visit, so that you can ask informed questions and can use the time to best advantage. Experts in
business, schools, and industry are other people you can interview for
information about topics you might be researching. Other members of
the community can help as well. If you are doing oral histories, for example, as Studs Terkel does (Chapter 3), you will be interviewing people to find out their stories or their attitudes about some part of their
lives.

To assemble background information about your topic, ask yourself some questions about what you know. Where did you first learn
about the topic? Do you have class materials or notes? Do you know
people who can serve as resources? And finally, how will you start
your library search strategy?

The first part of your search for information should help you to
develop a brief overview of the topic: important names, dates, and terminology associated with the topic; related subjects and terms to use
for searching for articles; and a list of potential sources for information. After collecting a basic list of core terms and key words, you are
ready to search.

Library Sources   Library sources, both print and other media, will
probably serve as your core materials for research, so it is important to
get to know your library system. You have probably already used reference materials and library books to find information you needed;
you may be less familiar with alternatives—electronic media, for example, including on-line, or networked, researching capabilities and CD-
ROMs, which store large amounts of information and are updated
frequently. Familiarize yourself with such data-gathering resources as
soon as possible, because they will become more and more prominent
in the future. Ask your instructor or a librarian for class or individual
instruction on using them. Some public libraries now have such
sources to search for magazine articles; generally, they are "user
friendly" and entail only punching a few clearly marked buttons.

Materials in the library fall into three categories. *Primary sources*
are original materials, such as interviews, survey data, oral histories,
photographs, posters, advertisements, paintings, and literary works.
What constitutes a primary resource depends on the field and context,

but generally they are the raw data about which others may write or which they may interpret. Examples of primary sources in this book are *Keep within Compass* and the writings of Frederick Douglass. Student writers Judy Ou and John Wu used statistical evidence as a primary source.

Secondary sources are materials written *about* the primary sources: authors describe, interpret, or otherwise integrate primary sources into their writings. Louise Erdrich's story "American Horse" in Chapter 5 is a primary source; a literary analysis of the short story is a secondary source. Paul Fussell uses primary sources to develop his thesis about stereotyping in "Type-casting" in Chapter 8; his essay is then a secondary source analyzing primary sources. A student analyzing propaganda materials could use both primary materials, such as posters, and secondary materials, such as Fussell's essay, to develop an analytical or argumentative essay about techniques of propaganda.

Tertiary sources are third-level materials, such as bibliographies, which list collections of both primary and secondary sources. *The Mexican American: A Selected and Annotated Bibliography* is a tertiary source.

Finding Sources   The sources you need will vary depending on the research stage. Initially, general sources, such as general or specialized encyclopedias, can provide an overview of the topic and identify the core concepts and issues. Encyclopedias range from the general, such as *Encyclopaedia Britannica*, to the specialized, such as encyclopedias of music, religion, social science, and the like. Encyclopedias and specialized dictionaries are shelved in the reference sections of the library, and they generally are listed in online catalogs as well. While you are doing basic general information gathering, look up your topic's key words in the Library of Congress Subject Headings reference guide, which should be available in the reference room as well. As online searches for materials become more and more important in conducting research, it is essential that you have a good working list of key words with which to conduct your searches. For example, people researching Latino studies may need to use key words such as *ethnic identity, Cuban Americans,* or *Puerto Rico—U.S.*

Once you have general background information, you can start digging for additional, more focused materials. Compile a list of selections in books, academic journals, and general interest magazines to help you find more detailed information.

To find books on your topic, consult either the card catalog or whatever on-line computer catalog your institution or local library uses. Start with the list of key words and browse for titles that look interesting. Consider both general and more specific levels of your topic, and pay special attention to any bibliographies or books that indicate that they include bibliographies.

To find articles, search periodical indexes in both print and media forms. You are probably familiar with the *Reader's Guide to Periodical Literature*, but you may not yet have used specialized indexes. Some important ones are the *Humanities Index, Social Science Index, General Science Index, Alternative Press Index, Index to Black Periodicals, Women's Studies Abstracts, Historical Abstracts, MLA Bibliography, PAIS International, Psych Abstracts,* and, for general information, a newspaper index such as *The New York Times Index.*

The electronic media include both general and specific magazine and journal indexes as well as reference sources. Lexis-Nexis, as one example, provides full texts of articles in business, general news, and law. Specialized sources you may have access to include *Bibliography of Native North Americans, EconLit, Psychlit, Art Index,* and the on-line *Oxford English Dictionary,* as well as duplication of print versions of *MLA Bibliography* and *Historical Abstracts.*

In addition to the general reference and research sources already outlined, your library may have some specialized sources for research on American themes. Following are some of the possible categories of specialized references and some examples of the kinds of material you may be able to find to help you investigate your subject.

General Sources for American Themes

American Writers before 1800

American Writers

American Drama Criticism: Interpretations, 1890–1977

MLA International Bibliography

American Humanities Index

The Democracy Reader: Classic and Modern Speeches, Essays, Poems, Declarations, and Documents on Freedom and Human Rights

The Bill of Rights: A Documentary History

Encyclopedia of the American Constitution

Documentary History of the Modern Civil Rights Movement

Slavery in the Courtroom: Annotated Bibliography of Cases

Black Slavery in the Americas

The American Civil Liberties Union: An Annotated Bibliography

Social Reform and Reaction in America: An Annotated Bibliography

Women's Rights Movement in the United States

Encyclopedia of the American Constitution

Index on Censorship

The Anthropology of War: A Bibliography

Encyclopedia of Military History

Peace Research Abstracts Journal

American Public Opinion Index

American Public Opinion Data

Public Opinion, 1935–1946

The Gallup Poll: Public Opinion (annual)

An American Profile: Opinions and Behavior, 1972–1989

Public Opinion Polls and Survey Research: Selective Annotated Bibliography of U.S. Guides and Studies from the 1980s

Statistical Abstracts of the United States (from the U.S. Census Bureau)

Historical Statistics of the United States: Colonial Times to 1970

Social Indicators III: Selected Data and Social Conditions and Trends in the United States

American Statistics Index

The Official Washington Post *Index*

Immigration and Ethnicity: A Guide to Information Sources

Statistical Abstracts of the United States

We the People: An Atlas of America's Ethnic Diversity
America: History and Life

Film Studies

The American Film Industry: A Historical Dictionary

The Film Encyclopedia

Blacks in American Films and Television

The Hispanic Image on the Silver Screen: An Interpretive Filmography from Silents

Contemporary Theatre, Film and Television

Who's Who in American Film

Film Study: An Analytical Bibliography

The New Film Index: A Bibliography of Magazine Articles in English, 1930–1970

Ethnic and Racial Images in American Film and Television: Historical Essays and Bibliography

Blacks in Film and Television: A Pan-African Bibliography of Films, Filmmakers, and Performers

Film Literature Index

New York Times *Film Reviews*

Film Review Index

Index to Critical Reviews

Americans of African Descent

Some key words for searching: Afro-Americans—Race-Identity; Afro-American Press; Afro-Americans—History; Black Power—United States; Civil Rights—United States; School Integration—United States.

The African American Encyclopedia

Dictionary of Afro-American Slavery

Encyclopedia of Black America

Encyclopedia of Southern Culture

Notable Black American Women

Black Women in America

The Harlem Renaissance: A Historical Dictionary

The Negro Almanac: A Reference Work on the Afro-American into Sound, 1898–1935

Women of Color and Southern Women: A Bibliography of Social Science Research

Afro-American Folk Culture

Afro-American History

Afro-American Reference: An Annotated Bibliography of Selected Resources

Black Adolescence: Current Issues and Annotated Bibliography

Black American Writers: Bibliographical Essays

The Black Family in the United States

Black Rhetoric: A Guide to Afro-American Communication

Index to Black Periodicals

Latino Studies

Some key words for searching: Mexican Americans—Ethnic Identity; Hispanic Americans—Ethnic Identity; Cuban Americans; Mexican American Women; Migrant Agricultural Laborers; Puerto Ricans—U.S.

> *Chicano Literature: A Reference Guide*
>
> *Dictionary of Mexican American History*
>
> *Bibliografia Chicana: A Guide to Information Sources*
>
> *A Bibliography of Criticism of Contemporary Chicano Literature*
>
> *Bibliography of Mexican American History*
>
> *Chicano Anthology Index: A Comprehensive Author, Title, and Subject Index to Chicano Anthologies, 1965–1987*
>
> *The Chicana Studies Index: Twenty Years of Gender Research, 1972–1991*
>
> *Latinos in the United States: A Historical Bibliography*
>
> *The Mexican American: A Selected and Annotated Bibliography*
>
> *Mexican American Biographies: A Historical Dictionary*
>
> *Statistical Handbook on US Hispanics*
>
> *The Chicano Index*
>
> *Latin American Studies*

American Indian Studies

The Library of Congress term for the aboriginal peoples of the Western Hemisphere, including the Inuit, is *Indians.* The Western Hemisphere is divided into regions: North America, Mexico, Central America, West Indies, and South America. Works on Indians of a particular region are listed as, for example, *Indians of North America.* Individual tribal names are used as appropriate, such as *Navaho Indians* or *Choctaw Indians.* Other key words include: Western Algonquin Indians; Athapascan Indians; Caddoan Indians; Eskimos; Mound-builders; Ojibwa Indians; Piegan Indians; Shoshoni Indians; Tinne Indians; United States—Civilization—Indian influences

> *Atlas of Ancient America*
>
> *Atlas of the North American Indian*
>
> *A Concise Dictionary of Indian Tribes of North America*
>
> *Dictionary of Daily Life of Indians of the Americas*

Dictionary of the American Indian

Encyclopedia of Native American Religions: An Introduction

Encyclopedia of Native American Tribes

Handbook of the American Frontier: Four Centuries of Indian-White Relationships

Handbook of North American Indians

Native American Almanac: A Portrait of Native America Today

American Indian Women: A Guide to Research

Native American Folklore, 1879–1979; An Annotated Bibliography

Native North Americans: Crime, Conflict, and Criminal Justice: A Research Bibliography

Southwest Native American Arts and Material Culture: A Guide to Research

Bibliography of Native North Americans on Disc (on CD-ROM)

Who Was Who in Native American History: Indians and Non-Indians from Early Contacts Through 1900

Native Women: A Statistical Overview

Reports of the American Indian Family History Project

Statistical Record of Native North Americans

Nations Within a Nation: Historical Statistics of American Indians

Research in Asian American Studies

The Library of Congress uses *Asian American*, but other headings include the following: American Literature—Asian American Authors, Chinese Americans, East Indians, Filipino American, Filipinos in the United States, Hawaiians, Japanese Americans, Korean Americans, Oceanian Americans, Pacific Islander Americans, Vietnamese Americans.

Asian-Americans Information Directory

The Chinese-American Heritage

The Chinese in America, 1920–1973

The Filipinos in America, 1898–1974

The Koreans in America, 1882–1974

Dictionary of Asian American History

Japanese American History: An A to Z Reference from 1868 to the Present

Harvard Encyclopedia of American Ethnic Groups

Refugees in the United States

Asian American Literature: An Annotated Bibliography

The Asian American Media Reference Guide, 2d ed.

Asian American Studies: An Annotated Bibliography and Research Guide

A Comprehensive Bibliography for the Study of American Minorities

Images of Color: A Guide to Media from and for Asian, Black, Latino and Native American Communities

Immigrant Women in the United States: A Selectively Annotated Multidisciplinary Bibliography

Pacific/Asian American Research

A Selected Bibliography on the Asians in America

South Asians in North America: An Annotated and Selected Bibliography (covers 1900–1986)

Biographical Sources

Chinese American Portraits: Personal Histories, 1828–1988

Who's Who Among Asian Americans

Statistical Record of Asian Americans

A number of sources already listed can also be good sources for information on Asian Americans.

Focusing the Search

Once you have found a general overview of your subject and a list of potential sources, deepen your search for materials. Many of the general and bibliographical sources are in the reference area of your library; your next step will probably be to collect some important books and periodical articles in the field.

In some fields, books will be your most important sources; a scholarly book has the advantage of being an in-depth examination of some issue or element in the field. A periodical, on the other hand, by virtue of the recurrent issuing of the material, offers less in-depth but more current information.

Books are generally spread out through the library storage system in what are commonly called *stacks*. Sometimes the stacks are closed, and you need to request books you want from the circulation desk. If stacks at your library are open, you can browse the shelves in your subject area. If the book you tracked down in a bibliography isn't available, perhaps another interesting book is. Or perhaps other nearby books on the shelves look helpful. You should plan on taking some time in the stacks and perusing tables of contents, introductory chapters, and bibliographies of books in the area of your topic.

Working with Sources

As you assemble general, preliminary, and increasingly specialized sources, you will need to keep track of your materials, both the original sources and your notes on them. Few experiences in academia are more frustrating than finding an excellent piece of information or an idea and then losing track of where you located it. Different writers approach notes and note taking in different ways.

First, you have to determine what you are looking for when you read sources. In addition to keeping in mind the general advice offered in Chapter 1 for reading critically, pay special attention to the following questions when critiquing sources:

1. What is the theme? What is the author's purpose in writing? Who are the intended audiences? What are the author's assumptions? Do you share those assumptions? Do the author's assumptions or emphasis indicate bias?

2. What is the overall idea the author develops? What is the primary organizing plan (cause-effect, problem-solution, definition, process)?

3. Is the evidence presented clearly? Is it persuasive? Do the author's conclusions logically follow from the evidence?

4. How does the selection connect with other readings? Does it provide information on other sources? Does it provide an example of a point made in another source? Does it contradict another source? Are there points of comparison or contrast with another source? What common threads run through the sources?

Taking Notes   As a fellow scholar in the academic community, you are expected not to take your sources at face value but to challenge and question them, to assess the merit of their arguments and the logic of their conclusions critically.

Be an active, assertive reader. Question information as you read it; argue with the text. If you own the book or you are using photocopies, make extensive marginal notes. Otherwise, use notecards, computer "notecards" (such as HyperCard files on a Macintosh), or notepaper to keep track of your information. Try to use a medium for taking notes that allows you to sort the notes by topic as you collect more information.

As you take notes, write down not only the information itself but key words, phrases, reactions to points the author makes, critical arguments and comments, and reactions you may have. *But take great care to keep track of exactly what information comes from the sources and which comments are your own reflections on the source.* When information or ideas appear in a number of sources (usually three or more), most writers will consider it common knowledge in the field and will not document the source. Until you have researched enough to know what will need citing, however, you should keep track of the sources in your notes.

There are three different types of notes we generally use to record our research of sources: summaries, paraphrase, and direct quotation. *Summaries* of information from the source help you to make sure you have digested the material and help you to translate the information into your own words. They pull out the key ideas of a source. *Paraphrases* are a kind of running commentary or translation of the original source; they capture essentially all of the material in the original. Paraphrase is a frequent suspect in plagiarism, the unacknowledged use of the ideas or phrases of others. The difference between summary and paraphrase can be seen in the following example, based on an excerpt from "The Gettysburg Address."

Original

Fourscore and seven years ago our fathers brought forth on this continent a new nation, conceived in liberty and dedicated to the proposition that all men are created equal.

Now we are engaged in a great civil war, testing whether that nation, or any nation so conceived and so dedicated, can long endure. We are met on a great battlefield of that war. We have come to dedicate a portion of that field, as a final resting place for those who here gave their lives that the nation might live. It is altogether fitting and proper that we should do this.

Summary

Eighty-seven years ago a country was founded on the principles of freedom and equality. We are now involved in a war that will test whether the nation and those principles will survive. Appropriately, we gather on a battlefield of that war to dedicate a cemetery for those who died here fighting for the nation's survival, and it is appropriate to do so.

Paraphrase

Eighty-seven years ago the founding fathers created on the American continent a new country, born in freedom and committed to the ideal that everyone is created equal.

We are now involved in a large-scale civil war that will determine if a nation with such ideals and such a purpose can last. We meet at the site of one of the great battles of that war and we are here to dedicate part of the battlefield as a cemetery for those who died here to save the nation. It is appropriate that we do so.

Direct quotations *must* be taken down exactly as written and put inside quotation marks. They should be saved for those occasions when the quotation so perfectly captures a concept, idea, or image that it would require a great deal more time and space to say the same thing that would have much less impact. They, too, need to be carefully documented. Sometimes you can summarize an author's point and then put key or specialized words into quotations. If you use only parts of a quotation by an author, be sure to use ellipses—three spaced dots—to indicate that you have left material out; be careful not to change the author's intended meaning. For a quotation within a quotation, use single quotation marks; if the author quotes someone else you want to quote directly, your citation would say, for example, "(Pritchard, qtd. in Garcia 32)." Keep careful track of who says what in your sources so that you can quote accurately.

Avoiding Plagiarism   Plagiarism is the unacknowledged use of the ideas or words of others. Whether accidental or intentional, plagiarism is a serious offense. To avoid plagiarism, some general guidelines should be followed.

Cite your sources in the following cases: an original idea from a source, whether you summarize it, paraphrase it, or quote it directly; factual information that is not common knowledge; any exact wording or unique phrasing taken from a source.

There is no need to cite when material is considered common knowledge; that is, it appears in a number of sources or can be verified by agreed-on measurement or criteria. How many sources must it appear in? Some scholars suggest a minimum of three sources; others say five. We have found that if the material is general background information and occurs in three sources or more, it can safely be considered common knowledge. But if you are writing about some scientific findings and it is relevant that a number of scientists duplicated certain results, then you would be better off citing even a large number of studies, since the confirmation of some findings by others is crucial to the information's credibility. Again, you need to develop judgment about audience, purpose, and subject as you make such decisions. Too many citations can interrupt the flow of your paper or give the impression that the sources' voices are taking over your paper, but when in doubt, it is better to cite rather than not.

Plagiarism is essentially the passing off of the ideas or words of others as your own. Keep in mind the spirit of the law and you will be guided by it as you make specific decisions about particular pieces of information in your essay.

Writing Drafts

As you collect information, review notes, and sift through ideas and evidence, connections should begin to form in your mind, and responses to your initial research question begin to suggest themselves. You can foster this process by reviewing notes as you collect new information, determining where the new sources fit with the material you already know. Take time at regular intervals to freewrite about your topic, either in a journal or in scheduled bursts of freewriting at the computer after a research session.

Some writers find it helpful to take notes from different sources and then begin to sort them by subtopic; or go back to their research question and divide the question into smaller questions; or review the working hypothesis, refine it, and divide it into categories. For example, a paper on the myth of the model minority could focus on the family ethos of work, the glass ceiling in corporations, the different patterns of immigration from Asia, the relative economic and educational status of each group, and so on. Sometimes a diagram or flowchart helps, with lines and circles connecting various parts of the material. Whatever your method, try to begin lining up the general elements of the material.

Consider the kinds of supporting assertions you can make based on your evidence; review your tentative thesis or hypothesis and refine it if needed based on your findings. Review your supporting assertions in the light of your refined thesis. Those supporting assertions can become your topic ideas. Line up those supporting assertions in the order in which your reader needs to hear them and in an order that links up one point to the next. Then draft a working outline based on the assertions you have identified and work through the material to find the support for your assertions and write a rough draft. At this stage, you are primarily interested in getting the basic structure down. While you should keep track of where your information is coming from, don't worry too much about the specifics of documentation or style: "(Smith 21)" or "(Smith teaching article p. 21)" in some form is sufficient at this stage, but try to keep track of article and page number. Checking spelling and worrying about specifics of grammar are tasks for a later stage of writing. Just get your core argument down. Save your file often if you are working on the computer! If you are writing out or typing your draft, photocopy it as you write large parts of it to guard against losing your work.

Revising the Draft

After you get the basic structure of the rough draft down, review the logic of your assertions. Determine whether they still support the thesis and whether the thesis still allows you to engage the parts of your topic that you want to cover. Thesis and support must remain connected and mutually reinforcing. Review your draft and determine if you need more evidence or if you should cut out parts that don't seem relevant. Peer feedback at this stage can be useful. Exchange drafts with a classmate and try to give each other "big picture" feedback on the thesis, basic structure, and supporting evidence. Then revise your essay as needed to attend to criticism from your peer. Remember, though, that as the author, you have the final decision over changes you make. Accept feedback, but use your own judgment in deciding how much and what kind of advice to take.

You should certainly spell-check your paper if you are using a computer to write it, but such tools do not find all the errors and lapses in good style that your draft may have. Peer feedback is also helpful for detecting errors that you may not find, since at this point in the draft your eyes may see what they expect to see (or want to see) rather than what is on the page. You and a peer should both go over your paper in fine detail, attending to issues of style, appropriateness of language, level of diction, proper syntax, and correct documentation style.

Documentation

When you converse in the academic community, you generally need to use the conventions of the various disciplines to communicate ideas and research findings. As you begin to think of yourself as a part of the scholarly community, you will see how citation forms work as a kind of shorthand that permits scholars to share their findings with others in the national and international academic communities and helps those scholars follow up on each other's work. The cooperative nature of research may help to explain the very specific formats used in different disciplines. In the social sciences, for example, the date of a research study is crucial, so the American Psychological Association (APA) format puts the date right after the author's name. In humanities fields, on the other hand, where the date of the findings is less important, the Modern Language Association (MLA) format for in-text citations contains a name or book title and page number. In the "Works Cited" list as well, the date comes last.

You may have been instructed to use a particular documentation style. Your instructor may provide guidance, or you can use a style book. Both MLA and APA have style books. Some examples of style manuals in other disciplines include *Council of Biology Editors Style Manual: A Guide for Authors, Editors, and Publishers; A Manual for Authors of Mathematical Papers;* and *Style Manual for Guidance in the Preparation of Papers.*

Most composition courses suggest following either the MLA or APA style. If you have a choice and you know you are interested in humanities or social science, you may want to start using the format you are likely to use in future classes and to buy the appropriate manual. Following are the general guidelines for documenting your essays and citing your sources.

How to Document   Most disciplines are moving toward parenthetical within-text citation, and that is the style we will use here. In APA style, supply the last name of the author(s) and the year of publication: (Garcia & Collins, 1988). In MLA style, if you are referring to a work by an author, cite the author's name and a page number: (Garcia 38). Note that in MLA style you don't need a comma or "p." to indicate page number. If Garcia's name or book or article title is implied in the context, you can simply use the page number (38) as the reference. If you are citing two works by Garcia, you can use a brief title of the work (Messages 28) to indicate to the reader which work this particular quotation comes from. Look at the documented student essays in this book for samples; both John Wu (Chapter 5) and Jody Ou (Chapter 6) documented their essays in correct MLA style. If you have substantive notes or "asides" to the reader, you can include those as footnotes or endnotes. If you use endnotes, place them at the end of the paper, but before your list of references.

References/Works Cited   Within the general guidelines for documentation, there are specific forms that should be followed for different types of sources. A "Works Cited" list is now commonly used with MLA style; it contains only the references actually cited in the paper. The APA style uses a "References" list with all relevant readings that may have influenced the paper.

Sample Documentation   The following lists provide samples of common works that you will use. Note that underlining may be substituted for italics if you are writing by hand or on a typewriter.

A book by one author

> *MLA:* Sowell, Thomas. *Ethnic America.* New York: Basic Books, 1981.
>
> *APA:* Sowell, T. (1981). *Ethnic America.* New York: Basic Books.

A book by two authors

> *MLA:* Neesom, Lisa, and George Madera. *Early American Art.* Englewood Cliffs, N.J.: Prentice-Hall, 1955.
>
> *APA:* Neesom, M., and Madera, G. (1955). *Early American art.* Englewood Cliffs, N.J.: Prentice-Hall.

A book by three authors

> *MLA:* Lewis, Peter, A. J. McGee, and Martin Washington. *American Folk Art.* 3rd ed. New York: McGraw-Hill, 1993.
>
> *APA:* Lewis, P., McGee, A. J., & Washington, M. (1993). *American folk art* (3rd ed.). New York: McGraw-Hill.

A book with more than three authors

> *MLA:* Isselbacher, Kurt J., et al. *Harrison's Principles of Internal Medicine.* 9th ed. New York: McGraw-Hill, 1980.
>
> *APA:* Isselbacher, K.J., Adams, D. A., Braunwald, E., Petersdorf, R. G., Wilson, J. D. (1980). *Harrison's Principles of internal medicine* (9th ed.) New York: McGraw-Hill.

The edited work of an author

> *MLA:* Hawthorne, Nathaniel. *The Portable Hawthorne.* Ed. Malcolm Cowley. New York: Viking, 1969.
>
> *APA:* Hawthorne, N. (1969). *The portable Hawthorne.* (M. Cowley, Ed.). New York: Viking Press.

A work in an anthology

> *MLA:* Hawthorne, Nathaniel. "Young Goodman Brown." *Heritage of American Literature, Volume 1.* Ed. James E. Miller, Jr., with Kathleen Farley. New York: Harcourt Brace, 1991. 1413–1421.
>
> *APA:* Hawthorne, N. (1991). Young Goodman Brown. In J. E. Miller, Jr. (Ed.), *Heritage of American literature, volume 1* (pp. 1413–1421). New York: Harcourt Brace.

A work in translation

> *MLA:* Pushkin, Aleksander. *Eugene Onegin,* 4 vols. Trans. Vladimir Nabokov. New York: Bollingen Foundation, 1964.

APA: Pushkin, A. (1964). *Eugene Onegin* (Vols. 1–4). (V. Nabokov, Trans.). New York: Bollingen Foundation

An article in a journal with separate pagination for each issue

MLA: Budd, Matthew A. "Human Suffering: Road to Illness or Gateway to Learning?" *Advances: The Journal of Mind-Body Health* 3 (Summer 1993): 28–35.

APA: Budd, M. A. (1993, Summer). Human suffering: Road to illness or gateway to learning? *Advances: The Journal of Mind-Body Health.* 28–35.

An article in a journal with continuous pagination

MLA: Frey, Olivia. "Beyond Literary Darwinism: Women's Voices and Critical Discourse." *College English* 52 (1990): 507–26.

APA: Frey, O. (1990). Beyond literary Darwinism: Women's voices and critical discourse. *College English 52,* 507–526.

An unsigned newspaper article or editorial

MLA: "Small Companies Earn Big Honors." *San Francisco Examiner* 20 May 1994: B-1.

APA: Small companies earn big honors. (1994, May 20). *San Francisco Examiner,* p. B-1.

A signed newspaper article or editorial

MLA: Ulrich, Allan. "Variations on a Gould-en Theme." *San Francisco Examiner* 20 May 1994: C-1.

APA: Ulrich. A. (1994, May 20). Variations on a Gould-en theme. *San Francisco Examiner,* p. C-1.

A public document:

MLA: United States Department of Health and Human Services, Administration for Children, Youth and Families, Children's Bureau. *Child Welfare Strategies in the Coming Years.* Washington: Office of Human Development Services, 1978.

APA: United States Department of Health and Human Services, Administration for Children, Youth and Families, Children's Bureau. (1978). *Child welfare strategies in the coming years.* Washington: Office of Human Development Services.

A film

> *MLA:* Kramer, Stanley, dir. *Judgment at Nuremberg.* United
> Artists, 1961.
> *APA:* Kramer, S. (Director). (1961). *Judgment at Nuremberg*
> [Film]. United Artists.

A lecture

> *MLA:* Rebholz, Ronald. "Shakespeare and the Power of an
> Idea." Centennial Lecture Series, Stanford U, 23 Sept.
> 1991.
> *APA:* Rebholz, Ronald. (1991, September). *Shakespeare and the*
> *power of an idea.* Lecture presented at the Centennial Lec-
> ture Series, Stanford University.

An interview

> *MLA:* Garcia, Juana. Personal interview. 3 Dec. 1993.
> *APA:* Garcia, J. (1993, December 3). (Interview).

A computer program

> *MLA:* Watters, Ann. *The Art of Persuasion.* Vers. 1.0. Computer
> software. Focus Interactive, 1995. Macintosh, CD-ROM.
> *APA:* Watters, A. (1995). *The art of persuasion* [computer soft-
> ware]. Menlo Park, CA: Focus Interactive. (Macintosh,
> CD-ROM)

Legal Cases

> Plessy v. Ferguson, 163 U.S. 537 (1896).

(Note: both the MLA and APA follow the style set forth in *A Uniform*
System of Citation, 15th edition, published by the Harvard Law Review
Association in 1991.)

Part Two

Argument in the
American Tradition

CHAPTER

3

IDENTITIES

Whom do you visualize when you hear the term *"American"*? Do you identify a specific gender, race, occupation, or age that you consider typical? Do you see a white male banker? An American Indian high school student? A family of migrant farmers? A Chinese American factory worker? All of these people can be American citizens, of course, but is there one that seems *more* American to you than the others?

America is a confluence of cultures: American Indians who have lived here for millennia; European and Asian immigrants who came here in search of a better life; people of African descent brought by force. Over time, these cultures have mingled and evolved into something new and recognizably American. How do all of these disparate identities come together to form an American identity?

In understanding American identities, we need to come to terms with unity and division, with separateness and common ground. The question, What do we mean by "American"? encompasses a host of related questions: Is there a distinctly American identity? Is there one overriding, generalized American culture? Or are there only disparate subcultures that form strategic alliances for survival? Should we retain the old metaphor of the melting pot, into which various cultures are tossed, melted down, and pulled out as generic Americans? If so, what are the characteristics of that generic American? If we reject the metaphor of the melting pot, what should we use as a more fitting metaphor: A mosaic? A puzzle?

Identity has always been a difficult question nagging the collective American mind. We wonder how much we have in common besides

69

living in the same country. We argue about a common culture, a shared set of values—whether there is one, whether we should try to hobble one together, whether we should try to revise one that has been thrust upon us or simply evolved. We debate whether it is more important for Americans of a particular ethnic, racial, or cultural heritage to celebrate that history or to feel part of mainstream America—or whether both can coexist.

The question of who or what is an American is clearly important on a personal level as each of us comes to terms with who we are. But it is also a pressing political issue because citizenship, government entitlements, voting rights, job protection, civil liberties, and every other advantage or opportunity that America offers depend ultimately upon whether a person is considered a true American.

American Identities through History

As long as there has been an America, Americans have wondered and argued about who they were. The dominant issues and topics have shifted over time, but the same concerns have surfaced time and time again. All of the authors in this chapter have taken part in the debate about Americans and American identities, about individuality and cohesion, on both personal and political levels.

One of the first issues was whether there was—or could be—a unified American identity at all. Before the American Revolution, European settlers typically thought of themselves as residents of their own colonies and subjects of European monarchs, not as part of a unified new nation. In the 1750s, however, with the French and Indian War looming, Benjamin Franklin and others began calling for a union of the colonies for mutual protection. Franklin's lithograph *Join or Die* is a graphic representation of the advantages of such unity: self-preservation rather than destruction.

After the Revolution, when political unity had been established, observers began offering assessments of the American character and culture, based almost exclusively on the Anglo Americans of the northeast and eastern seaboard. Alexis de Tocqueville attempts to define the American character by describing the political and social history of its most dominant group, and he identifies that group as English settlers, especially in New England. The approach that he takes—seeing the English character as the origin of true American culture—is one that almost all succeeding writers have had to address.

Although de Tocqueville and other historians at the time focused on the British ancestry of mainstream America, many other cultures were contributing to the American identity. Over the course of the nineteenth century, the American population became more and more

diverse: Irish fleeing famine; Jews and Catholics fleeing religious persecution; Italians, Swedes, Chinese, Russians, and others seeking jobs
and opportunities. How were all these people—whose looks, languages, and actions were generally quite different from the dominant
Anglo culture—to be incorporated into the American identity?

These immigrants generally favored assimilation. After arriving in
America, each group found itself faced with further hardship and discrimination because they were so easily identified as "foreign." Their
desire to succeed became a desire to escape the unwanted attention of
other groups, to merge with mainstream American culture. The dominant ideal became that of the melting pot, with foreign differences
melted away and identical Americans rolling off the assembly line.

At one time or another, every foreign element or influence associated with new immigrants was considered suspect. The artist who created *The U.S. Hotel* cartoon clearly wanted to preserve America for
Americans—that is, for the people who were already here and the few
newcomers who would completely accept those established cultural
values. At other times, especially when America was faced with an
outside enemy, all Americans were considered acceptable, regardless
of their heritage. The divisiveness of *The U.S. Hotel* is completely absent from the propagandistic posters from World War I, which
proudly presented a diverse but united America.

One name often missing even from a picture of multicultural
America is a recognizable American Indian. European immigrant
groups were not, of course, writing their history on a blank page. For
countless generations, American Indians had identified themselves
with the American land. Luther Standing Bear articulates the argument
that the true American is the Indian, identified with the essence of the
American continent. Another group struggling in the early twentieth
century to be recognized as full-fledged Americans were African
Americans. Because the American identity had always been defined in
terms of whites, African Americans were, as Ralph Ellison pointed out,
invisible. In the Prologue to *Invisible Man,* Ellison uses the metaphor of
invisibility to explore how the prevailing definition of "American" has
kept some groups dominant and others excluded.

By the mid twentieth century, the melting pot ideal was falling
into disfavor. Clearly, not all Americans had been accounted for, and
those who had been were beginning to challenge the value of assimilation. Critic Kenneth Burke suggests, "If men were not apart from one
another, there would be no need for the rhetorician to proclaim their
unity." John F. Kennedy, elected president in 1960, sought to unite the
divided nation by proclaiming its unity. In his inaugural address, he
defines a new American identity based on the nation's role in the international scene and its presumed unity of purpose.

In recent decades, many writers have focused on forging a coherent personal identity as Americans living within—and sometimes living as examples of—a cultural mosaic. In "Split at the Root," Adrienne Rich attempts to piece together an identity from seemingly disparate elements: a gentile, Jewish, Southern, lesbian mother in America. In her poem "Fire," Joy Harjo explores the very idea of personal identity and provides some clues as to what constitutes her identity as an American Indian woman. Playwright Frank Chin, as presented in Studs Terkel's oral history, struggles to provide a definition of his chosen identity as "an American of Chinese descent" and examines the subtle interplay among nondominant cultures in America. In "Chicana," the chapter's final selection, student writer Martha Serrano argues for her right to define her own identity, choosing a label that accurately reflects her heritage.

Creating Identity through Definition

Each exploration of American identity in this chapter is based on a definition of who an American is. A definition clarifies what something is and sets that something apart from all similar things. Good definitions are essential to good argumentation. Any argument should rest on a common understanding of what the issues are and how the relevant terms are being used. (For an argument about immigration, what is meant by the term "recent immigrant"? For an argument about cultural assimilation, what is meant by the term "mainstream American culture"?) If people arguing these topics cannot agree on definitions of the issues and terms, miscommunication and misunderstanding will result.

Sometimes those participating in a debate find it impossible to agree on definitions. Then the argument turns to one about the proper definition of a term. (Are only native-born citizens "real Americans"? What do we mean by "American"?) The authors in this chapter strive to be clear and persuasive in defining what an American is. The discussion of definition and methods of definition at the end of this chapter will help you make use of the appropriate argumentative strategies in your own writing.

As you read and reflect on the selections that follow, consider not only your own personal identity and cultural origins but also the social and political implications of your identity and that of others as you begin to take part in the obligations and privileges of citizenship: open debate, difference of opinion, and the need to take a stand on important issues. Ask yourself the questions that the readings pose: Who is an American? Who is entitled to what America has to offer? What are our common bonds, our goals, our ethics and beliefs as a society?

JOIN, OR DIE

1 7 5 4

Benjamin Franklin

Benjamin Franklin (1706–1790), American statesman, author, printer, inventor, was apprenticed at age twelve to his brother, a printer, and in 1723 went to Philadelphia, where he eventually set up his own paper and published Poor Richard's Almanack. *Franklin was active throughout the American Revolution and was a signer of the Declaration of Independence. "Join, or Die," considered the first American cartoon, was Franklin's contribution to the debate about unity among the colonies as the French and Indian War approached. Franklin was the delegate from Pennsylvania as seven colonies sent representatives to negotiate with the Iroquois Nation, but his argument for a union of colonies with "one general government" for common defense would serve in other crises as well. To make his point, Franklin draws upon a myth that is familiar to his audience: a cut-up snake that is reassembled before sundown will come back to life.*

For Journals

Some created images, such as the American flag or the Statue of Liberty, evoke a sense of America for many people. What images from nature, whether plant or animal, embody your sense of America?

For Discussion

1.   What is the primary argument of the cartoon? What does Franklin want the audience to do? Why?

2.   Woodcuts with a moral or lesson in text below a visual image date back centuries. What are some advantages of making an argument in both text and image? What audiences can an author hope to reach in this way?

3.   What are some of the advantages of visual argument over text, especially a simple design, as in this cartoon? Consider your own responses to other visual images, such as cartoons and advertisements, as well as the response you would expect of Franklin's contemporaries.

4.   Mid–twentieth century audiences may find the image of a snake threatening or disturbing, but what of the largely agrarian American population of the mid–eighteenth century? Do you suspect they had a similar response? Why might Franklin have wanted to identify the united colonies as a dangerous creature? Consider the use of other, similar slogans in early U.S. history, such as "don't tread on me," frequently accompanying an image of a coiled snake.

5.   If a separated snake can unite its parts before sundown and survive, to what symbolic, political sundown is Franklin drawing an analogy?

6.   What identity does Franklin foresee for the colonies? In what ways is this identity a precursor to other identities for America?

For Writing

1.   Look through some newspapers, especially in the editorial pages, and select a political cartoon dealing with some aspect of American identity (foreign policy or immigration, for example). Analyze the allusions or references in the cartoon that readers need to know in order to understand the point of it. Will audiences fifty, one hundred, or two hundred years from now understand the cartoon you have selected? Explain your answer.

2.   Research some aspect of American history or politics at the turn of this century by looking at cartoons from the era—during an election, for example. You could review old newspapers or look at a cartoon

collection at the library. Alternatively, browse through old newspapers or magazines and see what you can infer about the social or political debates of the times. To what extent do you understand the allusions or jokes? Why do you think this is so? Write up your findings in an analytical essay; if possible, include photocopies of the cartoons you analyze.

ORIGIN OF THE ANGLO-AMERICANS
1 8 3 9

Alexis de Tocqueville

 Count Alexis [Charles Henri Maurice Clerel] de Tocqueville (1805–1859), magistrate and political observer, held a number of positions in the French government. His observations of and writings on the workings of democracy in the United States, based on an extended visit to America, comprise the well-known work Democracy in America *(*Democratie en Amerique*), from which the following selection is excerpted. Written between 1835 and 1839, this work is considered a landmark study of American institutions and is often quoted to this day. It is valuable in studying both historical and contemporary aspects of American cultures.*

 After the birth of a human being, his early years are obscurely spent in the toils or pleasures of childhood. As he grows up, the world receives him, when his manhood begins, and he enters into contact with his fellows. He is then studied for the first time, and it is imagined that the germ of the vices and the virtues of his maturer years is then formed. This, if I am not mistaken, is a great error. We must begin higher up; we must watch the infant in his mother's arms; we must see the first images which the external world casts upon the dark mirror of his mind, the first occurrences which he witnesses; we must hear the first words which awaken the sleeping powers of thought, and stand by his earliest efforts,—if we would understand the prejudices, the habits, and the passions which will rule his life. The entire man is, so to speak, to be seen in the cradle of the child.

 The growth of nations presents something analogous to this; they all bear some marks of their origin. The circumstances which accompanied their birth and contributed to their development affect the whole term of their being. If we were able to go back to the elements of states, and to examine the oldest monuments of their history, I doubt not that we should discover in them the primal cause of the prejudices, the habits, the ruling passions, and, in short, of all that constitutes what is called the national character. We should there find the explanation of certain customs which now seem at variance with the prevailing manners; of such laws as conflict with established principles; and of such incoherent opinions as are here and there to be met with in society, like those fragments of broken chains which we sometimes see hanging from the vaults of an old edifice, and supporting nothing. This might explain the destinies of certain nations which seem borne on by an unknown force to ends of which they themselves are ignorant. But hitherto facts have been wanting to researches of this kind: the spirit of inquiry has only come upon communities in their latter days; and when they at length contemplated their origin, time had already obscured it, or ignorance and pride adorned it with truth-concealing fables.

America is the only country in which it has been possible to witness the natural and tranquil growth of society, and where the influence exercised on the future condition of states by their origin is clearly distinguishable. . . . America, consequently, exhibits in the broad light of day the phenomena which the ignorance or rudeness of earlier ages conceals from our researches. Near enough to the time when the states of America were founded, to be accurately acquainted with their elements, and sufficiently removed from that period to judge of some of their results, the men of our own day seem destined to see further than their predecessors into the series of human events. Providence has given us a torch which our forefathers did not possess, and has allowed us to discern fundamental causes in the history of the world which the obscurity of the past concealed from them. If we carefully examine the social and political state of America, after having studied its history, we shall remain perfectly convinced that not an opinion, not a custom, not a law, I may even say not an event, is upon record which the origin of that people will not explain. The readers of this book will find in the present chapter the germ of all that is to follow, and the key to almost the whole work.

The emigrants who came at different periods to occupy the territory now covered by the American Union differed from each other in many respects; their aim was not the same, and they governed themselves on different principles. These men had, however, certain features in common, and they were all placed in an analogous situation. The tie of language is, perhaps, the strongest and the most durable that can unite mankind. All the emigrants spoke the same tongue; they were all offsets from the same people. Born in a country which had been agitated for centuries by the struggles of faction, and in which all parties had been obliged in their turn to place themselves under the protection of the laws, their political education had been perfected in this rude school; and they were more conversant with the notions of right, and the principles of true freedom, than the greater part of their European contemporaries. At the period of the first emigrations, the township system, that fruitful germ of free institutions, was deeply rooted in the habits of the English; and with it the doctrine of the sovereignty of the people had been introduced into the bosom of the monarchy of the house of Tudor. . . .

Another remark, to which we shall hereafter have occasion to recur, is applicable not only to the English, but to . . . all the Europeans who successively established themselves in the New World. All these European colonies contained the elements, if not the development, of a complete democracy. Two causes led to this result. It may be said generally, that on leaving the mother country the emigrants had, in general, no notion of superiority one over another. The happy and the powerful do not go into exile, and there are no surer guaranties of equality among men than poverty and misfortune. It happened, however, on several occasions, that persons of rank were driven to America by political and religious quarrels. Laws were made to establish a gradation of ranks; but it was soon found that the soil of America was opposed to a territorial aristocracy. To bring that refractory land into cultivation, the constant and interested exertions of the owner himself were necessary; and when the ground was prepared, its produce was found to be insufficent to enrich a proprietor and a farmer at the same time. This land was then naturally broken up into small portions, which the proprietor cultivated for himself. Land is the basis of an aristocracy, which clings to the soil that supports it; for it is not by privileges alone, nor by birth, but by landed property handed down from generation to generation, that an aristocracy is constituted. A nation may present immense fortunes and extreme wretchedness; but unless those fortunes are territorial, there is no true aristocracy, but simply the class of the rich and that of the poor.

All the British colonies had then a great degree of family likeness at the epoch of their settlement. All of them, from their beginning, seemed destined to witness the growth, not of the aristocratic liberty of their mother country, but of that freedom of the middle and lower orders of which the history of the world had as yet furnished no complete example. In this general uniformity, however, several striking differences were discernible, which it is necessary to point out. Two branches may be distinguished in the great Anglo-American family, which have hitherto grown up without entirely commingling; the one in the South, the other in the North.

Virginia received the first English colony; the emigrants took possession of it in 1607. The idea that mines of gold and silver are the sources of national wealth was at that time singularly prevalent in Europe; a fatal delusion, which has done more to impoverish the European nations who adopted it, and has cost more lives in America, than the united influence of war and bad laws. The men sent to Virginia were seekers of gold, adventurers without resources and without character, whose turbulent and restless spirit endangered the infant colony, and rendered its progress uncertain. Artisans and agriculturists arrived afterwards; and, although they were a more moral and orderly race of men, they were hardly in any respect above the level of the inferior classes in England. No lofty views, no spiritual conception, presided over the foundation of these new settlements. The colony was scarcely established when slavery was introduced; this was the capital fact which was to exercise an immense influence on the character, the laws and the whole future of the South. Slavery . . . dishonors labor; it introduces idleness into society, and with idleness, ignorance and pride, luxury and distress. It enervates the powers of the mind, and benumbs the activity of man. The influence of slavery, united to the English character, explains the manners and the social condition of the Southern States.

In the North, the same English character . . . received totally different colors. Here . . . the two or three main ideas which now constitute the basis of the social theory of the United States were first combined. . . . They now extend their influence . . . over the whole American world. The civilization of New England has been like a beacon lit upon a hill, which, after it has diffused its warmth immediately around it, also tinges the distant horizon with its glow. . . .

The settlers who established themselves on the shores of New England all belonged to the more independent classes of their native country. Their union on the soil of America at once presented the singular phenomenon of a society containing neither lords nor common people, and we may almost say, neither rich nor poor. These men possessed, in proportion to their number, a greater mass of intelligence than is to be found in any European nation of our own time. All, perhaps without a single exception, had received a good education, and many of them were known in Europe for their talents and their acquirements. The other colonies had been founded by adventurers without families; the emigrants of New England brought with them the best elements of order and morality; they landed on the desert coast accompanied by their wives and children. But what especially distinguished them from all others was the aim of their undertaking. They had not been obliged by necessity to leave their country; the social position they abandoned was one to be regretted, and their means of subsistence were certain. . . . In facing the inevitable sufferings of exile, their object was the triumph of an idea.

The emigrants, or, as they deservedly styled themselves, the Pilgrims, belonged to that English sect the austerity of whose principles had acquired for them the name of Puritans. Puritanism was not merely a religious doctrine, but it corresponded in many points with the most absolute democratic and republican theories. It was this tendency which had aroused its most dangerous adversaries. Persecuted by the government of the mother country, and disgusted by the habits of a society which the rigor of their own principles condemned, the Puritans went forth to seek some rude and unfrequented part of the world, where they could live according to their own opinions, and worship God in freedom. . . . Puritanism . . . was scarcely less a political than a religious doctrine. No sooner had the emigrants landed on the barren coast . . . than it was their first care to constitute a society, by subscribing the [Mayflower Compact]:

"In the name of God. Amen. We, whose names are underwritten, the loyal subjects of our dread Sovereign Lord King James, &s, &c., Having undertaken for the glory of God, and advancement of the Christian Faith, and the honour of our King and country, a voyage to plant the first colony in the northern parts of Virginia; Do by these presents solemnly and mutually, in the presence of God and one another, covenant and combine ourselves together into a civil body politick, for our better ordering and preservation, and furtherance of the ends aforesaid: and by virtue hereof do enact, constitute, and frame such just and equal laws, ordinances, acts, constitutions, and offices, from time to time, as shall be thought most meet and convenient for the general good of the Colony: unto which we promise all due submission and obedience . . . "

This happened in 1620, and from that time forwards the emigration went on. The religious and political passions which ravaged the British empire during the whole reign of Charles I drove fresh crowds of sectarians every year to the shores of America. In England, the stronghold of Puritanism continued to be in the middle classes; and it was from the middle classes that most of the emigrants came. The population of New England increased rapidly; and whilst the hierarchy of rank despotically classed the inhabitants of the mother country, the colony approximated more and more the novel spectacle of a community homogeneous in all its parts. A democracy, more perfect than antiquity had dared to dream of, started in full size and panoply from the midst of an ancient feudal society.

For Journals

Whom do you think of as the first Americans?

For Discussion

1. Why do you think de Tocqueville frames his study of America and Americans using the analogy of studying the child to know the man? How does this image illuminate and clarify his purpose?

2. To what in the Anglo Americans' history does de Tocqueville attribute their knowledge of the principles of freedom? Are you persuaded by his conclusion? Do you think his contemporaries would have been?

3. How does de Tocqueville characterize New England and the Puritans? Pay special attention to the passages he cites to illuminate "the spirit of these pious adventurers." What conclusions does he draw from his evidence? Do you think his contemporary audience would have been convinced? Are you convinced of the Puritans' character based on the passage he cites?

4. According to de Tocqueville, what effects does slavery have on a society in general? What do you infer from his remark, "The influence of slavery, united to the English character, explains the manners and the social condition of the Southern states"?

5. De Tocqueville writes in paragraph 4, "The tie of language is, perhaps, the strongest and most durable that can unite mankind." What assumption is he making about language and culture? How does this approach to culture define "American"? Do you agree with his assumption and with this definition? How do you think his contemporaries would have reacted to his assertion?

For Writing

1. Drawing from your discussions in response to numbers 1 and 4 above, write an essay in which you compare and contrast de Tocqueville's treatment of North and South and the American identities that developed in each region. Which identity do you find more clearly articulated? Which assertions are more persuasive? Do you find his generalizations merited, based on the evidence he offers? How is your assessment of his argument biased by your own cultural or geographical identity?

2. De Tocqueville's discussion of a common language has had strong reverberations in recent debates over "English only" in schools and over policies establishing English as the official language of the United States. Research one of these issues, checking recent journal, newspaper, and magazine indexes for both educational journals and popular magazines, as well as books, so that you have up-to-date information. Develop a thesis about the topic and support it with well-reasoned arguments based on evidence from your research.

THE U.S. HOTEL BADLY NEEDS A BOUNCER
CA. 1890

This cartoon (on page 82) was published in Puck, *the first successful American weekly humor magazine.* Puck *was started in 1876 by Joseph Keppler, one of the well-known color cartoonists of the great age of political cartooning, which flourished from approximately 1870 to 1900. While other American magazines printed perhaps one cartoon per issue, Keppler published three a week in* Puck, *perhaps accounting in part for the magazine's popularity. Color cartoons at that time were larger than we are used to today.* Puck, *for example, included a full-page front cover and back-cover cartoon and a two-page spread. This golden age of cartooning and the production of* Puck, *which was published until 1918, coincided with a huge influx of European immigrants in America—some 14 million between 1869 and 1900. It is not surprising that issues of immigration, and American identity, appeared as the subject matter for such cartoons.*

For Journals

Do you think there are certain people who should be encouraged to come to America or discouraged from coming?

For Discussion

1. Study the cartoon, noting the figures and their appearance, their arrangement, the relationships between them, and their identities. What sorts of people are represented by which types of figures? Which are the "good" identities or qualities? Which are the undesirable traits?
2. Discuss the overall point of the cartoon. From what evidence, or examples, did you infer that point? What assumptions about America, Americans, and immigrants are implied? State the cartoon's argument in your own words.

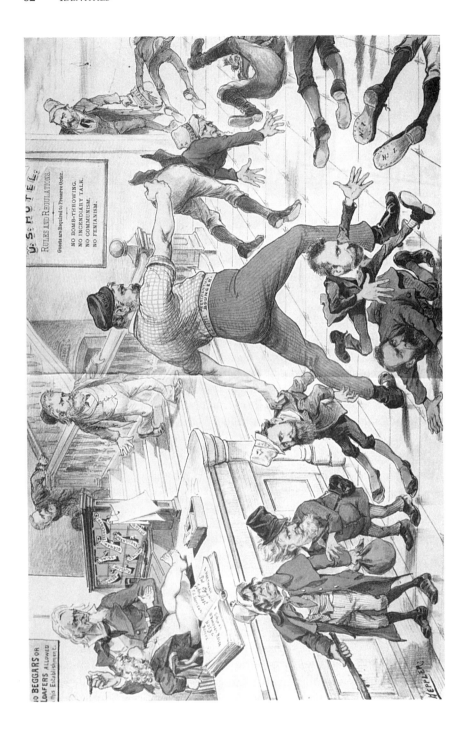

3. Why do you believe the artist chose the metaphor of the hotel? What effect does this metaphor have on the argument? Do you believe America should be a hotel rather than a home? Should bouncers be able to evict people?

4. How might the artist's contemporaries have reacted to the cartoon? Judgng from the artist's persuasive strategies, what can you infer from the cartoon about immigration issues of the times? About the cartoon's audiences and their beliefs and values? Does the message seem more directed at getting people to behave well or encouraging them to regulate the behavior of others?

For Writing

1. Compare the argument and assumptions in *U.S. Hotel,* with other selections in this chapter, such as Ralph Ellison's Prologue to *Invisible Man.* Alternatively, compare the persuasiveness of this cartoon with the posters in Chapter 8, "War and the Enemy." What common strategies or themes do you find?

2. Select a recent social or political cartoon—from the editorial pages of a newspaper, for example—on an issue related to American identities, such as immigration. Compare and contast the cartoon you choose with *U.S. Hotel,* focusing on strategies of persuasion and the artist's implicit assumptions about their audiences.

3. How do you think audiences have changed since this cartoon was published? In what ways have they remained the same? How have strategies or techniques of persuasion changed or remained the same?

VICTORY LIBERTY LOAN
1919

Howard Chandler Christy

> *World War I began in Europe in 1914, and the United States entered the war in 1917. In the year and a half following the U.S. declaration of war, civilian efforts to support the war included some 18 billion dollars in war-bond purchases. War bonds, or funds through which consumers lent money to the government at a modest interest rate, helped finance war material*

without harsh increases in federal income taxes; to some extent, bonds were said to help deal with currency inflation that can ensue when there are few consumer goods to buy. More important, though, Americans were also persuaded to "buy into" the war through purchasing bonds. William Gibbs McAdoo, who was then secretary of the treasury, wrote: "We went directly to the people, and that means to everybody—to business men, workmen, farmers, bankers, millionaires, school-teachers, laborers. We capitalized on the profound impulse called patriotism. It is the quality of coherence that holds a nation together; it is one of the deepest and most powerful of human motives." Artists such as Christy were commissioned to create posters to advertise the bonds, while film stars and others appeared at rallies to urge people to buy bonds—and to support the war.

For Journals

What visual symbols remind you of America? What kinds of symbols appeal to your sense of patriotism?

For Discussion

1. What draws your eye when you first look at the poster? What are the poster's most prominent features? What did the artist want the viewer to see and feel first? Why?

2. Is the clothing of the female figure in the poster what you expect for its era? How would you account for her style of dress?

3. What do the wreath, the gold star, and the honor roll symbolize? (In what other contexts have you seen these symbols?) The woman is literally draping herself in the American flag. What do her posture and gestures suggest?

4. Read the list of names under the heading "Honor Roll" carefully. What do you notice? What point is the artist trying to make?

5. Who do you think was the intended audience for this poster? Explain your answer.

For Writing

1. Compare and contrast the assumptions about the American identity evident in this poster and in the cartoon *The U.S. Hotel.* Are the assumptions similar or different? Explain your assessment.

2. Select a modern advertisement that tries to appeal to Americans with a variety of ethnic heritages. Write an essay analyzing the choice of persuasive strategies in the ad and their effectiveness.

3.   If you were asked to provide a poster or flyer to appeal to patriotism, what design choices would you make? Try to design such a poster or flyer (you may want to take an existing one and give it a patriotic edge), writing out the text and sketching the images you would use. Write an essay explaining your choices.

WHAT THE INDIAN MEANS TO AMERICA
1933

Luther Standing Bear

Luther Standing Bear (1868–1947), a member of a Teton Sioux tribe, attended the government Indian school at Carlyle, Pennsylvania, and later worked in jobs ranging from storekeeper to minister to performer in Buffalo Bill's Wild West Show. Having lived during and observed first hand the forcible removal of Indians to reservations during the rapid expansion of the West, Standing Bear found the government practices untenable. His views are set out in My People the Sioux *(1928),* My Indian Boyhood *(1931),* Stories of the Sioux *(1934), and* Land of the Spotted Eagle *(1933), from which the following selection is excerpted. In this essay, Standing Bear identifies the American Indian as the one who truly understands the American lands.*

The feathered and blanketed figure of the American Indian has come to symbolize the American continent. He is the man who through centuries has been moulded and sculpted by the same hand that shaped its mountains, forests, and plains, and marked the course of its rivers.

The American Indian is of the soil, whether it be the region of forests, plains, pueblos, or mesas. He fits into the landscape, for the hand that fashioned the continent also fashioned the man for his surroundings. He once grew as naturally as the wild sunflowers; he belongs just as the buffalo belonged.

With a physique that fitted, the man developed fitting skills—crafts which today are called American. And the body had a soul, also formed and moulded by the same master hand of harmony. Out of the Indian approach to existence there came a great freedom—an intense and absorbing love for nature; a respect for life; enriching faith in a

Supreme Power; and principles of truth, honesty, generosity, equity, and brotherhood as a guide to mundane relations. . . .

The white man does not understand the Indian for the reason that he does not understand America. He is too far removed from its formative processes. The roots of the tree of his life have not yet grasped the rock and soil. The white man is still troubled with primitive fears; he still has in his consciousness the perils of this frontier continent, some of its fastnesses not yet having yielded to his questing footsteps and inquiring eyes. He shudders still with the memory of the loss of his forefathers upon its scorching deserts and forbidding mountaintops. The man from Europe is still a foreigner and an alien. And he still hates the man who questioned his path across the continent.

But in the Indian the spirit of the land is still vested; it will be until other men are able to divine and meet its rhythm. Men must be born and reborn to belong. Their bodies must be formed of the dust of their forefathers' bones.   5

The attempted transformation of the Indian by the white man and the chaos that has resulted are but the fruits of the white man's disobedience of a fundamental and spiritual law. The pressure that has been brought to bear upon the native people, since the cessation of armed conflict, in the attempt to force conformity of custom and habit has caused a reaction more destructive than war, and the injury has not only affected the Indian, but has extended to the white population as well. Tyranny, stupidity, and lack of vision have brought about the situation now alluded to as the "Indian Problem."

There is, I insist, no Indian problem as created by the Indian himself. Every problem that exists today in regard to the native population is due to the white man's cast of mind, which is unable, at least reluctant, to seek understanding and achieve adjustment in a new and a significant environment into which it has so recently come.

The white man excused his presence here by saying that he has been guided by the will of his God; and in so saying absolved himself of all responsibility for his appearance in a land occupied by other men.

Then, too, his law was a written law; his divine decalogue reposed in a book. And what better proof that his advent into this country and his subsequent acts were the result of divine will! He brought the Word! There ensued a blind worship of written history, of books, of the written word, that has denuded the spoken word of its power and sacredness. The written word became established as a criterion of the superior man—a symbol of emotional fineness. The man who could write his name on a piece of paper, whether or not he possessed the spiritual fineness to honor those words in speech, was by some miraculous formula a more highly developed and sensitized person than the

one who had never had a pen in hand, but whose spoken word was in-
violable and whose sense of honor and truth was paramount. With
false reasoning was the quality of human character measured by man's
ability to make with an implement a mark upon paper. But granting
this mode of reasoning be correct and just, then where are to be placed
the thousands of illiterate whites who are unable to read and write?
Are they, too, "savages"? Is not humanness a matter of heart and
mind, and is it not evident in the form of relationship with men? Is not
kindness more powerful than arrogance; and truth more powerful
than the sword?

10   True, the white man brought great change. But the varied fruits of
his civilization, though highly colored and inviting, are sickening and
deadening. And if it be the part of civilization to maim, rob, and
thwart, then what is progress? . . .

After subjugation, after dispossession, there was cast the last abuse
upon the people who so entirely resented their wrongs and punishments, and that was the stamping and labeling of them as savages. To
make this label stick has been the task of the white race and the greatest salve that it has been able to apply to its sore and troubled conscience now hardened through the habitual practice of injustice.

But all the years of calling the Indian a savage has never made him
one; all the denial of his virtues has never taken them from him; and
the very resistance he has made to save the things inalienably his has
been his saving strength—that which will stand him in need when justice does make its belated appearance and he undertakes rehabilitation.

All sorts of feeble excuses are heard for the continued subjection of
the Indian. One of the most common is that he is not yet ready to accept the society of the white man—that he is not yet ready to mingle as
a social entity.

This, I maintain, is beside the question. The matter is not one of
making over the external Indian into the likeness of the white race—a
process detrimental to both races. Who can say that the white man's
way is better for the Indian? Where resides the human judgment with
the competence to weigh and value Indian ideals and spiritual concepts; or substitute for them other values?

15   Then, has the white man's social order been so harmonious and
ideal as to merit the respect of the Indian, and for that matter the thinking class of the white race? Is it wise to urge upon the Indian a foreign
social form? Let none but the Indian answer!

Rather, let the white brother face about and cast his mental eye
upon a new angle of vision. Let him look upon the Indian world as a
human world; then let him see to it that human rights be accorded to
the Indians. And this for the purpose of retaining for his own order of
society a measure of humanity. . . .

The spiritual health and existence of the Indian was maintained by song, magic, ritual, dance, symbolism, oratory (or council), design, handicraft, and folk-story.

Manifestly, to check or thwart this expression is to bring about spiritual decline. And it is in this condition of decline that the Indian people are today. There is but a feeble effort among the Sioux to keep alive their traditional songs and dances, while among other tribes there is but a half-hearted attempt to offset the influence of the Government school and at the same time recover from the crushing and stifling regime of the Indian Bureau.

One has but to speak of Indian verse to receive uncomprehending and unbelieving glances. Yet the Indian loved verse and into this mode of expression went his deepest feelings. Only a few ardent and advanced students seem interested; nevertheless, they have given in book form enough Indian translations to set forth the character and quality of Indian verse.

Oratory receives a little better understanding on the part of the white public, owing to the fact that oratorical complications include those of Indian orators.   20

Hard as it seemingly is for the white man's ear to sense the differences, Indian songs are as varied as the many emotions which inspire them, for no two of them are alike. For instance, the Song of Victory is spirited and the notes high and remindful of an unrestrained hunter or warrior riding exultantly over the prairies. On the other hand, the song of the *Cano unye* is solemn and full of urge, for it is meant to inspire the young men to deeds of valor. Then there are the songs of death and the spiritual songs which are connected with the ceremony of initiation. These are full of the spirit of praise and worship, and so strong are some of these invocations that the very air seems as if surcharged with the presence of the Big Holy.

The Indian loved to worship. From birth to death he revered his surroundings. He considered himself born in the luxurious lap of Mother Earth and no place was to him humble. There was nothing between him and the Big Holy. The contact was immediate and personal, and the blessings of Wakan Tanka flowed over the Indian like rain showered from the sky. Wakan Tanka was not aloof, apart, and ever seeking to quell evil forces. He did not punish the animals and the birds, and likewise He did not punish man. He was not a punishing God. For there was never a question as to the supremacy of an evil power over and above the power of Good. There was but one ruling power, and that was *Good.*

Of course, none but an adoring one could dance for days with his face to the sacred sun, and that time is all but done. We cannot have back the days of the buffalo and the beaver; we cannot win back our clean blood-stream and superb health, and we can never again expect the beautiful *rapport* we once had with Nature. The springs and lakes have dried and the mountains are bare of forests. The plow has changed the face of the world. Wi-wila is dead! No more may we heal our sick and comfort our dying with a strength founded on faith, for even the animals now fear us, and fear supplants faith.

And the Indian wants to dance! It is his way of expressing devotion, of communing with unseen power, and in keeping his tribal identity. When the Lakota heart was filled with high emotion, he danced. When he felt the benediction of the warming rays of the sun, he danced. When his blood ran hot with success of the hunt or chase, he danced. When his heart was filled with pity for the orphan, the lonely father, or bereaved mother, he danced. All the joys and exaltations of life, all his gratefulness and thankfulness, all his acknowledgments of the mysterious power that guided life, and all his aspirations for a better life, culminated in one great dance—the Sun Dance.

25   When the Indian has forgotten the music of his forefathers, when the sound of the tomtom is no more, when noisy jazz has drowned the melody of the flute, he will be a dead Indian. When the memory of his heroes are no longer told in story, and he forsakes the beautiful white bucksin for factory shoddy, he will be dead. When from him has been taken all that is his, all that he has visioned in nature, all that has come to him from infinite sources, he then, truly, will be a dead Indian. His spirit will be gone, and though he walk crowded streets, he will, in truth, be—*dead!*

But all this must not perish; it must live, to the end that America shall be educated no longer to regard native production of whatever tribe—folk-story, basketry, pottery, dance, song, poetry—as curios, and native artists as curiosities. For who but the man indigenous to the soil could produce its song, story, and folk-tale; who but the man who loved the dust beneath his feet could shape it and put it into undying, ceramic form; who but he who loved the reeds that grew beside still waters, and the damp roots of shrub and tree, could save it from seasonal death, and with almost superhuman patience weave it into enduring objects of beauty—into timeless art!

Regarding the "civilization" that has been thrust upon me since the days of reservation, it has not added one whit to my sense of justice; to my reverence for the rights of life; to my love for truth, honesty, and generosity; nor to my faith in Wakan Tanka—God of the Lakotas. For after all the great religions have been preached and expounded, or have been revealed by brilliant scholars, or have been written in books and embellished in fine language with finer covers, man—all man—is still confronted with the Great Mystery.

So if today I had a young mind to direct, to start on the journey of life, and I was faced with the duty of choosing between the natural way of my forefathers and that of the white man's present way of civilization, I would, for its welfare, unhesitatingly set that child's feet in the path of my forefathers. I would raise him to be an Indian!

For Journals

What do you know about the relationship between American Indians and the land?

For Discussion

1. How does Standing Bear establish the argument that the American Indian is not only the true symbol but also the essence of the American continent? In what ways do the American Indian and the land share an identity?

2. Standing Bear contrasts the American Indians and the whites in terms of their relationship with the land. What does he mean when he asserts that "in the Indian the spirit of the land is still vested"? How can others inherit that spirit?

3. According to Standing Bear, in what ways are whites foreigners in America? What kind of assimilation do white pepole need to undergo so as not to be aliens? How is this process similar to and different from other kinds of assimilation you have heard of?

4. How have the pressure and "conformity of custom" injured both American Indians and whites?

5. How do whites justify their presence in America and their subjugation of Indians? How does he refute these arguments? Standing Bear published this selection in 1933 as part of a larger work. How do you think his audiences responded to the initial arguments of whites and to Standing Bear's refutation? How do you respond?

For Writing

1. Write an essay summarizing Standing Bear's definition of a true American and then either offer support for or refute his position.

2. Research the Trail of Tears, the establishing of the reservation system, or some other specific issue in the history of Indian-white relations in America, and write a documented essay explaining the issue or event. Alternatively, investigate the current status of the relationship between one or more of the American Indian nations and the U.S.

government, focusing on the degree to which Indian-white relations have, or have not, changed since the publication of Standing Bear's books in the late 1920s and early 1930s.

PROLOGUE TO *INVISIBLE MAN*
1 9 4 7

Ralph Ellison

Born in Oklahoma in 1914 and educated at the Tuskegee Institute in Alabama, Ralph Ellison established his considerable reputation with his first and only novel, Invisible Man, *first published in 1947 and reprinted numerous times since, most recently in 1990. This selection from the Prologue is typical of Ellison's lyrical and unflinching portrayal of black identity in American society, an identity the novelist has fleshed out more fully in collections of essays like* Shadow and Act *(1964) and* Going to the Territory *(1986). Ellison lectured at Yale, Columbia, and New York universities, and remains a dominant figure on the American literary landscape even after his death in 1994.*

I am an invisible man. No, I am not a spook like those who haunted Edgar Allan Poe; nor am I one of your Hollywood-movie ectoplasms. I am a man of substance, of flesh and bone, fiber and liquids—and I might even be said to possess a mind. I am invisible, understand, simply because people refuse to see me. Like the bodiless heads you see sometimes in circus sideshows, it is as though I have been surrounded by mirrors of hard, distorting glass. When they approach me they see only my surroundings, themselves, or figments of their imagination—indeed, everything and anything except me.

Nor is my invisibility exactly a matter of a biochemical accident to my epidermis. That invisibility to which I refer occurs because of a peculiar disposition of the eyes of those with whom I come in contact. A matter of the construction of their *inner* eyes, those eyes with which they look through their physical eyes upon reality. I am not complaining, nor am I protesting either. It is sometimes advantageous to be unseen, although it is most often rather wearing on the nerves. Then too, you're constantly being bumped against by those of poor vision. Or again, you often doubt if you really exist. You wonder whether you aren't simply a phantom in other people's minds. Say, a figure in a nightmare which the sleeper tries with all his strength to destroy. It's when you feel like this that, out of resentment, you begin to bump people back. And, let me confess, you feel that way most of the time. You ache with the need to convince yourself that you do exist in the real world, that you're a part of all the sound and anguish, and you strike out with your fists, you curse and you swear to make them recognize you. And, alas, it's seldom successful.

One night I accidentally bumped into a man, and perhaps because of the near darkness he saw me and called me an insulting name. I sprang at him, seized his coat lapels and demanded that he apologize. He was a tall blond man, and as my face came close to his he looked insolently out of his blue eyes and cursed me, his breath hot in my face as he struggled. I pulled his chin down sharp upon the crown of my head, butting him as I had seen the West Indians do, and I felt his flesh tear and the blood gush out, and I yelled, "Apologize! Apologize!" But he continued to curse and struggle, and I butted him again and again until he went down heavily, on his knees, profusely bleeding. I kicked him repeatedly, in a frenzy because he still uttered insults though his lips were frothy with blood. Oh yes, I kicked him! And in my outrage I got out my knife and prepared to slit his throat, right there beneath the lamplight in the deserted street, holding him in the collar with one hand, and opening the knife with my teeth—when it occurred to me that the man had not *seen* me, actually; that he, as far as he knew, was in the midst of a walking nightmare! And I stopped the blade, slicing the air as I pushed him away, letting him fall back to the street. I stared at him hard as the lights of a car stabbed through the darkness. He lay there, moaning on the asphalt; a man almost killed by a phantom. It unnerved me. I was both disgusted and ashamed. I was like a drunken man myself, wavering about on weakened legs. Then I was amused: Something in this man's thick head had sprung out and beaten him within an inch of his life. I began to laugh at this crazy discovery. Would he have awakened at the point of death? Would Death himself have freed him for wakeful living? But I didn't linger. I ran away into the dark, laughing so hard I feared I might rupture myself. The next day I saw his picture in the *Daily News*, beneath a caption stating that he had been "mugged." Poor fool, poor blind fool, I thought with sincere compassion, mugged by an invisible man!

Most of the time (although I do not choose as I once did to deny the violence of my days by ignoring it) I am not so overtly violent. I remember that I am invisible and walk softly so as not to awaken the sleeping ones. Sometimes it is best not to awaken them; there are few things in the world as dangerous as sleepwalkers. I learned in time though that it is possible to carry on a fight against them without their realizing it. For instance, I have been carrying on a fight with Monopolated Light & Power for some time now. I use their service and pay them nothing at all, and they don't know it. Oh, they suspect that power is being drained off, but they don't know where. All they know is that according to the master meter back there in their power station a hell of a lot of free current is disappearing somewhere into the jungle of Harlem. The joke, of course, is that I don't live in Harlem but in a border area. Several years ago (before I discovered the advantages of being invisible) I went through the routine process of buying service and paying their outrageous rates. But no more. I gave up all that, along with my apartment, and my old way of life: That way based upon the fallacious assumption that I, like other men, was visible. Now, aware of my invisibility, I live rent-free in a building rented strictly to whites, in a section of the basement that was shut off and forgotten during the nineteenth century, which I discovered when I was trying to escape in the night from Ras the Destroyer. But that's getting too far ahead of the story, almost to the end, although the end is in the beginning and lies far ahead.

5   The point now is that I found a home—or a hole in the ground, as you will. Now don't jump to any conclusion that because I call my home a "hole" it is damp and cold like a grave; there are cold holes and warm holes. Mine is a warm hole. And remember, a bear retires to his hole for the winter and lives until spring; then he comes strolling out like the Easter chick breaking from its shell. I say all this to assure you that it is incorrect to assume that, because I'm invisible and live in a hole, I am dead. I am neither dead nor in a state of suspended animation. Call me Jack-the-Bear, for I am in a state of hibernation.

My hole is warm and full of light. Yes, *full* of light. I doubt if there is a brighter spot in all New York than this hole of mine, and I do not exclude Broadway. Or the Empire State Building on a photographer's dream night. But that is taking advantage of you. Those two spots are among the darkest of our whole civilization—pardon me, our whole *culture* (an important distinction, I've heard)—which might sound like a hoax, or a contradiction, but that (by contradiction, I mean) is how the world moves: Not like an arrow, but a boomerang. (Beware of those who speak of the *spiral* of history; they are preparing a boomerang. Keep a steel helmet handy.) I know; I have been boomeranged across my head so much that I now can see the darkness of lightness. And I love light. Perhaps you'll think it strange that an invisible man should need light, desire light, love light. But maybe it is exactly because I *am* invisible. Light confirms my reality, gives birth to my form. A beautiful girl once told me of a recurring nightmare in which she lay in the center of a large dark room and felt her face expand until it filled the whole room, becoming a formless mass while her eyes ran in bilious jelly up the chimney. And so it is with me. Without light I am not only invisible, but formless as well; and to be unaware of one's form is to live a death. I myself, after existing some twenty years, did not become alive until I discovered my invisibility.

For Journals

Are there groups of people in your community—ethnic minorities, older people, disabled people—whom you rarely notice?

For Discussion

1.   How is the notion of invisibility developed in this selection? Why do you think Ellison uses the idea of invisibility? What associations does it have? What could a person do—or not do—if invisible?

2.   The speaker notes that he found a home, a "hole in the ground," literally in a basement of a building restricted to whites. What is significant about his living in such a place? What is special, literally and metaphorically, about the light and the power company?

3.   In what sense is the invisible man's identity related to and developed by how others see him? Consider his growing awareness of being invisible, the incident with the blond stranger, and his relationship with the power company.

4.   In an introduction to *Invisible Man* that accompanied an edition printed in 1981, Ellison writes, "My task was one of revealing the human universals hidden within the plight of one who was both black and an American." What do you infer from this selection about the plight of those who live with this double identity?

For Writing

1.   Write an essay discussing the effects of others' perceptions on developing one's own identity, whether in terms of ethnicity, race, culture, nationality, or age. You could develop this assignment as a personal essay; alternatively, you could investigate and incorporate recent research on the subject, found in psychology or sociology books and journals.

2.   Ellison wrote that his task in *Invisible Man* was to deal with "the sheer rhetorical challenge involved in communicating across our barriers of race and religion, class, color, and region—barriers which consist of the many strategies of division that were designed, and still function, to prevent what would otherwise have been a more or less

natural recognition of the reality of blackness." How does he cope with the rhetorical challenges—obstacles to persuasion—he mentions here? In what ways do his metaphor of invisibility and the voice and tone of the speaker serve to meet those challenges?

INAUGURAL ADDRESS
1 9 6 1

John F. Kennedy

John Fitzgerald Kennedy was born in Brookline, Massachusetts, in 1917 and graduated from Harvard University. He served as a torpedo boat commander in the Pacific during World War II and received both the Navy Medal and the Purple Heart for his service. For his book Profiles in Courage *(1956) Kennedy won the Pulitzer Prize, and after a career in Congress he became the youngest ever and first Roman Catholic president. His administration was cut tragically short when rifle fire from an assassin in Dallas, Texas ended his life in 1963. Kennedy's famous inaugural address exemplifes the youth, vitality, and vision of a generation and remains a classic of American rhetoric.*

We observe today not a victory of party but a celebration of freedom—symbolizing an end as well as a beginning, signifying renewal as well as change. For I have sworn before you and Almighty God the same solemn oath our forebears prescribed nearly a century and three-quarters ago.

The world is very different now. For man holds in his mortal hands the power to abolish all forms of human poverty and all forms of human life. And yet the same revolutionary beliefs for which our forebears fought are still at issue around the globe: the belief that the rights of man come not from the generosity of the state but from the hand of God.

We dare not forget today that we are the heirs of that first revolution. Let the word go forth from this time and place, to friend and foe alike, that the torch has been passed to a new generation of Americans—born in this century, tempered by war, disciplined by a hard and bitter peace, proud of our ancient heritage—and unwilling to witness or permit the slow undoing of those human rights to which this nation has always been committed, and to which we are committed today at home and around the world.

Let every nation know, whether it wishes us well or ill, that we shall pay any price, bear any burden, meet any hardship, support any friend, oppose any foe to assure the survival and the success of liberty.

This much we pledge—and more.   5

To those old allies whose cultural and spiritual origins we share, we pledge the loyalty of faithful friends. United, there is little we cannot do in a host of cooperative ventures. Divided, there is little we can do—for we dare not meet a powerful challenge at odds and split asunder.

To those new states whom we welcome to the ranks of the free, we pledge our word that one form of colonial control shall not have passed away merely to be replaced by a far more iron tyranny. We shall not always expect to find them supporting our view. But we shall always hope to find them strongly supporting their own freedom—and to remember that, in the past, those who foolishly sought power by riding the back of the tiger ended up inside.

To those people in the huts and villages of half the globe struggling to break the bonds of mass misery, we pledge our best efforts to help them help themselves, for whatever period is required—not because the Communists may be doing it, not because we seek their votes, but because it is right. If a free society cannot help the many who are poor, it cannot save the few who are rich.

To our sister republics south of the border, we offer a special pledge: to convert our good words into good deeds—in a new alliance for progress—to assist free men and free governments in casting off the chains of poverty. But this peaceful revolution of hope cannot become the prey of hostile powers. Let all our neighbors know that we shall join with them to oppose aggression or subversion anywhere in the Americas. And let every other power know that this hemisphere intends to remain the master of its own house.

To that world assembly of sovereign states, the United Nations,   10
our last best hope in an age where the instruments of war have far outpaced the instruments of peace, we renew our pledge of support—to prevent it from becoming merely a forum for invective, to strengthen its shield of the new and the weak, and to enlarge the area in which its writ may run.

Finally, to those nations who would make themselves our adversary, we offer not a pledge but a request: that both sides begin anew the quest for peace, before the dark powers of destruction unleashed by science engulf all humanity in planned or accidental self-destruction.

We dare not tempt them with weakness. For only when our arms are sufficient beyond doubt can we be certain beyond doubt that they will never be employed.

But neither can two great and powerful groups of nations take comfort from our present course—both sides overburdened by the cost of modern weapons, both rightly alarmed by the steady spread of the deadly atom, yet both racing to alter that uncertain balance of terror that stays the hand of mankind's final war.

So let us begin anew, remembering on both sides that civility is not a sign of weakness, and sincerity is always subject to proof. Let us never negotiate out of fear. But let us never fear to negotiate.

15   Let both sides explore what problems unite us instead of belaboring those problems which divide us.

Let both sides, for the first time, formulate serious and precise proposals for the inspection and control of arms—and bring the absolute power to destroy other nations under the absolute control of all nations.

Let both sides seek to invoke the wonders of science instead of its terrors. Together let us explore the stars, conquer the deserts, eradicate disease, tap the ocean depths, and encourage the arts and commerce.

Let both sides unite to heed in all corners of the earth the command of Isaiah—to "undo the heavy burdens . . . [and] let the oppressed go free."

And if a beachhead of cooperation may push back the jungle of suspicion, let both sides join in creating a new endeavor, not a new balance of power, but a new world of law, where the strong are just and the weak secure and the peace preserved.

20   All this will not be finished in the first one hundred days. Nor will it be finished in the first one thousand days, nor in the life of this administration, nor even perhaps in our lifetime on this planet. But let us begin.

In your hands, my fellow citizens, more than mine, will rest the final success or failure of our course. Since this country was founded, each generation of Americans has been summoned to give testimony to its national loyalty. The graves of young Americans who answered the call to service surround the globe.

Now the trumpet summons us again—not as a call to bear arms, though arms we need; not as a call to battle, though embattled we are—but a call to bear the burden of a long twilight struggle, year in and year out, "rejoicing in hope, patient in tribulation," a struggle against the common enemies of man: tyranny, poverty, disease, and war itself.

Can we forge against these enemies a grand and global alliance, north and south, east and west, that can assure a more fruitful life for all mankind? Will you join in that historic effort?

In the long history of the world, only a few generations have been granted the role of defending freedom in its hour of maximum danger. I do not shrink from this responsibility—I welcome it. I do not believe that any of us would exchange places with any other people or any other generation. The energy, the faith, the devotion which we bring to this endeavor will light our country and all who serve it—and the glow from that fire can truly light the world.

And so, my fellow Americans: Ask not what your country can do for you—ask what you can do for your country.   25

My fellow citizens of the world: Ask not what America will do for you, but what together we can do for the freedom of man.

Finally, whether you are citizens of America or citizens of the world, ask of us here the same high standards of strength and sacrifice which we ask of you. With a good conscience our only sure reward, with history the final judge of our deeds, let us go forth to lead the land we love, asking His blessing and His help, but knowing that here on earth God's work must truly be our own.

For Journals

What have you learned, from people older than you or in the media, about the Kennedy administration? What images, expressions, and values come to mind?

For Discussion

1. Identify the audience for and purpose of an inaugural address. What special demands do they place on the speaker? Kennedy was not only the youngest and first-ever Catholic president elected; he also won by an exceedingly narrow margin. What additional demands did he need to meet? What strategies did he use to meet these demands? Was he successful?

2. How does Kennedy define his generation? How does he link these definitions to the goals of his administration?

3. What rhetorical strategies does Kennedy use to unite his audience and evoke a sense of shared purpose? Focus specifically on word choice and on literary or biblical allusions in the speech. How do you think most people in Kennedy's audiences reacted, either consciously or unconsciously, to his words? Do you think such a speech would be suitable for an audience of your contemporaries? Why or why not?

4.   Study the themes of the address. What do you infer about how Americans at that time defined their role in international affairs? In what ways does their identity rest on a contrast with the Soviet Union?

5.   Kennedy draws a particular portrait of America and Americans. Write out or discuss in your own words the visions, goals, and ideas either suggested by or articulated in the speech.

For Writing

1.   Choose a topic from one of the burning issues of the early 1960s—civil rights, space exploration, communism, youth culture, rock music, free speech, or something else—to explore. Develop a research question; then collect information by reading books and essays on the topic and also by finding and evaluating magazines, newspapers, television shows, radio broadcasts, and music lyrics or albums of the time that were written on the topic. Try to interview people who were young adults at the time. Develop your findings into a presentation to share with your peers.

2.   Communicating clearly through a speech is different from communicating through writing. Good public speakers must take advantage of word choice, strong organization, parallelism, rhythm, and other elements of style to make their points. In other words, they take many features of good prose and accentuate them. Write an essay analyzing the use of one or more of these stylistic features in Kennedy's address. Try to show how the president used stylistic devices to emphasize his themes.

FIRE

1 9 7 9

Joy Harjo

Joy Harjo (1951–   ), the daughter of a Creek father and a Cherokee-French mother, was born in Oklahoma and received her B.A. from the University of New Mexico and her M.F.A. from the University of Iowa. Currently a professor at the University of New Mexico, Albuquerque, she has held a number of teaching positions, and from 1980 to 1983 served as a writer and consultant for the Native American Public Broadcasting Consortium, the National Indian Youth Council, and the National Endowment for the Arts (which named her a fellow in 1978). Harjo has published a number of books of poetry, including The Last Song *(1975),* What Moon Drove Me to This? *(1980),* She Had Some Horses *(1983), and* In Mad Love and War *(1990). She also authored a film script,* Origin of Apache Crown Dance *(1985), and has contributed to several literary journals. Harjo's American Indian heritage is an important part of her writing. She says, "I write poetry because it is a way to travel into internal landscapes / starscapes which also become the external. It helps in traveling between many worlds and helps in speaking them."*

a woman can't survive
by her own breath
        alone
she must know
the voices of mountains   5
she must recognize
the foreverness of blue sky
she must flow
with the elusive
bodies   10
of night wind women
who will take her into
her own self
look at me
i am not a separate woman   15
i am a continuance
of blue sky
i am the throat
of the sandia mountains
a night wind woman   20
who burns
with every breath
she takes

For Journals

In what ways do you identify with nature? Do you think that connection with nature has been affected by your gender or ethnicity?

For Discussion

1.   The speaker in the poem never explicitly states that she is an American Indian who is writing from an American Indian perspective. Would you nonetheless have made this conclusion simply from reading the poem? If so, what clues are there in the poem that would have led you to this conclusion?

2.   The speaker's reflections both "take her into / her own self" and show her that "i am not a separate woman / i am a continuance." In other words, the speaker is both focused on her individual self and aware that she is not a distinct individual but part of a larger whole. How do you explain this paradox? What does it explain about the speaker's view of identity?

3.   With whom, and with what, does the speaker identify? Why do you think Harjo chose these particular people and things? What else might she have chosen?

4.   How does Harjo's view of identity compare with that of Luther Standing Bear's in the selection in this chapter? Is the difference due to the different times in which they wrote or the genres in which they chose to write?

5.   What is the poem asserting about American Indian women's identity? How does it develop that assertion? Why might the author have chosen a poem, rather than an essay or story, to develop her ideas? What are advantages and disadvantages of using poetry to convey an idea?

For Writing

1.   Compare and contrast the theme of oneness with nature as it is developed in this poem and in the selection by Luther Standing Bear previously in this chapter.

2.   In your college or public library, find a collection of Native American stories or myths, oratory, poems, or prose. (See the Native American list in the library resources at the end of Chapter 2.) Select several pieces, and write an essay analyzing the ways in which they develop themes of American Indian identities, particularly as they relate to the Indian relationship to nature or the way they contrast with white American identities.

SPLIT AT THE ROOT:
AN ESSAY ON JEWISH IDENTITY
1986

Adrienne Rich

*Adrienne Rich (1929–   ), poet, essayist, literary critic, MacArthur
Fellow, and professor of English and feminist studies at Stanford University,
is a major force in American poetry and in feminist theory. Her many writings include* Necessities of Life *(1966),* The Will to Change *(1971),* Diving into the Wreck *(1973), which won the National Book Award in 1974,
and* Of Woman Born *(1976). The following selection, from Rich's* Blood,
Bread, and Poetry: Selected Prose, 1979–1985 *(1986) draws from her
poetry and her experience as the daughter of a gentile mother and a Jewish
father in an effort to make sense of her divided identity.*

For about fifteen minutes I have been sitting chin in hand in front
of the typewriter, staring out at the snow. Trying to be honest with
myself, trying to figure out why writing this seems to be so dangerous
an act, filled with fear and shame, and why it seems so necessary. It
comes to me that in order to write this I have to be willing to do two
things: I have to claim my father, for I have my Jewishness from him
and not from my gentile mother; and I have to break his silence, his
taboos; in order to claim him I have in a sense to expose him.

And there is, of course, the third thing: I have to face the sources
and the flickering presence of my own ambivalence as a Jew; the daily,
mundane anti-Semitisms of my entire life.

These are stories I have never tried to tell before. Why now? Why,
I asked myself sometime last year, does this question of Jewish identity
float so impalpably, so ungraspably around me, a cloud I can't quite
see the outlines of, which feels to me to be without definition?

And yet I've been on the track of this longer than I think.

In a long poem written in 1960, when I was thirty-one years old, I   5
described myself as "Split at the root, neither Gentile nor Jew, / Yankee nor Rebel." I was still trying to have it both ways: to be
neither/nor, trying to live (with my Jewish husband and three children
more Jewish in ancestry than I) in the predominantly gentile Yankee
academic world of Cambridge, Massachusetts.

But this begins, for me, in Baltimore, where I was born in my father's workplace, a hospital in the Black ghetto, whose lobby contained an immense white marble statue of Christ.

My father was then a young teacher and researcher in the department of pathology at the Johns Hopkins Medical School, one of the very few Jews to attend or teach at that institution. He was from Birmingham, Alabama; his father, Samuel, was Ashkenazic, an immigrant from Austria-Hungary and his mother, Hattie Rice, a Sephardic Jew from Vicksburg, Mississippi. My grandfather had had a shoe store in Birmingham, which did well enough to allow him to retire comfortably and to leave my grandmother income on his death. The only souvenirs of my grandfather, Samuel Rich, were his ivory flute, which lay on our living-room mantel and was not to be played with; his thin gold pocket watch, which my father wore; and his Hebrew prayer book, which I discovered among my father's books in the course of reading my way through his library. In this prayer book there was a newspaper clipping about my grandparents' wedding, which took place in a synagogue.

My father, Arnold, was sent in adolescence to a military school in the North Carolina mountains, a place for training white southern Christian gentlemen. I suspect that there were few, if any, other Jewish boys at Colonel Bingham's, or at "Mr. Jefferson's university" in Charlottesville, where he studied as an undergraduate. With whatever conscious forethought, Samuel and Hatti sent their son into the dominant southern WASP culture to become an "exception," to enter the professional class. Never, in describing these experiences, did he speak of having suffered—from loneliness, cultural alienation, or outsiderhood. Never did I hear him use the word *anti-Semitism*.

It was only in college, when I read a poem by Karl Shapiro beginning "To hate the Negro and avoid the Jew / is the curriculum," that it flashed on me that there was an untold side to my father's story of his student years. He looked recognizably Jewish, was short and slender in build with dark wiry hair and deep-set eyes, high forehead and curved nose.

10   My mother is a gentile. In Jewish law I cannot count myself a Jew. If it is true that "we think back through our mothers if we are women" (Virginia Woolf)—and I myself have affirmed this—then even according to lesbian theory, I cannot (or need not?) count myself a Jew.

The white southern Protestant woman, the gentile, has always been there for me to peel back into. That's a whole piece of history in itself, for my gentile grandmother and my mother were also frustrated artists and intellectuals, a lost writer and a lost composer between them. Readers and annotators of books, note takers, my mother a good pianist still, in her eighties. But there was also the obsession with ancestry, with "background," the southern talk of family, not as people you would necessarily know and depend on, but as heritage, the guarantee of "good breeding." There was the inveterate romantic heterosexual fantasy, the mother telling the daughter how to attract men (my mother often used the word "fascinate"); the assumption that relations between the sexes could only be romantic, that it was in the woman's interest to cultivate "mystery," conceal her actual feelings. Survival tactics of a kind, I think today, knowing what I know about the white woman's sexual role in the southern racist scenario. Heterosexuality as protection, but also drawing white women deeper into collusion with white men.

It would be easy to push away and deny the gentile in me—that white southern woman, that social christian. At different times in my life I have wanted to push away one or the other burden of inheritance, to say merely *I am a woman; I am a lesbian.* If I call myself a Jewish lesbian, do I thereby try to shed some of my southern gentile white woman's culpability? If I call myself only through my mother, is it because I pass more easily through a world where being a lesbian often seems like outsiderhood enough?

According to Nazi logic, my two Jewish grandparents would have made me a *Mischling, first-degree*—nonexempt from the Final Solution.

The social world in which I grew up was christian virtually without needing to say so—christian imagery, music, language, symbols, assumptions everywhere. It was also a genteel, white, middle-class world in which "common" was a term of deep opprobrium. "Common" white people might speak of "niggers"; *we* were taught never to use that word—*we* said "Negroes" (even as we accepted segregation, the eating taboo, the assumption that Black people were simply of a separate species). Our language was more polite, distinguishing us from the "red-necks" or the lynch-mob mentality. But so charged with negative meaning was even the word "Negro" that as children we were taught never to use it in front of Black people. We were taught that any mention of skin color in the presence of colored people was treacherous, forbidden ground. In a parallel way, the word "Jew" was not used by polite gentiles. I sometimes heard my best friend's father, a Presbyterian minister, allude to "the Hebrew people" or "people of the Jewish faith." The world of acceptable folk was white, gentile (christian, really), and had "ideals" (which colored people, white "common" people, were not supposed to have). "Ideals" and "manners" included not hurting someone's feelings by calling her or him a

Negro or a Jew—naming the hated identity. This is the mental frame-work of the 1930s and 1940s in which I was raised.

15   (Writing this, I feel dimly like the betrayer: of my father, who did not speak the word; of my mother, who must have trained me in the messages; of my caste and class; of my whiteness itself.)

Two memories: I am in a play reading at school of *The Merchant of Venice.* Whatever Jewish law says, I am quite sure I was *seen* as Jewish (with a reassuringly gentile mother) in that double vision that bigotry allows. I am the only Jewish girl in the class, and I am playing Portia. As always, I read my part aloud for my father the night before, and he tells me to convey, with my voice, more scorn and contempt with the word "Jew": "Therefore, Jew . . ." I have to say the word out, and say it loudly. I was encouraged to pretend to be a non-Jewish child acting a non-Jewish character who has to speak the word "Jew" emphatically. Such a child would not have had trouble with the part. But *I* must have had trouble with the part, if only because the word itself was really taboo. I can see that there was a kind of terrible, bitter bravado about my father's way of handling this. And who would not dissociate from Shylock in order to identify with Portia? As a Jewish child who was also a female, I loved Portia—and, like every other Shakespearean heroine, she proved a treacherous role model.

A year or so later I am in another play, *The School for Scandal,* in which a notorious spendthrift is described as having "many excellent friends . . . among the Jews." In neither case was anything explained, either to me or to the class at large, about this scorn for Jews and the disgust surrounding Jews and money. Money, when Jews wanted it, had it, or lent it to others, seemed to take on a peculiar nastiness; Jews and money had some peculiar and unspeakable relation.

At this same school—in which we had Episcopalian hymns and prayers, and read aloud through the Bible morning after morning—I gained the impression that Jews were in the Bible and mentioned in English literature, that they had been persecuted centuries ago by the wicked Inquisition, but that they seemed not to exist in everyday life. These were the 1940s, and we were told a great deal about the Battle of Britain, the noble French Resistance fighters, the brave, starving Dutch—but I did not learn of the resistance of the Warsaw ghetto until I left home.

I was sent to the Episcopal church, baptized and confirmed, and attended it for about five years, though without belief. That religion seemed to have little to do with belief or commitment; it was liturgy that mattered, not spiritual passion. Neither of my parents ever en-tered that church, and my father would not enter *any* church for any reason—wedding or funeral. Nor did I enter a synagogue until I left Baltimore. When I came home from church, for a while, my father insisted on reading aloud to me from Thomas Paine's *The Age of Reason*—a diatribe against institutional religion. Thus, he explained, I would have a balanced view of these things, a choice. He—they—did not give me the choice to be a Jew. My mother explained to me when I was filling out forms for college that if any question was asked about "religion," I should put down "Episcopalian" rather than "none"—to seem to have no religion was, she implied, dangerous.

But it was white social christianity, rather than any particular   20
christian sect, that the world was founded on. The very word *Christian* was used as a synonym for virtuous, just, peace-loving, generous, etc., etc.* The norm was christian: "religion: none" was indeed not acceptable. Anti-Semitism was so intrinsic as not to have a name. I don't recall exactly being taught that the Jews killed Jesus—"Christ killer" seems too strong a term for the bland Episcopal vocabulary—but certainly we got the impression that the Jews had been caught out in a terrible mistake, failing to recognize the true Messiah, and were thereby less advanced in moral and spiritual sensibility. The Jews had actually allowed *moneylenders in the Temple* (again, the unexplained obsession with Jews and money). They were of the past, archaic, primitive, as older (and darker) cultures are supposed to be primitive; christianity was lightness, fairness, peace on earth, and combined the feminine appeal of "The meek shall inherit the earth" with the masculine stride of "Onward, Christian Soldiers."

Sometime in 1946, while still in high school, I read the newspaper that a theater in Baltimore was showing films of the Allied liberation of the Nazi concentration camps. Alone, I went downtown after school one afternoon and watched the stark, blurry, but unmistakable newsreels. When I try to go back and touch the pulse of that girl of sixteen, growing up in many ways so precocious and so ignorant, I am overwhelmed by a memory of despair, a sense of inevitability more enveloping than any I had ever known. Anne Frank's diary and many other personal narratives of the Holocaust were still unknown or unwritten. But it came to me that every one of those piles of corpses, mountains of shoes and clothing had contained, simply, individuals, who had believed, as I now believed of myself, that they were intended to live out a life of some kind of meaning, that the world possessed some kind of sense and order; yet *this* had happened to them. And I, who believed my life was intended to be so interesting and meaningful, was connected to those dead by something—not just mortality but a taboo name, a hated identity. Or was I—did I really have to be? Writing this now, I feel belated rage that I was so impoverished by

*In a similar way the phrase "That's white of you" implied that you were behaving with the superior decency and morality expected of white but not of Black people. {Author's note}

the family and social worlds I lived in, that I had to try to figure out by myself what this did indeed mean for me. That I had never been taught about resistance, only about passing. That I had no language for anti-Semitism itself.

When I went home and told my parents where I had been, they were not pleased. I felt accused of being morbidly curious, not healthy, sniffling around death for the thrill of it. And since, at sixteen, I was often not sure of the sources of my feelings or of my motives for doing what I did, I probably accused myself as well. One thing was clear: there was nobody in my world with whom I could discuss those films. Probably at the same time, I was reading accounts of the camps in magazines and newspapers; what I remember were the films and having questions that I could not even phrase, such as *Are those men and women "them" or "us"?*

To be able to ask even the child's astonished question *Why do they hate us so?* means knowing how to say "we." The guilt of not knowing, the guilt of perhaps having betrayed my parents or even those victims, those survivors, through mere curiosity—these also froze in me for years the impulse to find out more about the Holocaust.

1947: I left Baltimore to go to college in Cambridge, Massachusetts, left (I thought) the backward, enervating South for the intellectual, vital North. New England also had for me some vibration of higher moral rectitude, of moral passion even, with its seventeenth-century Puritan self-scrutiny, its nineteenth-century literary "flowering," its abolitionist righteousness, Colonel Shaw and his Black Civil War regiment depicted in granite on Boston Common. At the same time, I found myself, at Radcliffe, among Jewish women. I used to sit for hours over coffee with what I thought of as the "real" Jewish students, who told me about middle-class Jewish culture in America. I described my background—for the first time to strangers—and they took me on, some with amusement at my illiteracy, some arguing that I could never marry into a strict Jewish family, some convinced I didn't "look Jewish," others that I did. I learned the names of holidays and foods, which surnames are Jewish and which are "changed names"; about girls who had had their noses "fixed," their hair straightened. For these young Jewish women, students in the late 1940s, it was acceptable, perhaps even necessary, to strive to look as gentile as possible; but they stuck proudly to being Jewish, expected to marry a Jew, have children, keep the holidays, carry on the culture.

25   I felt I was testing a forbidden current, that there was danger in these revelations. I bought a reproduction of a Chagall portrait of a rabbi in striped prayer shawl and hung it on the wall of my room. I

was admittedly young and trying to educate myself, but I was also doing something that *is* dangerous: I was flirting with identity.

One day that year I was in a small shop where I had bought a dress with a too-long skirt. The shop employed a seamstress who did alterations, and she came in to pin up the skirt on me. I am sure that she was a recent immigrant, a survivor. I remember a short, dark woman wearing heavy glasses, with an accent so foreign I could not understand her words. Something about her presence was very powerful and disturbing to me. After marking and pinning up the skirt, she sat back on her knees, looked up at me, and asked in a hurried whisper: "You Jewish?" Eighteen years of training in assimilation sprang into the reflex by which I shook my head, rejecting her, and muttered, "No."

What was I actually saying "no" to? She was poor, older, struggling with a foreign tongue, anxious; she had escaped the death that had been intended for her, but I had no imagination of her possible courage and foresight, her resistance—I did not see in her a heroine who had perhaps saved many lives, including her own. I saw the frightened immigrant, the seamstress hemming the skirts of college girls, the wandering Jew. But I was an American college girl having her skirt hemmed. And I was frightened myself, I think, because she had recognized me ("It takes one to know one," my friend Edie at Radcliffe had said) even if I refused to recognize myself or her, even if her recognition was sharpened by loneliness or the need to feel safe with me.

But why should she have felt safe with me? I myself was living with a false sense of safety.

There are betrayals in my life that I have known at the very moment were betrayals: this was one of them. There are other betrayals committed so repeatedly, so mundanely, that they leave no memory trace behind, only a growing residue of misery, of dull, accreted self-hatred. Often these take the form not of words but of silence. Silence before the joke at which everyone is laughing: the anti-woman joke, the racist joke, the anti-Semitic joke. Silence and then amnesia. Blocking it out when the oppressor's language starts coming from the lips of one we admire, whose courage and eloquence have touched us: *She didn't really mean that; he didn't really say that.* But the accretions build up out of sight, like scale inside a kettle.

1948: I come home from my freshman year at college, flaming with 30 new insights, new information. I am the daughter who has gone out into the world, to the pinnacle of intellectual prestige, Harvard, fulfilling my father's hopes for me, but also exposed to dangerous influences. I have already been reproved for attending a rally for Henry Wallace and the Progressive party. I challenge my father: "Why haven't you told me that I am Jewish? Why do you never talk about being a Jew?" He answers measuredly, "You know that I have never denied that I am a Jew. But it's not important to me. I am a scientist, a deist. I have no use for organized religion. I choose to live in a world of many kinds of people. There are Jews I admire and others whom I despise. I am a person, not simply a Jew." The words are as I remember them, not perhaps exactly as spoken. But that was the message. And it contained enough truth—as all denial drugs itself on partial truth—so that it remained for the time being unanswerable, leaving me high and dry, split at the root, gasping for clarity, for air.

At that time Arnold Rich was living in suspension, waiting to be appointed to the professorship of pathology at Johns Hopkins. The appointment was delayed for years, no Jew ever having held a professional chair in that medical school. And he wanted it badly. It must have been a very bitter time for him, since he had believed so greatly in the redeeming power of excellence, of being the most brilliant, inspired man for the job. With enough excellence, you could presumably make it stop mattering that you were Jewish; you could become the *only* Jew in the gentile world, a Jew so "civilized," so far from "common," so attractively combining southern gentility with European cultural values that no one would ever confuse you with the raw, "pushy" Jews of New York, the "loud, hysterical" refugees from eastern Europe, the "overdressed" Jews of the urban South.

We—my sister, mother, and I—were constantly urged to speak quietly in public, to dress without ostentation, to repress all vividness or spontaneity, to assimilate with a world which might see us as too flamboyant. I suppose that my mother, pure gentile though she was, could be seen as acting "common" or "Jewish" if she laughed too loudly or spoke aggressively. My father's mother, who lived with us half the year, was a model of circumspect behavior, dressed in dark blue or lavender, retiring in company, ladylike to an extreme, wearing no jewelry except a good gold chain, a narrow brooch, or a string of pearls. A few times, within the family, I saw her anger flare, felt the passion she was repressing. But when Arnold took us out to a restaurant or on a trip, the Rich women were always tuned down to some WASP level my father believed, surely, would protect us all—maybe also make us unrecognizable to the "real Jews" who wanted to seize us, drag us back to the *shtetl*, the ghetto, in its many manifestations.

For, yes, that *was* a message—that some Jews would be after you, once they "knew," to rejoin them, to re-enter a world that was messy, noisy, unpredictable, maybe poor—"even though," as my mother once wrote me, criticizing my largely Jewish choice of friends in college, "some of them will be the most brilliant, fascinating people you'll ever meet." I wonder if that isn't one message of assimilation—of America—that the unlucky or the unachieving want to pull you backward, that to identify with them is to court downward mobility, lose the precious chance of passing, of token existence. There was always within this sense of Jewish identity a strong class discrimination. Jews might be "fascinating" as individuals but came with huge unruly families who "poured chicken soup over everyone's head" (in the phrase of a white southern male poet). Anti-Semitism could thus be justified by the bad behavior of certain Jews; and if you did not effectively deny family and community, there would always be a remote cousin claiming kinship with you who was the "wrong kind" of Jew.

I have always believed his attitude toward other Jews depended on who they were. . . . It was my impression that Jews of this background looked down on Eastern European Jews, including Polish Jews and Russian Jews, who generally were not as well educated. This from a letter written to me recently by a gentile who had worked in my father's department, whom I had asked about anti-Semitism there and in particular regarding my father. This informant also wrote me that it was hard to perceive anti-Semitism in Baltimore because the racism made so much more intense an impression: *I would almost have to think that blacks went to a different heaven than the whites, because the bodies were kept in a separate morgue, and some white persons did not even want blood transfusions from black donors.* My father's mind was predictably racist and misogynist; yet as a medical student he noted in his journal that southern male chivalry stopped at the point of any white man in a streetcar giving his seat to an old, weary Black woman standing in the aisle. Was this a Jewish insight—an outsider's insight, even though the outsider was striving to be on the inside?

Because what isn't named is often more permeating than what is, I believe that my father's Jewishness profoundly shaped my own identity and our family existence. They were shaped both by external anti-Semitism and my father's self-hatred, and by his Jewish pride. What Arnold did, I think, was call his Jewish pride something else: achievement, aspiration, genius, idealism. Whatever was unacceptable got left back under the rubric of Jewishness or the "wrong kind" of Jews—uneducated, aggressive, loud. The message I got was that we were really superior: nobody else's father had collected so many books, had traveled so far, knew so many languages. Baltimore was a musical city, but for the most part, in the families of my school friends, culture was for women. My father was an amateur musician, read poetry, adored encyclopedic knowledge. He prowled and pounced over my school papers, insisting I use "grown-up" sources; he criticized my poems for faulty technique and gave me books on rhyme and meter and form.

His investment in my intellect and talent was egotistical, tyrannical, opinionated, and terribly wearing. He taught me, nevertheless, to believe in hard work, to mistrust easy inspiration, to write and rewrite; to feel that I *was* a person of the book, even though a woman; to take ideas seriously. He made me feel, at a very young age, the power of language and that I could share in it.

The Riches were proud, but we also had to be very careful. Our behavior had to be more impeccable than other people's. Strangers were not to be trusted, nor even friends; family issues must never go beyond the family; the world was full of potential slanderers, betrayers, *people who could not understand.* Even within the family, I realize that I never in my whole life knew what my father was really feeling. Yet he spoke—monologued—with driving intensity. You could grow up in such a house mesmerized by the local electricity, the crucial meanings assumed by the merest things. This used to seem to me a sign that we were all living on some high emotional plane. It was a difficult force field for a favored daughter to disengage from.

Easy to call that intensity Jewish; and I have no doubt that passion is one of the qualities required for survival over generations of persecution. But what happens when passion is rent from its original base, when the white gentile world is softly saying "Be more like us and you can be almost one of us"? What happens when survival seems to mean closing off one emotional artery after another? His forebears in Europe had been forbidden to travel or expelled from one country after another, had special taxes levied on them if they left the city walls, had been forced to wear special clothes and badges, restricted to the poorest neighborhoods. He had wanted to be a "free spirit," to travel widely, among "all kinds of people." Yet in his prime of life he lived in an increasingly withdrawn world, in his house up on a hill in a neighborhood where Jews were not supposed to be able to buy property, depending almost exclusively on interactions with his wife and daughters to provide emotional connectedness. In his home, he created a private defense system so elaborate that even as he was dying, my mother felt unable to talk freely with his colleagues or others who might have helped her. Of course, she acquiesced in this.

The loneliness of the "only," the token, often doesn't feel like loneliness but like a kind of dead echo chamber. Certain things that ought to don't resonate. Somewhere Beverly Smith writes of women of color "inspiring the behavior" in each other. When there's nobody to "inspire the behavior," act out of the culture, there is an atrophy, a dwindling, which is partly invisible. . . .

Sometimes I feel I have seen too long from too many disconnected angles: white, Jewish, anti-Semite, racist, anti-racist, once-married, lesbian, middle-class, feminist, exmatriate southerner, *split at the root*—that I will never bring them whole. I would have liked, in this essay, to bring together the meanings of anti-Semitism and racism as I have experienced them and as I believe they intersect in the world beyond my life. But I'm not able to do this yet. I feel the tension as I think, make notes: *If you really look at the one reality, the other will waver and disperse.* Trying in one week to read Angela Davis and Lucy Davidowicz; trying to hold throughout to a feminist, a lesbian, perspective—what does this mean? Nothing has trained me for this. And sometimes I feel inadequate to make any statement as a Jew; I feel the history of denial within me like an injury, a scar. For assimilation has affected *my* perceptions; those early lapses in meaning, those blanks, are with me still. My ignorance can be dangerous to me and to others.

Yet we can't wait for the undamaged to make our connections for   40 us; we can't wait to speak until we are perfectly clear and righteous. There is no purity and, in our lifetimes, no end to this process.

This essay, then, has no conclusions: it is another beginning for me. Not just a way of saying, in 1982 Right Wing America, *I, too, will wear the yellow star.* It's a moving into accountability, enlarging the range of accountability. I know that in the rest of my life, the next half century or so, every aspect of my identity will have to be engaged. The middle-class white girl taught to trade obedience for privilege. The Jewish lesbian raised to be a heterosexual gentile. The woman who first heard oppression named and analyzed in the Black Civil Rights struggle. The woman with three sons, the feminist who hates male violence. The woman limping with a cane, the woman who has stopped bleeding are also accountable. The poet who knows that beautiful language can lie, that the oppressor's language sometimes sounds beautiful. The woman trying, as part of her resistance, to clean up her act.

For Journals

Do you have a sense of allegiance or heritage to more than one culture or group?

For Discussion

1.   Comment on Rich's metaphor, "split at the root," and on the next lines from her cited poem, "Neither Gentile nor Jew / Yankee nor Rebel." Does she develop both comparisons to a similar degree? Do you get a sense of which split was more difficult for her to deal with and why? What other splits does she write about?

2.   In what ways does Rich "flirt with identity"? What does she mean by this expression? She also writes of "moving into accountability," of

claiming both her heritage and her responsibility. For what, or for whom, does she feel she should be responsible? Why do you think claiming an identity or a heritage is so difficult and even dangerous for Rich?

3.   Identifying with another is seeing something of oneself in that person and something of that person in oneself. Rich was not eager to identify with the poor seamstress, nor her father with the "loud, pushy Jews of New York." Why not? What were the consequences of rejecting those identities? How did Rich feel about her and her father's choices? Why did it seem natural, at some stages of her life, for her and her father to suppress their identity in favor of a "white bread" American one?

4.   To what extent is Rich's dilemma a typically American one? What other dual identities exist in American cultures? Consider both immigrant Americans and American Indians in your response, and perhaps review the Ralph Ellison selection in this chapter.

5.   For whom, and for what purpose, is Rich writing? Do you think she would like to include her parents as one of her audiences?

For Writing

1.   Rich writes that she has seen the world from too many angles and cannot "bring them whole." Explore the different parts of your own identity, and as Rich does, develop and support your analysis with specifics—examples, images, dialogue, or anecdotes. With whom do you identify? How did your sense of identity develop? What roles did your family and friends play in the process? Have your choices changed as you have grown older? Have you had to deal with different splits, different allegiances?

2.   Rich writes of the invisibility of Jewishness, the belief that "it takes one to know one," of the very ability to "pass" and the conflicts that that ability brings in her search for identity. Compare and contrast Rich's notion of invisible identity with Ellison's in the selection from *Invisible Man*.

FRANK CHIN
1992

Studs Terkel

Studs (Louis) Terkel (1912–   ) was born in Chicago of working-class parents. A talented interviewer and author, Terkel earned an A.B. and a J.D. from the University of Chicago; he has worked as a radio and stage actor, sports columnist, news commentator, disk jockey, playwright, journalist, lecturer, talk-show host. He has been able to combine his talents as an interviewer and an author, and with the assistance of a tape recorder, he has compiled a number of studies of American life, recording and transcribing the lives of ordinary American men and women. His best-selling oral histories include Divison Street: America *(1966), focusing on conflict in urban America in the 1960s;* Hard Times: An Oral History of the Great Depression *(1970), which includes personal memories of the 1930s; and* Working *(1974), which taps into attitudes about and frustrations with work in America. The following selection, an oral history of playwright Frank Chin, is from Terkel's recent work,* Race: How Blacks and Whites Think and Feel about the American Obsession *(1992).*

A Chinese-American playwright and novelist.

"When I was a little kid, during World War II, I was raised by white folks: a retired vaudeville acrobat and a retired silent-screen bit player. We lived in a tarpaper shanty, outside Sacramento.

"A war veteran, with one eye missing and a few drinks, said to them, 'What are you doin' with that Jap kid?' I said, 'I'm no Jap kid. I'm an American of Chinese descent.' I didn't know what it was, but he didn't either. The rest of my life, I've been trying to find out exactly what it is." [Laughs.]

He later moved in with his grandmother and aunts in Oakland. "All we spoke in the family was Cantonese."

I hung out with blacks. I learned if I could make them laugh, I wouldn't get beat up and I could walk away and maintain my dignity. They actually came to respect me because I could talk my way out of fights in a way that would make them feel good. They would walk me to school.

Some people looked at this as a rejection of things Chinese. On the other hand, the blacks would say, and the whites, too, why was I talking about all this Chinese stuff? "We think of you as a member of the family." That always bothered me.

The Tower of Babel story always bothered me, too.

Oakland is the Tower of Babel. All these languages. And nobody even speaks English like everybody else. I've come to believe that monotheism encourages racism, whoever practices it. There is only one God and everyone else is an infidel, a pagan, or a goy. The Chinese look on all behavior as tactics and strategy. It's like war. You have to know the terrain. You don't destroy the terrain, you deal with it. We get along, not because we share a belief in God or Original Sin or a social contract, but because we make little deals and alliances with each other.

5   I like whites and blacks. I take them as individuals. I admire white culture: Shakespeare, the great ideas of Western Civilization. I also like black culture. In the sixties, it became a force in Asian-America. It always had a large presence in Oakland. I grew up with rhythm-and-blues, jazz, our original American art forms.

The fifties was still our age of innocence: the Eisenhower era. Everything was looking up: Perry Como. Since I grew up a loner, without any idea of parents, I thought Mommy and Daddy were just nicknames, like Shorty and Skinny. The idea that parents had a proprietary right over children was alien to me. A lot of the ideas of Chinese inferiority came late to me, from the outside. The one thing that saved me from being raised in the stereotype was my isolation during World War II, being raised by these white folks.

The sixties and the civil-rights movement came along, and the blacks were asserting themselves and getting our attention with phrases like "Power to the People." These wonderful black-leather jackets and the shades and the black berets were new even to the blacks themselves. It was like a parade, everyone in uniform.

As for the yellows, the civil-rights movement made us aware that we had no presence, no image in American culture as men, as people. We were perceived as being bright but with less physical prowess than the blacks and whites. We were more favored than the blacks, but we lacked their manhood. So a bunch of us began to appropriate "blackness." We'd wear the clothes, we'd affect the walk and we began talking black. We'd call our selves "Bro" and began talking Southern: "Hey, man."

We started talking about the sisters in the street and the brothers in the joint. I'd been in the joint and I didn't see any yellows there. I didn't see so many of our sisters walking the streets. That wasn't our thing. If it had been, we might have had a better sex life. [*Laughs.*]

10   [*He imitates the Black Panther rap.*] "Brothers and sisters, we've gotta organize, get together, and fight the *pig*. Brothers and sisters, Power to the People. Right on!" I said, "*What is this?* This isn't Chinese. It's a yellow minstrel show."

At this time, the government was throwing a lot of money at the gangs. The War on Poverty was on. Chinatown gangs, whose main business was being criminals, suddenly had social significance. They were perfectly happy to collect chump change.

I was teaching a class in Asian-American studies. My students were Chinese-Americans and Japanese-Americans. They were from the suburbs, outside Chinatown. My purpose was to break down stereotypes. So I decided to do an agit-prop thing, having them *play* the stereotypes.

We were rehearsing, doing a rock-and-roll version of

Ching-chong Chinaman,
sitting on a rail,
along come a choo-choo train,
cut off his tail.

Guitars, everything. The Lum gang walks in, walks up to the singer [*Simulates a deep, menacing voice.*]: "Stop singing that song. We don't like it." Lum comes up to me, he's holding his fist down, staring a hole through my chest. A student, a quiet little girl, who'd become a militant, is behind me saying, "Don't take no shit from nobody." I'm saying, "Shhh, shhh!" Porky, who's standing behind Lum, is yelling, "Kill 'im! Kill 'im!"

Lum is growling, "Stop singing that song. It makes fun of Chinese   15
people." I say, in my gentlest voice, "Have you ever heard of satire? We *know* it's a racist song. That's why we're singing it. We're making fun of the people who make fun of Chinese. Do you understand?" I could see I wasn't cutting it. Porky is hollering, "Kill 'im! Kill 'im!" Finally, in frustration, because I wasn't responding to a fight, they walk out.

The gang council decides that we're too controversial. They call me to a meeting. The leader of the Chinatown Red Guard taps me on the shoulder and says, "I want to talk to you." I turn around and just like in the movies, his fist is coming toward me. He knocks me down, my glasses go flying, he punches me in the stomach. Just like in the movies, he hits me in the back of the neck. While I'm on my hands and knees, he stomps on me and starts kicking me. I'm saying [*in a whining voice*], "This is the wrong movie, guys."

He says, "Identify with China!" I say, "Wait a minute. We're in America. This is where we are, where we live and where we're going to die. There's not going to be any revolution. That's crazy." He can't hit me anymore. He's already done that and it's not working. I've interrupted his speech. This had never happened to him before. He curls his lip and says, "You cultural nationalist!" I go, "*What?* What's a cultural nationalist? Don't you know how to swear? Call me mother-fucker, call me asshole, call me anything you want, but what's a cultural nationalist?" He doesn't know what to say to that, so they leave.

George Woo, a big guy, who's now teaching Asian-American Studies at San Francisco State, was pretty tight with the gangs then. He runs after the Red Guard and tells them if they ever beat me up again, he'll take it personally, that I'm his friend. All of a sudden, the leader of the gang council comes up to me and says, "I want to shake your hand. No one ever talked back to Alex that way before." We're all buddy-buddy now, because George said he'll take it personally.

The word flashes through Chinatown. Twenty-five minutes later, another gang of kids shows up. Must be fifteen, sixteen years old. One of them has a Tommy gun. "*Where are they? We heard someone beat up a friend of George's.*" [*Laughs.*] I said "No, no, that's not my style. Let's do it with words."

20   The civil-rights movement of the sixties affected the Chinese-American community in a number of ways. In ways that aren't very flattering to us. When I went to interview some Asian-American actors who played Charlie Chan's Number One, Two, Three, and Four sons, they were blaming the blacks for the yellows not getting more parts. "Here we've been good people, keeping our noses clean—" Suddenly they realized what I was up to and they saw *me* as a threat. I was making Chinese-Americans controversial by speaking out against racism.

It's an old story. The good Chinese were the Christian Chinese. The good Chinese were the ones who shucked all Chinese ways. They revere Pearl Buck and the missionaries that worked Chinatown. That's what bothered me, our history in Chinatown, San Francisco.

In Chinatown's twelve blocks, there are forty-two Christian churches. On the walls of Chinatown, there's a plaque honoring Ross Hunter, who produced *The Flower Drum Song;* a plaque honoring the song "Grant Avenue"; a plaque marking the birthplace of the first white child in San Francisco; a monument to the first white school. *Nothing* for the Chinese. There is one exception: a monument to Sun Yat Sen. He was a Christian.

Most in the community saw the civil-rights movement as a threat. They objected to school integration because they didn't want their children to be influenced by blacks. The fact is the mimicking of blacks that I experienced were of a few. White journalists have emphasized that aspect. As though the Chinese don't think of themselves as Chinese-Americans. As though we're an enclave, like Americans working for Aramco in Saudi Arabia.

Chinatown may be a stronghold of Chinese culture, but we're Chinese-Americans. We saw the movement as a threat because we might be identified as a minority. We were thinking of ourselves as being assimilated. We had worked so hard at being acculturated that we didn't know anything about China anymore.

During the Depression, my uncle was raised in a Chinese Baptist   25
Home for Boys. To raise money, they put on a show. It was the first Chinese-American blackface minstrel show in the history of the world. I came across the autobiography of the founder. I showed my uncle a picture in the book; the boys in blackface. He burst into tears. He was one of the Chung-mai minstrels. He got sad and I got angry. It was humiliating.

At the same time, we thought we were above the blacks. My family owned some property in the black district of Oakland. I once went with my mother to collect the rent. I said, "These places are terrible." She says, "Yeah, but they drive Cadillacs. It's what you call nigger-rich." That struck me so hard. I had never heard my folks put down blacks, denigrate people that way. Yet we were slumlords, taking advantage, exploiting them. It was a moment of moral confusion. I was eight at the time.

We feel because we're more civilized, quote unquote, because we're more middle-class, that we deserve more acceptance than the blacks. We don't riot, we don't make waves, we didn't protest, we're more American. We don't see that we've described ourselves as a race of Helen Kellers, mute, blind and deaf. We're the perfect minority.

We embrace Charlie Chan as an image of racist love. Most of us still think the good Chinaman is the Christian, Charlie Chan. There's a Chinese-American sociologist who said, "The Chinese, much to their credit, have never been overly bitter about racial prejudice. They have gone into jobs that reduced visibility and are moving out of population vortices of New York and San Francisco's Chinatown to outlying areas. Such a movement should be encouraged, because dispersion discourages visibility." The stereotype is embraced as a strategy for white acceptance.

The prejudice against blacks still continues, but we're smart enough to know it isn't quite civilized. We're also smart enough to use it to get our share. It happened to me. It was in the sixties. The railroads were taken to court for failing to integrate. They fell under ICC [Interstate Communication Commission] rules. So they put up a call: they were hiring brakemen. I was encouraged to apply. I was a clerk for a railroad company. It was the lowest of the low. I was fairly assured I'd be hired, implying I'd be more acceptable than a black. By default, I became the first Chinese-American brakeman on the Southern Pacific. I was the lesser of the two evils.

We believed what whites believed about blacks. We adopted all   30
the white prejudice. The blacks adopted the same prejudices about us. David Hilliard of the Black Panthers got up in Portsmouth Square—

luckily most Chinese there didn't understand English—and said, "You Chinese are the Uncle Toms of the colored peoples." It was apt. At the same time, the solution was not for us to become black.

The new immigrants, the Indochinese are a revelation. They still speak all the dialects of Indochina: Lao, Viet, or Cambodian. They pick up English as a matter of necessity, as a language of commerce. It's strategic. It's a white-man's world and you have to get along. Yet, all these languages are being spoken. They're using English as a dialect of Chinese and not following the rules. In Chinese-America, it is the new immigrants threatening our relationship with the whites, not the blacks. They are the unredeemed Chinese Chinese. It's an interesting, exciting time.

For Journals

Do you identify yourself more as having a particular ethnic heritage or as an American?

For Discussion

1.   With which different ethnic or cultural groups does Chin identify? What is his definition of "an American of Chinese descent"?

2.   When the Red Guard leader tells Chin, "Identify with China," Chin replies, "Wait a minute. We're in America. This is where we are, where we live and where we're going to die." What does this response imply about how Chin defines "American"? Can one be American and still "identify with China"?

3.   Chin says, "We get along, not because we share a belief in God or Original Sin or a social contract, but because we make little deals and alliances with each other." Compare this view with Benjamin Franklin's view of American unity.

4.   Chin describes the lack of presence of Chinese in American culture and cites a Chinese American sociologist who speaks approvingly of Chinese dispersion and "reduced visibility." How is this "invisibility" similar to and different from that of the narrator in *Invisible Man?* To the invisibility of Rich's Jewish identity in "Split at the Root"?

5.   What are the stereotypes about Chinese and blacks that Chin discusses? How do stereotypes affect a group's status as Americans? What do you think Chin would say?

6.   This selection is an oral history: Frank Chin told his story to Studs Terkel, who transcribed Chin's words and put them in the final form you see here. How does this fact affect your interpretation of the selection? Whose argument about American identity are you reading,

Terkel's or Chin's? In what ways do you think Chin shaped his words to appeal to Terkel? In what ways did Terkel shape Chin's words to appeal to you?

For Writing

1.   Individually or in small groups, interview two or three people, and ask them about their own ethnic and American identities and their views of racial issues. Write up the interviews, and share them with the class. What common ground do you find? What contrasts? What do you infer from the narratives?

2.   Research an ethnic stereotype, a piece of folklore, or ethnic jokes about your own ethnic group. You could do library research, and you may be able to interview a faculty member on your campus, especially in a social science department, who has some expertise in this area. Analyze the origins and process of such phenomena, paying special attention to the concept of "in" groups and "out" groups.

3.   Compare and contrast Chin's view of assimilation with that of another author represented in this chapter, perhaps Adrienne Rich in "Split at the Root."

CHICANA
1994

━━━━━

Martha Serrano

Martha Serrano grew up in Los Angeles. In her adolescent years she was a member of a gang but she dropped out of it to concentrate on high-school studies. Currently a college student majoring in American studies, she plans to attend law school and work on behalf of her people. As part of a first-year writing course, Serrano wrote the essay that follows in response to assignment number 2 at the end of this chapter.

Don't call me Hispanic. Don't call me Latina. Don't call me Mexican. Don't call me Mexican American. I want to be called Chicana. I am *mestiza*—indigenous and Spanish. My heritage is struggle and strength. I join my strength and struggle to that of my *hermanas*, my sisters. I am a woman of *Aztlan*, the southwestern United States. I don't want to be called Hispanic because I don't want people to tell me who I am and where I come from.

Most, if not all, of the people who call me Hispanic do not know that "Hispanic" is a term imposed on Americans of Latin descent by federal regulators, unprepared educators, and merchants who want our money but not us. In the mid 1970s, the U.S. Census Bureau first admitted that its 1970 census had seriously undercounted persons of Latin American descent in the United States. Under pressure from Latino activists to avoid a repetition of that mistake in the 1980 head count, the bureau searched for an all-encompassing word to describe the diverse assortment of Latin Americans living in this country: Mexican Americans and Mexican citizens, Puerto Ricans and Cuban Americans, and "other Hispanics" was the Census Bureau's solution.

The term "Hispanic" denies my cultural heritage. However, a Chicana is both Hispanic and Indian. For the Chicana, her world has been shaped by historical forces beyond the barrio and this country. My ancestors are the *conquistadores* and the conquered indigenous people of 1492. Our vanquished heritage has always haunted us and has been ignored by American historians.

The term "Chicana" is linked to my indigenous past. The roots of the word date back to the conquest of *El Valle de México*. Back then, Mexico was pronounced "meshico." The Spaniards had no letter or sound in their alphabet for the Nahuatl "sh" or hard "j" so they put an "x" in its place. In Meshico, "Mejico" became "Mexico" and "Tejas," "Texas." Mexico's Catholicism (which came from the encounter between Spaniards and Native Americans), and its food, art, and customs manifest Indian presence. Moreover, the Mexican dialect of Spanish, used to create world-famous prose and poetry, is influenced by Aztec words.

5   The first *mestizos* were born of Spanish soldiers and indigenous maidens. This scorned underclass was called Meshicanos and evolved to shicanos, Chicanos. Culturally, in the past, the word "Chicano" was a pejorative, class-bound adjective. Latinos used to associate the word "Chicano" with violent gangsters who had nothing better to do but hang out in the street and cause trouble. Now, however, it is the root idea of a new cultural identity for my people. It reveals a growing solidarity and the development of a common social praxis. Today, the widespread use of the word signals a rebirth of pride and confidence.

It embodies an ancient truth: "Man is never closer to his true self as when he is close to his community."

All Chicanos agree that being Chicano/a is more than being an American of Mexican descent; it is a way of thinking. It means being politically and culturally aware. It means knowing who you are and where you came from. It means being proud of your ethnic background and history. Most important of all, it means resisting assimilation into American mainstream society. Chicanos fight for self-determination and tackle issues facing the Chicano community. Chicanos struggle for the betterment of *La Raza,* the people.

Chicanos are *mestizos,* or the blending of two races and cultures. No matter what our differences may be, all Chicanos believe that education, especially higher education, leads to progress and the development of our community. We believe that once our people get educated, we can go to our own lawyers, doctors, architects, engineers, and others to help build a stronger and united Chicano community. However, we believe that education must contribute to the formation of a complete man or woman who truly values life and freedom. I am Chicana!

For Journals

Are there particular ways in which people categorize you that you dislike? What do you know about the origins of these labels?

For Discussion

1. Do your intellectual and emotional sides respond in the same way to Serrano's argument? If not, how do your reactions conflict? Do you find her introduction effective? Explain your answer.

2. What connections is Serrano making between the term "Chicana" and cultural identity? What is the connection between the individual, the community, and culture in forming identity?

3. Serrano describes the history of the terms "Chicana" and "Hispanic" to support her view that the former is the better term for her identity and her people. Are you persuaded by the information she provides? Could she offer other arguments to support her view?

4. Serrano rejects the term "Hispanic" as one imposed by others. Should people be able to name and define their own ethnicity and culture as they wish?

5. Serrano writes of resisting assimilation; some of the other readings in this chapter, however, assume that assimilation is good. Working in groups or pairs in class, argue that being American does or does not entail assimilation into mainstream American society. In the process, try to come up with a working definition of assimilation for contemporary Americans.

For Writing

1.   Compare and contrast Serrano's idea of cultural identity with Frank Chin's. Alternatively, construct a dialogue between Serrano and Adrienne Rich on claiming a cultural identity.

2.   Analyze the ways in which exposure to others of your ethnic group or national origin has, or has not, helped you to form an identity.

FILMS ON AMERICAN IDENTITIES

With a peer, in small groups, or as a class, view a video or film focusing on some aspect of American identities. Then discuss the ways in which it develops a particular theme, set of values, or perspective on American identity. The following films are suggested:

Sounder
Ballad of Gregorio Cortez
Roots
Coming to America
Dances with Wolves
Faces of the Enemy
Joy Luck Club
Daughters of the Dust
Avalon
Do the Right Thing

DEFINITION

Definition entails explaining or clarifying a word or expression. Defining terms accurately is crucial in argument; if writers and readers are to debate an issue, they must first understand each other and the basic terms of the discussion. If they do not establish a mutual understanding of the terms of debate, they are like two people talking to each other in different languages, conveying little except confusion. Agreeing on terms establishes common ground from which to launch a discussion.

Sometimes we can agree on common terms and proceed. When we cannot, the definitions themselves may become the argument. *American culture*, for example, has different meanings to de Tocqueville, Luther Standing Bear, and Frank Chin, not only because of the times in which they lived but also because of their different cultural perspectives. Explaining what they mean requires more than a sentence or two and more than one strategy of definition.

Defining terms effectively and appropriately requires a good sense of audience awareness. If writers define terms with which their audiences are already familiar, they waste time and space and try their readers' patience; they may also inadvertently insult readers' intelligence, which will undercut efforts to persuade. But writers should not assume that the audience knows specialized terms or understands a particular interpretation of an abstract term. Analyzing intended audiences—their education, experience, familiarity with the subject of discussion—must guide writers in determining how much they need to define.

Analyzing Definitions in Arguments

Because definitions are fundamental building blocks in argument, an essential step in analyzing persuasive writing is to identify and understand the definitions the writer has used. Because any discussion of American identities must include a definition of what is meant by "American," the writers and visual artists in this chapters have all used definitions. The type of definition used depends on the occasion, the audience, the purpose, and the subject matter.

Writers do not always call attention to the ways in which they are defining terms. Often the most important definitions are implicit. For example, Ralph Ellison, in the Prologue to *Invisible Man*, is apparently examining the phenomenon of cultural invisibility and its consequences for Americans of African descent. However, he is also providing an implicit definition of "American": in this term, Ellison would argue, we must include all those who live in and contribute to American society, whether they are powerful and white or excluded and black. Others are very explicit in defining key terms. The cartoonist who created *U.S. Hotel* quite clearly considered bomb throwing, incendiary talk, and communism—and all those who embrace these practices—to be un-American. Be alert to both implicit and explicit definitions.

When proposing a definition is the central purpose in a piece of persuasive writing, the writer must provide supporting evidence. The writers in this chapter have supported their definitions of the American identity in a variety of ways. Frank Chin, as quoted by Studs Terkel, defines himself initially as "an American of Chinese descent." The personal experiences he then relates explore and amplify what that statement means for a man of Chinese ethnicity raised by a non-Chinese family in an ethnically diverse neighborhood. Clearly the simple definition does not convey all that Chin intends. Adrienne Rich combines personal experience with analysis and reflection to express and support her perceived self-identity as someone who is "split at the root." In each case, the author has used the kind of evidence he or she thought would be most effective for the expected audience and purpose of the writing. When you read extended definitions supported by examples, facts, narratives, case histories, and so on, consider whether the evidence is strong enough to support the proposed definition.

Using Definitions in Arguments

When writing your own arguments, be careful to provide clear, effective definitions whenever they are needed. To decide whether a definition is needed, consider whether your readers are likely to know the term and whether they will be confused or misled if a definition is not provided.

Following are some common strategies used for defining terms. When you need to define terms only as the basis for an argument, one or two of these strategies should do. When you are arguing for the definition of a complex or abstract term—and when that term is controversial—you may find it useful to combine several strategies to persuade your reader that your definition and interpretation of the term are appropriate.

Essential Definition   An essential definition assigns the thing defined to a general class and then identifies the characteristics that distinguish it from every other member of this class: "An American is a person born in America." In this definition, the term defined is "an American," the general class is "person" and the distinguishing characteristic is "born in America." A person born in France would not be an American by this definition. A good essential definition is like a mathematical formula with the verb "is" acting as an equals sign; you should be able to turn it around and still have a true, logical statement: "A person born in America is an American."

Dictionary definitions are often essential definitions, and a good dictionary, such as *Webster's Third New International Dictionary* or the

Oxford English Dictionary, may provide you with precisely the definition you need. Sometimes definitions from specialized dictionaries—a dictionary of music or philosophy, for example—will help you to use and define particular technical terms. Using a dictionary definition is most useful when your readers are likely to agree with your definition or will accept the authority of the source.

Definition by Comparison   Comparison is a useful way to define when you can relate your term to something with which the reader is already familiar. Some comparisons are explicit and literal, as when Frank Chin compares the actions and attitudes of African Americans and Chinese Americans during the civil rights movement. "The Chinese American experience of this phenomenon," he would say, "is like the African American experience." Explicit comparisons are most useful when you expect readers to agree with your definition. If you think readers will disagree, you will be forced to provide enough evidence to support the validity of the comparison, which will distract you from the points you wanted to draw from the comparison.

Other comparisons used as definitions are implicit, often communicated through metaphors. For example, Ellison uses the metaphor of invisibility to define the experience of being a black American: being a black person in America is like being invisible. Implicit comparisons are useful when the reader is likely to be familiar with the concept or image you select for your metaphor and when other means of definition seem inadequate; it would be difficult for Ellison to convey literally the day-in and day-out inequities of being black in midtwentieth century America without inducing guilt or alienation on the part of his white readers. Metaphors and other implied comparisons allow you to present a potentially objectionable or problematic definition subtly and gradually; you must eventually provide evidence that the definition is a sound one, but readers will probably grant you more leeway.

Definition by Example   Examples are often used to define abstract or complex terms. When Adrienne Rich sought to define the nature of her ambivalence about her Jewish heritage, she used a series of brief anecdotes from her personal life. When Alexis de Tocqueville wanted to define the American character, he used examples drawn from legal and political history. Narratives and other examples can be effective in clarifying and explaining a complex term, but be sure that your readers will accept the examples you select. If they view the examples as atypical, irrelevant, or simply unclear, your definition will not be successful.

Stipulative Definition   A stipulative definition differentiates a specialized or temporary use of a term from its conventional or common usage. For example, the term "racism" is defined in the dictionary as the belief that race is the primary determinant of human traits and capacities. Many people, however, believe that the term cannot be applied to nonwhites because racism can be perpetuated only by those in power, and in America nonwhites lack the power to enforce racism institutionally. Such a writer would need to clarify that in his or her writing "racism" is the term that will apply to biased white people and "prejudiced" is the term that will apply to biased nonwhite people. A stipulative definition can help ensure that you and your reader understand each other when you use a term likely to have more than one meaning.

Negative Definition   Most definitions are stated in positive terms: "*x* is *y*." However, sometimes the most effective way to convey what something *is* is to define what it is *not*. The cartoonist who created *The U.S. Hotel* defined good Americans by identifying the traits they should *not* have: a penchant for bomb throwing, incendiarism, communism, and so on.

Often a negative definition can be used in conjunction with a positive definition, as when President Kennedy declared that his election was "not a victory of party, but a celebration of freedom." Martha Serrano used this strategy as well when she first established that she is not a Hispanic, not a Latina, and not a Mexican American; she is a Chicana. Such an approach is helpful when the reader is likely to have preconceived definitions of a term in mind and the writer needs to deal with those misconceptions before moving on to state what the term *does* mean.

WRITING ASSIGNMENTS

1.   Construct and argue for a fully developed definition on an issue raised in the readings, drawing on one or more of the strategies for definition just described. Make sure you select a term that is arguable rather than clearly conveyed with a brief or dictionary-style definition. You may need to do additional research—interviewing experts, looking in specialized dictionaries, developing examples as evidence—to define your term.

2.   Write a memoir, narrative, or autobiography that conveys a sense of your personal identity as an American and what the term "American" means to you. Review the Rich, Terkel, Ellison, and Serrano readings for ways in which these authors developed their self-definition or search for identity. Make sure you have a specific focus or claim about

your identity rather than stringing together examples or anecdotes without a persuasive intent.

3. Investigate past or contemporary issues in immigration policy. Examine how people are defined as American citizens, who is a citizen automatically and who must apply, what kinds of restrictions are in place, whether different categories of immigrants are able to enter in higher numbers and why. Some research questions you might consider include the following: What kinds of immigrants does American policy favor? How can definitions be used to favor particular groups? In what ways have policies changed over the years? Present your thesis and findings in an essay that documents this research.

4. Imagine that you are an advertising copywriter and you have been asked to create a public relations campaign for a political candidate that defines the best that America and Americans have to offer for an audience of U.S. citizens. Sketch out your strategy, and then propose your strategy to your client, a candidate who wants to identify himself or herself with that idealization of America, and argue that your strategy will be effective.

Alternatively, design a campaign for a U.S. tourism organization that will target an overseas audience from a country or region you designate. It might be interesting, for example, to devise a campaign for countries from the former Soviet Union.

5. Currently, scholars, activists, and students are discussing the notion of "identity politics"—or the belief that people from nondominant cultures should define themselves rather than having identities imposed on them by others. Martha Serrano's essay is an example of the kinds of debate revolving around conflicts between how people identify themselves and how others define them. Research this concept in recent periodicals, and write an essay explaining the concept to your classmates or other peer group. Alternatively, argue for a redefinition of an ethnic group or culture with which you identify.

AMERICAN DREAMS

$\mathcal{T}$he selections in this chapter revolve around the most familiar but elusive expression of the American national character, the American dream. It is an expression that turns up everywhere in our culture; open any newspaper or watch any news program, and you will probably find more samples like:

- An African-American banker helps provide mortgages to minority applicants. The headline of the newspaper story is "The American Dream"; the subtitle is "Doing Well by Doing Good."

- Three promising Navy officers, a woman and two men, are killed in a double murder and suicide. The news story focuses on the poignancy of the loss by pointing out that all three officers were on the way to achieving the American dream.

- A teenage television actor becomes wealthy and famous; a television magazine program reporting on his new-found stardom calls it an example of the American dream.

As these examples show, the American dream is so well established—both as an expression and an idea—that no one feels the need to define it; however, no one seems to agree on exactly what it means. Perhaps the closest we can come is to say that the American dream represents both what Americans believe themselves entitled to and what they believe themselves capable of. In other words, it is the promise inherent in the idea of America itself.

The idea of America actually began with a mistake; Renaissance Europeans in search of a route to the East Indies stumbled on it. As the famous naval historian Samuel Eliot Morison remarked, they spent the next fifty years trying to get around or through it. Actually finding such a continent, even by accident, had exciting and unsettling impact on the European imagination. As a result, early European dreams about America reflected a curious combination of fantasy and science fiction. Writers who had never been to America described Indians with feathers sprouting from their feet, precious stones growing out of their chests, heads that grew from below their shoulders, no government, no private property, a taste for cannibalism, and a life span of one-hundred-and-fifty years.

Of course the reality was very different, and dreams changed, from the discovery of golden cities to the acquisition of land for farming. But two early elements were fixed—that America represented the possibility of prosperity and that whoever came here could make a new start.

From the beginning, then, the American dream has existed as a series of evolving promises and discrepancies, of continuous conflicts and renewed possibilities for achievement: between faith in a glorious promise and the more difficult task of making that promise come true under less-than-ideal conditions. These contradictions are elements in a three-hundred–year debate that continues to this day, because, while most Americans believe in the American dream, there is much disagreement on its particulars. We argue about what the dream consists of—money, social equality, power, success, democratic ideals; we argue about the means to achieve it—hard work, luck, aggressiveness, drive, or the will to succeed at any cost; we argue about who is entitled to it: long-term residents, new immigrants, everyone, or just the lucky few. And finally, we argue over how much each person is entitled to—the complete fulfillment of his or her dream, or just the right to compete?

American Dreams through History

The selections in this chapter reflect this combination of reality and myth, of coexisting contradictions, of disappointing experience and renewed optimism and faith. Benjamin Franklin, who came of age along with his country in the eighteenth century, became the archetypal successful American; everything he tried—printing, foreign languages, scientific inventions, diplomacy, writing—he did, and he did brilliantly. His *Autobiography* (written in an agrarian America with only one major city, Philadelphia, and a small population) is still the model for all subsequent American success stories and contains the most famous coming-of-age scene in American history: a young Ben Franklin arriving in Philadelphia, walking down the main street with two rolls under his arm and the whole world before him. For him, and for his young country, anything is possible.

Not everyone in America could count on the availability of the American dream. Frederick Douglass, for example, was born a slave, and therefore excluded from the kind of opportunity that Franklin enjoyed. He wrote his autobiography after he escaped from his owners and made his way to freedom. Given his history, he could not help but be aware of a darker side of the dream; told explicitly that the dream was not for him, he rebelled and pursued it anyway, at enormous personal risk. Still, the American dream continued to have a powerful attraction for immigrants from other parts of the world and, drawn by the lure of western expansion, for residents and immigrants in other parts of the country, even though the results could not live up to everyone's glorious expectations. The unknown artist who drew the poster, *California, Cornucopia of the World,* counted on the promise of unlimited land and opportunity to draw population to California.

The immigrant who wrote most glowingly and confidently of the accessibility of the American dream was Mary Antin, who arrived in America in the 1890s as part of massive Russian-Jewish immigration to America to escape religious and economic persecution. Antin wrote her autobiography, *The Promised Land,* in 1912 when she was still a young woman and when anti-immigration sentiment was picking up steam in Congress. It is a defense of immigrants and of the "open-door" policy that made their coming possible.

Antin's book was a best-seller, but in 1924 Congress passed legislation closing the open door and eliminating easy immigration. At about the same time, Langston Hughes, an African-American poet, writer, and a leader of the great cultural explosion of the Harlem Renaissance, was questioning why the dream that was so clear to Antin was still so inaccessible to many other Americans. In a series of poems, including "Let America Be America Again," he underlined the contradictions between the dream of equal opportunity and a much grimmer reality, between what America promises and what it delivers. In 1963, thirty years after Hughes made his plea for a renewed commitment to the American dream, Martin Luther King, Jr., the leader of the modern civil rights movement, made the most famous American speech of the twentieth century: the largely extemporaneous address at the Lincoln Memorial, "I Have a Dream." At the time, most southern blacks could not share a water fountain, a beach, a bus seat, a school room, or a voting booth with southern whites. King, a believer in the power of nonviolent resistance, had already led a successful bus boycott in Montgomery, Alabama, and a long series of marches, demonstrations, and sit-ins at ordinary places like lunch counters; he had been arrested by southern sheriffs and was the frequent recipient of death threats. But a huge civil rights march in Washington, D.C., gave him the opportunity to address a larger American audience and to locate civil rights at the political center of the American dream, to make one the expression of the other.

As the United States has become more powerful, more technologically developed, and more urban, the conditions that originally attracted immigrants (like the promise of cheap land) have ceased to exist even as promises. But the dream of individual and collective fulfillment continues to tantalize people with its possibilities. During your lifetime, new immigrants fleeing persecution or seeking security have continued fighting great odds to reach America; no degree of discouragement has kept people from southeast Asia, from Central America, from Russia, even from Western Europe, from competing for the limited number of legal permits or from entering the country illegally; to them, America is still the only country where their dreams of a better life can come true.

As we approach the end of this century, Americans are confronting for the first time the problems of decreased space and natural resources, and there are new questions to be answered as to what we can reasonably expect from our dreams in our own lifetimes. Will we be able to achieve the standard of living that most Americans enjoyed after World War II? Will our jobs be secure enough to allow us to plan for the future?

The selections up to this point have focused on the possibilities for personal achievement and happiness inherent in the American dream, but Dolores Hayden, a professional architect and urban planner, examines a side of the dream so basic that it is usually taken for granted: How do Americans live? What is an American home like? What happens to the domestic side of the American dream now that women work outside the home and the typical American family does not have the house with a picket fence, two parents, a sufficient middle-class income, and a mother who can afford to stay in and do the housework? Why does it take more time to take care of a family of four today than it did in 1920? Hayden's argument is punctuated with two magazine advertisements from the high-flying 1920s and the Great Depression that illustrate cherished notions of how the American dream should be lived.

While the selections in this chapter provide many avenues of approach to gain an understanding of the American dream, the most important fact is that it continues to affect people's lives today and to function as a source of inspiration and passionate conflict. Caroline Mendoza's essay about her family's immigration from Peru and her parents' determination to make a better life for their children drama-tizes that power. So does the article from the San Francisco *Chronicle* by Suzanne Solis. The first in a series about pro- and anti-immigrant forces in California in the 1990s, it allows people on each side of the ar-gument to express what they want, what they are afraid of, and why they each feel that the custodianship of the American dream today be-longs to them.

All selections in this chapter, separated as they are by time and distance, speak to us in distinct and recognizable American voices. In Chapter 3, you read about Americans trying to establish their identities by defining, for themselves as much as for anyone else, who an Ameri-can is. This chapter's selections continue that process by trying to ex-press what Americans want and what they feel are their unique opportunities; the selections appeal to a common sense of possibility that both shapes our ambitions and survives our experience.

Expressing the American Dream through Examples

All the writers and artists in this chapter, despite considerable dif-ferences in style and content, use examples drawn from experience, often their own experience. Of course, in autobiographies we expect to hear the author's story; it's what an autobiography is. But there is something else at work here—writers who feel that their subject matter is so distinctly American that they must serve as their own role mod-els. It's not that they are not influenced by previous writers: Franklin read and imitated English essayists as a young man, Douglass read Franklin, Hughes read them both. But the intent of these writers is to communicate their ideas, in an informal way, about large American preoccupations; freedom, achievement, civil rights, and the American dream. By being particular, by using specific and personal examples from their own experience as evidence, they establish their credibility and make it possible for readers who have not shared their experience to identify with its underlying emotional effect.

As you read and reflect on the selections that follow, consider your own personal dreams. Are they very different than those in the selec-tions or those of people you know? Is your dream something you can achieve on your own—like educating yourself—something that needs other people—like raising a family—or something that requires a change in our culture—like eliminating racism? Is a dream worth pur-suing even though you may not be able to fulfill it?

FROM *AUTOBIOGRAPHY*

1771

Benjamin Franklin

Benjamin Franklin (1706–1790) made his fortune as an editor and printer, taught himself several languages, had a lifelong passionate involvement with science, started the first lending library and fire department in America, invented the Franklin stove, bifocals, and a new kind of clock, and improved the street lighting in Philadelphia. He founded the American Philosophical Society and the school that became the University of Pennsylvania. When he began writing the Autobiography, *he had already been involved in politics for many years and was shortly to become a member of the Continental Congress. Franklin helped draft the Declaration of Independence and then served as an enormously successful first American ambassador to France. He was a member of the 1787 Convention that produced the Constitution of the United States.*

My elder Brothers were all put Apprentices to different Trades. I was put to the Grammar School at Eight Years of Age, my Father intending to devote me as the Tithe of his Sons to the Service of the Church. My early Readiness in learning to read (which must have been very early, as I do not remember when I could not read) and the Opinion of all his Friends that I should certainly make a good Scholar, encourag'd him in this Purpose of his. My Uncle Benjamin too approv'd of it, and propos'd to give me all his Shorthand Volumes of Sermons I suppose as a Stock to set up with, if I would learn his Character. I continu'd however at the Grammar School not quite one Year, tho' in that time I had risen gradually from the Middle of the Class of that Year to be the Head of it, and farther was remov'd into the next Class above it, in order to go with that into the third at the End of the Year. But my Father in the mean time, from a View of the Expence of a College Education which, having so large a Family, he could not well afford, and the mean Living many so educated were afterwards able to obtain, Reasons that he gave to his Friends in my Hearing, altered his first Intention, took me from the Grammar School, and sent me to a School for Writing & Arithmetic kept by a then famous Man, Mr Geo. Brownell, very successful in his Profession generally, and that by mild encouraging Methods. Under him I acquired fair Writing pretty soon, but I fail'd in the Arithmetic, & made no Progress in it.—At Ten Years old, I was taken home to assist my Father in his Business, which was that of a Tallow Chandler and Sope-Boiler. A Business he was not bred to, but had assumed on his Arrival in New England & on finding his Dying Trade would not maintain his Family, being in little Request. Accordingly I was employed in cutting Wick for the Candles, filling the Dipping Mold, & the Molds for cast Candles, attending the Shop, going of Errands, &c.—I dislik'd the Trade and had a strong Inclination for the Sea; but my Father declar'd against it; however, living near the Water, I was much in and about it, learnt early to swim well, & to manage Boats, and when in a Boat or Canoe with other Boys I was commonly allow'd to govern, especially in any case of Difficulty; and upon other Occasions I was generally a Leader among the Boys, and sometimes led them into Scrapes, of wch. I will mention one Instance, as it shows an early projecting public Spirit, tho' not then justly conducted. There was a Salt Marsh that bounded part of the Mill Pond, on the Edge of which at Highwater, we us'd to stand to fish for Minews. By much Trampling, we had made it a mere Quagmire. My Proposal was to build a Wharf there fit for us to stand upon, and I show'd my Comrades a large Heap of Stones which were intended for a new House near the Marsh, and which would very well suit our Purpose. Accordingly in the Evening when the Workmen were gone, I assembled a Number of my Play-fellows, and working with them diligently like so many Emmets, sometimes two or three to a Stone, we brought them all away and built our little Wharff.—The next Morning the Workmen were surpriz'd at Missing the Stones; which were found in our Wharff; Enquiry was made after the Removers; we were discovered & complain'd of; several of us were corrected by our Fathers; and tho' I pleaded the Usefulness of the Work, mine convinc'd me that nothing was useful which was not honest.—

To return, I continu'd thus employ'd in my Father's Business for two Years, that is till I was 12 Years old; and my Brother John, who was bred to that Business having left my Father, married and set up for himself at Rhodeisland, there was all Appearance that I was destin'd to supply his Place and be a Tallow Chandler. But my Dislike to the Trade continuing, my Father was under Apprehensions that if he did not find one for me more agreable, I should break away and get to Sea, as his Son Josiah had done to his great Vexation. He therefore sometimes took me to walk with him, and see Joiners, Bricklayers, Turners, Braziers, &c. at their Work, that he might observe my Inclination, & endeavour to fix it on some Trade or other on Land.—It has ever since been a Pleasure to me to see good Workmen handle their Tools; and it has been useful to me, having learnt so much by it, as to be able to do little Jobs my self in my House, when a Workman could not readily be got; & to construct little Machines for my Experiments while the

Intention of making the Experiment was fresh & warm in my Mind. My Father at last fix'd upon the Cutler's Trade, and my Uncle Benjamin's Son Samuel who was bred to that Business in London being about that time establish'd in Boston, I was sent to be with him some time on liking. But his Expectations of a Fee with me displeasing my Father, I was taken home again.—

From a Child I was fond of Reading, and all the little Money that came into my Hands was ever laid out in Books. Pleas'd with the Pilgrim's Progress, my first Collection was of John Bunyan's Works, in separate little Volumes. I afterwards sold them to enable me to buy R. Burton's Historical Collections; they were small Chapmen's Books and cheap, 40 or 50 in all.—My Father's little Library consisted chiefly of Books in polemic Divinity, most of which I read, and have since often regretted, that at a time when I had such a Thirst for Knowledge, more proper Books had not fallen in my Way, since it was now resolv'd I should not be a Clergyman. Plutarch's Lives there was, in which I read abundantly, and I still think that time spent to great Advantage. There was also a Book of Defoe's called an Essay on Projects and another of Dr Mather's call'd Essays to do Good, which perhaps gave me a Turn of Thinking that had an Influence on some of the principal future Events of my Life.

This Bookish Inclination at length determin'd my Father to make me a Printer, tho' he had already one Son, (James) of that Profession. In 1717 my Brother James return'd from England with a Press & Letters to set up his Business in Boston. I lik'd it much better than that of my Father, but still had a Hankering for the Sea.—To prevent the apprehended Effect of such an Inclination, my Father was impatient to have me bound to my Brother. I stood out some time, but at last was persuaded and signed the Indentures, when I was yet but 12 Years old.—I was to serve as an Apprentice till I was 21 Years of Age, only I was to be allow'd Journeyman's Wages during the last Year. In a little time I made great Proficiency in the Business, and became a useful Hand to my Brother. I now had Access to better Books. An Acquaintance with the Apprentices of Booksellers, enabled me sometimes to borrow a small one, which I was careful to return soon & clean. Often I sat up in my Room reading the greatest Part of the Night, when the Book was borrow'd in the Evening & to be return'd early in the Morning lest it should be miss'd or wanted. . . .

5   My Brother had in 1720 or 21, begun to print a Newspaper. It was the second that appear'd in America, & was called *The New England Courant.* The only one before it, was *The Boston News Letter.* I remember his being dissuaded by some of his Friends from the Undertaking, as not likely to succeed, one Newspaper being in their Judgment enough for America.—At this time 1771 there are not less than five & twenty.—

He went on however with the Undertaking, and after having work'd in composing the Types & printing off the Sheets I was employ'd to carry the Papers thro' the Streets to the Customers.—He had some ingenious Men among his Friends who amus'd themselves by writing little Pieces for this Paper, which gain'd it Credit, & made it more in Demand; and these Gentlemen often visited us.—Hearing their Conversations, and their Accounts of the Approbation their Papers were receiv'd with, I was excited to try my Hand among them. But being still a Boy, & suspecting that my Brother would object to printing any Thing of mine in his Paper if he knew it to be mine, I contriv'd to disguise my Hand, & writing an anonymous Paper I put it in at Night under the Door of the Printing House. It was found in the Morning & communicated to his Writing Friends when they call'd in as Usual. They read it, commented on it in my Hearing, and I had the exquisite Pleasure, of finding it met with their Approbation, and that in their different Guesses at the Author none were named but Men of some Character among us for Learning & Ingenuity.—I suppose now that I was rather lucky in my Judges: And that perhaps they were not really so very good ones as I then esteem'd them. Encourag'd however by this, I wrote and convey'd in the same Way to the Press several more Papers, which were equally approv'd, and I kept my Secret till my small Fund of Sense for such Performances was pretty well exhausted, & then I discovered it; when I began to be considered a little more by my Brother's Acquaintance, and in a manner that did not quite please him, as he thought, probably with reason, that it tended to make me too vain. And perhaps this might be one Occasion of the Differences that we began to have about this Time. Tho' a Brother, he considered himself as my Master, & me as his Apprentice; and accordingly expected the same Services from me as he would from another; while I thought he demean'd me too much in some he requir'd of me, who from a Brother expected more Indulgence. Our Disputes were often brought before our Father, and I fancy I was either generally in the right, or else a better Pleader, because the Judgment was generally in my favour: But my Brother was passionate & had often beaten me, which I took extreamly amiss;* and thinking my Apprenticeship very tedious, I was continually wishing for some Opportunity of shortening it, which at length offered in a manner unexpected.

One of the Pieces in our News-Paper, on some political Point which I have now forgotten, gave Offence to the Assembly. He was taken up, censur'd and imprison'd for a Month by the Speaker's Warrant, I suppose because he would not discover his Author. I too was

---

*I fancy his harsh & tyrannical Treatment of me, might be a means of impressing me with that Aversion to arbitrary Power that has stuck to me thro' my whole Life.

taken up & examin'd before the Council; but tho' I did not give them any Satisfaction, they contented themselves with admonishing me, and dismiss'd me; considering me perhaps as an Apprentice who was bound to keep his Master's Secrets. During my Brother's Confinement, which I resented a good deal, notwithstanding our private Differences, I had the Management of the Paper, and I made bold to give our Rulers some Rubs in it, which my Brother took very kindly, while others began to consider me in an unfavourable Light, as a young Genius that had a Turn for Libelling & Satyr. My Brother's Discharge was accompany'd with an Order of the House, (a very odd one) *that James Franklin should no longer print the Paper called The New England Courant.* There was a Consultation held in our Printing House among his Friends what he should do in this Case. Some propos'd to evade the Order by changing the Name of the Paper; but my Brother seeing Inconveniences in that, it was finally concluded on as a better Way, to let it be printed for the future under the Name of *Benjamin Franklin.* And to avoid the Censure of the Assembly that might fall on him, as still printing it by his Apprentice, the Contrivance was, that my old Indenture should be return'd to me with a full Discharge on the Back of it, to be shown on Occasion; but to secure to him the Benefit of my Service I was to sign new Indentures for the Remainder of the Term, wch were to be kept private. A very flimsy Scheme it was, but however it was immediately executed, and the Paper went on accordingly under my Name for several Months. At length a fresh Difference arising between my Brother and me, I took upon me to assert my Freedom, presuming that he would not venture to produce the new Indentures. It was not fair in me to take this Advantage, and this I therefore reckon one of the first Errata of my Life: But the Unfairness of it weigh'd little with me, when under the Impressions of Resentment, for the Blows his Passion too often urg'd him to bestow upon me. Tho' He was otherwise not an ill-natur'd Man: Perhaps I was too saucy & provoking.—

When he found I would leave him, he took care to prevent my getting Employment in any other Printing-House of the Town, by going round & speaking to every Master, who accordingly refus'd to give me Work. I then thought of going to New York as the nearest Place where there was a Printer: and I was then rather inclin'd to leave Boston, when I reflected that I had already made my self a little obnoxious, to the governing Party. . . .

Walking in the Evening by the Side of the River a Boat came by, which I found was going towards Philadelphia, with several People in her. They took me in, and as there was no Wind, we row'd all the Way; and about Midnight not having yet seen the City, some of the Company were confident we must have pass'd it, and would row no farther, the others knew not where we were, so we put towards the Shore, got into a Creek, landed near an old Fence with the Rails of which we made a Fire, the Night being cold, in October, and there we remain'd till Daylight. Then one of the Company knew the Place to be Cooper's Creek a little above Philadelphia, which we saw as soon as we got out of the Creek, and arriv'd there about 8 or 9 a Clock, on the Sunday morning, and landed at the Market street Wharff.—

I have been the more particular in this Description of my Journey, & shall be so of my first Entry into that City, that you may in your Mind compare such unlikely Beginning with the Figure I have since made there. I was in my working Dress, my best Cloaths being to come round by Sea. I was dirty from my Journey; my Pockets were stuff'd out with Shirts & Stockings; I knew no Soul, nor where to look for Lodging. I was fatigu'd with Travelling, Rowing & Want of Rest. I was very hungry, and my whole Stock of Cash consisted of a Dutch Dollar and about a Shilling in Copper. The latter I gave the People of the Boat for my Passage, who at first refus'd it on Acc^t of my Rowing; but I insisted on their taking it, a Man being sometimes more generous when he has but a little Money than when he has plenty, perhaps thro' Fear of being thought to have but little. Then I walk'd up the Street, gazing about, till near the Market House I met a Boy with Bread. I had made many a Meal on Bread, & inquiring where he got it, I went immediately to the Baker's he directed me to in second Street; and ask'd for Bisket, intending such as we had in Boston, but they it seems were not made in Philadelphia, then I ask'd for a threepenny Loaf, and was told they had none such: so not considering or knowing the Difference of Money & the greater Cheapness nor the Names of his Bread, I bad him give me three pennyworth of any sort. He gave me accordingly three great Puffy Rolls. I was surpriz'd at the Quantity, but took it, and having no Room in my Pockets, walk'd off, with a Roll under each Arm, & eating the other. Thus I went up Market Street as far as fourth Street, passing by the Door of Mr Read, my future Wife's Father, when she standing at the Door saw me, & thought I made as I certainly did a most awkward ridiculous Appearance. Then I turn'd and went down Chestnut Street and part of Walnut Street, eating my Roll all the Way, and coming round found my self again at Market street Wharff, near the Boat I came in, to which I went for a Draught of the River Water, and being fill'd with one of my Rolls, gave the other two to a Woman & her Child that came down the River in the Boat with us and were waiting to go farther. Thus refresh'd I walk'd again up the Street, which by this time had many clean dress'd People in it who were all walking the same Way; I join'd them, and thereby was led into the great Meeting House of the Quakers near the Market. I sat down among them, and after looking round a while & hearing nothing said, being very drowzy thro' Labour & want of Rest the preceding Night, I fell fast asleep, and continu'd so till the Meeting broke up, when one was kind enough to rouse me. This was therefore the first House I was in or slept in, in Philadelphia. . . .

10

There are Croakers in every Country always boding its Ruin. Such a one then lived in Philadelphia, a Person of Note, an elderly Man, with a wise Look and very grave Manner of Speaking. His Name was Samuel Mickle. This Gentleman, a Stranger to me, stopt one Day at my Door, and ask'd me if I was the young Man who had lately opened a new Printing-house: Being answer'd in the Affirmative; He said he was sorry for me; because it was an expensive Undertaking, & the Expence would be lost, for Philadelphia was a sinking Place, the People already half Bankrupts or near being so; all Appearances of the contrary such as new Buildings & the Rise of Rents, being to his certain Knowledge fallacious, for they were in fact among the Things that would soon ruin us. And he gave me such a Detail of Misfortunes now existing or that were soon to exist, that he left me half-melancholy. Had I known him before I engag'd in this Business, probably I never should have done it.—This Man continu'd to live in this decaying Place, & to declaim in the same Strain, refusing for many Years to buy a House there, because all was going to Destruction, and at last I had the Pleasure of seeing him give five times as much for one as he might have bought it for when he first began his Croaking.—

I should have mention'd before, that in the Autumn of the preceding Year, I had form'd most of my ingenious Acquaintance into a Club, for mutual Improvement, which we call'd the Junto. We met on Friday Evenings. The Rules I drew up, requir'd that every Member in his Turn should produce one or more Queries on any Point of Morals, Politics or Natural Philosophy, to be discuss'd by the Company, and once in three Months produce and read an Essay of his own Writing on any Subject he pleased. Our Debates were to be under the Direction of a President, and to be conducted in the sincere Spirit of Enquiry after Truth, without fondness for Dispute, or Desire of Victory; and to prevent Warmth, all Expressions of Positiveness in Opinion, or of direct Contradiction, were after some time made contraband & prohibited under small pecuniary Penalties. The first Members were, Joseph Brientnal, a Copyer of Deeds for the Scriveners; a good-natur'd friendly middle-ag'd Man, a great Lover of Poetry, reading all he could meet with, & writing some that was tolerable; very ingenious in many little Nicknackeries, & of sensible Conversation. Thomas Godfrey, a self-taught Mathematician, great in his Way, & afterwards Inventor of what is now call'd Hadley's Quadrant. But he knew little out of his way, and was not a pleasing Companion, as like most Great Mathmaticians I have met with, he expected unusual Precision in every thing convenient to us to have them all together where we met, that upon Occasion they might be consulted; and By thus clubbing our Books to a common Library, we should, while we lik'd to keep them together, have each of us the Advantage of using the Books of all the other Members, which would be nearly as beneficial as if each owned the whole. It was lik'd and agreed to, & we fill'd one End of the Room with such Books as we could best spare. The Number was not so great as we expected; and tho' they had been of great Use, yet some Inconveniencies occurring for want of due Care of them, the Collection after about a Year was separated, & each took his Books home again.

And now I set on foot my first Project of a public Nature, that for a Subscription Library. I drew up the Proposals, got them put into Form by our great Scrivener Brockden, and by the help of my Friends in the Junto, procur'd Fifty Subscribers of 40/ each to begin with & 10/ a Year for 50 Years, the Term our Company was to continue. We afterwards obtain'd a Charter, the Company being increas'd to 100. This was the Mother of all the N American Subscription Libraries now so numerous. It is become a great thing itself, & continually increasing.— These Libraries have improv'd the general Conversation of the Americans, made the common Tradesmen & Farmers as intelligent as most Gentlemen from other Countries, and perhaps have contributed in some degree to the Stand so generally made throughout the Colonies in Defence of their Privileges. Finding the Advantage of this little Collection, I propos'd to render the Benefit from Books more common by commencing a Public Subscription Library. I drew a Sketch of the Plan and Rules that would be necessary, and got a skilful Conveyancer Mr Charles Brockden to put the whole in Form of Articles of Agreement to be subscribed, by which each Subscriber engag'd to pay a certain Sum down for the first Purchase of Books and an annual Contribution for encreasing them.—So few were the Readers at that time in Philadelphia, and the Majority of us so poor, that I was not able with great Industry to find more than Fifty Persons, mostly young Tradesmen, willing to pay down for this purpose Forty shillings each, & Ten Shillings per Annum. On this little Fund we began. The Books were imported. The Library was open one Day in the Week for lending them to the Subscribers, on their Promisory Notes to pay Double the Value if not duly returned. The Institution soon manifested its Utility, was imitated by other Towns and in other Provinces, the Librarys were augmented by Donations, Reading became fashionable, and our People having no publick Amusements to divert their Attention from Study became better acquainted with Books, and in a few Years were observ'd by Strangers to be better instructed & more intelligent than People of the same Rank generally are in other Countries. . . .

The Objections, & Reluctances I met with in Soliciting the Sub-
scriptions, made me soon feel the Impropriety of presenting one's self
as the Proposer of any useful Project that might be suppos'd to raise
one's Reputation in the smallest degree above that of one's Neighbours, when one has need of their Assistance to accomplish that Project. I therefore put my self as much as I could out of sight, and stated
it as a Scheme of *a Number of Friends,* who had requested me to go
about and propose it to such as they thought Lovers of Reading. In this
way my Affair went on more smoothly, and I ever after practis'd it on
such Occasions; and from my frequent Successes, can heartily recom-
mend it. The present little Sacrifice of your Vanity will afterwards be
amply repaid. If it remains a while uncertain to whom the Merit belongs, some one more vain than yourself will be encourag'd to claim it,
and then even Envy will be dispos'd to do you Justice, by plucking
those assum'd Feathers, & restoring them to their right Owner. This
Library afforded me the Means of Improvement by constant Study, for
which I set apart an Hour or two each Day; and thus repair'd in some
Degree the Loss of the Learned Education my Father once intended for
me.

For Journals

Before you read this selection, what did you know about Benjamin
Franklin?

For Discussion

1.   What were Franklin's dreams and ambitions when he was a boy?
What examples give an indication of the kind of man he was to become?

2.   The picture of Franklin entering Philadelphia, tired, dirty, and
alone, with a roll under each arm, is one of the most famous images of
arrival in American history. Why does he go into such detail? What do
you think he wants his audience to learn about him or his situation
from this description?

3.   Franklin gives several examples of his growing interest in both his
own intellectual development and in leadership in projects for the public good. Which ones do you think showed him behaving most effectively, and why? How do those projects help him achieve his dreams
for personal and public improvement?

4.   It has been said of Franklin that he made jokes about absolutely
everything except science. Find some examples of his sense of irony,

his ability to laugh at himself, and his tolerance for the behavior of others. How does his ability not to take himself too seriously help him make his narrative more persuasive?

5. Franklin was the original American do-it-yourself person. What examples does he give of untraditional means of teaching and learning? What examples in contemporary American life, including your own, do you see of the do-it-yourself mentality? Are any of those behaviors ones you associate with aspects of the American dream? Which aspects?

For Writing

1. Franklin was the most prolifically talented American of his time, with the possible exception of Thomas Jefferson. Write a paper in which you research one of the following topics: his inventions and their uses; his role as ambassador to France during the American Revolution and his celebrity status there; his other publications, including *Poor Richard's Almanac*; his contributions to the Declaration of Independence and the Constitutional Convention; his troubled relationship with his own son, who supported the British during the Revolution; his political satires; or his antislavery writings.

2. Different audiences and people read the same text very differently. In his book *Studies in Classic American Literature* (1923), the twentieth-century English writer D. H. Lawrence detested Franklin and wrote of him:

> The perfectability of Man! The perfectability of the Ford car! The perfectability of which man? I am many men. Which of them are you going to perfect? I am not a mechanical contrivance. Education! Which of the various me's do you propose to educate, and which do you propose to suppress? . . . Old Daddy Franklin will tell you. He'll rig him up for you, the pattern American. . . . He knew what he was about, the sharp little man. He set up the first dummy American.

Write an essay comparing Lawrence's impression of Franklin with your own view of him, and use Franklin's text for examples. Consider these questions: What values, positive or negative, does Franklin represent to Lawrence? What does Lawrence seem to think the American dream is? Do you think one has to be an American to appreciate Franklin? Why or why not?

FROM *THE LIFE AND TIMES OF FREDERICK DOUGLASS*
1 8 4 5

Frederick Douglass

    Frederick Douglass (1817–1895) is the author of the most famous slave narrative and one of the greatest autobiographies in American literature. He was born a slave in Maryland, the child of a black mother and an unknown white father. He learned to read and write, actions which were illegal for slaves, and at the age of twenty planned a successful escape from slavery. He edited an influential antislavery newspaper and became a famous abolitionist speaker. During the Civil War he organized regiments of black soldiers; his two sons served in them. Throughout Reconstruction and after he continued his work on behalf of civil rights for African Americans, serving in several posts, including ambassador to Haiti.

Learning to Read

    Established in my new home in Baltimore, I was not very long in perceiving that in picturing to myself what was to be my life there, my imagination had painted only the bright side, and that the reality had its dark shades as well as its light ones. The open country which had been so much to me was all shut out. Walled in on every side by towering brick buildings, the heat of the summer was intolerable to me, and the hard brick pavements almost blistered my feet. If I ventured out on to the streets, new and strange objects glared upon me at every step, and startling sounds greeted my ears from all directions. My country eyes and ears were confused and bewildered. Troops of hostile boys pounced upon me at every corner. They chased me, and called me "eastern-shore man," till really I almost wished myself back on the Eastern Shore. My new mistress happily proved to be all she had seemed, and in her presence I easily forgot all outside annoyances. Mrs. Sophia was naturally of an excellent disposition—kind, gentle, and cheerful. The supercilious contempt for the rights and feelings of others, and the petulance and bad humor which generally characterized slaveholding ladies, were all quite absent from her manner and bearing toward me.

    She had never been a slaveholder—a thing then quite unusual at the South—but had depended almost entirely upon her own industry for a living. To this fact the dear lady no doubt owed the excellent preservation of her natural goodness of heart, for slavery could change a saint into a sinner, and an angel into a demon. I hardly knew how to behave towards "Miss Sopha," as I used to call Mrs. Hugh Auld. I could not approach her even as I had formerly approached Mrs. Thomas Auld. Why should I hang down my head, and speak with bated breath, when there was no pride to scorn me, no coldness to repel me, and no hatred to inspire me with fear? I therefore soon came to regard her as something more akin to a mother than a slaveholding mistress. So far from deeming it impudent in a slave to look her straight in the face, she seemed ever to say, "Look up, child; don't be afraid." The sailors belonging to the sloop esteemed it a great privilege to be the bearers of parcels or messages for her, for whenever they came, they were sure of a most kind and pleasant reception. If little Thomas was her son, and her most dearly loved child, she made me something like his half-brother in her affections. If dear Tommy was exalted to a place on his mother's knee, "Freddy" was honored by a place at the mother's side. Nor did the slave-boy lack the caressing strokes of her gentle hand, soothing him into the consciousness that, though motherless, he was not friendless. Mrs. Auld was not only kind-hearted, but remarkably pious, frequent in her attendance at public worship and much given to reading the Bible and to chanting hymns of praise when alone.

Mr. Hugh was altogether a different character. He cared very little about religion, knew more of the world and was more a part of the world, than his wife. He doubtless set out to be, as the world goes, a respectable man and to get on by becoming a successful ship-builder, in that city of shipbuilding. This was his ambition, and it fully occupied him. I was of course of very little consequence to him, and when he smiled upon me, as he sometimes did, the smile was borrowed from his lovely wife, and like borrowed light, was transient, and vanished with the source whence it was derived. Though I must in truth characterize Master Hugh as a sour man of forbidding appearance, it is due to him to acknowledge that he was never cruel to me, according to the notion of cruelty in Maryland. During the first year or two, he left me almost exclusively to the management of his wife. She was my lawgiver. In hands so tender as hers, and in the absence of the cruelties of the plantation, I became both physically and mentally much more sensitive, and a frown from my mistress caused me far more suffering than had Aunt Katy's hardest cuffs. Instead of the cold, damp floor of my old master's kitchen, I was on carpets; for the corn bag in winter, I had a good straw bed, well furnished with covers; for the coarse corn meal in the morning, I had good bread and mush occasionally; for my old tow-linen shirt, I had good clean clothes. I was really well off. My employment was to run of errands, and to take care of Tommy, to prevent his getting in the way of carriages, and to keep him out of harm's way generally.

So for a time everything went well. I say for a time, because the fatal poison of irresponsible power, and the natural influence of slave customs, were not very long in making their impression on the gentle and loving disposition of my excellent mistress. She at first regarded me as a child, like any other. This was the natural and spontaneous thought; afterwards, when she came to consider me as property, our relations to each other were changed, but a nature so noble as hers could not instantly become perverted, and it took several years before the sweetness of her temper was wholly lost.

5   The frequent hearing of my mistress reading the Bible aloud, for she often read aloud when her husband was absent, awakened my curiosity in respect to this *mystery* of reading, and roused in me the desire to learn. Up to this time I had known nothing whatever of this wonderful art, and my ignorance and inexperience of what it could do for me, as well as my confidence in my mistress, emboldened me to ask her to teach me to read. With an unconscious and inexperience equal to my own, she readily consented, and in an incredibly short time, by her kind assistance, I had mastered the alphabet and could spell words of three or four letters. My mistress seemed almost as proud of my progress as if I had been her own child, and supposing that her husband would be as well pleased, she made no secret of what she was doing for me. Indeed, she exultingly told him of the aptness of her pupil and of her intention to persevere, as she felt it her duty to do, in teaching me, at least, to read the Bible. And here arose the first dark cloud over my Baltimore prospects, the precursor of chilling blasts and drenching storms. Master Hugh was astounded beyond measure and, probably for the first time, proceeded to unfold to his wife the true philosophy of the slave system, and the peculiar rules necessary in the nature of the case to be observed in the management of human chattels. Of course he forbade her to give me any further instruction, telling her in the first place that to do so was unlawful, as it was also unsafe, "for," said he, "if you give a nigger an inch he will take an ell. Learning will spoil the best nigger in the world. If he learns to read the Bible it will forever unfit him to be a slave. He should know nothing but the will of his master, and learn to obey it. As to himself, learning will do him no good, but a great deal of harm, making him disconsolate and unhappy. If you teach him how to read, he'll want to know how to write, and this accomplished, he'll be running away with himself." Such was the tenor of Master Hugh's oracular exposition, and it must be confessed that he very clearly comprehended the nature and the requirements of the relation of master and slave. His discourse was the

first decidedly anti-slavery lecture to which it had been my lot to listen. Mrs. Auld evidently felt the force of what he said, and, like an obedient wife, began to shape her course in the direction indicated by him. The effect of his words *on me* was neither slight nor transitory. His iron sentences, cold and harsh, sunk like heavy weights deep into my heart, and stirred up within me a rebellion not soon to be allayed.

This was a new and special revelation, dispelling a painful mystery against which my youthful understanding had struggled, and struggled in vain, to wit, the white man's power to perpetuate the enslavement of the black man. "Very well," thought I. "Knowledge unfits a child to be a slave." I instinctively assented to the proposition, and from that moment I understood the direct pathway from slavery to freedom. It was just what I needed, and it came to me at a time and from a source whence I least expected it. Of course I was greatly saddened at the thought of losing the assistance of my kind mistress, but the information so instantly derived, to some extent compensated me for the loss I had sustained in this direction. Wise as Mr. Auld was, he underrated my comprehension, and had little idea of the use to which I was capable of putting the impressive lesson he was giving to his wife. He wanted me to be a slave; I had already voted against that on the home plantation of Col. Lloyd. That which he most loved I most hated, and the very determination which he expressed to keep me in ignorance only rendered me the more resolute to seek intelligence. In learning to read, therefore, I am not sure that I do not owe quite as much to the opposition of my master as to the kindly assistance of my amiable mistress. I acknowledge the benefit rendered me by the one, and by the other, believing that but for my mistress I might have grown up in ignorance.

Growing in Knowledge

I lived in the family of Mr. Auld, at Baltimore, seven years, during which time, as the almanac makers say of the weather, my condition was variable. The most interesting feature of my history here was my learning, under somewhat marked disadvantages, to read and write. In attaining this knowledge I was compelled to resort to indirections by no means congenial to my nature, and which were really humiliating to my sense of candor and uprightness. My mistress, checked in her benevolent designs toward me, not only ceased instructing me herself, but set her face as a flint against my learning to read by any means. It is due to her to say, however, that she did not adopt this course in all its stringency at first. She either thought it unnecessary, or she lacked the depravity needed to make herself forget at once my human nature. She was, as I have said, naturally a kind and tender-hearted woman, and in the humanity of her heart and the simplicity of her mind, she set out, when I first went to live with her, to treat me as she supposed one human being ought to treat another.

Nature never intended that men and women should be either slaves or slaveholders, and nothing but rigid training long persisted in, can perfect the character of the one or the other.

Mrs. Auld was singularly deficient in the qualities of a slaveholder. It was no easy matter for her to think or to feel that the curly-headed boy, who stood by her side, and even leaned on her lap, who was loved by little Tommy, and who loved Tommy in turn, sustained to her only the relation of a chattel. I was more than that; she felt me to be more than that. I could talk and sing; I could laugh and weep; I could reason and remember; I could love and hate. I was human, and she, dear lady, knew and felt me to be so. How could she then treat me as a brute, without a mighty struggle with all the noblest powers of her soul? That struggle came, and the will and power of the husband were victorious. Her noble soul was overcome, and he who wrought the wrong was injured in the fall no less than the rest of the household. When I went into that household, it was the abode of happiness and contentment. The wife and mistress there was a model of affection and tenderness. Her fervent piety and watchful uprightness made it impossible to see her without thinking and feeling that "that woman is a Christian." There was no sorrow nor suffering for which she had not a tear, and there was no innocent joy for which she had not a smile. She had bread for the hungry, clothes for the naked, and comfort for every mourner who came within her reach.

10   But slavery soon proved its ability to divest her of these excellent qualities, and her home of its early happiness. Conscience cannot stand much violence. Once thoroughly injured, who is he who can repair the damage? If it be broken toward the slave on Sunday, it will be toward the master on Monday. It cannot long endure such shocks. It must stand unharmed, or it does not stand at all. As my condition in the family waxed bad, that of the family waxed no better. The first step in the wrong direction was the violence done to nature and to conscience in arresting the benevolence that would have enlightened my young mind. In ceasing to instruct me, my mistress had to seek to justify herself *to* herself, and once consenting to take sides in such a debate, she was compelled to hold her position. One needs little knowledge of moral philosophy to see where she inevitably landed. She finally became even more violent in her opposition to my learning to read than was Mr. Auld himself. Nothing now appeared to make her more angry than seeing me, seated in some nook or corner, quietly reading a book or newspaper. She would rush at me with the utmost fury, and snatch

the book or paper from my hand, with something of the wrath and consternation which a traitor might be supposed to feel on being discovered in a plot by some dangerous spy. The conviction once thoroughly established in her mind, that education and slavery were incompatible with each other, I was most narrowly watched in all my movements. If I remained in a separate room from the family for any considerable length of time, I was sure to be suspected of having a book, and was at once called to give an account of myself. But this was too late—the first and never-to-be-retraced step had been taken. Teaching me the alphabet had been the "inch" given, I was now waiting only for the opportunity to "take the ell."

Filled with the determination to learn to read at any cost, I hit upon many expedients to accomplish that much desired end. The plan which I mainly adopted, and the one which was the most successful, was that of using as teachers my young white playmates, with whom I met on the streets. I used almost constantly to carry a copy of *Webster's Spelling-Book* in my pocket, and when sent on errands, or when playtime was allowed me, I would step aside with my young friends and take a lesson in spelling. I am greatly indebted to these boys—Gustavus Dorgan, Joseph Bailey, Charles Farity, and William Cosdry.

Although slavery was a delicate subject and, in Maryland, very cautiously talked about among grown-up people, I frequently talked with the white boys about it, and that very freely. I would sometimes say to them, while seated on a curbstone or a cellar door, "I wish I could be free, as you will be when you get to be men." "You will be free, you know, as soon as you are twenty-one, and can go where you like, but I am a slave for life. Have I not as good a right to be free as you have?" Words like these, I observed, always troubled them, and I had no small satisfaction in drawing out from them, as I occasionally did, that fresh and bitter condemnation of slavery which ever springs from natures unseared and unperverted. Of all consciences, let me have those to deal with, which have not been seared and bewildered with the cares and perplexities of life. I do not remember ever while I was in slavery, to have met with a *boy* who defended the system, but I do remember many times, when I was consoled by them, and by them encouraged to hope that something would yet occur by which I would be made free. Over and over again, they have told me that "they believed I had as good a right to be free as *they* had," and that "they did not believe God ever made any one to be a slave." It is easily seen that such little conversations with my playfellows had no tendency to weaken my love of liberty, nor to render me contented as a slave.

When I was about thirteen years old, and had succeeded in learning to read, every increase of knowledge, especially anything respecting the free states, was an additional weight to the almost intolerable burden of my thought—"*I am a slave for life.*" To my bondage I could see no end. It was a terrible reality, and I shall never be able to tell how sadly that thought chafed my young spirit. Fortunately or unfortunately, I had, by blacking boots for some gentlemen, earned a little money with which I purchased of Mr. Knight, on Thames street, what was then a very popular school 'book, viz., *The Columbian Orator,* for which I paid fifty cents. I was led to buy this book by hearing some little boys say that they were going to learn some pieces out of it for the exhibition. This volume was indeed a rich treasure, and, for a time, every opportunity afforded me was spent in diligently perusing it. Among much other interesting matter, that which I read again and again with unflagging satisfaction was a short dialogue between a master and his slave. The slave is represented as having been recaptured in a second attempt to run away, and the master opens the dialogue with an upbraiding speech, charging the slave with ingratitude, and demanding to know what he has to say in his own defense. Thus upbraided and thus called upon to reply, the slave rejoins that he knows how little anything that he can say will avail, seeing that he is completely in the hands of his owner, and with noble resolution, calmly says, "I submit to my fate." Touched by the slave's answer, the master insists upon his further speaking, and recapitulates the many acts of kindness which he has performed toward the slave, and tells him he is permitted to speak for himself. Thus invited, the quondam slave made a spirited defense of himself, and thereafter the whole argument for and against slavery is brought out. The master was vanquished at every turn in the argument, and, appreciating the fact, he generously and meekly emancipates the slave, with his best wishes for his prosperity.

It is unnecessary to say that a dialogue with such an origin and such an end, read by me when every nerve of my being was in revolt at my own condition as a slave, affected me most powerfully. I could not help feeling that the day might yet come when the well-directed answers made by the slave to the master, in this instance, would find a counterpart in my own experience. This, however, was not all the fanaticism which I found in *The Columbian Orator*. I met there one of Sheridan's mighty speeches on the subject of Catholic Emancipation, Lord Chatham's speech on the American War, and speeches by the great William Pitt, and by Fox. These were all choice documents to me, and I read them over and over again, with an interest ever increasing, because it was ever gaining in intelligence, for the more I read them the better I understood them. The reading of these speeches added much to my limited stock of language, and enabled me to give tongue to many interesting thoughts which had often flashed through my mind and died away for want of words in which to give them utterance. The mighty power and heart-searching directness of truth, penetrating the heart of a slaveholder and compelling him to yield up his earthly interests to the claims of eternal justice, were finely illustrated in the dialogue, and from the speeches of Sheridan I got a bold and powerful denunciation of oppression and a most brilliant vindication of the rights of man.

Here was indeed a noble acquisition. If I had ever wavered under the consideration that the Almighty, in some way, had ordained slavery and willed my enslavement for His own glory, I wavered no longer. I had now penetrated to the secret of all slavery and of all oppression, and had ascertained their true foundation to be in the pride, the power, and the avarice of man. With a book in my hand so redolent of the principles of liberty, and with a perception of my own human nature and of the facts of my past and present experience, I was equal to a contest with the religious advocates of slavery, whether white or black, for blindness in this matter was not confined to the white people. I have met, at the South, many good, religious colored people who were under the delusion that God required them to submit to slavery and to wear their chains with meekness and humility. I could entertain no such nonsense as this, and I quite lost my patience when I found a colored man weak enough to believe such stuff. Nevertheless, eager as I was to partake of the tree of knowledge, its fruits were bitter as well as sweet. "Slaveholders," thought I, "are only a band of successful robbers, who, leaving their own homes, went into Africa for the purpose of stealing and reducing my people to slavery." I loathed them as the meanest and the most wicked of men. And as I read, behold! the very discontent so graphically predicted by Master Hugh had already come upon me. I was no longer the light-hearted, gleesome boy, full of mirth and play, that I was when I landed in Baltimore. Light had penetrated the moral dungeon where I had lain, and I saw the bloody whip for my back and the iron chain for my feet, and my *good, kind* master was the author of my situation. The revelation haunted me, stung me, and made me gloomy and miserable. As I writhed under the sting and torment of this knowledge I almost envied my fellow slaves their stupid indifference. It opened my eyes to the horrible pit, and revealed the teeth of the frightful dragon that was ready to pounce upon me, but alas, it opened no way for my escape. I wished myself a beast, a bird, anything rather than a slave. I was wretched and gloomy beyond my ability to describe. This everlasting thinking distressed and tormented me, and yet there was no getting rid of this subject of my thoughts. Liberty, as the inestimable birthright of every man, converted every object into an asserter of this right. I heard it in every sound, and saw it in every object. It was ever present to torment me with a sense of my wretchedness. The more beautiful and charming were the smiles of nature, the more horrible and desolate was my condition. I saw nothing without seeing it, and I heard nothing without hearing it. I do not exaggerate when I say that it looked at me in every star, smiled in every calm, breathed in every wind and moved in every storm.

I have no doubt that my state of mind had something to do with the change in treatment which my mistress adopted towards me. I can easily believe that my leaden, downcast, and disconsolate look was very offensive to her. Poor lady! She did not understand my trouble, and I could not tell her. Could I have made her acquainted with the real state of my mind and given her the reasons therefor, it might have been well for both of us. As it was, her abuse fell upon me like the blows of the false prophet upon his ass; she did not know that an angel stood in the way. Nature made us friends, but slavery had made us enemies. My interests were in a direction opposite to hers, and we both had our private thoughts and plans. She aimed to keep me ignorant, and I resolved to *know,* although knowledge only increased my misery. My feelings were not the result of any marked cruelty in the treatment I received; they sprung from the consideration of my being a slave at all. It was *slavery,* not its mere *incidents* that I hated. I had been cheated. I saw through the attempt to keep me in ignorance. I saw that slaveholders would have gladly made me believe that, in making a slave of me and in making slaves of others, they were merely acting under the authority of God, and I felt to them as to robbers and deceivers. The feeding and clothing me well could not atone for taking my liberty from me. The smiles of my mistress could not remove the deep sorrow that dwelt in my young bosom. Indeed, these came, in time, but to deepen the sorrow. She had changed, and the reader will see that I too, had changed. We were both victims to the same overshadowing evil, she as mistress, I as slave. I will not censure her harshly.

For Journals

What was your emotional response to Douglass's descriptions of growing up a slave?

For Discussion

1. Analyze Douglass's belief that oppression does as much harm to the slave owner as it does to the slave. Why do you think Douglass feels the way he does? What conclusion would you have expected from someone with his experiences?

2. Douglass says he might owe as much to Mr. Auld's cruelty to him as to Mrs. Auld's early kindness. Certainly Douglass is not arguing on

behalf of either slavery or cruelty, so in what way could Mr. Auld's mistreatment of him have helped Douglass's dreams of self-fulfillment to come true?

3. How does Douglass connect the dream of literacy to the dream of freedom? How does he attempt to persuade his audience that this dream is valid?

4. Douglass was writing for a mostly white northern audience not sympathetic to slavery but not necessarily willing to become militant antislavery activists either. What specific examples does he give of his experience that you think would have been particularly persuasive to that audience? Which examples are the most persuasive to you? Why?

5. In the last and longest edition of his autobiography, completed many years after the Civil War, Douglass says that he went back to visit Mr. Auld, an old man by then, and that Auld said to him, "Frederick, I always knew you were too smart to stay a slave." What do you think Auld meant? Why would Douglass have gone back to see him? Why do you think Douglass included this episode? Do you think he had a different audience of readers for this last edition than for the earlier ones? Different dreams for himself?

For Writing

1. Douglass says, "Established in my new home in Baltimore, I was not very long in perceiving that in picturing to myself what was to be my life there, my imagination had painted only the bright side and that the reality had its dark shades as well as its light ones" (paragraph 1). Write an essay analyzing this comment. Is there always a dark side to dreams, a price to pay? What do you think Douglass dreamed his life in Baltimore would be like? How was the reality different from both his previous experience and the way he imagined it would be? How did his time in Baltimore, including his work, affect his dreams of freedom?

2. For Douglass, as for Franklin, the key to the American dream is education. Write an essay in which you compare these two men with regard to how they got reading matter and what they read, the effect their reading had on their development and their ability to achieve what they wanted, and which texts were particularly meaningful to each man and why. Provide specific examples, in terms of what they read and in terms of their emotional and intellectual reactions to those texts.

CALIFORNIA, CORNUCOPIA OF THE WORLD
1 8 8 9

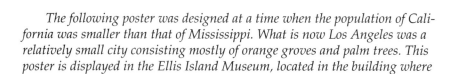

The following poster was designed at a time when the population of California was smaller than that of Mississippi. What is now Los Angeles was a relatively small city consisting mostly of orange groves and palm trees. This poster is displayed in the Ellis Island Museum, located in the building where millions of immigrants first set foot on American soil.

For Journals

When you think of California, what images come to your mind? How many of them are in this poster?

For Discussion

1.   Whom do you think was the audience here? What guesses can you make about their educational level? Their occupations? Their goals and dreams?

2.   What does the artist want the audience to learn about California? What kinds of positive facts are incorporated into the picture? What does the artist want the audience to overlook or remain ignorant of?

3.   The central image in the poster is the cornucopia overflowing with fruits, vegetables, and flowers. Why do you think this image was chosen? What associations does it bring to mind?

4.   There are gaps in the text of this poster. For example, what does "untaken" land mean if American Indians are living there? How can California be the cornucopia of the world if so many millions of its acres are still unfarmed? What other gaps can you find? What other kinds of information do you think the audience would want? Is this kind of advertising fair or unfair to the audience, and why?

For Writing

1.   Look through some travel magazines for advertisements about a particular American place to visit. Be sure there are both pictures and text. Then write an essay answering questions 1–4 above. You could begin with a visual exercise: Look at the picture, close your eyes, and try to visualize it again; then look at it again, put it away, and try to

write down everything you remember about it. What you remember—even incorrectly—will be a good guide for what in the advertisement made the biggest impression on you and will help you organize your ideas. Use examples from the text and images in the advertisement to support whatever conclusions you draw.

2.   In his cultural history of California, *Inventing the Dream,* historian Kevin Starr says that developments and transformations in California set the standard for the rest of the nation and that California, particularly southern California and Hollywood, has a fixed place in the "daydream of America." Write an essay analyzing this idea. Some questions to consider: What are your mental images of California? What examples (such as movies, television, and music) portray the California dream Starr speaks of? How much do you identify the idea of California with the idea of the American dream?

FROM *THE PROMISED LAND*
1912

Mary Antin

Mary Antin (1881–1949) was born to a Jewish family in Polotzk, Russia. As a result of business failure and religious persecution, her father emigrated to Boston in 1891, and the family followed him three years later. When Antin was sixteen she published From Plotzk to Boston, *a collection of letters she had written on the boat to America. Antin sought to emphasize immigrant contributions to American life, and wrote her memoir,* The Promised Land, *at a time when Congress was considering legislation to limit immigration. The story of one young woman's Americanization,* The Promised Land *became a best-seller, speaking eloquently to both immigrants and the native born.*

Our initiation into American ways began with the first step on the new soil. My father found occasion to instruct or correct us even on the way from the pier to Wall Street, which journey we made crowded together in a rickety cab. He told us not to lean out of the windows, not to point, and explained the word "greenhorn." We did not want to be "greenhorns," and gave the strictest attention to my father's instructions. I do not know when my parents found opportunity to review together the history of Polotzk in the three years past, for we children had no patience with the subject; my mother's narrative was constantly interrupted by irrelevant questions, interjections, and explanations.

The first meal was an object lesson of much variety. My father produced several kinds of food, ready to eat, without any cooking, from little tin cans that had printing all over them. He attempted to introduce us to a queer, slippery kind of fruit, which he called "banana," but had to give it up for the time being. After the meal, he had better luck with a curious piece of furniture on runners, which he called "rocking-chair." There were five of us newcomers, and we found five different ways of getting into the American machine of perpetual motion, and as many ways of getting out of it. One born and bred to the use of a rocking-chair cannot imagine how ludicrous people can make themselves when attempting to use it for the first time. We laughed immoderately over our various experiments with the novelty, which was a wholesome way of letting off steam after the unusual excitement of the day.

In our flat we did not think of such a thing as storing the coal in the bathtub. There was no bathtub. So in the evening of the first day my father conducted us to the public baths. As we moved along in a little procession, I was delighted with the illumination of the streets. So many lamps, and they burned until morning, my father said, and so people did not need to carry lanterns. In America, then, everything was free, as we had heard in Russia. Light was free; the streets were as bright as a synagogue on a holy day. Music was free; we had been serenaded, to our gaping delight, by a brass band of many pieces, soon after our installation on Union Place.

Education was free. That subject my father had written about repeatedly, as comprising his chief hope for us children, the essence of American opportunity, the treasure that no thief could touch, not even misfortune or poverty. It was the one thing that he was able to promise us when he sent for us; surer, safer than bread or shelter. On our second day I was thrilled with the realization of what this freedom of education meant. A little girl from across the alley came and offered to conduct us to school. My father was out, but we five between us had a few words of English by this time. We knew the word school. We understood. This child, who had never seen us till yesterday, who could not pronounce our names, who was not much better dressed than we, was able to offer us the freedom of the schools of Boston! No application made, no questions asked, no examinations, rulings, exclusions; no machinations, no fees. The doors stood open for every one of us. The smallest child could show us the way.

This incident impressed me more than anything I had heard in advance of the freedom of education in America. It was a concrete proof—almost the thing itself. One had to experience it to understand it.   5

It was a great disappointment to be told by my father that we were not to enter upon our school career at once. It was too near the end of the term, he said, and we were going to move to Crescent Beach in a week or so. We had to wait until the opening of the schools in September. What a loss of precious time—from May till September!

Not that the time was really lost. Even the interval on Union Place was crowded with lessons and experiences. We had to visit the stores and be dressed from head to foot in American clothing; we had to learn the mysteries of the iron stove, the washboard, and the speaking-tube; we had to learn to trade with the fruit peddler through the window, and not to be afraid of the policeman; and, above all, we had to learn English.

The kind people who assisted us in these important matters form a group by themselves in the gallery of my friends. If I had never seen them from those early days till now, I should still have remembered them with gratitude. When I enumerate the long list of my American teachers, I must begin with those who came to us on Wall Street and taught us our first steps. To my mother, in her perplexity over the cookstove, the woman who showed her how to make the fire was an angel of deliverance. A fairy godmother to us children was she who led us to a wonderful country called "uptown," where, in a dazzlingly beautiful palace called a "department store," we exchanged our hateful homemade European costumes, which pointed us out as "greenhorns" to the children on the street, for real American machine-made garments, and issued forth glorified in each other's eyes.

With our despised immigrant clothing we shed also our impossible Hebrew names. A committee of our friends, several years ahead of us in American experience, put their heads together and concocted American names for us all. Those of our real names that had no pleasing American equivalents they ruthlessly discarded, content if they retained the initials. My mother, possessing a name that was not easily translatable, was punished with the undignified nickname of Annie. Fetchke, Joseph, and Deborah issued as Frieda, Joseph, and Dora, respectively. As for poor me, I was simply cheated. The name they gave me was hardly new. My Hebrew name being Maryashe in full, Mashke for short, Russianized into Marya (*Mar-ya*), my friends said that it would hold good in English as *Mary;* which was very disappointing, as I longed to possess a strange-sounding American name like the others.

10 I am forgetting the consolation I had, in this matter of names, from the use of my surname, which I have had no occasion to mention until now. I found on my arrival that my father was "Mr. Antin" on the slightest provocation, and not, as in Polotzk, on state occasions alone. And so I was "Mary Antin," and I felt very important to answer to such a dignified title. It was just like America that even plain people should wear their surnames on week days.

As a family we were so diligent under instruction, so adaptable, and so clever in hiding our deficiencies, that when we made the journey to Crescent Beach, in the wake of our small wagon-load of household goods, my father had very little occasion to admonish us on the way, and I am sure he was not ashamed of us. So much we had achieved toward our Americanization during the two weeks since our landing.

Crescent Beach is a name that is printed in very small type on the maps of the environs of Boston, but a life-size strip of sand curves from Winthrop to Lynn; and that is historic ground in the annals of my family. The place is now a popular resort for holiday crowds, and is famous under the name of Revere Beach. When the reunited Antins made their stand there, however, there were no boulevards, no stately bath-houses, no hotels, no gaudy amusement places, no illuminations, no showmen, no tawdry rabble. There was only the bright clean sweep of sand, the summer sea, and the summer sky. At high tide the whole Atlantic rushed in, tossing the seaweeds in his mane; at low tide he rushed out, growling and gnashing his granite teeth. Between tides a baby might play on the beach, digging with pebbles and shells, till it lay asleep on the sand. The whole sun shone by day, troops of stars by night, and the great moon in its season. . . .

Thus courting the influence of sea and sky and variable weather, I was bound to have dreams, hints, imaginings. It was no more than this, perhaps: that the world as I knew it was not large enough to contain all that I saw and felt; that the thoughts that flashed through my mind, not half understood, unrelated to my utterable thoughts, concerned something for which I had as yet no name. Every imaginative growing child has these flashes of intuition, especially one that becomes intimate with some one aspect of nature. With me it was the growing time, that idle summer by the sea, and I grew all the faster because I had been so cramped before. My mind, too, had so recently been worked upon by the impressive experience of a change of country that I was more than commonly alive to impressions, which are the seeds of ideas.

Let no one suppose that I spent my time entirely, or even chiefly, in inspired solitude. By far the best part of my day was spent in play—frank, hearty, boisterous play, such as comes natural to American children. In Polotzk I had already begun to be considered too old for play, excepting set games or organized frolics. Here I found myself included with children who still played, and I willingly returned to childhood. There were plenty of playfellows. My father's energetic little partner had a little wife and a large family. He kept them in the little cottage next to ours; and that the shanty survived the tumultuous presence of that brood is a wonder to me to-day. The young Wilners included an assortment of boys, girls, and twins, of every possible variety of age, size, disposition, and sex. They swarmed in and out of the cottage all day long, wearing the door-sill hollow, and trampling the ground to powder. They swung out of windows like monkeys, slid up the roof like flies, and shot out of trees like fowls. Even a small person like me couldn't go anywhere without being run over by a Wilner; and I could never tell which Wilner it was because none of them ever stood still long enough to be identified; and also because I suspected that they were in the habit of interchanging conspicuous articles of clothing, which was very confusing.

15 You would suppose that the little mother must have been utterly lost, bewildered, trodden down in this horde of urchins; but you are mistaken. Mrs. Wilner was a positively majestic little person. She ruled her brood with the utmost coolness and strictness. She had even the biggest boy under her thumb, frequently under her palm. If they enjoyed the wildest freedom outdoors, indoors the young Wilners lived by the clock. And so at five o'clock in the evening, on seven days in the week, my father's partner's children could be seen in two long rows around the supper table. You could tell them apart on this occasion, because they all had their faces washed. And this is the time to count them: there are twelve little Wilners at table.

I managed to retain my identity in this multitude somehow, and while I was very much impressed with their numbers, I even dared to pick and choose my friends among the Wilners. One or two of the smaller boys I liked best of all, for a game of hide-and-seek or a frolic on the beach. We played in the water like ducks, never taking the trouble to get dry. One day I waded out with one of the boys, to see which of us dared go farthest. The tide was extremely low, and we had not wet our knees when we began to look back to see if familiar objects were still in sight. I thought we had been wading for hours, and still the water was so shallow and quiet. My companion was marching straight ahead, so I did the same. Suddenly a swell lifted us almost off our feet, and we clutched at each other simultaneously. There was a lesser swell, and little waves began to run, and a sigh went up from the sea. The tide was turning—perhaps a storm was on the way—and we were miles, dreadful miles from dry land.

Boy and girl turned without a word, four determined bare legs ploughing through the water, four scared eyes straining toward the land. Through an eternity of toil and fear they kept dumbly on, death at their heels, pride still in their hearts. At last they reach high-water mark—six hours before full tide.

Each has seen the other afraid, and each rejoices in the knowledge. But only the boy is sure of his tongue.

"You was scared, warn't you?" he taunts.

20 The girl understands so much, and is able to reply:—

"You can schwimmen, I not."

"Betcher life I can schwimmen," the other mocks.

And the girl walks off, angry and hurt.

"An' I can walk on my hands," the tormentor calls after her. "Say, you greenhorn, why don'tcher look?"

The girl keeps straight on, vowing that she would never walk with that rude boy again, neither by land nor sea, not even though waters should part at his bidding.

I am forgetting the more serious business which had brought us to Crescent Beach. While we children disported ourselves like mermaids and mermen in the surf, our respective fathers dispensed cold lemonade, hot peanuts, and pink popcorn, and piled up our respective fortunes, nickel by nickel, penny by penny. I was very proud of my connection with the public life of the beach. I admired greatly our shining soda fountain, the rows of sparkling glasses, the pyramids of oranges, the sausage chains, the neat white counter, and the bright array of tin spoons. It seemed to me that none of the other refreshment stands on the beach—there were a few—were half so attractive as ours. I thought my father looked very well in a long white apron and shirt sleeves. He dished out ice cream with enthusiasm, so I supposed he was getting rich. It never occurred to me to compare his present occupation with the position for which he had been originally destined; or if I thought about it, I was just as well content, for by this time I had by heart my father's saying, "America is not Polotzk." All occupations were respectable, all men were equal, in America.

If I admired the soda fountain and the sausage chains, I almost worshipped the partner, Mr. Wilner. I was content to stand for an hour at a time watching him make potato chips. In his cook's cap and apron, with a ladle in his hand and a smile on his face, he moved about with the greatest agility, whisking his raw materials out of nowhere, dipping into his bubbling kettle with a flourish, and bringing forth the finished product with a caper. Such potato chips were not to be had anywhere else on Crescent Beach. Thin as tissue paper, crisp as dry snow, and salt as the sea—such thirst-producing, lemonade-selling, nickel-bringing potato chips only Mr. Wilner could make. On holidays, when dozens of family parties came out by every train from town, he could hardly keep up with the demand for his potato chips. And with a waiting crowd around him our partner was at his best. He was as voluble as he was skilful, and as witty as he was voluble; at least so I guessed from the laughter that frequently drowned his voice. I could not understand his jokes, but if I could get near enough to watch his lips and his smile and his merry eyes, I was happy. That any one could talk so fast, and in English, was marvel enough, but that this prodigy should belong to *our* establishment was a fact to thrill me. I had never seen anything like Mr. Wilner, except a wedding jester; but then he spoke common Yiddish. So proud was I of the talent and good taste displayed at our stand that if my father beckoned to me in the crowd

25

and sent me on an errand, I hoped the people noticed that I, too, was connected with the establishment.

And all this splendor and glory and distinction came to a sudden end. There was some trouble about a license—some fee or fine—there was a storm in the night that damaged the soda fountain and other fixtures—there was talk and consultation between the houses of Antin and Wilner—and the promising partnership was dissolved. No more would the merry partner gather the crowd on the beach; no more would the twelve young Wilners gambol like mermen and mermaids in the surf. And the less numerous tribe of Antin must also say farewell to the jolly seaside life; for men in such humble business as my father's carry their families, along with their other earthly goods, wherever they go, after the manner of the gypsies. We had driven a feeble stake into the sand. The jealous Atlantic, in conspiracy with the Sunday law, had torn it out. We must seek our luck elsewhere.

In Polotzk we had supposed that "America" was practically synonymous with "Boston." When we landed in Boston, the horizon was pushed back, and we annexed Crescent Beach. And now, espying other lands of promise, we took possession of the province of Chelsea, in the name of our necessity.

30   In Chelsea, as in Boston, we made our stand in the wrong end of the town. Arlington Street was inhabited by poor Jews, poor Negroes, and a sprinkling of poor Irish. The side streets leading from it were occupied by more poor Jews and Negroes. It was a proper locality for a man without capital to do business. My father rented a tenement with a store in the basement. He put in a few barrels of flour and of sugar, a few boxes of crackers, a few gallons of kerosene, an assortment of soap of the "save the coupon" brands; in the cellar, a few barrels of potatoes, and a pyramid of kindling-wood; in the showcase, an alluring display of penny candy. He put out his sign, with a gilt-lettered warning of "Strictly Cash," and proceeded to give credit indiscriminately. That was the regular way to do business on Arlington Street. My father, in his three years' apprenticeship, had learned the tricks of many trades. He knew when and how to "bluff." The legend of "Strictly Cash" was a protection against notoriously irresponsible customers; while none of the "good" customers, who had a record for paying regularly on Saturday, hesitated to enter the store with empty purses.

If my father knew the tricks of the trade, my mother could be counted on to throw all her talent and tact into the business. Of course she had no English yet, but as she could perform the acts of weighing, measuring, and mental computation of fractions mechanically, she was able to give her whole attention to the dark mysteries of the language, as intercourse with her customers gave her opportunity. In this she made such rapid progress that she soon lost all sense of disadvantage, and conducted herself behind the counter very much as if she were back in her old store in Polotzk. It was far more cosey than Polotzk—at least, so it seemed to me; for behind the store was the kitchen, where, in the intervals of slack trade, she did her cooking and washing. Arlington Street customers were used to waiting while the storekeeper salted the soup or rescued a loaf from the oven.

Once more Fortune favored my family with a thin little smile, and my father, in reply to a friendly inquiry, would say, "One makes a living," with a shrug of the shoulders that added "but nothing to boast of." It was characteristic of my attitude toward bread-and-butter matters that this contented me, and I felt free to devote myself to the conquest of my new world. Looking back to those critical first years, I see myself always behaving like a child let loose in a garden to play and dig and chase the butterflies. Occasionally, indeed, I was stung by the wasp of family trouble; but I knew a healing ointment—my faith in America. My father had come to America to make a living. America, which was free and fair and kind, must presently yield him what he sought. I had come to America to see a new world, and I followed my own ends with the utmost assiduity; only, as I ran out to explore, I would look back to see if my house were in order behind me—if my family still kept its head above water.

In after years, when I passed as an American among Americans, if I was suddenly made aware of the past that lay forgotten,—if a letter from Russia, or a paragraph in the newspaper, or a conversation overheard in the street-car, suddenly reminded me of what I might have been,—I thought it miracle enough that I, Mashke, the granddaughter of Raphael the Russian, born to a humble destiny, should be at home in an American metropolis, be free to fashion my own life, and should dream my dreams in English phrases. But in the beginning my admiration was spent on more concrete embodiments of the splendors of America; such as fine houses, gay shops, electric engines and apparatus, public buildings, illuminations, and parades. My early letters to my Russian friends were filled with boastful descriptions of these glories of my new country. No native citizen of Chelsea took such pride and delight in its institutions as I did. It required no fife and drum corps, no Fourth of July procession, to set me tingling with patriotism. Even the common agents and instruments of municipal life, such as the letter carrier and the fire engine, I regarded with a measure of respect. I know what I thought of people who said that Chelsea was a very small, dull, unaspiring town, with no discernible excuse for a separate name or existence.

The apex of my civic pride and personal contentment was reached on the bright September morning when I entered the public school. That day I must always remember, even if I live to be so old that I cannot tell my name. To most people their first day at school is a memorable occasion. In my case the importance of the day was a hundred times magnified, on account of the years I had waited, the road I had come, and the conscious ambitions I entertained. . . .

35   Who were my companions on my first day at school? Whose hand was in mine, as I stood, overcome with awe, by the teacher's desk, and whispered my name as my father prompted? Was it Frieda's steady, capable hand? Was it her loyal heart that throbbed, beat for beat with mine, as it had done through all our childish adventures? Frieda's heart did throb that day, but not with my emotions. My heart pulsed with joy and pride and ambition; in her heart longing fought with abnegation. For I was led to the schoolroom, with its sunshine and its singing and the teacher's cheery smile; while she was led to the workshop, with its foul air, care-lined faces, and the foreman's stern command. Our going to school was the fulfillment of my father's best promises to us, and Frieda's share in it was to fashion and fit the calico frocks in which the baby sister and I made our first appearance in a public schoolroom. . . .

Father himself conducted us to school. He would not have delegated that mission to the President of the United States. He had awaited the day with impatience equal to mine, and the visions he saw as he hurried us over the sun-flecked pavements transcended all my dreams. Almost his first act on landing on American soil, three years before, had been his application for naturalization. He had taken the remaining steps in the process with eager promptness, and at the earliest moment allowed by the law, he became a citizen of the United States. It is true that he had left home in search of bread for his hungry family, but he went blessing the necessity that drove him to America. The boasted freedom of the New World meant to him far more than the right to reside, travel, and work wherever he pleased; it meant the freedom to speak his thoughts, to throw off the shackles of superstition, to test his own fate, unhindered by political or religious tyranny. He was only a young man when he landed—thirty-two; and most of his life he had been held in leading-strings. He was hungry for his untasted manhood.

Three years passed in sordid struggle and disappointment. He was not prepared to make a living even in America, where the day laborer eats wheat instead of rye. Apparently the American flag could not protect him against the pursuing Nemesis of his limitations; he must expiate the sins of his fathers who slept across the seas. He had been endowed at birth with a poor constitution, a nervous, restless temperament, and an abundance of hindering prejudices. In his boyhood his body was starved, that his mind might be stuffed with useless learning. In his youth this dearly gotten learning was sold, and the price was the bread and salt which he had not been trained to earn for himself. Under the wedding canopy he was bound for life to a girl whose features were still strange to him; and he was bidden to multiply himself, that sacred learning might be perpetuated in his sons, to the glory of the God of his fathers. All this while he had been led about as a creature without a will, a chattel, an instrument. In his maturity he awoke, and found himself poor in health, poor in purse, poor in useful knowledge, and hampered on all sides. At the first nod of opportunity he broke away from his prison, and strove to atone for his wasted youth by a life of useful labor; while at the same time he sought to lighten the gloom of his narrow scholarship by freely partaking of modern ideas. But his utmost endeavor still left him far from his goal. In business, nothing prospered with him. Some fault of hand or mind or temperament led him to failure where other men found success. Wherever the blame for his disabilities be placed, he reaped their bitter fruit. "Give me bread!" he cried to America. "What will you do to earn it?" the challenge came back. And he found that he was master of no art, of no trade; that even his precious learning was of no avail, because he had only the most antiquated methods of communicating it.

So in his primary quest he had failed. There was left him the compensation of intellectual freedom. That he sought to realize in every possible way. He had very little opportunity to prosecute his education, which, in truth, had never been begun. His struggle for a bare living left him no time to take advantage of the public evening school; but he lost nothing of what was to be learned through reading, through attendance at public meetings, through exercising the rights of citizenship. Even here he was hindered by a natural inability to acquire the English language. In time, indeed, he learned to read, to follow a conversation or lecture; but he never learned to write correctly, and his pronunciation remains extremely foreign to this day.

If education, culture, the higher life were shining things to be worshipped from afar, he had still a means left whereby he could draw one step nearer to them. He could send his children to school, to learn all those things that he knew by fame to be desirable. The common school, at least, perhaps high school; for one or two, perhaps even college! His children should be students, should fill his house with books and intellectual company; and thus he would walk by proxy in the Elysian Fields of liberal learning. As for the children themselves, he knew no surer way to their advancement and happiness.

So it was with a heart full of longing and hope that my father led   40
us to school on that first day. He took long strides in his eagerness, the rest of us running and hopping to keep up.

At last the four of us stood around the teacher's desk; and my father, in his impossible English, gave us over in her charge, with some broken word of his hopes for us that his swelling heart could no longer contain. I venture to say that Miss Nixon was struck by something un-common in the group we made, something outside of Semitic features and the abashed manner of the alien. My little sister was as pretty as a doll, with her clear pink-and-white face, short golden curls, and eyes like blue violets when you caught them looking up. My brother might have been a girl, too, with his cherubic contours of face, rich red color, glossy black hair, and fine eyebrows. Whatever secret fears were in his heart, remembering his former teachers, who had taught with the rod, he stood up straight and uncringing before the American teacher, his cap respectfully doffed. Next to him stood a starved-looking girl with eyes ready to pop out, and short dark curls that would not have made much of a wig for a Jewish bride.

All three children carried themselves rather better than the com-mon run of "green" pupils that were brought to Miss Nixon. But the figure that challenged attention to the group was the tall, straight fa-ther, with his earnest face and fine forehead, nervous hands eloquent in gesture, and a voice full of feeling. This foreigner, who brought his children to school as if it were an act of consecration, who regarded the teacher of the primer class with reverence, who spoke of visions, like a man inspired, in a common schoolroom, was not like other aliens, who brought their children in dull obedience to the law; was not like the native fathers, who brought their unmanageable boys, glad to be relieved of their care. I think Miss Nixon guessed what my fa-ther's best English could not convey. I think she divined that by the simple act of delivering our school certificates to her he took posses-sion of America.

For Journals

Imagine that someone of your age has just arrived in America from a foreign country. What aspects of American life do you think will be the strangest or the hardest for that person to get used to? What kind of advice and information can you offer that person?

For Discussion

1. Why are the Antins so anxious not to be "greenhorns"? What are they willing to give up to be more American? How do you think Mary Antin would define assimilation? How positive or negative would that concept be to her?

2. Not everyone in the Antin family shared Mary's experience—her older sister, Frieda, for example. How does she adjust her dreams for the sake of her family? How do you feel about the idea of sacrificing

your dreams for other members of your family? Has anyone in your family done that for you?

3. Antin is extremely aware of her father's dream. What does he hope for? How does America measure up to his expectations for himself and his children?

4. Discuss the last sentences in the chapter: "I think Miss Nixon guessed what my father's best English could not convey. I think she divined that by the simple act of delivering our school certificates to her he took possession of America." How has Mr. Antin's dream changed? How do you think that change will affect Mary Antin's own dreams?

5. Although she had personal reasons for writing her autobiography, one of Mary Antin's main purposes was to combat the anti-immigration mood in Congress. Judging from the examples she gives in this excerpt, how persuasive do you think her book was to those opposed to immigration?

For Writing

1. Mary Antin is keenly aware of her father's desire to find success in America. Write an essay in which you consider these questions: How does America measure up to Mr. Antin's expectations for himself and his children? How do your parents, or one of your parents, define the American dream for you, and how comfortable are you with that definition? In what ways, if any, would your own definition of the American dream differ from that of your parents or Mr. Antin?

2. Mary Antin wrote her book at a time of intense debate over whether open immigration should be continued. Conflict over who should be permitted to immigrate to America continues to this day. Argue *one* of the following:

- Anyone who wants to come to America today should be able to, even if that person has not been politically persecuted at home, is not a highly skilled worker, and would compete for jobs with native-born Americans.

- America should accept only immigrants who have strong educational and financial backgrounds and can prove that they will not be a drain on national resources.

Whichever side you choose, explain who you think is entitled to the American dream and how inclusive or exclusive that dream is. Be sure to include examples from your own background, or from newspaper and magazine articles, to support your argument.

TYPICAL OF THE 16,000 SMALL TOWNS
1936

Grit *Newspaper*

Grit *was a weekly, national newspaper focusing on the lives and events in small-town America. The following advertisement was placed in* Advertising Age, *a professional publication, to encourage businesses to place their ads in* Grit. *It focuses on a specific small town where* Grit *is sold, Mount Jewett, and stresses that its readers are financially well off enough to buy any goods the advertisers might want to sell.*

For Journals

Why would a weekly newspaper in the middle of the Great Depression call itself *Grit*? Why would that title be appealing?

For Discussion

1.   This advertisement is trying to convince those who want to sell goods and services to people living in small-town America to place ads in *Grit*. How does the advertisement make that argument? How do the words and pictures contribute to this message? How does an ideal of the American dream contribute to it?

2.   The advertisement ran in 1936, when the country was in the throes of the Great Depression. Does anything in the ad suggest that small-town America is economically depressed? Explain.

3.   Several photographs depicting businesses and homes in Mount Jewett are included, presumably to show that the American dream is alive in this town. What dream of small-town life do you see represented in these pictures? How does it compare to your own idea or your own experience of small-town life?

4.   The word *typical* is used as a highly positive term here: Mount Jewett is "typical" of small towns with buying power; the homes in the bottom picture are "typical" homes. Does this town and its homes seem typical to you? Why do you think the word *typical* was used this way? What values do you think this use of *typical* was trying to appeal to?

—typical of the 16,000 small towns where 500,000 families read GRIT every week

MAIN STREET BUSINESS SECTION

TANNERY EMPLOYS 185

GLASS WORKS EMPLOYS 125

TYPICAL HOMES

THE tannery is going full blast and so is the glass works. In a population of 1,379 there are only 290 families to provide workers for two large industries, so it is necessary to draw help from nearby towns.

Wages are good, living standards high. The local banker says business is better than it was in 1929.

Every week GRIT sells 155 copies in Mount Jewett—the broadest coverage in this town provided by any national publication.

Mount Jewett is just another of the 16,000 thriving, able-to-buy small towns where your business will be better when you put GRIT on your advertising schedules.

America's Greatest Weekly Newspaper

For Writing

1.   Write an advertisement for a product that you think is representative of some domestic aspect of your idea of the American dream—something related to home, family, or leisure time. Be sure that it uses both pictures or photographs and text.

2.   Find two ads drawn from two different decades dealing with domestic life, and write an essay that analyzes their use of examples, the effectiveness of their language and illustrations, and their ability to appeal to an audience by playing on some element of the American dream that the audience would recognize. Identify whom you think the audience is. You might want to choose ads that are in some way connected—for example, representing similar products or life-styles, marketing similar values, or making their audience want the same results (for example, to feel more attractive, more successful, or more independent).

LET AMERICA BE AMERICA AGAIN
1 9 3 8

Langston Hughes

   Langston Hughes (1902–1967) was one of the premier figures of the Harlem Renaissance—that jubilant outpouring of black art and culture in New York City in the 1920s. Hughes uses the rhythms of jazz, blues, and gospel music to celebrate and probe the role of black people in American society. His collections of verse include The Dream Keeper (1932), The Way of White Folks (1934), Shakespeare in Harlem (1941), and Montage of a Dream Deferred (1951).

   Let America be America again.
   Let it be the dream it used to be.
   Let it be the pioneer on the plain
   Seeking a home where he himself is free.

5   (America never was America to me.)

Let America be the dream the dreamers dreamed—
Let it be that great strong land of love
Where never kings connive nor tyrants scheme
That any man be crushed by one above.

(It never was America to me.)   10

O, let my land be a land where Liberty
Is crowned with no false patriotic wreath,
But opportunity is real, and life is free,
Equality is in the air we breathe.

(There's never been equality for me,   15
Nor freedom in this "homeland of the free.")

Say who are you that mumbles in the dark?
And who are you that draws your veil across the
    stars?

I am the poor white, fooled and pushed apart,
I am the red man driven from the land.   20
I am the refugee clutching the hope I seek—
But finding only the same old stupid plan

Of dog eat dog, of mighty crush the weak.
I am the Negro, "problem" to you all.
I am the people, humble, hungry, mean—   25
Hungry yet today despite the dream.
Beaten yet today—O, Pioneers!
I am the man who never got ahead,
The poorest worker bartered through the years.
Yet I'm the one who dreamt our basic dream   30
In that Old World while still a serf of kings,
Who dreamt a dream so strong, so brave, so true,
That even yet its mighty daring sings
In every brick and stone, in every furrow turned
That's made America the land it has become.   35
O, I'm the man who sailed those early seas
In search of what I meant to be my home—
For I'm the one who left dark Ireland's shore,
And Poland's plain, and England's grassy lea,
And torn from Black Africa's strand I came   40
To build a "homeland of the free."

The free?
Who said the free? Not me?
Surely not me? The millions on relief today?
45 The millions who have nothing for our pay
For all the dreams we've dreamed
And all the songs we've sung
And all the hopes we've held
And all the flags we've hung,
50 The millions who have nothing for our pay—
Except the dream we keep alive today.

O, let America be America again—
The land that never has been yet—
And yet must be—the land where every man is
    free.
55 The land that's mine—the poor man's, Indian's,
    Negro's, ME—
Who made America,
Whose sweat and blood, whose faith and pain,
Whose hand at the foundry, whose plow in the
    rain,
Must bring back our mighty dream again.

60   O, yes,
     I say it plain,
     America never was America to me,
And yet I swear this oath—
America will be!

For Journals

What do you know about the America of the 1930s and the Great Depression? What do you think they have to do with the subject of the
poem?

For Discussion

1. With whom, or with what, does Hughes identify the America that
is "the dream it used to be" (line 2)? In the first three stanzas, which examples of the dream does he celebrate?

2. In the second half of the poem (beginning with line 52), Hughes
gives examples of the people he thinks of as the real source of the

American dream, a dream that must be "the poor man's, Indian's, Negro's, ME" (line 55) in order to be valid. How can this viewpoint co-exist with the idea of an America exemplified by the founding fathers, including Franklin?

3.   Analyze the poem as an argument. What are the two sides? What are they fighting over? What points does each side makes? Where does the poem "turn"? How would you describe the tone of the speaker? Optimistic? Cheerful? Bitter? What do you consider the most persuasive part of the poem?

4.   What does it mean for America to be America again, as the title says, if it never was in the first place? Since the population of America is almost all descended from people who came from somewhere else, including all the nationalities Hughes mentions, is there any evidence in the poem to support the possibility of change? Where would it come from?

5.   Considering how much of the American dream revolves around success, how do you respond to the fact that Hughes identifies the dream with examples of people who are not successful—"I am the man who never got ahead, / The poorest worker bartered through the years" (lines 28–29)? Do you think he is distorting the definition of the dream, or redefining it? Why?

For Writing

1.   Write an essay that provides a persuasive answer to the following questions: If the people who originated the American dream are left out of it, what about the dream is still worthwhile to them? Why do they still want it? Read several newspaper or magazine articles about the problems and attitudes that prospective immigrants to America currently encounter. Support your essay with examples and, if possible, with actual quotations from immigrants about their desires to come to this country.

2.   Hughes was active as a writer both during and after the Harlem Renaissance. Research and write an essay on one of the following: the historical and social background for the Harlem Renaissance; the work of any of the artists, musicians, and writers involved in the Renaissance, for example, Jean Toomer, Zora Neale Hurston, Duke Ellington, Richard Wright, Countee Cullen, or Lou Jones; the history of the Cotton Club and the entertainers who worked there; the story of the Apollo Theater; or other work by Langston Hughes, including his great short stories, *The Best of Simple.*

I HAVE A DREAM
1963

Martin Luther King, Jr.

Martin Luther King, Jr. (1929–1968) was the leader of the nonviolent civil rights struggle. A minister from a family of ministers, he became a public figure while still in his twenties when he led a bus boycott in Montgomery, Alabama. Frequently threatened or arrested, he was the main organizer of sit-ins and marches in segregated southern towns and cities, particularly Birmingham, Alabama, in 1963. That summer he addressed a huge audience of civil rights workers who had marched in protest in Washington, D.C. His speech, delivered from the steps of the Lincoln Memorial, is one of the most famous of the century. King received the Nobel Prize for Peace in 1964, the youngest person ever to do so. He was assassinated in Memphis, Tennessee, in 1968.

Five score years ago, a great American, in whose symbolic shadow we stand, signed the Emancipation Proclamation. This momentous decree came as a great beacon light of hope to millions of Negro slaves who had been seared in the flames of withering injustice. It came as a joyous daybreak to end the long night of captivity.

But one hundred years later, we must face the tragic fact that the Negro is still not free. One hundred years later, the life of the Negro is still sadly crippled by the manacles of segregation and the chains of discrimination. One hundred years later, the Negro lives on a lonely island of poverty in the midst of a vast ocean of material prosperity. One hundred years later, the Negro is still languishing in the corners of American society and finds himself an exile in his own land. So we have come here today to dramatize an appalling condition.

In a sense we have come to our nation's Capitol to cash a check. When the architects of our republic wrote the magnificent words of the Constitution and the Declaration of Independence, they were signing a promissory note to which every American was to fall heir. This note was a promise that all men would be guaranteed the unalienable rights of life, liberty, and the pursuit of happiness.

It is obvious today that America has defaulted on this promissory note insofar as her citizens of color are concerned. Instead of honoring this sacred obligation, America has given the Negro people a bad check; a check which has come back marked "insufficient funds." But we refuse to believe that the bank of justice is bankrupt. We refuse to believe that there are insufficient funds in the great vaults of opportunity of this nation. So we have come to cash this check—a check that will give us upon demand the riches of freedom and the security of justice. We have also come to this hallowed spot to remind America of the fierce urgency of *now*. This is no time to engage in the luxury of cooling off or to take the tranquilizing drug of gradualism. *Now* is the time to make real the promises of Democracy. *Now* is the time to rise from the dark and desolate valley of segregation to the sunlit path of racial justice. *Now* is the time to open the doors of opportunity to all of God's children. *Now* is the time to lift our nation from the quicksands of racial injustice to the solid rock of brotherhood.

It would be fatal for the nation to overlook the urgency of the moment and to underestimate the determination of the Negro. This sweltering summer of the Negro's legitimate discontent will not pass until there is an invigorating autumn of freedom and equality. 1963 is not an end, but a beginning. Those who hope that the Negro needed to blow off steam and will now be content will have a rude awakening if the nation returns to business as usual. There will be neither rest nor tranquility in America until the Negro is granted his citizenship rights. The whirlwinds of revolt will continue to shake the foundations of our nation until the bright day of justice emerges.

But there is something I must say to my people who stand on the warm threshold which leads into the palace of justice. In the process of gaining our rightful place we must not be guilty of wrongful deeds. Let us not seek to satisfy our thirst for freedom by drinking from the cup of bitterness and hatred. We must forever conduct our struggle on the high plane of dignity and discipline. We must not allow our creative protest to degenerate into physical violence. Again and again we must rise to the majestic heights of meeting physical force with soul force. The marvelous new militancy which has engulfed the Negro community must not lead us to a distrust of all white people, for many of our white brothers, as evidenced by their presence here today, have come to realize that their destiny is tied up with our destiny and their freedom is inextricably bound to our freedom. We cannot walk alone.

And as we walk, we must make the pledge that we shall march ahead. We cannot turn back. There are those who are asking the devotees of civil rights, "When will you be satisfied?" We can never be satisfied as long as the Negro is the victim of the unspeakable horrors of police brutality. We can never be satisfied as long as our bodies, heavy with the fatigue of travel, cannot gain lodging in the motels of the highways and the hotels of the cities. We cannot be satisfied as long as the Negro's basic mobility is from a smaller ghetto to a larger one. We can never be satisfied as long as a Negro in Mississippi cannot vote and a Negro in New York believes he has nothing for which to vote. No, no, we are not satisfied, and we will not be satisfied until justice rolls down like waters and righteousness like a mighty stream.

I am not unmindful that some of you have come here out of great trials and tribulations. Some of you have come fresh from narrow jail cells. Some of you have come from areas where your quest for freedom left you battered by the storms of persecution and staggered by the winds of police brutality. You have been the veterans of creative suffering. Continue to work with the faith that unearned suffering is redemptive.

Go back to Mississippi, go back to Alabama, go back to South Carolina, go back to Georgia, go back to Louisiana, go back to the slums and ghettoes of our northern cities, knowing that somehow this situation can and will be changed. Let us not wallow in the valley of despair.

10 I say to you today, my friends, that in spite of the difficulties and frustrations of the moment I still have a dream. It is a dream deeply rooted in the American dream.

I have a dream that one day this nation will rise up and live out the true meaning of its creed: "We hold these truths to be self-evident; that all men are created equal."

I have a dream that one day on the red hills of Georgia the sons of former slaves and the sons of former slaveowners will be able to sit down together at the table of brotherhood.

I have a dream that the state of Mississippi, a desert state sweltering with the heat of injustice and oppression, will be transformed into an oasis of freedom and justice.

I have a dream that my four little children will one day live in a nation where they will not be judged by the color of their skin but by the content of their character.

15 I have a dream today.

I have a dream that the state of Alabama, whose governor's lips are presently dripping with the words of interposition and nullification, will be transformed into a situation where little black boys and black girls will be able to join hands with little white boys and white girls and walk together as sisters and brothers.

I have a dream today.

I have a dream that one day every valley shall be exalted, every hill and mountain shall be made low, the rough places will be made plain, and the crooked places will be made straight, and the glory of the Lord shall be revealed, and all flesh shall see it together.

This is our hope. This is the faith with which I return to the South. With this faith we will be able to hew out of the mountain of despair a stone of hope. With this faith we will be able to transform the jangling discords of our nation into a beautiful symphony of brotherhood. With this faith we will be able to work together, to pray together, to struggle together, to go to jail together, to stand up for freedom together, knowing that we will be free one day.

This will be the day when all of God's children will be able to sing   20
with new meaning.

> My country, tis of thee
> Sweet land of liberty,
>   Of thee I sing:
> Land where my fathers died,
> Land of the pilgrims' pride,
> From every mountainside
>   Let freedom ring.

And if America is to be a great nation this must become true. So let freedom ring from the prodigious hilltops of New Hampshire. Let freedom ring from the mighty mountains of New York. Let freedom ring from the heightening Alleghenies of Pennsylvania!

Let freedom ring from the snowcapped Rockies of Colorado!

Let freedom ring from the curvaceous peaks of California!

But not only that; let freedom ring from Stone Mountain of Georgia!

Let freedom ring from Lookout Mountain of Tennessee!   25

Let freedom ring from every hill and molehill of Mississippi. From every mountainside, let freedom ring.

When we let freedom ring, when we let it ring from every village and every hamlet, from every state and every city, we will be able to speed up that day when all of God's children, black men and white men, Jews and Gentiles, Protestants and Catholics, will be able to join hands and sing in the words of the old Negro spiritual, "Free at last! free at last! thank God almighty, we are free at last!"

For Journals

What have you heard or read about the civil rights movement? About Martin Luther King, Jr.? If you have seen film or newsreels of the struggle between civil rights advocates and segregationists, how did you react to them?

For Discussion

1. What is King trying to convince African Americans they should do about segregation? What is he trying to convince white Americans to do?

2. King gave this speech at the Lincoln Memorial. Aside from the obvious location, why does he begin with a line reminiscent of the beginning of Lincoln's Gettysburg Address, "Four score and seven years ago"? What associations might he be trying to raise in the minds of his audience?

3. In order to identify the consequences of racial injustice in American life, King uses both unusual figures of speech, like the promissory note of equality (paragraph 3), and examples of the effects of prejudice in ordinary life, like not being able to get into a hotel (paragraph 7). Go through the speech and look for some more examples of both unusual language and ordinary experience. What do you think he gains from using both kinds of examples? How do the two together help make his argument more persuasive?

4. King says his dream is deeply rooted in the American dream. But he also uses Judeo-Christian references that are part of his background as a minister. Divide the speech up into sections; with two of your peers, look through the speech for examples of religious and biblical language. What values or ideas are expressed in those examples and in the American dream, as you see it?

5. King also has to address the frustrated dreams of African Americans in the civil rights movement who thought progress was too slow and the irritation of northerners who thought it was too fast. Look at the section of the speech starting with, "We have also come to this hallowed spot to remind America of the fierce urgency of *now*" (the middle of the fourth paragraph). What examples does he use to address each group? Which examples advocate patience, and which ones express determination? Do you recognize the sources of any of his metaphorical examples?

6. The video of King's speech is available in many college libraries. If it is in yours, watch it in class. If not, read the speech out loud in class. In the last and most famous part of the speech, King begins paragraphs with the word, "I have a dream," and then "Let freedom ring." What kinds of fulfillment does he dream about in these passages? You might want to paraphrase his language to see how many kinds of dreams he evokes here.

For Writing

1. King gave this speech in the summer of 1963. Using contemporary newspaper and magazine reports and at least one biography of King or a history of the civil rights movement (Taylor Branch's *Parting the Waters* is a good example), write a researched paper on the circumstances that preceded the march. Some points to include: Who was

against it? Why were there fears about what would happen at the
march? What was the response of the audience? The press? What was
the aftermath? Did people who heard King's speech talk about their
own dreams for America in response?

2.   This speech is remarkable for the number of other texts it borrows
from, rephrases, or uses for its own purposes—the Bible, the Declaration of Independence, the Gettysburg Address, Shakespeare, spiritu-
als, and others. Write an essay in which you identify at least three
examples of these borrowed texts, and explain why you think King
picked them, what point they were used to make, and how persuasive
you think they are. Then try to come up with examples of contemporary texts or songs that you would borrow from if you were delivering
this speech today.

HOME, MOM, AND APPLE PIE
1 9 8 4

Dolores Hayden

    *Dolores Hayden (1945–   ) is a professor of architecture and urban
planning at the University of California at Los Angeles. Her research interests include American cities, neighborhoods and houses and how Americans
have lived, live now, and might live in the future. This selection is from her
award-winning book,* Redesigning the American Dream: The Future of
Housing, Work, and Family Life.

    Home is where the heart is. Home, sweet home. Whoever speaks
of housing must also speak of home; the word means both the physical
space and the nurturing that takes place there. In American life, it is
hard to separate the ideal of home from the ideals of mom and apple
pie, of mother love and home cooking. Rethinking home life involves
rethinking the spatial, technological, cultural, social, and economic di-
mensions of sheltering, nurturing, and feeding society, activities often
discussed as if they had existed unchanged from the beginning of time,
unsmirched by capitalist development, technological manipulation, or
social pressures. Social scientists, despite an interest in careful histori-

cal and economic analysis of family life, have scarcely explored the realities of domestic work. Yet among feminists, mother love and home cooking have been celebrated targets provoking witty slogans, and it is understood that "home, sweet home, has never meant housework, sweet housework," as Charlotte Perkins Gilman put it in the 1890s. It has also been clear that mothering is political. Lily Braun, the German feminist, wrote: "After the birth of my son, the problems of women's liberation were no longer mere theories. They cut into my own flesh." But there has been no clear contemporary agreement in the United States, much less in the rest of the world, about what constitutes a fully egalitarian political position on domestic life, since male participation in nurturing work is in some ways incompatible with full recognition of female skills.

Nurturing men and children has traditionally been woman's work. A brief analysis of such work in this country reveals the many separate tasks involved. Home cooking requires meals prepared to suit the personal likes and dislikes of family members. It is also one of the most satisfying and creative aesthetic activities for many women and men. House-cleaning requires sweeping, vacuuming, washing, polishing, and tidying the living space. Laundry requires sorting, washing, drying, folding or ironing, and putting away clean clothes and linens. Health care begins at home, and home remedies and prescribed medicines are distributed there. Mental health also begins at home when homemakers smooth out worries and provide emotional support so that all family members make successful connections and adjustments to the larger society. This is crucial not only for the education of young, but also for adults, who must sustain the pressures of earning a living, and for the aged, who need emotional support in their declining years.

Equally important are those ties to kin and community that maintain the social status and ethnic identity of the household. Maintenance of these ties often includes cultural rituals—the preparation of Thanksgiving dinners, Seders, Cinco de Mayo celebrations—with all the food, clothing, and special objects associated with each event. Recreation is another home task: arranging for children's play, family vacations, team sports for the young, parties and socials for adolescents. In urban societies, recreation also means arranging family experiences of nature, such as visits to parks or camping trips.

A good home life for a family of four took about sixty hours of nurturing work per week in 1982. That work may have been more physically arduous in the past, but never more complex than now. Beyond the house and the immediate neighborhood, home life in most urban industrial societies today includes the management of extensive relationships with stores, banks, and other commercial service facilities, and with public institutions such as schools, hospitals, clinics, and government offices. Part of homemaking involves seeing that each family member's myriad personal needs are fully met. The new dress must be the right size; the new fourth grade teacher must understand a child's history of learning difficulties. Sometimes relationships with stores or institutions turn into adversarial ones. If the new car is a lemon; if the grade school isn't teaching reading fast enough, if the hospital offers an incorrect diagnosis, if the social security benefit check is late, then the stressful nature of the homemaker's brokering work between home, market, and state is exacerbated. . . .

While "man's home is his castle," a woman often lacks any private   5
space in her home. Society defines the ideal home as a warm, supportive place for men and children, but for homemakers it has always been a workplace, where a "woman's work is never done." While women may have gourmet kitchens, sewing rooms, and so-called "master" bedrooms to inhabit, even in these spaces the homemaker's role is to service, not to claim autonomy and privacy. There has been little nurturing for homemakers themselves unless they break down. In crises, women have looked to other women for emotional support. This may be the informal help acknowledged by homemaker and author Erma Bombeck, who dedicated one of her books to the other homemakers in her car pool: the women who, "when I was drowning in a car pool threw me a line. . . . always a funny one." Women's support may also come from mothers, sisters, female friends, and female kin, who traditionally rally in crises. It may come from the range of services provided by the feminist movement, such as discussion groups, crisis centers, health centers, and hostels. Or it may come from husbands and children who finally notice when their wives and mothers break down. . . .

American urban design, social policy planning, and housing design have seldom taken the complexity of homemaking into account. To rethink private life, it is essential to be explicit about the range of needs that homes and homemakers fulfill. Home life is the source of great cultural richness and diversity in an immigrant nation. Home life is also the key to social services—education, health, mental health. And home life is the key to successful urban design, in the patterning of residential space, commercial space, and institutional space, so that the linkages between home, market, and state can be sustained without undue hardship.

Yet in the last thirty years, the cultural strength of home has been debated: the success of the family in providing socialization for children has been challenged; the failure of many residential neighborhoods has been noted. In light of the extensive literature on such topics as divorce and family violence, it is surprising to see how few alternative models of home life are discussed in a serious, sustained way. Many critics fail to distinguish between the traditional patriarchal

family and other models of family life. Others welcome new models
but fail to record the struggles to transform the patriarchal family that
feminists have waged for at least two hundred years. Innovative, egalitarian housing strategies that lead to new forms of housing cannot be
developed without a reformulation of the traditional family and its
gender division of nurturing work. Americans experiencing demographic changes need to make ideological changes, but before considering these let us examine the history of three alternative models of
home, mom, and apple pie.

In the years between 1870 and 1930, home life provoked a phe-
nomenal amount of political debate. Because this topic linked the
Woman Question to the Labor Question, it attracted the attention of
housewives, feminist activists, domestic servants, inventors, economists,
architects, urban planners, utopian novelists, visionaries, and efficiency
experts. Housework, factory work, and home were all susceptible to
restructuring in the industrial city. Women and men of all political per-
suasions generally agreed that household work, as it had been carried
out in the pre-industrial houses of the first half of the nineteenth century, left most women little time to be good wives and mothers. Industrial development was transforming all other work and workplaces,
and it was expected that domestic work, and residential environments
would be transformed as well. Activists raised fundamental questions
about the relationships between women and men, households and servants. They explored the economic and social definitions of "woman's
work." They also raised basic questions about household space, public
space, and the relationship between economic policies and family life
concretized in domestic architecture and residential neighborhoods.

Many proposed solutions drew, in one way or another, on the possibilities suggested by new aspects of urban and industrial life: new
forms of specialization and division of labor, new technologies, new
concentrations of dwelling units in urban apartment houses or suburban neighborhoods. But all of the domestic theorists also had to deal
with a number of unwelcome consquences of these new developments:
hierarchy in the workplace; replacement of hand craft skills by mecha-
nization; erosion of privacy in crowded urban dwellings; development
of conspicuous domestic consumption in bourgeois neighborhoods.
Although life in the isolated household was burdensome, inefficient,
and stifling, many reformers feared that the socialization of domestic
work would deprive industrial society of its last vestige of uncapital-
ized, uncompetitive, standard work: that is, of mother love and home
cooking. . . .

10   The leading exponent of the home as haven was the domestic advice giver Catharine Beecher. In *The American Woman's Home* (1869)
and earlier books, she not only explained the technological and archi-

tectural basis of a refined suburban home. She also proposed to increase the effectiveness of the isolated housewife and to glorify woman's traditional sphere of work. Released from some of her fomer drudgery by better design, the housewife, always a maker of perfect pies, would be newly equipped with a better pastry counter and flour bin, and a better oven, so she could devote more of her labor to becoming an emotional support for her husband and an inspiring mother for her children. Self-sacrifice would be her leading virtue. The home, a spiritual and physical shelter from the competition and exploitation of industrial capitalist society, and a training ground for the young, would become a haven in a heartless world. Beecher believed this division of labor between men and women would blunt the negative effects of industrial society on male workers. She argued that both rich and poor women, removed from competition with men in paid work, would find gender a more engrossing identification than class.

For Beecher, it was extremely important that the housewife do all the work of nurturing with her own two hands. As she performed many different tasks each day, she was to be a sacred figure, above and beyond the cash nexus; her personal services as wife and mother were beyond price. Thus the biological mother was presented as the only focus for her children's needs; the virtuous wife was presented as the only one who could meet her husband's needs as well. The spatial envelope for all of this exclusive nurturing was the little cottage in a garden: nature surrounding the home reinforced the belief in woman's natural, biologically determined role within it.

The industrial strategy, as articulated by the German Marxist August Bebel in his classic book *Women Under Socialism* (1883), was to move most traditional household work into the factory, abolishing women's domestic sphere entirely. Bebel argued: "The small private kitchen is, just like the workshop of the small master mechanic, a transition stage, an arrangement by which time, power and material are senselessly squandered and wasted. . . . in the future the domestic kitchen is rendered wholly superfluous by all the central institutions for the preparation of food. . . . He also predicted that just as factory kitchens would prepare dinners, and large state bakeries would bake pies, so mechanical laundries would wash clothes and cities would provide central heating. Children would be trained in public institutions from their earliest years. Women would take up industrial employment outside the household, and the household would lose control of many private activities. The effects of industrialization would be general, and women would share in the gains and losses with men, although their new factory work would probably be occupationally segregated labor in the laundry or the pie factory. A life of dedication to greater industrial production and the socialist state would reward personal sacrifice in the Marxist version of the industrial strategy.

In Bebel's version of home life, both nature and biology disappear in favor of industrial efficiency. Bebel believed that nurturing work should be done by women, but he tended to see women as interchangeable service workers. The patriarchal demand that women nurture with a personal touch, so central to Beecher, was replaced by a sense that any day-care worker could offer a substitute for mother love and any canteen worker could serve up a substitute for home cooking. The spatial container for this interchangeable, industrial nurturing was to be the apartment house composed of industrial components and equipped with large mess halls, recreation clubs, child-care centers, and kitchenless apartments. Of course, service workers would need to be constantly on duty to keep these residential complexes running, but Bebel did not consider this service as labor of any particular value or skill; in fact, he underestimated the importance of the socialized home as workplace, even as he recognized the private home as workshop.

Midway between the haven strategy and the industrial strategy, there was a third strategy. The material feminists led by Melusina Fay Peirce wanted to socialize housework under women's control through neighborhood networks. . . . Peirce, the most important material feminist theorist in the United States between 1868 and 1884, argued that "it is just as necessary, and just as honorable for a wife to earn money as it is for her husband," but she criticized the traditional arrangement of domestic work as forcing the housewife to become a "jack-of-all-trades."

15   Peirce's proposed alternative was the producers' cooperative, including former housewives and former servants, all doing cooking, baking, laundry, and sewing in one technologically well-equipped neighborhood workplace. They would send the freshly baked pies, the clean laundry, or the mended garments home to their own husbands (or their former male employers) for cash on delivery. Peirce planned to overcome the isolation and economic dependency inherent in the haven approach, and the alienation inherent in the industrial approach. While revering woman's traditional nurturing skills and neighborhood networks, the material basis of women's sphere, Peirce proposed to transform these skills and networks into a new kind of economic power for women by elevating nurturing to the scale of several dozen united households.

Peirce also overcame another great flaw in the haven approach: in the early 1870s, there were very few technological advances, aside from Beecher's own little inventions and architectural refinements, to help the housewife who worked alone. Almost all of the major advances such as clothes-washing machines, dishwasher, refrigerators, and new kinds of stoves were being developed for commercial laundries, breweries, hotels, hospitals, and apartment houses. They were designed to serve fifty to five hundred people, not one family. Peirce proposed, like Bebel, to use this technology, but to use it at the neighborhood scale, in a community workplace with a series of open courtyards set apart from kitchenless houses in a landscaped setting or integrated with kitchenless apartments. Peirce experimented with both as building types. . . .

When Catharine Beecher, August Bebel, and Melusina Peirce framed their views of what the industrial revolution should mean to domestic life, they set up models of women's work and family life marked by all the hopes and fears of the mid-nineteenth century. In particular, they accepted gender stereotypes so strong that not one of these models incorporated any substantial male responsibility for housework and child care. Yet Beecher's and Bebel's models of home continued to shape home life and public policy for over a century. The haven strategy and the industrial strategy became the ruling paradigms for domestic life in capitalist and in state socialist societies where the paid employment of women was a fact, not a hope or a fear. Neither model of home life incorporated any substantial critique of male exclusion from the domestic scene; both models disconnected household space from other parts of the industrial city and its economy. Attempts to repair their conceptual difficulties accelerated in the years after World War I, but neither model has undergone the total revision that would enable planners of housing, jobs, and services to create the spatial settings for modern societies where the paid employment of women is essential. . . .

What is astonishing is that . . . inventions eroded the autonomy of women at least as much as they contributed to saving women's labor. Eventually the haven strategy produced not a skilled housewife happy at home, supported by her husband's "family" wage, but a harried woman constantly struggling to keep up standards.

The years since 1900 have seen the production of privately owned clothes washers, clothes dryers, refrigerators, gas and electric stoves, freezers, dishwashers, toasters, blenders, electric ovens, food processors, vacuum cleaners, and electric brooms. Many of these appliances were the result of an extended campaign to miniaturize earlier hotel technology in the post–World War I era, and their potential for lightening household labor was tremendous. Unfortunately manufacturers began their sales of all such appliances and home improvements by advertising in women's magazines with themes of fear and guilt. "For the health of your family . . . keep your foods sweet and pure, free from odors, impurities, and contamination," read the copy for McCray Sanitary Refrigerators. "Don't apologize for your toilet! Modernize it," said Pfau Manufacturing Company. Women were also told that liberation could be bought: "Electricity has brought to women a new freedom [represented by the figure of Liberty, wearing a crown and classical drapery] . . . the easy scientific method of cleaning with the Western Electric Vacuum cleaner." The ideal of the "laboratory-clean home" was only part of the pseudo science the housewife had to achieve.

While household engineers made women guilty for not doing tasks fast enough, advertisers made both men and women guilty when they sold through the emotional blackmail of love. Men were told that if they loved their wives, they owed it to them to buy particular appliances. Women were told that if they bought certain items, men would love them more. "Man seeks no club, when the home has a Hub," wrote one stove manufacturer. The American response to such ad campaigns was extensive purchasing, but researchers who have studied time budgets find that conflicts within the home continued and the work of the "haven" housewives was still "never done." Jo Ann Vanek reported in her extensive survey in *Scientific American* that household standards have risen but women's time has not been saved. To take just one example, Vanek shows that the full-time urban or rural housewife spent more hours doing laundry in the 1970s than in the 1920s, despite all the new washing machines, dryers, bleaches, and detergents, because her family had more clothes and wanted them cleaner. The familiar "ring around the collar" commercials dramatize the conflict: a husband and his five-year-old son jeer at a woman for using a detergent that can't remove the stains on their shirt collars. Her guilty response exemplifies the ways that conflict within a family can be exploited by advertisers.

20   The popularity of gourmet cooking, the expansion of the size of houses, and the increasing complexity of home furnishings have also contributed to an increasing demand for female labor hours in the home. Another development launched in the 1920s and continued through the 1980s was the creation of a culture of mothering which demanded intense attention to children at every stage of their development. Although the numbers of children were shrinking, mothers were expected to spend more time with each one. When American technology finally produced a baby-sitting machine (TV), many households used it over six hours per day. However, television created as many problems as it solved, since children listened to endless commercials for candy and toys.

Clearly, family values must be more carefully integrated with research, development, and marketing before new technological inventions can aid the homemaker and parent in a substantial, lasting way. Clothes washers, dishwashers, refrigerators, and reliable stoves are valuable inventions, but the context for their use can be improved, and their environmental efficiency can be improved. Other "inventions" are better eliminated from home life, or should be developed at the neighborhood scale. To measure the "standard of living," as the U.S. Census now does, in terms of the number of families owning a particular appliance is misleading.

For Journals

How much housework do you do at your home? How many people in your family participate in the work? Who does most of this housework? Why?

For Discussion

1.   Hayden deals with a subject that is seldom analyzed critically: American domestic life. Why do you think social scientists have paid so little attention to such an obvious subject that is part of everyone's experience?

2.   Hayden gives three examples of how a woman's role could help realize the American dream at home: Catharine Beecher's woman as nurturer and icon; August Bebel's woman as industrial worker, professional server, and nurturer for other families; and Melusina Fay Peirce's woman as cooperative worker with other women. With two of your classmates, divide up these three theories; each of you should read one theory and explain its main points to the other two. Which elements of each plan do you find most interesting? Most peculiar? Most radical? Most likely to work?

3.   Think about the following sayings. What does it mean to say, "home, Mom, and apple pie"? What about "A man's home is his castle," or "A man's castle is woman's factory," or "Today's woman gets what she wants . . . The right to a career. Soap to match her bathroom's color scheme," or "You've come a long way, baby!"? How do you respond to these phrases? Do you react more positively to some than to others? What assumptions do you think these phrases make about Americans' values?

4.   Hayden says that taking care of an American family of four requires about sixty hours of work per week, which is more time than it took in the 1920s. Considering all the examples Hayden gives of time-saving inventions since 1900, such as clothes washers and dryers, toast-

ers, blenders, and food processors, why do you think this work is still so time-consuming?

5. Go through the text with a couple of your classmates and find Hayden's main thesis about the reality of women's housework. What conclusions does she draw about the problematic nature of home life for women today? What examples does she give as evidence? How persuasive are her examples to you? Why? What other examples can you devise to support or argue against her position?

For Writing

1. Hayden mentions that for many years advertisements tended to make husbands feel guilty for not buying their wives all the new labor-saving devices and tended to make wives feel guilty for not keeping perfect houses. Research issues of one or two older magazines published anywhere from the 1920s to the 1960s, such as *Woman's Day, McCall's, Good Housekeeping, Harper's, Life, Look,* or the original *Cosmopolitan* or *Vanity Fair,* for examples of advertisements about the home and women's role in it. Then research any contemporary magazines of your choice for examples of how home life and women's role in relation to home is portrayed today. Write an essay comparing the ads with respect to the following: the images they use; the values they represent; the expectations they express about women; and whether the recent advertisements reveal any great change in women's roles in the home or just variations on old ones. Use specific examples from the ads as evidence: what people in the ad are doing, how they are dressed, what their attitudes seem to be, and so forth.

2. Using examples from the three plans Hayden describes or from your own experience, devise your own model for a home that fulfills your idea of the American dream. Draw up the plan for either a family with two parents and two children or a single parent with two children. Assume that the adults in the family, male or female, have jobs outside the home. Include examples of how the following chores should be managed: Who does the housework? Cooking? Shopping for clothing and food? Who cleans up? Does the laundry or the smaller house repairs? Who pays for what? If there are children, do they help too?

3. What are the family values, the beliefs, the ethics that you grew up with? Select one of your core values—perhaps one relating to work or success—and write either a reflective personal essay or a researched essay that explores the value or belief and the ways in which it reflects your ethnic group or socioeconomic class.

DIVIDED WE STAND: THE IMMIGRATION BACKLASH
1 9 9 4

Suzanne Espinosa Solis

Susan Espinosa Solis (1962–   ) is a writer for the San Francisco Chronicle. *This selection is from a four-part series that ran in the* Chronicle *in March and April 1994. It is the latest chapter in the never-ending debate about whether immigrants are good for America.*

When Rudi DiPrima went to the Department of Motor Vehicles to apply for a new driver's license, the first thing the clerk wanted from him was proof that he had a legal right to be in the United States.

DiPrima happened to have his birth certificate, but as a blond San Francisco native, he couldn't believe that the state was asking to see it. He waited at the desk while three clerks checked and rechecked his documents. And by the time they sent him on to the next clerk, he was steamed.

"Pretty soon they'll start tattooing numbers on us at birth," he muttered.

The DMV document check was a brief bureaucratic aggravation for DiPrima, but it was something more, too: one of the most visible signs of a cultural and political backlash against immigrants that is unprecedented in modern California history.

In the past year, long-simmering frustration with immigration—illegal and legal—has boiled over in the state. Where before immigration had caused modest concerns, suddenly a broad political opposition has risen against it.   5

Some, wearied by recession, argue that the immigrants take away jobs and impose a burden on welfare, schools and other government programs. Some environmentalists argue that California lacks the water and other natural resources to support the rapid growth caused by immigration. Other people worry that with so many new residents coming from so many foreign cultures, the familiar American culture will be diluted or lost.

"Unfortunately, it's become an ideological thing," says businessman Mike Scott, a member of the Orange County-based Citizens for Responsible Immigration. "It's a heart-gripping problem because you're dealing with human beings, but it can't go on. I'm afraid it's reached a flash point."

Already, the impact is apparent.

Illegal immigrants devastated by January's Northridge earthquake have been denied earthquake-repair aid, although many have lived and paid taxes in the state for years. Children have been turned out of California schools along the border with Mexico. Activists are gathering signatures for the "Save Our State" initiative that would deny illegal immigrants access to public schools, hospitals and other social services.

10   Critics of the movement say the reaction is too strong and spreads too far. The sting of the backlash is being felt not just by illegal immigrants, they say, but by those who are here legally.

The descendants of Mexicans, Chinese and Japanese who came to California generations ago say they hear slurs and insults on the street. Some have been threatened. A few have been beaten.

"We are at a point where civil rights, particularly of immigrants, are in danger," warned Cruz Reynoso, a former California Supreme Court justice who is now vice chairman of the U.S. Commission on Civil Rights.

As it has been with many social movements, California seems to be at the front of a national anti-immigrant wave that is expected to crest as this year's elections approach.

Polarized and angry, the nation has come to a crossroads: Will we remain a haven for the poor of the world, as the Statue of Liberty promises, or will we close the door?

15   Either way, there will be a price to pay.

A History of Hostility

The United States has been at this crossroads before. Almost every decade in the nation's history, a new exodus of immigrants has arrived, and almost every decade there has been a hostile reaction.

In the 1840s, Roman Catholic immigrants from Ireland and Germany were the targets of Protestants who had settled in the country generations earlier. Later in the century, Italians and Jews were greeted with anger. From the time of the Gold Rush through the end of World War II, Chinese and Japanese immigrants endured prejudice that was sometimes legally sanctioned.

Today, the number of people on the move is staggering. A United Nations report issued last year estimated that at least 100 million people, or about 2 percent of the world's population, are international migrants. As the gap has widened between rich nations and poor, migratory pressures have increased, the report found.

And although some nations have tried to crack down, the report concluded that "where legal channels are closed, migrants will enter by whatever means are available."

Between 1982 and 1992, 9.5 million foreigners obtained legal permission to call the United States home, according to the Immigration and Naturalization Service. An additional 3.2 million reside here illegally, but experts admit that number is an educated guess.   20

Those arriving in the United States these days find their new neighbors offer a cool welcome, or no welcome at all.

A Time magazine/CNN poll late last year found that 85 percent of the public wanted tougher federal laws on illegal immigrants. Sixty percent wanted reduced legal immigration. Across the state, polls have found that three of four Californians favor stationing National Guard troops along the U.S.-Mexico border.

Said Annelise Anderson, a senior research fellow at Stanford University's Hoover Institution: "We do have relatively more immigrants that are foreign-born than in the 1950s, and people are aware of it because it is Asian and Hispanic, rather than European."

"Of course, people have always objected to immigrants," she said. "But earlier groups have now been absorbed and now are viewed as part of the population that isn't foreign-born and doesn't strike us as different."

Economic and Political Pressures

No single factor explains the profound change in public opinion.   25
Instead, many experts trace it primarily to economic worries, aggravated by news events and political rhetoric.

In November, economist Donald L. Huddle of Rice University asserted that legal and illegal immigrants take thousands of jobs away from U.S. citizens. In 1992, he concluded, 7.2 million legal and illegal immigrants residing in California cost $18 billion more for public services than they paid in taxes.

But in a report released last month, Jeffrey Passel of the Urban Institute in Washington charged that Huddle's research was flawed. Passel reported that immigrants in California actually generate net government revenue of more than $12 billion.

Compounding the disagreement, the Alexis de Tocqueville Institute in Virginia reported last week that immigration does not lead to higher unemployment rates and may even reduce joblessness.

Many economists admit that, in fact, nobody knows exactly what effect the immigrants have had—for better or for worse.

The truth may well be in the middle. But in the debate over immigration, little middle ground exists.   30

Last year, in a time of deep anxiety over the state's economy, Governor Wilson took the offensive: He suggested that illegal immigrants cost the state close to $3 billion in public education, health, social and law enforcement services.

Although the statistics were widely disputed, they struck a chord with the public. Polls showed a dramatic improvement in Wilson's popularity, and the governor has continued to stress the immigration issue.

Meanwhile, among some grassroots activists who are pressing for immigration restrictions, another concern may be as important as the economy, but it is far more politically sensitive: the rise of a multicultural society.

The melting pot is not only full but overflowing, they say, and the dominant culture cannot assimilate so many people from so many different cultures so quickly.

35   "I think every nation is entitled to defend its own culture," says Lynn Young, a coordinator of the Cupertino-based South Bay Citizens for Immigration Reform. "It seems weird to me that some countries come under attack for that. If you say you'd like to maintain Tibetan culture, everybody says that's wonderful."

DMV Law an Indicator

The passage of last year's DMV bill in California was the sum of these strains of public opinion.

On March 1, the day the new law took effect, the San Francisco DMV office resembled an immigration checkpoint at an international airport. A crowd gathered in front of a desk at the entryway, and anxious applicants slapped down passports and birth certificates and flashed green cards and other immigration documents.

In the first 90 minutes, 17 people were turned away because they were unable to prove legal residency.

Most said they were U.S.-born citizens or legal residents who simply did not bring their birth certificates or immigration documentation with them. Two—a domestic worker from El Salvador and a tortilla factory worker from Mexico—conceded they were undocumented.

40   "I came here to work, not for anything else," said the Mexican worker, identifying himself only as Jose. He said that an hour's wage in the United States is equivalent to a day's pay in Mexico and that his work here helps to support his family back home.

A French biology student at the University of California at San Francisco also was turned away. She panicked when a state employee told her that her French passport was not acceptable and that she could not get her driver's license.

"I do not know what I will do," she said, tears brimming in her eyes.

Even as California awaited the implementation of the DMV law, the federal government and other states also were intervening against illegal immigration.

Florida Governor Lawton Chiles, who contends that illegal immigration is costing his state millions of dollars, has threatened to lead a lawsuit on behalf of his state, California and several others against the federal government for funds to pay the bills. In Congress, at least 150 pieces of legislation are pending to punish illegal immigration or reduce legal immigration.

The federal government already has erected a border blockade in   45
Texas to make passage to El Paso from the adjoining Mexican city of Juarez more difficult. And along the California-Mexico border, some stretches have come to resemble a military zone.

Fear and Humiliation

No one can say yet whether the crackdown has had an effect on the numbers of new illegal immigrants. But among immigrants already living in the United States, the new laws and angry rhetoric have left a profound impression.

While some struggle to mount a political counterattack, immigrants inside the taquerias, Laundromats and neighborhood centers of San Francisco's Mission District talk about their immense fear and humiliation.

Sylvia, an undocumented secretary at a local community center, is the mother of two boys, ages 5 and 6.

"I stopped sending my sons to school," she said. "I did not understand what everybody was talking about, but I kept hearing that the schools were going to be raided by the *migra* [U.S. Immigration Service—ed.].

"My friends call me at home, and they cry. They will be watching   50
the television and hearing all these things about immigrants and how they are being blamed for all these problems here. And they know it's not true."

What worries many immigrant-rights groups is that the same suspicion easily extends to anyone who looks "different."

Doreena Wong, a hate-violence researcher for the Asian Law Caucus, fears that the climate can lead to attacks against any person of color who is believed to be an immigrant.

"I think the more 'foreign-looking' you appear, the more you're associated with immigrants, and assumptions are made that all immigrants are here illegally," Wong said. "As far as a lot of people are concerned, we're all the same—we don't belong here. That's what we're worried about."

Pre-Election Debate

These are not new issues in the American story. In a nation both populated by immigrants and deeply suspicious of them, the issues are never far from the surface. But many observers believe that the debate—and the suspicions and the fears—will become more intense as Election Day approaches this fall.

55   In California, immigrant groups have begun to stage small protests against the backlash. At the same time, anti-immigrant groups in the state are collecting signatures for a ballot initiative. And politicians are appealing for votes with high-intensity rhetoric.

"It is difficult to introduce any balance into the debate," said Stan Mark, an attorney with the Asian American Legal Defense Fund in New York. "It is an election year, and many politicians see this as an issue that can be effectively exploited."

For Journals

Do you favor limitations on immigration or unlimited immigration? If you favor some intermediate position, what is it? Who would you allow in, and who would you keep out?

For Discussion

1.   What reasons does the author give for the rising political opposition in California to immigrants?

2.   If the opponents of immigration are correct in saying that "the melting pot is overflowing . . . and the dominant culture cannot assimilate so many people from so many cultures so quickly," how will the American dream be changed? How important is the idea of America as a haven for refugees and immigrants to the American dream?

3.   This is a news article, designed to set up both sides of the problem. How well do you think the author accomplishes the job of being even-handed? What are the most persuasive examples the author presents as evidence for each side? How strong is the evidence provided by these examples? Are there any examples that you think are unfair or biased?

4.   What difference, if any, does it make that exclusionary policies are now most frequently aimed at illegal immigrants, or at people who emigrate temporarily for economic reasons? What is their relationship

to the traditional American dream of having the opportunity to improve oneself?

5.   The article makes the point that in an election year, politicians are inclined to exploit anti-immigrant sentiment. Why is immigration a particularly useful issue for galvanizing voters? What other examples of controversial issues can you think of that could be used to influence public opinion?

6.   Look again at the *California, Cornucopia of the World* poster in this chapter, which invited people to move to California, and the *The U.S. Hotel Badly Needs a Bouncer* cartoon in Chapter 3, which depicts nineteenth-century opposition to immigration. How do the sentiments expressed in these two pictures resemble or differ from the examples of attitudes toward immigrants that Solis discusses in this article?

For Writing

1.   The article gives examples of several immigrant groups—Irish, Italians, Jews, Chinese, Japanese—that have experienced prejudice when they immigrated to America. Research any one aspect of immigration involving a particular immigrant group, past or present, and write up your results. Some possible subjects could be: the emigration of the Irish in the 1840s as a result of the potato famine; the emigration of Russian Jews beginning in 1881 to escape persecution; the Chinese Exclusion Act of 1882; the emigration of Central Americans or Mexicans in the last twenty years; the history of the Immigration and Nationalization Service and/or its contemporary policies on admitting immigrants.

2.   Mary Antin (this chapter) wrote a book about immigrants, *They Who Knock at Our Gates.* Alexis de Tocqueville (whom you read in Chapter 3) wrote about the character of Americans from other countries who settled here in his book *Democracy in America.* Read a couple of chapters from Antin's or from de Tocqueville's books, and then write an essay in which you analyze their main arguments about immigration and compare them to the ideas expressed in this article, both pro and con.

THE AMERICAN IMMIGRANTS
1994

Caroline Mendoza

*Caroline Mendoza was born in San Francisco after her family emigrated
to California from Peru in the 1970s. She is a student at a university in
northern California and is studying to be a doctor. Mendoza wrote this essay
in response to writing assignment number 2 at the end of this chapter, asking
her to argue for her idea of what the American dream means and how she sees
it in herself and her family.*

"*Voy a viajar a Los Estados Unidos para mejorar mi vida y para hacer
mis suenos realidad.*" This statement flashes across the minds of many
Latin Americans who come to the United States. It was the belief that
my father embedded in his heart the day he chose to come to America.
Translated from Spanish it means, "I will travel to the United States to
make my life better and to make my dreams a reality."

My parents decided to come to the United States twenty-two years
ago. My mother and father had stable jobs working for the government
and a comfortable home, but our economic situation was not improving and there was little future for my three brothers and sister in Peru.
America, the land where you can achieve "the American Dream," offered hope, promise of a better life. My parents knew that the American dream promised happiness for Alberto, Jorge, Carlos, and Patricia,
perhaps the material wealth that did not exist in Peru.

My father traveled to the United States before my mother. He
came with an old green suitcase we still keep, and no knowledge of
English, but a determined heart. He had a difficult time adjusting to
his new life in San Francisco. Accustomed to eating my mother's *arroz
con pollo, papa a la huancaina, papas rellenas*, or *aji de gallina*, my father
was forced to eat "American" foods he disliked, like hamburgers, hot
dogs, and even his own cooking. He worked as a delivery boy at a
bakeshop during the morning and afternoon. At night he would leave
for work as the supervising night porter at the Olympic Club. He had
two jobs and enough time to sleep between them so that he could
dream of the family he had left behind. Five years passed before my father and mother were reunited, five years before my family could
come to this "land of opportunity," five years before my brother would
have to leave the university, five years before my mother would leave

her secure government job—five years before the American dream would turn into the American nightmare.

I was born in San Francisco, but grew up an "American immigrant" watching my family struggle. Out of the foggy window of an old dilapidated apartment in the San Francisco Mission District, I would watch my brothers and sister catch a bus to a school in a "better" neighborhood, Millbrae, at 6:00 A.M. My mother would come home tired from her job as a housekeeper only to find more chores and my eldest brother waiting to go to night school, eager to learn English. I would contrast my mother's crying with her reassuring hand, stroking my head confident that better things awaited us.

Like Mary Antin, I grew up in innocence, never completely aware   5
of the sacrifices my parents had made. I did not sufficiently appreciate my father treating me to the zoo. The time that he should have spent resting, he spent with his family. I did not comprehend the hesitation when my parents' jobs were described as "honest." Working in an office all her life, my mother was not accustomed to manual labor. I did not know that my mother associated pride with working in her former office, that she felt inferior having to admit she was a housekeeper. I did not know that she had been offered a chance to further her education in Peru with all costs paid. She rejected the offer so that she could work in the United States, and help pay for our education.

I have seen how differently coming to America affected my family in relation to their ages. My eldest brother came at the age of eighteen, mature enough to understand the reasons for leaving home and suppressing his fears of the new land. My two other brothers came at an age when they understood the motives for leaving Peru but were still attached to the security of their former home. My sister, age nine at the time, was too young to understand and face a new life when she was just beginning her life in Peru. I was born here, and grew up watching them, learning to understand their characters and learning to define myself not as an immigrant to America but as an American immigrant.

Over the years, I have come to the realization that being American does not mean physically traveling to the United States. Immigration does not occur as a journey to America or as a journey in America; it exists within oneself. We are immigrants into our hearts and spirits, searching for a definition of ourselves as Americans. In the United States, we come into contact with various cultures, beliefs, and religions, some of which we combine with our own, some of which we refuse to accept. Only after we encounter these differences and question their compatibility with our own existences are we able to define ourselves. When we recognize who we are, we can specify what it means to be an American. America provides the potential for wealth which attracts the immigrant, but it also provides the impediments, hardships, perhaps the unfairness in the immigrants' journey. The difficulties we encounter serve to remind us that our accomplishments are the dreams we sought before coming to the United States. The hardships make us value our achievements. Because we find a meaning of who we are and obtain our dreams in America, we call ourselves "Americans" who obtain the "American dream." The immigrant must accept who he was, what might have been, and who he has become. He must understand any changes he has undergone, all aspects of his native culture as well as the new life he has formed in America. Independent of whether the immigrant is first generation or native born, each individual needs to incorporate new and old traditions as best he can. Even when the Hispanic immigrant says, "I will travel to the United States to make *my* life better and to make *my* dreams a reality," the dreams and life belong to him. His life as an "American" and his "American dream" are what he ultimately makes them.

I look back and see two worlds within one family. I see the love of freedom, the belief and hope of equality among men. I also see the old traditions of attending Spanish mass, celebrating a *quincenera,* even singing "Happy Birthday" in Spanish.

At the root of this I see my parents' sacrificing their own dreams in their native country to make their children's dream possible. I finally understand that what I think is sacrifice on their part is, to them, love of their children. I look at my brothers and sister and I contrast them to what I saw as a child. I saw my eldest brother, Alberto, struggling to learn English, and now I see him working as a research chemist graduated from Berkeley. I saw my second brother, Jorge, crying for friends and now see him smiling as a manager graduated from San Francisco State University. I saw my youngest brother, Carlos, struggling over geometry and now see him a naval officer graduated from Berkeley as a civil engineer. When I look out a window, I still see a small girl running after a bus in the darkness: my sister, Patricia, who is now a registered nurse.

I remember all that my family has been through, and I see myself writing this paper as I reflect on my childhood and what it has meant to me. I do not hesitate in speaking of an "honest" job or speaking to "honest-working" people. When I tutor a young child or an adult participating in the Stanford Literacy Improvement Project, I put forth an extra effort. Children waiting for a bus in the darkness awaken my old feelings of standing powerless, behind a window. I find myself trying to treat everyone as I wish my family would have been treated upon their arrival. I observe this journey into myself and refer to myself as an "American immigrant." I am an American citizen but I am an immigrant into my own spirit and heart as I search for a definition of myself—a definition which combines the identity of my family and of myself into one.

For Journals

Have you encountered hardships like the ones experienced by Caroline Mendoza's father and mother, or by her brothers and sisters, when they arrived in America? If not, how do you think you would cope with such hardships?

For Discussion

1.   Look at the quotation in the first paragraph. How does the American dream it expresses compare to others you have encountered in this chapter?

2.   How do you respond to the idea that what immigrant parents do is sacrifice their own dreams so that their children might achieve theirs? Judging from the author's examples, in what ways do you think the experience of immigration is harder for parents?

3.   Do Mendoza's examples persuade you that the relative ages at which people emigrate determine their reactions to what they find in their new country?

4.   Mendoza was born in America. Why do you think she refers to herself as an immigrant?

5.   Analyze Mendoza's statement that "immigration does not occur as a journey in America or a journey to America; it occurs within oneself." What occurs within oneself? What do you think Americanization means to this writer? to her family?

For Writing

1.   Compare Mendoza's essay with Mary Antin's autobiography (this chapter) and write an essay in which you examine them both for mood, attitude toward becoming an American, the roles of parents versus children, the fate of younger children versus older children, and the dreams of each generation.

2.   Write a reflective essay in which you discuss your reaction to Mendoza's statement that being an American is an internal process of making an internal journey. Whether or not there are recent immigrants in your family, think of how your sense of yourself as a citizen is shaped by a variety of factors—your family background, your education, the beliefs you were raised with, and so on.

FILMS ON AMERICAN DREAMS

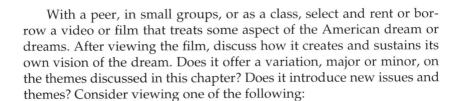

With a peer, in small groups, or as a class, select and rent or borrow a video or film that treats some aspect of the American dream or dreams. After viewing the film, discuss how it creates and sustains its own vision of the dream. Does it offer a variation, major or minor, on the themes discussed in this chapter? Does it introduce new issues and themes? Consider viewing one of the following:

Hester Street

Avalon

Diary of a Mad Housewife

Glory

It's a Wonderful Life

Sullivan's Travels

Boyz 'n' the Hood

Raisin in the Sun

Wall Street

American Dream

Crimes and Misdemeanors

EXAMPLE

Technically, an example is a single part chosen to show the nature or character of a whole, or a sample of a larger unit, or a typical sample of something; George Washington is an example of an American president, and Sister Souljah is an example of a rap musician.

Practically, though, examples fulfill two crucial functions in writing. First, they enable an audience to identify emotionally and/or intellectually with the writer or the writer's subject. This is especially important if the writer wants to move the audience to action, or knows that the audience is hostile or indifferent or just unfamiliar with the material. For instance, in "I Have a Dream," Martin Luther King, Jr., included examples of how prejudice affected the lives of African Americans doing ordinary things—like trying to book a hotel room or get a seat on a bus—to explain the effects of racial segregation to an audience many of whose members had no personal experience of segregation. These common and easily understandable examples help to persuade through *identification*—identification between King and his audience, between the people he is talking about and the people he is talking to.

The second role that example fills is to support persuasion through *evidence;* examples can act as proof for general statements or assertions. Just as abstractions without examples are emotionally uninvolving, assertions without examples are unconvincing. Examples are as essential to a persuasive argument as results are to an experiment.

The following two paragraphs show the difference between a paragraph without clear examples and the same paragraph rewritten by the author to include examples. The argument concerns whether dropping the atom bomb on Japan hastened the end of World War II. The writer, Paul Fussell, is criticizing John Kenneth Galbraith, the economist, who thought that the atom bomb made no difference.

Without Examples

On the other hand, John Kenneth Galbraith is persuaded that the Japanese would have surrendered by November without an invasion. He thinks the atomic bombs were not decisive in bringing about the surrender and he implies that their use was unjustified. What did he do in the war? He was in the Office of Price Administration in Washington, and then he was director of the United States Strategic Bombing Survey. He was thirty-seven in 1945, and I don't demand that he experience having his ass shot off. I just note that he didn't. In saying this I'm aware of its offensive implications ad hominem. But here I think that approach justified. What's at stake in an infantry assault is so entirely unthinkable to those without any experience of one, even if they possess very wide-ranging imaginations and sympathies, that experience is crucial in this case.

With Examples

On the other hand, John Kenneth Galbraith is persuaded that the Japanese would have surrendered surely by November without an invasion. He thinks the A-bombs were unnecessary and unjustified because the war was ending anyway. The A-bombs meant, he says, "a difference, at most, of two or three weeks." But at the time, with no indication that surrender was on the way, the kamikazes were sinking American vessels, the *Indianapolis* was sunk (880 men killed), and Allied casualties were running to over 7,000 per week. "Two or three weeks," says Galbraith. Two weeks more means 14,000 more killed and wounded, three weeks more, 21,000. Those weeks mean the world if you're one of those thousands or related to one of them. During the time between the dropping of the Nagasaki bomb on August 9 and the actual surrender on the 15th, the war pursued its accustomed course: on the 12th of August eight captured American fliers

were executed (heads chopped off); the fifty-first United States sub-
marine, *Bonefish,* was sunk (all aboard drowned); the destroyer
Callaghan went down, the seventieth to be sunk, and the Destroyer
Escort *Underhill* was lost. That's a bit of what happened in six days of
the two or three weeks posited by Galbraith. What did he do in the
war? He worked in the Office of Price Administration in Washington. I don't demand that he experience having his ass shot off. I
merely note that he didn't.

The first paragraph gives no evidence to support or refute Galbraith's
contention that the use of the bombs was unnecessary. The second,
with its example upon example of the numbers and types of casualties
that occurred in the last days of the war, certainly puts the writer in a
stronger position to persuade the reader that Galbraith was wrong.

Analyzing Examples in Arguments

The most effective examples are both genuine expressions of an
author's temperament and suited to his or her audience and purpose.
Any successful piece of persuasive writing, whether framed as a narrative, an exposition, or an argument, comes from a writer who knows
his or her audience, at least well enough to strike a chord of recognition; it reaches for some common emotional bond, shared beliefs,
shared hopes. But a writer seeking common ground will be effective
only if there is something else as well—a powerful sense of his or her
individuality. One of the great paradoxes of writing, art, film, or good
conversation is that the only way to have a general effect is to be particular. Abstractions don't move people and don't convince them. If
you want to communicate powerfully, you must find a way to connect
to your audience directly, and that's what good, specific examples do.

In choosing and presenting examples, bear in mind the types of
experiences an audience is likely to sympathize with and understand;
examples far removed from the experience of most people generally
do not work well. Benjamin Franklin needed a way to communicate
his extraordinary successes without overwhelming his readers. Given
his pragmatic, problem-solving nature, he used several techniques, including irony and casual understatement (I decided to learn languages,
so first I learned French and then I started on Italian), but he also includes examples of his own mistakes and bad behavior, such as the
time he organized his friends to steal building materials to make a
wharf for swimming. Franklin's original readers, who knew how
many public works he started in Philadelphia—hospitals, places of
worship, the fire department, the lending library—would have appreciated his example of theft as his "first act of public service." Modern
writers as well can see that he doesn't take himself too seriously; thus,

his use of a common example fosters a sense of amused comradeship between Franklin and his audience.

When a writer's audience has not shared his or her experiences at all, the examples chosen should be touchstones, which evoke shared human feeling. The nineteenth-century white audience that read Frederick Douglass's autobiography had no direct experience of slavery; moreover, it was unlikely to believe that an ex-slave could write at all. Douglass, in fact, had to have a white man write an introduction asserting that Douglass had written the book himself. Beyond that, however, Douglass used examples from his own experience—his mother's walking all night to see him for a few hours; learning to read when reading was illegal for slaves; the sadism of the overseer who beat him—to establish his authenticity, to counteract any doubts his audience might have, and to establish a level of common humanity. No one reading the autobiography could doubt the anguish of Douglass's experiences—or deny the extraordinary human being who had emerged from them.

Mary Antin wanted her story of immigrant experience to stand for the stories of all immigrants who never got a chance to tell theirs: in a way she wanted to serve as an example. She chose a title that framed the whole book—*The Promised Land.* Her audience would have recognized a parallel to the exodus of the Jews from Egypt and their entry into the promised land. But to bridge the gap between the weighty biblical reference and to give immediacy to the story of a young immigrant girl, Antin studded her narrative with examples of her own experience. To illustrate how embedded anti-semitism was in Russia, she tells an anecdote of a neighborhood boy who routinely spat at her. When she wants to explain how pleasantly mysterious America was to her at first, she gives the example of trying to figure out how to eat a banana, a fruit she had never seen before.

Examples are just as important when the subject isn't a personal experience. Dolores Hayden, writing about what happens to the American dream of domesticity when someone has to do the laundry and clean the bathroom, bases her whole argument on examples. She gives three examples of models for running the home, illustrates each with examples of how they were supposed to help women or fulfill some domestic ideal, and follows up with more examples, some of them statistical, to show how much time women really spend taking care of their homes and families, and which "labor-saving" devices increase their work load and their families' expectations. Together, these examples constitute her proof for her thesis; without them, she would have theories but no evidence.

Examples are not difficult for the reader to recognize in a text or for a viewer to recognize in a picture (see the examples of wealth in the

California, Cornucopia of the World poster). As the writer or speaker, your purpose is to find examples that are comfortable to you, appropriate to your material, and create the best emotional connections among you, your material, and your audience.

Using Examples in Arguments

How you select examples is determined by your audience, your purpose, and the medium in which you are working—all of which together form your rhetorical framework. Suppose you want to tell your closest friend about a fight you had with your father. You might say, "My father and I had a disagreement." That might be accurate but is completely uncommunicative and not very interesting. Besides, you want your friend to know exactly how you felt—why you thought you were right and your father wrong—and exactly what you said and what your father said, what you did and what he did. You must give examples. No matter what you are writing about, when you want your audience to know exactly what you mean and to believe you, specific examples are the best and easiest way of helping you to make a direct connection. This is true whether your audience is personally sympathetic and known to you, indifferent, or even hostile. It is also true whether your subject is your personal experience, a research topic, or an argument in your dormitory about the house rules.

The following categories give some of the most useful sources of examples.

Personal Experience and Observation   Your first source of examples is you: your own experience, your relationships with your family and friends, your own conflicts, your own education, and your own temperament. If you are writing about yourself, those elements are relevant as examples and will form a natural part of your subject matter. Suppose you are writing a paper on the dreams of people trying to immigrate to America today, and you or your immediate family are first-generation immigrants. You will probably write some general statements about political freedom, or opportunity, or equality. But if you really want to explain dreams of coming to America, you need specific examples, drawn from you and your family's own experience—what you thought your new home would look like, whether the smells and the foods were different, how tired your parents looked, what the furniture in your first American house was like, what frightened you, what you thought about and said. The use of such examples requires that you have the courage to look at yourself honestly, but the attention you pay to accuracy and to details pays off in vivid writing that both pleases and persuades your readers.

Field Research   Your ability to draw examples from your own experience extends to observations of people who are strangers to you and to situations in which you participate by getting information from sources other than yourself. Suppose you are writing a research paper on contemporary immigration, and as part of your research you attend a hearing of the Immigration and Naturalization Service to listen to the testimony of a man asking for asylum because he is afraid of persecution and torture in his home country. You would take notes on the testimony, including quotes from the dialogue and conversation. But you would also pay attention to tones of voice, the body language of the applicant, the temperature in the hearing room, the number of spectators, their manner of dress, and other matters.

As an alternative, you might interview a new arrival in this country and ask questions about why the person came, how hard it was, what they miss about home, and so on. In your paper, you would want to draw some conclusions about reasons for their coming to America, but you would support them with some of the dialogue between you and your subject. You would note the comments of the lawyers, tones of their voices, the tension. You will be able to draw on all of these observations when you state your thesis or make your general statements. In fact, the formulation of your general statements could be heavily influenced by the observations you have already made in the course of the interview; they may change the direction of your research and the conclusions you draw.

Library Research   Library research is primarily the result of the experiences and observations of other people, so in a sense the examples you find through library research are drawn from the work someone else has already done. But it's up to you to determine which elements to choose, how to order and connect them, and what ideas of yours they can support. Evaluating library materials is like evidence in a trial; it has to be sifted and weighed, so you can separate out pertinent examples from a much larger body of information.

Suppose that in your research project about immigration you need to learn about the background of the U.S. Immigration and Naturalization Service (INS). You can look in the government documents section for INS regulations; and you can look in a law school library or the local courthouse library for examples of immigration cases. Consult the *Congressional Record* for the legislative history of immigration laws and examples of how attitudes toward immigration policy have changed over the years. Check the microfiche index for old newspaper articles about immigration that give examples of immigrants' personal experience; read the first-person accounts of recent immigrants or the autobiographies of earlier ones; find old photographs and read diaries immigrants or their families kept; and use newspapers, magazines, and movies to see how different ethnic groups are portrayed in the time period you are researching.

Sometimes students early in their college writing careers have an unfortunate tendency to think that if they use big words and grandiose sentences and, especially, if they make broad and inclusive generalizations about enormous subjects, the results will sound more impressive. Actually, the opposite is true. If you write about a subject you know well because it is close to you, or if you write about an unfamiliar area you have gotten to know because you researched it, and you support either subject with specific and honest examples, you will produce something of quality.

There is no formula to follow here. Whatever examples you choose will emerge from your subject, your ideas, your experience, and your willingness to stay aware of what you want your audience to take away. The more you learn to be observant and the more energy you are willing to invest in looking for examples, the better your writing will be. Good, specific examples can prove that you can express yourself in understandable terms, that your writing has substance, that you have evaluated the evidence, and that you respect the intelligence of your audience.

WRITING ASSIGNMENTS

1.   Find an advertisement in a magazine or newspaper that uses examples of American symbols directly (e.g., advertising U.S. savings bonds by showing the emblem of the American bald eagle) or indirectly (e.g., savings bank using Benjamin Franklin's portrait as a logo, or a jeans company that embroiders an American flag on the pocket). There are many such examples; you also might want to look at CD covers and movie advertisements. Write an analysis of the ad in which you consider the following: Who is the audience? Why do you think that advertiser included an example of American symbolism in the ad? Why was the particular example chosen? How effective is that example in conveying American values? How successful or unsuccessful do you think this approach is?

2.   The selections in this chapter express some element of the American dream. Write an essay in which you argue for your own idea of what the American dream means—both what you think it means to most Americans and what it means to you. How do you see the American dream in members of your family? In yourself? What elements are crucial to it? Because you are dealing with a broad idea, it is especially

important that you include specific examples of what you believe the dream to be and of how it manifests itself in you and your family. Do not confine yourself to generalizations like "My parents want me to have a better life than they have." Use your examples to explain what their life is, including disappointments or worries, and to show what you really dream of for yourself.

3. Langston Hughes was vitally interested in the promise of the American dream and in the importance of making it accessible to all Americans. With his work in mind, listen to and read the lyrics of contemporary songs, including rap lyrics, that talk about American dreams and nightmares. Write an analytical essay in which you discuss the vision of American life, especially urban life, set forth in these songs, including what they say about dreams for the future. Cite examples from the lyrics to support your assertions. You can use Hughes as a point of comparison if you want.

4. Imagine that you have to explain the American dream to an English-speaking visitor from another country and that you have to compose a popular culture curriculum featuring contemporary materials that would make the dream clearer to a stranger. Prepare a list of examples for this visitor drawn from each of the following categories: four movies to see; two to four musicians to listen to; two works of fiction and two works of nonfiction to read; and two magazines to read. After each selection, write a paragraph explaining why this particular example says something about the American dream, and what that is.

5. Go to the newsstand or your library and pick up the following: one issue of what is usually known as a women's magazine (*Family Circle, Ladies' Home Journal,* and so on), one issue of a magazine addressed to different women's interests (*Cosmopolitan, Mademoiselle,* and so on), and one issue of a magazine addressed largely to men (*GQ, Esquire,* and so on). Be sure that the magazines you choose have *at least one article apiece* on the home (entertaining at home, decorating the home, cooking for friends or family, spending time with children at home, and so on.), Write an essay comparing the images of house and home you find in these publications. What dreams of American home life do you think they advertise? Do the dreams of home revealed in articles in a men's magazine differ from those in the articles for women? If so, in what ways? Are any of the articles more informative than others? If they include photographs, how do the illustrations function to support the articles' points of view and to persuade readers to accept them?

CHAPTER

5

FAMILY VALUES

$\mathcal{A}$t the core of American identities and American dreams lies the family. Whether a colonial-era farm household, an immigrant extended family, a native clan or tribe, an urban domestic partnership, or a suburban nuclear family, families serve as a connection between the individual and the outside world. The individual's identity, his or her dreams, in large part depend on the family of origin or a family of choice. The individual is shaped through beliefs, values, and assumptions that the family holds about the world and that are based on the family members' experiences and collective memory. The family itself, in turn, derives its value from the social, cultural, political, and philosophical assumptions and beliefs and the economic needs of the larger culture.

Questions about the family are omnipresent in contemporary American society: What is the "definition" of a family? Who can belong to a family? What are appropriate gender roles within families? What restraints does the concept of family place on women? On men? What happens to a society in which the nuclear family is no longer the dominant configuration? What are "family values"? Are they positive beliefs and aspirations that optimize growth and diversity for all, or narrow-minded strictures and intolerances that seek to shut out differences of approach or opinion? The debates over these issues are increasingly rancorous.

And yet this kind of conflict is not altogether new. The history of our country is one of uneasy inequality between men and women.

211

Revolutionary-era rhetoric depended heavily on a philosophy that was based on equality and on political rights, but those concepts applied to men only. Industrialization brought with it manufacturing and manufactured goods but also exploitation of children for labor. World War I saw tremendous support for the war effort and for social services from women, but although women finally gained the vote in 1920, they received few additional rights thereafter. World War II brought new and demanding jobs for women to support the war effort, but as soon as the men returned from war, society's needs for employment for men and for social stability issued a new message to women: go home, stay home, and raise children. The civil rights and women's movements of the sixties and seventies brought attention to gross civil injustices, but the Equal Rights Amendment failed to pass. Women have made some strides in business and government, but cries from the media, to politicians, to the religious right have declared that feminism and women's liberation have brought women in particular and society in general nothing but grief.

Despite this inequality of the sexes, the idea of the stable American family—and, concomitantly, a stable American society—has been with us for a long time. Recent debates decry the "decline" of the family and blame societal ills on a perceived lack of family stability. But to some degree we have idealized the family of the past. The current divorce rate is 50 percent of first marriages within forty years, but in the colonial era, marriages averaged only twelve years or less because of the death of one spouse. We deplore the numbers of absentee parents, but up to half of all colonial-era children lost at least one parent before the age of twenty-one, and before the 1920s, divorced fathers had no legal obligation to pay child support. We are rightfully concerned about problems in educating youth, but in the 1940s fewer than half of the students entering high school were able to finish. We mourn the death of the extended family, yet children are now more likely than at any earlier time in our history to have living grandparents and to be in contact with them. Many factories in the nineteenth century employed children under the age of eleven, and during the early industrial period, from 1850 to 1885, children worked at home, in tenement sweatshops, in mines and mills. Domestic workers supported middle-class nurturing and mothering, but their own children frequently served as maids or garment workers. During the years of the Great Depression, in the 1930s, families united for their own collective survival, but incompatible people who were stuck together in this manner, with few resources and little hope, would sometimes produce phenomena all too familiar in other eras: withdrawn or violent men; exhausted, overextended women; children with no resources with which to face the future.

Family Values through History

Early recorded history of the colonies and the Revolution suggests that while the United States was founded on principles of equality, women were either invisible or were assumed to absorb the political views of their husbands or male relatives, just as their husbands were able to absorb their property upon marriage. They were expected to support economic embargoes against Britain and to supply provisions and support for the war, and they could be tried for treason during the Revolution. Men were expected to carry out the public duties of government and commerce. Some early Republicans and philosophers may have noticed the contradictions in promoting arguments about equal rights while restricting those rights to male landowners, but few questioned assumptions that women's work should be restricted to the home (though in the largely rural society, work at home was substantial). Women's sphere was the domestic arena; men participated in and ruled the public domain and debated affairs of state. One way to cope with this dichotomy was to state that the two realms were different but equal. As we examine this discussion, we will question just how equal those realms truly were, both in actuality and in perception.

The first selection in the chapter, the etching *Keep within Compass,* comes from the early post-Revolutionary period and taps into the notion of the dual spheres for men and women. As such, it is part of a long-standing tradition of defining women's roles by circumscribing them and fostering a desire for stability. One change that did result from the Revolution, however, was that divorce was slightly easier for women to obtain, which may help explain why the etching contrasts the contented "virtuous woman" with images of what can happen to her if she steps outside her role.

In the nineteenth century, little challenged the assumptions of the twin spheres of domesticity and public realm, though domestic life, particularly in rural areas, certainly entailed labor, since families generally produced their own food and household goods and sometimes bartered for other needed commodities. Industrialization brought with it goods produced outside the home or farm, and along with increasing industry came the need for cheap labor. Immigrants, women, and children were part of that massive work force. In the mid-nineteenth century, as household production decreased, wage labor and professional occupations developed, giving rise to an increasing middle class. Upper- and middle-class women could maintain a role focused on domesticity while men earned the family income, but the cost was borne by the laborers, often slaves and other men, women, and children, in mills, fields, and factories. The next selection, from *Life among the Paiutes,* describes some of the values and family customs of the

Paiute Indians. Sara Winnemucca Hopkins, who published her book in 1883, hoped that it would serve as an argument and as evidence to persuade white Americans to recognize their unjust treatment of the first Americans. Challenging centuries of misperceptions about "savages," Hopkins writes of her democratic, community-oriented tribe whose value of women, children, and parenthood contrasts sharply with the ills visited upon many American families in the name of progress.

The second decade of the twentieth century saw worldwide turmoil brought about by World War I and social turmoil as women agitated for the vote, which they finally obtained in 1920. In a society in which women were assumed to carry on the emotional, sentimental, and moral needs of society as men pursued individualistic and public pursuits, women were to give love and nurturing freely, uncontaminated by the market forces of the newly industrial society. But if the men were the financial support of the family, economically dependent women could hardly have been "freely" offering their emotional support. H. L. Mencken, bombastic wordsmith and social commentator, exploited this dichotomy in his treatise on the relationship between men and women, *In Defense of Women*. The short selections included in this chapter cast a hard, satiric look at the "business" of marriage and the crucial role it played in women's lives.

In addition to their role as breadwinners, men were assumed to be strong heroes and to protect women and children. War-era rhetoric and propaganda in particular appealed to such manly attributes as physical strength and a muscular build. Advertisements for the Charles Atlas technique of bodybuilding became legendary. The example included in this chapter, published in 1944 during the height of America's involvement in World War II, uses classic appeals focusing on the shame of weakness and on men's desire to be real "red-blooded" Americans—with fame, and the admiration of women, as the ultimate prize.

In the years that followed the civil rights and free speech movements of the 1960s, the women's movement increasingly argued for equality for women in society, especially in the home and workplace. Progress was slow, and within even liberal to left-wing social and political movements such as the Student Nonviolent Coordinating Committee, male leaders typically assigned women to clerical or support duties rather than leadership roles. In the family, increasing numbers of women in the workplace, relative to the postwar era of the 1950s and early 1960s, brought changes in the stable (to some, but stultifying to others) nuclear family. Long-standing assumptions that the nuclear family is the core of American communities underlie much of mainstream culture and affect how some Americans perceive cultures based on concepts and family values that differ from the mainstream. In the short story "American Horse," Louise Erdrich offers a view into the clashing cultures, values, assumptions, and expectations as a white social worker armed with a court order comes to take away a young American Indian boy from his mother.

Assumptions and values about what a family is or should be extend even to the zoning codes of local communities. The late attorney Keenan Peck, arguing from personal experience as well as from statutes and other legal evidence, articulates the hidden assumptions and challenges their applicability and their role in determining what does, and what does not, constitute a legal family. His essay, "When 'Family' Is Not a Household Word," argues that not only two-parent married couples with children but also people who are not blood relatives yet care about and support each other constitute a family. Historically, unrelated people often lived together; boarding houses, to cite just one example, often brought strangers into a household. The term "alternative family" has been gaining currency among some Americans, but assumptions about marriage and family run deep, and, as Peck points out, change can be frightening.

In the late 1980s and early 1990s, on the heels of the social changes of the previous two decades, gay and lesbian rights movements further challenged the concept and value of the heterosexual nuclear family; moreover, they brought the debate over homosexual marriages into the open. Thomas Stoddard, attorney and gay rights leader, argues that "Marriage Is a Fundamental Right" and that same-gender marriages are a civil rights issue. Attorney Bruce Fein's essay, "Reserve Marriage for Heterosexuals," cites legal precedent, as does Stoddard, but also draws on our fears for children and our assumptions about two-parent families to make his case.

As the century has progressed, women have appeared to make gains in politics, economics, the workplace, and society generally. But despite these gains—or, according to author Susan Faludi, because of them—women don't "have it all." In fact, women have never been worse off, according to her view. Faludi reports on her extensive study of the negative reaction to women's modest gains of the 1970s and 1980s in her book, *Backlash: The Undeclared War Against Women.* In the introduction to the book, entitled, "Blame It on Feminism," Faludi articulates the assumptions made by those castigating the ill effects of feminism and then challenges them with reasoning as well as evidence and statistics.

The post–civil rights movement era also shows increasing concern over the needs of children. Some 20 percent of children still grow up in poverty, abuse, and neglect; some are born addicted to drugs and alcohol. One battle for children's rights is being fought through the courts, with child advocates arguing for increased legal rights for young people. An adult who has worked on behalf of children's rights for years, child advocate and Children's Defense Fund founder Marian Wright Edelman, explains the values, assumptions, and beliefs that led her to her life's work on behalf of children. Edelman's essay, "A Family Legacy," describes the family and extended family of community from which she learned the values of hard work, discipline, doing for others, repaying the privileges of intellectual and material gifts by serving the community.

The final selection in the chapter looks at the values of Asian American families. In a researched essay, "Making and Unmaking the 'Model Minority'," student writer John Wu studies a label once applied to Jewish immigrants and now applied to Asian Americans and analyzes assumptions and beliefs about the values transmitted through families about family, work, and success, and about the values assumed by society to be held by American families of Asian descent.

Creating Family Values Through Assumptions

Discussions about family issues delve into deeply felt values, beliefs, and assumptions. An *assumption* is something that is accepted or taken to be true without question or analysis. Those who participate in the debate about the meaning of families and family values need to understand the assumptions they and their audiences hold, to sense when to use those assumptions as part of the argument, and to know when to supplement assumptions with reasons for drawing a conclusion, before moving on to the rest of the argument. *Premise,* a related term, is something taken as a given. It is an assumption, a generalization or statement of general principle from which we derive conclusions or other generalizations. Different authors define and use the term in different ways. In this text, specifically in this chapter, we use the term *assumption* rather than *premise* to reiterate the idea that many of the beliefs and ideas we take as given—or accept as general truth—are ideas we *assume* to be true. We assume, for example, that men or women are supposed to act in a certain way, that certain kinds of families are preferable to others, and so forth. In argument, we seldom start from scratch; we take certain ideas as given, we assume a certain shared understanding and proceed from that point. The discussion of assumptions and premises at the end of this chapter is designed to help you to analyze the assumptions in what you read and to take care with the assumptions you hold and the premises on which you base arguments.

As you read the following selections, reflect on your own ideas about what a family consists of and what the role of each member within it should be. Try also to identify and articulate the deeper assumptions on which these ideas are based. Do you think your ideas and assumptions are typical for an American? Are you comfortable with the fact that other Americans may have different family values?

KEEP WITHIN COMPASS
CA. 1790

A metaphor that surfaces decade after decade in conveying social worlds is that of the circle, or in some cases, the three-dimensional sphere. Sometimes referring to a social class, other times to occupations, the image is frequently used, from the late 1700s through to the twentieth century, to describe the designated and circumscribed roles for men and women: men's world of greater economic, industrial, and political society, and women's world of the home.

This etching (on the following page) draws upon a centuries-old tradition of emblems, which are a combination of a visual element and a moral lesson. Combining a didactic picture with a textual moral statement, the etching depicts four unpleasant scenes with which the "virtuous" woman is threatened if she does not remain within her own sphere or circle: raising a child in poverty and misery, working as a domestic or tavern worker, selling in the street, and prostituting herself to soldiers. Such scenes contrast with the well-dressed, happy-looking gentlewoman depicted next to flowers and a large home.

For Journals

Write about what you imagine to be the daily life of eighteenth-century American women: women of means, with landed or wealthy families, and women without family or financial support.

For Discussion

1. What is your overall impression of the etching? What draws your eye? What is emphasized? Why do you think the etching was drawn to create this impression and this emphasis? Relative to the entire circle, how much space is allotted to the virtuous woman?

2.   Who are the intended audiences? Do different elements of the etching appeal to different audiences? To different audience concerns?

3.   Why do you think the artist used a compass to make his point? In the late eighteenth century, who would have been likely to wield a compass? Who, then, would be setting the limits on women?

4.   Analyze the etching as a moral lesson or argument with supporting subtopics and evidence, including the smaller pictures and the ad-

ditional printed messages. Write out a text outline of the argument. What is inside the compass? What are "good" women supposed to do? What is outside the compass? What are women not supposed to do? Is this what you would expect?

5.   Why is it important that a woman be "a crown to her husband"? Do you think the authors of this etching would expect a man to be a crown to his wife? What associations does the crown bring to mind?

6.   In what ways might the assumptions apparent in this etching be relevant today? Do you see any connections between this two-hundred-year-old image and arguments about date rape today?

For Writing

1.   In what ways are gender roles still restricted today? Draw a contemporary version of this etching for men or for women. Then write an essay explaining your diagram.

2.   Argue that women are no longer restricted by gender roles—or that men are more restricted in their choices and behavior than women.

3.   Do research in art or literature of the American colonial period on the role of women or home life. Examine art books from your library, primary materials such as diaries if they are available, or secondary sources about the period. What do you conclude about women's or men's role in the home or in society during this period? Write a documented essay reporting your conclusions.

FROM *LIFE AMONG THE PAIUTES*
1883

Sarah Winnemucca Hopkins

Sarah Winnemucca Hopkins (1844–1891) was born and educated in Nevada. The descendent of Paiute chiefs, her people lived in small family groups, coming together for ceremonies and for hunting. Hopkins traveled with relatives to California and had contact with many white settlers; she became fluent in English and served for many years as a translator between her tribe and settlers and the military. In 1879 she toured the East, giving a number of lectures protesting federal policies toward American Indians. One of her Eastern supporters, educator Elizabeth Peabody Mann, edited Hopkins's manuscript Life among the Paiutes: Their Wrongs and Claims, *published in 1883. While Hopkins had hoped for a reconciliation between American Indians and whites, Mann had hoped, apparently in vain, that the book would serve as argument and evidence to spur white American society to recognize their mistreatment of and duty to the original Americans. In the excerpt that follows, Hopkins writes of the customs and values that encompass family life, courtship rituals, child rearing, and community relations and governance.*

Our children are very carefully taught to be good. Their parents tell them stories, traditions of old times, even of the first mother of the human race; and love stories, stories of giants, and fables; and when they ask if these last stories are true, they answer, "Oh, it is only coyote," which means that they are make-believe stories. Coyote is the name of a mean, crafty little animal, half wolf, half dog, and stands for everything low. It is the greatest term of reproach one Indian has for another. Indians do not swear,—they have no words for swearing till they learn them of white men. The worst they call each is bad or coyote; but they are very sincere with one another, and if they think each other in the wrong they say so.

We are taught to love everybody. We don't need to be taught to love our fathers and mothers. We love them without being told to. Our tenth cousin is as near to us as our first cousin; and we don't marry into our relations. Our young women are not allowed to talk to any young man that is not their cousin, except at the festive dances, when both are dressed in their best clothes, adorned with beads, feathers or shells, and stand alternately in the ring and take hold of hands. These are very pleasant occasions to all the young people.

Many years ago, when my people were happier than they are now, they used to celebrate the Festival of Flowers in the spring. I have been to three of them only in the course of my life.

Oh, with what eagerness we girls used to watch every spring for the time when we could meet with our hearts' delight, the young men, whom in civilized life you call beaux. We would all go in company to see if the flowers we were named for were yet in bloom, for almost all the girls are named for flowers. We talked about them in our wigwams, as if we were the flowers, saying, "Oh, I saw myself today in full bloom!" We would talk all the evenings in this way in our families with such delight, and such beautiful thoughts of the happy day when we should meet with those who admired us and would help us to sing our flower-songs which we made up as we sang. But we were always sorry for those that were not named after some flower, because we knew they could not join in the flower-songs like ourselves, who were named for flowers of all kinds.

At last one evening came a beautiful voice, which made every 5 girl's heart throb with happiness. It was the chief, and every one hushed to hear what he said to-day.

"My dear daughters, we are told that you have seen yourselves in the hills and in the valleys, in full bloom. Five days from to-day your festival day will come. I know every young man's heart stops beating while I am talking. I know how it was with me many years ago. I used to wish the Flower Festival would come every day. Dear young men and young women, you are saying, 'Why put it off five days?' But you all know that is our rule. It gives you time to think, and to show your sweetheart your flower."

All the girls who have flower-names dance along together, and those who have not go together also. Our fathers and mothers and grandfathers and grandmothers make a place for us where we can dance. Each one gathers the flower she is named for, and then all weave them into wreaths and crowns and scarfs, and dress up in them.

Some girls are named for rocks and are called rock-girls, and they find some pretty rocks which they carry; each one such a rock as she is named for, or whatever she is named for. If she cannot, she can take a branch of sage-brush, or a bunch of rye-grass, which have no flower.

They all go marching along, each girl in turn singing of herself; but she is not a girl any more,—she is a flower singing. She sings of herself, and her sweetheart, dancing along by her side, helps her sing the song she makes.

I will repeat what we say of ourselves. "I, Sarah Winnemucca, am 10 a shell-flower, such as I wear on my dress. My name is Thocmetony. I am so beautiful! Who will come and dance with me while I am so beautiful? Oh, come and be happy with me! I shall be beautiful while the earth lasts. Somebody will always admire me; and who will come and be happy with me in the Spirit-land? I shall be beautiful forever there. Yes, I shall be more beautiful than my shell-flower, my Thocmetony! Then, come, oh come, and dance and be happy with me!" The young men sing with us as they dance beside us.

Our parents are waiting for us somewhere to welcome us home. And then we praise the sage-brush and the rye-grass that have no flower, and the pretty rocks that some are named for; and then we present our beautiful flowers to these companions who could carry none. And so all are happy; and that closes the beautiful day.

My people have been so unhappy for a long time they wish now to *disincrease*, instead of multiply. The mothers are afraid to have more children, for fear they shall have daughters, who are not safe even in their mother's presence.

The grandmothers have the special care of the daughters just before and after they come to womanhood. The girls are not allowed to get married until they have come to womanhood; and that period is recognized as a very sacred thing, and is the subject of a festival, and has peculiar customs. The young woman is set apart under the care of two of her friends, somewhat older, and a little wigwam, called a teepee, just big enough for the three, is made for them, to which they retire. She goes through certain labors which are thought to be strengthening, and these last twenty-five days. Every day, three times a day, she must gather, and pile up as high as she can, five stacks of wood. This makes fifteen stacks a day. At the end of every five days the attendants take her to a river to bathe. She fasts from all flesh-meat during these twenty-five days, and continues to do this for five days in every month all her life. At the end of the twenty-five days she returns to the family lodge, and gives all her clothing to her attendants in payment for their care. Sometimes the wardrobe is quite extensive.

It is thus publicly known that there is another marriageable woman, and any young man interested in her, or wishing to form an alliance, comes forward. But the courting is very different from the courting of the white people. He never speaks to her, or visits the family, but endeavors to attract her attention by showing his horsemanship, etc. As he knows that she sleeps next to her grandmother in the lodge, he enters in full dress after the family has retired for the night, and seats himself at her feet. If she is not awake, her grandmother wakes her. He does not speak to either young woman or grandmother, but when the young woman wishes him to go away, she rises and goes and lies down by the side of her mother. He then leaves as silently as he came in. This goes on sometimes for a year or longer, if the young woman has not made up her mind. She is never forced by her parents to marry against her wishes. When she knows her own mind, she makes a confidant of her grandmother, and then the young man is summoned by the father of the girl, who asks him in her presence, if he really loves his daughter, and reminds him, if he says he does, of all the duties of a husband. He then asks his daughter the same question, and sets before her minutely all her duties. And these duties are not slight. She is to dress the game, prepare the food, clean the buckskins, make his moccasins, dress his hair, bring all the wood,—in short, do all the household work. She promises to "be himself," and she fulfils her promise. Then he is invited to a feast and all his relatives with him. But after the betrothal, a teepee is erected for the presents that pour in from both sides.

At the wedding feast, all the food is prepared in baskets. The 15 young woman sits by the young man, and hands him the basket of food prepared for him with her own hands. He does not take it with his right hand; but seizes her wrist, and takes it with the left hand. This constitutes the marriage ceremony, and the father pronounces them man and wife. They go to a wigwam of their own, where they live till the first child is born. This event also is celebrated. Both father and mother fast from all flesh, and the father goes through the labor of piling the wood for twenty-five days, and assumes all his wife's household work during that time. If he does not do his part in the care of the child, he is considered an outcast. Every five days his child's basket is changed for a new one, and the five are all carefully put away at the end of the days, the last one containing the navel-string, carefully wrapped up, and all are put up into a tree, and the child put into a new and ornamented basket. All this respect shown to the mother and child makes the parents feel their responsibility, and makes the tie between parents and children very strong. The young mothers often get together and exchange their experiences about the attentions of their husbands; and inquire of each other if the fathers did their duty to their children, and were careful of their wives' health. When they are married they give away all the clothing they have ever worn, and dress themselves anew. The poor people have the same ceremonies, but do not make a feast of it, for want of means.

Our boys are introduced to manhood by their hunting of deer and mountain-sheep. Before they are fifteen or sixteen, they hunt only small game, like rabbits, hares, fowls, etc. They never eat what they kill themselves, but only what their father or elder brothers kill. When a boy becomes strong enough to use larger bows made of sinew, and arrows that are ornamented with eagle-feathers, for the first time, he kills game that is large, a deer or an antelope, or a mountain-sheep. Then he brings home the hide, and his father cuts it into a long coil which is wound into a loop, and the boy takes his quiver and throws it on his back as if he was going on a hunt, and takes his bow and arrows in his hand. Then his father throws the loop over him, and he jumps through it. This he does five times. Now for the first time he eats the flesh of the animal he has killed, and from that time he eats whatever he kills but he has always been faithful to his parents' command not to eat what he has killed before. He can now do whatever he likes, for now he is a man, and no longer considered a boy. If there is a war he can go to it; but the Paiutes, and other tribes west of the Rocky Mountains, are not fond of going to war. I never saw a war-dance but once. It is always the whites that begin the wars, for their own selfish purposes. The government does not take care to send the good men; there are a plenty who would take pains to see and understand the chiefs and learn their characters, and their good will to the whites. But the whites have not waited to find out how good the Indians were, and what ideas they had of God, just like those of Jesus, who called him Father, just as my people do, and told men to do to others as they would be done by, just as my people teach their children to do. My people teach their children never to make fun of any one, no matter how they look. If you see your brother or sister doing something wrong, look away, or go away from them. If you make fun of bad persons, you make yourself beneath them. Be kind to all, both poor and rich, and feed all that come to your wigwam, and your name can be spoken of by every one far and near. In this way you will make many friends for yourself. Be kind both to bad and good, for you don't know your own heart. This is the way my people teach their children. It was handed down from father to son for many generations. I never in my life saw our children rude as I have seen white children and grown people in the streets.

The chief's tent is the largest tent, and it is the council-tent, where every one goes who wants advice. In the evenings the head men go there to discuss everything, for the chiefs do not rule like tyrants; they discuss everything with their people, as a father would in his family. Often they sit up all night. They discuss the doings of all, if they need to be advised. If a boy is not doing well they talk that over, and if the women are interested they can share in the talks. If there is not room enough inside, they all go out of doors, and make a great circle. The men are in the inner circle, for there would be too much smoke for the women inside. The men never talk without smoking first. The women sit behind them in another circle, and if the children wish to hear, they can be there too. The women know as much as the men do, and their advice is often asked. We have a republic as well as you. The council-tent is our Congress, and anybody can speak who has anything to say, women and all. They are always interested in what their husbands are doing and thinking about. And they take some part even in the wars. They are always near at hand when fighting is going on, ready to snatch their husbands up and carry them off if wounded or killed. One splendid woman that my brother Lee married after his first wife died, went out into the battle-field after her uncle was killed, and went into the front ranks and cheered the men on. Her uncle's horse was dressed in a splendid robe made of eagles' feathers and she snatched it off and swung it in the face of the enemy, who always carry off everything they find, as much as to say, "You can't have that—I have it safe"; and she staid and took her uncle's place, as brave as any of the men. It means something when the women promise their fathers to make their husbands *themselves.* They faithfully keep with them in all the dangers they can share. They not only take care of their children together, but they do everything together; and when they grow blind, which I am sorry to say is very common, for the smoke they live in destroys their eyes at last, they take sweet care of one another. Marriage is a sweet thing when people love each other. If women could go into your Congress I think justice would soon be done to the Indians. I can't tell about all Indians; but I know my own people are kind to everybody that does not do them harm; but they will not be imposed upon, and when people are too bad they rise up and resist them. This seems to me all right. It is different from being revengeful. There is nothing cruel about our people. They never scalped a human being.

The chiefs do not live in idleness. They work with their people, and they are always poor for the following reason. It is the custom with my people to be very hospitable. When people visit them in their tents, they always set before them the best food they have, and if there is not enough for themselves they go without.

The chief's tent is the one always looked for when visitors come, and sometimes many come the same day. But they are all well received. I have often felt sorry for my brother, who is now the chief, when I saw him go without food for this reason. He would say, "We will wait and eat afterwards what is left." Perhaps little would be left, and when the agents did not give supplies and rations, he would have to go hungry.

At the council, one is always appointed to repeat at the time every- 20 thing that is said on both sides, so that there may be no misunderstanding, and one person at least is present from every lodge, and after it is over, he goes and repeats what is decided upon at the door of the lodge, so all may be understood. For there is never any quarrelling in the tribe, only friendly counsels. The sub-chiefs are appointed by the great chief for special duties. There is no quarrelling about that, for neither sub-chief or great chief has any salary. It is this which makes the tribe so united and attached to each other, and makes it so dreadful to be parted. They would rather all die at once than be parted. They believe that in the Spirit-land those that die still watch over those that are living. When I was a child in California, I heard the Methodist minister say that everybody that did wrong was burned in hell forever. I was so frightened it made me very sick. He said the blessed ones in heaven looked down and saw their friends burning and could not help them. I wanted to be unborn, and cried so that my mother and the others told me it was not so, that it was only here that people did wrong and were in the hell that it made, and that those that were in the Spirit-land saw us here and were sorry for us. But we should go to them when we died, where there was never any wrongdoing, and so no hell. That is our religion.

My people capture antelopes by charming them, but only some of the people are charmers. My father was one of them, and once I went with him on an antelope hunt.

The antelopes move in herds in the winter, and as late in the spring as April. At this time there was said to be a large herd in a certain place, and my father told all his people to come together in ten days to go with him in his hunt. He told them to bring their wives with them, but no small children. When they came, at the end of ten days, he chose two men, who he said were to be his messengers to the antelopes. They were to have two large torches made of sage-brush bark, and after he had found a place for his camp, he marked out a circle around which the wigwams were to be placed, putting his own in the middle of the western side, and leaving an opening directly opposite in the middle of the eastern side, which was towards the antelopes.

The people who were with him in the camp then made another circle to the east of the one where their wigwams were, and made six mounds of sage-brush and stones on the sides of it, with a space of a hundred yards or more from one mound to the next one, but with no fence between the mounds. These mounds were made high, so that they could be seen from far off.

The women and boys and old men who were in the camp, and who were working on the mounds, were told to be very careful not to drop anything and not to stumble over a sage-brush root, or a stone, or anything, and not to have any accident, but to do everything perfectly and to keep thinking about the antelopes all the time, and not to let their thoughts go away to anything else. It took five days to charm the antelopes, and if anybody had an accident he must tell of it.

25   Every morning early, when the bright morning star could be seen, the people sat around the opening to the circle, with my father sitting in the middle of the opening, and my father lighted his pipe and passed it to his right, and the pipe went round the circle five times. And at night they did the same thing.

After they had smoked the pipe, my father took a kind of drum, which is used in this charming, and made music with it. This is the only kind of musical instrument which my people have, and it is only used for this antelope-charming. It is made of a hide of some large animal, stuffed with grass, so as to make it sound hollow, and then wound around tightly from one end to the other with a cord as large as my finger. One end of this instrument is large, and it tapers down to the other end, which is small, so that it makes a different sound on the different parts. My father took a stick and rubbed this stick from one end of the instrument to the other, making a penetrating, vibrating sound, that could be heard afar off, and he sang, and all his people sang with him.

After that the two men who were messengers went out to see the antelopes. They carried their torches in their right hands, and one of them carried a pipe in his left hand. They started from my father's wigwam and went straight across the camp to the opening; then they crossed, and one went around the second circle to the right and the other went to the left, till they met on the other side of the circle. Then they crossed again, and one went round the herd of antelopes one way and the other went round the other way, but they did not let the antelopes see them. When they met on the other side of the herd of antelopes, they stopped and smoked the pipe, and then they crossed, and each man came back on the track of the other to the camp, and told my father what they saw and what the antelopes were doing.

This was done every day for five days, and after the first day all the men and women and boys followed the messengers, and went around the circle they were to enter. On the fifth day the antelopes were charmed, and the whole herd followed the tracks of my people and entered the circle where the mounds were, coming in at the entrance, bowing and tossing their heads, and looking sleepy and under a powerful spell. They ran round and round inside the circle just as if there was a fence all around it and they could not get out, and they staid there until my people had killed every one. But if anybody had dropped anything, or had stumbled and had not told about it, then when the antelopes came to the place where he had done that, they threw off the spell and rushed wildly out of the circle at that place.

My brother can charm horses in the same way.

The Indian children amuse themselves a great deal by modelling   30
in mud. They make herds of animals, which are modelled exceedingly well, and after setting them up, shoot at them with their little bows and arrows. They also string beads of different colors and show natural good taste.

For Journals

What did you learn in elementary school about American Indian family life? Is your sense that it is similar to, or quite different from, other American ethnic groups?

For Discussion

1.   The Paiute tell their children stories to teach them about the values of their culture. What are some of the moral lessons they learn? How do the lessons compare with those you have learned from your own family?

2.   What assumptions about whites did Hopkins have as she was growing up? Which assumptions were revised as she came to know them, and which remained? What similar impressions might white settlers have had about the Paiutes?

3.　Are there aspects of Paiute courtship that strike you as similar to, or different from, the dating and courtship of your family or peers? How do their courtship rituals strengthen the sense of community and kinship in their tribe?

4.　The Paiute father questions his daughter and her suitor about the responsibilities and duties that accompany marriage, and the daughter's wishes in a suitor are respected. From this practice and other Paiute customs, what do you learn about their attitudes toward marriage? Toward the obligations of parenthood and the value of children? Toward the role of elders or grandparents? What assumptions about kinship, about the value and strength of the tribe, and about the interconnectedness of their daily lives do such beliefs convey?

5.　How do Paiutes transmit to young couples their community values about children? About the marriage relationship? In what ways are such customs and values similar to or different from Anglo American values and customs?

6.　Hopkins describes a belief that the Paiute wife must "be himself" to her husband. What do you understand the phrase to mean? Does Hopkins's narrative of the wife who goes to battle after her fallen husband illuminate the concept more fully? Does the belief strike you as consistent with practices in Anglo culture of the times? With contemporary American culture?

7.　The Paiutes believe in the Spirit-land and in dead relatives watching over the living; yet, they believe in Jesus and His ways of treating others, but they reject the doctrines of Hell and eternal punishment. How do you think contemporary white Christians would have responded to these beliefs? How do you think Hopkins tries to correct their assumptions?

8.　Compare and contrast the men's roles and women's roles in the tribal community with those expressed or implied in *Keep within Compass.*

For Writing

1.　Hopkins states, "The Council-tent is our Congress, and anybody can speak who has anything to say, women and all." Based on Hopkins's essay, analyze the tribe's system of government, practice of public discussion, inclusion of all members of the tribe, and practice of unpaid chiefs and subchiefs. Write an essay in which you either support or argue with her assessment.

FROM *IN DEFENSE OF WOMEN*
1 9 1 7

H. L. Mencken

H[enry] L[ewis] Mencken (1880–1956) was an American journalist, editor, and critic who worked for the Baltimore Herald *and then the* Baltimore Sun *(from 1906), where he stayed for the rest of his life. He edited a magazine, the* Smart Set, *and cofounded another magazine, the* American Mercury; *he was noted for debunking popular beliefs and middle-class values of those whom he termed "the Booboisie." Mencken was adept at insults and cast them, by turns, at Puritans, communists, Christians, Jews, the Ku Klux Klan, and others. His books include critical works, such as* George Bernard Shaw *(1905) and* The Philosophy of Friedrich Nietzsche *(1917), as well as* Notes on Democracy *(1926) and* Treatise of the Gods *(1930). Mencken was widely read and highly influential for some years, especially among college students in his heyday, but his popularity diminished after the early 1930s. The selection that follows is from his book* In Defense of Women, *a work he later found embarrassing on the event of his marriage late in life.*

How Marriages Are Arranged

I've said that women are not sentimental, i.e., not prone to permit mere emotion and illusion to corrupt their estimation of a situation. The doctrine, perhaps, will raise a protest. The theory that they are is itself a favourite sentimentality, one sentimentality will be brought up to substantiate another; dog will eat dog. But an appeal to a few obvious facts will be enough to sustain my contention, despite the vast accumulation of romantic rubbish to the contrary.

Turn, for example, to the field in which the two sexes come most constantly into conflict, and in which, as a result, their habits of mind are most clearly contrasted—to the field, to wit, of monogamous marriage. Surely no long argument is needed to demonstrate the superior competence and effectiveness of women here, and therewith their greater self-possession, their saner weighing of considerations, their higher power of resisting emotional suggestion. The very fact that marriages occur at all is a proof, indeed, that they are more cool-headed than men, and more adept in employing their intellectual resources, for it is plainly to a man's interest to avoid marriage as long as possible, and as plainly to a woman's interest to make a favourable marriage as soon as she can. The efforts of the two sexes are thus directed, in one of the capital concerns of life, to diametrically antagonistic ends. Which side commonly prevails? I leave the verdict to the jury. All normal men fight the thing off; some men are successful for relatively long periods; a few extraordinarily intelligent and courageous men (or perhaps lucky ones) escape altogether. But, taking one generation with another, as every one knows, the average man is duly married and the average woman gets a husband. Thus the great majority of women, in this clear-cut and endless conflict, make manifest their substantial superiority to the great majority of men.

Not many men, worthy of the name, gain anything of net value by marriage, at least as the institution is now met with in Christendom. Even assessing its benefits at their most inflated worth, they are plainly overborne by crushing disadvantages. When a man marries it is no more than a sign that the feminine talent for persuasion and intimidation—i.e., the feminine talent for survival in a world of clashing concepts and desires, the feminine competence and intelligence—has forced him into a more or less abhorrent compromise with his own honest inclinations and best interests. Whether that compromise be a sign of his relative stupidity or of his relative cowardice it is all one: the two things, in their symptoms and effects, are almost identical. In the first case he marries because he has been clearly bowled over in a combat of wits; in the second he resigns himself to marriage as the safest form of liaison. In both cases his inherent sentimentality is the chief weapon in the hand of his opponent. It makes him cherish the fiction of his enterprise, and even of his daring, in the midst of the most crude and obvious operations against him. It makes him accept as real the bold play-acting that women always excel at, and at no time more than when stalking a man. It makes him, above all, see a glamour of romance in a transaction which, even at its best, contains almost as much gross trafficking, at bottom, as the sale of a mule.

A man in full possession of the modest faculties that nature commonly apportions to him is at least far enough above idiocy to realize that marriage is a bargain in which he gets the worse of it, even when, in some detail or other, he makes a visible gain. He never, I believe, wants *all* that the thing offers and implies. He wants, at most, no more than certain parts. He may desire, let us say, a housekeeper to protect his goods and entertain his friends—but he may shrink from the thought of sharing his bathtub with any one, and home cooking may be downright poisonous to him. He may yearn for a son to pray at his tomb—and yet suffer acutely at the mere approach of relatives-in-law. He may dream of a beautiful and complaisant mistress, less exigent and mercurial than any a bachelor may hope to discover—and stand aghast at admitting her to his bank-book, his family-tree and his secret ambitions. He may want company and not intimacy, or intimacy and not company. He may want a cook and not a partner in his business, or a partner in his business and not a cook. But in order to get the precise thing or things that he wants, he has to take a lot of other things that he doesn't want—that no sane man, in truth, could imaginably want—and it is to the enterprise of forcing him into this almost Armenian bargain that the woman of his "choice" addresses herself. Once the game is fairly set, she searches out his weaknesses with the utmost delicacy and accuracy, and plays upon them with all her superior resources. He carries a handicap from the start. His sentimental and unintelligent belief in theories that she knows quite well are not true—e.g., the theory that she shrinks from him, and is modestly appalled by the banal carnalities of marriage itself—give her a weapon against him which she drives home with instinctive and compelling art. The moment she discerns this sentimentality bubbling within him—that is, the moment his oafish smirks and eye-rollings signify that he has achieved the intellectual disaster that is called falling in love—he is hers to do with as she will. Save for acts of God, he is forthwith as good as married.

The Feminine Attitude

This sentimentality in marriage is seldom, if ever, observed in women. For reasons that we shall examine later, they have much more to gain by the business than men, and so they are prompted by their cooler sagacity to enter upon it on the most favourable terms possible, and with the minimum admixture of disarming emotion. Men almost invariably get their mates by the process called falling in love; save among the aristocracies of the North and Latin men, the marriage of convenience is relatively rare; a hundred men marry "beneath" them to every woman who perpetrates the same folly. And what is meant by this so-called falling in love? What is meant by it is a procedure whereby a man accounts for the fact of his marriage, after feminine initiative and generalship have made it inevitable, by enshrouding it in a purple maze of romance—in brief, by setting up the doctrine that an obviously self-possessed and mammalian woman, engaged deliberately in the most important adventure of her life, and with the keenest understanding of its utmost implications, is a naive, tender, moony and almost disembodied creature, enchanted and made perfect by a passion that has stolen upon her unawares, and which she could not acknowledge, even to herself, without blushing to death. By this preposterous doctrine, the defeat and enslavement of the man is made glorious, and even gifted with a touch of flattering naughtiness. The sheer horsepower of his wooing has assailed and overcome her maiden modesty; she trembles in his arms; he has been granted a free franchise to work his wicked will upon her. Thus do the ambulant images of God cloak their shackles proudly, and divert the judicious with their boastful shouts.

Women, it is almost needless to point out, are much more cautious about embracing the conventional hocus-pocus of the situation. They never acknowledge that they have fallen in love, as the phrase is, until the man has formally avowed the delusion, and so cut off his retreat; to do otherwise would be to bring down upon their heads the mocking and contumely of all their sisters. With them, falling in love thus appears in the light of an afterthought, or, perhaps more accurately, in the light of a contagion. The theory, it would seem, is that the love of the man, laboriously avowed, has inspired it instantly, and by some unintelligible magic; that it was non-existent until the heat of his own flames set it off. This theory, it must be acknowledged, has a certain element of fact in it. A woman seldom allows herself to be swayed by emotion while the principal business is yet afoot and its issue still in doubt; to do so would be to expose a degree of imbecility that is confined only to the half-wits of the sex. But once the man is definitely committed, she frequently unbends a bit, if only as a relief from the strain of a fixed purpose, and so, throwing off her customary inhibitions, she indulges in the luxury of a more or less forced and mawkish sentiment. It is, however, almost unheard of for her to permit herself this relaxation before the sentimental intoxication of the man is assured. To do otherwise—that is, to confess, even *post facto*, to an anterior descent,—would expose her, as I have said, to the scorn of all other women. Such a confession would be an admission that emotion had got the better of her at a critical intellectual moment, and in the eyes of women, as in the eyes of the small minority of genuinely intelligent men, no treason to the higher cerebral centres could be more disgraceful.

The Male Beauty

This disdain of sentimental weakness, even in those higher reaches where it is mellowed by aesthetic sensibility, is well revealed by the fact that women are seldom bemused by mere beauty in men. Save on the stage, the handsome fellow has no appreciable advantage in amour over his more Gothic brother. In real life, indeed, he is viewed with the utmost suspicion by all women save the most stupid. In him the vanity native to his sex is seen to mount to a degree that is positively intolerable. It not only irritates by its very nature; it also throws about him a sort of unnatural armour, and so makes him resistant to the ordinary approaches. For this reason, the matrimonial enterprises of the more reflective and analytical sort of women are almost always directed to men whose lack of pulchritude makes them easier to bring down, and, what is more important still, easier to hold down. The weight of opinion among women is decidedly against the woman who falls in love with an Apollo. She is regarded, at best, as a flighty creature, and at worst, as one pushing bad taste to the verge of indecency. Such weaknesses are resigned to women approaching senility, and to the more ignoble variety of women labourers. A shop girl, perhaps, may plausibly fall in love with a moving-picture actor, and a half-idiotic old widow may succumb to a youth with shoulders like the Parthenon, but no woman of poise and self-respect, even supposing her to be transiently flustered by a lovely buck, would yield to that madness for an instant, or confess it to her dearest friend. Women know how little such purely superficial values are worth. The voice of their order, the first taboo of their freemasonry, is firmly against making a sentimental debauch of the serious business of marriage.

This disdain of the pretty fellow is often accounted for by amateur psychologists on the ground that women are anaesthetic to beauty—that they lack the quick and delicate responsiveness of man. Nothing could be more absurd. Women, in point of fact, commonly have a far keener aesthetic sense than men. Beauty is more important to them; they give more thought to it; they crave more of it in their immediate surroundings. The average man, at least in England and America, takes a sort of bovine pride in his anaesthesia to the arts; he can think of them only as sources of tawdry and somewhat discreditable amusement; one seldom hears of him showing half the enthusiasm for any beautiful thing that his wife displays in the presence of a fine fabric, an effective colour, or a graceful form, say in millinery. The truth is that women are resistant to so-called beauty in men for the simple and sufficient reason that such beauty is chiefly imaginary. A truly beautiful man, indeed, is as rare as a truly beautiful piece of jewelry. What men mistake for beauty in themselves is usually nothing save a certain hollow gaudiness, a revolting flashiness, the superficial splendour of a prancing animal. The most lovely moving-picture actor, considered in the light of genuine aesthetic values, is no more than a piece of vulgarity; his like is to be found, not in the Uffizi gallery or among the harmonies of Brahms, but among the plush sofas, rococo clocks and hand-painted oil-paintings of a third-rate auction-room. All women, save the least intelligent, penetrate this imposture with sharp eyes. They know that the human body, except for a brief time in infancy, is not a beautiful thing, but a hideous thing. Their own bodies give them no delight; it is their constant effort to disguise and conceal them; they never expose them aesthetically, but only as an act of the grossest sexual provocation. If it were advertised that a troupe of men of easy virtue were to appear half-clothed upon a public stage, exposing their chests, thighs, arms and calves, the only women who would go to the entertainment would be a few delayed adolescents, a psychopathic old maid or two, and a guard of indignant members of the parish Ladies Aid Society.

For Journals

Do you think the marketplace is an appropriate metaphor for courtship and marriage? Explain why you agree or disagree.

For Discussion

1.   Mencken's core premise is that women have more to gain from marriage than men do. What reasons does he give for this conclusion? Outline the assumptions and conclusion of his argument.

2.   If marriage were advantageous to women, why might this have been the case in 1917? In your response, consider Mencken's statement in paragraph 3 that women look to "survival in a world of clashing concepts and desires." Does anyone argue today that marriage benefits women more than men? Or men more than women? How so?

3.   According to Mencken (in paragraph 2), why is the fact that "marriages occur at all" proof that women's cooler heads and "superior competence" prevail?

4.   What do you infer from Mencken's claims about the relative power of men and women in the society? To what social classes do you think his essay is directed?

5.   Mencken claims that men do not really want all that marriage offers, but only parts. What does his list of what men want and don't want suggest about the expectations for women of his era?

6.   Mencken's assertions are unflattering to women. Are they more, or less, critical of men? Cite reasons from Mencken's argument to support your view.

7.   How might Mencken react to *Keep within Compass*? To the Charles Atlas advertisement (this chapter)?

For Writing

1.   Mencken argues that women are less concerned with male beauty than with the "serious business" of marriage. Argue that contemporary American women are, or are not, less concerned than men are with the physical appearance of potential partners; or argue that

women are, or are not, more concerned than men are with social and economical advantages.

2.   Write a critical analysis of Mencken's argument and style of writing, paying special attention to the assumptions buried within his arguments and to his highly inflammatory language.

FAME INSTEAD OF SHAME
1944

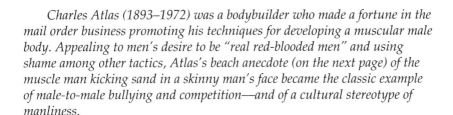

Charles Atlas (1893–1972) was a bodybuilder who made a fortune in the mail order business promoting his techniques for developing a muscular male body. Appealing to men's desire to be "real red-blooded men" and using shame among other tactics, Atlas's beach anecdote (on the next page) of the muscle man kicking sand in a skinny man's face became the classic example of male-to-male bullying and competition—and of a cultural stereotype of manliness.

For Journals

What kinds of appeals dominate advertisements for men in the magazines you read?

For Discussion

1.   List several assumptions that the author of this advertisement makes about the readers. Do such assumptions seem realistic? What is assumed about what men want? About what women want in a man? About attractiveness, maturity, competition? What expectations of men are conveyed?

2.   How does Atlas define "a real man"? Examine the language, the physique of the cartoon figures, the appeals to emotion, the appeals to authority. How persuasive do you think this advertisement was in 1944? To what degree is it significant that the ad appeared during World War II? Do you think the ad would be effective today? Why or why not? How would an advertisement for a similar product be marketed today?

3.   The advertisement contains a number of enthymemes (concise deductive arguments with conclusions that depend on the assumptions of its audience in order to make sense). (For a fuller discussion of enthymemes, see Chapter 1.) Identify one or two; state them and supply the missing assumption.

4.   Do you detect any appeals to logos, or logic, in the text? What are they? What is the evidence supplied to support the appeals? (See discussion of appeals to logos in Chapter 1.)

5.   Considering both images and text, compare and contrast the stereotypical roles conveyed in *Keep within Compass* and in this advertisement. Which gender seems to have a more narrowly defined role in society? Have times changed for either gender?

For Writing

1.   Write an essay arguing that expectations for men and their role in American society have, or have not, changed since this advertisement was published. You can focus on this advertisement, or you can find a related contemporary advertisement and compare and contrast the two.

2.   Review a variety of magazines from the 1920s through the 1960s, looking for advertisements that convey gender roles or expectations. What is assumed in them about men's and women's roles? About children or children's gender roles? Write an essay developing your position. If possible, include photocopies of the advertisements you use.

AMERICAN HORSE

1983

Louise Erdrich

Louise Erdrich (1954–   ), a contemporary novelist and poet who is part American Indian, is the author of Love Medicine *(1986),* The Beet Queen *(1986), and* Tracks *(1988), three best-selling novels, as well as two collections of poetry,* Jacklight *(1984) and* Baptism of Desire *(1990). Her most recent work,* The Crown of Columbus *(1991), was cowritten with her husband, writer Michael Dorris. The following story weaves threads of American Indian lore about children being spirited away and bewitched in with contemporary social issues about family life in American cultures.*

The woman sleeping on the cot in the woodshed was Albertine American Horse. The name was left over from her mother's short marriage. The boy was the son of the man she had loved and let go. Buddy was on the cot too, sitting on the edge because he'd been awake three hours watching out for his mother and besides, she took up the whole cot. Her feet hung over the edge, limp and brown as two trout. Her long arms reached out and slapped at things she saw in her dreams.

5   Buddy had been knocked awake out of hiding in a washing machine while herds of policemen with dogs searched through a large building with many tiny rooms. When the arm came down, Buddy screamed because it had a blue cuff and sharp silver buttons. "Tss," his mother mumbled, half awake, "wasn't nothing." But Buddy sat up after her breathing went deep again, and he watched.

There was something coming and he knew it.

It was coming from very far off but he had a picture of it in his mind. It was a large thing made of metal with many barbed hooks, points, and drag chains on it, something like a giant potato peeler that rolled out of the sky, scraping clouds down with it and jabbing or crushing everything that lay in its path on the ground.

Buddy watched his mother. If he woke her up, she would know what to do about the thing, but he thought he'd wait until he saw it for sure before he shook her. She was pretty, sleeping, and he liked knowing he could look at her as long and close up as he wanted. He took a strand of her hair and held it in his hands as if it was the rein to a delicate beast. She was strong enough and could pull him along like the horse their name was.

Buddy had his mother's and his grandmother's name because his father had been a big mistake.

"They're all mistakes, even your father. But *you* are the best thing that ever happened to me."

That was what she said when he asked.

Even Kadie, the boyfriend crippled from being in a car wreck, was not as good a thing that had happened to his mother as Buddy was. "He was a medium-sized mistake," she said. "He's hurt and I shouldn't even say that, but it's the truth." At the moment, Buddy knew that being the best thing in his mother's life, he was also the reason they were hiding from the cops.

10   He wanted to touch the satin roses sewed on her pink T-shirt, but he knew he shouldn't do that even in her sleep. If she woke up and found him touching the roses, she would say, "Quit that, Buddy." Sometimes she told him to stop hugging her like a gorilla. She never said that in the mean voice she used when he oppressed her, but when she said that he loosened up anyway.

There were times he felt like hugging her so hard and in such a special way that she would say to him, "Let's get married." There were also times he closed his eyes and wished that she would die, only a few times, but still it haunted him that his wish might come true. He and Uncle Lawrence would be left alone. Buddy wasn't worried, though, about his mother getting married to somebody else. She had said to her friend, Madonna, "All men suck," when she thought Buddy wasn't listening. He had made an uncertain sound, and when they heard him they took him in their arms.

"Except for you, Buddy," his mother said. "All except for you and maybe Uncle Lawrence, although he's pushing it."

"The cops suck the worst, though," Buddy whispered to his mother's sleeping face, "because they're after us." He felt tired again, slumped down, and put his legs beneath the blanket. He closed his eyes and got the feeling that the cot was lifting up beneath him, that it was arching its canvas back and then traveling, traveling very fast and in the wrong direction for when he looked up he saw the three of them were advancing to meet the great metal thing with hooks and barbs and all sorts of sharp equipment to catch their bodies and draw their blood. He heard its insides as it rushed toward them, purring softly like a powerful motor and then they were right in its shadow. He pulled the reins as hard as he could and the beast reared, lifting him. His mother clapped her hand across his mouth.

"Okay," she said. "Lay low. They're outside and they're gonna hurt."

She touched his shoulder and Buddy leaned over with her to look   15
through a crack in the boards.

They were out there all right, Albertine saw them. Two officers and that social worker woman. Vicki Koob. There had been no whistle, no dream, no voice to warn her that they were coming. There was only the crunching sound of cinders in the yard, the engine purring, the dust sifting off their car in a fine light brownish cloud and settling around them.

The three people came to a halt in their husk of metal—the car emblazoned with the North Dakota State Highway Patrol emblem which is the glowing profile of the Sioux policeman, Red Tomahawk, the one who killed Sitting Bull. Albertine gave Buddy the blanket and told him that he might have to wrap it around him and hide underneath the cot.

"We're gonna wait and see what they do." She took him in her lap and hunched her arms around him. "Don't you worry," she whispered against his ear. "Lawrence knows how to fool them."

Buddy didn't want to look at the car and the people. He felt his mother's heart beating beneath his ear so fast it seemed to push the satin roses in and out. He put his face to them carefully and breathed the deep, soft powdery woman smell of her. That smell was also in her little face cream bottles, in her brushes, and around the washbowl after she used it. The satin felt so unbearably smooth against his cheek that he had to press closer. She didn't push him away, like he expected, but hugged him still tighter until he felt as close as he had ever been to back inside her again where she said he came from. Within the smells of her things, her soft skin, and the satin of her roses, he closed his eyes then, and took his breaths softly and quickly with her heart.

20   They were out there, but they didn't dare get out of the car yet because of Lawrence's big, ragged dogs. Three of these dogs had loped up the dirt driveway with the car. They were rangy, alert, and bounced up and down on their cushioned paws like wolves. They didn't waste their energy barking, but positioned themselves quietly, one at either car door and the third in front of the bellied-out screen door to Uncle Lawrence's house. It was six in the morning but the wind was up already, blowing dust, ruffling their short moth-eaten coats. The big brown one on Vicki Koob's side had unusual black and white markings, stripes almost, like a hyena and he grinned at her, tongue out and teeth showing.

"Shoo!" Miss Koob opened her door with a quick jerk.

The brown dog sidestepped the door and jumped before her, tiptoeing. Its dirty white muzzle curled and its eyes crossed suddenly as if it was zeroing its cross-hair sights in on the exact place it would bite her. She ducked back and slammed the door.

"It's mean," she told Officer Brackett. He was printing out some type of form. The other officer, Harmony, a slow man, had not yet reacted to the car's halt. He had been sitting quietly in the back seat, but now he rolled down his window and with no change in expression unsnapped his holster and drew his pistol out and pointed it at the dog on his side. The dog smacked down on its belly, wiggled under the car and was out and around the back of the house before Harmony drew his gun back. The other dogs vanished with him. From wherever they had disappeared to they began to yap and howl, and the door to the low shoebox-style house fell open.

"Heya, what's going on?"

25   Uncle Lawrence put his head out the door and opened wide the one eye he had in working order. The eye bulged impossibly wider in outrage when he saw the police car. But the eyes of the two officers and Miss Vicki Koob were wide open too because they had never seen Uncle Lawrence in his sleeping get-up or, indeed, witnessed anything like it. For his ribs, which were cracked from a bad fall and still mending, Uncle Lawrence wore a thick white corset laced up the front with a striped sneakers' lace. His glass eye and his set of dentures were still out for the night so his face puckered here and there, around its absences and scars, like a damaged but fierce little cake. Although he had a few gray streaks now, Uncle Lawrence's hair was still thick, and because he wore a special contraption of elastic straps around his head

every night, two oiled waves always crested on either side of his middle part. All of this would have been sufficient to astonish, even without the most striking part of his outfit—the smoking jacket. It was made of black satin and hung open around his corset, dragging a tasseled belt. Gold thread dragons struggled up the lapels and blasted their furry red breath around his neck. As Lawrence walked down the steps, he put his arms up in surrender and the gold tassels in the inner seams of his sleeves dropped into view.

"My heavens, what a sight." Vicki Koob was impressed.

"A character," apologized Officer Harmony.

As a tribal police officer who could be counted on to help out the State Patrol, Harmony thought he always had to explain about Indians or get twice as tough to show he did not favor them. He was slow-moving and shy but two jumps ahead of other people all the same, and now, as he watched Uncle Lawrence's splendid approach, he gazed speculatively at the torn and bulging pocket of the smoking jacket. Harmony had been inside Uncle Lawrence's house before and knew that above his draped orange-crate shelf of war medals a blue-black German luger was hung carefully in a net of flat-headed nails and fishing line. Thinking of this deadly exhibition, he got out of the car and shambled toward Lawrence with a dreamy little smile of welcome on his face. But when he searched Lawrence, he found that the bulging pocket held only the lonesome-looking dentures from Lawrence's empty jaw. They were still dripping denture polish.

"I had been cleaning them when you arrived," Uncle Lawrence explained with acid dignity.

He took the toothbrush from his other pocket and aimed it like a   30
rifle.

"Quit that, you old idiot." Harmony tossed the toothbrush away. "For once you ain't done nothing. We came for your nephew."

Lawrence looked at Harmony with a faint air of puzzlement.

"Ma Frere, listen," threatened Harmony amiably, "those two white people in the car came to get him for the welfare. They got papers on your nephew that give them the right to take him."

"Papers?" Uncle Lawrence puffed out his deeply pitted cheeks. "Let me see them papers."

The two of them walked over to Vicki's side of the car and she   35
pulled a copy of the court order from her purse. Lawrence put his teeth back in and adjusted them with busy workings of his jaw.

"Just a minute," he reached into his breast pocket as he bent close to Miss Vicki Koob. "I can't read these without I have in my eye."

He took the eye from his breast pocket delicately, and as he popped it into his face the social worker's mouth fell open in a consternated O.

"What is this," she cried in a little voice.

Uncle Lawrence looked at her mildly. The white glass of the eye was cold as lard. The black iris was strangely charged and menacing.

40   "He's nuts," Bracket huffed along the side of Vicki's neck. "Never mind him."

Vicki's hair had sweated down her nape in tiny corkscrews and some of the hairs were so long and dangly now that they disappeared into the zippered back of her dress. Brackett noticed this as he spoke into her ear. His face grew red and the backs of his hands prickled. He slid under the steering wheel and got out of the car. He walked around the hood to stand with Leo Harmony.

"We could take you in too," said Brackett roughly. Lawrence eyed the officers in what was taken as defiance. "If you don't cooperate, we'll get out the handcuffs," they warned.

One of Lawrence's arms was stiff and would not move until he'd rubbed it with witch hazel in the morning. His other arm worked fine though, and he stuck it out in front of Brackett.

"Get them handcuffs," he urged them. "Put me in a welfare home."

45   Brackett snapped one side of the handcuffs on Lawrence's good arm and the other to the handle of the police car.

"That's to hold you," he said. "We're wasting our time. Harmony, you search that little shed over by the tall grass and Miss Koob and myself will search the house."

"My rights is violated!" Lawrence shrieked suddenly. They ignored him. He tugged at the handcuff and thought of the good heavy file he kept in his tool box and the German luger oiled and ready but never loaded, because of Buddy, over his shelf. He should have used it on these bad ones, even Harmony in his big-time white man job. He wouldn't last long in that job anyway before somebody gave him what for.

"It's a damn scheme," said Uncle Lawrence, rattling his chains against the car. He looked over at the shed and thought maybe Albertine and Buddy had sneaked away before the car pulled into the yard. But he sagged, seeing Albertine move like a shadow within the boards. "Oh, it's all a damn scheme," he muttered again.

"I want to find that boy and salvage him," Vicki Koob explained to Officer Brackett as they walked into the house. "Look at his family life—the old man crazy as a bedbug, the mother intoxicated somewhere."

50   Brackett nodded, energetic, eager. He was a short hopeful redhead who failed consistently to win the hearts of women. Vicki Koob in-

trigued him. Now, as he watched, she pulled a tiny pen out of an ornamental clip on her blouse. It was attached to a retractable line that would suck the pen back, like a child eating one strand of spaghetti. Something about the pen on its line excited Brackett to the point of discomfort. His hand shook as he opened the screendoor and stepped in, beckoning Miss Koob to follow.

They could see the house was empty at first glance. It was only one rectangular room with whitewashed walls and a little gas stove in the middle. They had already come through the cooking lean-to with the other stove and washstand and rusty old refrigerator. That refrigerator had nothing in it but some wrinkled potatoes and a package of turkey necks. Vicki Koob noted that in her perfect-bound notebook. The beds along the walls of the big room were covered with quilts that Albertine's mother, Sophie, had made from bits of old wool coats and pants that the Sisters sold in bundles at the mission. There was no one hiding beneath the beds. No one was under the little aluminum dinette table covered with a green oilcloth, or the soft brown wood chairs tucked up to it. One wall of the big room was filled with neatly stacked crates of things—old tools and springs and small half-dismantled appliances. Five or six television sets were stacked against the wall. Their control panels spewed colored wires and at least one was cracked all the way across. Only the topmost set, with coathanger antenna angled sensitively to catch the bounding signals around Little Shell, looked like it could possibly work.

Not one thing escaped Vicki Koob's trained and cataloguing gaze. She made note of the cupboard that held only commodity flour and coffee. The unsanitary tin oil drum beneath the kitchen window, full of empty surplus pork cans and beer bottles, caught her eye as did Uncle Lawrence's physical and mental deteriorations. She quickly described these "benchmarks of alcoholic dependency within the extended family of Woodrow (Buddy) American Horse" as she walked around the room with the little notebook open, pushed against her belly to steady it. Although Vicki had been there before, Albertine's presence had always made it difficult for her to take notes.

"Twice the maximum allowable space between door and threshold," she wrote now. "Probably no insulation. Two three-inch cracks in walls inadequately sealed with whitewashed mud." She made a mental note but could see no point in describing Lawrence's stuffed reclining chair that only reclined, the shadeless lamp with its plastic orchid in the bubble glass base, or the three-dimensional picture of Jesus that Lawrence had once demonstrated to her. When plugged in, lights rolled behind the water the Lord stood on so that he seemed to be strolling although he never actually went forward, of course, but only pushed the glowing waves behind him forever like a poor tame rat in a treadmill.

Brackett cleared his throat with a nervous rasp and touched Vicki's shoulder.

55   "What are you writing?"

She moved away and continued to scribble as if thoroughly absorbed in her work. "Officer Brackett displays an undue amount of interest in my person," she wrote. "Perhaps?"

He snatched playfully at the book, but she hugged it to her chest and moved off smiling. More curls had fallen, wetted to the base of her neck. Looking out the window, she sighed long and loud.

"All night on brush rollers for this. What a joke."

Brackett shoved his hands in his pockets. His mouth opened slightly, then shut with a small throttled cluck.

60   When Albertine saw Harmony ambling across the yard with his big brown thumbs in his belt, his placid smile, and his tiny black eyes moving back and forth, she put Buddy under the cot. Harmony stopped at the shed and stood quietly. He spread his arms to show her he hadn't drawn his big police gun.

"Ma Cousin," he said in the Michif dialect that people used if they were relatives or sometimes if they needed gas or a couple of dollars, "why don't you come out here and stop this foolishness?"

"I ain't your cousin," Albertine said. Anger boiled up in her suddenly. "I ain't related to no pigs."

She bit her lip and watched him through the cracks, circling, a big tan punching dummy with his boots full of sand so he never stayed down once he fell. He was empty inside, all stale air. But he knew how to get to her so much better than a white cop could. And now he was circling because he wasn't sure she didn't have a weapon, maybe a knife or the German luger that was the only thing that her father, Albert American Horse, had left his wife and daughter besides his name. Harmony knew that Albertine was a tall strong woman who took two big men to subdue when she didn't want to go in the drunk tank. She had hard hips, broad shoulders, and stood tall like her Sioux father, the American Horse who was killed threshing in Belle Prairie.

"I feel bad to have to do this," Harmony said to Albertine. "But for godsakes, let's nobody get hurt. Come on out with the boy, why don't you? I know you got him in there."

65   Albertine did not give herself away this time. She let him wonder. Slowly and quietly she pulled her belt through its loops and wrapped it around and around her hand until only the big oval buckle with turquoise chunks shaped into a butterfly stuck out over her knuckles. Harmony was talking but she wasn't listening to what he said. She was

listening to the pitch of his voice, the tone of it that would tighten or tremble at a certain moment when he decided to rush the shed. He kept talking slowly and reasonably, flexing the dialect from time to time, even mentioning her father.

"He was a damn good man. I don't care what they say, Albertine, I knew him."

Albertine looked at the stone butterfly that spread its wings across her fist. The wings looked light and cool, not heavy. It almost looked like it was ready to fly. Harmony wanted to get to Albertine through her father but she would not think about American Horse. She concentrated on the sky blue stone.

Yet the shape of the stone, the color, betrayed her.

She saw her father suddenly, bending at the grille of their old gray car. She was small then. The memory came from so long ago it seemed like a dream—narrowly focused, snapshot-clear. He was bending by the grille in the sun. It was hot summer. Wings of sweat, dark blue, spread across the back of his work shirt. He always wore soft blue shirts, the color of shade cloudier than this stone. His stiff hair had grown out of its short haircut and flopped over his forehead. When he stood up and turned away from the car, Albertine saw that he had a butterfly.

"It's dead," he told her. "Broke its wings and died on the grille."   70

She must have been five, maybe six, wearing one of the boy's T-shirts Mama bleached in Hilex-water. American Horse took the butterfly, a black and yellow one, and rubbed it on Albertine's collarbone and chest and arms until the color and the powder of it were blended into her skin.

"For grace," he said.

And Albertine had felt a strange lightening in her arms, in her chest, when he did this and said, "For grace." The way he said it, grace meant everything the butterfly was. The sharp delicate wings. The way it floated over grass. The way its wings seemed to breathe fanning in the sun. The wisdom of the way it blended into flowers or changed into a leaf. In herself she felt the same kind of possibilities and closed her eyes almost in shock or pain, she felt so light and powerful at that moment.

Then her father had caught her and thrown her high into the air. She could not remember landing in his arms or landing at all. She only remembered the sun filling her eyes and the world tipping crazily behind her, out of sight.

"He was a damn good man," Harmony said again.   75

Albertine heard his starched uniform gathering before his boots hit the ground. Once, twice, three times. It took him four solid jumps to get right where she wanted him. She kicked the plank door open when he reached for the handle and the corner caught him on the jaw. He faltered, and Albertine hit him flat on the chin with the butterfly. She hit him so hard the shock of it went up her arm like a string pulled taut. Her fist opened, numb, and she let the belt unloop before she closed her hand on the tip end of it and sent the stone butterfly swooping out in a wide circle around her as if it was on the end of a leash. Harmony reeled backward as she walked toward him swinging the belt. She expected him to fall but he just stumbled. And then he took the gun from his hip.

Albertine let the belt go limp. She and Harmony stood within feet of each other, breathing. Each heard the human sound of air going in and out of the other person's lungs. Each read the face of the other as if deciphering letters carved into softly eroding veins of stone. Albertine saw the pattern of tiny arteries that age, drink, and hard living had blown to the surface of the man's face. She saw the spoked wheels of his iris and the arteries like tangled threads that sewed him up. She saw the living net of springs and tissue that held him together, and trapped him. She saw the random, intimate plan of his person.

She took a quick shallow breath and her face went strange and tight. She saw the black veins in the wings of the butterfly, roads burnt into a map, and then she was located somewhere in the net of veins and sinew that was the tragic complexity of the world so she did not see Officer Brackett and Vicki Koob rushing toward her, but felt them instead like flies caught in the same web, rocking it.

"Albertine!" Vicki Koob had stopped in the grass. Her voice was shrill and tight. "It's better this way, Albertine. We're going to help you."

80   Albertine straightened, threw her shoulders back. Her father's hand was on her chest and shoulders lightening her wonderfully. Then on wings of her father's hands, on dead butterfly wings, Albertine lifted into the air and flew toward the others. The light powerful feeling swept her up the way she had floated higher, seeing the grass below. It was her father throwing her up into the air and out of danger. Her arms opened for bullets but no bullets came. Harmony did not shoot. Instead, he raised his fist and brought it down hard on her head.

Albertine did not fall immediately, but stood in his arms a moment. Perhaps she gazed still farther back behind the covering of his face. Perhaps she was completely stunned and did not think as she sagged and fell. Her face rolled forward and hair covered her features, so it was impossible for Harmony to see with just what particular expression she gazed into the head-splitting wheel of light, or blackness, that overcame her.

* * *

Harmony turned the vehicle onto the gravel road that led back to town. He had convinced the other two that Albertine was more trouble than she was worth, and so they left her behind, and Lawrence too. He stood swearing in his cinder driveway as the car rolled out of sight. Buddy sat between the social worker and Officer Brackett. Vicki tried to hold Buddy fast and keep her arm down at the same time, for the words she'd screamed at Albertine had broken the seal of antiperspirant beneath her arms. She was sweating now as though she'd stored up an ocean inside of her. Sweat rolled down her back in a shallow river and pooled at her waist and between her breasts. A thin sheen of water came out on her forearms, her face. Vicki gave an irritated moan but Brackett seemed not to take notice, or take offense at least. Air-conditioned breezes were sweeping over the seat anyway, and very soon they would be comfortable. She smiled at Brackett over Buddy's head. The man grinned back. Buddy stirred. Vicki remembered the emergency chocolate bar she kept in her purse, fished it out, and offered it to Buddy. He did not react, so she closed his fingers over the package and peeled the paper off one end.

The car accelerated. Buddy felt the road and wheels pummeling each other and the rush of the heavy motor purring in high gear. Buddy knew that what he'd seen in his mind that morning, the thing coming out of the sky with barbs and chains, had hooked him. Somehow he was caught and held in the sour tin smell of the pale woman's armpit. Somehow he was pinned between their pounds of breathless flesh. He looked at the chocolate in his hand. He was squeezing the bar so hard that a thin brown trickle had melted down his arm. Automatically he put the bar in his mouth.

As he bit down he saw his mother very clearly, just as she had been when she carried him from the shed. She was stretched flat on the ground, on her stomach, and her arms were curled around her head as if in sleep. One leg was drawn up and it looked for all the world like she was running full tilt into the ground, as though she had been trying to pass into the earth, to bury herself, but at the last moment something had stopped her.

85   There was no blood on Albertine, but Buddy tasted blood now at the sight of her, for he bit down hard and cut his own lip. He ate the chocolate, every bit of it, tasting his mother's blood. And when he had the chocolate down inside him and all licked off his hands, he opened his mouth to say thank you to the woman, as his mother had taught him. But instead of a thank you coming out he was astonished to hear a great rattling scream, and then another, rip out of him like pieces of his own body and whirl onto the sharp things all around him.

For Journals

What beliefs do you hold about the value of nuclear families versus alternative or single-parent families?

For Discussion

1. As you are drawn into the narrative, what kind of picture are you forming about Buddy and his family life? Does the image change as you read on?

2. The social worker says, "I want to find that boy and salvage him. Look at his family life—the old many crazy as a bedbug, the mother intoxicated somewhere" (paragraph 49). Unpack the assumptions in Vicki Koob's assessment of Buddy's family life and her own abilities.

3. Do you find yourself identifying with a particular character or point of view? To what degree is that identification a product of the author's ability to convey multiple points of view, your own cultural assumptions, or some other factors?

4. Koob observes the house and draws conclusions about alcohol dependency. Do her conclusions logically follow from her observations? In what ways are her assumptions shaping her conclusions? If you were her supervisor, would you accept her assessment? How might Albertine respond?

5. What is the role of Officer Harmony? Is he a necessary factor in this interaction? Can you draw any conclusions about his values and beliefs?

6. When Albertine read Harmony's face she saw "the complexity of the world" and how she and Koob and Brackett were all "caught in the same web" (paragraph 77). Explain your interpretation of her comment.

7. Examine the imagery of Buddy's dream and Albertine's memories. In what ways do the images underscore themes in the story?

For Writing

1. Argue that different assumptions about family life and intercultural misperceptions do or do not lead to the resolution of Buddy's case by his removal from the family.

2. Assume the role of Albertine's attorney at a custody hearing, and draft the argument you will make to the presiding judge. Remember to evaluate your audience's assumptions, values, and beliefs and to include reasons and evidence to support your view. You will also need to refute the points you assume the opposition will make.

WHEN "FAMILY" IS NOT A HOUSEHOLD WORD
1988

Keenan Peck

Keenan Peck (1960–1990), attorney, activist, and member of The Progressive *editorial board, was educated at the University of Wisconsin where he received his bachelor's degree and law degree. He also served as counsel to Senator Herbert Kohl (D-Wisconsin) and was chair of his local chapter of the American Civil Liberties Union. Peck's articles for* The Progressive *include an exposé of the Federal Emergency Management Agency. Peck, who worked diligently on behalf of human and civil rights died of an aneurysm at the age of 29. The article that follows was published in September, 1988, also in* The Progressive, *and draws from Peck's personal experience as well as from his research.*

If my friends had been married, the three of us could have lived in peace. Instead, the authorities ordered us to vacate our home. In my neighborhood, it turned out, three unrelated people could not live together legally. Never mind that we were good, quiet neighbors. Never mind that we enjoyed the area. No marriage license, no occupancy. There might as well have been a sign at the end of our street: ALTERNATIVE FAMILIES, KEEP OUT.

I was sharing a three-bedroom house in Madison, Wisconsin, with an unmarried couple—a man and a woman who intended to make a life together but didn't want to get married just yet. Our arrangement was illegal because Madison, like many other cities, prohibits occupancy by more than two unrelated persons in neighborhoods designated for families. It's called "single-family zoning," and it's a pernicious form of discrimination against those in loving but unorthodox relationships.

When Madison told us to move, we sued the city. We argued that the ordinance violated our right to associate with one another. We pointed out that it in no way advanced the admirable goals of residential stability and tranquility. A person's marital status has nothing to do with his or her compatibility with the neighbors, we said. Consanguinity and lawn mowing are not connected. The city should regulate the *use* of dwellings, not the users.

We lost in the trial court (the case is now on appeal), but the experience offered a lesson in civil rights. We discovered that we were part of a growing legal debate over the definition of "family." Increasingly, Americans who live in groupings they regard as families but who are not related by blood, marriage, or adoption are pressing courts, legislatures, and employers for the same rights claimed by traditional families. Although the media have concentrated on the steamy (or contagious) aspects of the sexual revolution, that revolution has also led to a struggle over such mundane but important matters as insurance, housing, and inheritance.

5   In our case, my roommates and I asserted the simple right to live where and with whom we wanted. But in 1974, the U.S. Supreme Court had held that the Constitution does not stop municipalities from restricting households composed of unrelated persons. The strength of one's rights in these situations turns on the interpretation of each state's constitution by its own judiciary. The high courts of New Jersey, California, New York, and Michigan have used their states' constitutions to protect alternative families; courts in Missouri, New Hampshire, and Hawaii have ruled against nontraditional living arrangements.

To reach their decisions, all of the courts grappled with the same essential questions: When does a household become, in lawyer's jargon, the "functional equivalent" of a family? And should the law treat the functional equivalent the same as the real item? The rise of the alternative family makes it essential to find answers.

The term "alternative family" refers to several kinds of living situations, the most common of which is the unmarried heterosexual couple. In 1980, the year of the last census, some 1.8 million Americans were living as cohabiting couples, a 300 percent increase from the number in 1970. The Census Bureau called them POSSLQs—Persons of Opposite Sex Sharing Living Quarters. According to two University of Wisconsin sociologists, Larry Bumpass and James Sweet, the proportion of persons cohabiting before their first marriage has quadrupled (to 44 percent) over the past two decades.

"Cohabitation has not simply become increasingly common," they said upon the release of their $4.5 million study. "If recent trends continue, it will soon be the majority experience."

"Alternative family" also encompasses gay and lesbian couples and the dependents of all unmarried couples. In all, there are about ten million people in the United States who can be classified as belonging to alternative families, reports Steven Ruggles, a demographer at the University of Minnesota. Looked at from the other side of the numbers, fewer than 30 percent of us live in a traditional nuclear family, defined as a married couple with children.

10   The law has lagged behind changes in our lifestyle. Twenty states have repealed laws against adultery, but cohabitators in some states

still live under the threat of prosecution. Only one state, Wisconsin, prohibits discrimination on the basis of sexual orientation, and no state permits persons of the same sex to marry. Thus, gay and lesbian couples are denied the legal benefits of marriage, such as the automatic passing of property to the surviving partner when the other one dies without a will. To make matters worse, the U.S. Supreme Court ruled in 1986 that Georgia could enforce a law against "homosexual sodomy." (Actually, the law prohibited anal intercourse between men and women as well, but the homophobic majority ignored that fact.)

Like state governments, employers and insurance companies often refuse to treat unmarried or unadopted loved ones as family for the purposes of various benefits. A union contract can help, but only if the union is enlightened enough to deal with the problem in the first place.

Law professor Barbara Cox, writing in the *Wisconsin Women's Law Journal,* has catalogued the entitlements that are extended to nuclear families but withheld from alternative families: "They include the opportunity to live in neighborhoods zoned for single families; receive employment-based health insurance, bereavement and sick leave, pensions, moving expenses, library and recreational privileges, and low-cost day care and travel packages; sue for loss of consortium, worker's compensation or unemployment compensation; visit family members in hospitals and authorize their emergency medical treatment; and receive low-cost family rates from organizations such as health clubs, museums, and art centers."

What is the motive for perpetuating such discrimination? In the field of housing, opposition to alternative families is often really bias against college students who, local governments fear, will wreak havoc in communes. This was the unspoken justification for Madison's ordinance, and it figures in much of the litigation over zoning (including the 1974 U.S. Supreme Court case).

College students, to be sure, can put strain on a family-oriented neighborhood. Still, in the words of a recent New Jersey court opinion, students should not be "required to govern their lifestyle to meet the dictates of those who disapprove of their ways." The same judge hinted at another reason behind hostility toward alternative families: the generation gap. People who set rules and policies are likely to hark back to an era when sexual taboos limited alternative living arrangements. And homophobia afflicts politicians and employers, too. Employers and insurance companies, moreover, don't want to spend the money to cover children and lovers who are deemed family in expanded benefits plans.

But there seems to be a more fundamental concern behind the opposition to alternative families—the feeling that the *nuclear* family forms society's bedrock. New types of loving relationships are per-   15 ceived as a threat to the very order of things. The problem with this objection is that it ignores the negative attributes of nuclear families and the positive characteristics of alternative families. Something in the nuclear family is wrong if almost half of new marriages end in divorce; and what is wrong with an alternative relationship that's lasting and loving?

Steven Ruggles, the Minnesota demographer, found no significant differences between married and unmarried couples "in terms of satisfaction, commitment, sexual satisfaction, communication, or psychological adjustment." What's more, half of the cohabitants in the University of Wisconsin study married within three years, suggesting that an alternative status is frequently temporary.

A happy or sad, healthy or abusive relationship will not be made less or more so with a marriage certificate. The law should focus on the societal interest, which is in long-term, supportive relationships. Although blood relation, marriage, and adoption have served as useful shorthands for "family," the legal establishment must now find categories that can accommodate new living arrangements without losing all definition.

Two cities have attempted to do so. In Santa Cruz, California, city workers and their loved ones may sign an "Affidavit of Domestic Partnership" to qualify the partners for health benefits. Under penalty of perjury, the two affirm, "We are each other's sole domestic partner and intend to remain so indefinitely and are responsible for our common welfare." The Santa Cruz personnel department indicates that 2 percent of the municipal work force has signed on the dotted line.

In West Hollywood, California, domestic partners can swear out a form indicating that they "share the common necessities of life," "are each other's sole domestic partner," and "agree to be responsible for each other's welfare." In addition to providing benefits for partners of municipal workers, the ordinance also requires hospitals and jails to permit visitation by partners. About 15 per cent of the work force has signed up in West Hollywood, which has a large gay population.

20   Following the example of the California cities, a member of the Madison Common Council proposed a similar plan. Partners would be allowed to file an affidavit with the city stating that they are in a relationship of "mutual support, caring, and commitment." The form would make partners and dependents eligible for the benefits given to nuclear families. Despite the support of the Madison Equal Opportunities Commission, however, the proposal encountered resistance in the usually liberal town. As of this writing, the plan has not been adopted.

When I try to fathom why the Madison plan fell flat—and, for that matter, why the city tried to oust three people from their home—one word comes to mind: fright. The powers that be are frightened by the prospect of yet another unfamiliar constituency demanding legal recognition. In Madison and elsewhere, officials are whispering, "Enough is enough." To them, alternative families don't need to live in family-oriented neighborhoods; gay couples don't need to marry; partners don't need benefits that accrue to their lovers.

By the same token, though, blacks didn't need to ride in the front of the bus; women didn't need membership in formerly all-male clubs; poor people didn't need the vote. But in each of those instances, the aggrieved segment of the population persuaded the rest of us that "equal rights" means what it says. In the coming years, many Americans will be asking for equal rights for the ten million members of alternative families.

In the meantime, I'll be asking for nothing more than the right to live with unmarried friends in a house of my choosing.

For Journals

Should there be regulations about who lives in your neighborhood— about unmarried couples living together, or domestic partners, or groups of unrelated people?

For Discussion

1.   Study Peck's introduction. Why do you think he begins with a personal anecdote? With this particular anecdote?

2.   What is the fundamental issue in controlling residents based on marital status? How does it relate to society's assumptions about marriage and families? How does it reflect assumptions about nonmarried people living together? Why are the courts involved in this issue? To what extent do society's needs or interests dictate the rules and regulations governing cohabitation?

3.   Analyze the support the author uses to convince his readers of his assertion. What types of evidence and appeals seem most convincing? Consider statistics, personal experience, definition, analogy, comparison and contrast, cites to authorities, appeals to emotion and to ethos, or values and beliefs.

4.   How does Peck define family? In what ways is it like, or unlike, your own definition of family? On what assumptions is Peck's definition based? On what assumptions is your definition based? What does Peck's community appear to believe about what creates a family? In what ways is Peck's small group like, and unlike, a family?

5.   Do you agree with Peck's assertion that laws restricting alternative families exist, in large part, to restrict college students? Or do you believe they are a result of a more pervasive bias or fear in society of non–nuclear family relationships?

6.   Are you convinced by Peck's argument that fostering long-term, stable relationship of various kinds is in society's best interest? Would Thomas Stoddard agree? What about Bruce Fein? (Both selections to follow.)

For Writing

1.   Stoddard and Peck both cite civil rights to support their arguments. Compare and contrast the readings, examining the persuasiveness and appropriateness of the premise that their issues are civil rights issues, keeping in mind their audiences: Stoddard—general readers and lawyers; Fein—lawyers; Peck—the liberal readership of *The Progressive.* (Alternatively, argue that Peck's case is, or is not, a civil rights issue.)

2.   Research zoning laws pertaining to group or alternative-family housing in your college community. You could get in touch with City Hall offices or other local authorities, or your campus housing office may have such information about the campus and nearby areas. Do the regulations only support traditional nuclear families, or do they allow for alternative arrangements? Write a documented essay based on your findings and share it with your classmates. If your campus housing office does not already have this information, they may be interested in getting a copy of your report.

3.   Argue that communities do, or do not, have a right to enforce the kind of restrictions against which Peck is arguing. Examine the assumptions on which you are basing your argument. Be sure to support your assertion with reasons, evidence, and examples.

MARRIAGE IS A FUNDAMENTAL RIGHT
1989

Thomas Stoddard

Thomas Stoddard (1948–   ) is an attorney and serves as executive director of the Lambda Defense and Education Fund, a gay rights organization.

He is the author of The Rights of Gay People *(1983) and frequently speaks out on gay civil rights issues. In the essay that follows, which first appeared in the* New York Times, *Stoddard argues on behalf of a controversial but fundamental issue: the rights of same-gender couples to marry.*

"In sickness and in health, 'til death do us part." With those words, millions of people each year are married, a public affirmation of a private bond that both society and the newlyweds hope will endure. Yet for nearly four years, Karen Thompson was denied the company of the one person to whom she had pledged life-long devotion.

Her partner is a woman, Sharon Kowalski, and their home state of Minnesota, like every other in the United States, refuses to permit same-sex marriages.

Karen Thompson and Sharon Kowalski are spouses in every respect except the legal. They exchanged vows and rings. They lived together until November 13, 1983—when Kowalski, as the result of an automobile accident, was rendered unable to walk and barely able to speak.

Thompson sought a ruling granting her guardianship over her partner, but Kowalski's parents opposed the petition and obtained sole guardianship. They then moved Kowalski to a nursing home 300 miles away from Thompson and forbade all visits between the two women.

In February 1989, in the wake of a reevaluation of Kowalski's mental competence, Thompson was permitted to visit her partner again. But the prolonged injustice and anguish inflicted on both women hold a moral for everyone.   5

Marriage, the Surpeme Court declared in 1967 in *Loving* v. *Virginia,* is "one of the basic civil rights of man" (and, presumably, of woman as well). The freedom to marry, said the Court, is "essential to the orderly pursuit of happiness."

Marriage is far more than a symbolic state. It can be the key to survival—emotional and financial. Marriage triggers a universe of rights, privileges and presumptions. In every jurisdiction in this country, a married person can share in a spouse's estate even when there is no will. She typically has access to the group insurance and pension programs offered by the spouse's employer, and she enjoys tax advantages.

The decision whether or not to marry belongs properly to individuals, not to the government. While marriage historically has required a male and a female partner, history alone cannot sanctify injustice.

If tradition were the only measure, most states still would limit matrimony to partners of the same race. As recently as 1967, before the

Supreme Court declared in *Loving* that miscegenation statutes are unconstitutional, sixteen states still prohibited marriages between a white person and a black person. When all the excuses were stripped away, it was clear that the only purpose of those laws was to maintain white supremacy.

10   Those who argue against reforming the marriage statutes because they believe that same-sex marriage would be "anti-family" overlook the obvious: Marriage creates families and promotes social stability. In an increasingly loveless world, those who wish to commit themselves to a relationship founded upon devotion should be encouraged, not scorned. Government has no legitimate interest in how that love is expressed.

And it can no longer be argued—if it ever could—that marriage is fundamentally a procreative unit. Otherwise, states would forbid marriage between those who, by reason of age or infertility, cannot have children, as well as those who elect not to.

The case of Sharon Kowalski and Karen Thompson demonstrates that sanctimonious illusions can lead directly to the suffering of others. Denied the right to marry, these women were left to the whims and prejudices of others, and of the law.

It is time for the marriage statutes to incorporate fully the concept of equal protection of the law by extending to the many millions of gay Americans the right to marry.

For Journals

Freewrite for five or ten minutes on your assumptions about or biases toward same-gender marriages or domestic partnerships.

For Discussion

1.   Why do you think Stoddard begins with an anecdote? Why do you think he focuses on women? On the issue of caring for sick loved ones? How does this strategy shift the focus of the debate?

2.   How does Stoddard's introductory strategy counter his readers' assumptions about the issue of gay marriage?

3.   Stoddard's assertion is that same-gender marriage is not anti-family, as some have charged, but rather pro-family. Does he adequately counter the anti-family arguments? Does he adequately support his assertions that same-gender marriage "creates families and promotes stability" (paragraph 10)? In what ways is he transforming traditional definitions of family to do so?

4.   What appeals to values and beliefs does Stoddard make? What appeals to emotion? To logic? Which do you find most persuasive?

5. Although this essay was first published in the *New York Times*, a newspaper with a general rather than legal audience, Stoddard (who is an attorney) is comfortable citing legal precedent to support his argument. Do you think his evidence is convincing to a diverse audience? Stoddard's article was later reprinted in the *Journal of the American Bar Association*. Do you think that audience is more, or less, likely to accept the arguments he makes?

For Writing

1. Write a rebuttal to Stoddard, arguing with the specific points he makes, challenging his assumptions or premises, and making any additional points to support the opposing view. You may develop your argument using appeals to ethos, pathos, or logos, or appeals to values and beliefs, to emotion and empathy, to logic and evidence. (See Chapter 1, "Reading and Analyzing Arguments" on ethos, pathos, and logos.) Or you may wish to integrate evidence from outside sources into your arguments. If you do, be sure to read on both sides of the issue and to use your evidence to represent the opposing views fairly and ethically and in accord with the author's intended meaning. See Chapter 2, "Writing and Research," for additional information on research.

2. With a peer or in groups, write a dialogue between two people debating this topic or another controversial social issue. Then exchange dialogues with another peer or group. Evaluate the assumptions, premises, and appeals used in the dialogues. Summarize your findings, and share them with your class.

RESERVE MARRIAGE FOR HETEROSEXUALS
1990

Bruce Fein

Bruce Fein, a Washington, D.C., attorney, is the author of Significant Decisions of the Supreme Court *(1979–1980). He has contributed articles to the* National Review *and* American Legion Magazine. *Fein's article first appeared in the* Journal of the American Bar Association, *which also reprinted the preceding selection by Thomas Stoddard.*

Authorizing the marriage of homosexuals, like sanctioning polygamy, would be unenlightened social policy. The law should reserve the celebration of marriage vows for monogamous male-female attachments to further the goal of psychologically, emotionally and educationally balanced offspring.

As Justice Oliver Wendell Holmes noted, the life of the law has not been logic, it has been experience. Experience confirms that child development is skewed, scarred or retarded when either a father or mother is absent in the household.

In the area of adoption, married couples are favored over singles. The recent preferences for joint child-custody decrees in divorce proceedings tacitly acknowledges the desirability of child intimacies with both a mother and father.

As Supreme Court Justice Byron White recognized in *Taylor* v. *Louisiana* (1975): "[T]he two sexes are not fungible; a community made up exclusively of one is different from a community of both; the subtle interplay of influence one on the other is among the imponderables" (quoting from *Ballard* v. *United States*).

5   A child receives incalculable benefits in the maturing process by the joint instruction, consolation, oversight and love of a father and mother—benefits that are unavailable in homosexual households. The child enjoys the opportunity to understand and respect both sexes in a uniquely intimate climate. The likelihood of gender prejudice is thus reduced, an exceptionally worthy social objective.

The law should encourage male-female marriage vows over homosexual attachments in the interests of physically, mentally, and psychologically healthy children, the nation's most valuable asset.

Crowning homosexual relationships with the solemnity of legal marriage would wrongly send social cues that male-female marriages are not preferable. And there is no constitutional right to homosexual marriage since homosexual sodomy can be criminalized. See *Bowers* v. *Hardwick* (1986).

The fact that some traditional marriages end in fractious divorce, yield no offspring, or result in families with mistreated children does not discredit limiting marriage to monogamous female-male relationships. Anti-polygamy laws are instructive. They seek to discourage female docility, male autocracy, and intra-family rancor and jealousies that are promoted by polygamous marriages. That some might not exhibit such deplorable characteristics is no reason for their repeal or a finding of constitutional infirmity.

To deny the right of homosexual marriage is not an argument for limiting other rights to gays, because of community animosity or vengeance. These are unacceptable policy motivations if law is to be civilized.

Several states and localities protect homosexuals against discrimi-   10
nation in employment or housing. In New York, a state law confers on
a homosexual the rent-control benefits of a deceased partner. Other ju-
risdictions have eschewed special legal rights for homosexuals, and the
military excludes them. Experience will adjudge which of the varied
legal approaches to homosexual rights has been the most enlightened.

Sober debate over homosexual rights is in short supply. The subject challenges deep-rooted and passionately held images of manhood,
womanhood and parenthood, and evokes sublimated fears of community ostracism or degradation.

Each legal issue regarding homosexuality should be examined dis-
cretely with the recognition that time has upset many fighting faiths
and with the goal of balancing individual liberty against community
interests. With regard to homosexual marriage, that balance is negative.

For Journals

Freewrite for five to ten minutes on the assumptions about marriage
you had as a child and now have as an adult. How do children fit into
the image you have in mind?

For Discussion

1.   What kinds of appeals does Fein make? Consider particularly his
core assertion: that children will suffer from same-gender marriages.
What assumptions about the purpose of marriage does his argument
rest on? Is the argument that children are the key consideration in marriage laws one that would be as persuasive to general audiences as
Fein believes it will be to lawyers?

2.   In addition to citing legal cases, Fein cites authorities such as
Oliver Wendell Holmes. But he then states that "experience confirms
that child development is skewed, scarred or retarded when either a
father or mother is absent in the household" (paragraph 2). Are you
persuaded by his citing of "experience"? If not, what additional evidence could he offer that might be more convincing?

3.   Fein's overall organizational pattern is direct: he asserts and then
supports. How might writing for an audience of lawyers have dictated
this pattern? Would it have been equally effective writing for a general
audience?

4.   Fein also argues by making an analogy to polygamous marriages.
How convincing is the analogy? How appropriate is it to the argument?

5.   Fein differentiates and separates this issue from other civil rights
issues. Do you accept his premise that marriage rights differ fundamentally from other civil rights?

6. Examine the logic of Fein's arguments, such as the one in paragraph 7. It may be helpful to outline the premises and conclusion for each argument he makes. Which of his arguments stand up to the analysis? Which ones are weak? Which ones could be strengthened with evidence?

For Writing

1. Write a letter of rebuttal to Fein. Use a different approach and different arguments than Thomas Stoddard (this chapter) uses in "Marriage Is a Fundamental Right." Remember to keep in mind the biases and assumptions you wrote about in your journal assignment for the Stoddard article.

2. Compare and contrast Fein's and Stoddard's arguments, focusing on the effectiveness of appeals, their use of evidence, and their patterns of development. Which argument makes more appeals to emotion? To logic? To traditions, values, beliefs? Keeping in mind your own biases and attitudes toward the topic, which argument seems more sound?

BLAME IT ON FEMINISM
1991

Susan Faludi

Susan Faludi (1959–   ) graduated summa cum laude from Harvard University in 1981. Ten years later she won the Pulitzer Prize for an article about the leveraged buyout of Safeway supermarkets and the National Book Critics Circle Award for Backlash: The Undeclared War Against American Women *(1991), an extensive study of the social and political reaction against feminism and women's modest progress toward equal rights. Faludi is a regular contributor to the magazines* Ms. *and* Mother Jones, *and her writing sometimes skeptically examines the status of women in contemporary society. She describes* Backlash *as a book that "arms women with information and a good dose of cynicism," adding, "It's also very large, so it can be thrown at misogynists."*

To be a woman in America at the close of the 20th century—what good fortune. That's what we keep hearing, anyway. The barricades have fallen, politicians assure us. Women have "made it," Madison Avenue cheers. Women's fight for equality has "largely been won," *Time* magazine announces. Enroll at any university, join any law firm, apply for credit at any bank. Women have so many opportunities now, corporate leaders say, that we don't really need equal opportunity policies. Women are so equal now, lawmakers say, that we no longer need an Equal Rights Amendment. Women have "so much," former President Ronald Reagan says, that the White House no longer needs to appoint them to higher office. Even American Express ads are saluting a woman's freedom to charge it. At last, women have received their full citizenship papers.

And yet . . .

Behind this celebration of the American woman's victory, behind the news, cheerfully and endlessly repeated, that the struggle for women's rights is won, another message flashes. You may be free and equal now, it says to women, but you have never been more miserable.

This bulletin of despair is posted everywhere—at the newsstand, on the TV set, at the movies, in advertisements and doctors' offices and academic journals. Professional women are suffering "burnout" and succumbing to an "infertility epidemic." Single women are grieving from a "man shortage." The *New York Times* reports: Childless women are "depressed and confused" and their ranks are swelling. *Newsweek* says: Unwed women are "hysterical" and crumbling under a "profound crisis of confidence." The health advice manuals inform: High-powered career women are stricken with unprecedented outbreaks of "stress-induced disorders," hair loss, bad nerves, alcoholism, and even heart attacks. The psychology books advise: Independent women's loneliness represents "a major mental health problem today." Even founding feminist Betty Friedan has been spreading the word: she warns that women now suffer from a new identity crisis and "new 'problems that have no name.'"

How can American women be in so much trouble at the same time   5
that they are supposed to be so blessed? If the status of women has never been higher, why is their emotional state so low? If women got what they asked for, what could possibly be the matter now?

The prevailing wisdom of the past decade has supported one, and only one, answer to this riddle: it must be all that equality that's causing all that pain. Women are unhappy precisely *because* they are free. Women are enslaved by their own liberation. They have grabbed at the gold ring of independence, only to miss the one ring that really matters. They have gained control of their fertility, only to destroy it.

They have pursued their own professional dreams—and lost out on the greatest female adventure. The women's movement, as we are told time and again, has proved women's own worst enemy.

"In dispensing its spoils, women's liberation has given my generation high incomes, our own cigarette, the option of single parenthood, rape crisis centers, personal lines of credit, free love, and female gynecologists," Mona Charen, a young law student, writes in the *National Review,* in an article titled "The Feminist Mistake." "In return it has effectively robbed us of one thing upon which the happiness of most women rests—men." The *National Review* is a conservative publication, but such charges against the women's movement are not confined to its pages. "Our generation was the human sacrifice" to the women's movement, *Los Angeles Times* feature writer Elizabeth Mehren contends in a *Time* cover story. Baby-boom women like her, she says, have been duped by feminism: "We believed the rhetoric." In *Newsweek,* writer Kay Ebeling dubs feminism "the Great Experiment That Failed" and asserts "women in my generation, its perpetrators, are the casualties." Even the beauty magazines are saying it: *Harper's Bazaar* accuses the women's movement of having "lost us [women] ground instead of gaining it."

In the last decade, publications from the *New York Times* to *Vanity Fair* to the *Nation* have issued a steady stream of indictments against the women's movement, with such headlines as WHEN FEMINISM FAILED OR THE AWFUL TRUTH ABOUT WOMEN'S LIB. They hold the campaign for women's equality responsible for nearly every woe besetting women, from mental depression to meager savings accounts, from teenage suicides to eating disorders to bad complexions. The "Today" show says women's liberation is to blame for bag ladies. A guest columnist in the *Baltimore Sun* even proposes that feminists produced the rise in slasher movies. By making the "violence" of abortion more acceptable, the author reasons, women's rights activists made it all right to show graphic murders on screen.

At the same time, other outlets of popular culture have been forging the same connection: in Hollywood films, of which *Fatal Attraction* is only the most famous, emancipated women with condominiums of their own slink wild-eyed between bare walls, paying for their liberty with an empty bed, a barren womb. "My biological clock is ticking so loud it keeps me awake at night," Sally Field cries in the film *Surrender,* as, in an all too common transformation in the cinema of the '80s, an actress who once played scrappy working heroines is now showcased groveling for a groom. In prime-time television shows, from *thirtysomething* to *Family Man,* single, professional, and feminist women are humiliated, turned into harpies, or hit by nervous breakdowns; the wise ones recant their independent ways by the closing sequence. In popular novels, from Gail Parent's *A Sign of the Eighties* to Stephen King's *Misery*, unwed women shrink to sniveling spinsters or inflate to fire-breathing she-devils; renouncing all aspirations but marriage, they beg for wedding bands from strangers or swing axes at reluctant bachelors. We "blew it by waiting," a typically remorseful careerist sobs in Freda Bright's *Singular Women*; she and her sister professionals are "condemned to be childless forever." Even Erica Jong's high-flying independent heroine literally crashes by the end of the decade, as the author supplants *Fear of Flying*'s saucy Isadora Wing, a symbol of female sexual emancipation in the '70s, with an embittered careerist-turned-recovering-"co-dependent" in *Any Woman's Blues*—a book that is intended, as the narrator bluntly states, "to demonstrate what a deadend the so-called sexual revolution had become, and how desperate so-called free women were in the last few years of our decadent epoch."

Popular psychology manuals peddle the same diagnosis for con-   10
temporary female distress. "Feminism, having promised her a stronger sense of her own identity, has given her little more than an identity *crisis*," the best-selling advice manual *Being a Woman* asserts. The authors of the era's self-help classic *Smart Women/Foolish Choices* proclaim that women's distress was "an unfortunate consequence of feminism," because "it created a myth among women that the apex of self-realization could be achieved only through autonomy, independence, and career."

In the Reagan and Bush years, government officials have needed no prompting to endorse this thesis. Reagan spokeswomen Faith Whittlesey declared feminism a "straitjacket" for women, in the White House's only policy speech on the status of the American female population—entitled "Radical Feminism in Retreat." Law enforcement officers and judges, too, have pointed a damning finger at feminism, claiming that they can chart a path from rising female independence to rising female pathology. As a California sheriff explained it to the press, "Women are enjoying a lot more freedom now, and as a result, they are committing more crimes." The U.S. Attorney General's Commission on Pornography even proposed that women's professional advancement might be responsible for rising rape rates. With more women in college and at work now, the commission members reasoned in their report, women just have more opportunities to be raped.

Some academics have signed on to the consensus, too—and they are the "experts" who have enjoyed the highest profiles on the media circuit. On network news and talk shows, they have advised millions of women that feminism has condemned them to "a lesser life." Legal scholars have railed against "the equality trap." Sociologists have claimed that "feminist-inspired" legislative reforms have stripped women of special "protections." Economists have argued that well-paid working women have created "a less stable American family." And demographers, with greatest fanfare, have legitimated the prevailing wisdom with so-called neutral data on sex ratios and fertility trends; they say they actually have the numbers to prove that equality doesn't mix with marriage and motherhood.

Finally, some "liberated" women themselves have joined the lamentations. In confessional accounts, works that invariably receive a hearty greeting from the publishing industry, "recovering Superwomen" tell all. In *The Cost of Loving: Women and the New Fear of Intimacy*, Megan Marshall, a Harvard-pedigreed writer, asserts that the feminist "Myth of Independence" has turned her generation into unloved and unhappy fast-trackers, "dehumanized" by careers and "uncertain of their gender identity." Other diaries of mad Superwomen charge that "the hard-core feminist viewpoint," as one of them puts it, has relegated educated executive achievers to solitary nights of frozen dinners and closet drinking. The triumph of equality, they report, has merely given women hives, stomach cramps, eye-twitching disorders, even comas.

But what "equality" are all these authorities talking about?

15   If American women are so equal, why do they represent two-thirds of all poor adults? Why are more than 80 percent of full-time working women making less than $20,000 a year, nearly double the male rate? Why are they still far more likely than men to live in poor housing and receive no health insurance, and twice as likely to draw no pension? Why does the average working woman's salary still lag as far behind the average man's as it did twenty years ago? Why does the average female college graduate today earn less than a man with no more than a high school diploma (just as she did in the '50s)—and why does the average female high school graduate today earn less than a male high school dropout? Why do American women, in fact, face the worst gender-based pay gap in the developed world?

If women have "made it," then why are nearly 80 percent of working women still stuck in traditional "female" jobs—as secretaries, administrative "support" workers and salesclerks? And, conversely, why are they less than 8 percent of all federal and state judges, less than 6 percent of all law partners, and less than one half of 1 percent of top corporate managers? Why are there only three female state governors, two female U.S. senators, and two Fortune 500 chief executives? Why are only nineteen of the four thousand corporate officers and directors women—and why do more than half the boards of Fortune companies still lack even one female member?

If women "have it all," then why don't they have the most basic requirements to achieve equality in the work force? Unlike virtually all other industrialized nations, the U.S. government still has no family-leave and child care programs—and more than 99 percent of American private employers don't offer child care either. Though business leaders say they are aware of and deplore sex discrimination, corporate America has yet to make an honest effort toward eradicating it. In a 1990 national poll of chief executives at Fortune 1000 companies, more than 80 percent acknowledged that discrimination impedes female employees' progress—yet, less than 1 percent of these same companies regarded *remedying* sex discrimination as a goal that their personnel departments should pursue. In fact, when the companies' human resource officers were asked to rate their department's priorities, women's advancement ranked last.

If women are so "free," why are their reproductive freedoms in greater jeopardy today than a decade earlier? Why do women who want to postpone childbearing now have fewer options than ten years ago? The availability of different forms of contraception has declined, research for new birth control has virtually halted, new laws restricting abortion—or even *information* about abortion—for young and poor women have been passed, and the U.S. Supreme Court has shown little ardor in defending the right it granted in 1973.

Nor is women's struggle for equal education over; as a 1989 study found, three-fourths of all high schools still violate the federal law banning sex discrimination in education. In colleges, undergraduate women receive only 70 percent of the aid undergraduate men get in grants and work-study jobs—and women's sports programs receive a pittance compared with men's. A review of state equal-education laws in the late '80s found that only thirteen states had adopted the minimum provisions required by the federal Title IX law—and only seven states had anti-discrimination regulations that covered all education levels.

Nor do women enjoy equality in their own homes, where they still   20 shoulder 70 percent of the household duties—and the only major change in the last fifteen years is that now middle-class men *think* they do more around the house. (In fact, a national poll finds the ranks of women saying their husbands share equally in child care shrunk to 31 percent in 1987 from 40 percent three years earlier.) Furthermore, in thirty states, it is still generally legal for husbands to rape their wives; and only ten states have laws mandating arrest for domestic violence—even though battering was the leading cause of injury of women in the late '80s. Women who have no other option but to flee find that isn't much of an alternative either. Federal funding for battered women's shelters has been withheld and one third of the 1 million battered women who seek emergency shelter each year can find none. Blows from men contributed far more to the rising numbers of "bag ladies" than the ill effects of feminism. In the '80s, almost half of all homeless women (the fastest growing segment of the homeless) were refugees of domestic violence.

The word may be that women have been "liberated," but women themselves seem to feel otherwise. Repeatedly in national surveys, majorities of women say they are still far from equality. Nearly 70 percent of women polled by the *New York Times* in 1989 said the movement for women's rights had only just begun. Most women in the 1990 Virginia Slims opinion poll agreed with the statement that conditions for their sex in American society had improved "a little, not a lot." In poll after poll in the decade, overwhelming majorities of women said they needed equal pay and equal job opportunities, they needed an Equal Rights Amendment, they needed the right to an abortion without government interference, they needed a federal law guaranteeing maternity leave, they needed decent child care services. They have none of these. So how exactly have we "won" the war for women's rights?

Seen against this background, the much ballyhooed claim that feminism is responsible for making women miserable becomes absurd—and irrelevant. . . . The afflictions ascribed to feminism are all myths. From "the man shortage" to "the infertility epidemic" to "female burnout" to "toxic day care," these so-called female crises have had their origins not in the actual conditions of women's lives but rather in a closed system that starts and ends in the media, popular culture, and advertising—an endless feedback loop that perpetuates and exaggerates its own false images of womanhood.

Women themselves don't single out the women's movement as the source of their misery. To the contrary, in national surveys 75 to 95 percent of women credit the feminist campaign with *improving* their lives, and a similar proportion say that the women's movement should keep pushing for change. Less than 8 percent think the women's movement might have actually made their lot worse.

What actually is troubling the American female population, then? If the many ponderers of the Woman Question really wanted to know, they might have asked their subjects. In public opinion surveys, women consistently rank their own *inequality,* at work and at home, among their most urgent concerns. Over and over, women complain to pollsters about a lack of economic, not marital, oppportunities; they protest that working men, not working women, fail to spend time in the nursery and the kitchen. The Roper Organization's survey analysts find that men's opposition to equality is "a major cause of resentment and stress" and "a major irritant for most women today." It is justice for their gender, not wedding rings and bassinets, that women believe to be in desperately short supply. When the *New York Times* polled women in 1989 aobut "the most important problem facing women today," job discrimination was the overwhelming winner; none of the crises the media and popular culture had so assiduously promoted even made the charts. In the 1990 Virginia Slims poll, women were most upset by their lack of money, followed by the refusal of their men to shoulder child care and domestic duties. By contrast, when the women were asked where the quest for a husband or the desire to hold a "less pressured" job or to stay at home ranked on their list of concerns, they placed them at the bottom.

As the last decade ran its course, women's unhappiness with in-   25
equality only mounted. In national polls, the ranks of women protesting discriminatory treatment in business, political, and personal life climbed sharply. The proportion of women complaining of unequal employment opportunities jumped more than ten points from the '70s, and the number of women complaining of unequal barriers to job advancement climbed even higher. By the end of the decade, 80 percent to 95 percent of women said they suffered from job discrimination and unequal pay. Sex discrimination charges filed with the Equal Employment Opportunity Commission rose nearly 25 percent in the Reagan years, and charges of general harassment directed at working women climbed 208 percent. In the decade, complaints of sexual harassment jumped 70 percent. At home, a much increased proportion of women complained to pollsters of male mistreatment, unequal relationships, and male efforts to, in the words of the Virginia Slims poll, "keep women down." The share of women in the Roper surveys who agreed that men were "basically kind, gentle, and thoughtful" fell from almost 70 percent in 1970 to 50 percent by 1990. And outside their homes, women felt more threatened, too: in the 1990 Virginia Slims poll, 72 percent of women said they felt "more afraid and uneasy on the streets today" than they did a few years ago. Lest this be attributed only to a general rise in criminal activity, by contrast only 49 percent of men felt this way.

While the women's movement has certainly made women more cognizant of their own inequality, the rising chorus of female protest shouldn't be written off as feminist-induced "oversensitivity." The monitors that serve to track slippage in women's status have been working overtime since the early '80s. Government and private surveys are showing that women's already vast representation in the lowliest occupations is rising, their tiny presence in higher-paying trade and craft jobs stalled or backsliding, their minuscule representation in upper management posts stagnant or falling, and their pay dropping in the very occupations where they have made the most "progress." The status of women lowest on the income ladder has plunged most perilously; government budget cuts in the first four years of the Reagan administration alone pushed nearly 2 million female-headed families and nearly 5 million women below the poverty line. And the prime target of government rollbacks has been one sex only: one-third of the Reagan budget cuts, for example, came out of programs that predominantly serve women—even more extraordinary when one considers that all these programs combined represent only 10 percent of the federal budget.

The alarms aren't just going off in the work force. In national politics, the already small numbers of women in both elective posts and political appointments fell during the '80s. In private life, the average amount that a divorced man paid in child support fell by about 25 percent from the late '70s to the mid' 80s (to a mere $140 a month). Domestic-violence shelters recorded a more than 100 percent increase in the numbers of women taking refuge in their quarters between 1983 and 1987. And government records chronicled a spectacular rise in sexual violence against women. Reported rapes more than doubled from the early '70s—at nearly twice the rate of all other violent crimes and four times the overall crime rate in the United States. While the homicide rate declined, sex-related murders rose 160 percent between 1976 and 1984. And these murders weren't simply the random, impersonal by-product of a violent society; at least one-third of the women were killed by their husbands or boyfriends, and the majority of that group were murdered just after declaring their independence in the most intimate manner—by filing for divorce and leaving home.

By the end of the decade, women were starting to tell pollsters that they feared their sex's social status was once again beginning to slip. They believed they were facing an "erosion of respect," as the 1990 Virginia Slims poll summed up the sentiment. After years in which an increasing percentage of women had said their status had improved from a decade earlier, the proportion suddenly shrunk by 5 percent in the last half of the '80s, the Roper Organization reported. And it fell most sharply among women in their thirties—the age group most targeted by the media and advertisers—dropping about ten percentage points between 1985 and 1990.

Some women began to piece the picture together. In the 1989 *New York Times* poll, more than half of black women and one-fourth of white women put it into words. They told pollsters they believed men were now trying to retract the gains women had made in the last twenty years. "I wanted more autonomy," was how one woman, a thirty-seven-year-old nurse, put it. And her estranged husband "wanted to take it away."

30   The truth is that the last decade has seen a powerful counterassault on women's rights, a backlash, an attempt to retract the handful of small and hard-won victories that the feminist movement did manage to win for women. This counterassault is largely insidious: in a kind of

pop-culture version of the Big Lie, it stands the truth boldly on its head and proclaims that the very steps that have elevated women's position have actually led to their downfall.

The backlash is at once sophisticated and banal, deceptively "progressive" and proudly backward. It deploys both the "new" findings of "scientific research" and the dime-store moralism of yesteryear; it turns into media sound bites both the glib pronouncements of pop-psych trend-watchers and the frenzied rhetoric of New Right preachers. The backlash has succeeded in framing virtually the whole issue of women's rights in its own language. Just as Reaganism shifted political discourse far to the right and demonized liberalism, so the backlash convinced the public that women's "liberation" was the true contemporary American scourge—the source of an endless laundry list of personal, social, and economic problems.

But what has made women unhappy in the last decade is not their "equality"—which they don't yet have—but the rising pressure to halt, and even reverse, women's quest for that equality. The "man shortage" and the "infertility epidemic" are not the price of liberation; in fact, they do not even exist. But these chimeras are the chisels of a society-wide backlash. They are part of a relentless whittling-down process—much of it amounting to outright propaganda—that has served to stir women's private anxieties and break their political wills. Identifying feminism as women's enemy only furthers the ends of a backlash against women's equality, simultaneously deflecting attention from the backlash's central role and recruiting women to attack their own cause.

Some social observers may well ask whether the current pressures on women actually constitute a backlash—or just a continuation of American society's long-standing resistance to women's rights. Certainly hostility to female independence has always been with us. But if fear and loathing of feminism is a sort of perpetual viral condition in our culture, it is not always in an acute stage; its symptoms subside and resurface periodically. And it is these episodes of resurgence, such as the one we face now, that can accurately be termed "backlashes" to women's advancement. If we trace these occurrences in American history . . . , we find such flare-ups are hardly random; they have always been triggered by the perception—accurate or not—that women are making great strides. These outbreaks are backlashes because they have always arisen in reaction to women's "progress," caused not simply by a bedrock of misogyny but by the specific efforts of contemporary women to improve their status, efforts that have been interpreted time and again by men—especially men grappling with real threats to their economic and social well-being on other fronts—as spelling their own masculine doom.

The most recent round of backlash first surfaced in the late '70s on the fringes, among the evangelical right. By the early '80s, the fundamentalist ideology had shouldered its way into the White House. By the mid-'80s, as resistance to women's rights acquired political and social acceptability, it passed into the popular culture. And in every case, the timing coincided with signs that women were believed to be on the verge of breakthrough.

35   Just when women's quest for equal rights seemed closest to achieving its objectives, the backlash struck it down. Just when a "gender gap" at the voting booth surfaced in 1980, and women in politics began to talk of capitalizing on it, the Republican party elevated Ronald Reagan and both political parties began to shunt women's rights off their platforms. Just when support for feminism and the Equal Rights Amendment reached a record high in 1981, the amendment was defeated the following year. Just when women were starting to mobilize against battering and sexual assaults, the federal government stalled funding for battered-women's programs, defeated bills to fund shelters, and shut down its Office of Domestic Violence—only two years after opening it in 1979. Just when record numbers of younger women were supporting feminist goals in the mid '80s (more of them, in fact, than older women) and a majority of all women were calling themselves feminists, the media declared the advent of a younger "postfeminist generation" that supposedly reviled the women's movement. Just when women racked up their largest percentage ever supporting the right to abortion, the U.S. Supreme Court moved toward reconsidering it.

In other words, the antifeminist backlash has been set off not by women's achievement of full equality but by the increased possibility that they might win it. It is a preemptive strike that stops women long before they reach the finish line. "A backlash may be an indication that women really have had an effect," feminist psychiatrist Dr. Jean Baker Miller has written, "but backlashes occur when advances have been small, before changes are sufficient to help many people. . . . It is almost as if the leaders of backlashes use the fear of change as a threat before major change has occurred." In the last decade, some women did make substantial advances before the backlash hit, but millions of others were left behind, stranded. Some women now enjoy the right to legal abortion—but not the 44 million women, from the indigent to the military work force, who depend on the federal government for their medical care. Some women can now walk into high-paying professional careers—but not the more than 19 million still in the typing pools or behind the department store sales counters. (Contrary to popular myth about the "have-it-all" baby-boom women, the largest percentage of women in this generation remain typists and clerks.)

As the backlash has gathered force, it has cut off the few from the many—and the few women who have advanced seek to prove, as a social survival tactic, that they aren't so interested in advancment after all. Some of them parade their defection from the women's movement, while their working-class peers founder and cling to the splintered remains of the feminist cause. While a very few affluent and celebrity women who are showcased in news articles boast about having "found my niche as Mrs. Andy Mill" and going home to "bake bread," the many working-class women appeal for their economic rights—flocking to unions in record numbers, striking on their own for pay equity and establishing their own fledgling groups for working women's rights. In 1986, while 41 percent of upper-income women were claiming in the Gallup poll that they were not feminists, only 26 percent of low-income women were making the same claim.

Women's advances and retreats are generally described in military terms; battles won, battles lost, points and territory gained and surrendered. The metaphor of combat is not without its merits in this context and, clearly, the same sort of martial accounting and vocabulary is already surfacing here. But by imagining the conflict as two battalions neatly arrayed on either side of the line, we miss the entangled nature, the locked embrace, of a "war" between women and the male culture they inhabit. We miss the reactive nature of a backlash, which, by definition, can exist only in response to another force.

In times when feminism is at a low ebb, women assume the reactive role—privately and most often covertly struggling to assert themselves against the dominant cultural tide. But when feminism itself becomes the tide, the opposition doesn't simply go along with the reversal: it digs in its heels, brandishes its fists, builds walls and dams. And its resistance creates countercurrents and treacherous undertows.

The force and furor of the backlash churn beneath the surface,   40
largely invisible to the public eye. On occasion in the last decade, they have burst into view. We have seen New Right politicians condemn women's independence, antiabortion protesters fire-bomb women's clinics, fundamentalist preachers damn feminists as "whores" and "witches." Other signs of the backlash's wrath, by their sheer brutality, can push their way into public consciousness for a time—the sharp increase in rape, for example, or the rise in pornography that depicts extreme violence against women.

More subtle indicators in popular culture may receive momentary, and often bemused, media notice, then quickly slip from social awareness: A report, for instance, that the image of women on prime-time TV shows has suddenly degenerated. A survey of mystery fiction finding the numbers of female characters tortured and mutilated mysteriously multiplying. The puzzling news that, as one commentator put it, "So many hit songs have the B-word [bitch] to refer to women that some rap music seems to be veering toward rape music." The ascendancy of virulently misogynist comics like Andrew Dice Clay—who called women "pigs" and "sluts" and strutted in films in which women were beaten, tortured, and blown up—or radio hosts like Rush Limbaugh, whose broadsides against "femi-Nazi" feminists made his syndicated program the most popular radio talk show in the nation. Or word that in 1987, the American Women in Radio & Television couldn't award its annual prize for ads that feature women positively: it could find no ad that qualified.

These phenomena are all related, but that doesn't mean they are somehow coordinated. The backlash is not a conspiracy, with a council dispatching agents from some central control room, nor are the people who serve its ends often aware of their role: some even consider themselves feminists. For the most part, its workings are encoded and internalized, diffuse and chameleonic. Not all of the manifestations of the backlash are of equal weight or significance either; some are mere ephemera, generated by a culture machine that is always scrounging for a "fresh" angle. Taken as a whole, however, these codes and cajolings, these whispers and threats and myths, move overwhelmingly in one direction: they try to push women back into their "acceptable" roles—whether as Daddy's girl or fluttery romantic, active nester or passive love object.

Although the backlash is not an organized movement, that doesn't make it any less destructive. In fact, the lack of orchestration, the absence of a single string-puller, only makes it harder to see—and perhaps more effective. A backlash against women's rights succeeds to the degree that it appears *not* to be political, that it appears not to be a struggle at all. It is most powerful when it goes private, when it lodges inside a woman's mind and turns her vision inward, until she imagines the pressure is all in her head, until she begins to enforce the backlash, too—on herself.

In the last decade, the backlash has moved through the culture's secret chambers, traveling through passageways of flattery and fear. Along the way, it has adopted disguises: a mask of mild derision or the painted face of deep "concern." Its lips profess pity for any woman who won't fit the mold, while it tries to clamp the mold around her ears. It pursues a divide-and-conquer strategy: single versus married women, working women versus homemakers, middle- versus working-class. It manipulates a system of rewards and punishments, elevating women who follow its rules, isolating those who don't. The backlash remarkets old myths about women as new facts and ignores all appeals to reason. Cornered, it denies its own existence, points an accusatory finger at feminism, and burrows deeper underground.

Backlash happens to be the title of a 1947 Hollywood movie in which a man frames his wife for a murder he's committed. The backlash against women's rights works in much the same way: its rhetoric charges feminists with all the crimes it perpetrates. The backlash line blames the women's movement for the "feminization of poverty"—while the backlash's own instigators in Washington pushed through the budget cuts that helped impoverish millions of women, fought pay equity proposals, and undermined equal opportunity laws. The backlash line claims the women's movement cares nothing for children's rights—while its own representatives in the capital and state legislatures have blocked one bill after another to improve child care, slashed billions of dollars in federal aid for children, and relaxed state licensing standards for day care centers. The backlash line accuses the women's movement of creating a generation of unhappy single and childless women—but its purveyors in the media are the ones guilty of making single and childless women feel like circus freaks.

To blame feminism for women's "lesser life" is to miss entirely the point of feminism, which is to win women a wider range of experience. Feminism remains a pretty simple concept, despite repeated—and enormously effective—efforts to dress it up in greasepaint and turn its proponents into gargoyles. As Rebecca West wrote sardonically in 1913, "I myself have never been able to find out precisely what feminism is: I only know that people call me a feminist whenever I express sentiments that differentiate me from a doormat."

The meaning of the word "feminist" has not really changed since it first appeared in a book review in the *Athenaeum* of April 27, 1895, describing a woman who "has in her the capacity of fighting her way back to independence." It is the basic proposition that, as Nora put it in Ibsen's *A Doll's House* a century ago, "Before everything else I'm a human being." It is the simply worded sign hoisted by a little girl in the 1970 Women's Strike for Equality: I AM NOT A BARBIE DOLL. Feminism asks the world to recognize at long last that women aren't decorative ornaments, worthy vessels, members of a "special-interest group." They are half (in fact, now more than half) of the national population, and just as deserving of rights and opportunities, just as capable of participating in the world's events, as the other half. Feminism's agenda is basic: It asks that women not be forced to "choose" between public justice and private happiness. It asks that women be free to define themselves—instead of having their identity defined for them, time and again, by their culture and their men.

The fact that these are still such incendiary notions should tell us

45

that American women have a way to go before they enter the promised land of equality.

For Journals

How do you define the term *feminism*?

For Discussion

1.   According to Faludi, what is the real reason for women's unhappiness in contemporary American society? What role do men play in this
reason?

2.   Reread the first two paragraphs of the selection. In what ways
does the introduction set the approach, direction, and tone for the rest
of the argument?

3.   Faludi's basic assertion is that there has been a backlash, or resistance, against gains in women's rights. Examine her key points and
supporting evidence. Are you persuaded by her assertions and her
supporting evidence that there is, indeed, a backlash? Explain the reasons for your answer.

4.   What are the implications for the American family of what Faludi
is discussing? For example, she cites recent reports in the popular press
about a "man shortage," an "infertility epidemic," and "hysterical"
unwed women (paragraph 4). To what degree are concerns about the
future and stability of families feeding the backlash? Do you think
those fears are unfounded or appropriate?

5.   Faludi cites a range of sources, first to summarize the backlash argument that it is "all that equality that's causing all the pain" (paragraph 6) and then to question what "equality" is under discussion.
Analyze Faludi's use of statistics and sources, in both her representation of the opposing view and in support of her own assertions.

6.   Faludi cites Mona Charen, writing in the conservative *National Review,* who says that feminism has effectively "robbed us of one thing
upon which the happiness of most women rests—men" (paragraph 7).
Do you think a male writer would be likely to make such an assertion
about feminism?

For Writing

1.   Write a dialogue between Faludi and the author of *Keep within
Compass,* Mencken, or Charles Atlas, asserting arguments consistent
with each author's position and refuting the opposing view in the way
you think each author might. Considering your reading of these three

authors and others represented in the chapter, to what degree have the arguments over women's and men's roles changed over the years?

2.   The author cites Rebecca West, who wrote in 1913 that "people call me a feminist whenever I express sentiments that differentiate me from a doormat" (paragraph 45). Drawing from your journal writings, this article, other readings you have done, or conversations and experiences you have had, define what you mean by "feminist" and argue that feminism is, or is not, ultimately beneficial to women, men, and families.

A FAMILY LEGACY
1992

Marian Wright Edelman

Marian Wright Edelman (1939–   ), attorney and founding president of the Children's Defense Fund, is one of five children of a Baptist minister. She graduated from Spelman College, a historically black institution, and Yale Law School; she was the first woman to pass the state bar exam in Mississippi. Edelman has spent her professional life as an activist for disadvantaged Americans, especially children. She has received many honors and awards, and her writings include Children out of School in America *(1974),* Black and White Children in America *(1980), and* Families in Peril: An Agenda for Social Change *(1987). The essay that follows is the first chapter of her book* The Measure of Our Success: A Letter to My Children and Yours.

South Carolina is my home state and I am the aunt, granddaughter, daughter, and sister of Baptist ministers. Service was as essential a part of my upbringing as eating and sleeping and going to school. The church was a hub of Black children's social existence, and caring Black adults were buffers against the segregated and hostile outside world that told us we weren't important. But our parents said it wasn't so, our teachers said it wasn't so, and our preachers said it wasn't so. The message of my racially segregated childhood was clear: let no man or woman look down on you, and look down on no man or woman.

We couldn't play in public playgrounds or sit at drugstore lunch counters and order a Coke, so Daddy built a playground and canteen behind the church. In fact, whenever he saw a need, he tried to respond. There were no Black homes for the aged in Bennettsville, so he began one across the street for which he and Mama and we children cooked and served and cleaned. And we children learned that it was our responsibility to take care of elderly family members and neighbors, and that everyone was our neighbor. My mother carried on the home after Daddy died, and my brother Julian has carried it on to this day behind our church since our mother's death in 1984.

Finding another child in my room or a pair of my shoes gone was far from unusual, and twelve foster children followed my sister and me and three brothers as we left home.

Child-rearing and parental work were inseparable. I went everywhere with my parents and was under the watchful eye of members of the congregation and community who were my extended parents. They kept me when my parents went out of town, they reported on and chided me when I strayed from the straight and narrow of community expectations, and they basked in and supported my achievements when I did well. Doing well, they made clear, meant high academic achievement, playing piano in Sunday school or singing or participating in other church activities, being helpful to somebody, displaying good manners (which is nothing more than consideration toward others), and reading. My sister Olive reminded me recently that the only time our father would not give us a chore ("Can't you find something constructive to do?" was his most common refrain) was when we were reading. So we all read a lot! We learned early what our parents and extended community "parents" valued. Children were taught—not by sermonizing, but by personal example—that nothing was too lowly to do. I remember a debate my parents had when I was eight or nine as to whether I was too young to go with my older brother, Harry, to help clean the bed and bedsores of a very sick, poor woman. I went and learned just how much the smallest helping hands and kindness can mean to a person in need.

5   The ugly external voices of my small-town, segregated childhood (as a very young child I remember standing and hearing former South Carolina Senator James Byrnes railing on the local courthouse lawn about how Black children would never go to school with whites) were tempered by the internal voices of parental and community expectation and pride. My father and I waited anxiously for the *Brown* v. *Board of Education* decision in 1954. We talked about it and what it would mean for my future and for the future of millions of other Black children. He died the week before *Brown* was decided. But I and other children lucky enough to have caring and courageous parents and other

adult role models were able, in later years, to walk through the new and heavy doors that *Brown* slowly and painfully opened—doors that some are trying to close again today.

The adults in our churches and community made children feel valued and important. They took time and paid attention to us. They struggled to find ways to keep us busy. And while life was often hard and resources scarce, we always knew who we were and that the measure of our worth was inside our heads and hearts and not outside in our possessions or on our backs. We were told that the world had a lot of problems; that Black people had an extra lot of problems, but that we were able and obligated to struggle and change them; that being poor was no excuse for not achieving; and that extra intellectual and material gifts brought with them the privilege and responsibility of sharing with others less fortunate. In sum, we learned that service is the rent we pay for living. It is the very purpose of life and not something you do in your spare time.

When my mother died, an old white man in my hometown of Bennettsville asked me what I do. In a flash I realized that in my work at the Children's Defense Fund I do exactly what my parents did—just on a different scale. My brother preached a wonderful sermon at Mama's funeral, but the best tribute was the presence in the back pew of the town drunk, whom an observer said he could not remember coming to church in many years.

The legacies that parents and church and teachers left to my generation of Black children were priceless but not material: a living faith reflected in daily service, the discipline of hard work and stick-to-it-ness, and a capacity to struggle in the face of adversity. Giving up and "burnout" were not part of the language of my elders—you got up every morning and you did what you had to do and you got up every time you fell down and tried as many times as you had to to get it done right. They had grit. They valued family life, family rituals, and tried to be and to expose us to good role models. Role models were of two kinds: those who achieved in the outside world (like Marian Anderson, my namesake) and those who didn't have a whole lot of education or fancy clothes but who taught us by the special grace of their lives the message of Christ and Tolstoy and Gandhi and Heschel and Dorothy Day and Romero and King that the Kingdom of God was within—in what you are, not what you have. I still hope I can be half as good as Black church and community elders like Miz Lucy McQueen, Miz Tee Kelly, and Miz Kate Winston, extraordinary women who were kind and patient and loving with children and others and who, when I went to Spelman College, sent me shoeboxes with chicken and biscuits and greasy dollar bills.

It never occurred to any Wright child that we were not going to college or were not expected to share what we learned and earned with the less fortunate. I was forty years old before I figured out, thanks to my brother Harry's superior insight, that my Daddy often responded to our requests for money by saying he didn't have any change because he *really* didn't have any rather than because he had nothing smaller than a twenty dollar bill.

10   I was fourteen years old the night my Daddy died. He had holes in his shoes but two children out of college, one in college, another in divinity school, and a vision he was able to convey to me as he lay dying in an ambulance that I, a young Black girl, could be and do anything; that race and gender are shadows; and that character, self-discipline, determination, attitude, and service are the substance of life.

I have always believed that I could help change the world because I have been lucky to have adults around me who did—in small and large ways. Most were people of simple grace who understood what Walker Percy wrote: You can get all As and still flunk life.

Life was not easy back in the 1940s and 1950s in rural South Carolina for many parents and grandparents. We buried children who died from poverty (and I can't stand it that we still do). Little Johnny Harrington, three houses down from my church parsonage, stepped on and died from a nail because his grandmother had no doctor to advise her, nor the money to pay for health care. (Half of all low-income urban children under two are still not fully immunized against preventable childhood diseases like tetanus and polio and measles.) My classmate, Henry Munnerlyn, broke his neck when he jumped off the bridge into the town creek because only white children were allowed in the public swimming pool. I later heard that the creek where Blacks swam and fished was the hospital sewage outlet. (Today thousands of Black children in our cities and rural areas are losing their lives to cocaine and heroin and alcohol and gang violence because they don't have enough constructive outlets.) The migrant family who collided with a truck on the highway near my home and the ambulance driver who refused to take them to the hospital because they were Black still live in my mind every time I hear about babies who die or are handicapped from birth when they are turned away from hospitals in emergencies or their mothers are turned away in labor because they have no health insurance and cannot pay pre-admission deposits to enter a hospital. I and my brothers and sister might have lost hope—as so many young people today have lost hope—except for the stable, caring, attentive adults in our family, school, congregation, civic and political life who struggled with and for us against the obstacles we faced and provided us positive alternatives and the sense of possibility we needed.

At Spelman College in Atlanta, I found my Daddy and Mama's values about taking responsibility for your own learning and growth reinforced in the daily (except Saturday) chapel service. Daily chapel attendance was compulsory and enforced by the threat of points taken off one's earned grade average as a result of truancy. For all my rebellion then, I remember now far more from the chapel speakers who came to talk to us about life and the purpose of education than from any class. And during my tenure as chairwoman of Spelman's board, I advocated reinstitution of some compulsory assemblies (monthly, not daily!) so our young women would have to hear what we adults think is important.

Many of my mentors and role models, such as Dr. Benjamin Mays, then president of Morehouse College, Whitney Young, dean of the School of Social Work at Atlanta University and later National Urban League head, M. Carl Holman, a professor at Clark College, later head of the National Urban Coalition, Dr. Howard Thurman, dean of the Chapel at Boston University, and Dr. King, all conveyed the same message as they spoke in Sisters Chapel at Spelman: education is for improving the lives of others and for leaving your community and world better than you found it. Other important influences during my Spelman years—Ella Baker, Septima Clark, Howard Zinn, Charles E. Merrill, Jr., and Samuel Dubois Cook—stretched my vision of the future and of one person's ability to help shape it. I'm still trying to live up to their teachings and to the examples of the extraordinary ordinary people whom I had the privilege to serve and learn from after law school during my civil rights sojourn in Mississippi between 1963 and 1968.

Fannie Lou Hamer, Amzie Moore, Winson and Dovie Hudson, Mae Bertha Carter, school desegregation and voting rights pioneers in Mississippi, and Unita Blackwell, who rose from sharecropper to mayor of rural Mayersville, Mississippi—and countless courageous men and women who gave their voices and homes and lives to get the right to vote and to secure for their children a better life than they had—guide and inspire me still. Those largely unknown and usually unlettered people of courage and commitment, along with my parents, remind me each day to keep trying and to let my little light shine, as Mrs. Hamer sang and did through her inspiring life. In a D.C. neighborhood church, I recently saw a banner that reminded me "there is not enough darkness in the world to snuff out the light of even one small candle."

I have always felt extraordinarily blessed to live in the times I have. As a child and as an adult—as a Black woman—I have had to struggle to understand the world around me. Most Americans remember Dr. King as a great leader. I do too. But I also remember him as someone able to admit how often he was afraid and unsure about his next step. But faith prevailed over fear and uncertainty and fatigue and depression. It was his human vulnerability and his ability to rise above it that I most remember. In this, he was not different from many Black adults whose credo has been to make "a way out of no way."

The Children's Defense Fund was conceived in the cauldron of Mississippi's summer project of 1964 and in the Head Start battles of 1965, where both the great need for and limits of local action were apparent. As a private civil rights lawyer, I learned that I could have only limited, albeit important, impact on meeting epidemic family and child needs in that poor state without coherent national policy and investment strategies to complement community empowerment strategies. I also learned that critical civil and political rights would not mean much to a hungry, homeless, illiterate child and family if they lacked the social and economic means to exercise them. And so children—my own and other people's—became the passion of my personal and professional life. For it is they who are God's presence, promise, and hope for humankind.

For Journals

How do you think American families measure their success? What kinds of achievements or possessions are often used to measure success?

For Discussion

1. The subtitle of Edelman's book, of which this selection is the first chapter, is "A Letter to My Children and Yours." Why do you believe Edelman is addressing her remarks to these audiences? How do the audiences shape her message?

2. Edelman and the children of her community grew up knowing that they were valued and important. How did the adults of the community transmit these beliefs? What were the adults' expectations of the children? What did the children assume about their role in the community?

3. Edelman writes of the legacies from her family and community— of service, of doing for others, of making the most of intellectual and material gifts. How have such legacies changed her life? How have they influenced her work?

4. Edelman concludes, "Service is the rent we pay for living" (paragraph 6). What are the assumptions on which she bases this statement?

5. Edelman's community served as an extended family in supporting her and other children. In what ways was her upbringing like, and unlike, that of children growing up in the 1980s and 1990s? What has changed for the better? For the worse? What has not changed?

6. Edelman writes that her father died with "holes in his shoes but two children out of college, one in college, another in divinity school, and a vision" (paragraph 10). How does Edelman's measure of her father's success compare to, and contrast with, statements of family values and beliefs evident in other readings in this book? (Look, for example, at the excerpt from Mary Antin's *The Promised Land* and Martin Luther King, Jr.'s "I Have a Dream," both in Chapter 4.)

For Writing

1. Write an essay examining, and explaining, the values and beliefs with which you were raised. What did you learn about your role in the family? In the community? What were the expectations of your parents and any extended family you have? You could focus on education, community involvement, music, or some other aspect of your youth.

2. Research a current issue in children's rights—for example, health care, legal protection, or issues of abuse. In addition to drawing on books, periodicals, and government documents, try to interview people in your community who work on behalf of children in the area you are researching. What are the controversies? Write up your research in a documented essay.

3. Write a letter to the children you have or expect to have, or to nieces or nephews or other relatives. Explain to them the legacies that you grew up with and that you hope you will pass on to them.

MAKING AND UNMAKING THE "MODEL MINORITY"

1994

John Wu

John Wu is a college student who was born in Taipei, Taiwan, and lived there until 1983. His family then moved to Arcadia, California, where they still live. Wu hopes to pursue a career in film and television; his parents still hope that he will go into law. Wu wrote this researched essay in response to writing assignment number 6, at the end of this chapter, asking him to examine assumptions about his identity and his family values.

Asians in America used to be the "yellow peril" and were considered unassimilable. Today, Asian Americans are the "model minority" and are seemingly assimilating into the white, middle-class mainstream. This change in public perception affirms the improving fortune of Asian Americans as a group in recent years. Rosy pictures, however, do not capture the full realities facing this diverse and aggregate population under the rubric of "Asian American." Labeling an entire group overlooks the individuality of its members. Labels lead to generalizations and stereotypes. Generalizations and stereotypes lead to prejudice. And prejudice is the seed of racism. For this reason, many Asian Americans reject the model minority label despite its complimentary nature.

Whether celebrated or renounced, the model minority label carries with it expectations that are uncomfortably familiar to second-generation Asian Americans whose immigrant parents want nothing less for their children than for them to be the "model minority." This familiarity is the source of unease and ambivalence about the outright rejection of the model minority image. Because the sense of familial duty and filial piety is deeply embedded in most Asian cultures, second-generation Asian Americans often feel obligated to live up to the visions of the immigrant parents and to fulfill the American dream.

There are many explanations for why the model minority story emerged. Bob Suzuki, in what is considered the first major rebuttal to the model minority thesis, titled "Education and the Socialization of Asian Americans: A Revisionist Analysis of the 'Model Minority' Thesis," suggests that the timing which coincided with the racial crisis of the sixties was not accidental. He writes: "The activists charged that the actual status of Asian Americans was being deliberately distorted to fit the 'model minority' image in an attempt to discredit the protests and demands for social justice of other minority groups by admonishing them to follow the 'shining example' set by Asian Americans" (Suzuki 24). The concept of model minority absolves the guilt of the white majority for the bleak condition which other minority groups face. It permits white Americans to feel better about America and its history of flagrant racial discrimination and botched race relations.

More important, the model minority story keeps the American dream alive. Americans hold dear the idea that an individual, regardless of any disadvantaged background, can succeed in this society as long as he or she works hard. Commenting on the need of the model minority myth, Ronald Takaki, professor of ethnic studies at the University of California at Berkeley, explains: "Here is a society that is very nervous about the black underclass and gloomy about the economy. These are tough economic times . . . you need a model minority to reassure people, they need to be told the American dream still works . . . 'look at these immigrants, they can still do it'" (qtd. in Kamen). Thus the success of Asian Americans reassures the dominant culture that the American dream is still realizable.

Within the Asian American community, the current debate is no longer whether Asian Americans are the model minority; rather, it is over whether we should completely discard the label or take pride in its positive aspects. What almost all commentators agree on is that the expectations brought about by the model minority stereotype present problems for Asian Americans. Consider the following description in the Washington Post: "Armed with little more than a will to succeed, they open stores where no other entrepreneur will venture. They streak to the top in the technical worlds of computers and mathematics. Their workers are the most dedicated and tireless, their children are the smartest. They are wealthy and self-sufficient" (Kamen). This near-mythical description is an example of the overall depiction of Asian Americans by the media "as industrious and intelligent, enterprising and polite, with good values and strong families, equally successful as children in school and as adults in business and medicine and science and engineering" (Shaw).

These popular media stereotypes create expectations of how Asian Americans are supposed to be. Ironically, these expectations are the same ones that immigrant parents often have of their children. In school, Asian American students are expected to excel. Placing much hope on education as the key to success, parents want and expect their children to work extra hard in school. They accept nothing but the best marks and the highest scores as evidence of hard work and success. Educators also expect Asian American students to be brilliant in the classroom, particularly in math and science. These two sources of high expectations create an enormous pressure for Asian American students. Those who cannot deliver perfect scores and top marks often suffer from low self-esteem and low confidence. Some community activists believe that the expectations of the society and the parents are a contributing factor to an increase in suicides among Asian American youth (Kamen).

As adults, Asian Americans have limited career choices because of the model minority label and of parental expectations. Stereotypes of Asian Americans as good in technical fields are not bad in and of themselves. The implication, though, is that Asian Americans are not good in anything else. Hence we see few successful Asian Americans in areas like politics, sports, and entertainment. In fact, many doors to nontechnical fields are virtually dead-bolted to Asian Americans. This limited career track is also enforced by many Asian parents who push their children in certain directions. Having self-sacrificed by leaving a familiar home, immigrant parents place all of their hopes on their children to succeed, to be better than they. They tend to encourage their children to stick to safe fields where success is rewarded by hard work and not by luck.

Asian Americans are also seen as people who "do not rock the boat." This expectation is usually entangled with the stereotype of being quiet and unassertive. Many non-Asians regard Asian Americans as people who are easy to work with but are not leaders, which may explain why few Asian Americans are in the top management level despite the high percentage of professionals in the corporate world. The emphasis on stoicism in many Asian cultures is the other source for the "do not rock the boat" expectation. Immigrant parents usually teach their children not to fight back against harassment or not to complain about academic pressures (Lee). In the same way, the society expects Asian Americans to overcome any obstacles of racism and discrimination. As Leonard Downie, managing editor of the Washington Post, observes, "These are just quiet people who come here, go to work and go to school and do a good job and don't ask for coverage and don't make themselves very visible in the community" (qtd. in Shaw).

Beyond these expectations, the dominant culture and new immigrants share one more thing in common—the American dream. The dominant culture, still embracing the American dream, wishes to believe that American society is colorblind and that individualism is a practicable principle (Chan 171). The model minority tale grants them that wish: Asian Americans are living the American dream because they have the initiative and they work hard. Children of immigrant parents are well aware of the American dream. It is the reason, at least partially, many Asian immigrants have come to the United States. They come in search of better opportunities. With expectations of success conjured by the American dream, immigrant parents self-sacrifice so their children can have a better education, a better career, and a better life. Knowing the sacrifices of the immigrant parents, second-generation Asian Americans feel obligated to work hard to meet the expectations and, in a way, repay the first generation. These are the same expectations as those of the society on Asian Americans in general as a model minority.

10   These expectations exact a psychological toll on Asian Americans. Suzuki explains that "over-anxious attempts by Asian Americans to gain acceptance have stripped them of their dignity and have caused many of them to suffer from severe psychological disorders characterized by lack of confidence, low self-esteem, expressive conformity and alienation" (25). This situation is especially acute among Asian American students. Feeling obligated to succeed, they work extremely hard in school. Their diligence, though praised by teachers, is frowned upon

by non-Asian peers. As a result, Asian American students often feel isolated and alienated. This situation is compounded when Asian American students cannot meet the expectations demanded of them. In essence, they are "doubly burdened" (Shaw). On the one hand, they are attempting to meet the standards of their parents and end up feeling isolated from the peer community. On the other, their inability to meet those standards distances them from their parents.

Because of the pluralist nature of American society, every minority group member feels as if he or she is serving as a model for the group as a whole. As Asian Americans, we constantly feel as if we have to prove ourselves to white Americans that we are just as "good." Perhaps we have achieved our goal because we are now a model minority. But because we do not have our individuality, we are not as "good" as they.

Labels and stereotypes hinder individuality. The model minority myth precludes the possibility that some Asian Americans may not be upwardly mobile and successful. Yet our parents expect us to become upwardly mobile and successful. Our parents' expectations personalize the society's model minority expectations for us. For second-generation Asian Americans, the Asian sense of duty to the family and filial piety still runs strong. We feel obligated to live up to the goals of our parents. At the same time, we want to be our own person; we want to be successful on our own terms. We want to reject the labels and the stereotypes but we cannot deny the positive achievements of Asian Americans. We are in a schizophrenic state of trying to become the "model minority" for our parents while trying to unmake the "model minority" of white America.

Works Cited

Chan, Sucheng. *Asian Americans: An Interpretive History.* Boston: Twayne, 1991.
Kamen, Al. "Myth of 'model minority' haunts Asian Americans." *Washington Post,* June 22, 1992, A1.
Lee, Felicia. "'Model minority' label taxes Asian youths." *New York Times,* March 20, 1990, B1.
Shaw, David. "Asian-Americans chafe against stereotype of 'model citizen.'" *Los Angeles Times,* December 11, 1990, A31.
Suzuki, Bob. "Education and the socialization of Asian Americans: A revisionist analysis of the 'model minority' thesis." *Amerasia* 4:2 (1977), 23–51.

For Journals

Do people make assumptions about you, based on your ethnicity or gender?

For Discussion

1. Identify the main idea and key supporting points in Wu's essay. To what extent do his own assumptions link and support the evidence to his main idea?

2. What assumptions of society is Wu questioning? Of white American society? Of Asian Americans and their families?

3. To what extent are the values Wu writes about transmitted through families? Through society?

4. If you were to exchange drafts with Wu in peer review, what suggestions would you make for a revision?

For Writing

1. Select a social issue of concern and interest to you and, as Wu does, challenge the assumptions with reasoning and evidence.

2. Do others make assumptions about your family values and beliefs? Write an essay explaining your value system to others with the goal of clarifying misperceptions and communicating what you consider to be a true picture of your value system.

FILMS ON FAMILY VALUES

Although themes about family pervade both early and contemporary films, some films are particularly interesting to examine in view of the assumptions and premises they make or refute about family issues. Select a film with your peers or on your own that you think would provide a rich example, and develop a discussion after reviewing the film. The following list is a starting point:

Housekeeping
It's a Wonderful Life
Little Women
Making Mr. Right
Thelma and Louise
Parenthood
The Good Mother
The Little Foxes

Terms of Endearment
The Prince of Tides
Kramer vs. Kramer
The Color Purple
The Great Santini
Ordinary People
Shoot the Moon
Mermaids
Fried Green Tomatoes
The Joy Luck Club

ASSUMPTIONS

In everyday life we make countless assumptions: that the water will flow out of the tap when we turn it on, that the bus will come more or less on time to take us to school or work. That sometimes the water main breaks or the bus is quite late does not change the fact that we take these things for granted. When we arrive at school, we assume that a paper we turn in will be read and evaluated; we assume that the data we obtain from reliable sources—books, reputable journals, people we trust—are reported accurately. Sometimes we explicitly state the assumptions on which we are operating; for example, we might say, "With inflation holding steady for the rest of the quarter, we predict stable interest rates."

Assumptions are the unseen glue in an argument, providing the connection between the evidence or proof and the conclusions drawn from that proof. They are underlying principles on which we base our claims and part of the shared values or wisdom of a community, whether a society, culture, workplace, or academic discipline. We might conclude, for example, that a family might be dysfunctional based on our own criteria for functional families. Or we might assume that nuclear families have always been the norm, until we reflect on other community structures such as clans, tribes, and the like, or research alternative families in American history.

There is nothing inherently bad about assumptions; life would be extremely difficult if we had to start from scratch every day. But critical readers and careful writers do need to recognize assumptions in arguments, particularly those that are unstated. Careful readers question assumptions in the arguments they read, interrogating the text (or image) and writing notes in the margins or a notebook: "Who says? Why do you say that? Do you have any proof? Why did you draw that conclusion?" They will check for missing links between evidence and claim, or a jump from reason to conclusion that does not seem warranted by the reason itself. In addition to asking questions, one can diagram a selection by blocking out on paper the conclusion and the specific reasons that support it, and then examine them for underlying assumptions.

Analyzing Assumptions in Arguments

The American family is a subject that taps into our emotions, values, beliefs, and principles. Ongoing arguments about the form and role of families, marriage, and children, about relations within and between families, nearly always rest on assumptions with which we were raised in our own families, whether the core issue is power, or control of sexuality, or the treatment of children as property and potential labor, or the transmission of property and family names.

Within this chapter, the arguments, both verbal and visual, depend on assumptions as their taking-off point. Sometimes writers or illustrators assume that an assumption is so deep-seated in the society that most readers or viewers will concur with an argument based on that assumption. *Keep within Compass* aimed at defining proper behavior for women; the author depends on assumptions about the image of women that women—and men—would find appealing: the woman industriously doing needlework as she walks on the grounds of a pleasant estate. Contrasted with this assumption about how women *should* behave are fairly lurid portrayals of what the Fates have in store for unvirtuous women. The Charles Atlas advertisement assumes that men want muscular bodies and that women prefer such men; its creators also hoped that readers would assume that the Atlas system would work as it apparently did for Atlas. Bruce Fein assumes that readers share his assumptions that two-parent, two-gender nuclear families are best for children. Marian Wright Edelman writes movingly of the assumptions of her childhood family and community and the ways in which those assumptions, or shared values and beliefs, have guided her life and her life's work.

Often, arguments about families in America have focused on challenging or refuting assumptions. Sara Winnemucca Hopkins's persuasive purpose, for example, is to challenge the assumptions of white Americans about American Indians. H. L. Mencken articulates and explodes assumptions that women are sentimental and romantic, arguing instead that they are the opposite—pragmatic to the point of being calculating. Keenan Peck, too, challenges readers' assumptions about what makes a family a family—questioning the very definition of the word "family" and developing a new definition based on different assumptions. In her short story "American Horse," Louise Erdrich illustrates the clash between assumptions and expectations of a white social worker and the outside society she represents, and the values of the American Indian family she comes to "save." Susan Faludi spends considerable effort and evidence challenging two core assumptions—that women are unhappy and that they are "equal"—in order to question the conclusion drawn by critics of feminism that "all that equality" must be making women unhappy.

Using Assumptions in Arguments

Your own argumentation will likely involve one of the noted strategies: relying on assumptions to make your argument and to support your reasoning from the evidence to the conclusion; and challenging assumptions made by others in their arguments. Be careful in relying on assumptions. Your most basic step will be analyzing your audience. If you and they share assumptions, beliefs, and values, your efforts to persuade can focus on establishing that common ground, in the same way that you establish common definitions of terms as the basis for argument. Perhaps you will need to remind the audience of those shared values. In doing so, you will increase your audience's identification with you and encourage them to listen to you and to your argument. As you proceed, gauge when to offer additional support of your view and when to assume that the audience shares your view and needs no further convincing.

In academic writing, you should be alert to appropriate and inappropriate assumptions about knowledge and procedure. If, for example, you are writing a researched essay about string theory or dark matter for your writing course, you should not assume that your instructor has more than a generalist's familiarity with the concepts of physics; nor would you be especially persuasive if you assumed your physics instructor would understand an analogy made to the theory of archetypes in literary criticism. Each discipline has its own set of assumptions and beliefs, and familiarizing yourself with those beliefs is part of your training as a scholar.

If you are writing for an audience whose assumptions and values you are not familiar with or if you are communicating to audiences with diverse values, you need to spend more time supporting the claims you make as you go, never assuming that your audiences agree with you and always checking to see if you are offering enough evidence and reasons to support your view. For example, if you want to persuade your classmates that money from your residence hall or living group discretionary or social funds should not be used to pay for alcohol for dorm events, you need to figure out what your fellow students' assumptions are. Do they believe that social funds should pay for social events, and that social events for college students must necessarily offer alcoholic beverages? Do they assume that fees collected from everyone should support the drinking habits of some residents, in the manner that everyone pays taxes even if they don't support government policy? Do they assume that laws governing consumption of alcohol by minors should be suspended for college social functions?

When you are writing to refute assumptions, you need to be particularly careful to inform yourself fully about what you are trying to disprove. Why do people hold on to this or that particular belief? What in their experiences might account for their assumptions? How fixed are the assumptions? Are they movable or unmovable? Do you need to do research to arm yourself with data to counter what you believe are frequently held but generally unexamined assumptions?

Usually you will need to be direct when writing to refute assumptions. Lay out your argument within the first couple of paragraphs, including a clear summary of the idea you are trying to disprove and a powerful statement of your own thesis. Support each point you make—*for* your argument, *against* the assumption under discussion—with reasons backed by evidence, logical as well as emotional. Look carefully at your argument and that of your opposition to make sure that no assumptions go unstated. Spell out your own points, and, if necessary, make a list of all the assumptions, both explicitly stated and implicit, in the opposing argument. You probably do not need to present every item on that list in your own argument, but having made it will ensure that you do not overlook important nuances of the structure and substance of the opposing argument.

WRITING ASSIGNMENTS

1.   Select a reading in this chapter, and diagram it for the assumptions on which it rests. Put the main point in a box at the top of the page and then draw boxes and connecting lines showing the supporting assumptions and reasons. How do you think the writer selected which assumptions to state explicitly and which ones would be understood or automatically accepted by the audience?

2.   Examine a piece of artwork that appears in another chapter in this book. Articulate the implicit and explicit assumptions, and write an

essay analyzing what such assumptions tell us about the audiences for the image.

3.   Develop your own argument on the subject of women's or men's proper role in society, or on same-gender domestic partnerships, on interracial adoption, or on some other social issue of concern to you. Exchange essays with a peer, preferably one who has taken an opposing view or has written on a different subject. Write refutations of each other's essays, and turn in both originals and refutations. Did you find yourselves refuting primarily the assumptions, the reasons, the conclusions drawn, or some of each part of the argument in equal amounts?

4.   Examine your own assumptions about family and gender. Do some private freewriting, reflecting on how you have come to hold those values and beliefs. What are your assumptions about family life? The work ethic? Dating roles? Parental roles? Friendship between genders? Marriage/partnership roles? Write a reflective essay exploring the process through which you have come to hold these particular beliefs or assumptions.

5.   Interview your parents or grandparents or other people of their generations; ask them about the assumptions they grew up with about dating, gender roles, or family and parental duties. Do they still hold those assumptions? What do they think of current assumptions? Write an essay summarizing your findings and share it with other class members. Alternatively, compare the assumptions held by the people you interviewed with those you hold, and analyze the similarities and differences.

6.   In a group, and if everyone is willing to share, put up butcher paper around the classroom and have everyone write his or her name, ethnic background, parents' and grandparents' occupations, their sayings, proverbs, legacies (ideas/things they've passed down to you). After everyone has written the above and other items you all may wish to add, silently review the material, looking for connections, themes, values, assumptions that emerge. Discuss as a class, or write up your reflections, privately, or to share.

7.   Design a flyer to inform an audience about a social issue. Write an essay explaining your design, focusing on the assumptions you made about your audience and the premises on which your flyer is based.

CHAPTER

WORK AND SUCCESS

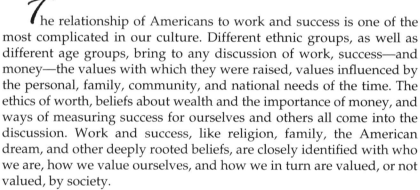

$\mathscr{T}$he relationship of Americans to work and success is one of the most complicated in our culture. Different ethnic groups, as well as different age groups, bring to any discussion of work, success—and money—the values with which they were raised, values influenced by the personal, family, community, and national needs of the time. The ethics of worth, beliefs about wealth and the importance of money, and ways of measuring success for ourselves and others all come into the discussion. Work and success, like religion, family, the American dream, and other deeply rooted beliefs, are closely identified with who we are, how we value ourselves, and how we in turn are valued, or not valued, by society.

Americans believe that everyone deserves at least the chance to be successful; perhaps that's how most would interpret the Declaration of Independence's guarantee of the pursuit of happiness. But they have never agreed on how success is to be achieved or measured and are torn between the Protestant work ethic—a belief in hard work and diligence rewarded by middle-class prosperity—and the fantasy of wealth gained without any work, through the blind luck of buying a winning lottery ticket or marrying the boss's only child.

Between those two extremes, Americans have historically entertained a variety of beliefs about work and success, some of them mutually inconsistent. The Calvinist theology that prevailed in early New England believed that God chooses to save some unworthy souls as a sign of infinite mercy; these fortunate few are called the elect. Gradually that austere faith turned into an assumption that someone living the comfortable life must be doing it with God's help; thus, outward success was viewed proof of good work habits. Calvinism has long since ceased to function as a measure of spirituality, but the connection of high pay, status, and success on the one hand, and personal self-worth, on the other, has remained embedded in American culture and consciousness.

Industrialization, especially after the Civil War, brought factory jobs and long hours. The fortunate few—the elect of industrial America—were the robber barons, railroad, mine, and factory owners who came from poor or ordinary backgrounds and made inconceivably vast amounts of money. Poorer Americans both resented and worshipped them; low pay and terrible working conditions were the reality for most Americans, and their highest goal was to become middle class, but their secret dream was that perhaps their children would do better—much better.

In this century, the traditional American belief that work leads to success remains. However, it is accompanied by a degree of cynicism and even disillusionment prompted by a series of convulsive political and social developments: two world wars; the financial irresponsibility of the 1920s followed by the devastating unemployment and displacement of the Great Depression; the entry of women into the workplace in wartime and their forced return to the home when the wars were over; the first and second waves of the women's movement; the influx of millions of immigrants; and widespread corporate "restructuring" that has led to the loss of many thousands of white-collar jobs.

The most significant American writing about work and money is both a response to and a reflection on the values behind them and the national experience that shaped them. The selections in this chapter sample a spectrum of those values and that experience and provide different answers to an underlying set of questions: Is independence possible without financial security? Is money the best or the only measure of success? Is a high-paying job proof of success in itself? Is middle-class existence enough? Should it be? How much opportunity to succeed do women really have? Is a job with pay a proof of self-worth in America, and, if so, can a woman ever be successful if her financial security is derived solely from her husband's work outside the home rather than from her own work inside it? Can a life dedicated to making money, and only to making money, be deemed successful?

Work and Success Through History

This peculiarly American combination of confidence and questioning, in which dreams of work, money, and success are perpetually adjusted and reinvented, finds expression in this chapter's selections. We follow Ben Franklin as he works overtime to build his printing business, lives frugally, and takes every opportunity to improve himself. But he also makes time for friends and public service, and when he gets rich, purely as a result of his own skill, he quits his work and spends the rest of his life giving money away, practicing international diplomacy, and doing science. He is either the most or the least typical example of the American faith in meritocracy, with talent, intelligence, and hard work inevitably rewarded with both money and success.

The opportunities for American women, however, even decades later at the end of the nineteenth century, remained far more constricted by finances, cultural considerations, or both. The jobs open to poor women were limited to factory and domestic work. The most that educated single women could hope for were jobs as teachers or governesses. And married middle-class women, like Charlotte Perkins Gilman, were barred by Victorian social norms from working outside the home at all. Gilman's analysis of the frustration experienced by talented and ambitious women who were not allowed to compete for money or success in the same arenas as men is an important document in American economics, but it's also a record of her personal experience.

By the time Gilman died in 1934, America was just a few years past the excesses and the self-centered materialism of the 1920s, variously referred to as the Roaring Twenties or, in F. Scott Fitzgerald's term, the Jazz Age. Whatever they were called, the 1920s was a period of great financial prosperity for many Americans; factory production was up, the stock market was up, living standards were up, Prohibition had created a huge black market for illegal liquor, and the possibility of becoming rich and successful without spending a lifetime devoted to the Protestant work ethic had never before seemed so close.

Fitzgerald, who understood the enormous energy behind the American love of success and experienced it himself when he became a very young best-selling author, created in *The Great Gatsby* a hero who could never be anything but American. Gatsby starts poor, gets rich—not through thirty years of working in a bank but through five years of illegal business—and remains a strangely innocent believer in the American ideals of hard work and reward. He knows that getting rich quick isn't easy, but he tries to ignore the cost because he thinks money is the only way to win the woman he loves. For Gatsby, as for Franklin, money is a means to an end, and success is the chance to do what he wants.

By 1937, Fitzgerald was forgotten, drinking too much and writing about disintegration—his own and that of the easy dream of success that had fueled American ambition before the stock market crash of 1929 wiped out 15 million jobs. The poor got poorer, and more than at any other time in our history, the middle class, the primary carrier of our beliefs in the rewards of hard work and the inevitability of success, found itself largely unemployed. The savings of a lifetime were gone when banks failed; frugality and honesty weren't rewarded; confidence in one's ability to mold the future was destroyed.

The Great Depression made an indelible impression on Americans and challenged all their beliefs about the permanence of either money or success. Margaret Bourke-White, a famous photographer for *Time* and *Life* magazines, took many pictures of Americans coping with the terrors of the depression; one of her best photographs, the ironically titled *There's No Way Like the American Way*, captures an image of poor people next to an image of a richer, more secure America than the one they knew.

America didn't fully recover from the Great Depression until the beginning of World War II, when the need for war material put factories on overtime and created an immense need for laborers. Another side effect of the war was that millions of women who had never expected to work outside the home suddenly found themselves recruited for well-paying jobs vacated by the men who had joined the armed forces. For the first time, many found themselves in business, earning money and feeling successful in ways that had traditionally been reserved for men.

As soon as the war ended and the men returned, though, women were rerouted back into domestic life with a vengeance. Magazines like *Woman's Day* emphasized not their lost earning power but their ability to make a good tuna casserole. Men, on the other hand, were expected to provide more and more material proof of their own success at the office: the split-level ranch house in the suburbs, the healthy 2.3 children, and an ever-changing model of American-made car. The Edsel advertisement from 1958 is a classic example of 1950s expectations in this mode.

A more offbeat—and intentionally funnier—examination of how Americans can and do behave when they succeed is Tom Wolfe's description of two midwestern couples on vacation in that monument to conspicuous consumption, Las Vegas. The architecture, the neon lights, the bad taste, the invitation to misbehave, are to Wolfe bizarre manifestations of American materialism packaged to attract people whose values should have kept them away. Wolfe is interested in the work ethic as a force for repression of wilder impulses, and Las Vegas is the perfect place for him to dissect what happens when people who embody that ethic cut loose from it, at least temporarily.

Today many Americans tend to remember the 1950s as a safe time, when men and women knew their roles and America's economic power in the world was unchallenged. But the cracks began to appear early, with the beginnings of the modern civil rights movement and its gradual extension into the mid 1960s, and the turmoil of the Vietnam War. By the mid-1970s, women were reentering the work force for financial reasons—middle-class life was no longer manageable on one income—and a feminist movement, descended from the one Charlotte Perkins Gilman articulated, began to argue for a broadening of women's sphere to include opportunities for more work and more money and the status that went with them.

Gloria Steinem, one of the major spokespersons for this movement, examines the value and importance of work for both men and women. She rejects the notion that men work because they like it and women work only because they have to, a stance she claims evades the issue of personal satisfaction and achievement, which is true for both men and women. Steinem also harks back to Gilman when she addresses the issue of women working at home without financial compensation and says that "the real work revolution won't come until all productive work is rewarded."

Phyllis Rose, on the other hand, composed a tongue-in-cheek paen of praise to the ubiquitous manifestation of Americans' ability to enjoy the rewards of financial success: the shopping mall. Writing as a middle-class woman with a career and financial independence, she dwells on what she calls the spiritual pleasure of shopping—not buying, which bespeaks a need for something, but looking and not needing anything and therefore being able to enjoy how much there is. Whether Gilman had mall worship in mind when she argued for women's financial rights is another question. But Rose, like Wolfe, understands that for Americans, one of the rewards of earning money and feeling successful is the pleasure of reveling in one's power to consume at leisure what society has to offer.

Another recurrent element in the continuing argument about what constitutes success in America and how work should be valued turns up in Alfred Lubrano's "Bricklayer's Boy," a moving memoir by a man raised by a blue-collar father he respects but from whom he is separated, financially and educationally, by his rise into the middle class and the world of white-collar work and values. Like Fitzgerald, Lubrano recognizes the darker side of the work ethic. Like Steinem, although from an entirely different perspective, he is an example of the way contemporary writers reevaluate that ethic.

Finally, because factory work is still the entry level for Americans trying to inch up the ladder, particularly women without education or skill, and because success in America is still a dream for so many Americans, this chapter closes with a student essay by Judy Ou on the employment and exploitation of Asian women in the garment industry today.

Justifying Work and Success through Assertions

The writers of the selections in this chapter all tend to express their ideas about work and money as assertions—strong positive statements not necessarily supported by evidence but said with great confidence. Every culture has subjects that are particularly sensitive, and for Americans one of those subjects is work and success: who has them, who doesn't, how society excludes someone who lacks them, and how far someone is willing to go to get them. Perhaps because questions of value—blue collar versus white collar, women's work at home or in the marketplace, what people want for themselves and for their children, what makes them feel that they have succeeded—are the result of our upbringing, our parents' experiences, and enormous social pressures, they are not susceptible to obvious proofs but arouse profound feelings.

Feelings about work and success are articulated in this chapter in various forms, but the intensity with which these authors assert their ideas is itself an article of faith—faith in limitless opportunity, an ability to overcome obstacles, and even a willingness to confront the ambition, materialism, and competitiveness that live in the darker side of the American dream. As you read these selections, think about your own ideals of work and success: What are they? Where did they come from? Why are they important to you?

FROM *AUTOBIOGRAPHY*
1771

Benjamin Franklin

Benjamin Franklin (1706–1790) had established himself as a printer, writer, and public servant in Philadelphia by the time he was twenty-four years old. He was so successful that he retired from business at the age of forty-two and spent the next forty-two years of his life in the service of philanthropy, science, and the young country he had helped to found. Franklin wrote his Autobiography *in 1771. (See Chapter 4 for another excerpt.) The excerpt that follows describes how he started his printing business, with type shipped over from London, and how he built the business, his reputation, and his fortune. It also shows him in one of his many experiments—this one personal rather than scientific—which he recounts with characteristic self-mockery.*

We had not been long return'd to Philadelphia, before the New Types arriv'd from London—We settled with Keimer, & left him by his Consent before he heard of it.—We found a House to hire near the Market, and took it. To lessen the Rent, (which was then but 24£ a Year tho' I have since known it let for 70) We took in Tho§Godfrey a Glazier, & his Family, who were to pay a considerable Part of it to us, and we to board with them. We had scarce opened our Letters & put our Press in Order, before George House, an Acquaintance of mine, brought a Countryman to us; whom he had met in the Street enquiring for a Printer. All our Cash was now expended in the Variety of Particulars we had been obliged to procure, & this Countryman's Five Shillings, being our First Fruits & coming so seasonably, gave me more Pleasure than any Crown I have since earn'd; and from the Gratitude I felt towards House, has made me often more ready than perhaps I should otherwise have been to assist young Beginners. . . .

Brientnal particularly procur'd us from the Quakers, the Printing 40 Sheets of their History, the rest being to be done by Keimer: and upon this we work'd exceeding hard, for the Price was low. . . . I compos'd of it a Sheet a Day, and Meredith work'd it off at Press. It was often 11 at Night and sometimes later, before I had finish'd my Distribution for the next days Work: For the little Jobbs sent in by our other Friends now & then put us back. But so determin'd I was to continue doing a Sheet a Day of the Folio, that one Night when having impos'd my Forms, I thought my Days Work over, one of them by accident was broken and two Pages reduc'd to Pie. I immediately distributed & compos'd it over again before I went to bed. And this Industry visible to our Neighbours began to give us Character and Credit; particularly I was told, that mention being made of the new Printing Office at the Merchants Every-night-Club, the general Opinion was that it must fail, there being already two Printers in the Place, Keimer & Bradford; but Doctor Baird . . . gave a contrary Opinion; for the Industry of that Franklin, says he, is superior to any thing I ever saw of the kind: I see him still at work when I go home from Club; and he is at Work again before his Neighbours are out of bed. This struck the rest, and we soon after had Offers from one of them to supply us with Stationary. But as yet we did not chuse to engage in Shop Business.

I soon after obtain'd, thro' my Friend Hamilton, the Printing of the NewCastle Paper Money, another profitable Jobb, as I then thought it; small Things appearing great to those in small Circumstances. And these to me were really great Advantages, as they were great Encouragements.—He procured me also the Printing of the Laws and Votes of that Government which continu'd in my Hands as long as I follow'd the Business.—

I now open'd a little Stationer's Shop. I had in it Blanks of all Sorts the correctest that ever appear'd among us, being assisted in that by my Friend Brientnal; I had also Paper, Parchment, Chapmen's Books, &c. One Whitemash a Compositor I had known in London, an excellent Workman now came to me & work'd with me constantly & diligently, and I took an Apprentice the Son of Aquila Rose. I began now gradually to pay off the Debt I was under. . . . In order to secure my Credit and Character as a Tradesmen, I took care not only to be in *Reality* Industrious & frugal, but to avoid all *Appearances* of the Contrary. I drest plainly; I was seen at no Places of idle Diversion; I never went out a-fishing or shooting; a Book, indeed, sometimes debauch'd me from my Work; but that was seldom, snug, & gave no Scandal: and to show that I was not above my Business, I sometimes brought home the Paper I purchas'd at the Stores, thro' the Streets on a Wheelbarrow. Thus being esteem'd an industrious thriving young Man, and paying duly for what I bought, the Merchants who imported Stationary solicited my Custom, others propos'd supplying me with Books, & I went on swimmingly.—In the mean time Keimer's Credit & Business declining daily, he was at last forc'd to sell his Printing-house to satisfy his Creditors. He went to Barbadoes, & there lived some Years, in very poor Circumstances.

5   But now another Difficulty came upon me, which I had never the least Reason to expect. Mr. Meredith's Father, who was to have paid for our Printing House according to the Expectations given me, was able to advance only one Hundred Pounds, Currency, which had been paid, & a Hundred more was due to the Merchant; who grew impatient & su'd us all. We gave Bail, but saw that if the Money could not be rais'd in time, the Suit must come to a Judgment & Execution, & our hopeful Prospects must with us be ruined, as the Press & Letters must be sold for Payment, perhaps at half-Price.—In this Distress two true Friends whose Kindness I have never forgotten nor ever shall forget while I can remember any thing, came to me separately unknown to each other, and without any Application from me, offering each of them to advance me all the Money that should be necessary to enable me to take the whole Business upon my self if that should be practicable, but they did not like my continuing the Partnership with Meredith, who as they said was often seen drunk in the Streets, & playing at low Games in Alehouses, much to our Discredit. These two Friends were *William Coleman* & *Robert Grace*. I told them I could not propose a Separation while any Prospect remain'd of the Merediths fulfilling

their Part of our Agreement. Because I thought my self under great Obligations to them for what they had done & would do if they could. But if they finally fail'd in their Performance, & our Partnership must be dissolv'd, I should then think myself at Liberty to accept the Assistance of my Friends. Thus the matter rested for some time. When I said to my Partner, perhaps your Father is dissatisfied at the Part you have undertaken in this Affair of ours, and is unwilling to advance for you & me what he would for you alone: If that is the Case, tell me, and I will resign the whole to you & go about my Business. No—says he, my Father has really been disappointed and is really unable; and I am unwilling to distress him farther. I see this is a Business I am not fit for. I was bred a Farmer, and it was a Folly in me to come to Town & put my self at 30 Years of Age an Apprentice to learn a new Trade. Many of our Welsh People are going to settle in North Carolina where Land is cheap: I am inclin'd to go with them, & follow my old Employment. You may find Friends to assist you. If you will take the Debts of the Company upon you, return to my Father the hundred Pound he has advanc'd, pay my little personal Debts, and give me Thirty Pounds & a new Saddle, I will relinquish the Partnership & leave the whole in your Hands. I agreed to this Proposal. It was drawn up in Writing, sign'd & seal'd immediately. I gave him what he demanded & he went soon after to Carolina; from whence he sent me next Year two long Letters, containing the best Account that had been given of that Country, the Climate, Soil, Husbandry, &c. for in those Matters he was very judicious. I printed them in the Papers, and they gave grate Satisfaction to the Publick.

As soon as he was gone, I recurr'd to my two Friends; and because I would not give an unkind Preference to either, I took half what each had offered & I wanted, of one, & half of the other; paid off the Company Debts, and went on with the Business in my own Name, advertising that the Partnership was dissolved. I think this was in or about the Year 1729. . . .

It was about this time that I conceiv'd the bold and arduous Project of arriving at moral Perfection. I wish'd to live without committing any Fault at any time; I would conquer all that either Natural Inclination, Custom, or Company might lead me into. As I knew, or thought I knew, what was right and wrong, I did not see why I might not *always* do the one and avoid the other. But I soon found I had undertaken a Task of more Difficulty than I had imagined: While my Care was employ'd in guarding against one Fault, I was often surpriz'd by another. . . .

The Precept of *Order* requiring that *every Part of my Business should have its allotted Time,* one Page in my little Book contain'd the following Scheme of Employment for the Twenty-four Hours of a natural Day,

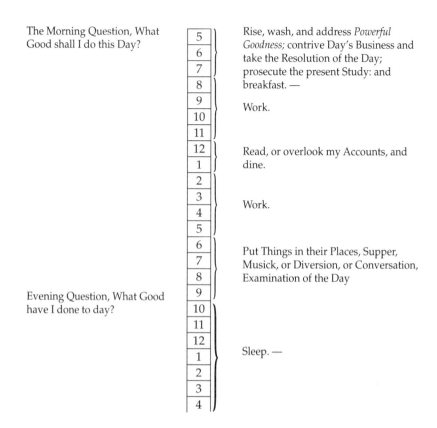

The Morning Question, What
Good shall I do this Day?

5	Rise, wash, and address *Powerful*
6	*Goodness;* contrive Day's Business and
7	take the Resolution of the Day;
8	prosecute the present Study: and
	breakfast. —
9	
10	Work.
11	
12	Read, or overlook my Accounts, and
1	dine.
2	
3	
4	Work.
5	
6	Put Things in their Places, Supper,
7	Musick, or Diversion, or Conversation,
8	Examination of the Day
9	

Evening Question, What Good
have I done to day?

10	
11	
12	
1	Sleep. —
2	
3	
4	

. . . My Scheme of Order, gave me the most Trouble, and I found, that tho' it might be practicable where a Man's Business was such as to leave him the Disposition of his Time, that of a Journey-man Printer for instance, it was not possible to be exactly observ'd by a Master, who must mix with the World, and often receive People of Business at their own Hours.—*Order* too, with regard to Places for Things, Papers, &c. I found extreamly difficult to acquire. I had not been early accustomed to it, & having an exceeding good Memory, I was not so sensible of the Inconvenience attending Want of Method. This Article therefore cost me so much painful Attention & my Faults in it vex'd me so much, and I made so little Progress in Amendment, & had such frequent Relapses, that I was almost ready to give up the Attempt, and content my self with a faulty Character in that respect. Like the Man who in buying an Ax of a Smith my Neighbour, desired to have the whole of its Surface as bright as the Edge; the Smith consented to grind it bright for him if he would turn the Wheel. He turn'd while the Smith press'd the broad Face of the Ax hard & heavily on the Stone, which made the

Turning of it very fatiguing. The Man came every now & then from the Wheel to see how the Work went on; and at length would take his Ax as it was without farther Grinding. No, says the Smith, Turn on, turn on; we shall have it bright by and by; as yet 'tis only speckled. Yes, says the Man; but—*I think I like a speckled Ax best.*—And I believe this may have been the Case with many who having for want of some such Means as I employ'd found the Difficulty of obtaining good, & breaking bad Habits, in other Points of Vice & Virtue, have given up the Struggle, & concluded that *a speckled Ax was best.* . . . In Truth I found myself incorrigible with respect to *Order*; and now I am grown old, and my Memory bad, I feel very sensibly the want of it. But on the whole, tho' I never arrived at the Perfection I had been so ambitious of obtaining, but fell far short of it, yet I was by the Endeavour made a better and a happier Man than I otherwise should have been, if I had not attempted it.

For Journals

Do you think Franklin would succeed in a business today if he were starting one? Would his skills still be useful?

For Discussion

1. How would you describe Franklin's work ethic? Why does he work hard? What does he get out of his efforts? What are his own assertions about work? Look for supporting evidence in the text—either quotations or accounts of his work experience.

2. What role does friendship play in Franklin's ability to build a business? What assumptions do you think his friends make about him when they bring him business or loan him money? Do you think his experiences with friends were only helpful in an open society with relatively little competition, like colonial America? Would any of the same patterns be helpful to a businessperson today?

3. Franklin was very open about promoting his reputation as a hard-working and industrious young man. He says, "In order to secure my credit and character as a tradesman, I took care not only to be in reality industrious and frugal, but to avoid all appearances to the contrary" (paragraph 4). What relationship do you think there is between his public advertisement of his hard work and his private success? Could he have one without the other? If he did, would that make his achievements less valuable to him? To you?

4. What do you think was Franklin's attitude toward success? How do you think he would have defined it? Would you define it differently? How much of Franklin's definition do you think has to do with money? Would you describe Franklin's idea of success as typically American? Atypically? Why?

5.   How does the anecdote Franklin tells about the man who took his ax to a smith to be polished, but eventually took it back partly polished, support or not support the assertions he makes about self-improvement? Why would Franklin tell this story about himself?

6.   Franklin believed, at least for a while, that he could get rid of all his bad habits and develop good ones instead. Look at his chart of how he wanted to spend his time every day (paragraph 10). How much of this activity do you regard as work?

For Writing

1.   Write an essay about your own work ethic. Whatever assertions you make about what you think of work and why it is or isn't important to you, try to be aware of the assumptions you are basing your ideas on. Consider the following questions: How important is making money to you? Is that why you work? Would you work if you didn't need the money? What would you do instead? It might be interesting to make up a chart like Franklin's using your own assessment of how your time should be divided up daily for you to get the most out of it.

2.   Starting with Franklin's *Autobiography*, research and write a paper on Philadelphia in the eighteenth century. Consider, for example, what people did for a living, what cultural institutions there were (aside from the ones that Franklin started himself), the role of the Quaker community, what food people ate, and what houses looked like and how they were furnished.

FROM *WOMEN AND ECONOMICS*
1 8 9 8

Charlotte Perkins Gilman

   Born in Hartford, Connecticut, in 1860, Charlotte Perkins Gilman supported herself as an artist, teacher, and governess before discovering her gift for writing. In the 1890s she escaped destitution by publishing short stories

*like "Similar Cases" and "The Yellow Wall Paper," the latter a harrowing
fictionalization of her own experience of nervous breakdown.* Women and
Economics *appeared in 1898 and was hailed as the most important work of
its kind since John Stuart Mill's* Subjugation of Women. *Gilman committed suicide in 1934. She is recognized as one of the intellectual leaders of the
women's movement in American history.*

What we do modifies us more than what is done to us. The freedom of expression has been more restricted in women than the freedom of impression, if that be possible. Something of the world she
lived in she has seen from her barred windows. Some air has come
through the purdah's folds, some knowledge has filtered to her eager
ears from the talk of men. Desdemona learned somewhat of Othello.
Had she known more, she might have lived longer. But in the ever-
growing human impulse to create, the power and will to make, to do,
to express one's new spirit in new forms,—here she has been utterly
debarred. She might work as she had worked from the beginning,—at
the primitive labors of the household; but in the inevitable expansion
of even those industries to professional levels we have striven to hold
her back. To work with her own hands, for nothing, in direct body-
service to her own family,—this has been permitted,—yes, compelled.
But to be and to do anything further from this she has been forbidden.
Her labor has not been limited in kind, but in degree. Whatever she
has been allowed to do must be done in private and alone, the firsthand industries of savage times. . . .

It is painfully interesting to trace the gradual cumulative effect of
these conditions upon women: first, the action of large natural laws,
acting on her as they would act on any other animal; then the evolution of social customs and laws (with her position as the active cause),
following the direction of mere physical forces, and adding heavily to
them; then, with increasing civilization, the unbroken accumulation of
precedent, burnt into each generation by the growing force of education, made lovely by art, holy by religion, desirable by habit; and,
steadily acting from beneath, the unswerving pressure of economic necessity upon which the whole structure rested. These are strong modi-
fying conditions indeed.

The process would have been even more effective and far less
painful but for one important circumstance. Heredity has no Salic law.
Each girl child inherits from her father a certain increasing percentage
of human development, human power, human tendency; and each boy
as well inherits from his mother the increasing percentage of sex-devel-
opment, sex-power, sex-tendency. The action of heredity has been to

equalize what every tendency of environment and education made to differ. This has saved us from such a female as the gypsy moth. It has held up the woman, and held down the man. It has set iron bounds to our absurd effort to make a race with one sex a million years behind the other. But it has added terribly to the pain and difficulty of human life,—a difficulty and a pain that should have taught us long since that we were living on wrong lines. Each woman born, re-humanized by the current of race activity carried on by her father and re-womanized by her traditional position, has had to live over again in her own person the same process of restriction, repression, denial; the smothering "no" which crushed down all her human desires to create, to discover, to learn, to express, to advance. . . .

To the young man confronting life the world lies wide. Such powers as he has he may use, must use. If he chooses wrong at first, he may choose again, and yet again. Not effective or successful in one channel, he may do better in another. The growing, varied needs of all mankind call on him for the varied service in which he finds his growth. What he wants to be, he may strive to get. What he wants to get, he may strive to get. Wealth, power, social distinction, fame,—what he wants he can try for.

5   To the young woman confronting life there is the same world beyond, there are the same human energies and human desires and ambition within. But all that she may wish to have, all that she may wish to do, must come through a single channel and a single choice. Wealth, power, social distinction, fame,—not only these, but home and happiness, reputation, ease and pleasure, her bread and butter,—all, must come to her through a small gold ring. This is a heavy pressure. It has accumulated behind her through heredity, and continued about her through environment. It has been subtly trained into her through education, till she herself has come to think it a right condition, and pours its influence upon her daughter with increasing impetus. Is it any wonder that women are oversexed? But for the constant inheritance from the more human male, we should have been queen bees, indeed, long before this. But the daughter of the soldier and the sailor, of the artist, the inventor, the great merchant, has inherited in body and brain her share of his development in each generation, and so stayed somewhat human for all her femininity.

For Journals

What is your response to Gilman's first assertion: "What we do modifies us more than what is done to us" (paragraph 1)?

For Discussion

1. According to Gilman, what different kinds of conditions have combined to make women dependent? Do you agree with her? If you do not, would you substitute other reasons to support her conclusion?

2. How do you respond to Gilman's views on heredity and its consequences for creativity in both men and women? Identify her central assertion about heredity, and rephrase it in your own terms. Do you accept her reasoning? What evidence do you have, personal or otherwise, to support or deny it?

3. What assertions does Gilman make about the effect of marriage on women's independence? Why is a gold wedding ring such a heavy burden to her? What do you think she would consider a successful woman's life?

4. Gilman is talking about the situation of middle- and upper-middle-class Victorian women. How valid or invalid do you find her assertions about women, independence, and the need for work today? How do you think women who work entirely in the home today feel about their independence or the value of their work?

5. What is your evaluation of Gilman's belief that a young man confronting life can try for anything he wants, do any kind of work he wants, and keep getting new opportunities if the work he is doing doesn't suit him? Do you agree? Why or why not?

6. In her book on the history of American housework, *Never Done,* Susan Strasser writes, "When Charlotte Perkins Gilman described the food of her ideal future, she envisioned kitchenless houses; individuals and families would patronize establishments that served hot cooked food ready to eat, produced according to the industrial principles of the division of labor and economies of scale. Eighty years later her dream has come true at McDonald's." From what you have read of Gilman and what you know of McDonald's, how valid is Strasser's assertion?

For Writing

1. Write an essay in which you analyze a major compromise made by your mother, another female relative, a friend, or you for the sake of financial security. The choice can be personal or professional, and you can argue either for or against it, but, even if you disagree with the result, try to be objective. What reasons or assertions were given or assumed in making the trade-off? What values or beliefs supported it?

What pressures, economic or otherwise, were brought to bear on the person who made the compromise?

2.   Research and write a report to share with your peers about a Victorian American woman who found a way to combine work and marriage, or one who chose work over marriage (for example, political activists Susan B. Anthony and Carrie Chapman Catt, or writers such as Harriet Beecher Stowe, Louisa May Alcott, Kate Chopin, and Edith Wharton). Pay special attention to the economic and social obstacles these women had to struggle with in order to find fulfilling work.

FROM *THE GREAT GATSBY*
1924

F. Scott Fitzgerald

While still in his twenties, F. Scott Fitzgerald (1897–1940) was already famous for his stories and novels. An extremely careful prose stylist, he was never prolific, but he had to produce a lot of short stories for magazines to pay for the expensive life-style he and wife had become accustomed to. By the time he died in 1940 of a heart attack, he had survived years of alcoholism and the decline of his reputation. But he had produced three remarkable novels: The Great Gatsby, Tender Is the Night, *and the unfinished* The Last Tycoon. *Since his death, he has become one of the most widely read and written-about of all American novelists.* The Great Gatsby, *his story of a self-made millionaire with a mysterious background who gives lavish parties in order to pursue a tragic love affair, is his finest creation.*

The story is narrated by Nick Carraway, a young stockbroker originally from the Midwest who lives in a tiny house next to Gatsby's mansion. The first two selections, from Chapters Three and Four, depict the preparations for one of Gatsby's parties and the people who came to them; they intimate that he has made his fortune quickly and illegally. The next excerpt, from Chapter Six, reveals who Gatsby really was and how he got started. The excerpt from Chapter Nine begins after Gatsby, taking the blame for a hit-and-run accident that his lover, Daisy, is responsible for, is murdered by the distraught husband of the victim. Nick is left trying to round up people for the funeral.

Chapter Three

There was music from my neighbor's house through the summer nights. In his blue gardens men and girls came and went like moths among the whisperings and the champagne and the stars. At high tide in the afternoon I watched his guests diving from the tower of his raft or taking the sun on the hot sand of his beach while his two motor boats slit the waters of the Sound, drawing aquaplanes over cataracts of foam. On week-ends his Rolls-Royce became an omnibus, bearing parties to and from the city, between nine in the morning and long past midnight, while his station wagon scampered like a brisk yellow bug to meet all trains. And on Mondays eight servants including an extra gardener toiled all day with mops and scrubbing-brushes and hammers and garden shears, repairing the ravages of the night before.

Every Friday five crates of oranges and lemons arrived from a fruiterer in New York—every Monday these same oranges and lemons left his back door in a pyramid of pulpless halves. There was a machine in the kitchen which could extract the juice of two hundred oranges in half an hour, if a little button was pressed two hundred times by a butler's thumb.

At least once a fortnight a corps of caterers came down with several hundred feet of canvas and enough colored lights to make a Christmas tree of Gatsby's enormous garden. On buffet tables, garnished with glistening hors d'œuvre, spiced baked hams crowded against salads of harlequin designs and pastry pigs and turkeys bewitched to a dark gold. In the main hall a bar with a real brass rail was set up, and stocked with gins and liquors and with cordials so long forgotten that most of his female guests were too young to know one from another.

By seven o'clock the orchestra has arrived—no thin five piece affair but a whole pit full of oboes and trombones and saxophones and viols and cornets and piccolos and low and high drums. The last swimmers have come in from the beach now and are dressing upstairs; the cars from New York are parked five deep in the drive, and already the halls and salons and verandas are gaudy with primary colors and hair shorn in strange new ways and shawls beyond the dreams of Castile. The bar is in full swing and floating rounds of cocktails permeate the garden outside until the air is alive with chatter and laughter and casual innuendo and introductions forgotten on the spot and enthusiastic meetings between women who never knew each other's names.

The lights grow brighter as the earth lurches away from the sun   5
and now the orchestra is playing yellow cocktail music and the opera of voices pitches a key higher. Laughter is easier, minute by minute,

spilled with prodigality, tipped out at a cheerful word. The groups change more swiftly, swell with new arrivals, dissolve and form in the same breath—already there are wanderers, confident girls who weave here and there among the stouter and more stable, become for a sharp, joyous moment the center of a group and then excited with triumph glide on through the sea-change of faces and voices and color under the constantly changing light.

Suddenly one of these gypsies in trembling opal seizes a cocktail out of the air, dumps it down for courage and moving her hands like Frisco dances out alone on the canvas platform. A momentary hush; the orchestra leader varies his rhythm obligingly for her and there is a burst of chatter as the erroneous news goes around that she is Gilda Gray's understudy from the "Follies." The party has begun.

I believe that on the first night I went to Gatsby's house I was one of the few guests who had actually been invited. People were not invited—they went there. They got into automobiles which bore them out to Long Island and somehow they ended up at Gatsby's door. Once there they were introduced by somebody who knew Gatsby and after that they conducted themselves according to the rules of behavior associated with amusement parks. Sometimes they came and went without having met Gatsby at all, came for the party with a simplicity of heart that was its own ticket of admission. . . .

Chapter Four

On Sunday morning while church bells rang in the villages along shore the world and its mistress returned to Gatsby's house and twinkled hilariously on his lawn.

"He's a bootlegger," said the young ladies, moving somewhere between his cocktails and his flowers. "One time he killed a man who had found out that he was nephew to von Hindenburg and second cousin to the devil. Reach me a rose, honey, and pour me a last drop into that there crystal glass."

10   Once I wrote down on the empty spaces of a time-table the names of those who came to Gatsby's house that summer. It is an old time-table now, disintegrating at its folds and headed "This schedule in effect July 5th, 1922." But I can still read the grey names and they will give you a better impression than my generalities of those who accepted Gatsby's hospitality and paid him the subtle tribute of knowing nothing whatever about him.

From East Egg, then, came the Chester Beckers and the Leeches and a man named Bunsen whom I knew at Yale and Doctor Webster Civet who was drowned last summer up in Maine. And the Hornbeams and the Willie Voltaires and a whole clan named Blackbuck who always gathered in a corner and flipped up their noses like goats at whosoever came near. And the Ismays and the Chrysties (or rather Hubert Auerbach and Mr. Chrystie's wife) and Edgar Beaver whose hair they say turned cotton-white one winter afternoon for no good reason at all.

Clarence Endive was from East Egg, as I remember. He came only once, in white knickerbockers, and had a fight with a bum named Etty in the garden. From farther out on the Island came the Cheadles and the O. R. P. Schraeders and the Stonewall Jackson Abrams of Georgia and the Fishguards and the Ripley Snells. Snell was there three days before he went to the penitentiary, so drunk out on the gravel drive that Mrs. Ulysses Swett's automobile ran over his right hand. The Dancies came too and S. B. Whitebait, who was well over sixty, and Maurice A. Flink and the Hammerheads and Beluga the tobacco importer and Beluga's girls.

From West Egg came the Poles and the Mulreadys and Cecil Roebuck and Cecil Schoen and Gulick, the state senator, and Newton Orchid who controlled Films Par Excellence and Eckhaust and Clyde Cohen and Don S. Schwartze (the son) and Arthur McCarty, all connected with the movies in one way or another. And the Catlips and the Bembergs and G. Earl Muldoon, brother to that Muldoon who afterwards strangled his wife. Da Fontano the promoter came there and Ed Legros and James B. ("Rot-gut") Ferret and the de Jongs and Ernest Lilly—they came to gamble and when Ferret wandered into the garden it meant he was cleaned out and Associated Traction would have to fluctuate profitably next day.

A man named Klipspringer was there so often and so long that he became known as "the boarder"—I doubt if he had any other home. Of theatrical people there were Gus Waize and Horace O'Donavan and Lester Myer and George Duckweed and Francis Bull. Also from New York were the Chromes and the Backhyssons and the Dennickers and Russel Betty and the Corrigans and the Kellehers and the Dewars and the Scullys and S. W. Belcher and the Smirkes and the young Quinns, divorced now, and Henry L. Palmetto who killed himself by jumping in front of a subway train in Times Square.

Benny McClenahan arrived always with four girls. They were never   15
quite the same ones in physical person but they were so identical one with another that it inevitably seemed they had been there before. I have forgotten their names—Jaqueline, I think, or else Consuela or Gloria or Judy or June, and their last names were either the melodious names of flowers and months or the sterner ones of the great American capitalists whose cousins, if pressed, they would confess themselves to be.

In addition to all these I can remember that Faustina O'Brien came there at least once and the Baedeker girls and young Brewer who had his nose shot off in the war and Mr. Albrucksburger and Miss Haag, his fiancée, and Ardita Fitz-Peters, and Mr. P. Jewett, once head of the American Legion, and Miss Claudia Hip with a man reputed to be her chauffeur, and a prince of something whom we called Duke and whose name, if I ever knew it, I have forgotten.

All these people came to Gatsby's house in the summer. . . .

Chapter Six

About this time an ambitious young reporter from New York arrived one morning at Gatsby's door and asked him if he had anything to say.

"Anything to say about what?" inquired Gatsby politely.

20 "Why,—any statement to give out."

It transpired after a confused five minutes that the man had heard Gatsby's name around his office in a connection which he either wouldn't reveal or didn't fully understand. This was his day off and with laudable initiative he had hurried out "to see."

It was a random shot, and yet the reporter's instinct was right. Gatsby's notoriety, spread about by the hundreds who had accepted his hospitality and so become authorities upon his past, had increased all summer until he fell just short of being news. Contemporary legends such as the "underground pipe-line to Canada" attached themselves to him, and there was one persistent story that he didn't live in a house at all, but in a boat that looked like a house and was moved secretly up and down the Long Island shore. Just why these inventions were a source of satisfaction to James Gatz of North Dakota, isn't easy to say.

James Gatz—that was really, or at least legally, his name. He had changed it at the age of seventeen and at the specific moment that witnessed the beginning of his career—when he saw Dan Cody's yacht drop anchor over the most insidious flat on Lake Superior. It was James Gatz who had been loafing along the beach that afternoon in a torn green jersey and a pair of canvas pants, but it was already Jay Gatsby who borrowed a row-boat, pulled out to the *Tuolomee* and informed Cody that a wind might catch him and break him up in half an hour.

I suppose he'd had the name ready for a long time, even then. His parents were shiftless and unsuccessful farm people—his imagination had never really accepted them as his parents at all. The truth was that Jay Gatsby, of West Egg, Long Island, sprang from his Platonic conception of himself. He was a son of God—a phrase which, if it means anything, means just that—and he must be about His Father's Business, the service of a vast, vulgar and meretricious beauty. So he invented just the sort of Jay Gatsby that a seventeen year old boy would be likely to invent, and to this conception he was faithful to the end.

For over a year he had been beating his way along the south shore 25 of Lake Superior as a clam digger and a salmon fisher or in any other capacity that brought him food and bed. His brown, hardening body lived naturally through the half fierce, half lazy work of the bracing days. He knew women early and since they spoiled him he became contemptuous of them, of young virgins because they were ignorant, of the others because they were hysterical about things which in his overwhelming self-absorption he took for granted.

But his heart was in a constant, turbulent riot. The most grotesque and fantastic conceits haunted him in his bed at night. A universe of ineffable gaudiness spun itself out in his brain while the clock ticked on the wash-stand and the moon soaked with wet light his tangled clothes upon the floor. Each night he added to the pattern of his fancies until drowsiness closed down upon some vivid scene with an oblivious embrace. For a while these reveries provided an outlet for his imagination; they were a satisfactory hint of the unreality of reality, a promise that the rock of the world was founded securely on a fairy's wing.

An instinct toward his future glory had led him, some months before, to the small Lutheran college of St. Olaf in southern Minnesota. He stayed there two weeks, dismayed at its ferocious indifference to the drums of his destiny, to destiny itself, and despising the janitor's work with which he was to pay his way through. Then he drifted back to Lake Superior, and he was still searching for something to do on the day that Dan Cody's yacht dropped anchor in the shallows along shore.

Cody was fifty years old then, a product of the Nevada silver fields, of the Yukon, of every rush for metal since Seventy-five. The transactions in Montana copper that made him many times a millionaire found him physically robust but on the verge of softmindedness, and suspecting this an infinite number of women tried to separate him from his money. The none too savory ramifications by which Ella Kaye, the newspaper woman, played Madame de Maintenon to his weakness and sent him to sea in a yacht, were common knowledge to the turgid journalism of 1902. He had been coasting along all too hospitable shores for five years when he turned up as James Gatz's destiny in Little Girl Bay.

To young Gatz, resting on his oars and looking up at the railed deck, that yacht represented all the beauty and glamor in the world. I suppose he smiled at Cody—he had probably discovered that people liked him when he smiled. At any rate Cody asked him a few questions (one of them elicited the brand new name) and found that he was quick, and extravagantly ambitious. A few days later he took him to Duluth and bought him a blue coat, six pair of white duck trousers and a yachting cap. And when the *Tuolomee* left for the West Indies and the Barbary Coast Gatsby left too.

30   He was employed in a vague personal capacity—while he remained with Cody he was in turn steward, mate, skipper, secretary and even jailor, for Dan Cody sober knew what lavish doings Dan Cody drunk might soon be about and he provided for such contingencies by reposing more and more trust in Gatsby. The arrangement lasted five years during which the boat went three times around the continent. It might have lasted indefinitely except for the fact that Ella Kaye came on board one night in Boston and a week later Dan Cody inhospitably died.

I remember the portrait of him up in Gatsby's bedroom, a grey, florid man with a hard empty face—the pioneer debauchee who during one phase of American life brought back to the eastern seaboard the savage violence of the frontier brothel and saloon. It was indirectly due to Cody that Gatsby drank so little. Sometimes in the course of gay parties women used to rub champagne into his hair; for himself he formed the habit of letting liquor alone.

And it was from Cody that he inherited money—a legacy of twenty-five thousand dollars. He didn't get it. He never understood the legal device that was used against him but what remained of the millions went intact to Ella Kaye. He was left with his singularly appropriate education; the vague contour of Jay Gatsby had filled out to the substantiality of a man. . . .

Chapter Nine

. . . I think it was on the third day that a telegram signed Henry C. Gatz arrived from a town in Minnesota. It said only that the sender was leaving immediately and to postpone the funeral until he came.

It was Gatsby's father, a solemn old man very helpless and dismayed, bundled up in a long cheap ulster against the warm September day. His eyes leaked continuously with excitement and when I took the bag and umbrella from his hands he began to pull so incessantly at his sparse grey beard that I had difficulty in getting off his coat. He was on the point of collapse so I took him into the music room and made him sit down while I sent for something to eat. But he wouldn't eat and the glass of milk spilled from his trembling hand.

35   "I saw it in the Chicago newspaper," he said. "It was all in the Chicago newspaper. I started right away."

"I didn't know how to reach you."

His eyes, seeing nothing, moved ceaselessly about the room.

"It was a mad man," he said. "He must have been mad."

"Wouldn't you like some coffee?" I urged him.

"I don't want anything. I'm all right now, Mr.—"   40

"Carraway."

"Well, I'm all right now. Where have they got Jimmy?"

I took him into the drawing room where his son lay, and left him there. Some little boys had come up on the steps and were looking into the hall; when I told them who had arrived they went reluctantly away.

After a little while Mr. Gatz opened the door and came out, his mouth ajar, his face flushed slightly, his eyes leaking isolated and unpunctual tears. He had reached an age where death no longer has the quality of ghastly surprise, and when he looked around him now for the first time and saw the height and splendor of the hall and the great rooms opening out from it into other rooms his grief began to be mixed with an awed pride. I helped him to a bedroom upstairs; while he took off his coat and vest I told him that all arrangements had been deferred until he came.

"I didn't know what you'd want, Mr. Gatsby—"   45

"Gatz is my name."

"—Mr. Gatz. I thought you might want to take the body west."

He shook his head.

"Jimmy always liked it better down East. He rose up to his position in the East. Were you a friend of my boy's, Mr.—?"

"We were close friends."   50

"He had a big future before him, you know. He was only a young man but he had a lot of brain power here."

He touched his head impressively and I nodded.

"If he'd of lived he'd of been a great man. A man like James J. Hill. He'd of helped build up the country."

"That's true," I said uncomfortably.

He fumbled at the embroidered coverlet, trying to take it from the   55 bed, and lay down stiffly—was instantly asleep. . . .

. . . After changing my clothes I went next door and found Mr. Gatz walking up and down excitedly in the hall. His pride in his son and in his son's possessions was continually increasing and now he had something to show me.

"Jimmy sent me this picture." He took out his wallet with trembling fingers. "Look there."

It was a photograph of the house, cracked in the corners and dirty with many hands. He pointed out every detail to me eagerly. "Look there!" and then sought admiration from my eyes. He had shown it so often that I think it was more real to him now than the house itself.

"Jimmy sent it to me. I think it's a very pretty picture. It shows up well."

60   "Very well. Had you seen him lately?"

"He come out to see me two years ago and bought me the house I live in now. Of course we was broke up when he run off from home but I see now there was a reason for it. He knew he had a big future in front of him. And ever since he made a success he was very generous with me."

He seemed reluctant to put away the picture, held it for another minute, lingeringly, before my eyes. Then he returned the wallet and pulled from his pocket a ragged old copy of a book called "Hopalong Cassidy."

"Look here, this is a book he had when he was a boy. It just shows you."

He opened it at the back cover and turned it around for me to see. On the last fly-leaf was printed the word SCHEDULE, and the date September 12th, 1906. And underneath:

Rise from bed	.6.00	A.M.
Dumbbell exercise and wall-scaling	.6.15–6.30	"
Study electricity, etc.	.7.15–8.15	"
Work	.8.30–4.30	P.M.
Baseball and sports	.4.30–5.00	"
Practice elocution, poise and how to attain it	.5.00–6.00	"
Study needed inventions	7.00–9.00	"

GENERAL RESOLVES

No wasting time at Shafters or [a name, indecipherable]
No more smokeing or chewing
Bath every other day
Read one improving book or magazine per week
Save $5.00 [crossed out] $3.00 per week
Be better to parents

"I come across this book by accident," said the old man. "It just shows you, don't it?"

65   "It just shows you."

"Jimmy was bound to get ahead. He always had some resolves like this or something. Do you notice what he's got about improving his mind? He was always great for that. He told me I et like a hog once and I beat him for it."

He was reluctant to close the book, reading each item aloud and then looking eagerly at me. I think he rather expected me to copy down the list for my own use.

A little before three the Lutheran minister arrived from Flushing and I began to look involuntarily out the windows for other cars. So did Gatsby's father. And as the time passed and the servants came in and stood waiting in the hall his eyes began to blink anxiously and he spoke of the rain in a worried uncertain way. The minister glanced several times at his watch so I took him aside and asked him to wait for half an hour. But it wasn't any use. Nobody came. . . .

Gatsby's house was still empty when I left—the grass on his lawn had grown as long as mine. One of the taxi drivers in the village never took a fare past the entrance gate without stopping for a minute and pointing inside; perhaps it was he who drove Daisy and Gatsby over to East Egg the night of the accident and perhaps he had made a story about it all his own. I didn't want to hear it and I avoided him when I got off the train.

I spent my Saturday nights in New York because those gleaming, dazzling parties of his were with me so vividly that I could still hear the music and the laughter faint and incessant from his garden and the cars going up and down his drive. One night I did hear a material car there and saw its lights stop at his front steps. But I didn't investigate. Probably it was some final guest who had been away at the ends of the earth and didn't know that the party was over. 70

On the last night, with my trunk packed and my car sold to the grocer, I went over and looked at that huge incoherent failure of a house once more. On the white steps an obscene word, scrawled by some boy with a piece of brick, stood out clearly in the moonlight and I erased it, drawing my shoe raspingly along the stone. Then I wandered down to the beach and sprawled out on the sand.

Most of the big shore places were closed now and there were hardly any lights except the shadowy, moving glow of a ferryboat across the Sound. And as the moon rose higher the inessential houses began to melt away until gradually I became aware of the old island here that flowered once for Dutch sailors' eyes—a fresh, green breast of the new world. Its vanished trees, the trees that had made way for Gatsby's house, had once pandered in whispers to the last and greatest of all human dreams; for a transitory enchanted moment man must have held his breath in the presence of this continent, compelled into an æsthetic contemplation he neither understood nor desired, face to face for the last time in history with something commensurate to his capacity for wonder.

And as I sat there, brooding on the old unknown world, I thought of Gatsby's wonder when he first picked out the green light at the end of Daisy's dock. He had come a long way to this blue lawn and his dream must have seemed so close that he could hardly fail to grasp it. He did not know that it was already behind him, somewhere back in

that vast obscurity beyond the city, where the dark fields of the republic rolled on under the night.

Gatsby believed in the green light, the orgastic future that year
by year recedes before us. It eluded us then, but that's no matter—tomorrow we will run faster, stretch out our arms farther.... And one
fine morning—

75   So we beat on, boats against the current, borne back ceaselessly
into the past.

For Journals

Fitzgerald wrote *The Great Gatsby* in the middle of what is now known
as the Roaring Twenties or the Jazz Age. How would you interpret
them? If you had to give a name to the 1980s–1990s, what would it be?

For Discussion

1.   Gatsby makes his money through bootlegging (selling illegal or
spoiled liquor), engaging in questionable bond deals, and getting business favors from gangsters, including a man who fixed the World Series in 1919. He does so not for the money but for the love of a woman.
In what ways do his reasons for seeking money or success to impress a
woman support or contradict your understanding of the American
work ethic?

2.   Reread the description of the preparations for the party, looking
closely at the language—for example, the clean-up crew repairs "the
ravages" of the party (paragraph 1); the used oranges form a "pyramid" (paragraph 2); the caterers come in a "corps" (paragraph 3); the
roast turkeys are "bewitched to a dark gold" (paragraph 3); the orchestra plays "yellow cocktail music" (paragraph 5). How does Fitzgerald's
language support his assertions about luxury and conspicuous consumption?

3.   Read out loud the "party list" of the names of people who came to
Gatsby's house (paragraphs 11–16). What is unusual about them?
What does Fitzgerald think of these people? How do the names he
gives the guests reinforce the assertions he makes about these people?

4.   Fitzgerald was a passionate student of American history, and he
kept Franklin's *Autobiography* in mind in writing *Gatsby*. Go back to the
Franklin selection in this chapter and find the page from his notebook
on time management, success, and self-improvement (paragraph 10).
Compare it to the page from Gatsby's notebook that Gatsby's father
and Nick find after Gatsby's murder (paragraph 63). In what ways
does Gatsby fulfill Franklin's legacy, and in what ways does he pervert
it?

5.   In what ways is Gatsby's story of changing from James Gatz to Jay Gatsby a typical American success story?

6.   The last two pages of the excerpt you've read epitomize for many people America as the land of opportunity. Reread the excerpt (beginning with paragraph 68) and express in your own words Fitzgerald's assertions about the American dream. What is your response to the ideas in this passage?

For Writing

1.   Fitzgerald's most famous assertion about money was his remark, "The rich are different from you and me," to which Ernest Hemingway responded, "Yes, they have more money." Write an essay in which you argue *either* that Fitzgerald was right—the possession of a lot of money creates deep differences—or that Hemingway was right. Give your own interpretation of both remarks. You can use readings from this or previous chapters—Franklin, Fitzgerald himself, Sam Keen, Tom Wolfe, Gloria Steinem—as well as your personal experience, to support your assertions.

2.   The 1920s was a time of great prosperity and excess for many Americans. Research some aspect of the decade using books and periodicals as sources, and write a documented paper on a topic such as Prohibition and bootlegging, the stock market crash of 1929, or the Teapot Dome scandal.

THERE'S NO WAY LIKE THE AMERICAN WAY
1937

Margaret Bourke-White

Margaret Bourke-White (1904–1971) was a photojournalist who covered major news stories for Life *magazine when that publication was home to the world's best photographers. As well as the work she did on the Great Depression, she is famous for her photographs of the invasion of Russia in World War II and the liberation of concentration camps.*

One of Bourke-White's most famous photographs (on the next page) is this picture of Americans in 1937, during the Great Depression, standing in line at an emergency relief station in the aftermath of an Ohio flood that killed hundreds of people and left thousands of others homeless.

For Journals

What do you know about the Great Depression of the 1930s? Was anyone in your family affected by it?

For Discussion

1. From looking at this photo, what would you say was the image of the ideal American family in 1937? How is that image affected by the fact that in 1937 the Depression was in full force, with roughly 15 million Americans out of work?

2. There are two verbal assertions in this photograph, both of them slogans on the billboard. How does the rest of the photograph, including the line of people, support or refute those statements?

3. What do you suppose would have been the response of the people in the line to the billboard behind them if they had turned and looked at it? What is your response?

4. The composition of a great photograph is never accidental. Since the line of people was longer than the billboard, what do you think were Bourke-White's reasons for taking a photograph of those particular people under that particular billboard? Would it have different impact if the flood victims were white? Is their color or their economic situation more important?

5. If you had to translate this photo into a verbal assertion about life in America in 1937, what would it be? What details of the photograph would you choose to support your statement?

For Writing

1. Today America still has problems of homelessness and unemployment. Look in recent newspapers or magazines for a picture or pictures of homeless or unemployed Americans. Write a reflective essay in which you consider the following: whether you could imagine yourself or your family in a similar situation and whether your choice of your major in school is affected by your concerns for the future.

2. Bourke-White took this photograph from a particular point of view. Using back copies of magazines, contemporary magazines, or books of photographs, find an American photograph from a historic event—for example, the Civil War, the Great Depression, one of the world wars, a political assassination, the civil rights struggle in the south, a presidential campaign—in which the photographer makes a judgment about the event through the image. Research the background of the event to be sure you understand the historical context.

Then write an essay in which you respond to the following questions: What is the photo's impact on you? Has the meaning of the photo changed over time? What biases or values or assumptions do you think the photographer is expressing? What details in the photograph support your assertions?

THEY'LL KNOW YOU'VE ARRIVED
1958

Ford Motor Co.

The Edsel car was one of the most embarrassing debacles in the automotive industry generally, and for the Ford motor company specifically, in the 1950s. Decades later, middle-aged and older Americans still allude to the Edsel in describing a colossal mistake, particularly in product development. But as the advertisement here suggests, the Edsel was marketed as a part of post–World War II prosperity, and ads such as this appeared in mainstream, middle-class magazines.

For Journals

What kinds of advertisements do you find most appealing? Do some types draw your eyes more than others? Do some appeal to your desire for status and success?

For Discussion

1.   Who are the active people in the advertisement? Who are the passive onlookers? Where are the people in the photograph relative to the product being displayed? What do these positions in the photograph convey to you about gender roles, power, and targeted audiences for the advertisement?

2.   The headline plays on the word *arrived* to indicate not only transportation but status and success. Examine the smaller text at the bottom of the ad. In what ways does it reinforce the connection made in the headline between success, money, and consumption?

They'll know you've *arrived*

when you drive up in an Edsel

Step into an Edsel and you'll learn where the excitement is this year.
Other drivers spot that classic vertical grille a block away—and never fail to take a long look at this year's most exciting car.

On the open road, your Edsel is watched eagerly for its already-famous performance.

And parked in front of your home, your Edsel always gets even more attention—because it always says a lot about you. It says you chose elegant styling, luxurious comfort and such exclusive features as Edsel's famous Teletouch Drive—only shift that puts the buttons where they belong, on the steering-wheel hub.

Your Edsel also means you made a wonderful buy. For of all medium-priced cars, this one really new car is actually priced the lowest.* See your Edsel Dealer this week.

*Based on comparison of suggested retail delivered prices of the Edsel Ranger and similarly equipped cars in the medium-price field.

Above: Edsel Citation 2-door Hardtop. Engine: the E-475, with 10.5 to one compression ratio, 345 hp, 475 ft.-lb. torque. Transmission: Automatic with Teletouch Drive. Suspension: Ball-joint with optional air suspension. Brakes: self-adjusting.

EDSEL DIVISION · FORD MOTOR COMPANY

1958 EDSEL

Of all medium-priced cars, the one that's really new is the lowest-priced, too!

3. What assertions does the advertisement make about success? What appeals to ethos, or credibility and shared values; to pathos, or emotions; to logos, or logic, do the text and photograph make? Do both parts of the ad rely on the same types of appeals?

4. The Edsel became a notoriously unpopular car and the butt of many jokes. Is there a car or other type of product today that you think may become the "Edsel" of tomorrow despite currently being considered a status symbol?

For Writing

1.   In her article, "You've Come a Long Way, Madison Avenue" in *Lear's* magazine, author Betsy Sharkey has argued that ads sell sex to men and style to women. Browse through some current popular magazines, and find several advertisements you think are directed at men and several directed at women. Does the evidence you find support or refute Sharkey's assertion? Develop an argument in which you agree or disagree with Sharkey, drawing on the visual and textual evidence of the advertisements to support your view.

2.   For many years, cigarettes were advertised for their ability to help depress the appetite and even for their good health side effects. Lucky Strike, for example, used to run an ad that said, "Reach for a Lucky—instead of a sweet" and "It's toasted—No Throat Irritation—No Cough." Find an advertisement that you think is particularly misleading or unrealistic, and write an essay in which you argue specifically against elements of the ad you find most dubious.

3.   In *Satisfaction Guaranteed,* her book on American consumerism, Susan Strasser says that Americans had to be trained to want products and to believe that they needed them so that they would go out and buy things and spend money. Based on your own observations and experience, do you agree or disagree with Strasser? Develop your argument into an essay supported by examples and details you have observed or experienced.

LAS VEGAS (WHAT?)
1 9 6 5

Tom Wolfe

   Tom Wolfe (1931–   ), *whose real name is Thomas Kennerly, writes about popular culture in a style so distinctive that it has given its name to a whole school of writing: New Journalism. Wolfe's approach is to write in a way that brings the reader very close to the experience he's describing: the acid culture in* The Electric KoolAid Acid Test *(1968), American architecture and art in* From Bauhaus to Our House *(1981) the space program in* The Right Stuff *(1982), and corporate greed in* The Bonfire of the Vanities *(1987). The hallmarks of his style include everything from sound effects and comic book exclamations to multiple narratives and historical asides—all directed, he says, "to give the reader the feeling of being inside the character's mind." This selection is from his first collection of essays,* The Kandy-Colored Tangerine Flake Streamlined Baby *(1965).*

Hernia, hernia, hernia, hernia, hernia, hernia, hernia, hernia, hernia, hernia, hernia, hernia, hernia, HERNia, hernia, HERNia, hernia, hernia, hernia, hernia, HERNia, HERNia, hernia, hernia, hernia, hernia, hernia, hernia, hernia, eight is the point, the point is eight; hernia, hernia, HERNia; hernia, hernia, hernia, hernia, all right, hernia, hernia, hernia, hernia, hard eight, hernia, hernia, hernia, HERNia, hernia, hernia, hernia, HERNia, hernia, hernia, hernia, HERNia, hernia, hernia, hernia, hernia.

"What is all this *hernia hernia* stuff?"

This was Raymond talking to the wavy-haired fellow with the stick, the dealer, at the craps table about 3:45 Sunday morning. The stickman had no idea what this big wiseacre was talking about, but he resented the tone. He gave Raymond that patient arch of the eyebrows known as a Red Hook brush-off, which is supposed to convey some such thought as, I am a very tough but cool guy, as you can tell by the way I carry my eyeballs low in the pouches, and if this wasn't such a high-class joint we would take wiseacres like you out back and beat you into jellied madrilene.

At this point, however, Raymond was immune to subtle looks.

The stickman tried to get the game going again, but every time he   5
would start up his singsong, by easing the words out through the nose, which seems to be the style among craps dealers in Las Vegas—"All right, a new shooter . . . eight is the point, the point is eight" and so on—Raymond would start droning along with him in exactly the same tone of voice, "Hernia, hernia, hernia; hernia, HERNia, HERNia, hernia; hernia, hernia, hernia."

Everybody at the craps table was staring in consternation to think that anybody would try to needle a tough, hip, elite *soldat* like a Las Vegas craps dealer. The gold-lamé odalisques of Los Angeles were staring. The Western sports, fifty-eight-year-old men who wear Texas string ties, were staring. The old babes at the slot machines, holding Dixie Cups full of nickels, were staring at the craps tables, but cranking away the whole time.

Raymond, who is thirty-four years old and works as an engineer in Phoenix, is big but not terrifying. He has the sort of thatchwork hair that grows so low all along the forehead there is no logical place to part it, but he tries anyway. He has a huge, prognathous jaw, but it is

as smooth, soft and round as a melon, so that Raymond's total effect is
that of an Episcopal divinity student.

The guards were wonderful. They were dressed in cowboy uniforms like Bruce Cabot in *Sundown* and they wore sheriff's stars.

"Mister, is there something we can do for you?"

"The expression is 'Sir,'" said Raymond. "You said 'Mister.' The
expression is 'Sir.' How's your old Cosa Nostra?"

Amazingly, the casino guards were easing Raymond out peaceably, without putting a hand on him. I had never seen the fellow before, but possibly because I had been following his progress for the last
five minutes, he turned to me and said, "Hey, do you have a car? This
wild stuff is starting again."

The gist of it was that he had left his car somewhere and he
wanted to ride up the Strip to the Stardust, one of the big hotel-casinos.
I am describing this big goof Raymond not because he is a typical Las
Vegas tourist, although he has some typical symptoms, but because he
is a good example of the marvelous impact Las Vegas has on the
senses. Raymond's senses were at a high pitch of excitation, the only
trouble being that he was going off his nut. He had been up since
Thursday afternoon, and it was now about 3:45 A.M. Sunday. He had
an envelope full of pep pills—amphetamine—in his left coat pocket
and an envelope full of Equanils—meprobamate—in his right pocket,
or were the Equanils in the left and the pep pills in the right? He could
tell by looking, but he wasn't going to look anymore. He didn't care to
see how many were left.

He had been rolling up and down the incredible electric-sign
gauntlet of Las Vegas' Strip, U.S. Route 91, where the neon and the par
lamps—bubbling, spiraling, rocketing, and exploding in sunbursts ten
stories high out in the middle of the desert—celebrate one-story casinos. He had been gambling and drinking and eating now and again at
the buffet tables the casinos keep heaped with food day and night, but
mostly hopping himself up wtih good old amphetamine, cooling himself down with meprobamate, then hooking down more alcohol, until
now, after sixty hours, he was slipping into the symptoms of toxic
schizophrenia.

He was also enjoying what the prophets of hallucinogen call "consciousness expansion." The man was psychedelic. He was beginning to
isolate the components of Las Vegas' unique bombardment of the
senses. He was quite right about this *hernia hernia* stuff. Every casino in
Las Vegas is, among the other things, a room full of craps tables with
dealers who keep up a running singsong that sounds as though they
are saying "hernia, hernia, hernia, hernia, hernia" and so on. There
they are day and night, easing a running commentary through their
nostrils. What they have to say contains next to no useful instruction.

Its underlying message is, We are the initiates, riding the crest of chance. That the accumulated sound comes out "hernia" is merely an unfortunate phonetic coincidence. Actually, it is part of something rare and rather grand: a combination of baroque stimuli that brings to mind the bronze gongs, no larger than a blue plate, that Louis XIV, his ruff collars larded with the lint of the foul Old City of Byzantium, personally hunted out in the bazaars of Asia Minor to provide exotic acoustics for his new palace outside Paris.

The sounds of the craps dealer will be in, let's say, the middle register. In the lower register will be the sound of the old babes at the slot machines. Men play the slots too, of course, but one of the indelible images of Las Vegas is that of the old babes at the row upon row of slot machines. There they are at six o'clock Sunday morning no less than at three o'clock Tuesday afternoon. Some of them pack their old hummocky shanks into Capri pants, but many of them just put on the old print dress, the same one day after day, and the old hob-heeled shoes, looking like they might be going out to buy eggs in Tupelo, Mississippi. They have a Dixie Cup full of nickels or dimes in the left hand and an Iron Boy work glove on the right hand to keep the callouses from getting sore. Every time they pull the handle, the machine makes a sound much like the sound a cash register makes before the bell rings, then the slot pictures start clattering up from left to right, the oranges, lemons, plums, cherries, bells, bars, buckaroos—the figure of a cowboy riding a bucking bronco. The whole sound keeps churning up over and over again in eccentric series all over the place, like one of those random-sound radio symphonies by John Cage. You can hear it at any hour of the day or night all over Las Vegas. You can walk down Fremont Street at dawn and hear it without even walking in a door, that and the spins of the wheels of fortune, a boring and not very popular sort of simplified roulette, as the tabs flap to a stop. As an overtone, or at times simply as a loud sound, comes the babble of the casino crowds, with an occasional shriek from the craps tables, or, anywhere from 4 P.M. to 6 A.M., the sound of brass instruments or electrified string instruments from the cocktail-lounge shows.

The crowd and band sounds are not very extraordinary, of course. But Las Vegas' Muzak is. Muzak pervades Las Vegas from the time you walk into the airport upon landing to the last time you leave the casinos. It is piped out to the swimming pool. It is in the drugstores. It is as if there were a communal fear that someone, somewhere in Las Vegas, was going to be left with a totally vacant minute on his hands.

Las Vegas has succeeded in wiring an entire city with this electronic stimulation, day and night, out in the middle of the desert. In the automobile I rented, the radio could not be turned off, no matter which dial you went after. I drove for days in a happy burble of Action

15

Checkpoint News, "Monkey No. 9," "Donna, Donna, the Prima Donna," and picking-and-singing jingles for the Frontier Bank and the Fremont Hotel.

One can see the magnitude of the achievement. Las Vegas takes what in other American towns is but a quixotic inflammation of the senses for some poor salary mule in the brief interval between the flagstone rambler and the automatic elevator downtown and magnifies it, foliates it, embellishes it into an institution.

For example, Las Vegas is the only town in the world whose skyline is made up neither of buildings, like New York, nor of trees, like Wilbraham, Massachusetts, but signs. One can look at Las Vegas from a mile away on Route 91 and see no buildings, no trees, only signs. But such signs! They tower. They revolve, they oscillate, they soar in shapes before which the existing vocabulary of art history is helpless. I can only attempt to supply names—Boomerang Modern, Palette Curvilinear, Flash Gordon Ming-Alert Spiral, McDonald's Hamburger Parabola, Mint Casino Elliptical, Miami Beach Kidney. Las Vegas' sign makers work so far out beyond the frontiers of conventional studio art that they have no names themselves for the forms they create. Vaughan Cannon, one of those tall, blond Westerners, the builders of places like Las Vegas and Los Angeles, whose eyes seem to have been bleached by the sun, is in the back shop of the Young Electric Sign Company out on East Charleston Boulevard with Herman Boernge, one of his designers, looking at the model they have prepared for the Lucky Strike Casino sign, and Cannon points to where the sign's two great curving faces meet to form a narrow vertical face and says:

20   "Well, here we are again—what do we call that?"

"I don't know," says Boernge. "It's sort of a nose effect. Call it a nose."

Okay, a nose, but it rises sixteen stories high above a two-story building. In Las Vegas no farseeing entrepreneur buys a sign to fit a building he owns. He rebuilds the building to support the biggest sign he can get up the money for and, if necessary, changes the name. The Lucky Strike Casino today is the Lucky Casino, which fits better when recorded in sixteen stories of flaming peach and incandescent yellow in the middle of the Mojave Desert. In the Young Electric Sign Co. era signs have become the architecture of Las Vegas, and the most whimsical, Yale-seminar-frenzied devices of the two late geniuses of Baroque Modern, Frank Lloyd Wright and Eero Saarinen, seem rather stuffy business, like a jest at a faculty meeting, compared to it. Men like Boernge, Kermit Wayne, Ben Mitchem and Jack Larsen, formerly an artist for Walt Disney, are the designer-sculptor geniuses of Las Vegas, but their motifs have been carried faithfully throughout the town by lesser men, for gasoline stations, motels, funeral parlors, churches, public buildings, flophouses and sauna baths.

Then there is a stimulus that is both visual and sexual—the Las Vegas buttocks décolletage. This is a form of sexually provocative dress seen more and more in the United States, but avoided like Broadway message–embroidered ("Kiss Me, I'm Cold") underwear in the fashion pages, so that the euphemisms have not been established and I have no choice but clinical terms. To achieve buttocks décolletage a woman wears bikini-style shorts that cut across the round fatty masses of the buttocks rather than cupping them from below, so that the outer-lower edges of these fatty masses, or "cheeks," are exposed. I am in the cocktail lounge of the Hacienda Hotel, talking to managing director Dick Taylor about the great success his place has had in attracting family and tour groups, and all around me the waitresses are bobbing on their high heels, bare legs and décolletage-bare backsides, set off by pelvis-length lingerie of an uncertain denomination. I stare, but I am new here. At the White Cross Rexall drugstore on the Strip a pregnant brunette walks in off the street wearing black shorts with buttocks décolletage aft and illusion-of-cloth nylon lingerie hanging fore, and not even the old mom's-pie pensioners up near the door are staring. They just crank away at the slot machines. On the streets of Las Vegas, not only the show girls, of which the town has about two hundred fifty, bona fide, in residence, but girls of every sort, including, especially, Las Vegas' little high-school buds, who adorn what locals seeking roots in the sand call "our city of churches and schools," have taken up the chic of wearing buttocks décolletage step-ins under flesh-tight slacks, with the outline of the undergarment showing through fashionably. Others go them one better. They achieve the effect of having been dipped once, briefly, in Helenca stretch nylon. More and more they look like those wonderful old girls out of Flash Gordon who were wrapped just once over in Baghdad pantaloons of clear polyethylene with only Flash Gordon between them and the insane red-eyed assaults of the minions of Ming. It is as if all the hip young suburban gals of America named Lana, Deborah and Sandra, who gather wherever the arc lights shine and the studs steady their coiffures in the plate-glass reflection, have convened in Las Vegas with their bouffant hair above and anatomically stretch-pant-swathed little bottoms below, here on the new American frontier. But exactly!

None of it would have been possible, however, without one of those historic combinations of nature and art that creates an epoch. In this case, the Mojave Desert plus the father of Las Vegas, the late Benjamin "Bugsy" Siegel.

25   Bugsy was an inspired man. Back in 1944 the city fathers of Las Vegas, their Protestant rectitude alloyed only by the giddy prospect of gambling revenues, were considering the sort of ordinance that would have preserved the town with a kind of Colonial Williamsburg dinkiness in the motif of the Wild West. All new buildings would have to have at least the facade of the sort of place where piano players used to wear garters on their sleeves in Virginia City around 1880. In Las Vegas in 1944, it should be noted, there was nothing more stimulating in the entire town than a Fremont Street bar where the composer of "Deep in the Heart of Texas" held forth and the regulars downed fifteen-cent beer.

Bugsy pulled into Las Vegas in 1945 with several million dollars that, after his assassination, was traced back in the general direction of gangster-financiers. Siegel put up a hotel-casino such as Las Vegas had never seen and called it the Flamingo—all Miami Modern, and the hell with piano players with garters and whatever that was all about. Everybody drove out Route 91 just to gape. Such shapes! Boomerang Modern supports, Palette Curvilinear bars, Hot Shoppe Cantilever roofs and a scalloped swimming pool. Such colors! All the new electrochemical pastels of the Florida littoral: tangerine, broiling magenta, livid pink, incarnadine, fuchsia demure. Congo ruby, methyl green, viridine, aquamarine, phenosafranine, incandescent orange, scarlet-fever purple, cyanic blue, tessellated bronze, hospital-fruit-basket orange. And such signs! Two cylinders rose at either end of the Flamingo—eight stories high and covered from top to bottom with neon rings in the shape of bubbles that fizzed all eight stories up into the desert sky all night long like an illuminated whisky-soda tumbler filled to the brim with pink champagne.

The business history of the Flamingo, on the other hand, was not such a smashing success. For one thing, the gambling operation was losing money at a rate that rather gloriously refuted all the recorded odds of the gaming science. Seigel's backers apparently suspected that he was playing both ends against the middle in collusion with professional gamblers who hung out at the Flamingo as though they had liens on it. What with one thing and another, someone decided by the night of June 20, 1947, that Benny Siegel, lord of the Flamingo, had had it. He was shot to death in Los Angeles.

Yet Siegel's aesthetic, psychological and cultural insights, like Cézanne's, Freud's and Max Weber's, could not die. The Siegel vision and the Siegel aesthetic were already sweeping Las Vegas like gold fever. And there were builders of the West equal to the opportunity. All over Las Vegas the incredible electric pastels were repeated. Overnight the Baroque Modern forms made Las Vegas one of the few architecturally unified cities of the world—the style was Late

American Rich—and without the bother and bad humor of a City Council ordinance. No enterprise was too small, too pedestrian or too solemn for The Look. The Supersonic Carwash, the Mercury Jetaway, Gas Vegas Village and Terrible Herbst gasoline stations, the Par-a-Dice Motel, the Palm Mortuary, the Orbit Inn, the Desert Moon, the Blue Onion Drive-In—on it went, like Wildwood, New Jersey, entering Heaven.

The atmosphere of the six-mile-long Strip of hotel-casinos grips even those segments of the population who rarely go near it. Barely twenty-five-hundred feet off the Strip, over by the Convention Center, stands Landmark Towers, a shaft thirty stories high, full of apartments, supporting a huge circular structure shaped like a space observation platform, which was to have contained the restaurant and casino. Somewhere along the way Landmark Towers went bankrupt, probably at that point in the last of the many crises when the construction work- ers *still* insisted on spending half the day flat on their bellies with their heads, tongues and eyeballs hanging over the edge of the tower, look- ing down into the swimming pool of the Playboy Apartments below, which has a "nudes only" section for show girls whose work calls for a tan all over.

Elsewhere, Las Vegas' beautiful little high-school buds in their   30 buttocks-décolletage stretch pants are back on the foam-rubber uphol- stery of luxury broughams peeling off the entire chick ensemble long enough to establish the highest venereal-disease rate among high- school students anywhere north of the yaws-rotting shanty jungles of the Eighth Parallel. The Negroes who have done much of the construc- tion work in Las Vegas' sixteen-year boom are off in their ghetto on the west side of town, and some of them are smoking marijuana, eating peyote buttons and taking horse (heroin), which they get from Tijuana. I mean it's simple, baby, right through the mails and old Raymond, the Phoenix engineer, does not have the high life to himself.

I am on the third floor of the Clark County Courthouse talking to Sheriff Captain Ray Gubser, another of these strong, pale-eyed West- ern-builder types, who is obligingly explaining to me law enforcement on the Strip, where the problem is not so much the drunks, crooks or roughhousers, but these nuts on pills who don't want to ever go to bed, and they have hallucinations and try to bring down the casinos like Samson. The county has two padded cells for them. They cool down after three or four days and they turn out to be somebody's earnest breadwinner back in Denver or Minneapolis, loaded with the right credentials and pouring soul and apologiae all over the county cops before finally pulling out of never-never land for good by plane. Captain Gubser is telling me about life and eccentric times in Las

Vegas, but I am distracted. The captain's office has windows out on the corridor. Coming down the corridor is a covey of girls, skipping and screaming, giggling along, their heads exploding in platinum-and-neon-yellow bouffants or beehives or raspberry-silk scarves, their eyes appliquéd in black like mail-order decals, their breasts aimed up under their jerseys at the angle of anti-aircraft automatic weapons, and, as they swing around the corner toward the elevator, their glutei maximi are bobbing up and down with their pumps in the inevitable buttocks décolletage pressed out against black, beige and incarnadine stretch pants. This is part of the latest shipment of show girls to Las Vegas, seventy in all, for the "Lido de Paris" revue at the Stardust, to be entitled *Bravo!*, replacing the old show, entitled *Voilà*. The girls are in the county courthouse getting their working papers, and fifteen days from now these little glutei maximi and ack-ack breasts with stars pasted on the tips will be swinging out over the slack jaws and cocked-up noses of patrons sitting at stageside at the Stardust. I am still listening to Gubser, but somehow it is a courthouse where mere words are beaten back like old atonal Arturo Toscanini trying to sing along with the NBC Symphony. There he would be, flapping his little toy arms like Tony Galento shadowboxing with fate, bawling away in the face of union musicians who drowned him without a bubble. I sat in on three trials in the courthouse, and it was wonderful, because the courtrooms are all blond-wood modern and look like sets for TV panel discussions on marriage and the teen-ager. What the judge has to say is no less formal and no more fatuous than what judges say everywhere, but inside of forty seconds it is all meaningless because the atmosphere is precisely like a news broadcast over Las Vegas' finest radio station, KORK. The newscast, as it is called, begins with a series of electronic wheeps out on that far edge of sound where only quadrupeds can hear. A voice then announces that this is Action Checkpoint News. "The news—all the news—flows first through Action Checkpoint!—then reaches You! at the speed of Sound!" More electronic wheeps, beeps and lulus, and then an item: "Cuban Premier Fidel Castro nearly drowned yesterday." Urp! Wheep! Lulu! No news a KORK announcer has ever brought to Las Vegas at the speed of sound, or could possibly bring, short of word of the annihilation of Los Angeles, could conceivably compete within the brain with the giddiness of this electronic jollification.

The wheeps, beeps, freeps, electronic lulus. Boomerang Modern and Flash Gordon sunbursts soar on through the night over the billowing hernia-hernia sounds and the old babes at the slots—until it is 7:30 A.M. and I am watching five men at a green-topped card table playing poker. They are sliding their Bee-brand cards into their hands and squinting at the pips with a set to the lips like Conrad Veidt in a tunic collar studying a code message from S.S. headquarters. Big Sid Wyman, the old Big-Time gambler from St. Louis, is there, with his eyes looking like two poached eggs engraved with a road map of West Virginia after all night at the poker table. Sixty-year-old Chicago Tommy Hargan is there with his topknot of white hair pulled back over his little pink skull and a mountain of chips in front of his old caved-in sternum. Sixty-two-year-old Dallas Maxie Welch is there, fat and phlegmatic as an Indian Ocean potentate. Two los Angeles biggies are there exhaling smoke from candela-green cigars into the gloom. It looks like the perfect vignette of every Big Time back room, "athletic club," snooker house and floating poker game in the history of the guys-and-dolls lumpen-bourgeoisie. But what is all this? Off to the side, at a rostrum, sits a flawless little creature with bouffant hair and Stridex-pure skin who looks like she is polished each morning with a rotary buffer. Before her on the rostrum is a globe of coffee on a hot coil. Her sole job is to keep the poker players warmed up with coffee. Meantime, numberless uniformed lackeys are cocked and aimed about the edges to bring the five Big Timers whatever else they might desire, cigarettes, drinks, napkins, eyeglass-cleaning tissues, plug-in telephones. All around the poker table, at a respectful distance of ten feet, is a fence with the most delicate golden pickets. Upon it, even at this narcoleptic hour, lean men and women in their best clothes watching the combat of the titans. The scene is the charmed circle of the casino of the Dunes Hotel. As everyone there knows, or believes, these fabulous men are playing for table stakes of fifteen or twenty thousand dollars. One hundred dollars rides on a chip. Mandibles gape at the progress of the battle. And now Sid Wyman, who is also a vice-president of the Dunes, is at a small escritoire just inside the golden fence signing a stack of vouchers for such sums as $4500, all printed in the heavy Mondrianesque digits of a Burroughs business check-making machine. It is as if America's guys-and-dolls gamblers have somehow been tapped upon the shoulders, knighted, initiated into a new aristocracy.

Las Vegas has become, just as Bugsy Siegel dreamed, the American Monte Carlo—without any of the inevitable upper-class baggage of the Riviera casinos. At Monte Carlo there is still the plush mustiness of the nineteenth century noble lions—of Baron Bleichroden, a big winner at roulette who always said, "My dear friends, it is so easy on Black." Of Lord Jersey, who won seventeen maximum bets in a row—on black, as a matter of fact—nodded to the croupier, and said, "Much obliged, old sport, old sport," took his winnings to England, retired to the country and never gambled again in his life. Or of the old Duc de Dinc who said he could win only in the high-toned Club Privé, and who won very heavily one night, saw two Englishmen gaping at his good fortune, threw them every mille-franc note he had in his hands and said, "Here. Englishmen without money are altogether odious." Thousands of Europeans from the lower orders now have the money to go to the Riviera, but they remain under the century-old status pall of the aristocracy. At Monte Carlo there are still Wrong Forks, Deficient Accents, Poor Tailoring, Gauche Displays, Nouveau Richness, Cultural Aridity—concepts unknown in Las Vegas. For the grand debut of Monte Carlo as a resort in 1879 the architect Charles Garnier designed an opera house for the Place du Casino; and Sarah Bernhardt read a symbolic poem. For the debut of Las Vegas as a resort in 1946 Bugsy Siegel hired Abbott and Costello, and there, in a way, you have it all.

I am in the office of Major A. Riddle—Major is his name—the president of the Dunes Hotel. He combs his hair straight back and wears a heavy gold band on his little finger with a diamond sunk into it. As everywhere else in Las Vegas, someone has turned on the air conditioning to the point where it will be remembered, all right, as Las Vegas–style air conditioning. Riddle has an appointment to see a doctor at 4:30 about a crimp in his neck. His secretary, Maude McBride, has her head down and is rubbing the back of her neck. Lee Fisher, the P.R. man, and I are turning ours from time to time to keep the pivots from freezing up. Riddle is telling me about "the French war" and moving his neck gingerly. The Stardust bought and imported a version of the Lido de Paris spectacular, and the sight of all those sequined giblets pooning around on flamingo legs inflamed the tourists. The Tropicana fought back with the Folies Bergère, the New Frontier installed "Paree Ooh La La," the Hacienda reached for the puppets "Les Poupées de Paris," and the Silver Slipper called in Lili St. Cyr, the stripper, which was going French after a fashion. So the Dunes has bought up the third and last of the great Paris girlie shows, the Casino de Paris. Lee Fisher says, "And we're going to do things they *can't* top. In this town you've got to move ahead in quantum jumps."

35   Quantum? But exactly! The beauty of the Dunes' Casino de Paris show is that it will be beyond art, beyond dance, beyond spectacle, even beyond the titillations of the winking crotch. The Casino de Paris will be a behemoth piece of American calculus, like Project Mercury.

"This show alone will cost us two and a half million a year to operate and one and a half million to produce," Major A. Riddle is saying. "The costumes alone will be fantastic. There'll be more than five hundred costumes and—well, they'll be fantastic.

"And this machine—by the time we get through expanding the stage, this machine will cost us $250,000."

"Machine?"

"Yes. Sean Kenny is doing the staging. The whole set moves electronically right in front of your eyes. He used to work with this fellow Lloyd Wright."

"Frank Lloyd Wright?"   40

"Yes. Kenny did the staging for *Blitz*. Did you see it? Fantastic. Well, it's all done electronically. They built this machine for us in Glasgow, Scotland, and it's being shipped here right now. It moves all over the place and creates smoke and special effects. We'll have everything. You can stage a bombardment with it. You'll think the whole theatre is blowing up.

"You'll have to program it. They had to use the same mechansim that's in the Skybolt Missile to build it. It's called 'Celson' or something like that. That's how complicated this thing is. They have to have the same thing as the Skybolt Missile."

As Riddle speaks, one gets a wonderful picture of sex riding the crest of the future. Whole tableaux of bare-bottomed Cosmonaughties will be hurtling around the Casino de Paris Room of the Dunes Hotel at fantastic speed in elliptical orbits, a flash of the sequined giblets here, a blur of the black-rimmed decal eyes there, a wink of the crotch here and there, until, with one vast Project Climax for our times, Sean Kenny, who used to work with this fellow Frank Lloyd Wright, presses the red button and the whole yahooing harem, shrieking ooh-la-la amid the din, exits in a mushroom cloud.

The allure is most irresitible not to the young but the old. No one in Las Vegas will admit it—it is not the modern, glamorous notion—but Las Vegas is a resort for old people. In those last years, before the tissue deteriorates and the wires of the cerebral cortex hang in the skull like a clump of dried seaweed, they are seeking liberation.

At eight o'clock Sunday morning it is another almost boringly   45
sunny day in the desert, and Clara and Abby, both about sixty, and their husbands, Earl, sixty-three, and Ernest, sixty-four, come squinting out of the Mint Casino onto Fremont Street.

"I don't know what's wrong with me," Abby says. "Those last three drinks, I couldn't even feel them. It was just like drinking fizz. You know what I mean?"

"Hey," says Ernest, "how about that place back 'ere? We ain't been back 'ere. Come on."

The others are standing there on the corner, squinting and looking doubtful. Abby and Clara have both entered old babehood. They have that fleshy, humped-over shape across the back of the shoulders. Their torsos are hunched up into fat little loaves supported by bony, atrophied leg stems sticking up into their hummocky hips. Their hair has been fried and dyed into improbable designs.

"You know what I mean? After a while it just gives me gas," says Abby. "I don't even feel it."

50   "Did you see me over there?" says Earl. "I was just going along, nice and easy, not too much, just riding along real nice. You know? And then, boy, I don't know what happened to me. First thing I know I'm laying down fifty dollars. . . ."

Abby lets out a great belch. Clara giggles.

"Gives me gas," Abby says mechanically.

"Hey, how about that place back 'ere?" says Ernest.

". . . Just nice and easy as you please. . . ."

55   ". . . get me all fizzled up. . . ."

"Aw, come on. . . ."

And there at eight o'clock Sunday morning stand four old parties from Albuquerque, New Mexico, up all night, squinting at the sun, belching from a surfeit of tall drinks at eight o'clock Sunday morning, and—marvelous!—there is no one around to snigger at what an old babe with decaying haunches looks like in Capri pants with her heels jacked up on decorated wedgies.

"Where do we *come* from?" Clara said to me, speaking for the first time since I approached them on Fremont Street. "He wants to know where we come from. I think it's past your bedtime, sweets."

"Climb the stairs and go to bed," said Abby.

60   Laughter all around.

"Climb the stairs" was Abby's finest line. At present there are almost no stairs to climb in Las Vegas. Avalon homes are soon to go up, advertising "Two-Story Homes!" as though this were an incredibly lavish and exotic concept. As I talked to Clara, Abby, Earl and Ernest, it came out that "climb the stairs" was a phrase they brought along to Albuquerque with them from Marshalltown, Iowa, those many years ago, along with a lot of other baggage, such as the entire cupboard of Protestant taboos against drinking, lusting, gambling, staying out late, getting up late, loafing, idling, lollygagging around the streets and wearing Capri pants—all designed to deny a person short-term pleasures so he will center his energies on bigger, long-term goals.

"We was in 'ere"—the Mint—"a couple of hours ago, and that old boy was playing the guitar, you know. 'Walk right in, set right down,' and I kept hearing an old song I haven't heard for twenty years. It has this little boy and his folks keep telling him it's late and he has to go to bed. He keeps saying, 'Don't make me go to bed and I'll be good.' Am I *good*, Earl? Am I *good*?"

The liberated cortex in all its glory is none other than the old babes at the slot machines. Some of them are tourists whose husbands said, *Here is fifty bucks, go play the slot machines,* while they themselves went off to more complex pleasures. But most of these old babes are part of the permanent landscape of Las Vegas. In they go to the Golden Nugget or the Mint, with their Social Security check or their pension check from the Ohio telephone company, cash it at the casino cashier's, pull out the Dixie Cup and the Iron Boy work glove, disappear down a row of slots and get on with it. I remember particularly talking to another Abby—a widow, sixty-two years old, built short and up from the bottom like a fire hydrant. After living alone for twelve years in Canton, Ohio, she had moved out to Las Vegas to live with her daughter and her husband, who worked for the Army.

"They were wonderful about it," she said. "Perfect hypocrites. She kept saying, you know, 'Mother, we'd be delighted to have you, only we don't think you'll *like* it. It's practically a frontier town,' she says. 'It's so *garish*,' she says. So I said, I told her, 'Well, if you'd rather I didn't come . . .' 'Oh, no!' she says. I wish I could have heard what her husband was saying. He calls me 'Mother.' '*Mother*,' he says. Well, once I was here, they figured, well I *might* make a good baby-sitter and dishwasher and duster and mopper. The children are nasty little things. So one day I was in town for something or other and I just played a slot machine. It's fun—I can't describe it to you. I suppose I lose. I lose a little. And *they* have fits about it. 'For God's sake, Grandmother,' and so forth. They always say '*Grand*mother' when I am supposed to 'act my age' or crawl through a crack in the floor. Well, I'll tell you, the slot machines are a *whole lot* better than sitting in that little house all day. They kind of get you; I can't explain it."

The childlike megalomania of gambling is, of course, from the same cloth as the megalomania of the town. And, as the children of the liberated cortex, the old guys and babes are running up and down the Strip around the clock like everybody else. It is not by chance that much of the entertainment in Las Vegas, especially the second-stringers who perform in the cocktail lounges, will recall for an aging man what was glamorous twenty-five years ago when he had neither the money nor the freedom of spirit to indulge himself in it. In the big theatre-dining room at the Desert Inn, The Painted Desert Room, Eddie Fisher's act is on and he is saying cozily to a florid guy at a table right next to the stage, "Manny, you know you shouldn'a sat this close— you know you're in for it now, Manny, baby," while Manny beams with fright. But in the cocktail lounge, where the idea is chiefly just to keep the razzle-dazzle going, there is Hugh Farr, one of the stars of another era in the West, composer of two of the five Western songs the Library of Congress has taped for posterity, "Cool Water" and "Tumbling Tumbleweed," when he played the violin for the Sons of the Pioneers. And now around the eyes he looks like an aging Chinese savant, but he is wearing a white tuxedo and powder-blue leather boots and playing his sad old Western violin with an electric cord plugged in it

65

for a group called The Country Gentlemen. And there is Ben Blue, looking like a waxwork exhibit of vaudeville, doffing his straw skimmer to reveal the sculptural qualities of his skull. And down at the Flamingo cocktail lounge—Ella Fitzgerald is in the main room—there is Harry James, looking old and pudgy in one of those toy Italian-style show-biz suits. And the Ink Spots are at the New Frontier and Louis Prima is at the Sahara, and the old parties are seeing it all, roaring through the dawn into the next day, until the sun seems like a par lamp fading in and out. The casinos, the bars, the liquor stores are open every minute of every day, like a sempiternal wading pool for the childhood ego.". . . Don't make me go to bed. . . ."

For Journals

Have you ever been to Las Vegas? Is it a place you would want to go to have a good time? Why or why not?

For Discussion

1.   Reread Wolfe's encounter with the two tourist couples, Clara and Earl and Abby and Ernest, and the woman named Abby who lives in Las Vegas and plays the slot machines (paragraphs 45–64). What assertions does he make about them, their appearance, their taste? What do you think his opinion of them is? Find some specific examples that support your evaluation.

2.   How do you think the two couples would react to Wolfe's assertions about them? How do you think they view themselves? Their work ethic? Choice of entertainment? Values? What reasons do you think they would give for wanting to gamble in Las Vegas?

3.   What assertions, positive or negative, does Wolfe make about the difference between Las Vegas and Monte Carlo? Discuss specific examples. Which do you think he prefers? Why? How do his examples of what Monte Carlo is show what he thinks Las Vegas is not?

4.   *The Encyclopedia of Bad Taste* says Las Vegas is "the most equal-opportunity place on earth: any slob, however low his social standing, however ugly his clothes, and no matter how uncouthly he may behave, gets treated like royalty if he has money to spend." Does Wolfe support or contradict this view? Does he approve of this lowest-common-denominator democracy? What evidence does he give either way?

5.   Wolfe's style of writing—a continuous barrage of information, sound effects, exclamation points, lists—is at least as famous as his subject matter. He even makes up names for people, buildings, and so forth. Find three or four samples of Wolfe's unique descriptive language and take turns in class reading them out loud. How do these examples provide support for his opinions and convey to you his sense of Las Vegas?

6. Americans from the Midwest, the central location of Protestant population and the heartland of the work ethic, are among the most frequent visitors to Las Vegas. Why do you think people whose values are considered the most representative of solid American work habits and family values would be attracted to a place as openly materialistic and garish as Las Vegas?

For Writing

1. If you have ever been to Disneyland, Disneyworld, Atlantic City, or any similar place that large numbers of Americans visit for leisure or vacation, write a description of your visit. Include your opinion on who goes there and why, how they behave, whether you thought the buildings and atmosphere were in good taste or poor taste, and your own response to the experience. Use details from your observations as supporting evidence for your ideas.

2. Both Fitzgerald and Wolfe write about people with the time and money to enjoy themselves. Write an essay in which you choose one episode from Wolfe's "Las Vegas (What?)" and compare it with Fitzgerald's description of the party episode in *The Great Gatsby* and the list of partygoers' names. In each case, what judgments or assertions are being made about these people? Are the assertions negative or positive? How does each writer use language to support his view? Refer to specific examples to support your conclusions.

THE IMPORTANCE OF WORK

1983

Gloria Steinem

> *Born in Toledo, Ohio, Gloria Steinem (1934–   ) was educated at Smith College and went on to study at the University of Delhi and the University of Calcutta, India. She is the editor and cofounder of* Ms. magazine

and has played an important part in the women's movement. Steinem's works include Outrageous Acts and Everyday Rebellions *(1983),* Revolution from Within *(1992), and* Moving Beyond Words *(1994). In her essay "The Importance of Work," she examines the relationship between personal and professional fulfillment.*

Toward the end of the 1970s, the *Wall Street Journal* devoted an eight-part front-page series to "the working woman"—that is, the influx of women into the paid-labor force—as the greatest change in American life since the Industrial Revolution.

Many women readers greeted both the news and the definition with cynicism. After all, women have always worked. If all the productive work of human maintenance that women do in the home were valued at its replacement cost, the gross national product of the United States would go up by 26 percent. It's just that we are now more likely than ever before to leave our poorly rewarded, low-security, high-risk job of homemaking (though we're still trying to explain that it's a perfectly good one and that the problem is male society's refusal both to do it and to give it an economic value) for more secure, independent and better-paid jobs outside the home.

Obviously, the real work revolution won't come until all productive work is rewarded—including child rearing and other jobs done in the home—and men are integrated into so-called women's work as well as vice versa. But the radical change being touted by the *Journal* and other media is one part of that long integration process: the unprecedented flood of women into salaried jobs, that is, into the labor force as it has been male-defined and previously occupied by men. We are already more than 41 percent of it—the highest proportion in history. Given the fact that women also make up a whopping 69 percent of the "discouraged labor force" (that is, people who need jobs but don't get counted in the unemployment statistics because they've given up looking), plus an official female unemployment rate that is substantially higher than men's, it's clear that we could expand to become fully half of the national work force by 1990.

Faced with this determination of women to find a little independence and to be paid and honored for our work, experts have rushed to ask: "Why?" It's a question rarely directed at male workers. Their basic motivations of survival and personal satisfaction are taken for granted. Indeed, men are regarded as "odd" and therefore subjects for sociological study and journalistic reports only when they *don't* have work, even if they are rich and don't need jobs or are poor and can't find them. Nonetheless, pollsters and sociologists have gone to great expense to prove that women work outside the home because of dire financial need, or if we persist despite the presence of a wage-earning male, out of some desire to buy "little extras" for our families, or even out of good old-fashioned penis envy.

Job interviewers and even our own families may still ask salaried   5 women the big "Why?" If we have small children at home or are in some job regarded as "men's work," the incidence of such questions increases. Condescending or accusatory versions of "What's a nice girl like you doing in a place like this?" have not disappeared from the workplace.

How do we answer these assumptions that we are "working" out of some pressing or peculiar need? Do we feel okay about arguing that it's as natural for us to have salaried jobs as for our husbands whether or not we have young children at home? Can we enjoy strong career ambitions without worrying about being thought "unfeminine"? When we confront men's growing resentment of women competing in the work force (often in the form of such guilt-producing accusations as "You're taking men's jobs away" or "You're damaging your children"), do we simply state that a decent job is a basic human right for everybody?

I'm afraid the answer is often no. As individuals and as a movement, we tend to retreat into some version of a tactically questionable defense: "Womenworkbecausewehaveto." The phrase has become one word, one key on the typewriter—an economic form of the socially "feminine" stance of passivity and self-sacrifice. Under attack, we still tend to present ourselves as creatures of economic neccessity and familial devotion. "Womenworkbecausewehaveto" has become the easiest thing to say.

Like most truisms, this one is easy to prove with statistics. Economic need *is* the most consistent work motive—for women as well as men. In 1976, for instance, 43 percent of all women in the paid-labor force were single, widowed, separated, or divorced, and working to support themselves and their dependents. An additional 21 percent were married to men who had earned less than ten thousand dollars in the previous year, the minimum then required to support a family of four. In fact, if you take men's pensions, stocks, real estate, and various forms of accumulated wealth into account, a good statistical case can be made that there are more women who "have" to work (that is, who have neither the accumulated wealth, nor husbands whose work or wealth can support them for the rest of their lives) than there are men with the same need. If we were going to ask one group "Do you really need this job?" we should ask men.

But the first weakness of the whole "have to work" defense is its deceptiveness. Anyone who has ever experienced dehumanized life on welfare or any other confidence-shaking dependency knows that a paid job may be preferable to the dole, even when the handout is coming from a family member. Yet the will and self-confidence to work on one's own can diminish as dependency and fear increase. That may explain why—contrary to the "have to" rationale—wives of men who earn less that three thousand dollars a year are actually *less* likely to be employed than wives whose husbands make ten thousand dollars a year or more.

10   Furthermore, the greatest proportion of employed wives is found among families with a total household income of twenty-five to fifty thousand dollars a year. This is the statistical underpinning used by some sociologists to prove that women's work is mainly important for boosting families into the middle or upper middle class. Thus, women's incomes are largely used for buying "luxuries" and "little extras": a neat double-whammy that renders us secondary within our families, and makes our jobs expendable in hard times. We may even go along with this interpretation (at least, up to the point of getting fired so a male can have our job). It preserves a husbandly ego-need to be seen as the primary breadwinner, and still allows us a safe "feminine" excuse for working.

But there are often rewards that we're not confessing. As noted in *The Two-Career Couple,* by Francine and Douglas Hall: "Women who hold jobs by choice, even blue-collar routine jobs, are more satisfied with their lives than are the full-time housewives."

In addition to personal satisfaction, there is also society's need for all its members' talents. Suppose that jobs were given out on only a "have to work" basis to both women and men—one job per household. It would be unthinkable to lose the unique abilities of, for instance, Eleanor Holmes Norton, the distinguished chair of the Equal Employment Opportunity Commission. But would we then be forced to question the important work of her husband, Edward Norton, who is also a distinguished lawyer? Since men earn more than twice as much as women on the average, the wife in most households would be more likely to give up her job. Does that mean the nation could do as well without millions of its nurses, teachers, and secretaries? Or that the rare man who earns less than his wife should give up his job?

It was this kind of waste of human talents on a society-wide scale that traumatized millions of unemployed or underemployed Americans during the Depression. Then, a one-job-per-household rule seemed somewhat justified, yet the concept was used to displace women workers only, create intolerable dependencies, and waste female talent that the country needed. That Depression experience, plus the energy and example of women who were finally allowed to work during the manpower shortage created by World War II, led Congress to reinterpret the meaning of the country's full-employment goal in its Economic Act of 1946. Full employment was officially defined as "the employment of those who want to work, without regard to whether their employment is, by some definition, necessary. This goal applies equally to men and women." Since bad economic times are again creating a resentment of employed women—as well as creating more need for women to be employed—we need such a goal more than ever. Women are again being caught in a tragic double bind: We are required to be strong and then punished for our strength.

Clearly, anything less than government and popular commitment to this 1946 definition of full employment will leave the less powerful groups, whoever they may be, in danger. Almost as important as the financial penalty paid by the powerless is the suffering that comes from being shut out of paid and recognized work. Without it, we lose much of our self-respect and our ability to prove that we are alive by making some difference in the world. That's just as true for the suburban woman as it is for the unemployed steel worker.

But it won't be easy to give up the passive defense of "weworkbe-   15
causewehaveto."

When a woman who is struggling to support her children and grandchildren on welfare sees her neighbor working as a waitress, even though that neighbor's husband has a job, she may feel resentful; and the waitress (of course, not the waitress's husband) may feel guilty. Yet unless we establish the obligation to provide a job for everyone who is willing and able to work, that welfare woman may herself be penalized by policies that give out only one public-service job per household. She and her daughter will have to make a painful and divisive decision about which of them gets that precious job, and the whole household will have to survive on only one salary.

A job as a human right is a principle that applies to men as well as women. But women have more cause to fight for it. The phenomenon of the "working woman" has been held responsible for everything from an increase in male impotence (which turned out, incidentally, to be attributable to medication for high blood pressure) to the rising cost of steak (which was due to high energy costs and beef import restrictions, not women's refusal to prepare the cheaper, slower-cooking cuts). Unless we see a job as part of every citizen's right to autonomy and personal fulfillment, we will continue to be vulnerable to someone else's idea of what "need" is, and whose "need" counts the most.

In many ways, women who do not have to work for simple sur-

vival, but who choose to do so nonetheless, are on the frontier of asserting this right for all women. Those with well-to-do husbands are
dangerously easy for us to resent and put down. It's easier still to resent women from families of inherited wealth, even though men generally control and benefit from that wealth. (There is no Rockefeller
Sisters Fund, no J. P. Morgan & Daughters, and sons-in-law may be
the ones who really sleep their way to power.) But to prevent a woman
whose husband or father is wealthy from earning her own living, and
from gaining the self-confidence that comes with that ability, is to keep
her needful of that unearned power and less willing to disperse it.
Moreover, it is to lose forever her unique talents.

Perhaps modern feminists have been guilty of a kind of reverse
snobbism that keeps us from reaching out to the wives and daughters
of wealthy men; yet it was exactly such women who refused the restrictions of class and financed the first wave of feminist revolution.

20   For most of us, however, "womenworkbecausewehaveto" is just
true enough to be seductive as a personal defense.

If we use it without also staking out the larger human right to a
job, however, we will never achieve that right. And we will always be
subject to the false argument that independence for women is a luxury
affordable only in good economic times. Alternatives to layoffs will not
be explored, acceptable unemployment will always be used to frighten
those with jobs into accepting low wages, and we will never remedy
the real cost, both to families and to the country, of dependent women
and a massive loss of talent.

Worst of all, we may never learn to find productive, honored work
as a natural part of ourselves and as one of life's basic pleasures.

For Journals

Why do you believe women work? Do they work for different reasons
than men do?

For Discussion

1. Steinem writes that "the real work revolution won't come until all
productive work is rewarded—including child rearing and other jobs
done in the home—and men are integrated into so-called women's
work as well as vice versa" (paragraph 3). Do you believe that, a
decade later, this revolution has begun? If so, to what do you attribute
the change? If not, why not? Specify the assumptions and evidence on
which you are basing your assertion.

2. Steinem takes issue with the "womenworkbecausewehaveto"
(paragraph 7) rejoinder that has so often answered those who criticize

women for holding down paid jobs outside the home. What is her counter assertion, and how does she support it? Do you find her argument convincing?

3. Do you believe the "womenworkbecausewehave to" (paragraph 7) argument is valid? Support your point of view with specific examples, narrative, or other support.

4. Consider the following two quotations, the first from Gilman's *Women and Economics* (this chapter):

> But all that she may wish to have, all that she may wish to do, must come through a single channel and a single choice. Wealth, power, social distinction, fame—not only these, but home and happiness, reputation, ease, and pleasure, her bread and butter—all must come to her through a gold ring. (paragraph 5).

the second from Steinem's essay:

> "Womenworkbecausewehaveto." The phrase has become one word, one key on the typewriter—an economic form of the socially "feminine" stance of passivity and self-sacrifice. Under attack, we still tend to present ourselves as creatures of economic necessity and familial devotion. (paragraph 7).

Compare these two quotations by examining the different assumptions behind them, the evidence the authors provide to support them, and the extent to which they represent gender and work issues of their respective times.

5. Analyze the evidence on which Steinem bases her assertions. Do you agree with the conclusions she draws? Do you accept the evidence she cites?

For Writing

1. What is the importance of work to you? Write an essay arguing that the role and value of work is, or is not, determined by gender.

2. Compare the assertions about work and gender that Steinem makes with either Gilman or Ou (both this chapter). You may want to create a dialogue between the two writers in responding to the assignment.

SHOPPING AND OTHER SPIRITUAL ADVENTURES

1984

Phyllis Rose

Phyllis Rose (1942–   ) is an editor and writer whose varied works include biographies of both Virginia Woolf and Josephine Baker, the book Parallel Lives: Five Victorian Marriages *(1983), and a collection of her essays. Her work has also appeared in the* New York Times *and other notable periodicals.*

Last year a new Waldbaum's Food Mart opened in the shopping mall on Route 66. It belongs to the new generation of superdupermarkets open twenty-four hours that have computerized checkout. I went to see the place as soon as it opened and I was impressed. There was trail mix in Lucite bins. There was freshly made pasta. There were coffee beans, four kinds of tahini, ten kinds of herb teas, raw shrimp in shells and cooked shelled shrimp, fresh-squeezed orange juice. Every sophistication known to the big city, even goat's cheese covered with ash, was now available in Middletown, Connecticut. People raced from the warehouse aisle to the bagel bin to the coffee beans to the fresh fish market, exclaiming at all the new things. Many of us felt elevated, graced, complimented by the presence of this food palace in our town.

This is the wonderful egalitarianism of American business. Was it Andy Warhol who said that the nice thing about Coke is, no can is any better or worse than any other? Some people may find it dull to cross the country and find the same chain stores with the same merchandise from coast to coast, but it means that my town is as good as yours, my shopping mall as important as yours, equally filled with wonders.

Imagine what people ate during the winter as little as seventy-five years ago. They ate food that was local, long-lasting and dull, like acorn squash, turnips and cabbage. Walk into an American supermarket in February and the world lies before you: grapes, melons, artichokes, fennel, lettuce, peppers, pistachios, dates, even strawberries, to say nothing of ice cream. Have you ever considered what a triumph of civilization it is to be able to buy a pound of chicken livers? If you lived on a farm and had to kill a chicken when you wanted to eat one, you wouldn't ever accumulate a pound of chicken livers.

Another wonder of Middletown is Caldor, the discount department store. Here is man's plenty: tennis racquets, pantyhose, luggage,
glassware, records, toothpaste, Timex watches, Cadbury's chocolate,
corn poppers, hair dryers, warm-up suits, car wax, light bulbs, television sets. All good quality at low prices with exchanges cheerfully
made on defective goods. There are worse rules to live by. I feel good
about America whenever I walk into this store, which is almost every
midwinter Sunday afternoon, when life elsewhere has closed down. I
go to Caldor the way English people go to pubs: out of sociability. To
get away from my house. To widen my horizons. For culture's sake.
Caldor provides me too with a welcome sense of seasonal change.
When the first outdoor grills and lawn furniture appear there, it's as
exciting a sign of spring as the first crocus or robin.

Someone told me about a Soviet émigré who practices English   5
by declaiming, at random, sentences that catch his fancy. One of his
favorites is, "Fifty percent off all items today only." Refugees from
Communist countries appreciate our supermarkets and discount department stores for the wonders they are. An Eastern European scientist visiting Middletown wept when she first saw the meat counter at
Waldbaum's. On the other hand, before her year in America was up,
her pleasure turned sour. She wanted everything she saw. Her approach to consumer goods was insufficiently abstract, too materialistic.
We Americans are beyond a simple, possessive materialism. We're
used to abundance and the possibility of possessing things. The things,
and the possibility of possessing them, will still be there next week,
next year. So today we can walk the aisles calmly.

It is a misunderstanding of the American retail store to think we
go there necessarily to buy. Some of us shop. There's a difference.
Shopping has many purposes, the least interesting of which is to acquire new articles. We shop to cheer ourselves up. We shop to practice
decision-making. We shop to be useful and productive members of our
class and society. We shop to remind ourselves how much is available
to us. We shop to remind ourselves how much is to be striven for. We
shop to assert our superiority to the material objects that spread themselves before us.

Shopping's function as a form of therapy is widely appreciated.
You don't really need, let's say, another sweater. You need the feeling
of power that comes with buying or not buying it. You need the feeling
that someone wants something you have—even if it's just your money.
To get the benefit of shopping, you needn't actually purchase the
sweater, any more than you have to marry every man you flirt with. In
fact, window-shopping, like flirting, can be more rewarding, the same
high without the distressing commitment, the material encumbrance.
The purest form of shopping is provided by garage sales. A connois-

seur goes out with no goal in mind, open to whatever may come his or her way, secure that it will cost very little. Minimum expense, maximum experience. Perfect shopping.

I try to think of the opposite, a kind of shopping in which the object is all-important, the pleasure of shopping at a minimum. For example, the purchase of blue jeans. I buy new blue jeans as seldom as possible because the experience is so humiliating. For every pair that looks good on me, fifteen look grotesque. But even shopping for blue jeans at Bob's Surplus on Main Street—no frills, bare-bones shopping—is an event in the life of the spirit. Once again I have to come to terms with the fact that I will never look good in Levi's. Much as I want to be mainstream, I never will be.

In fact, I'm doubly an oddball, neither Misses nor Junior, but Misses Petite. I look in the mirror, I acknowledge the disparity between myself and the ideal, I resign myself to making the best of it: I will buy the Lee's Misses Petite. Shopping is a time of reflection, assessment, spiritual self-discipline.

10   It is appropriate, I think, that Bob's Surplus has a communal dressing room. I used to shop only in places where I could count on a private dressing room with a mirror inside. My impulse then was to hide my weaknesses. Now I believe in sharing them. There are other women in the dressing room at Bob's Surplus trying on blue jeans who look as bad as I do. We take comfort from one another. Sometimes a woman will ask me which of two items looks better. I always give a definite answer. It's the least I can do. I figure we are all in this together, and I emerge from the dressing room not only with a new pair of jeans but with a renewed sense of belonging to a human community.

When a Solzhenitsyn rants about American materialism, I have to look at my digital Timex and check what year this is. Materialism? Like conformism, a hot moral issue of the 50s, but not now. How to spread the goods, maybe. Whether the goods are the Good, no. Solzhenitsyn, like the visiting scientist who wept at the beauty of Waldbaum's meat counter but came to covet everything she saw, takes American materialism too materialistically. He doesn't see its spiritual side. Caldor, Waldbaum's, Bob's Surplus—these, perhaps, are our cathedrals.

For Journals

How do you respond to the title of the essay? How could shopping be a spiritual experience? What are the other spiritual experiences to which Rose refers?

For Discussion

1.   How does Rose support her assertion that shopping fulfills a completely different purpose for Americans than it does for people from less wealthy societies, or even for Americans of earlier generations?

2.   Rose speaks of how "we" Americans feel about shopping, and that "we" shop to cheer ourselves up. What assumptions about the composition of her audience is she making in these statements? To which Americans is she addressing herself? Do you count yourself among them?

3.   How do you think Alfred Lubrano's working-class father (selection this chapter) would respond to Rose's assertions that we shop for therapy, or to establish our superiority to the material objects before us, or for self-fulfillment?

4.   Why do you think Rose doesn't mention money in this essay? Is money irrelevant to the shopping experience she describes? What would you expect the spiritual experience of shopping would be for someone out of work?

5.   Charlotte Perkins Gilman said she wanted women to have financial independence. How do you think her notions of money and leisure differ from or resemble Rose's?

6.   How do you respond to Rose's statement that stores are our cathedrals? If Americans believe in the work ethic, what would they be worshipping in a shopping center?

For Writing

1.   Go to a shopping mall or a garage sale on a Saturday or Sunday, and write up your observations. Be sure to take notes on the appearance and demeanor of the shoppers. Make some educated guesses about their financial status. Do they browse? Do they appear to be engaged in the pursuit of a pleasurable leisure activity? Keep Rose's assertions about the psychological satisfaction of shopping in mind, and see if the behaviors you observe support or refute her argument. You can pick individual assertions out of her essay and then respond to them with the material from your observations if you wish.

Alternatively, test Rose's assertions by interviewing some of your peers about their attitudes toward shopping. Prepare a short questionnaire, and sample both male and female opinions to see if the attitudes about shopping differ by gender.

2.   Rose asserts that Americans of seventy-five years ago could never have imagined the prolific nature of today's shopping experience. In your school library, find the recently reissued *Sears, Roebuck Catalogue* of 1902. Its advertisements are organized by type of products. Pick three or four categories of goods—cameras, bicycles, fishing and hunting equipment, musical instruments—that draw your eye. Read the advertisements; look for variety of goods and variety of uses (e.g., advertisements for both work and leisure-related activities). Then write an essay in which you consider the following questions: What kinds of products were available? How wide was the selection within categories? How closely related do you think ordering from or browsing through a Sears catalog in 1902 is to shopping in a suburban mall today? Given the decline in the value of the dollar since 1902, how affordable do you think these products would have been to most Americans?

BRICKLAYER'S BOY
1 9 8 9

Alfred Lubrano

Alfred Lubrano is a reporter for New York Newsday *and is a contributor to* Gentleman's Quarterly, *where this essay originally appeared. Lubrano frequently writes about issues of personal relationships and family life. In the memoir that follows, he writes about the family and work values gained from his blue collar upbringing and the ways in which they are, or are not, reconciled with the ways in which he lives his adult life.*

My father and I were college buddies back in the mid 1970s. While I was in class at Columbia, struggling with the esoterica du jour, he was on a bricklayer's scaffold not far up the street, working on a campus building.

Sometimes we'd hook up on the subway going home, he with his tools, I with my books. We didn't chat much about what went on during the day. My father wasn't interested in Dante, I wasn't up on arches. We'd share a *New York Post* and talk about the Mets.

My dad has built lots of places in New York City he can't get into: colleges, condos, office towers. He makes his living on the outside. Once the walls are up, a place takes on a different feel for him, as if he's not welcome anymore. It doesn't bother him, though. For my father, earning the dough that paid for my entrée into a fancy, bricked-in institution was satisfaction enough, a vicarious access.

We didn't know it then, but those days were the start of a branching off, a redefining of what it means to be a workingman in our family. Related by blood, we're separated by class, my father and I. Being the white-collar son of a blue-collar man means being the hinge on the door between two ways of life.

It's not so smooth jumping from Italian old-world style to U.S. yuppie in a single generation. Despite the myth of mobility in America, the true rule, experts say, is rags to rags, riches to riches. According to Bucknell University economist and author Charles Sackrey, maybe 10 percent climb from the working to the professional class. My father has had a tough time accepting my decision to become a mere newspaper reporter, a field that pays just a little more than construction does. He wonders why I haven't cashed in on that multi-brick education and taken on some lawyer-lucrative job. After bricklaying for thirty years, my father promised himself I'd never pile bricks and blocks into walls for a living. He figured an education—genielike and benevolent—would somehow rocket me into the consecrated trajectory of the upwardly mobile, and load some serious loot into my pockets. What he didn't count on was his eldest son breaking blue-collar rule No. 1: Make as much money as you can, to pay for as good a life as you can get.

He'd tell me about it when I was nineteen, my collar already fading to white. I was the college boy who handed him the wrong wrench on help-around-the-house Saturdays. "You better make a lot of money," my blue-collar handy dad wryly warned me as we huddled in front of a disassembled dishwasher I had neither the inclination nor the aptitude to fix. "You're gonna need to hire someone to hammer a nail into a wall for you."

In 1980, after college and graduate school, I was offered my first job, on a now-dead daily paper in Columbus, Ohio. I broke the news in the kitchen, where all the family business is discussed. My mother wept as if it were Vietnam. My father had a few questions: "Ohio? Where the hell is Ohio?"

I said it's somewhere west of New York City, that it was like Pennsylvania, only more so. I told him I wanted to write, and these were the only people who'd take me.

"Why can't you get a good job that pays something, like in advertising in the city, and write on the side?"

"Advertising is lying," I said, smug and sanctimonious, ever the unctuous undergraduate. "I wanna tell the truth."

"The truth?" the old man exploded, his face reddening as it does when he's up twenty stories in high wind. "What's truth?" I said it's real life, and writing about it would make me happy. "You're happy with your family," my father said, spilling blue-collar rule No. 2. "That's what makes you happy. After that, it all comes down to dollars and cents. What gives you comfort besides your family? Money, only money."

During the two weeks before I moved, he reminded me that newspaper journalism is a dying field, and I could do better. Then he pressed advertising again, though neither of us knew anything about it, except that you could work in Manhattan, the borough with the water-beading high gloss, the island polished clean by money. I couldn't explain myself, so I packed, unpopular and confused. No longer was I the good son who studied hard and fumbled endearingly with tools. I was hacking people off.

One night, though, my father brought home some heavy tape and that clear, plastic bubble stuff you pack your mother's second-string dishes in. "You probably couldn't do this right," my father said to me before he sealed the boxes and helped me take them to UPS. "This is what he wants," my father told my mother the day I left for Columbus in my grandfather's eleven-year-old gray Cadillac. "What are you gonna do?" After I said my good-byes, my father took me aside and pressed five $100 bills into my hands. "It's okay," he said over my weak protests. "Don't tell your mother."

When I broke the news about what the paper was paying me, my father suggested I get a part-time job to augment the income. "Maybe you could drive a cab." Once, after I was chewed out by the city editor for something trivial, I made the mistake of telling my father during a visit home. "They pay you nothin', and they push you around too much in that business," he told me, the rage building. "Next time, you gotta grab the guy by the throat and tell him he's a big jerk."

15   "Dad, I can't talk to the boss like that."

"Tell him. You get results that way. Never take any shit." A few years before, a guy didn't like the retaining wall my father and his partner had built. They tore it down and did it again, but the guy still bitched. My father's partner shoved the guy into the freshly laid bricks. "Pay me off," my father said, and he and his partner took the money and walked. Blue-collar guys have no patience for office politics and corporate bile-swallowing. Just pay me off and I'm gone. Eventually, I moved on to a job in Cleveland, on a paper my father has heard of. I think he looks on it as a sign of progress, because he hasn't mentioned advertising for a while.

When he was my age, my father was already dug in with a trade, a wife, two sons and a house in a neighborhood in Brooklyn not far from where he was born. His workaday, family-centered life has been very much in step with his immigrant father's. I sublet what the real-estate people call a junior one-bedroom in a dormlike condo in a Cleveland suburb. Unmarried and unconnected in an insouciant, perpetual-student kind of way, I rent movies during the week and feed single women in restaurants on Saturday nights. My dad asks me about my dates, but he goes crazy over the word "woman." "A girl," he corrects. "You went out with a girl. Don't say 'woman.' It sounds like you're takin' out your grandmother."

I've often believed blue-collaring is the more genuine of lives, in greater proximity to primordial manhood. My father is provider and protector, concerned only with the basics: food and home, love and progeny. He's also a generation closer to the heritage, a warmer spot nearer the fire that forged and defined us. Does heat dissipate and light fade further from the source? I live for my career, and frequently feel lost and codeless, devoid of the blue-collar rules my father grew up with. With no baby-boomer groomer to show me the way, I've been choreographing my own tentative shuffle across the wax-shined dance floor on the edge of the Great Middle Class, a different rhythm in a whole new ballroom.

I'm sure it's tough on my father, too, because I don't know much about bricklaying, either, except that it's hell on the body, a daily sacrifice. I idealized my dad as a kind of dawn-rising priest of labor, engaged in holy ritual. Up at five every day, my father has made a religion of responsibility. My younger brother, a Wall Street white-collar guy with the sense to make a decent salary, says he always felt safe when he heard Dad stir before him, as if Pop were taming the day for us. My father, fifty-five years old, but expected to put out as if he were three decades stronger, slips on machine-washable vestments of khaki cotton without waking my mother. He goes into the kitchen and turns on the radio to catch the temperature. Bricklayers have an occupational need to know the weather. And because I am my father's son, I can recite the five-day forecast at any given moment.

My father isn't crazy about this life. He wanted to be a singer and   20
actor when he was young, but that was frivolous doodling to his Italian family, who expected money to be coming in, stoking the stove that kept hearth fires ablaze. Dreams simply were not energy-efficient. My dad learned a trade, as he was supposed to, and settled into a life of pre-scripted routing. He says he can't find the black-and-white publicity glossies he once had made.

Although I see my dad infrequently, my brother, who lives at home, is with the old man every day. Chris has a lot more blue-collar in him than I do, despite his management-level career; for a short time, he wanted to be a construction worker, but my parents persuaded him to go to Columbia. Once in a while he'll bag a lunch and, in a nice wool suit, meet my father at a construction site and share sandwiches of egg salad on semolina bread.

It was Chris who helped my dad most when my father tried to change his life several months ago. My dad wanted a civil-service bricklayer foreman's job that wouldn't be so physically demanding. There was a written test that included essay questions about construction work. My father hadn't done anything like it in forty years. Why the hell they needed bricklayers to write essays I have no idea, but my father sweated it out. Every morning before sunrise, Chris would be ironing a shirt, bleary-eyed, and my father would sit at the kitchen table and read aloud his practice essays on how to wash down a wall, or how to build a tricky corner. Chris would suggest words and approaches.

It was so hard for my dad. He had to take a Stanley Kaplan–like prep course in a junior high school three nights a week after work for six weeks. At class time, the outside men would come in, twenty-five construction workers squeezing themselves into little desks. Tough blue-collar guys armed with No. 2 pencils leaning over and scratching out their practice essays, cement in their hair, tar on their pants, their work boots too big and clumsy to fit under the desks.

"Is this what finals felt like?" my father would ask me on the phone when I pitched in to help long-distance. "Were you always this nervous?" I told him yes. I told him writing's always difficult. He thanked Chris and me for the coaching, for putting him through school this time. My father thinks he did okay, but he's still awaiting the test results. In the meantime, he takes life the blue-collar way, one brick at a time.

25   When we see each other these days, my father still asks how the money is. Sometimes he reads my stories; usually he likes them, although he recently criticized one piece as being a bit sentimental: "Too schmaltzy," he said. Some psychologists say that the blue-white-collar gap between fathers and sons leads to alienation, but I tend to agree with Dr. Al Baraff, a clinical psychologist and director of the Men-Center in Washington, D.C. "The core of the relationship is based on emotional and hereditary traits," Baraff says. "Class [distinctions] just get added on. If it's a healthful relationship from when you're a kid, there's a respect back and forth that'll continue."

Nice of the doctor to explain, but I suppose I already knew that. Whatever is between my father and me, whatever keeps us talking and keeps us close, has nothing to do with work and economic class.

During one of my visits to Brooklyn not long ago, he and I were in the car, on our way to buy toiletries, one of my father's weekly routines. "You know, you're not as successful as you could be," he began, blue-collar blunt as usual. "You paid your dues in school. You deserve better restaurants, better clothes." Here we go, I thought, the same old stuff. I'm sure every family has five or six similar big issues that are re-played like well-worn videotapes. I wanted to fast-forward this thing when we stopped at a red light.

Just then my father turned to me, solemn and intense. His knees were aching and his back muscles were throbbing in clockable inter-vals that registered in his eyes. It was the end of a week of lifting fifty-pound blocks. "I envy you," he said quietly. "For a man to do something he likes and get paid for it—that's fantastic." He smiled at me before the light changed, and we drove on. To thank him for the understanding, I sprang for the deodorant and shampoo. For once, my father let me pay.

For Journals

To what extent do you think your ideas about work are based on your social class?

For Discussion

1.   What is your response to the voice and tone of the essay? Do the author and his family seem like people you would like to meet? Do any of the family members have beliefs and values that you share?

2.   Summarize the author's assessment of his father's values and his own values. Are the assertions Lubrano makes about blue-collar values based on assumptions he has grown up with, or are they generalized from evidence or experience?

3.   Lubrano discusses "blue-collar" rules. What do you think would be his "white-collar" rules? Develop your assertions about what these rules would be, and support them with examples.

4.   The essay is full of rich language and metaphor. Select some of the more vivid metaphors, and discuss the ways in which they underscore and reinforce Lubrano's assertions about values.

5.   What is the myth of mobility discussed in this essay? What is the connection of this myth to class values?

For Writing

1.   Lubrano asserts that generally life is rags to rags and riches to riches and that upward mobility is a myth. Based on your readings in this chapter so far—Franklin, Fitzgerald, Steinem, and the others—write an essay supporting or refuting his assertion.

2.   Lubrano writes, "I've often believed blue-collaring is the more genuine of lives, in greater proximity to primordial manhood" (paragraph 18). What do you think Rich's, Gilman's, or Rose's response to this assertion would be? Create a conversation between two of the writers focusing on the role of work in men's lives.

EXPLOITATION OF ASIAN WOMEN IMMIGRANT GARMENT WORKERS
1994

Judy Ou

Judy Ou is a college student in northern California. She wrote this essay in her first-year expository writing class as a documented response to the first question at the end of this chapter on the subject of Americans and work.

An Asian immigrant garment worker toils endlessly with her dilapidated sewing machine. She is working above a dirty floor littered with scraps of fabric. The air is thick with dust, the lights are very dim, and the crowded room is unbearably hot. The woman continues to work hard so she can finish sewing a dress. She will receive a mere two dollars for her work. She began working at 8:00 A.M. and will not go home until 7:00 P.M. She endures the hardships at work because it is the only job she can find.

The plight of this Asian immigrant worker is not uncommon. Asian immigrant garment workers make up a large percentage of the garment industry in areas such as San Francisco, Los Angeles, Orange County, New York, Boston, Philadelphia, Dallas, and Hawaii (Louie 25). According to federal law enforcement officials, Asians represent 5 to 70 percent (average of 35 percent) of garment workers in the United States (Louie 7). In the San Francisco Bay Area alone, women Asian garment workers make up 53 percent of workers (Textile 284). Despite their large population, many Asian women immigrant garment workers unfortunately suffer from labor abuses of the industry. The garment industry exploits these workers in order to capitalize on its profits. To understand fully why exploitation of Asian women immigrant garment workers still occurs today, we must examine their post-1965 history in the United States, the labor abuses they suffer, and laws or actions brought forth to combat labor abuses.

Many Asian immigrant women first came to the United States under the Immigration Act of 1965. Before this time, most Asians in the United States were single men because "of previous patterns of male labor importation from Asia" (Takaki qtd in Petras 88). Women had been "barred entry under the National Origins Act of 1924" (Takaki qtd in Petras 88). Since the 1965 Immigration Act "ended the discriminatory national origins provision" (Kwong 22), Asian women were allowed to immigrate. These women joined their husbands or relatives in America with the "Uniting the Family" provision of the 1965 Immigration Act. The influx of Asian immigrant women became a new labor pool in the United States.

After 1978, another influx of Asian immigrants came to the United States. This second wave of immigrants were mainly refugees from Southeast Asia or immigrants from areas such as China, Taiwan, and Hong Kong. The Southeast Asian refugees came as a result of the Vietnam War. "Between 1980 and 1985, nearly 800,000 refugees from Indochina (Southeast Asia)" (Petras 88) came to the United States. The immigrants from China, Taiwan, and Hong Kong came for other reasons. They feared the unification of Taiwan with China, they were uncertain about the future of Hong Kong when China takes over in 1997, or they were wary of the Tiananmen Square situation (Hay B4). All these immigrants fled from unfavorable conditions in their countries and had to look for jobs in the United States.

When Asian women immigrants looked for jobs in the United States, many found themselves working in the garment industry. The garment industry was attractive because it offered jobs that did not require them to speak English. These non-English-speaking immigrants "were willing to work for low wages" (Kwong 30) and endure bad conditions because as recent immigrants they could not find better jobs. Since they needed to help their husbands support the family (Louie 5), they accepted the conditions at the garment shops. These Asian immigrant women became the cheap labor that the industry needed.

The garment industry has always looked for cheap labor. Throughout history it has employed immigrants due to their acceptance of low wages and bad working conditions. The industry has never lacked this supply of labor. Even in New York during the 1960s when Italians, East Europeans, and Puerto Ricans were unwilling to work in low-wage sweatshops (Kwong 30), Asian immigrant workers were able to supply labor. Due to the 1965 Immigration Act, Asian immigrants continued to provide the industry with cheap labor.

The demand for these workers has recently gone up because some manufacturers have returned to the United States from overseas production. Previously, many manufacturers had brought their operations overseas because it was cheaper to produce apparel. This overseas "departure of U.S. garment manufacturing began during the 1960s, initially to Hong Kong and Taiwan, and then on to Korea, Singapore, Malaysia, Mexico, and, later, to Thailand and the Phillippines" (Petras 83). However, the "decision of American manufacturers to shift their production orders back to the U.S. as cost-cutting measure" (Petras 93) has caused sweatshops to proliferate in the United States. Although numerous manufacturers still produce overseas, some have ventured back to the United States because of cost-cutting measures such as expediency and the availability of cheap labor.

Manufacturers have come back to the United States because expediency and cheap labor are crucial to business. A quicker turnaround time for locally produced goods provides a competitive edge in the fashion industry. For example, bulk orders have to be placed far in advance by overseas manufacturers because of the distance and time needed to export the goods. By the time the apparel reaches the United States, American consumers may have changed their current style in clothing, forcing the manufacturers to mark down prices in order to sell the out-of-style clothes. Producing clothes in the United States reduces this problem and in the long run saves the manufacturers money. Along with this expediency, "Economists also cite quota restrictions and shipping costs as reasons why manufacturers are returning" (Louie 6) to production in America. Clothing manufacturers, such as Perry Ellis, had their production overseas but today "40% of their clothing is manufactured in the U.S." (Petras 93). The increase of American manufacturers has directly increased the demand for labor. Companies know they can profit by relying on expediency and the availability of cheap Asian immigrant workers.

Asian immigrant workers needed jobs, and American-based manufacturers needed workers. These two groups seemed to be a perfect match for each other. One supplied labor, and the other supplied work. The situation seemed ideal. However, when the working situations of the Asian immigrant garment worker are analyzed, one will discover how labor abuses still seem to plague the industry. A closer investigation of the pyramid structure of the garment industry can shed light on why abuses occur in this industry.

10   The pyramid structure of the garment industry displays how the industry operates. Retailers, manufacturers, contractors, and workers

function in the industry by making up the four levels in the pyramid. At the bottom of the pyramid are the garment workers. These workers are often employed under subminimum wage by small sewing shops known as contractors. Contractors make up the second level of this pyramid. These contractors compete with each other to acquire contracts from manufacturers. They are "legally responsible for any labor law violations" (Louie 80). Manufacturers are on the third level. These manufacturers vie for sales to big name retailers such as Macy's or Saks Fifth Avenue. They design the garments, determine how much the material should cost, how much the retail price is, and their profit margin. They are not legally accountable for labor law violations. Retailers are at the apex of the pyramid. They are the ones who buy the garments from the manufacturers and sell it to the consumer. Each level has a part in the overall production and distribution of apparel. However, since each level functions under the control of the upper level, the lowest level, the garment workers, falls victim to results of competition within the industry. Since the contractors receive only "rock-bottom dollar—or less" (Bernstein D3) from contracts with the manufacturers, they violate their workers' rights in order to survive financially. In a pyramid-structured industry where "a skirt that brings the retailer $85 and the manufacturer $40 typically brings the small contractors who directly employ the workers only $5, and the workers earn $2.50" (Bernstein D3), contractors have little choice in maintaining labor laws. Thus the structure of the pyramid contributes to the labor abuses that occur in the industry.

These labor abuses affect almost every conceivable aspect of work for Asian immigrant garment workers. Not only do labor abuses affect the wages and hours of workers, but they also affect their working conditions. In addition to the horrible working conditions, workers also have to take sewing home illegally. Although many of these abuses violate legal laws, they nonetheless flourish within the industry.

Violation of a worker's right to minimum wage is prevalent in the industry. Since "wages in the shops are usually paid by the piece, a woman may receive $1.20 to $3.00 for a garment that takes up to one hour to sew" (Petras 99). These wages fall below the minimum wage that all employees are legally entitled to receive under federal and state minimum wage laws. Former President Bush had "signed legislation to raise the federal minimum wage to $4.25 an hour" (Efron, "Sweatshops," A38) by 1991. This made it mandatory for employers to adhere to this law. Contractors, however, often do not take heed of the minimum wage laws.

These contractors instead blatantly disregard overtime pay in addition to being oblivious to minimum wage laws. Under law, "garment workers, like other non-salaried employees, must be paid time-and-a-half if they work more than eight hours a day or forty hours a week" (Efron A38). Despite this law, many Asian immigrant garment workers will "report to work at 8 A.M. They will log their usual ten or eleven hours without overtime" (Wills L38). It is expected that these Asian immigrant garment workers will work long hours without fair and decent pay. These contractors knowingly underpay their workers.

Back wages is another form of exploitation associated with wages of Asian immigrant garment workers. Cases recounted by an ILGWU (International Ladies' Garment Worker's Union) spokesperson describe situations where women were not paid on time or what they have been promised. The loss of back wages could be devastating to the workers. An example occurred when "a group of women working in Queens from 7 A.M. to 11 P.M. was promised $15 a day. When the employer finally paid the women, the checks bounced" (Petras 100). Not only had the contractor delayed in paying the women; he also presented them with bad checks. He had taken advantage of these workers by using their labor for free.

15   Although problems regarding wages are terrible, those concerning the working conditions of Asian immigrant garment workers are just as deplorable. Workers are frequently subjected to working conditions that are unsafe and unsanitary. Women work in small, cramped, areas that are not meant to be used to produce apparel. Ventilation is poor, and shops are often freezing cold in the winter and boiling hot in the summer. Plumbing problems include leaks, broken toilets, and a lack of hot water. Most sprinklers and fire alarm systems do not work (Bao 51–53). In one New York shop, "The women wear improvised dust masks, pieces of white fabric draped over their ears and noses. The windows are barred with iron gates, and the fire door is blocked by boxes and a metal bar" (Hays B4). These conditions are similar to those that existed in the 1911 Triangle Shirtwaist Factory. Conditions such as the blockage of fire escapes contributed to the death of one hundred and forty-six workers in a fire at the Triangle Shirtwaist Factory (Stein 195). Even though seventy-two years have passed, garment factories today still have work safety violations. The working conditions of these workers are horrendous, but the contractors have done little about it.

These contractors have instead promoted another deplorable aspect of the garment industry, that of home sewing. Contractors often make their workers take sewing home. This is illegal because "in 1942, the government banned home-based work" with women's clothing because "enforcement of the minimum wage law was difficult" ("Unfinished Homework," A12). When contractors tell their workers to sew at home, minimum wage is often not enforced. Sewing at home also causes health problems. Respiratory problems have risen because "women who sew in such homes risk inhaling dust and fibers from the heaps of cut fabric in poorly ventilated spaces" (Efron A38). The contractors not only exploit the workers on the job but also indirectly exploit them at home.

Asian immigrant garment workers have endured abuses of their industry. Although they face these injustices, most workers have not done anything about the abuses. They either do not know their rights because they cannot speak English or they are simply afraid to fight for their rights. They do not complain or fight for rights because they fear deportation (if they are illegal immigrants), they fear the reactions of their bosses, they have a disdain for structured unionization, or they are receiving public assistance while working. Those who fear deportation feel vulnerable. They feel vulnerable because "contractors sometimes use the threat of deportation to retain women in abusive conditions at work" (Petras 101). Those who fear their bosses do so because "owners have an effective weapon—the blacklist. Troublemakers are fired and unable to find another job in Chinatown" (Kwong 139). Some workers disdain fighting for their rights because of their experiences with unions that exist in the country they came from. In countries such as "Korea, unions have traditionally been viewed as communist organizations. Likewise, Chinese immigrant women . . . view them as an extension of the Communist Party" (Schuyler 14). Finally, some women cannot complain because they are illegally receiving public welfare checks while working. All of these Asian immigrant workers have justified reasons to avoid complaint and fight.

Although the workers infrequently complain about their sufferings, the industry itself has been made to recognize the abuses of the Asian immigrant garment workers. Contractors and manufacturers have been specifically targeted to deal with the labor abuses. Since contractors are legally accountable for the labor abuse, they are supposed to address and improve these problems. However, instead of eliminating labor abuses, the contractors have responded by saying that they cannot do anything about these problems. For example, these sweatshop owners "insist they will be bankrupt if they pay the minimum wage (and do go under at the rate of up to 30% a year)" (Efron A18). Shops close down often and "contractors readily admit that they violate labor laws just to stay in business" (Henry 22). These contractors instead transfer blame to the manufacturer. They contend that manufacturers force them to violate labor laws since they "control wages and working conditions throughout the industry" (Efron A18). The manufacturers, on the other hand, "put the blame for abuses in the system on retailers who . . . 'demand' low prices—and on consumers" (Henry 23). Even though most manufacturers are in a "system that allows them to maximize their profits" (Nutter B6), they lay the blame on someone else. Few in the garment industry have taken responsibility for the exploitation of the Asian immigrant garment workers.

Since few in the industry seem to be taking any responsibility for the labor abuses, some government officials and labor activists have tried to place more responsibility on contractors and manufacturers. Numerous steps have been taken against labor abuses in California. Since the labor abuses in California have been growing due to the expanding Asian immigrant population in southern California (about 100,000 Vietnamese have settled since 1975) (Efron A38), bills and actions specifically aimed at the garment industry have been raised to address these problems. Legislation such as the Hayden bill (AB3930), the "ditch and stitch" bill (AB1542), the Montoya Act of 1981, and the "hot goods" statute have all been brought up to fight the labor abuses of Asian immigrant garment workers.

20   The Hayden bill and the "ditch and stitch" bill were introduced as legislation at different times, but both included the same proposal. In order to curb labor abuse, both bills proposed to make "manufacturers and contractors jointly liable for worker pay and conditions" (Henry 38). These bills aimed to make manufacturers more careful in selecting their contractors. They would have ideally hired only those who did not participate in abuse. Labor abuses could then be reduced. However, the Hayden bill was vetoed by former California governor Deukmejian in 1990 because he believed the "measure would have placed an 'inappropriate emphasis on garment manufacturers to monitor and control independent contractors'" (Frammolino A29). The "ditch and stitch" bill was also vetoed by Pete Wilson in 1992 for similar reasons. The government had rejected legislation that could have aided in ending labor abuse.

The Montoya Act was a law enacted to help curtail labor abuse. Under this act "all garment contractors must register with the state and pass a licensing exam that covers all applicable laws. The 1981 law requires shops to keep wage and hour records" (Efron 38). This law tried to make shops comply with legal labor conditions. However, many shops circumvented this law by ignoring it. In southern California, Department of Industrial Relations Bureau of Field Enforcement regional manager Roger Miller said that many shops were not even registered (Louie 14). In addition to defaulting in registration, in one sweatshop, "thick clots of dust line the boxes where time cards are supposed to be, and the clock stopped long ago" (Hays B4). Even in shops that pay their workers by the hour, these workers do not get paid by the clock because contractors do not want to pay overtime. A law made to curtail labor abuse did not work.

As new legal legislation seemed to fail in stopping labor abuses, an obscure statute was revitalized to combat such mistreatment. The "hot goods" statute was a provision of the 1938 U.S. Fair Labor Standards Act (Henry 24). This statute "forbids the shipping across state lines of any product made in violation of federal labor laws" (Efron A3). Since it is important for manufacturers to ship their apparel across state lines, some have hired contractors who do not violate federal labor laws. By engaging in this practice, they will never be impeded by the "hot goods" law. A small victory for decent working situations has been attained.

Some legislation has worked and some has not in the battle to end labor abuses. Although the proposed "joint liability" act failed to become law, another minor victory was obtained when the first major manufacturer, Guess? Inc., voluntarily complied in 1992 to become responsible for the wages and working conditions of workers its contractors hire. With this new agreement,

> Guess? will regularly inspect its contractors' workshops, review their payroll records and interview some of their employees to make sure there have been no labor law violations. In addition, Guess? pledged to compensate employees who in the future are illegally underpaid by contractors. The company has already paid the Labor Department $573,000 to cover back wages owed to some of its contractors' employees. (Silverstein, Efron A1)

Guess? Inc. realized that it had a moral and social responsibility to help end the labor abuses. As a manufacturing giant that "has annual revenues of $750 million" (Silverstein, Efron A1), it established a precedent to combat labor abuses that affect workers such as the Asian immigrant garment workers.

Although progress has been slow, exploitation of Asian immigrant garment workers has been slowly diminishing. However, further reduction in labor abuses can be accomplished by educating Asian immigrants about their rights and encouraging them to voice their rights. Even though most Asian immigrants are reluctant to voice their opinions due to their various fears, AIWA (Asian Immigrant Women Advocates) has helped them to become more vocal. AIWA, an Oakland-based organization, "has been successful in educating Asian immigrant women about their rights" (Schuyler 14). Although "it has been harder to prompt the women to act on those rights" (Schuyler 14), some Asian women have started to voice their rights. Some of these women participated in their first San Francisco rally led by AIWA in March 1992 to voice their injustices of not being paid back wages by their contractor (Henry 21). By showing their strength, some Asian immigrant women have made a first step in helping themselves curb the abuse of the industry.

25   Labor abuses have long affected Asian women immigrant garment workers. Although most of these workers endured their conditions, some workers have spoken out against these abuses. Community-based organizations such as AIWA have slowly tried to encourage women to take a stand and overcome their fear of voicing their rights. The establishment of such organizations seems to be the next step in the fight against labor abuse. In the past, laws have been the major weapon used to eliminate labor abuses against Asian women immigrant workers. Since some of these laws have been effective while others have not, the workers themselves need to assert their rights. Only with a combination of workers' activism and laws can changes be brought about to end the exploitation of Asian women immigrant garment workers.

Works Cited

Bao, Xialan. *"Holding Up More Than Half the Sky": A History of Women Garment Workers in New York's Chinatown, 1948–1991*. Diss. New York University, 1991. Ann Arbor: UMI, 1983. 9213217.

Bernstein, Harry. "Sweatshops a Complex Problem." *Los Angeles Times* 10 July 1990, West L.A. ed.: D3.

Efron, Sonni. "Sweatshops Expanding into Orange County." *Los Angeles Times* 26 November 1989, Orange County ed.: A1, A38.

Efron, Sonni. "'Hot Goods' Law Revived as Anti-Sweatshop Tool." *Los Angeles Times* 28 November 1989, West L.A. ed.: A3, A18, A19.

Frammolino, Ralph. "Legislation Targeting Sweatshops Vetoed." *Los Angles Times* 25 August 1990, West L.A. ed.: A29.

Hays, Constance L. "Immigrants Strain Chinatown's Resources." *New York Times* 30 May 1990, Natl. ed.: B1, B4.

Henry, Sarah. "Labor and Lace." *Los Angeles Times Magazine* 1 August 1993: 21–24, 38.

Kwong, Peter. *The New Chinatown*. New York: Hill and Wang, 1987.

Louie, Miriam Ching. "Immigrant Asian Women in Bay Area Garment Sweatshops: 'After Sewing Laundry, Cleaning and Cooking, I Have No Breath Left to Sing.'" *Ameriasia Journal* 18 (1992): 1–26.

Nutter, Steve. Letter. *Los Angeles Times* 14 December 1989, West L.A. ed.: B:6.

Petras, Elizabeth McLean. "The Shirt on Your Back: Immigrant Workers and the Reorganization of the Garment Industry." *Social Justice* 19 (1992): 76–107.

Schuyler, Nina. "Asian Women Come Out Swinging." *Progressive* (May 1993): 14.

Silverstein, Stuart, and Efron, Sonni. "Guess? Accepts Pact to Curb Labor Violations." *Los Angeles Times* 5 August 1992, West L.A. ed.: A+.

Stein, Leon. *Out of the Sweatshop*. New York: Quadrangle/New Times Book Co., 1977.

Textile Workers in the San Francisco Bay Area by Sex. Chart. Detroit: Gale Research, 1993.

Wills, Kendall J. "Garment Sweatshops Are Spreading." *New York Times* 6 September 1987, natl. ed.: L38.

"Unfinished Homework." Editorial. *Wall Street Journal* 6 January 1993, natl. ed.: A12.

For Journals

Have you worked for minimum wage or less? How did your low salary affect how you perceived your employers and yourself? If you haven't worked for low wages, how do you think you would respond to the previous question?

For Discussion

1.   Examine Ou's first paragraph. Is the anecdote effective at drawing the reader in? Does she adequately prepare the reader for her focused topic? Does the background presented indicate the importance and relevance of her topic?

2.   Analyze the evidence Ou cites. Do her examples and statistics persuade you of the merit of her assertions? Cite specific examples from the essay to support your view.

3.   Does Ou's language support her point of view, or does it undermine her credibility?

4.   What attitudes about work and worth are conveyed by the workers, by the people who hire the workers, by Ou herself? What connections can you draw between this reading and other selections in this chapter?

For Writing

1.   Investigate some aspect of labor as it pertains to your region, your ethnic group, your gender, or your future career. You could focus on immigrant labor, as Ou does, or on the ways in which certain ethnic groups have historically been associated with particular types of work.

2.   Some Americans claim that immigrants are "taking jobs away from real Americans," while others argue that many new immigrants do work that native-born Americans would refuse. Research this issue in journals and other periodicals, in books, and among employers and workers in your local community if feasible. Develop an assertion that immigrants do or do not contribute more to the American economy than they use.

FILMS ON WORK AND SUCCESS

There are many American films that have success and/or work as principal subjects. The following is a starter list from which to choose a film for viewing with your peers. *Citizen Kane* is invariably voted the greatest American movie by film critics, partly because it was extremely innovative, partly because it is highly entertaining, and partly because it is one of the strongest American movie statements on both money and power. *The Great Gatsby* has been made into a movie several times; the one with Robert Redford as Gatsby is probably the most readily available. Watch one or two of the listed films as points of departure for your discussion of the themes in this chapter. You may also want to compare one of the films on this list with a film of your choice that deals with American ideas of work, success, and money in a creative way.

Citizen Kane

The Great Gatsby

Risky Business

Still Killing Us Softly

Wall Street

The Sweet Smell of Success

The Color of Money

The Hustler

Greed

Take the Money and Run

Modern Times

The Gold Rush

Material Girl

ASSERTIONS

Assertions are the conclusions one draws based on some combination of reasons and assumptions. The main assertion in an essay is often referred to as a *thesis statement*. Reasons are the support the writer offers—the evidence on which she or he has based those assertions. Assumptions, as we noted in Chapter 5, are the often unstated beliefs, values, and principles we hold that interplay with other assumptions and reasons. Some writers refer to assumptions and reasons as premises; the term *premise* is prominent in discussions of formal logic and the syllogism, or deductive argument in outline form. (See Chapter 1 for further discussion.) For the sake of clarity, we will use *assertions* consistently throughout this text but will note synonyms that other writers sometimes use.

Analyzing Assertions in Arguments

Assertions vary in tone and in language because of differences in the assumptions that underlie them and because of differences in temperament, background, and purpose. Some assertions are factual; some are statements of values; some are drawn from research; and some are meant as calls to action, to suggest changes in policy or procedure.

Had he chosen, Franklin could have made assertions about anything he wanted; his genius gave him more latitude, but his good sense gave him restraint. So even his most definite assertions are couched in modest terms and phrased in such a way as to be useful to other people without drumming in the fact that he was smarter than anyone he might have been talking to. For example, in explaining how he taught himself to stop overpowering other people in conversation, he says mildly that he has learned how *not* to assert himself: "I made it a rule to forbear all direct contradiction to the sentiments of others, and all positive assertion of my own. . . . When another asserted something that I thought an error, I denied myself the pleasure of contradicting him abruptly." Franklin's security and self-knowledge are clear; he can assert without trying to dominate, and in doing so he is more forceful than if he had been argumentative.

But Charlotte Perkins Gilman, writing out of a feeling of powerlessness and frustration, makes her assertions sharply and with a point: "All that [a woman] may wish to have, all that she may wish to do, must come through a single channel and a single choice. Wealth, power, social distinction, fame . . . ease and pleasure, her bread and butter—all must come to her through a small gold ring. This is a heavy pressure." Gilman's values—those of a woman who wants an active and atypical role in pursuit of financial and personal independence—are at variance with the role for which she was trained, and the conflict she feels is clear in her list of dependencies, combined with the short, angry assertion at the end: "This [marriage] is a heavy pressure."

When the purpose of an assertion is to question policies or propose new ones, it tends to be direct because the author wants to be sure that the point comes across. For example, when Gloria Steinem attacks the idea that women still pretend to work only because they need the money for their families and not because they like it, she says: "A job as a human right is a principle that applies to men as well as women. But women have more cause to fight for it." There are no metaphors or figures of speech here—only the bare assertion, said clearly and distinctly.

In argumentative papers based largely on research, the same directness may inform assertions about the subject, because they will be drawn partly from authorities and partly from the writer's understanding of the material and purpose in choosing it. In her paper on the exploitation of Asian women garment workers, student Judy Ou uses both outside sources and her own opinion in making her assertions: " 'The decision of American manufacturers to shift their production orders back to the United States as a cost cutting measure' (Petras 93) has caused sweatshops to proliferate in the United States. Although numerous manufacturers still produce overseas, some have ventured back to the United States because of cost-cutting measures such as expediency and the availability of cheap labor." The point of such an approach is to use outside authorities as validation for the writer's ideas, not a substitution for the writer's ability to sort through and identify relevant information.

Finally, some assertions are intended neither to convey research, nor to affect policy, or to express personal opinions so much as to affect the decision making of the reader or viewer. This is usually the case with advertisements, which may appeal to the reader's value system directly or indirectly but only with the intention of getting him or her to buy something. The Edsel advertisement, for example, spreads its primary assertion across the top of the page: "They'll know you've *arrived* when you drive up in an Edsel." Here the assertion is clearly an appeal to the prospective buyer's vanity, to the desire not just to keep up with the Joneses but to take a big step ahead of them. The advertisement succeeds only if its author has gauged the reader's value system correctly, which is what makes assertions in advertising such a delicate business.

Using Assertions in Arguments

In college writing as well as in personal writing and writing on the job, you will generally be asserting a position or a point of view. Assertions are derived from some interplay of assumptions and evidence; sometimes you argue a point based on long-standing belief or values; other times you generalize from observation, experience, or other types of evidence such as statistics or surveys. When you argue *inductively,* you are drawing your assertion from the evidence; when you argue *deductively,* you are taking a general principle or belief or assumption, (sometimes called a premise), and applying it to a particular situation. In either case, in your writing you will most often introduce your topic, state your general assertion, and then support that assertion with evidence. In other words, you assert your conclusion or finding first, and then present the evidence that led to that conclusion.

Assertions About Facts   Assertions about facts are generally supported by evidence rather than by other types of reasons and assumptions. Assertions about facts, less prominent in many arguments than other types of assertions, state that a thing does or does not exist, that something is or is not true. Since they are supported by factual evidence, they can generally be proved or disproved by reliable outside sources. A social scientist making claims about the makeup of contemporary U.S. households can find verification (or refutation) in the U.S. census and other demographic sources. Sometimes, however, assertions about facts, particularly in research and scientific arenas, are disputed or revised. A scientist asserting that HIV does not cause AIDS is stating a "fact" that many others currently dispute and will need convincing research data to support such an assertion.

Assertions About Values   Sometimes assertions are intended to evaluate or offer a judgment about things, ideas, or people. The painting *American Gothic,* one might assert, is aesthetically pleasing (or appallingly ugly). *Moby Dick* is a fine piece of literature (or a long, plodding yarn). Richard Nixon was an outstanding president (or an embarrassment). Blue-collar values are admirable (or not), you might argue, based on Lubrano's "Bricklayer's Boy" in this chapter. Corporate life is punishing for both men and women, so the workplace itself needs to change. Nevertheless, corporate life ought to be more accessible to women, you might respond.

Value is the core of the term *evaluating,* or measuring the worth of something by comparing it to some predetermined criteria, principles, or ideas about what is good. To argue successfully about the painting, the book, or the president, we need to operate from a set of standards that either we argue for or can agree on with the audience. Frequently, an argument about value will have to set forth criteria, either early on in the essay or as each point is made.

Once you have set forth your criteria, you still have the task of persuading your reader that your judgment is correct; that is, the object in question does or does not meet the criteria set forth. For example, some graffiti in the women's rest room at one college stated, "Fur is murder." The writer's argument contains the assumption about values that killing an animal is the equivalent of willfully killing a human being, an act most of us would call murder. The writer also relies on audience agreement about certain facts: that fur is from animals, that taking the fur requires the death of the animal. The writer, in effect, states that for humans to wear fur is not merely extravagant but morally reprehensible. For some in the audience, her criteria for judging an act to be murder are highly arguable.

Assertions That Propose Action   Assertions intended to move people to action, to change a situation, or to argue about policy are often called proposals. One could argue, for example, that corporations should change the way they treat people—or that people should avoid working for corporations. People should or should not work if they don't have to. There should be no minimum wage, and employers should be able to pay workers whatever the market will bear. There should be protection against piece-work garment labor. Any such proposal would require a careful consideration of various options: Why hasn't the proposal in question been tried before? What are the objections? What are the pros and cons of each side? How will this particular proposal or plan be different? Audience awareness will guide not only the arguments selected but also the order in which supporting evidence is presented. If multiple projects have been tried and have failed, or if considerable controversy surrounds your idea, you may need to acknowledge the facts or deal with objections up front, before making your proposal. If you believe your proposal will get a fair hearing and that your readers mainly need to hear the specifics of how you will carry out your plan, then you can introduce your proposal and support it with evidence, dealing with any lingering concerns later in the essay. A helpful pattern for writing proposals is to explain the problem, clarify why action is needed, and detail how such action will resolve the issue, dealing with objections to the plan and supporting your proposal with evidence at the most feasible points in the essay for doing so.

A core premise of argumentation is the expression, "He who asserts must prove." Whether you are making an assertion about facts, about values, or about a course of action, you need to support your view with evidence, standards by which to judge merit, or specific proposals for action. Any assertion will also need to rely on shared assumptions about acceptable evidence or criteria for judgment. The writing assignments that follow encourage you to practice developing and asserting a point of view and then supporting that view with evidence appropriate to the topic, the assertion being made, and the context of argument.

WRITING ASSIGNMENTS

1.   Why do people work? Or more specifically, why do you or will you work? After brainstorming, reading, discussing, and recollecting some of the points made in class and in your readings, develop a core assertion as to the meaning, value, or purpose of work—to people in your family, to people of a certain class, to people of a certain ethnic

culture or gender. Avoid vague generalizations. Focus on a specific assertion and strong support for it.

2.   Research advertisements or political cartoons from times gone by—from nineteenth-century publications to back issues of *Life* or other popular magazines from the 1940s. Analyze the values implied and the assertions made about work in the images. Alternatively, view television comedies from the 1950s and 1960s, and analyze the values, assumptions, and assertions they convey, particularly those about work and gender.

3.   Record oral histories of three different workers talking about what work means to them. (To review this form of communication, look at the "Frank Chin" selection by Studs Terkel in Chapter 3, or get Terkel's book, *Working,* a collection of oral histories.) Draft several questions to get your interview started and to suggest a focus. After the interviews, compare and contrast the views of your interviewees, looking for common and diverse threads among the histories. Develop a core claim or thesis, using the material from the interviews and, if you want, from the readings in this chapter and your own experience to support your view.

4.   Examine the assertions made about blue-collar work or the importance of work in women's lives by this chapter's authors, especially Lubrano, Gilman, and Steinem. Do particular types of factual assertions, evaluative assertions, or proposals dominate either topic or selection? Which types are most persuasive? Write an analytical paper discussing your findings.

5.   Write a proposal for change in a program at your college or in your community: a change in the curriculum, such as revising the language or writing requirements; a change in scholarship or work-study funding; a change in alcohol policy in your residence; or a campus or community recycling program. Write the proposal in the form of a letter to the appropriate administrator, or for a more general audience, as a letter to the editor.

6.   Write an argumentative essay asserting your own view of the value of work, success, money, education, or some other belief that you hold. Pay special attention to the assumptions you are making and the evidence you are selecting to support your view, and be sure to back up any assumptions you make that your audience may not share or accept.

CHAPTER

JUSTICE AND CIVIL LIBERTIES

*E*very morning, millions of American schoolchildren recite the pledge of allegiance to the flag, which ends, "With liberty and justice for all." That phrase refers to more people today than it has in the past; today it includes women, children, ethnic minorities, the aged, and the disabled. This is a country proudly self-conscious that its political system was established to be something new, that it offered a readjustment of rights and privileges more profound than anything that had ever been attempted before. So standards and expectations for justice and civil liberties have always been higher here, at least in theory, than anywhere else.

Given our ideals, however, the fact that for two hundred fifty years African Americans were bought and sold like furniture could not be easily explained, nor could the denial of their civil rights into modern times. So, more often than not, a consideration of social justice in America starts with racial justice.

Many of the high and low points associated with racial justice are attempts of whites to deny or to correct past wrongs, and the attempts of African Americans to claim the promise of liberty and the American dream from which they had been excluded. At times, individual leaders—like Frederick Douglass—have taken upon themselves the role of spokespersons and protest leaders. Their job has been simultaneously to educate white Americans about the everyday injustices in African American life and to organize their constituencies to effect change.

The fact that laws did not change quickly, or that the laws did but attitudes did not, has led to a continuing and sometimes violent debate over what justice is, who is entitled to justice (and how much), and whether there is a way to compensate citizens for past wrongs. These issues raise profound questions for Americans about the depth of their commitment to ideals of freedom, opportunity, and political participation.

Race is not the only social struggle in America. As the definitions of justice and freedom became gradually more inclusive in the nineteenth century, one of the offshoots of the first struggle for civil rights was the increased consciousness in other segments of the population that they too were discriminated against. Foremost among these other groups were women—mostly white and middle class—who began organizing for the right to vote. Many of them had been abolitionists, and they turned the self-confidence and political skills they had honed during the fight against slavery to the fight for universal suffrage.

In Victorian America, however, constrained expectations of women as domestic goddesses who knew their place (at home with husband and children) meant that most men and many women were horrified by the open political participation of women and criticized them for being disobedient, unfeminine, and threatening to the status quo. Like African Americans who demanded to be treated equally, the suffragettes were viewed as unnatural and ungrateful deviants from the norm who had forgotten their traditional virtues of deference and meekness.

In recent decades the gay rights movement has gained considerable momentum, though its members too have often been castigated as deviants from the norm who should stay in their place and not demand equal rights. Although gays have essentially secured civil liberties in such arenas as housing and employment, the ongoing debate about their presence in the armed forces indicates that the struggle is not fully resolved.

Indeed, complete civil liberties for ethnic and sexual minorities and women are still a long way from being assured as the twentieth century draws to a close. Unpopular causes and new ideas frequently make audiences angry, and while we all demand the right to say what we want, we are better at defending the speech of people who agree with us than that of people we think are wrong, misguided, extreme, disloyal, or simply very different. Fortunately, however, at all points in our history, this country has been graced by the presence of Americans who were willing to stand up—by themselves, if necessary—to defend the civil liberties in which they believed, particularly the freedoms of speech and press guaranteed by the First Amendment to the Constitution.

Justice and Civil Liberties through History

The writers and artists in this chapter all engaged in an ongoing argument in which the interpretations about the extent of civil liberties and the meaning of justice in America varied wildly. The values in question were established first in the Declaration of Independence in 1776, then the Constitution and the Bill of Rights in 1787, in the subsequent amendments to the Constitution, in two hundred years of legal decisions, in reform movements and political debates, in the trauma of a Civil War in which 618,000 Americans died at each other's hands, and in the words and lives of individuals who have made civil liberties and justice their personal business.

The men who dominated the American Revolution do not fit the usual image of revolutionaries. They were not poverty-stricken peasants revolting against an insensitive aristocracy but established, educated, and powerful men whose earliest loyalties were to England. Over time, however, they had come to feel capable of managing their own government; finally, they began to think of themselves differently—as Americans. But if they were not radical in the traditional sense, their great contribution to political history, a representative democracy headed by an elected leader, was a radical political development, and its first major expression, the Declaration of Independence, is a remarkable document. Like the Constitution that followed it eleven years later, it is written with such foresight and flexibility that it has stretched to accommodate the needs of later generations and previously excluded constituencies. Much of subsequent American political argument refers back to it or to its promise. Whenever the subject of justice, equality, or civil liberties comes up, either the phrases of the Declaration or the spirit—or both—hover over the discussion. For example, in the years before the Civil War, issues of equality and freedom were slowly if inexorably working their way to the forefront of American political consciousness, and some Americans were more sensitive than others to the impossibility of supporting slavery in a growing democracy with continental ambitions. Among those Americans were William Sidney Mount, Henry David Thoreau, and Frederick Douglass. Examples of their work in this chapter are all, in differing degrees, early warning signals for the conflagration of the coming Civil War. William Sidney Mount was an artist who specialized in portraits and paintings of country life. His painting, *The Power of Music,* completed in 1846, with the war still fourteen years in the future, was one of a series about slave life and illustrates the enormous psychological difference separating free whites and slaves.

A contemporary of Mount, Henry David Thoreau had a more direct sense of the evils of slavery, and he interpreted the Declaration not only as an ideal for collective rebellion against injustice but as an injunction to every single American to heed his or her conscience, even if that meant disobeying the government. Thoreau's most famous piece on dissent, *On Civil Disobedience,* which first appeared in 1849, has been a cattle prod to American complacency and self-satisfaction ever since.

Thoreau spoke publicly against slavery because he was an abolitionist—a member of the movement that campaigned for the immediate end to slavery. The abolitionist movement was considered a collection of radicals by most northerners, but like all other campaigns it depended on good speakers to attract attention, audiences, and public support. Thoreau was not in the same class as Frederick Douglass as an orator—nobody was—although he was once called upon to substitute for Douglass at a meeting in Boston.

Douglass, a former slave and a brilliant activist and writer, also had a charismatic presence as a speaker. His powerful intellect and emotion come through intensely in his 1851 Independence Day speech in Rochester, New York, in which he forcefully reminded his white audience of the meaninglessness of the phrase "all men are created equal" for Americans who were enslaved.

Once the Civil War was over, racial division remained, but the political energy that had previously been concentrated on the abolition of slavery began to find its way into other protest movements, particularly the movement for women's right to vote. The intellectual leader and spokesperson of the suffrage movement, Susan B. Anthony, gave her famous speech, "Women's Right to Vote," after she was arrested for trying to register to vote in a presidential election. Like Douglass, also a supporter of women's rights, she was adept at turning the language of the Declaration of Independence and the Constitution back on her audience to prove her point.

By 1896, all the southern states had passed segregation laws against African Americans for the explicit purpose of undoing the civil rights they had won as a result of the Civil War, especially the Thirteenth, Fourteenth, and Fifteenth Amendments to the Constitution, which ended slavery, granted equal protection under the law, and the right to vote. The Supreme Court undermined those amendments when, in 1896, it sided with the state of Louisiana in a case called *Plessy* v. *Ferguson,* and declared that black Americans who were forced to ride in separate train cars from whites were not being deprived of equal protection under the law. This is what became known as the "separate but equal" doctrine. Technically, the *Plessy* decision applied only to railroads, but its real effect was to institutionalize segregation in every area of southern public life: transportation, restaurants, beaches, churches, schools. The lone dissenter to the Court's ruling in *Plessy* was Justice John Harlan, a former slave owner who foresaw the tragic consequences of the decision very clearly.

The Supreme Court's interpretation of any case becomes the law of the land, until or unless the law changes or the interpretation changes. In the case of *Plessy*, the worst effects of segregation continued to make themselves felt everywhere in the ordinary experience, the psyches, and the economic suffering of African Americans in the South.

Roughly half a century, two world wars, and a depression after *Plessy*, Justice Harlan's lonely dissent was finally vindicated in what is probably the most famous Supreme Court decision of the twentieth century, *Brown* v. *Board of Education* (1954). In *Brown*, the Warren Court declared, in an unusual unanimous decision, that the "separate but equal" standard approved in *Plessy* is a contradiction in terms. Like *Plessy*, *Brown* was technically about only one kind of public segregation—in this instance, public schools. Like *Plessy*, however, it had a domino effect: the outlawing of segregation of children at school began, slowly, to dismantle segregation in the South.

But resistance to integration was fierce and change was irregular and slow, opposed at every step by southern legislatures, governors, sheriffs, and private citizens who met peaceful efforts to integrate public facilities with hatred and often violence. The medium through which most Americans became acquainted with southern segregation and the civil rights movement was television. Pictures of police turning water cannons or attack dogs on unarmed marchers, including elderly men and women, or on college students asking for service at a lunch counter or a drink of water at a fountain marked "WHITES ONLY," made a powerful impression on Americans who had never been below the Mason-Dixon line and whose only image of the South probably came from watching *Gone with the Wind.*

Martin Luther King, Jr., the leader of the civil rights movement, was frequently arrested. During one incarceration in Birmingham, Alabama, King took the opportunity to respond to some of his critics, who had taken out an advertisement in the local paper criticizing him and his followers. Ironically, these particular opponents were not Ku Klux Klan members or other white supremacists but southern clergymen—and mostly black clergymen at that. King's answer, "Letter from Birmingham Jail," immediately became an unofficial primer for the ideology of nonviolent resistance.

In the 1970s, a whole new series of arguments about justice and individual rights arose: for or against the Vietnam War, a new wave of the feminist movement, sex education in schools, gays in the military. College student Neha Gupta argues in her essay for one of the many issues that are still unresolved: the question of whether gay soldiers should be able to serve openly in the armed forces.

As long as Americans continue to believe in the ideals of the Declaration of Independence and the Constitution, they will recognize, intermittently and with considerable discomfort, that justice and civil liberty are easy to support but hard to practice. The tension between equality and conformity, individuality and difference, can lead to prejudice. Americans do not always welcome the artists, writers, or political leaders who remind them of the American promise or of how much they have fallen short. Yet even for its harshest critics, America's promise of justice for all survives.

Building Justice and Civil Liberties Using Refutation

You will notice as you read the selections in this chapter that all the authors seem to be constantly arguing with great zest against a person or an idea; and these are writers who aim cheerfully for the rhetorical jugular vein. This use of refutation has a long history in American discourse. Some, but not all, of this combativeness is inherent in our legal system. When a case is presented, there are always two sides, and their relationship is adversarial: only one can win. So a lawyer trying to convince a court to rule favorably cannot simply present information; the victor is often the one who also destroys the opponent's case by refuting its major premises. That is certainly true of a trained lawyer like Thomas Jefferson, the Supreme Court justices in *Plessy* and *Brown,* and the attorneys who argued the cases before them.

This insistence on refuting the opposition, and the level of intensity accompanying it, are also evident in the speeches of Susan B. Anthony and Frederick Douglass, and in Martin Luther King, Jr.'s letter. The most obvious explanation is that they all had personal experience of persecution and were determined to communicate it to a larger audience. But the deeper connection is their belief that they have both a right and a privilege, granted to them by the Declaration and the Constitution, to object when the ideals in those documents are violated, and they will criticize anyone, including the government itself, who tries to stop them. They take the ideas of justice and civil liberties personally; argumentation and refutation are the weapons they use in defense of the rights of others as well as their own.

As you read the sections in this chapter, keep in mind that dissenters can be very lonely and extremely unpopular, though eventually they may be regarded as heroes. Take the time to imagine how much it cost them to hold to their principles in a hostile environment: cold silence, disapproval, threats, arrest and imprisonment, the sudden loss of friendships and jobs. Is there any principle, any idea, you could care enough about to put yourself at risk of losing everything? Would you have the courage to take an unpopular stand if you believed you were in the right, or even the courage to support a friend who does so, when the choice is between your conscience and a comfortable life, or between safe conformity and dangerous independence?

THE DECLARATION OF INDEPENDENCE
1776

Thomas Jefferson

The author of the Declaration was thirty-two-year-old Thomas Jefferson (1743–1826) who could, in the words of a contemporary, "break a horse, play the violin, dance the minuet" and of whom the usually acerbic John Adams said, he had a "reputation for literature, science, and a happy talent of composition. His writings were remarkable for their felicity of expression." Jefferson was, in succession, a member of the Continental Congress, governor of Virginia, ambassador to France, the first secretary of state, vice-president, and then president for two terms, during which he authorized the Louisiana Purchase, doubling the size of the United States. He founded the University of Virginia; designed it and his home, Monticello, and collected the books that formed the basis for the Library of Congress. In 1962, when President Kennedy invited a group of Nobel Prize winners to dinner, he said it was the greatest concentration of intellect in the White House since the evenings when Thomas Jefferson dined there alone. Jefferson died on July 4, 1826— fifty years to the day after he wrote the Declaration of Independence. In the text that follows, the underlined words and phrases were in the first draft but were removed in the final draft. The words and phrases in the margin are those that appeared in the final version.

A DECLARATION BY THE REPRESENTATIVES OF THE UNITED STATES OF AMERICA, IN GENERAL CONGRESS ASSEMBLED.

When in the course of human events, it becomes necessary for one people to dissolve the political bands which have connected them with another, and to assume among the powers of the earth the separate and equal station to which the laws of nature and of nature's God entitle them, a decent respect to the opinions of mankind requires that they should declare the causes which impel them to the separation.

We hold these truths to be self evident: that all men are created equal, that they are endowed by their Creator with <u>inherent and in-</u>   certain alienable rights; that among these are life, liberty, and the pursuit of happiness; that to secure these rights, governments are instituted among men, deriving their just powers from the consent of the governed; that whenever any form of government becomes destructive of these ends, it is the right of the people to alter or to abolish it, and to institute new government, laying its foundation on such principles, and organizing its powers in such form, as to them shall seem most likely to effect their safety and happiness. Prudence, indeed, will dictate that governments long established should not be changed for light and transient causes; and accordingly all experience hath shown that mankind are more disposed to suffer while evils are sufferable, than to right themselves by abolishing the forms to which they are accustomed. But when a long train of abuses and usurpations, <u>begun at a distinguished period and</u> pursuing invariably the same object, evinces a design to reduce them under absolute despotism, it is their right, it is their duty to throw off such government, and to provide new guards for their future security. Such has been the patient sufferance of these colonies; and such is now the necessity which constrains them to <u>expunge</u> their former systems of government. The history of the pres-   alter ent king of Great Britain is a history of <u>unremitting</u> injuries and   repeated usurpations, <u>among which appears no solitary fact to contradict the</u>   all having <u>uniform tenor of the rest, but all have</u> in direct object the establishment of an absolute tyranny over these states. To prove this, let facts be submitted to a candid world <u>for the truth of which we pledge a faith yet unsullied by falsehood.</u>

He has refused his assent to laws the most wholesome and necessary for the public good.

5   He has forbidden his governors to pass laws of immediate and pressing importance, unless suspended in their operation till his assent should be obtained; and, when so suspended, he has utterly neglected to attend to them.

He has refused to pass other laws for the accommodation of large districts of people, unless those people would relinquish the right of representation in the legislature, a right inestimable to them, and formidable to tyrants only.

He has called together legislative bodies at places unusual, uncomfortable, and distant from the depository of their public records, for the sole purpose of fatiguing them into compliance with his measures.

He has dissolved representative houses repeatedly <u>and continually</u>

for opposing with manly firmness his invasions on the rights of the people.

He has refused for a long time after such dissolutions to cause others to be elected, whereby the legislative powers, incapable of annihilation, have returned to the people at large for their exercise, the state remaining, in the meantime, exposed to all the dangers of invasion from without and convulsions within.

He has endeavored to prevent the population of these states: for that purpose obstructing the laws for naturalization of foreigners, refusing to pass others to encourage their migrations hither, and raising the conditions of new appropriations of lands.   `10`

He has suffered the administration of justice totally to cease in some of these states refusing his assent to laws for establishing judiciary powers.   `obstructed by`

He has made our judges dependent on his will alone for the tenure of their offices, and the amount and payment of their salaries.

He has erected a multitude of new offices, by a self-assumed power and sent hither swarms of new officers to harass our people and eat out their substance.

He has kept among us in times of peace standing armies and ships of war without the consent of our legislatures.

He has affected to render the military independent of, and superior to, the civil power.   `15`

He has combined with others to subject us to a jurisdiction foreign to our constitutions and unacknowledged by our laws, giving his assent to their acts of pretended legislation for quartering large bodies of armed troops among us; for protecting them by a mock trial from punishment for any murders which they should commit on the inhabitants of these states; for cutting off our trade with all parts of the world; for imposing taxes on us without our consent; for depriving [   ] us of the benefits of trial by jury; for transporting us beyond seas to be tried for pretended offenses; for abolishing the free system of English laws in a neighboring province, establishing therein an arbitrary government, and enlarging its boundaries, so as to render it at once an example and fit instrument for introducing the same absolute rule into these states; for taking away our charters, abolishing our most valuable laws, and altering fundamentally the forms of our governments; for suspending our own legislatures, and declaring themselves invested with power to legislate for us in all cases whatsoever.   `in many cases`   `in many cases`   `colonies`

He has abdicated government here withdrawing his governors, and declaring us out of his allegiance and protection.   `by declaring us out of his protection and`

He has plundered our seas, ravaged our coasts, burnt our towns, and destroyed the lives of our people.   `waging war against us`

He is at this time transporting large armies of foreign mercenaries to complete the works of death, desolation and tyranny already begun with circumstances of cruelty and perfidy [   ] unworthy the head of a civilized nation. *scarcely parallele[d] in the mo[st] barbarou[s] ages, and totally*

20 He has constrained our fellow citizens taken captive on the high seas, to bear arms, against their country, to become the executioners of their friends and brethren, or to fall themselves by their hands.

He has [   ] endeavored to bring on the inhabitants of our frontiers, the merciless Indian savages, whose known rule of warfare is an undistinguished destruction of all ages, sexes and conditions of existence. *excited d[o]mestic in[sur]surrectio[ns] among u[s] and has*

He has incited treasonable insurrections of our fellow citizens, with the allurements of forfeiture and confiscation of our property

He has waged cruel war against human nature itself, violating its most sacred rights of life and liberty in the persons of a distant people who never offended him, captivating and carrying them into slavery in another hemisphere, or to incur miserable death in their transportation thither. This piratical warfare, the opprobrium of INFIDEL powers, is the warfare of the CHRISTIAN king of Great Britain. Determined to keep open a market where MEN should be bought and sold, he has prostituted his negative for suppressing every legislative attempt to prohibit or to restrain this execrable commerce. And that this assemblage of horrors might want no fact of distinguished die, he is now exciting those very people to rise in arms among us, and to purchase that liberty of which he has deprived them, by murdering the people on whom he also obtruded them: thus paying off former crimes committed against the LIBERTIES of one people, with crimes which he urges them to commit against the LIVES of another.

In every stage of these oppressions we have petitioned for redress in the most humble terms: our repeated petitions have been answered only by repeated injuries.

25 A prince whose character is thus marked by every act which may define a tyrant is unfit to be the ruler of a [   ] people who mean to be free. Future ages will scarcely believe that the hardiness of one man adventured, within the short compass of twelve years only, to lay a foundation so broad and so undisguised for tyranny over a people fostered and fixed in principles of freedom. *free*

Nor have we been wanting in attentions to our British brethren. We have warned them from time to time of attempts by their legislature to extend a jurisdiction over these our states. We have reminded them of the circumstances of our emigration and settlement here, no one of which would warrant so strange a pretension: that these were effected at the expense of our own blood and treasure, unassisted by *an/unwa[r]rantable/us* the wealth or the strength of Great Britain: that in constituting indeed our several forms of government, we had adopted one common king, thereby laying a foundation for perpetual league and amity with them: but that submission to their parliament was no part of our constitution, nor ever in idea, if history may be credited: and, we [   ] appealed to their native justice and magnanimity as well as to the ties of our common kindred to disavow these usurpations which were likely to interrupt our connection and correspondence. They too have been deaf to the voice of justice and of consanguinity, and when occasions have been given them, by the regular course of their laws, of removing from their councils the disturbers of our harmony, they have, by their free election, reestablished them in power. At this very time too, they are permitting their chief magistrate to send over not only soldiers of our common blood, but Scotch and foreign mercenaries to invade and destroy us. These facts have given the last stab to agonizing affection, and manly spirit bids us to renounce forever these unfeeling brethren. We must endeavor to forget our former love for them, and hold them as we hold the rest of mankind, enemies in war, in peace friends. We might have been a free and a great people together; but a communication of grandeur and of freedom, it seems, is below their dignity. Be it so, since they will have it. The road to happiness and to glory is open to us, too. We will tread it apart from them, and acquiesce in the necessity which denounces our eternal separation [   ]!

We therefore the representatives of the United States of America in General Congress assembled, do in the name, and by the authority of the good people of these states reject and renounce all allegiance and subjection to the kings of Great Britain and all others who may hereafter claim by, through or under them; we utterly dissolve all political connection which may heretofore have subsisted between us and the people or parliament of Great Britain: and finally we do assert and declare these colonies to be free and independent states, and that as free and independent states, they have full power to levy war, conclude peace, contract alliances, establish commerce, and to do all other acts and things which independent states may of right do.

And for the support of this declaration, we mutually pledge to each other our lives, our fortunes, and our sacred honor.

We, therefore, the representatives of the United States of America in General Congress assembled, appealing to the supreme judges of the world for the rectitude of our intentions, do in the name, and by the authority of the good people of these colonies, solemnly publish and declare, that these united colonies are, and of right ought to be free and independent states; that they are absolved from all allegiance to the British crown, and that all political connection between them

Margin notes: have | and we have conjured them by would inevitably | We must therefore | and hold them as we hold the rest of mankind, enemies in war, in peace friends

and the state of Great Britain is, and ought to be, totally dissolved; and that as free and independent states, they have full power to levy war, conclude peace, contract alliances, establish commerce, and to do all other acts and things which independent states may of right do.

30   And for the support of this declaration, with a firm reliance on the protection of divine providence, we mutually pledge to each other our lives, our fortunes, and our sacred honor.

For Journals

Is the content of the Declaration of Independence what you expected it would be? What parts of it, if any, were familiar to you?

For Discussion

1.   Read the entire Declaration out loud, with each person in the class reading part of it. Then do five minutes worth of freewriting. Using your freewriting as a basis, compare your thoughts about the Declaration with those of your peers.

2.   The Declaration was the justification for the idea of a democratic republic when no such republic had ever existed before. Working with someone else in your class, find three good examples of Jefferson's argument for the form of government he wants. What is the main point in each example? What is the supporting evidence? What isthe conclusion?

3.   The two most famous phrases in the Declaration of Independence declare that "all men are created equal" and that we are endowed by our Creator with the rights to "life, liberty, and the pursuit of happiness." What do you think those particular phrases mean? What does it mean to be created equal? Equal in what way? Equa spiritually? Equa legally? Equa intellectually? How do you think an American pursues happiness?

4.   Jefferson, who was trained as a lawyer, was accustomed to framing arguments. Reread the Declaration as though you were a member of a jury listening to a trial lawyer's closing statement on behalf of his client. How does he refute the idea that George III is a just king and that Americans owe him their loyalty under any circumstances? What kind of evidence does he present about the injustices committed by the King and Great Britain to prove that Americans are entitled to decide on their own?

5.   Many Americans disagreed with the Revolution and remained loyal to the English government. What arguments do you think they might have made to refute Jefferson's assertions? What holes would they have tried to find in his argument?

6. What do you think Jefferson wanted an American audience to take away from the Declaration? What do you think he wanted a British audience to learn?

For Writing

1. Look at the underlined phrases that were in the first version of the Declaration but were eliminated or changed in the final version and at the words in the margin that replaced them. For example, in the first draft, Jefferson included a long denunciation of slavery; in the final draft it is taken out because the southern slave states would not vote for a document that included it. Write an essay in which you respond to the following: What changes were the most surprising to you? Are there any cases in which you prefer the first version over the final one? Which ones do you think present a stronger argument against British injustice? Why?

2. There were many lawyers among the Founding Fathers; while they were all opposed to British rule, at least one of them was willing to defend British soldiers in court in the name of justice and civil liberties. Research and write a documented paper on the story of how John Adams defended British soldiers accused of murdering five colonials during the Boston Massacre. Include his reasons for taking on the case, what the colonial community thought of Adams's decision, and what your own reaction is.

THE POWER OF MUSIC

1 8 4 7

William Sidney Mount

 William Sidney Mount (1807–1868) grew up in rural Stony Brook, Long Island, and spent much of his career there. Although he began as a portrait painter, he is better known for his paintings of country life. Mount is the first significant white American painter to portray African Americans sympathetically. Interested in capturing everyday existence, he also pursued a lifelong interest in perspective and geometry, evident in the careful design of his paintings.

For Journals

Why do you think Mount titled this painting *The Power of Music*? If you didn't know the title, what would you guess the painting would be called? Why?

For Discussion

1.   Mount was interested in mathematics, and particularly in geometry, optics, and design, and those interests are reflected in his art work. Look at this painting again, and then describe its design: the arrangement of the figures, the spaces between those figures, their posture, the vertical and horizontal divisions on the canvas. Where do you look first? How does the design move your gaze around the picture?

2. What difference does it make that this painting was painted before the Civil War and that the man standing outside is a slave? If he were white, do you think the impact of the painting would be any different?

3. Mount has been praised as a sympathetic portrayer of slave life and at the same time criticized as a purveyor of sentimental ideas. What stereotypes do you think he supports or refutes in this painting? Look the painting over carefully. What details in the painting contribute to your evaluation?

4. What audiences do you think the painting was aimed at? What emotional response do you think Mount was hoping to get from his audience? What is your response?

5. Consider the following view of the painting written by one of Mount's contemporaries: Very expressive and clever are Mount's happy delineations of the arch, quaint, gay, and rustic humors seen among the primitive people of his native place; they are truly American. What is your response to this evaluation?

For Writing

1. Write a reflective essay comparing Mount's painting with one of the reading selections in this chapter that deals with a similar or related theme. Which one do you find more expressive? Which one do you think is more successful? Which is easier to understand? Why? Which medium do you think is better suited to communicating the ideas in it?

2. Most books on nineteenth-century American art have illustrations of Mount's work. Find another painting of his—for example, *The Haymakers,* which portrays a slave child listening to music, or *Dancing on the Barn Floor,* which portrays two young country people—both white—dancing as another young man plays the fiddle. Write a paper comparing one of these, or another of Mount's related paintings, to *The Power of Music.* Consider these questions: What is the mood of each picture? Who are the people in it? What are they doing, and where are they in relation to each other? What point do you think the artist is trying to make? Is it any different from the one made in *The Power of Music?* In what way?

FROM *ON CIVIL DISOBEDIENCE*
1 8 5 0

Henry David Thoreau

Henry David Thoreau (1817–1862) spent almost his entire life in and around Concord, Massachusetts, and found there all the subject matter he needed. An ardent abolitionist, diarist, nature writer, and natural scientist, he challenged American materialism and complacency as no other writer has before or since. Always an individualist, he wrote his most famous book, Walden *(1854), while living alone for two years at Walden Pond, where he said he could live a life of "simplicity, independence, magnanimity, trust." It was at Walden that he was arrested—willingly—and spent a night in jail for having refused to pay taxes supporting slavery and the Mexican-American war.* On Civil Disobedience, *which explains Thoreau's theory of passive resistance, challenged his neighbors—and us—to examine our lives and our ethics, and to act.*

I heartily accept the motto—"That government is best which governs least;" and I should like to see it acted up to more rapidly and systematically. Carried out, it finally amounts to this, which also I believe,—"That government is best which governs not at all;" and when men are prepared for it, that will be the kind of government which they will have. Government is at best but an expedient; but most governments are usually, and all governments are sometimes, inexpedient. The objections which have been brought against a standing army, and they are many and weighty, and deserve to prevail, may also at last be brought against a standing government. The standing army is only an arm of the standing government. The government itself, which is only the mode which the people have chosen to execute their will, is equally liable to be abused and perverted before the people can act through it. Witness the present Mexican war, the work of comparatively a few individuals using the standing government as their tool; for, in the outset, the people would not have consented to this measure.

This American government,—what is it but a tradition, though a recent one, endeavoring to transmit itself unimpaired to posterity, but each instant losing some of its integrity? It has not the vitality and force of a single living man; for a single man can bend it to his will. It is a sort of wooden gun to the people themselves; and, if ever they should use it in earnest as a real one against each other, it will surely split. But it is not the less necessary for this; for the people must have some complicated machinery or other, and hear its din, to satisfy that idea of government which they have. Governments show thus how successfully men can be imposed on, even impose on themselves, for their own advantage. It is excellent, we must all allow; yet this government never of itself furthered any enterprise, but by the alacrity with which it got out of its way. *It* does not keep the country free. *It* does not settle the West. *It* does not educate. The character inherent in the American people has done all that has been accomplished; and it would have done somewhat more, if the government had not sometimes got in its way. For government is an expedient by which men would fain succeed in letting one another alone; and, as has been said, when it is most expedient, the governed are most let alone by it. Trade and commerce, if they were not made of india rubber, would never manage to bounce over the obstacles which legislators are continually putting in their way; and, if one were to judge these men wholly by the effects of their actions, and not partly by their intentions, they would deserve to be classed and punished with those mischievous persons who put obstructions on the railroads.

But, to speak practically and as a citizen, unlike those who call themselves no-government men, I ask for, not at once no government, but *at once* a better government. Let every man make known what kind of government would command his respect, and that will be one step toward obtaining it.

After all, the practical reason why, when the power is once in the hands of the people, a majority are permitted, and for a long period continue, to rule, is not because this seems fairest to the minority, but because they are physically the strongest. But a government in which the majority rule in all cases cannot be based on justice, even as far as men understand it. Can there not be a government in which majorities do not virtually decide right and wrong, but conscience?—in which majorities decide only those questions to which the rule of expediency is applicable? Must the citizen ever for a moment, or in the least degree, resign his conscience to the legislator? Why has every man a conscience, then? I think that we should be men first, and subjects afterward. It is not desirable to cultivate a respect for the law, so much as for the right. The only obligation which I have a right to assume, is to do at any time what I think right. . . .

How does it become a man to behave toward this American government to-day? I answer that he cannot without disgrace be associated with it. I cannot for an instant recognize that political organization as *my* government which is the *slave's* government also. 5

All men recognize the right of revolution; that is, the right to refuse allegiance to and to resist the government, when its tyranny or its inefficiency are great and unendurable. But almost all say that such is not the case now. But such was the case, they think, in the Revolution of '75. If one were to tell me that this was a bad government because it taxed certain foreign commodities brought to its ports, it is most probable that I should not make an ado about it, for I can do without them; all machines have their friction; and possibly this does enough good to counterbalance the evil. At any rate, it is a great evil to make a stir about it. But when the friction comes to have its machine, and oppression and robbery are organized, I say, let us not have such a machine any longer. In other words, when a sixth of the population of a nation which has undertaken to be the refuge of liberty are slaves, and a whole country is unjustly overrun and conquered by a foreign army, and subject to military law, I think that it is not too soon for honest men to rebel and revolutionize. What makes this duty the more urgent is the fact, that the country so overrun is not our own, but ours is the invading army. . . .

Practically speaking, the opponents to a reform in Massachusetts are not a hundred thousand politicans at the South, but a hundred thousand merchants and farmers here, who are more interested in commerce and agriculture than they are in humanity, and are not prepared to do justice to the slave and to Mexico, *cost what it may.* I quarrel not with far-off foes, but with those who, near at home, co-operate with, and do the bidding of those far away, and without whom the latter would be harmless. We are accustomed to say, that the mass of men are unprepared; but improvement is slow, because the few are not materially wiser or better than the many. It is not so important that many should be as good as you, as that there be some absolute goodness somewhere; for that will leaven the whole lump. There are thousands who are *in opinion* opposed to slavery and to the war, who yet in effect do nothing to put an end to them; who, esteeming themselves children of Washington and Franklin, sit down with their hands in their pockets, and say that they know not what to do, and do nothing; who even postpone the question of freedom to the question of free-trade, and quietly read the prices-current along with the latest advices from Mexico, after dinner, and, it may be, fall asleep over them both. . . .

The American has dwindled into an Old Fellow,—one who may be known by the development of his organ of gregariousness, and a manifest lack of intellect and cheerful self-reliance; whose first and chief concern, on coming into the world, is to see that the alms-houses are in good repair; and, before yet he has lawfully donned the virile garb, to collect a fund for the support of the widows and orphans that may be; who, in short, ventures to live only by the aid of the mutual insurance company, which has promised to bury him decently. . . .

Unjust laws exist: shall we be content to obey them, or shall we endeavor to amend them, and obey them until we have succeeded, or shall we transgress them at once? Men generally, under such a government as this, think that they ought to wait until they have persuaded the majority to alter them. They think that, if they should resist, the remedy would be worse than the evil. But it is the fault of the government itself that the remedy *is* worse than the evil. *It* makes it worse. Why is it not more apt to anticipate and provide for reform? Why does it not cherish its wise minority? Why does it cry and resist before it is hurt? Why does it not encourage its citizens to be on the alert to point out its faults, and *do* better than it would have them? Why does it always crucify Christ, and excommunicate Copernicus and Luther, and pronounce Washington and Franklin rebels? . . .

If the injustice is part of the necessary friction of the machine of   10 government, let it go, let it go: perchance it will wear smooth,—certainly the machine will wear out. If the injustice has a spring, or a pulley, or a rope, or a crank, exclusively for itself, then perhaps you may consider whether the remedy will not be worse than the evil; but if it is of such a nature that it requires you to be the agent of injustice to another, then, I say, break the law. Let your life be a counter friction to stop the machine. What I have to do is to see, at any rate, that I do not lend myself to the wrong which I condemn.

As for adopting the ways which the State has provided for remedying the evil, I know not of such ways. They take too much time, and a man's life will be gone. I have other affairs to attend to. I came into this world, not chiefly to make this a good place to life [*sic*], but to live in it, be it good or bad. A man has not everything to do, but something; and because he cannot do *every thing*, it is not necessary that he should do *something* wrong. It is not my business to be petitioning the governor or the legislature any more than it is theirs to petition me; and if they should not hear my petition, what should I do then? But in this case the State has provided no way: its very Constitution is the evil. This may seem to be harsh and stubborn and unconciliatory; but it is to treat with the utmost kindness and consideration the only spirit that can appreciate or deserves it. So is all change for the better, like birth and death which convulse the body.

I do not hesitate to say, that those who call themselves abolitionists should at once effectually withdraw their support, both in person and property, from the government of Massachusetts, and not wait till they constitute a majority of one, before they suffer the right to prevail through them, I think that it is enough if they have God on their side, without waiting for that other one. Moreover, any man more right than his neighbors constitutes a majority of one already. . . .

Under a government which imprisons any unjustly, the true place for a just man is also in prison. The proper place to-day, the only place which Massachusetts has provided for her freer and less desponding spirits, is in her prisons, to be put out and locked out of the State by her own act, as they have already put themselves out by their principles. It is there that the fugitive slave, and the Mexican prisoner on parole, and the Indian come to plead the wrongs of his race, should find them; on that separate, but more free and honorable ground, where the State places those who are not *with* her, but *against* her,—the only house in a slave-state in which a free man can abide with honor. If any think that their influence would be lost there, and their voices no longer afflict the ear of the State, that they would not be as an enemy within its walls, they do not know by how much truth is stronger than error, nor how much more eloquently and effectively he can combat injustice who has experienced a little in his own person. Cast your whole vote, not a strip of paper merely, but your whole influence. A minority is powerless while it conforms to the majority; it is not even a minority then; but it is irresistible when it clogs by its whole weight. If the alternative is to keep all just men in prison, or give up war and slavery, the State will not hesitate which to choose. If a thousand men were not to pay their tax-bills this year, that would not be a violent and bloody measure, as it would be to pay them, and enable the State to commit violence and shed innocent blood. This is, in fact, the definition of a peaceable revolution, if any such is possible. If the tax-gatherer, or any other public officer, asks me, as one has done, "But what shall I do?" my answer is, "If you really wish to do anything, resign our office." When the subject has refused allegiance, and the officer has resigned his office, then the revolution is accomplished. But even suppose blood should flow. Is there not a sort of blood shed when the conscience is wounded? Through this wound a man's real manhood and immortality flow out, and he bleeds to an everlasting death. I see this blood flowing now. . . .

I have paid no poll-tax for six years. I was put into a jail once on this account, for one night; and, as I stood considering the walls of solid stone, two or three feet thick, the door of wood and iron, a foot thick, and the iron grating which strained the light, I could not help being struck with the foolishness of that institution which treated me as if I were mere flesh and blood and bones, to be locked up. I wondered that it should have concluded at length that this was the best use it could put me to, and had never thought to avail itself of my services in some way. I saw that, if there was a wall of stone between me and my townsmen, there was a still more difficult one to climb or break through, before they could get to be as free as I was. I did not for a moment feel confined, and the walls seemed a great waste of stone and mortar. I felt as if I alone of all my townsmen had paid my tax. They plainly did not know how to treat me, but behaved like persons who are underbred. In every threat and in every compliment there was a blunder; for they thought that my chief desire was to stand the other side of that stone wall. I could not but smile to see how industriously they locked the door on my meditations, which followed them out again without let or hinderance, and *they* were really all that was dangerous. As they could not reach me, they had resolved to punish my body; just as boys, if they cannot come at some person against whom they have a spite, will abuse his dog. I saw that the State was half-witted, that it was timid as a lone woman with her silver spoons, and that it did not know its friends from its foes, and I lost all my remaining respect for it, and pitied it.

Thus the State never intentionally confronts a man's sense, intellectual or moral, but only his body, his senses. It is not armed with superior wit or honesty, but with superior physical strength. I was not born to be forced. I will breathe after my own fashion. Let us see who is the strongest. What force has a multitude? They only can force me who obey a higher law than I. They force me to become like themselves. I do not hear of *men* being *forced* to live this way or that by masses of men. What sort of life were that to live? When I meet a government which says to me, "Your money or your life," why should I be in haste to give it my money? It may be in a great strait, and not know what to do: I cannot help that. It must help itself; do as I do. It is not worth the while to snivel about it. I am not responsible for the successful working of the machinery of society. I am not the son of the engineer. I perceive that, when an acorn and a chestnut fall side by side, the one does not remain inert to make way for the other, but both obey their own laws, and spring and grow and flourish as best they can, till one, perchance, overshadows and detroys the other. If a plant cannot live according to its nature, it dies; and so a man. . . . 15

I do not wish to quarrel with any man or nation. I do not wish to split hairs, to make fine distinctions, or set myself up as better than my neighbors. I seek rather, I may say, even an excuse for conforming to the laws of the land. I am but too ready to conform to them. Indeed I have reason to suspect myself on his head; and each year, as the tax-gatherer comes round, I find myself disposed to review the acts and position of the general and state governments, and the spirit of the people, to discover a pretext for conformity. I believe that the State will soon be able to take all my work of this sort out of my hands, and then I shall be no better a patriot than my fellow-countrymen. Seen from a lower point of view, the Constitution, with all its faults, is very good; the law and the courts are very respectable; even this State and this American government are, in many respects, very admirable and rare things, to be thankful for, such as a great many have described them; but seen from a point of view a little higher, they are what I have described them; seen from a higher still, and the highest, who shall say that they are, or that they are worth looking at or thinking of at all?

However, the government does not concern me much, and I shall bestow the fewest possible thoughts on it. It is not many moments that I live under a government, even in this world. If a man is thought-free, fancy-free, imagination-free, that which *is not* never for a long time appearing *to be* to him, unwise rulers or reformers cannot fatally interrupt him. . . .

The authority of government, even such as I am willing to submit to,—for I will cheerfully obey those who know and can do better than I, and in many things even those who neither know nor can do so well,—is still an impure one: to be strictly just, it must have the sanction and consent of the governed. It can have no pure right over my person and property but what I concede to it. The progress from an absolute to a limited monarchy, from a limited monarchy to a democracy, is a progress toward a true respect for the individual. Is a democracy, such as we know it, the last improvement possible in government? Is it not possible to take a step further towards recognizing and organizing the rights of man? There will never be a really free and enlightened State, until the State comes to recognize the individual as a higher and independent power, from which all its own power and authority are derived, and treats him accordingly. I please myself with imagining a State at last which can afford to be just to all men, and to treat the individual with respect as a neighbor, which even would not think it inconsistent with its own repose, if a few were to live aloof from it, not meddling with it, nor embraced by it, who fulfilled all the duties of neighbors and fellowmen. A State which bore this kind of fruit, and suffered it to drop off as fast as it ripened, would prepare the way for a still more perfect and glorious State, which also I have imagined, but not yet anywhere seen.

For Journals

Thoreau states that the government which governs best is the one which governs least. What functions does he seem to think government should stay out of? Which areas today would you want government to stay out of, and which do you think it should pursue more actively?

For Discussion

1. What is your response to Thoreau's ideas that an individual American following his or her conscience is a majority of one, and that fighting injustice by persuading the majority to change the law takes too long? What traditional ideas of good government and citizenship does he refute in these statements?

2. Thoreau says that the government does not keep the country free, that it does not settle the West, that it does not educate. In his opinion, then, what does it do?

3. Democracy is supposed to be governed by the rule of the majority, but Thoreau says that his only obligation is "to do what I think is right." How do you respond to this assertion? Do you think that the two principles—majority rule and individual conscience—are compatible or mutually incompatible? Why?

4. Thoreau refused to pay a poll tax as a protest against slavery and the war America was waging against Mexico. Do you find withholding taxes or going to jail reasonable ways of protesting injustice? If not, what would you say to refute Thoreau's belief in civil disobedience? Are there any principles for which you would be willing to break the law, willing to go to jail, or otherwise practice civil disobedience yourself?

5. What does Thoreau think constitute the responsibilities of a good citizen? Why does he think most Americans, even the ones opposed to slavery, are not truly good citizens?

6. How would the government function if everyone followed his or her conscience the way Thoreau did? Do you see him as an extremist? A patriot? Both?

For Writing

1. Write an essay in which you compose your own definition of patriotism. Be sure to identify the principles—political, personal, or ethical—on which your definition is based. You can refer to Thoreau, the Declaration, or any other readings, and either refute these arguments or draw on them to support your own views.

2. Read one of Thoreau's other works, for example, *On Walden Pond,* the diary of his year-long adventure of living alone and being self-sufficient; or *A Week on the Concord and Merrimack Rivers,* an account of his canoeing trip in the American wilderness. Write a review critiquing Thoreau's skill as a naturalist and observer; and share the review with your peers; you should use secondary library sources (articles, biographies, etc.) if possible.

INDEPENDENCE DAY SPEECH AT ROCHESTER
1852

Frederick Douglass

At the time Frederick Douglass (see Chapter 5) gave this speech, he had been living in Rochester, New York, for several years and editing his abolitionist newspaper, the Northern Star. *His autobiography had been published in 1845, after he escaped from slavery, and he subsequently spent two years in England lecturing and earning money to buy his freedom so that he could not be captured and returned to the South. He had a remarkable career as a diplomat, civil rights leader before and after the Civil War, marshal of the District of Columbia, organizer of black combat units, campaigner for women's rights, newspaper editor, and writer. He was asked to deliver the Fourth of July speech in Rochester in 1852. Fourth of July speeches were already an old American political tradition. Like parades and fireworks, the speeches on such occasions are usually celebratory, uncritical, and immediately forgettable. Douglass's speech, made nine years before the start of the Civil War, is the exception.*

Fellow citizens, pardon me, allow me to ask, why am I called upon to speak here today? What have I, or those I represent, to do with your national independence? Are the great principles of political freedom and of natural justice, embodied in that Declaration of Independence, extended to us? and am I, therefore, called upon to bring our humble offering to the national altar, and to confess the benefits and express devout gratitude for the blessings resulting from your independence to us?

Would to God, both for your sakes and ours, that an affirmative answer could be truthfully returned to these questions! Then would my task be light, and my burden easy and delightful. For who is there so cold that a nation's sympathy could not warm him? Who so obdurate and dead to the claims of gratitude that would not thankfully acknowledge such priceless benefits? Who so stolid and selfish that would not give his voice to swell the hallelujahs of a nation's jubilee, when the chains of servitude had been torn from his limbs? I am not that man. In a case like that the dumb might eloquently speak and the "lame man leap as an hart."

But such is not the state of the case. I say it with a sad sense of the disparity between us. I am not included within the pale of this glorious anniversary! Your high independence only reveals the immeasurable distance between us. The blessings in which you, this day, rejoice are not enjoyed in common. The rich inheritance of justice, liberty, prosperity, and independence bequeathed by your fathers is shared by you, not by me. The sunlight that brought light and healing to you has brought stripes and death to me. This Fourth of July is yours, not mine. You may rejoice, I must mourn. To drag a man in fetters into the grand illuminated temple of liberty, and call upon him to join you in joyous anthems, were inhuman mockery and sacrilegious irony. Do you mean, citizens, to mock me by asking me to speak today? If so, there is a parallel to your conduct. And let me warn you that it is dangerous to copy the example of a nation whose crimes, towering up to heaven, were thrown down by the breath of the Almighty, burying that nation in irrevocable ruin! I can today take up the plaintive lament of a peeled and woe-smitten people!

"By the rivers of Babylon, there we sat down. Yea! we wept when we remembered Zion. We hanged our harps upon the willows in the midst thereof. For there, they that carried us away captive, required of us a song; and they who wasted us required of us mirth, saying, Sing us one of the songs of Zion. How can we sing the Lord's song in a strange land? If I forget thee, O Jerusalem, let my right hand forget her cunning. If I do not remember thee, let my tongue cleave to the roof of my mouth."

Fellow citizens, above your national, tumultuous joy, I hear the   5
mournful wail of millions! whose chains, heavy and grievous yesterday, are, today, rendered more intolerable by the jubilee shouts that reach them. If I do forget, if I do not faithfully remember those bleeding children of sorrow this day, "may my right hand forget her cunning, and may my tongue cleave to the roof of my mouth"! To forget them, to pass lightly over their wrongs, and to chime in with the popular theme would be treason most scandalous and shocking, and would make me a reproach before God and the world. My subject, then, fellow citizens, is *American slavery*. I shall see this day and its popular characteristics from the slave's point of view. Standing there identified with the American bondman, making his wrongs mine. I do not hesitate to declare with all my soul that the character and conduct of this nation never looked blacker to me than on this Fourth of July! Whether we turn to the declarations of the past or to the professions of the present, the conduct of the nation seems equally hideous and revolting. America is false to the past, false to the present, and solemnly binds herself to be false to the future. Standing with God and the crushed and bleeding slave on this occasion, I will, in the name of humanity which is outraged, in the name of liberty which is fettered, in the name of the Constitution and the Bible which are disregarded and trampled

upon, dare to call in question and to denounce, with all the emphasis I can command, everything that serves to perpetuate slavery—the great sin and shame of America! "I will not equivocate, I will not excuse;" I will use the severest language I can command; and yet not one word shall escape me that any man, whose judgment is not blinded by prejudice, or who is not at heart a slaveholder, shall not confess to be right and just.

But I fancy I hear someone of my audience say, "It is just in this circumstance that you and your brother abolitionists fail to make a favorable impression on the public mind. Would you argue more and denounce less, would you persuade more and rebuke less, your cause would be much more likely to succeed." But, I submit, where all is plain, there is nothing to be argued. What point in the antislavery creed would you have me argue? On what branch of the subject do the people of this country need light? Must I undertake to prove that the slave is a man? That point is conceded already. Nobody doubts it. The slaveholders themselves acknowledge it in the enactment of laws for their government. They acknowledge it when they punish disobedience on the part of the slave. There are seventy-two crimes in the state of Virginia which, if committed by a black man (no matter how ignorant he be), subject him to the punishment of death; while only two of the same crimes will subject a white man to the like punishment. What is this but the acknowledgment that the slave is a moral, intellectual, and responsible being? The manhood of the slave is conceded. It is admitted in the fact that the Southern statute books are covered with enactments forbidding, under severe fines and penalties, the teaching of the slave to read or to write. When you can point to any such laws in reference to the beasts of the field, then I may consent to argue the manhood of the slave. When the dogs in your streets, when the fowls of the air, when the cattle on your hills, when the fish of the sea and the reptiles that crawl shall be unable to distinguish the slave from a brute, then will I argue with you that the slave is a man!

For the present, it is enough to affirm the equal manhood of the Negro race. Is it not astonishing that, while we are plowing, planting, and reaping, using all kinds of mechanical tools, erecting houses, constructing bridges, building ships, working in metals of brass, iron, copper, silver, and gold; that, while we are reading, writing, and ciphering, acting as clerks, merchants, and secretaries, having among us lawyers, doctors, ministers, poets, authors, editors, orators, and teachers; that, while we are engaged in all manner of enterprises common to other men, digging gold in California, capturing the whale in the Pacific, feeding sheep and cattle on the hillside, living, moving, acting, thinking, planning, living in families as husbands, wives, and children, and, above all, confessing and worshiping the Christian's God, and looking hopefully for life and immortality beyond the grave, we are called upon to prove that we are men!

Would you have me argue that man is entitled to liberty? That he is the rightful owner of his own body? You have already declared it. Must I argue the wrongfulness of slavery? Is that a question for republicans? Is it to be settled by the rules of logic and argumentation, as a matter beset with great difficulty, involving a doubtful application of the principle of justice, hard to be understood? How should I look today, in the presence of Americans, dividing and subdividing a discourse, to show that men have a natural right to freedom? speaking of it relatively and positively, negatively and affirmatively? To do so would be to make myself ridiculous and to offer an insult to your understanding. There is not a man beneath the canopy of heaven that does not know that slavery is wrong for him.

What, am I to argue that it is wrong to make men brutes, to rob them of their liberty, to work them without wages, to keep them ignorant of their relations to their fellow men, to beat them with sticks, to flay their flesh with the lash, to load their limbs with irons, to hunt them with dogs, to sell them at auction, to sunder their families, to knock out their teeth, to burn their flesh, to starve them into obedience and submission to their masters? Must I argue that a system thus marked with blood, and stained with pollution, is wrong? No! I will not. I have better employment for my time and strength than such arguments would imply.

What, then, remains to be argued? Is it that slavery is not divine; that God did not establish it; that our doctors of divinity are mistaken? There is blasphemy in the thought. That which is inhuman cannot be divine! Who can reason on such a proposition? They that can may; I cannot. The time for such argument is past.   10

At a time like this, scorching iron, not convincing argument, is needed. O! had I the ability, and could I reach the nation's ear, I would today pour out a fiery stream of biting ridicule, blasting reproach, withering sarcasm, and stern rebuke. For it is not light that is needed, but fire; it is not the gentle shower, but thunder. We need the storm, the whirlwind, and the earthquake. The feeling of the nation must be quickened; the conscience of the nation must be roused; the propriety of the nation must be startled; the hypocrisy of the nation must be exposed; and its crimes against God and man must be proclaimed and denounced.

What, to the American slave, is your Fourth of July? I answer: a day that reveals to him, more than all other days in the year, the gross injustice and cruelty to which he is the constant victim. To him, your celebration is a sham; your boasted liberty, an unholy license; your national greatness, swelling vanity; your sounds of rejoicing are empty and heartless; your denunciation of tyrants, brass-fronted impudence; your shouts of liberty and equality, hollow mockery; your prayers and hymns, your sermons and thanksgivings, with all your religious parade and solemnity, are, to Him, mere bombast, fraud, deception, impiety, and hypocrisy—a thin veil to cover up crimes which would disgrace a nation of savages. There is not a nation of savages. There is not a nation on the earth guilty of practices more shocking and bloody than are the people of the United States at this very hour.

Go where you may, search where you will, roam through all the monarchies and despotisms of the Old World, travel through South America, search out every abuse, and when you have found the last, lay your facts by the side of the everyday practices of this nation, and you will say with me that, for revolting barbarity and shameless hypocrisy, America reigns without a rival.

For Journals

Was Independence Day an appropriate time for Douglass to make his speech? Why or why not?

For Discussion

1. What do you think were the expectations of Douglass's audience when he began his speech? At what point in the speech do you think he begins to move toward his real topic?

2. Review Douglass's speech with one or two other people in your class, and identify the main points of his argument. (You might begin by identifying the crucial sentence in each paragraph.) What are his conclusions? What do you think he wants his audience to take away with them?

3. Refutation in Douglass's case is not only logically precise but full of emotion. Where in this speech do you find examples of Douglass's anger? Irony? Sarcasm? To what purpose does he express these? How do they help him make his point?

4. What evidence does Douglass accumulate to justify his conclusion that a slave is indeed a man? How would the argument be weaker without this proof? Are there any pieces of evidence that you would add?

5. Which phrases does Douglass quote or paraphrase from the language of the Declaration of Independence? How does he make use of those quotations to support his argument against slavery and to refute the idea that he should be celebrating July Fourth?

6. Douglass uses the technique of raising objections his audience might bring up and then refuting them himself. Find two or three examples of this strategy. Why do you think he employs it? In what ways is it effective in strengthening his argument?

For Writing

1. Douglass revised his autobiography, *The Life and Times of Frederick Douglass,* three times, adding information each time. For example, the first version, written before the Civil War, gives very few details about the people who helped him escape from slavery because Douglass didn't want to jeopardize anyone. The last version of the book, written many years later, is much more explicit. Write a research paper in which you compare elements of one version with another—for example, Douglass's childhood, his experiences as a slave, his education, his escape, or his relations with the Auld family. Consider these questions: What did Douglass add about a certain episode? Which version do you think is more effective? How was your initial response to the injustices Douglass fought against affected by reading the later version?

2. Following the pattern of Douglass's speech, write a speech, for delivery at a formal occasion, about a political or social cause you believe in and which your audience may be hostile to or not enthusiastic about. Be sure to identify your audience—your parents, the people who came to your high school graduation, a historical figure (living or dead), a friend or acquaintance. Begin by making the conventional remarks expected on the occasion, and then focus on what you really want to speak about. Anticipate the objections of your audience, and then refute these objections.

WOMEN'S RIGHT TO VOTE
1 8 7 3

Susan B. Anthony

Susan B. Anthony (1820–1906) grew up in a Quaker family with strong abolitionist beliefs. A campaigner for women's rights even as a teenager, she was an early advocate of equal pay for woman teachers and of coed education. At a time when women had almost no legal rights, she helped a bill through the New York legislature that gave women some control over their children and their earnings: both had previously been controlled by the husband. She

*supported the emancipation of slaves and was an active abolitionist, but de-
voted her life mainly to the fight for women's right to vote. In 1872, during a
presidential election, she decided to test whether the Fourteenth Amendment
to the Constitution—equal protection under the law—applied to women. She
tried to register and was arrested and fined; the fine was never collected. This
is the speech she gave to explain her views.*

I stand before you under indictment for the alleged crime of having voted at the last presidential election, without having a lawful right
to vote. It shall be my work this evening to prove to you that in thus
doing, I not only committed no crime, but instead simply exercised my
citizen's rights, guaranteed to me and all United States citizens by the
National Constitution beyond the power of any State to deny.

Our democratic-republican government is based on the idea of the
natural right of every individual member thereof to a voice and a vote
in making and executing the laws. We assert the province of government to be to secure the people in the enjoyment of their inalienable
rights. We throw to the winds the old dogma that government can give
rights. No one denies that before governments were organized each individual possessed the right to protect his own life, liberty and property. When 100 to 1,000,000 people enter into a free government they
do not barter away their natural rights; they simply pledge themselves
to protect each other in the enjoyment of them through prescribed judicial and legislative tribunals. They agree to abandon the methods of
brute force in the adjustment of their differences and adopt those of
civilization. . . . The Declaration of Independence, the United States
Constitution, the constitutions of the several States and the organic
laws of the Territories, all alike propose to *protect* the people in the exercise of their God-given rights. Not one of them pretends to bestow
rights.

> All men are created equal, and endowed by their Creator with certain
> inalienable rights. Among these are life, liberty and the pursuit of
> happiness. To secure these, governments are instituted among men,
> deriving their just powers from the consent of the governed.

Here is no shadow of government authority over rights, or exclusion of any class from their full and equal enjoyment. Here is pronounced the right of all men, and "consequently," as the Quaker
preacher said, "of all women," to a voice in the government. And here,

in this first paragraph of the Declaration, is the assertion of the natural right of all to the ballot; for how can "the consent of the governed" be given, if the right to vote be denied? . . . The women, dissatisfied as they are with this form of government, that enforces taxation without representation—that compels them to obey laws to which they never have given their consent—that imprisons and hangs them without a trial by a jury of their peers—that robs them, in marriage, of the custody of their own persons, wages, and children—are this half of the people who are left wholly at the mercy of the other half, in direct violation of the spirit and letter of the declarations of the framers of this government, every one of which was based on the immutable principle of equal rights to all. By these declarations, kings, popes, priests, aristocrats, all were alike dethroned and placed on a common level, politically, with the lowliest born subject or serf. By them, too, men, as such, were deprived of their divine right to rule and placed on a political level with women. By the practice of these declarations all class and caste distinctions would be abolished, and slave, serf, plebeian, wife, woman, all alike rise from their subject position to the broader platform of equality.

The preamble of the Federal Constitution says:

> We, the people of the United States, in order to form a more perfect union, establish justice, insure domestic tranquillity, provide for the common defence, promote the general welfare and secure the blessings of liberty to ourselves and our posterity, do ordain and establish this Constitution for the United States of America.

It was we, the people, not we, the white male citizens, nor we, the male citizens; but we, the whole people, who formed this Union. We formed it not to give the blessings of liberty but to secure them; not to the half of ourselves and the half of our prosperity, but to the whole people—women as well as men. It is downright mockery to talk to women of their enjoyment of the blessings of liberty while they are denied the only means of securing them provided by this democratic-republican government—the ballot. . . .

When, in 1871, I asked [Senator Charles Sumner] to declare the power of the United States Constitution to protect women in their right to vote—as he had done for black men—he handed me a copy of all his speeches during that reconstruction period, and said:

> Put "sex" where I have "race" or "color," and you have here the best and strongest argument I can make for woman. There is not a doubt but women have the constitutional right to vote, and I will never vote for a Sixteenth Amendment to guarantee it to them. I voted for both

5

the Fourteenth and Fifteenth under protest; would never have done it but for the pressing emergency of that hour; would have insisted that the power of the original Constitution to protect all citizens in the equal enjoyment of their rights should have been vindicated through the courts. But the newly-made freedmen had neither the intelligence, wealth nor time to await that slow process. Women do possess all these in an eminent degree, and I insist that they shall appeal to the courts and through them establish the powers of our American magna charta to protect every citizen of the republic.

But, friends, when in accordance with Senator Sumner's counsel I went to the ballot-box, last November, and exercised my citizen's right to vote, the courts did not wait for me to appeal to them—they appealed to me, and indicted me on the charge of having voted illegally. . . .

For any State to make sex a qualification, which must ever result in the disfranchisement of one entire half of the people, is to pass a bill of attainder, an ex post facto law, and is therefore a violation of the supreme law of the land. By it the blessings of liberty are forever withheld from women and their female posterity. For them, this government has no just powers derived from the consent of the governed. For them this government is not a democracy; it is not a republic. It is the most odious aristocracy ever established on the face of the globe. An oligarchy of wealth, where the rich govern the poor; an oligarchy of learning, where the educated govern the ignorant; or even an oligarchy of race, where the Saxon rules the African, might be endured; but this oligarchy of sex which makes father, brothers, husband, sons, the oligarchs over the mother and sisters, the wife and daughters of every household; which ordains all men sovereigns, all women subjects—carries discord and rebellion into every home of the nation. . . .

It is urged that the use of the masculine pronouns *he, his* and *him* in all the constitutions and laws, is proof that only men were meant to be included in their provisions. If you insist on this version of the letter of the law, we shall insist that you be consistent and accept the other horn of the dilemma, which would compel you to exempt women from taxation for the support of the government and from penalties for the violation of laws. There is no *she* or *her* or *hers* in the tax laws, and this is equally true of all the criminal laws.

10   Take for example, the civil rights law which I am charged with having violated; not only are all the pronouns in it masculine, but everybody knows that it was intended expressly to hinder the rebel men from voting. It reads, "If any person shall knowingly vote without *his* having a lawful right.". . . I insist if government officials may thus manipulate the pronouns to tax, fine, imprison and hang women, it is

their duty to thus change them in order to protect us in our right to vote. . . .

Though the words persons, people, inhabitants, electors, citizens, are all used indiscriminately in the national and State constitutions, there was always a conflict of opinion, prior to the war, as to whether they were synonymous terms, but whatever room there was for doubt, under the old regime, the adoption of the Fourteenth Amendment settled that question forever in its first sentence:

> All persons born or naturalized in the United States, and subject to the jurisdiction thereof, are citizens of the United States, and of the State wherein they reside.

The second settles the equal status of all citizens:

> No State shall make or enforce any law which shall abridge the privileges or immunities of citizens of the United States; nor shall any State deprive any person of life, liberty or property without due process of law, or deny to any person within its jurisdiction the equal protection of the laws.

The only question left to be settled now is: Are women persons? I scarcely believe any of our opponents will have the hardihood to say they are not. Being persons, then, women are citizens, and no State has a right to make any new law, or to enforce any old law, which shall abridge their privileges or immunities. Hence, every discrimination against women in the constitutions and laws of the several States is today null and void, precisely as is every one against negroes.

Is the right to vote one of the privileges or immunities of citizens? I think the disfranchised ex-rebels and ex-State prisoners all will agree that it is not only one of them, but the one without which all the others are nothing. Seek first the kingdom of the ballot and all things else shall be added, is the political injunction. . . .

However much the doctors of the law may disagree as to whether 15 people and citizens, in the original Constitution, were one and the same, or whether the privileges and immunities in the Fourteenth Amendment include the right of suffrage, the question of the citizen's right to vote is forever settled by the Fifteenth Amendment. "The right of citizens of the United States to vote shall not be denied or abridged by the United States, or by any State, on account of race, color or previous condition of servitude." How can the State deny or abridge the right of the citizen, if the citizen does not possess it? There is no escape from the conclusion that to vote is the citizen's right, and the specifications of race, color or previous condition of servitude can in no way impair the force of that emphatic assertion that the citizen's right to vote shall not be denied or abridged. . . .

If, however, you will insist that the Fifteenth Amendment's emphatic interdiction against robbing United States citizens of their suffrage "on account of race, color or previous condition of servitude," is a recognition of the right of either the United States or any State to deprive them of the ballot for any or all other reasons, I will prove to you that the class of citizens for whom I now plead are, by all the principles of our government and many of the laws of the States, included under the term "previous conditions of servitude."

Consider first married women and their legal status. What is servitude? "The condition of a slave." What is a slave? "A person who is robbed of the proceeds of his labor; a person who is subject to the will of another." By the laws of Georgia, South Carolina and all the States of the South, the negro had no right to the custody and control of his person. He belonged to his master. If he were disobedient, the master had the right to use correction. If the negro did not like the correction and ran away, the master had the right to use coercion to bring him back. By the laws of almost every State in this Union today, North as well as South, the married woman has no right to the custody and control of her person. The wife belongs to the husband; and if she refuse obedience he may use moderate correction, and if she do not like his moderate correction and leave his "bed and board," the husband may use moderate coercion to bring her back. The little word "moderate," you see, is the saving clause for the wife, and would doubtless be overstepped should her offended husband administer his correction with the "cat-o'-nine-tails," or accomplish his coercion with blood-hounds.

Again the slave had no right to the earnings of his hands, they belonged to his master; no right to the custody of his children, they belonged to his master; no right to sue or be sued, or to testify in the courts. If he committed a crime, it was the master who must sue or be sued. In many of the States there has been special legislation, giving married women the right to property inherited or received by bequest, or earned by the pursuit of any avocation outside the home; also giving them the right to sue and be sued in matters pertaining to such separate property; but not a single State of this Union has ever secured the wife in the enjoyment of her right to equal ownership of the joint earnings of the marriage copartnership. And since, in the nature of things, the vast majority of married women never earn a dollar by work outside their families, or inherit a dollar from their fathers, it follows that from the day of their marriage to the day of the death of their husbands not one of them ever has a dollar, except it shall please her husband to let her have it. . . .

Is anything further needed to prove woman's condition of servitude sufficient to entitle her to the guarantees of the Fifteenth Amendment? Is there a man who will not agree with me that to talk of freedom without the ballot is mockery to the women of this republic, precisely as New England's orator, Wendell Phillips, at the close of the late war declared it to be to the newly emancipated black man? I admit that, prior to the rebellion, by common consent, the right to enslave, as well as to disfranchise both native and foreign born persons, was conceded to the States. But the one grand principle settled by the war and the reconstruction legislation, is the supremacy of the national government to protect the citizens of the United States in their right to freedom and the elective franchise, against any and every interference on the part of the several States; and again and again have the American people asserted the triumph of this principle by their overwhelming majorities for Lincoln and Grant.

The one issue of the last two presidential elections was whether 20
the Fourteenth and Fifteenth Amendments should be considered the irrevocable will of the people; and the decision was that they should be, and that it is not only the right, but the duty of the national government to protect all United States citizens in the full enjoyment and free exercise of their privileges and immunities against the attempt of any State to deny or abridge. . . .

It is upon this just interpretation of the United States Constitution that our National Woman Suffrage Association, which celebrates the twenty-fifth anniversary of the woman's rights movement next May in New York City, has based all its arguments and action since the passage of these amendments. We no longer petition legislature or Congress to give us the right to vote, but appeal to women everywhere to exercise their too long neglected "citizen's right." We appeal to the inspectors of election to receive the votes of all United States citizens, as it is their duty to do. We appeal to United States commissioners and marshals to arrest, as is their duty, the inspectors who reject the votes of United States citizens, and leave alone those who peform their duties and accept these votes. We ask the juries to return verdicts of "not guilty" in the cases of law-abiding United States citizens who cast their votes, and inspectors of election who receive and count them.

We ask the judges to render unprejudiced opinions of the law, and wherever there is room for doubt to give the benefit to the side of liberty and equal rights for women, remembering that, as Sumner says, "The true rule of intepretation under our National Constitution, especially since its amendments, is that anything *for* human rights is constitutional, everything *against* human rights unconstitutional." It is on this line that we propose to fight our battle for the ballot—peaceably but nevertheless persistently—until we achieve complete triumph and all United States citizens, men and women alike, are recognized as equals in the government.

For Journals

What was your reaction to the first sentence in Anthony's speech?

For Discussion

1. Almost all men in Victorian America, and many women, thought that women should not have the right to vote. What would you guess the arguments were against women's suffrage? What would the opponents of suffrage have been worried about if women did secure the right to vote?

2. How do Anthony's infrequent references to the language of the Declaration of Independence, the Constitution, and the Fourteenth and Fifteenth amendments help her refute the belief that women should not be allowed to vote? Why do you think she chooses those particular quotations?

3. How does Anthony see the political condition of women in her own time as compared to the role of American men in the Revolution? As compared to the condition of former slaves? Considering your own knowledge, how valid do you find her comparisons?

4. Evaluate Anthony's argument that if laws refer only to "he" and "him," women shouldn't have to pay taxes to support the government or go to jail for breaking the law. What are the strengths and weaknesses of this argument? How would you make it stronger? What would Thoreau think of it?

5. Anthony argues that women are "persons" within the legal meaning stated by the Constitution. In an earlier selection in this chapter, Douglass argued that African Americans are men. Look back at Douglass's argument and compare it to Anthony's. Do they argue in similar ways or differently? Why do they feel compelled to argue these points at all?

6. Like Douglass, Anthony poses questions in her argument and then refutes them. What do you think are the advantages or disadvantages of this strategy? Which of her own questions do you think she answers best? In her place, what other questions would you ask? How would you answer them?

For Writing

1.   Write a paper in which you argue either for or against one of the following:

   a. An American teenager today has as much right to emancipation from parental control as a married woman in Anthony's time had with respect to her husband's control.

   b. Women should be allowed to serve in combat units in the armed forces.

   c. The women's movement has become too aggressive and does more harm than good.

Whichever issue or side you take, follow Anthony's example in using the Constitution and the Declaration of Independence for your argument. Keep in mind what someone who disagrees with you would say, so that you can anticipate some of the serious objections and refute them.

2.   Using recent biographies of Anthony or *The Life and Works of Susan B. Anthony*, write a documented paper on one of the following topics:

   a. The influence of her Quaker upbringing on her activism; her early fights for equal pay for women teachers.

   b. Her support of emancipation during the Civil War.

   c. Her refusal to support the vote for freed slaves because it did not include a vote for women.

   d. The circumstances surrounding her attempt to register to vote and her subsequent arrest.

PLESSY v. FERGUSON

1894

U.S. Supreme Court

   After the Civil War and Reconstruction, southern legislatures began passing Jim Crow laws, which reinstituted segregation against African Americans. In an earlier decision, the Court had repealed the Civil Rights Act of 1875, and the majority decision in Plessy *effectively made discrimination legal. Justice John Harlan, who had grown up as a slaveholder but who had become one of a long line of distinguished Supreme Court dissenters, was the only justice to vote against the decision.*

Majority Opinion (by Justice Henry Billings Brown)

Mr. Justice Brown, . . . delivered the opinion of the court.

This case turns upon the constitutionality of an Act of the general assembly of the state of Louisiana, passed in 1890, providing for separate railway carriages for the white and colored races.

The first section of the statute enacts "that all railway companies carrying passengers in their coaches in this state, shall provide equal but separate accommodations for the white, and colored races,

. . . [Plessy argued that he] was seven-eighths Caucasian and one-eighth African blood; that the mixture of colored blood was not discernible in him; and that he was entitled to every right, privilege, and immunity secured to citizens of the United States of the white race; and that, upon such theory, he took possession of a vacant seat in a coach where passengers of the white race were accommodated, and was ordered by the conductor to vacate said coach and take a seat in another, assigned to persons of the colored race, and, having refused to comply with such demand, he was forcibly ejected, with the aid of a police officer, and imprisoned in the parish jail to answer a charge of having violated the above act.

5   The constitutionality of this act is attacked upon the ground that it conflicts both with the Thirteenth Amendment of the Constitution abolishing slavery, and the Fourteenth Amendment, which prohibits certain restrictive legislation on the part of the states.

1. That it does not conflict with the Thirteenth Amendment, which abolished slavery and involuntary servitude, except as a punishment for crime, is too clear for argument. Slavery implies involuntary servitude,—a state of bondage; the ownership of mankind as a chattel, or, at least, the control of the labor and services of one man for the benefit of another, and the absence of a legal right to the disposal of his own person, property, and services.

. . . "It would be running the slavery question into the ground," said Mr. Justice Bradley, "to make it apply to every act of discrimination which a person may see fit to make as to the guests he will entertain, or as to the people he will take into his coach or cab or car, or admit to his concert or theater, or deal with in other matters of intercourse or business."

A statute which implies merely a legal distinction between the white and colored races—a distinction which is founded in the color of the two races, and which must always exist so long as white men are distinguished from the other race by color—has no tendency to destroy the legal equality of the two races, or re-establish a state of involuntary servitude. . . .

2. By the Fourteenth Amendment, all persons born or naturalized in the United States, and subject to the jurisdiction thereof, are made citizens of the United States and of the state wherein they reside; and the states are forbidden from making or enforcing any law which . . . shall deprive any person of life, liberty, or property without due process of law, or deny to any person . . . equal protection of the laws.

The object of the Amendment was undoubtedly to enforce the absolute equality of the two races before the law, but in the nature of things, it could not have been intended to abolish distinctions based upon color, or to enforce social, as distinguished from political, equality, or a commingling of the two races upon terms unsatisfactory to either. Laws permitting, and even requiring, their separation, in places where they are liable to be brought into contact, do not necessarily imply the inferiority of either race to the other. . . . The most common instance of this is connected with the establishment of separate schools for white and colored children. . . .

So far, then, as a conflict with the Fourteenth Amendment is concerned, the case reduces itself to the question whether the statute of Louisiana is a reasonable regulation, and with respect to this there must necessarily be a large discretion on the part of the legislature. In determining the question of reasonableness, it is at liberty to act with reference to the established usages, customs, and traditions of the people, and with a view to the promotion of their comfort, and the preservation of the public peace and good order. Gauged by this standard, we cannot say that a law which authorizes or even requires the separation of the two races in public conveyances is unreasonable, or more obnoxious to the Fourteenth Amendment than the acts of Congress requiring separate schools for colored children in the District of Columbia, the constitutionality of which does not seem to have been questioned, or the corresponding acts of state legislatures.

We consider the underlying fallacy of the plaintiff's argument to consist in the assumption that the enforced separation of the two races stamps the colored race with a badge of inferiority. If this be so, it is not by reason of anything found in the act, but solely because the colored race chooses to put that construction upon it. The argument necessarily assumes that if, as has been more than once the case, and is not unlikely to be so again, the colored race should become the dominant power in the state legislature, and should enact a law in precisely similiar terms, it would thereby relegate the white race to an inferior position. We imagine that the white race, at least, would not acquiesce in this assumption. The argument also assumes that social prejudices may be overcome by legislation, and that equal rights cannot be secured to the Negro except by an enforced commingling of the two

10

races. We cannot accept this proposition. If the two races are to meet upon terms of social equality, it must be the result of natural affinities, a mutual appreciation of each other's merits, and a voluntary consent of individuals. . . . Legislation is powerless to eradicate racial instincts, or to abolish distinctions based upon physical differences, and the attempt to do so can only result in accentuating the difficulties of the present situation. If the civil and political rights of both races be equal, one cannot be inferior to the other civilly or politically. If one race be inferior to the other socially, the Constitution of the United States cannot put them upon the same plane.

Dissenting Opinion (by Justice John Harlan)

. . . In respect of civil rights common to all citizens, the Constitution of the United States does not, I think, permit any public authority to know the race of those entitled to be protected in the enjoyment of such rights. Every true man has pride of race, and under appropriate circumstances when the rights of others, his equals before the law, are not to be affected, it is his privilege to express such pride and to take such action based upon it as to him seems proper. But I deny that any legislative body or judicial tribunal may have regard to the race of citizens when the civil rights of those citizens are involved. Indeed, such legislation, as that here in question, is inconsistent not only with the equality of rights which pertains to citizenship, national and state, but with the personal liberty enjoyed by every one within the United States. . . .

The white race deems itself to be the dominant race in this country. And so it is, in prestige, in achievements, in education, in wealth and in power. So, I doubt not, it will continue to be for all time, if it remains true to its great heritage and holds fast to the principles of constitutional liberty. But in view of the Constitution, in the eye of the law, there is in this country no superior, dominant, ruling class of citizens. There is no caste here. Our Constitution is color-blind, and neither knows nor tolerates classes among citizens. In respect of civil rights, all citizens are equal before the law. The humblest is the peer of the most powerful. The law regards man as man, and takes no account of his surroundings or of his color when his civil rights as guaranteed by the supreme law of the land are involved. It is, therefore, to be regretted that this high tribunal, the final expositor of the fundamental law of the land, has reached the conclusion that it is competent for a State to regulate the enjoyment by citizens of their civil rights solely upon the basis of race. . . .

The arbitrary separation of citizens, on the basis of race, while they 15 are on a public highway, is a badge of servitude wholly inconsistent with the civil freedom and the equality before the law established by the Constitution. It cannot be justified upon any legal grounds.

If evils will result from the commingling of the two races upon public highways established for the benefit of all, they will be infinitely less than those that will surely come from state legislation regulating the enjoyment of civil rights upon the basis of race. We boast of the freedom enjoyed by our people above all other peoples. But it is difficult to reconcile that boast with a state of the law which, practically, puts the brand of servitude and degradation upon a large class of our fellow-citizens, our equals before the law. The thin disguise of "equal" accommodations for passengers in railroad coaches will not mislead any one, nor atone for the wrong this day done.

For Journals

In your own words, what did the Court decide in this case? Who won? Who lost?

For Discussion

1. Mr. Plessy argued that denying him the right to ride in the white railway carriage was a violation of the Thirteenth Amendment, which prohibits slavery, and the Fourteenth Amendment, which grants equal protection under the law. What reasons does Justice Brown give to refute Plessy's argument? Why does he think the two amendments do not apply to this case?

2. How does the Court define "separate but equal"?

3. In the "Majority Opinion," Justice Brown says that equality before the law doesn't have to mean social equality. Do you think it is possible to be equal before the law but not in any other way? What is your definition of equality?

4. How would you refute the Court's statement that if blacks felt inferior because they were forced to ride in a separate railway carriage, it was their fault because they chose to look at it that way?

5. In his "Minority Opinion," what does Justice Harlan think is the real meaning of the separate-but-equal laws as far as the future of black–white relations is concerned? What kinds of injustices does he foresee in a segregated South?

6. Why do you think Harlan sees dangers to other minorities besides African Americans in the *Plessy* decision? Why does he say that the decision would not mislead anyone and not atone for the wrong done? Do you agree with him?

For Writing

1.   Research the term "Jim Crow." Write a documented paper in which you discuss the origins of the term and how Jim Crow laws affected the lives of southern blacks (give specific examples of segregation in everyday life). If you know someone who had firsthand experience with the Jim Crow laws, interview him or her for your paper.

2.   Both Justice Harlan in *Plessy* and Thoreau in *On Civil Disobedience* believed, with very different results, that legislation is not a good way to change people's behavior. Write an essay in which you argue for or against the proposition that injustice cannot be changed through legislation and that trying to eradicate differences through legislation can only make a situation worse. Focus your argument around an injustice you think needs changing. Use Thoreau, *Plessy,* or both, to back up your assertions.

BROWN v. BOARD OF EDUCATION
1954

U.S. Supreme Court

Brown *v.* Board of Education *is the landmark decision of the Supreme Court, under Chief Justice Earl Warren, in this century. Its official result was to declare segregation in public schools unconstitutional and to overturn the* Plessy *doctrine of separate but equal facilities. It followed on the heels of other cases that had outlawed segregation in professional schools. Its effect was to take away the legal underpinnings of segregation in all areas, and it began a process of dismantling segregation that has had a profound effect on American life.*

These cases come to us from the states of Kansas, South Carolina, Virginia, and Delaware. They are premised on different facts and different local conditions, but a common legal question justifies their consideration together in this consolidated opinion.

In each of the cases, minors of the Negro race, through their legal representatives, seek the aid of the courts in obtaining admission to the public schools of their community on a nonsegregated basis. In each instance, they have been denied admission to schools attended by white children under laws requiring or permitting segregation according to race. This segregation was alleged to deprive the plaintiffs of the equal protection of the laws under the Fourteenth Amendment. In each of the cases other than the Delaware case, a three-judge federal district court denied relief to the plaintiffs on the so-called "separate but equal" doctrine announced by this Court in *Plessy* v. *Ferguson*. . . . Under that doctrine, equality of treatment is accorded when the races are provided substantially equal facilities, even though these facilities be separate. . . .

The plaintiffs contend that segregated public schools are not "equal" and cannot be made "equal," and that hence they are deprived of the equal protection of the laws. Because of the obvious importance of the question presented, the Court took jurisdiction. . . .

There are findings below that the Negro and white schools involved have been equalized, or are being equalized, with respect to buildings, curricula, qualifications and salaries of teachers, and other "tangible" factors. Our decision, therefore, cannot turn on merely a comparison of these tangible factors in the Negro and white schools involved in each of the cases. We must look instead to the effect of segregation itself on public education.

In approaching this problem, we cannot turn the clock back to   5
1868 when the Amendment was adopted, or even to 1896 when *Plessy* v. *Ferguson* was written. We must consider public education in the light of its full development and its present place in American life throughout the nation. Only in this way can it be determined if segregation in public schools deprives these plaintiffs of the equal protection of the laws.

Today, education is perhaps the most important function of state and local governments. Compulsory school attendance laws and the great expenditures for education both demonstrate our recognition of the importance of education to our democratic society. It is required in the performance of our most basic public responsibilities, even service in the armed forces. It is the very foundation of good citizenship. Today it is a principal instrument in awakening the child to cultural values, in preparing him for later professional training, and in helping him to adjust normally to his environment. In these days, it is doubtful that any child may reasonably be expected to succeed in life if he is denied the opportunity of an education. Such an opportunity, where the state has undertaken to provide it, is a right which must be made available to all on equal terms.

We come then to the question presented: Does segregation of children in public schools solely on the basis of race, even though the physical facilities and other "tangible" factors may be equal, deprive the children of the minority group of equal educational opportunities? We believe that it does.

In *Sweatt* v. *Painter*, . . . in finding that a segregated law school for Negroes could not provide them equal educational opportunities, this Court relied in large part on "those qualities which are incapable of objective measurement but which make for greatness in a law school." In *McLaurin* v. *Oklahoma State Regents*, . . . the Court, in requiring that a Negro admitted to a white graduate school be treated like all other students, again resorted to intangible considerations: ". . . his ability to study, to engage in discussions and exchange views with other students, and, in general, to learn his profession." Such considerations apply with added force to children in grade and high schools. To separate them from others of similar age and qualifications solely because of their race generates a feeling of inferiority as to their status in the community that may affect their hearts and minds in a way unlikely ever to be undone. The effect of this separation on their educational opportunities was well stated by a finding in the Kansas case by a court which nevertheless felt compelled to rule against the Negro plaintiffs:

> Segregation of white and colored children in public schools has a detrimental effect upon the colored children. The impact is greater when it has the sanction of the law; for the policy of separating the races is usually interpreted as denoting the inferiority of the Negro group. A sense of inferiority affects the motivation of a child to learn. Segregation with the sanction of law, therefore, has a tendency to retard the educational and mental development of Negro children and to deprive them of some of the benefits they would receive in a racially integrated school system.

Whatever may have been the extent of psychological knowledge at the time of *Plessy* v. *Ferguson*, this finding is amply supported by modern authority. Any language in *Plessy* v. *Ferguson* contrary to this finding is rejected.

We conclude that in the field of public education the doctrine of "separate but equal" has no place. Separate educational facilities are inherently unequal. Therefore, we hold that the plaintiffs and others similarly situated for whom the actions have been brought are, by reason of the segregation complained of, deprived of the equal protection of the laws guaranteed by the Fourteenth Amendment. . . .

For Journals

Summarize the decision in the case. In your own words, write what you think the decision was.

For Discussion

1.   In American law, precedent—what has been determined in previous legal decisions—is very important, so refuting the ruling of *Plessy* after almost fifty years required considerable justification. How does the Warren Court in *Brown* get around the fact that *Plessy* had stood since it was declared good law in 1896?

2.   What are the Court's main points in its argument that education today and education right after the Civil War are so different that a new interpretation of *Plessy* is appropriate?

3.   Analyze what the Court says about the harmful effects of segregated schooling on black children. What injustice does the Court in *Brown* see in segregation that the Court in *Plessy* did not? Why wouldn't a school for black children do as good a job as an integrated school?

4.   The decision of a court is called a ruling. In refuting *Plessy*, the Warren Court made a ruling that separate public schools could not also be equal. Why did the Court think that separate but equal was a contradiction?

5.   If you had to pick one crucial sentence from this ruling, what would it be? Why?

6.   The Court says that if it only took into account "tangible" factors like buildings and curriculum for segregated schools, it would fail to see the situation in its entirety. What kinds of "intangibles" do you think the Warren Court considers in reaching its decision in *Brown?*

For Writing

1.   Research one of the following and, in a documented essay, discuss its significance for civil liberties in the United States:

a. The life and career of Thurgood Marshall, who argued *Brown* and later became solicitor general of the United States and then the first African American justice of the Supreme Court.

b. Marshall's strategy, as leading attorney for the NAACP, in challenging segregation through the courts instead of in state legislatures, and in picking elementary school education as the point of attack.

c. The significance of the cases before *Brown* that are mentioned by Chief Justice Warren, especially *Sweatt* v. *Painter* and *McLaurin* v. *Oklahoma State Regents*.

2. Chief Justice Warren wrote that we must look at the intangibles to get a complete picture. Write an essay in which you compare the *Brown* decision and its use of intangible factors to either Douglass's Independence Day speech or Anthony's "Women's Right to Vote" speech. What tangible and intangibles do the authors consider in arguing against injustice? Which category is more important to them? Which do you think is more important? Use examples from the selections as proof for your conclusions.

LETTER FROM BIRMINGHAM JAIL
1963

Martin Luther King, Jr.

The strategy developed by the modern civil rights movement and its leader, the young Atlanta minister Martin Luther King, Jr., (see Chapter 4) was the policy of nonviolent resistance. Based on the teachings of the Bible, Mahatma Gandhi, and Thoreau, it revolved around peaceful marches, sit-ins at lunch counters, and economic boycotts of buses and businesses. In 1963, while leading demonstrations in Montgomery, Alabama, King was arrested. In jail he wrote a letter of justification and explanation addressed to eight southern clergymen who had issued a public statement objecting to the demonstrations King led and to demonstrations as a method for dealing with racial problems. Both letters are reprinted here.

Clergymen's Letter

We the undersigned clergymen are among those who, in January, issued "An Appeal for Law and Order and Common Sense," in dealing with racial problems in Alabama. We expressed understanding that honest convictions in racial matters could properly be pursued in the courts, but urged that decisions of those courts should in the meantime be peacefully obeyed.

Since that time there had been some evidence of increased forbearance and a willingness to face facts. Responsible citizens have undertaken to work on various problems which cause racial friction and unrest. In Birmingham, recent public events have given indication that we all have opportunity for a new constructive and realistic approach to racial problems.

However, we are now confronted by a series of demonstrations by some of our Negro citizens, directed and led in part by outsiders. We recognize the natural impatience of people who feel that their hopes are slow in being realized. But we are convinced that these demonstrations are unwise and untimely.

We agree rather with certain local Negro leadership which has called for honest and open negotiation of racial issues in our area. And we believe this kind of facing of issues can best be accomplished by citizens of our own metropolitan area, white and Negro, meeting with their knowledge and experience of the local situation. All of us need to face that responsibility and find proper channels for its accomplishment.

Just as we formerly pointed out that "hatred and violence have no 5 sanction in our religious and political traditions," we also point out that such actions as incite to hatred and violence, however technically peaceful those actions may be, have not contributed to the resolution of our local problems. We do not believe that these days of new hope are days when extreme measures are justified in Birmingham.

We commend the community as a whole, and the local news media and the law enforcement officials in particular, on the calm manner in which these demonstrations have been handled. We urge the public to continue to show restraint should the demonstrations continue, and the law enforcement officials to remain calm and continue to protect our city from violence.

We further strongly urge our own Negro community to withdraw support from these demonstrations, and to unite locally in working peacefully for a better Birmingham. When rights are consistently denied, a cause should be pressed in the courts and in negotiations among local leaders, and not in the streets. We appeal to both our white and Negro citizenry to observe the principles of law and order and common sense.

Signed by:

C. C. J. *Carpenter*, D.D., LL.D., Bishop of Alabama
Joseph A. Durick, D.D., Auxiliary Bishop, Diocese of Mobile,
    Birmingham
Milton L. Grafman, Rabbi, Temple Emanu-El, Birmingham, Alabama

Paul Hardin, Bishop of the Alabama–West Florida Conference of the
  Methodist Church
Nolan B. Harmon, Bishop of the North Alabama Conference of the
  Methodist Church
George M. Murray, D.D., LL.D., Bishop Coadjutor, Episcopal Diocese of
  Alabama
Edward V. Ramage, Moderator, Synod of the Alabama Presbyterian
  Church in the United States.
Earl Stallings, Pastor, First Baptist Church, Birmingham, Alabama

King's Letter

April 16, 1963

My Dear Fellow Clergymen:

While confined here in the Birmingham city jail, I came across your recent statement calling my present activities "unwise and untimely." Seldom do I pause to answer criticism of my work and ideas. If I sought to answer all the criticisms that cross my desk, my secretaries would have little time for anything other than such correspondence in the course of the day, and I would have no time for constructive work. But since I feel that you are men of genuine good will and that your criticisms are sincerely set forth, I want to try to answer your statement in what I hope will be patient and reasonable terms.

10   I think I should indicate why I am here in Birmingham, since you have been influenced by the view which argues against "outsiders coming in." I have the honor of serving as president of the Southern Christian Leadership Conference, an organization operating in every southern state, with headquarters in Atlanta, Georgia. We have some eighty-five affiliated organizations across the South, and one of them is the Alabama Christian Movement for Human Rights. Frequently we share staff, educational and financial resources with our affiliates. Several months ago the affiliate here in Birmingham asked us to be on call to engage in a nonviolent direct-action program if such were deemed necessary. We readily consented, and when the hour came we lived up to our promise. So I, along with several members of my staff, am here because I was invited here. I am here because I have organizational ties here.

But more basically, I am in Birmingham because injustice is here. Just as the prophets of the eighth century B.C. left their villages and carried their "thus saith the Lord" far beyond the boundaries of their home towns, and just as the Apostle Paul left his village of Tarsus and carried the gospel of Jesus Christ to the far corners of the Greco-Roman world, so am I compelled to carry the gospel of freedom beyond my own home town. Like Paul, I must constantly respond to the Macedonian call for aid.

Moreover, I am cognizant of the interrelatedness of all communities and states. I cannot sit idly by in Atlanta and not be concerned about what happens in Birmingham. Injustice anywhere is a threat to justice everywhere. We are caught in an inescapable network of mutuality, tied in a single garment of destiny. Whatever affects one directly, affects all indirectly. Never again can we afford to live with the narrow, provincial "outside agitator" idea. Anyone who lives inside the United States can never be considered an outsider anywhere within its bounds.

You deplore the demonstrations taking place in Birmingham. But your statement, I am sorry to say, fails to express a similar concern for the conditions that brought about the demonstrations. I am sure that none of you would want to rest content with the superficial kind of social analysis that deals merely with effects and does not grapple with underlying causes. It is unfortunate that demonstrations are taking place in Birmingham, but it is even more unfortunate that the city's white power structure left the Negro community with no alternative.

In any nonviolent campaign there are four basic steps: collection of the facts to determine whether injustices exist; negotiation; self-purification; and direct action. We have gone through all these steps in Birmingham. There can be no gainsaying the fact that racial injustice engulfs this community. Birmingham is probably the most thoroughly segregated city in the United States. Its ugly record of brutality is widely known. Negroes have experienced grossly unjust treatment in the courts. There have been more unsolved bombings of Negro homes and churches in Birmingham than in any other city in the nation. These are the hard, brutal facts of the case. On the basis of these conditions, Negro leaders sought to negotiate with the city fathers. But the latter consistently refused to engage in good-faith negotiation.

Then, last September, came the opportunity to talk with leaders of 15 Birmingham's economic community. In the course of the negotiations, certain promises were made by the merchants—for example, to remove the stores' humiliating racial signs. On the basis of these promises, the Reverend Fred Shuttlesworth and the leaders of the Alabama Christian Movement for Human Rights agreed to a moratorium on all demonstrations. As the weeks and months went by, we realized that we were the victims of a broken promise. A few signs, briefly removed, returned; the others remained.

As in so many past experiences, our hopes had been blasted, and the shadow of deep disappointment settled upon us. We had no alternative except to prepare for direct action, whereby we would present our very bodies as a means of laying our case before the conscience of the local and the national community. Mindful of the difficulties involved, we decided to undertake a process of self-purification. We began a series of workshops on nonviolence, and we repeatedly asked ourselves: "Are you able to accept blows without retaliating?" "Are you able to endure the ordeal of jail?" We decided to schedule our direct-action program for the Easter season, realizing that except for Christmas, this is the main shopping period of the year. Knowing that a strong economic-withdrawal program would be the by-product of direct action, we felt that this would be the best time to bring pressure to bear on the merchants for the needed change.

Then it occurred to us that Birmingham's mayoral election was coming up in March, and we speedily decided to postpone action until after election day. When we discovered that the Commissioner of Public Safety, Eugene "Bull" Connor, had piled up enough votes to be in the run-off, we decided again to postpone action until the day after the run-off so that the demonstrations could not be used to cloud the issues. Like many others, we waited to see Mr. Connor defeated, and to this end we endured postponement after postponement. Having aided in this community need, we felt that our direct-action program could be delayed no longer.

You may well ask: "Why direct action? Why sit-ins, marches and so forth? Isn't negotiation a better path?" You are quite right in calling for negotiation. Indeed, this is the very purpose of direct action. Nonviolent direct action seeks to create such a crisis and foster such a tension that a community which has constantly refused to negotiate is forced to confront the issue. It seeks so to dramatize the issue that it can no longer be ignored. My citing the creation of tension as part of the work of the nonviolent-resister may sound rather shocking. But I must confess that I am not afraid of the word "tension." I have earnestly opposed violent tension, but there is a type of constructive, nonviolent tension which is necessary for growth. Just as Socrates felt that it was necessary to create a tension in the mind so that individuals could rise from the bondage of myths and half-truths to the unfettered realm of creative analysis and objective appraisal, so must we see the need for nonviolent gadflies to create the kind of tension in society that will help men rise from the dark depths of prejudice and racism to the majestic heights of understanding and brotherhood.

The purpose of our direct-action program is to create a situation so crisis-packed that it will inevitably open the door to negotiation. I therefore concur with you in your call for negotiation. Too long has our beloved Southland been bogged down in a tragic effort to live in monologue rather than dialogue.

20   One of the basic points in your statement is that the action that I and my associates have taken in Birmingham is untimely. Some have

asked: "Why didn't you give the new city administration time to act?" The only answer that I can give to this query is that the new Birmingham administration must be prodded about as much as the outgoing one, before it will act. We are sadly mistaken if we feel that the election of Albert Boutwell as mayor will bring the millennium to Birmingham. While Mr. Boutwell is a much more gentle person than Mr. Connor, they are both segregationists, dedicated to maintenance of the status quo. I have hope that Mr. Boutwell will be reasonable enough to see the futility of massive resistance to desegregation. But he will not see this without pressure from devotees of civil rights. My friends, I must say to you that we have not made a single gain in civil rights without determined legal and nonviolent pressure. Lamentably, it is an historical fact that privileged groups seldom give up their privileges voluntarily. Individuals may see the moral light and voluntarily give up their unjust posture; but, as Reinhold Niebuhr has reminded us, groups tend to be more immoral than individuals.

We know through painful experience that freedom is never voluntarily given by the oppressor; it must be demanded by the oppressed. Frankly, I have yet to engage in a direct-action campaign that was "well timed" in the view of those who have not suffered unduly from the disease of segregation. For years now I have heard the word "Wait!" It rings in the ear of every Negro with piercing familiarity. This "Wait" has almost always meant "Never." We must come to see, with one of our distinguished jurists, that "justice too long delayed is justice denied."

We have waited for more than three hundred forty years for our constitutional God-given rights. The nations of Asia and Africa are moving with jetlike speed toward gaining political independence, but we still creep at horse-and-buggy pace toward gaining a cup of coffee at a lunch counter. Perhaps it is easy for those who have never felt the stinging darts of segregation to say, "Wait." But when you have seen vicious mobs lynch your mothers and fathers at will and drown your sisters and brothers at whim; when you have seen hate-filled policemen curse, kick, and even kill your black brothers and sisters; when you see the vast majority of your twenty million Negro brothers smothering in an airtight cage of poverty in the midst of an affluent society; when you suddenly find your tongue twisted and your speech stammering as you seek to explain to your six-year-old daughter why she can't go to the public amusement park that has just been advertised on television, and see tears welling up in her eyes when she is told that Funtown is closed to colored children, and see ominous clouds of inferiority beginning to form in her little mental sky, and see her beginning to distort her personality by developing an unconscious bitterness toward white people; when you have to concoct an answer for a five-year-old son who is asking: "Daddy, why do white people treat colored people so mean?"; when you take a cross-country drive and find it necessary to sleep night after night in the uncomfortable corners of your automobile because no motel will accept you; when you are humiliated day in and day out by nagging signs reading "white" and "colored"; when your first name becomes "nigger," your middle name becomes "boy" (however old you are) and your last name becomes "John," and your wife and mother are never given the respected title "Mrs."; when you are harried by day and haunted by night by the fact that you are a Negro, living constantly at tiptoe stance, never quite knowing what to expect next, and are plagued with inner fears and outer resentments; when you are forever fighting a degenerating sense of "nobodiness"—then you will understand why we find it difficult to wait. There comes a times when the cup of endurance runs over, and men are no longer willing to be plunged into the abyss of despair. I hope, sirs, you can understand our legitimate and unavoidable impatience.

You express a great deal of anxiety over our willingness to break laws. This is certainly a legitimate concern. Since we so diligently urge people to obey the Supreme Court's decision of 1954 outlawing segregation in the public schools, at first glance it may seem rather paradoxical for us consciously to break laws. One may well ask: "How can you advocate breaking some laws and obeying others?" The answer lies in the fact that there are two types of laws: just and unjust. I would be the first to advocate obeying just laws. One has not only a legal but a moral responsibility to obey just laws. Conversely, one has a moral responsibility to disobey unjust laws. I would agree with St. Augustine that "an unjust law is no law at all."

Now, what is the difference between the two? How does one determine whether a law is just or unjust? A just law is a man-made code that squares with the moral law or the law of God. An unjust law is a code that is out of harmony with the moral law. To put it in the terms of St. Thomas Aquinas: An unjust law is a human law that is not rooted in eternal law and natural law. Any law that uplifts human personality is just. Any law that degrades human personality is unjust. All segregation statutes are unjust because segregation distorts the soul and damages the personality. It gives the segregator a false sense of superiority and the segregated a false sense of inferiority. Segregation, to use the terminology of the Jewish philosopher Martin Buber, substitutes an "I–it" relationship for an "I–thou" relationship and ends up relegating persons to the status of things. Hence, segregation is not only politically, economically and sociologically unsound, it is morally wrong and sinful. Paul Tillich has said that sin is separation. Is not segregation an existential expression of man's tragic separation, his awful estrangement, his terrible sinfulness? Thus it is that I can urge men to obey the 1954 decision of the Supreme Court, for it is morally right; and I can urge them to disobey segregation ordinances, for they are morally wrong.

Let us consider a more concrete example of just and unjust laws.   25 An unjust law is a code that a numerical or power majority group compels a minority group to obey but does not make binding on itself. This is *difference* made legal. By the same token, a just law is a code that a majority compels a minority to follow and that it is willing to follow itself. This is *sameness* made legal.

Let me give another explanation. A law is unjust if it is inflicted on a minority that, as a result of being denied the right to vote, had no part in enacting or devising the law. Who can say that the legislature of Alabama which set up that state's segregation laws was democratically elected? Throughout Alabama all sorts of devious methods are used to prevent Negroes from becoming registered voters, and there are some counties in which, even though Negroes constitute a majority of the population, not a single Negro is registered. Can any law enacted under such circumstances be considered democratically structured?

Sometimes a law is just on its face and unjust in its application. For instance, I have been arrested on a charge of parading without a permit. Now, there is nothing wrong in having an ordinance which requires a permit for a parade. But such an ordinance becomes unjust when it is used to maintain segregation and to deny citizens the First-Amendment privilege of peaceful assembly and protest.

I hope you are able to see the distinction I am trying to point out. In no sense do I advocate evading or defying the law, as would the rabid segregationist. That would lead to anarchy. One who breaks an unjust law must do so openly, lovingly, and with a willingness to accept the penalty. I submit that an individual who breaks a law that conscience tells him is unjust, and who willingly accepts the penalty of imprisonment in order to arouse the conscience of the community over its injustice, is in reality expressing the highest respect for law.

Of course, there is nothing new about this kind of civil disobedience. It was evidenced sublimely in the refusal of Shadrach, Meshach and Abednego to obey the laws of Nebuchadnezzar, on the ground that a higher moral law was at stake. It was practiced superbly by the early Christians, who were willing to face hungry lions and the excruciating pain of chopping blocks rather than submit to certain unjust laws of the Roman Empire. To a degree, academic freedom is a reality today because Socrates practiced civil disobedience. In our own nation, the Boston Tea Party represented a massive act of civil disobedience.

30   We should never forget that everything Adolf Hitler did in Germany was "legal" and everything the Hungarian freedom fighters did in Hungary was "illegal." It was "illegal" to aid and comfort a Jew in Hitler's Germany. Even so, I am sure that, had I lived in Germany at the time, I would have aided and comforted my Jewish brothers. If today I lived in a Communist country where certain principles dear to the Christian faith are suppressed I would openly advocate disobeying that country's antireligious laws.

I must make two honest confessions to you, my Christian and Jewish brothers. First, I must confess that over the past few years I have been gravely disappointed with the white moderate. I have almost reached the regrettable conclusion that the Negro's great stumbling block in his stride toward freedom is not the White Citizen's Counciler or the Ku Klux Klanner, but the white moderate, who is more devoted to "order" than to justice; who prefers a negative peace which is the presence of tension to a positive peace which is the presence of justice; who constantly says: "I agree with you in the goal you seek, but I cannot agree with your methods of direct action"; who paternalistically believes he can set the timetable for another man's freedom; who lives by a mythical concept of time and who constantly advises the Negro to wait for a "more convenient season." Shallow understanding from people of good will is more frustrating than absolute misunderstanding from people of ill will. Lukewarm acceptance is much more bewildering than outright rejection.

I had hoped that the white moderate would understand that law and order exist for the purpose of establishing justice and that when they fail in this purpose they become the dangerously structured dams that block the flow of social progress. I had hoped that the white moderate would understand that the present tension in the South is a necessary phase of the transition from an obnoxious negative peace, in which the Negro passively accepted his unjust plight, to a substantive and positive peace, in which all men will respect the dignity and worth of human personality. Actually, we who engage in nonviolent direct action are not the creators of tension. We merely bring to the surface the hidden tension that is already alive. We bring it out in the open, where it can be seen and dealt with. Like a boil that can never be cured so long as it is covered up but must be opened with all its ugliness to the natural medicines of air and light, injustice must be exposed, with all the tension its exposure creates, to the light of human conscience and the air of national opinion before it can be cured.

In your statement you assert that our actions, even though peaceful, must be condemned because they precipitate violence. But is this a logical assertion? Isn't this like condemning a robbed man because his possession of money precipitated the evil act of robbery? Isn't this like condemning Socrates because his unswerving commitment to truth and his philosophical inquiries precipitated the act by the misguided populace in which they made him drink hemlock? Isn't this like condemning Jesus because his unique God-consciousness and never-ceasing devotion to God's will precipitated the evil act of crucifixion? We must come to see that, as the federal courts have consistently affirmed, it is wrong to urge an individual to cease his efforts to gain his basic constitutional rights because the quest may precipitate violence. Society must protect the robbed and punish the robber.

I had also hoped that the white moderate would reject the myth concerning time in relation to the struggle for freedom. I have just received a letter from a white brother in Texas. He writes: "All Christians know that the colored people will receive equal rights eventually, but it is possible that you are in too great a religious hurry. It has taken Christianity almost two thousand years to accomplish what it has. The teachings of Christ take time to come to earth." Such an attitude stems from a tragic misconception of time, from the strangely irrational notion that there is something in the very flow of time that will inevitably cure all ills. Actually, time itself is neutral; it can be used either destructively or constructively. More and more I feel that the people of ill will have used time much more effectively than have the people of good will. We will have to repent in this generation not merely for the hateful words and actions of the bad people but for the appalling silence of the good people. Human progress never rolls in on wheels of inevitability; it comes through the tireless efforts of men willing to be co-workers with God, and without this hard work, time itself becomes an ally of the forces of social stagnation. We must use time creatively, in the knowledge that the time is always ripe to do right. Now is the time to make real the promise of democracy and transform our pending national elegy into a creative psalm of brotherhood. Now is the time to lift our national policy from the quicksand of racial injustice to the solid rock of human dignity.

You speak of our activity in Birmingham as extreme. At first I was 35 rather disappointed that fellow clergymen would see my nonviolent efforts as those of an extremist. I began thinking about the fact that I stand in the middle of two opposing forces in the Negro community. One is a force of complacency, made up in part of Negroes who, as a result of long years of oppression, are so drained of self-respect and a sense of "somebodiness" that they have adjusted to segregation; and in part of a few middle-class Negroes who, because of a degree of academic and economic security and because in some ways they profit by segregation, have become insensitive to the problems of the masses. The other force is one of bitterness and hatred, and it comes perilously close to advocating violence. It is expressed in the various black nationalists groups that are springing up across the nation, the largest and best-known being Elijah Muhammad's Muslim movement. Nourished by the Negro's frustration over the continued existence of racial discrimination, this movement is made up of people who have lost faith in America, who have absolutely repudiated Christianity, and who have concluded that the white man is an incorrigible "devil."

I have tried to stand between these two forces, saying that we need emulate neither the "do-nothingism" of the complacent nor the hatred and despair of the black nationalist. For there is the more excellent way of love and nonviolent protest. I am grateful to God that, through the influence of the Negro church, the way of nonviolence became an integral part of our struggle.

If this philosophy had not emerged, by now many streets of the South would, I am convinced, be flowing with blood. And I am further convinced that if our white brothers dismiss as "rabble-rousers" and "outside agitators" those of us who employ nonviolent direct action, and if they refuse to support our nonviolent efforts, millions of the Negroes will, out of frustration and despair, seek solace and security in black-nationalist ideologies—a development that would inevitably lead to a frightening racial nightmare.

Oppressed people cannot remain oppressed forever. The yearning for freedom eventually manifests itself, and that is what has happened to the American Negro. Something within has reminded him of his birthright of freedom, and something without has reminded him that it can be gained. Consciously or unconsciously, he has been caught up by the *Zeitgeist,* and with his black brothers of Africa and his brown and yellow brothers of Asia, South America and the Caribbean, the United States Negro is moving with a sense of great urgency toward the promised land of racial justice. If one recognizes this vital urge that has engulfed the Negro community, one should readily understand why public demonstrations are taking place. The Negro has many pent-up resentments and latent frustrations, and he must release them. So let him march; let him make prayer pilgrimages to the city hall; let him go on freedom rides—and try to undertand why he must do so. If his repressed emotions are not released in nonviolent ways, they will seek expression through violence; this is not a threat but a fact of history. So I have not said to my people: "Get rid of your discontent." Rather, I have tried to say that this normal and healthy discontent can be channeled into the creative outlet of nonviolent direct action. And now this approach is being termed extremist.

But though I was initially disappointed at being categorized as an extremist, as I continued to think about the matter I gradually gained a measure of satisfaction from the label. Was not Jesus an extremist for love: "Love your enemies, bless them that curse you, do good to them

that hate you, and pray for them which despitefully use you, and per-
secute you." Was not Amos an extremist for justice: "Let justice roll
down like waters and righteousness like an ever-flowing stream." Was
not Paul an extremist for the Christian gospel: "I bear in my body the
marks of the Lord Jesus." Was not Martin Luther an extremist: "Here I
stand; I cannot do otherwise, so help me God." And John Bunyan: "I
will stay in jail to the end of my days before I make a butchery of my
conscience." And Abraham Lincoln: "This nation cannot survive half
slave and half free." And Thomas Jefferson: "We hold these truths to
be self-evident, that all men are created equal. . . ." So the question is
not whether we will be extremists, but what kind of extremists we will
be. Will we be extremists for hate or for love? Will we be extremists for
the preservation of injustice or for the extension of justice? In that dramatic scene on Calvary's hill three men were crucified. We must never
forget that all three were crucified for the same crime—the crime of ex-
tremism. Two were extremists for immorality, and thus fell below their
environment. The other, Jesus Christ, was an extremist for love, truth
and goodness, and thereby rose above his environment. Perhaps the
South, the nation and the world are in dire need of creative extremists.

I had hoped that the white moderate would see this need. Perhaps I   40
was too optimistic; perhaps I expected too much. I suppose I should
have realized that few members of the oppressor race can understand
the deep groans and passionate yearnings of the oppressed race, and
still fewer have the vision to see that injustice must be rooted out by
strong, persistent and determined action. I am thankful, however, that
some of our white brothers in the South have grasped the meaning of
this social revolution and committed themselves to it. They are still all
too few in quantity, but they are big in quality. Some—such as Ralph
McGill, Lillian Smith, Harry Golden, James McBride Dabbs, Ann Braden
and Sarah Patton Boyle—have written about our struggle in eloquent
and prophetic terms. Others have marched with us down nameless
streets of the South. They have languished in filthy, roach-infested jails,
suffering the abuse and brutality of policemen who view them as "dirty
nigger-lovers." Unlike so many of their moderate brothers and sisters,
they have recognized the urgency of the moment and sensed the need
for powerful "action" antidotes to combat the disease of segregation.

Let me take note of my other major disappointment. I have been so
greatly disappointed with the white church and its leadership. Of
course, there are some notable exceptions. I am not unmindful of the
fact that each of you has taken some significant stands on this issue. I
commend you, Reverend Stallings, for your Christian stand on this
past Sunday, in welcoming Negroes to your worship service on a nonsegregated basis. I commend the Catholic leaders of this state for integrating Spring Hill College several years ago.

But despite these notable exceptions, I must honestly reiterate that I have been disappointed with the church. I do not say this as one of those negative critics who can always find something wrong with the church. I say this as a minister of the gospel, who loves the church; who was nurtured in its bosom; who has been sustained by its spiritual blessings and who will remain true to it as long as the cord of life shall lengthen.

When I was suddenly catapulted into the leadership of the bus protest in Montgomery, Alabama, a few years ago, I felt we would be supported by the white church. I felt that the white ministers, priests and rabbis of the South would be among our strongest allies. Instead, some have been outright opponents, refusing to understand the freedom movement and misrepresenting its leaders; all too many others have been more cautious than courageous and have remained silent behind the anesthetizing security of stained-glass windows.

In spite of my shattered dreams, I came to Birmingham with the hope that the white religious leadership of this community would see the justice of our cause and, with deep moral concern, would serve as the channel through which our just grievances could reach the power structure. I had hoped that each of you would understand. But again I have been disappointed.

45   I have heard numerous southern religious leaders admonish their worshipers to comply with a desegregation decision because it is the law, but I have longed to hear white ministers declare: "Follow this decree because integration is morally right and because the Negro is your brother." In the midst of blatant injustices inflicted upon the Negro, I have watched white churchmen stand on the sideline and mouth pious irrelevancies and sanctimonious trivialities. In the midst of a mighty struggle to rid our nation of racial and economic injustice, I have heard many ministers say: "Those are social issues, with which the gospel has no real concern." And I have watched many churches commit themselves to a completely otherworldly religion which makes a strange, un-Biblical distinction between body and soul, between the sacred and the secular.

I have traveled the length and breadth of Alabama, Mississippi and all the other southern states. On sweltering summer days and crisp autumn mornings I have looked at the South's beautiful churches with their lofty spires pointing heavenward. I have beheld the impressive outlines of her massive religious-education buildings. Over and over I have found myself asking: "What kind of people worship here? Who is their God? Where were their voices when the lips of Governor Barnett dripped with words of interposition and nullification? Where were they when Governor Wallace gave a clarion call for defiance and hatred? Where were their voices of support when bruised and weary

Negro men and women decided to rise from the dark dungeons of complacency to the bright hills of creative protest?"

Yes, these questions are still in my mind. In deep disappointment I have wept over the laxity of the church. But be assured that my tears have been tears of love. There can be no deep disappointment where there is not deep love. Yes, I love the church. How could I do otherwise? I am in the rather unique position of being the son, the grandson, and the great-grandson of preachers. Yes, I see the church as the body of Christ. But, oh! How we have blemished and scarred that body through social neglect and through fear of being nonconformists.

There was a time when the church was very powerful—in the time when the early Christians rejoiced at being deemed worthy to suffer for what they believed. In those days the church was not merely a thermometer that recorded the ideas and principles of popular opinion; it was a thermostat that transformed the mores of society. Whenever the early Christians entered a town, the people in power became disturbed and immediately sought to convict the Christians for being "disturbers of the peace" and "outside agitators." But the Christians pressed on, in the conviction that they were "a colony of heaven," called to obey God rather than man. Small in number, they were big in commitment. They were too God-intoxicated to be "astronomically intimidated." By their effort and example they brought an end to such ancient evils as infanticide and gladiatorial contests.

Things are different now. So often the contemporary church is a weak, ineffectual voice with an uncertain sound. So often it is an archdefender of the status quo. Far from being disturbed by the presence of the church, the power structure of the average community is consoled by the church's silent—and often even vocal—sanction of things as they are.

But the judgment of God is upon the church as never before. If today's church does not recapture the sacrificial spirit of the early church, it will lose its authenticity, forfeit the loyalty of millions, and be dismissed as an irrelevant social club with no meaning for the twentieth century. Every day I meet young people whose disappointment with the church has turned into outright disgust. 50

Perhaps I have once again been too optimistic. Is organized religion too inextricably bound to the status quo to save our nation and the world? Perhaps I must turn my faith to the inner spiritual church, the church within the church, as the true *ekklesia* and the hope of the world. But again I am thankful to God that some noble souls from the ranks of organized religion have broken loose from the paralyzing chains of conformity and joined us as active partners in the struggle for freedom. They have left their secure congregations and walked the streets of Albany, Georgia, with us. They have gone down the highways of the South on tortuous rides for freedom. Yes, they have gone to jail with us. Some have been dismissed from their churches, have lost the support of their bishops and fellow ministers. But they have acted in the faith that right defeated is stronger than evil triumphant. Their witness has been the spiritual salt that has preserved the true meaning of the gospel in these troubled times. They have carved a tunnel of hope through the dark mountain of disappointment.

I hope the church as a whole will meet the challenge of this decisive hour. But even if the church does not come to the aid of justice, I have no despair about the future. I have no fear about the outcome of our struggle in Birmingham, even if our motives are at present misunderstood. We will reach the goal of freedom in Birmingham and all over the nation, because the goal of America is freedom. Abused and scorned though we may be, our destiny is tied up with America's destiny. Before the pilgrims landed at Plymouth, we were here. Before the pen of Jefferson etched the majestic words of the Declaration of Independence across the pages of history, we were here. For more than two centuries our forebears labored in this country without wages; they made cotton king; they built the homes of their masters while suffering gross injustice and shameful humiliation—and yet out of a bottomless vitality they continued to thrive and develop. If the inexpressible cruelties of slavery could not stop us, the opposition we now face will surely fail. We will win our freedom because the sacred heritage of our nation and the eternal will of God are embodied in our echoing demands.

Before closing I feel impelled to mention one other point in your statement that has troubled me profoundly. You warmly commended the Birmingham police force for keeping "order" and "preventing violence." I doubt that you would have so warmly commended the police force if you had seen its dogs sinking their teeth into unarmed, nonviolent Negroes. I doubt that you would so quickly commend the policemen if you were to observe their ugly and inhumane treatment of Negroes here in the city jail; if you were to watch them push and curse old Negro women and young Negro girls; if you were to see them slap and kick old Negro men and young boys; if you were to observe them, as they did on two occasions, refuse to give us food because we wanted to sing our grace together. I cannot join you in your praise of the Birmingham police department.

It is true that police have exercised a degree of discipline in handling the demonstrators. In this sense they have conducted themselves rather "nonviolently" in public. But for what purpose? To preserve the evil system of segregation. Over the past few years I have consistently preached that nonviolence demands that the means we use must be as pure as the ends we seek. I have tried to make clear that it is wrong to use immoral means to attain moral ends. But now I must affirm that it is just as wrong, or perhaps even more so, to use moral means to preserve immoral ends. Perhaps Mr. Connor and his policemen have been rather nonviolent in public, as was Chief Pritchett in Albany, Georgia, but they have used the moral means of nonviolence to maintain the immoral end of racial injustice. As T. S. Eliot has said: "The last temptation is the greatest treason: To do the right deed for the wrong reason."

I wish you had commended the Negro sit-inners and demonstrators of Birmingham for their sublime courage, their willingness to suffer and their amazing discipline in the midst of great provocation. One day the South will recognize its real heroes. They will be the James Merediths, with the noble sense of purpose that enables them to face jeering and hostile mobs, and with the agonizing loneliness that characterizes the life of the pioneer. They will be old, oppressed, battered Negro women, symbolized in a seventy-two-year-old woman in Montgomery, Alabama, who rose up with a sense of dignity and with her people decided not to ride segregated buses, and who responded with ungrammatical profundity to one who inquired about her weariness: "My feets is tired, but my soul is at rest." They will be the young high school and college students, the young ministers of the gospel and a host of their elders, courageously and nonviolently sitting in at lunch counters and willingly going to jail for conscience' sake. One day the South will know that when these disinherited children of God sat down at lunch counters, they were in reality standing up for what is best in the American dream and for the most sacred values in our Judaeo-Christian heritage, thereby bringing our nation back to those great wells of democracy which were dug deep by the founding fathers in their formulation of the Constitution and the Declaration of Independence.

Never before have I written so long a letter. I'm afraid it is much too long to take your precious time. I can assure you that it would have been much shorter if I had been writing from a comfortable desk, but what else can one do when he is alone in a narrow jail cell, other than write long letters, think long thoughts and pray long prayers?

If I have said anything in this letter that overstates the truth and indicates an unreasonable impatience, I beg you to forgive me. If I have said anything that understates the truth and indicates my having a patience that allows me to settle for anything less than brotherhood, I beg God to forgive me.

I hope this letter finds you strong in faith. I also hope that circumstances will soon make it possible for me to meet each of you, not as an integrationist or a civil-rights leader but as a fellow clergyman and a Christian brother. Let us all hope that the dark clouds of racial prejudice will soon pass away and the deep fog of misunderstanding will be

lifted from our fear-drenched communities, and in some not too distant tomorrow the radiant stars of love and brotherhood will shine
over our great nation with all their scintillating beauty.

Yours for the cause of Peace and Brotherhood
MARTIN LUTHER KING, JR.

For Journals

What does King mean, in response to accusations that the civil rights
demonstrations have not come to Birmingham at the right time, that he
"has never yet engaged in a direct-action movement that was 'well
timed' " (paragraph 21)?

For Discussion

1.   Why do you think the black clergymen opposed to King were so
worried about the civil rights activists? Since they were subject to the
same prejudice as King, why wouldn't they join in the demonstrations
themselves?

2.   How does King refute the accusations that he is an outsider in
Birmingham?

3.   What is your response to King's argument that there are legitimate
reasons for breaking the law if it is unjust? What are his bases for deciding if a law is unjust? What basis would you use to decide if a law is
unjust?

4.   King says that one reason injustice is so powerful is not the actions
of bad people but the "appalling silence of good people" (paragraph
34). Do you think he is right? What is the responsibility of ordinary
people when faced with an evil in their society?

5.   Why do you think it pleases King to be referred to by his religious
opponents as an extremist?

6.   What do King's criticisms of the contemporary church tell you
about what he thinks the role an effective clergy should be in promoting justice in American society? How does King refute the idea that an
uninvolved clergy is better than an active one? How does he make the
transition from discussing unheroic clergy to heroic activists?

For Writing

1.   Write an essay or a speech on a public topic that makes you angry.
Use Douglass and King as models. Be very explicit about who your
audience is; you can choose to address yourself to any audience you
want. State the point of view that you disagree with; then refute it. If

you want, write your essay as a letter to the editor of a local newspaper; mail it to the newspaper for possible publication.

2.   Like Thoreau, King spent time in jail for his beliefs, although Thoreau was never in danger of being killed and King was. Review Thoreau's *On Civil Disobedience,* and write an essay in which you discuss the way both men approach and implement political resistance. Include a consideration of the following questions: What is Thoreau's definition of nonviolent resistance, and how does it compare with King's? What does King owe Thoreau in the development of his own philosophy? How does each man argue for the need to sometimes go to jail?

GAYS IN THE MILITARY
1994

Neha Gupta

Neha Gupta's family emigrated to the United States from India; she grew up in the Midwest and attends college in California, where she intends to pursue a career in the sciences. This essay was written as a response to a question about how a contemporary controversial issue could be treated in an argument.

Since the birth of our nation, there have been many conflicts over who can join the military, from the blacks during the Civil War period to gays in more recent times. Strong feelings have always been centered around the military because of our country's dependence on its quality and performance on the battlefield. The current uproar is about whether men who have publicly acknowledged their homosexuality should be allowed to serve in the military.

Several reasons against allowing gays in the military have come up. According to "Gays in Arms" (*New Republic,* Feb. 19, 1990), these reasons include a need to "ensure the integrity of the system of rank and command," a need to maintain "discipline, good order, and morale," and the uncomfortableness due to the lack of privacy in the army. In these arguments, the main refutation that gays have already been serving successfully in the military for years is ignored. The one common thread that ties these arguments together is fear: the fear that people with different sexual orientations are very different in other important ways also. People are afraid that the presence of homosexuals would compromise the quality and experience of the military.

One of the arguments against gays—the fear that the integrity of the system of rank and command would be compromised by allowing gays into the military—is fueled by the speculation that heterosexuals would refuse to take orders from homosexual commanders. This is an argument that dates from the time before racial integration, when there was a fear that white soldiers would not take orders from a black commander. While some did refuse and were court-martialed, the majority of whites realized that even if they did not like taking orders from a black commander, they had no choice about it after Truman made his executive order in 1948. Realistically, this is what would probably happen today with the gays. Heterosexuals would realize that listening to homosexual commanders is simply another command to follow. No damage occurred because of racial integration, and nothing will happen if uncloseted gays are integrated into the military.

The second argument, on the need to maintain "discipline, good order, and morale," is a constant concern for officers in the military at all times, whether homosexuals are allowed to serve or not. Yet this concern gains greater importance if gays are allowed in the military because of the general feeling that discipline, good order, and morale would all decrease with homosexuals in the units. Commanding officers in the military feel that the open recognition of sexual feelings would change the nature of the unit and not spur the men to bind together and fight and die for their country. Overlooked, once again, is the fact that gays have always been in the military and the military has not suffered because of their presence yet, so who's to say the military will suffer once the gays are recognized? The anti-gay argument states that the openly gay soldiers would be disruptive, while the closeted gays would maintain order by keeping their sexual identity secret. However, "friends and commanding officers often know [the homosexuals] are gay and most pass through the services without trouble" ("Arms" 20). According to Sandra Lowe, an attorney with the Lambda Legal Defense and Education fund, "Ninety-nine percent go through and do very well."

5   The fear of the officers really lies in the idea that having gays in the military would add homosexual overtones to the bonding and cama-

raderie, suggesting a loss of "manliness." This has not been a problem with the countries that do allow gays in the military, such as Italy, Sweden, Norway, Denmark, and the Netherlands, and it really should not pose a problem for the U.S. army. Homosexuals are no different from heterosexuals in their ability to have a great sense of loyalty to their country and a deep sense of respect for their officers. They also pledge their lives for the sake of their fellow citizens. Just the fact that they volunteered shows that they have the first step in what it takes to be a good soldier: discipline.

The last argument, on the lack of privacy in the army, is a genuine concern of the soldiers performing military duty with homosexuals in their units. "Soldiers and sailors say they don't want to be regarded with sexual interest when they are naked in common showers or asleep in common barracks" ("Arms" 21). The truth is that there are plenty of gays in the showers. For years closeted gays have been serving in the military without any problems of sexuality ever occurring. It's highly unlikely that the soldiers did not know that someone in their unit was gay. They seem to just get over the fact that there are homosexuals in their unit and move on with more important issues. While the heterosexual soldiers are able to deal with the issue that there are gays in the barracks, the overwhelming fear that underlies this argument is that giving the gays official recognition would allow the homosexuals to stare freely and be more open and aggressive in their advances. Yet no one is suggesting that the rules of the military about harassment or fraternization be changed. Sexual advances and activity have always been and will always be prohibited on duty. The heterosexual soldiers need simply to realize that 10 percent of the U.S. population is gay and they need to overcome their fears and accept the reality that there is no way they can keep themselves from coming into contact with gays. This will happen in some way, whether gays are recognized or not.

The arguments presented are but a few examples of the many others that exist in protesting gays in the military. Underlying the arguments is the genuine, though unsupported, fear of homosexuals. People, in general, are unsure about homosexuals. People feel that if a person's sexual orientation is different, he must be different in some other way also. They do not realize that homosexuals are people also, with similar feelings of joy, sadness, anger, and fear. What the adversaries of having gays in the military need to realize is that the question is not whether gays should be allowed to serve but whether the already present gays should have their sexual orientation officially recognized. Nothing would change by giving the homosexuals recognition; the military would simply be facing reality. Homosexuals are a part of society that cannot be ignored, for they too are citizens of the United States and must also fight for the protection of others.

For Journals

What is your attitude toward gays in the military?

For Discussion

1. Do you think the question Gupta raises is one of military discipline or civil liberties? Why?

2. What do you think is Gupta's strongest argument for allowing gay men to serve openly in the armed forces?

3. How does Gupta use an analogy to days when the armed forces were segregated racially to refute the idea that soliders today would not take orders from a commander they knew to be gay? How convincing is this analogy to you?

4. How did you respond to Gupta's assertion that the real objection to gays in the military is based on the fear that people who are different sexually are different in other ways also?

5. How do you think someone opposed to gays in the military would refute Gupta's argument that morale and discipline are not adversely affected by the presence of gays in a unit?

For Writing

1. Depending on your own point of view, write *one* of the following: an essay in which you refute Gupta's argument in favor of gays in the military or an essay in which you present an argument for or against another unsolved question, for example, the rights of women in the armed forces to take combat roles. For either topic, follow Gupta's pattern of recognizing opposing views and presenting a refutation for each of them.

2. Find another selection from this or previous chapters—an essay, a poem, a story, a cartoon, or a political document—which takes a strong position on a controversial issue. Write an essay in which you analyze what the issue is; what side its creator argues for; how he or she characterizes the opposing point of view; and what details are included to refute or criticize the opponent. Two possible examples are Langston Hughes's poem, "Let America Be America Again," and the cartoon, *The U.S. Hotel Needs a Bouncer.*

FILMS ON JUSTICE AND CIVIL LIBERTIES

The following films dramatize some of the themes in this chapter. View at least one of them with your class. If you have time, try to see two of them for purposes of comparison. *Eyes on the Prize* is a multipart public television documentary presentation about the struggle for civil rights. It is available on individual videos, so you can choose one or more parts to watch. *Judgment at Nuremburg, Gideon's Trumpet, Inherit the Wind,* and *The Thurgood Marshall Story* are all dramatizations of real events. With your classmates, discuss how successfully themes and characterizations are developed in the film or films you saw, and how the ideas of justice and injustice can be dramatized.

To Kill a Mockingbird

Gideon's Trumpet

The Thurgood Marshall Story

The Long Walk Home

The Verdict

Do the Right Thing

Judgment at Nuremburg

And Justice for All

Eyes on the Prize

The Ox-Bow Incident

Inherit the Wind

Glory

REFUTATION

Refutation is proof that an argument or statement is wrong. It comes into existence only when there is an opponent or another side. Refutation means that someone else has gone first; it is the answer to an assumption, or a point of view, or a statement with which one disagrees.

In one sense, then, refutation is not a completely independent rhetorical strategy; it needs something to bounce off and argue against.

The emphasis in refutation is less on stating one's own principles than on taking the material presented by an opponent and dismantling it.

In another sense, refutation is based on instinct, on the impulse to react negatively when we hear an idea that infuriates us or strikes us as stupid or unethical or unjust. But refutation is more disciplined than that. An artful, well-prepared writer or speaker uses refutation as a lever to overturn an opponent's argument or to take its ideas and reverse them to advantage.

It is possible to refute an argument logically without necessarily having a deep intellectual belief in the view expressed by refuting it. For example, an excellent logician could refute the argument of someone he or she agrees with by pointing up inconsistencies; a member of a debating team could be randomly assigned either side of an argument and would be expected to find ways to damage the other side's approach. And criminal attorneys are routinely expected to fulfill their duty of defending people whom they dislike, distrust, or even believe to be guilty, mostly by refuting the prosecution's evidence and raising doubt in the mind of a jury or judge.

The higher forms of refutation, however, are neither mechanical nor uncommitted. They come from one's involvement with an issue or a principle, and they do more than decimate the opposing viewpoint; they can change the way people think and move them to action.

In extraordinary cases—like Thoreau's, Douglass's or King's—refutation can acquire a significant symbolic authority, which resonates over time to larger and more distant audiences. It can even move and inspire otherwise ordinary people to risk their own security and freedom in the name of an idea. Thoreau, for example, argued so powerfully for the effectiveness of nonviolent resistance over the use of force that both Mahatma Gandhi and Martin Luther King, Jr., were able to apply his approach to two of the most powerful civil rights movements of the twentieth century.

Analyzing Refutation in Arguments

The writers in this chapter spent their lives challenging accepted beliefs in the public arena; the ability to use refutation successfully was a professional requirement for them. As a rule, they were less likely to spend their time refuting individual opponents than in arguing against established beliefs and ideas. For example, when Douglass argued in his Fourth of July speech that Independence Day was an insult to slaves who had never had any independence, he was not debating a particular person but disproving an assumption: that the Fourth of July holds the same meaning for all Americans.

In the same way, when Susan B. Anthony argued for women's

right to vote, she was arguing against a whole set of established stereotypes about women's weakness, their need to be told what to do by their husbands, their inability to function outside the home, and so on. To refute those beliefs, she used the one body of evidence that was valid to both her and her opponents: the Declaration of Independence, the Constitution, and the Fourteenth and Fifteenth Amendments. But while her opponents used that evidence to prove that women were not entitled to equal protection under the law, Anthony used it to demonstrate that excluding women from the vote was both philosophically illogical and silly. She was so effective that her career functioned as a sort of living refutation to the idea that women were too weak and helpless to use the vote intelligently.

In *Brown,* however, Chief Justice Warren wanted to refute not only a previous Supreme Court ruling on the separate but equal doctrine that had survived for fifty years but, by implication, the whole structure of segregation that it supported. He needed more ammunition than he could get from a refutation based purely on logic. His solution was to broaden the kinds of evidence on which the refutation could be based. He accepted testimony from sociologists and psychologists on the damage segregation did to the self-esteem of young black children in the South and used it to show that, in fact, separate schooling could never be equal. In effect, since the doctrine he wanted to refute was immovable if taken on its own terms, he succeeded in refuting it by changing the terms of the debate.

Finally, in "Letter from Birmingham Jail," Martin Luther King, Jr., used a broad base of evidence to refute the criticism of black clergy who were frightened by civil rights activism. His evidence was of a very different kind from Justice Warren's; as a minister arguing with other ministers, he used biblical analogies, theological references, and philosophical teachings, as well as the Declaration of Independence and the Constitution, contemporary history, and his own forceful presentation. But his problem was similar: how to refute a theory of political nonintervention that masks a deep-seated reluctance to change.

Using Refutation in Arguments

If argument assumes more than one point of view and if refutation results from a previously articulated difference of opinion, most of the essays you have written and perhaps most of the conversations you have had with your peers have elements of one, or the other, or both. But refutation in an argument about principles is something more: a combination of discipline and creativity. The following strategies will help you formulate your refutation.

1.   *Familiarize yourself with the ideas of the opposing side, concentrating on its strongest argumentative elements.* The natural tendency is to state your own position and ignore anyone else's, but recognizing and respecting the strengths of your opponent's ideas is the best basis for successful refutation. This can be a difficult strategy to practice if your opponent's views are so unpleasant or so infuriating that you would rather not make a detailed study of them. But it is when you have the strongest emotional reaction to another viewpoint that you have to pay the most attention to it. Frederick Douglass must have found it difficult, as a former slave, to have to refute pro-slavery propositions one at a time when the immorality of slavery was so obvious to him. And Susan B. Anthony was frustrated at having to review ad infinitum all the arguments against women's capabilities. But even if the point of view you are opposing seems easy to criticize, you still need to identify what its difficulties are, and, unless you have a photographic memory, take notes.

2.   *Know what you believe and what principles you are supporting.* This strategy may seen obvious, but it is crucial. No matter how many holes you can poke in someone else's argument, your refutation will be successful only in direct proportion to how much it reflects your own ideas and reinforces your own argument.

3.   *Have factual material that you can use as evidence for the points you want to make.* The ability to refute someone else depends on your being well prepared yourself, with whatever kinds of information the situation demands, such as statistics, analogies, and historical and contemporary references. If you were disagreeing about how much trade the United States does with China, you would recognize that your opponent was understating the financial value of this trade only if you knew what the value was yourself. Lacking evidence, you may find yourself with the vague feeling that somewhere there is a good point you could have made, and you will leave the impression that your opponent's argument is much stronger than it actually is.

4.   *Look for factual mistakes in the opposing argument*—not only statistical errors but the deeper errors that come from relying too heavily on a narrow band of information and ignoring other relevant material. For example, keep in mind the difference between the very narrow grounds on which *Plessy* was decided and the much broader grounds that the Warren Court in *Brown* used to refute it.

5.   *Look for sweeping, glittering generalities in the opposing argument.* These are the easiest and most substantive kinds of mistakes to refute. Sentences that begin with overboard classifications—all children are impossible; all parents are inconsistent—are often good candidates for refutation; so are general statements about particular groups or about historical events or eras.

    6. *Look for logical inconsistencies or lapses.* These usually take the form of changes in the pattern of an argument. For example, the reasons an opposing argument proposes to use in justifying a conclusion may disappear somewhere in the course of argument and never be heard from again, or two previously unconnected ideas may be suddenly yoked together.

    7. *Be specific about what points in the opposing argument you want to refute.* Quote them if possible; go through the points one at a time so that everyone understands what is being refuted and why. That way you will simultaneously organize your counterargument and weaken your opponent's case.

    8. *Conclude with your own views.* Once you have refuted as much as you can of the opposing argument, remember that the animating force behind good refutation is a struggle over principle. No matter what anyone else's argument is, you must understand and put forth what you really believe in.

    Successful refutation requires that you pay close attention to the position or the ideas you want to attack. But you have leeway. You are not required to take each opposing point in the order in which it was given, and you do not have to accept all the terms of someone else's argument. The way you order your points, the consistency and tightness of your logic, your ability to vary your tone, and, above all, your power to argue more persuasively than someone who has not thought the issue through—all draw heavily on your imagination, your spirit, and your creativity.

WRITING ASSIGNMENTS

1. Write an analytical essay comparing Frederick Douglass's Independence Day speech with Martin Luther King's "Letter from Birmingham Jail." Consider the audience each man was addressing; the way in which each criticizes his audience and why; the sources of their anger; and how successful each one is at refuting the argument of his opponents. Do Douglass and King have any persuasive or argumentative points in common? Do they evoke in you similar or different responses?

2. Investigate some of the Victorian stereotypes about women's behavior, weakness, and dependence that Susan B. Anthony had to refute in her efforts to secure the vote. Use periodicals and books, but, if
they are available at your library, also look at nineteenth-century wom-
en's magazines, etiquette books, and so on. Write an essay on your
findings.

3. Visit the nearest federal, state, or city courthouse, and sit in on a
trial for a couple of hours. Call or write the court clerk in advance so
that you will know what kinds of trials are scheduled for that week
and can pick a case that interests you. Family court and juvenile court,
for example, deal in emotional issues that are both immediate and
comprehensible. Take notes on what you see and hear: the behavior of
the judge and attorneys, the demeanor of the defendants, the issues
being raised. Write a paper analyzing the experience: what you saw
and learned, whether the trial was different from what you've learned
to expect from television, and how effectively each attorney refuted the
other's arguments.

4. Devise your own favorite example of American individualism
coming up against either government regulations or majority opinion—anything from whether the government can make you fight a war
to whether it can force you to wear a helmet when you're riding a mo-
torcycle. Write an argumentative paper in favor of your opinion, and
include quotations or ideas from *On Civil Disobedience* as support for
your refutation.

5. During the Civil War, Frederick Douglass petitioned President
Lincoln for the formation of black army units. Eventually the Fifty-
Fourth Regiment was formed, and two of Douglass's sons fought in it.
Write a documented research paper on the history of this unit or on
Douglass's role in getting it established. Alternatively, compare the re-
sults of your research with the way the unit is developed in the film
Glory. Does the film support or refute the version you found during
your research? Why or why not?

6. The U.S. armed forces remained officially segregated until President Truman integrated them by executive order in 1947. Research this
decision, and write a paper on your findings. What were the arguments against integration? What ideas were advanced to refute them?
What was the immediate reaction of the military? How was integration
put into practice?

CHAPTER

WAR AND THE ENEMY

*I*n the introduction to the film *Faces of the Enemy,* narrator Sam Keen notes, "Before we make war, even before we make weapons, we make an idea of the enemy." As we make an image of the enemy, we clarify who we are and set ourselves in opposition to that enemy: we are good, they are evil; our cause is just, theirs is unjust; we are human, they are animals. There is a certain peace of mind accompanying that clarity; suicide rates go down in wartime, people feel they have a common purpose, citizens rally to the cause, gray tones disappear in an increasingly black and white world where there is a good side (us) and a bad side (them).

As we identify and characterize an enemy, we more clearly establish our own national identity. Our leaders then appeal to that identity and to the desire to belong in order to rally the nation to support the war effort. In encouraging the citizenry to identify with national goals and in vilifying the enemy, politicians and officials, and often private commercial interests, use primarily appeals to ethos and pathos. Appeals to *ethos* commonly establish a sense of values and ideals to which true Americans would subscribe; those wishing to be considered real Americans support the efforts identified as essential to the common good. Leaders can also appeal to ethos to establish their credibility and their sense of leadership and authority, to appear "presidential" and offer an image of stability and steadfastness in the face of potential chaos.

Appeals to *pathos* convince us to suffer for the common good. On the home front, such appeals urge us to support the war politically, to work in factories, to conserve petroleum products, to do without luxuries, and sometimes necessities, to support the war effort in any way possible. Even more difficult can be the appeal to offer one's time and loss of independence and income through military service. Along with such service comes the risk of losing one's life, and appeals must be strong indeed to urge men and women to be prepared to give their lives for their country and the "American way of life."

War and the Enemy through History

Throughout recorded history on the American continent, conflicts between economic forces, between cultures and ways of life, and between competing claims on the land have created divergent views about whose rights to the land, to the resources, to political and economic power, should be superior. White settlements intruded on the indigenous peoples of America, and European settlers from various countries fought over land and resources.

Most notable in mainstream American history is the Revolutionary War against Britain. In the first selection, Thomas Paine writes persuasively about the kind of American whom Americans would not want to be—the "summer soldier and sunshine patriot"—and the kind with whom they want to identify—"he whose heart is firm, and whose conscience approves his conduct, will pursue his principles unto death." Intertwined with his appeals to support American independence in its most desperate hour are his descriptions of the enemy, "A sottish, stupid, stubborn, worthless, brutish man." In setting up oppositions—of supporting America or not, of courage or fear—Paine relies on parallel phrasing and balanced sentences to outline and reinforce the choices Americans will need to make.

Speaking about the Civil War—a war that many argue was primarily economic yet pitted "brother against brother"—Abraham Lincoln sought, in "The Gettysburg Address," not to divide but to unite, by linking the themes of birth and death, the deaths of Gettysburg in exchange for "a new birth of freedom." Lincoln predicted in his address that "the world will little note nor long remember what we say here," but about that he was wrong: The world rightly sees "The Gettysburg Address" as a perhaps unparalleled statement of the poignance of war.

Just as each side in the Civil War saw itself as the rightful victor, so do we frequently need to see ourselves as good and the other side as bad; we need to avoid seeing the enemy as anything but dangerous and worthy of extinction. Mark Twain, a sharp if humorous critic of American society, lacerates the tendency to simplify the waging of war in "The War Prayer," a short satirical piece countering piety with the grim reminder that victory for one side brings with it defeat and blighted lives for the other.

Once we have created an image of an enemy and determined the need to go to war, and once society has endorsed that war, popular culture often takes on the selling of that war back to society, through posters, advertisements, opinion pieces, and other media that implore us to enlist, to conserve, to contribute. In the same media, we see not advertisers selling the war but war selling the products, whether or not such products have anything to do with the war effort. In *"We Smash 'Em HARD,"* an advertisement published in 1918, we see association, innuendo, and appeals to the emotion of hatred as well as an appeal to the desire to be manly and the association of masculinity with tobacco products. A very different image, an anti-Nazi poster entitled *Deliver Us from Evil*, appeals to emotion and to values in order to move its audience—not merely to buy bonds but to sacrifice for the innocent victims of war.

The act of asking Congress to declare war is probably the most solemnn occasion at which a sitting president can speak, and President Franklin Delano Roosevelt's "Pearl Harbor Address" on December 8, 1941, after the bombings of Pearl Harbor and other bases on Oahu, Hawaii, is a prime example of a difficult rhetorical situation and the ways in which a nation's leader can use such an occasion to unite his citizens against a common enemy. In asking for a formal declaration of war, Roosevelt's speech required appeals to patriotism and a strong characterization of a treacherous enemy.

The rhetoric of war entails, perhaps of necessity, often crude stereotyping of friend and enemy alike.

Paul Fussell's essay, "Type-casting," on the stereotyping endemic to World War II, provides some background for examining the verbal rhetoric and characterization of the enemy that suffuse Roosevelt's speech, as well as the visual persuasion in the media that evokes hatred of the enemy and protectiveness of the vulnerable.

Sometimes in creating an enemy, we see something of ourselves in the enemy and something of the enemy in ourselves. The two Vietnam War–era photographs included in this chapter illustrate contradictions of that war. In *Saigon Execution*, Americans are brought painfully close to the actuality of the war and to the confusion about friends and enemies that characterized it. In *The Terror of War*, war's most horrifying damage—to innocent children—challenged political arguments and domino theories of spreading communism and had a profound effect on Americans' perceptions of the war.

Simple, straightforward narratives of war hold their own compelling power as well and can teach us something memorable about suffering. Jacqueline Navarra Rhoads's narrative, "Nurses in Vietnam," is a story of healing in the midst of massive casualties and war waging. Rhoads's account of her tour of duty in Vietnam also reminds us of the power of the personal voice in bringing the pain and tragedy of massive warfare to an individual level.

Language is one of the weapons of war, but it is also a weapon of justifying war. George Lakoff examines politicians' use of metaphors to justify war in his essay, "Metaphor and the Gulf War," which was distributed over the electronic network shortly before the Gulf War against Iraq began. Reading Lakoff's essay in view of the preceding materials in this chapter can provide an illuminating perspective on the use of persuasion before, during, and after a war to identify the "good" side and the "bad" side, to recruit troops and rally the home front, and to write the history of the war and set it in the context of America's image of itself. Student writer Jeremy Kassis looks, from his vantage point of the 1990s, at the rhetorical strategies Roosevelt used to bring America into World War II and to unite all Americans in support for that war.

Creating War and the Enemy through Persuasive Language

Each of the selections in this chapter is an argument: to unite against a common threat; to renounce an enemy; to embrace a former enemy and "bind up the nation's wounds"; to unite as a people to defeat a treacherous foe; to challenge our assumptions about who our political friends and enemies are. The arguments about war, and about waging war, appeal to the ethos of Americans—to fair play, to leadership in the free world, to protecting the innocent—and to logic—to protecting American and allies' interests. They also appeal to pathos—to empathy for the weak and hurt, to manliness and virility, to hatred of the less-than-human enemy. These appeals are made through language: word choice, syntax or sentence structure, emphasis, and allusions or references that evoke images to which we respond. (See Chapter 1 for further explanation.)

The authors in this chapter are all highly attentive to the power of language to move people's emotions and to move them to action. The discussion after the reading selections will help you to analyze persuasive language in what you read, to develop persuasive strategies of language in your own writing, and to appreciate the power of language to unite and to divide.

As you read and reflect on the selections in this chapter, consider the changes, even over your own lifetime, that have created the context in which questions about war must now be asked. In the last years of the twentieth century, given the changing world political order that has resulted from the breakup of the Soviet Union and the end of the Cold War, Americans increasingly look upon war—and this nation's role in establishing and maintaining world peace—with skepticism. There may no longer be a clearly definable, monolithic "enemy"—communism for example—but there are nevertheless desperate, devastating ethnic, political, and religious struggles all over the globe, from the Middle East to Bosnia to Rwanda to Haiti. Acutely aware of our own democratic problems—a soaring national deficit, inadequate health care coverage, unacceptable levels of poverty, illiteracy, unemployment, and perceived deterioration of standards of living—we increasingly decline to commit our national involvement and American lives to the affairs of other nations, no matter how grievous the situation. The questions, then, intensify: What are America's vital interests? When is war not merely justifiable but necessary? Are there situations so grave that it is our moral imperative to wage war to eradicate them?

THESE ARE THE TIMES THAT TRY MEN'S SOULS

1 7 7 6

Thomas Paine

Thomas Paine (1737–1809) came to America from England in 1774. A political radical and active writer and supporter of the American Revolution, Paine worked in a variety of occupations and held several official posts in the colonies, but it is for his crusades on behalf of democratic principles and rights, both in America and abroad, that he is best remembered. Paine's writings include Common Sense *(1776),* The American Crisis *(1776–1783),* Public Good *(1780),* The Rights of Man *(1791–1792), and* The Age of Reason *(1794–1796), a book for which he was denounced as an atheist. The* American Crisis, *a series of sixteen pamphlets supporting the American Revolution, was widely distributed in the American colonies. The selection that follows is from the famous first pamphlet in the series, which was read to American troops on the eve of the battle of Trenton by order of General Washington.*

These are the times that try men's souls. The summer soldier and the sunshine patriot will, in this crisis, shrink from the service of his country; but he that stands it NOW, deserves the love and thanks of man and woman. Tyranny, like hell, is not easily conquered: yet we have this consolation with us, that the harder the conflict, the more glorious the triumph. What we obtain too cheap, we esteem too lightly: 'tis dearness only that gives every thing its value. Heaven knows how to put a proper price upon its goods: and it would be strange indeed, if so celestial an article as FREEDOM should not be highly rated. Britain, with an army to enforce her tyranny, has declared that she has a right (*not only to* TAX) but "to BIND *us in* ALL CASES WHATSOEVER," and if being *bound in that manner,* is not slavery, then is there no such a thing as slavery upon earth. Even the expression is impious, for so unlimited a power can belong only to God. . . .

I have as little superstition in me as any man living, but my secret opinion has ever been, and still is, that God Almighty will not give up a people to military destruction, or leave them unsupportedly to perish, who have so earnestly and so repeatedly sought to avoid the calamities of war, by every decent method which wisdom could invent. Neither have I so much of the infidel in me, as to suppose that He has relinquished the government of the world, and given us up to the care of devils, and as I do not, I cannot see on what grounds the king of Britain can look up to Heaven for help against us: a common murderer, a highwayman, or a housebreaker, has as good a pretence as he. . . .

I call not upon a few, but upon all: not on *this* state or *that* state, but on *every* state; up and help us; lay your shoulders to the wheel; better have too much force than too little, when so great an object is at stake. Let it be told to the future world, that in the depth of winter, when nothing but hope and virtue could survive, that the city and the country, alarmed at one common danger, came forth to meet and to repulse it. Say not that thousands are gone, turn out your tens of thousands: throw not the burden of the day upon Providence, but "*show your faith by your works,*" that God may bless you. It matters not where you live, or what rank of life you hold, the evil or the blessing will reach you all. The far and the near, the home counties and the back, the rich and the poor, will suffer or rejoice alike. The heart that feels not now, is dead: the blood of his children will curse his cowardice, who shrinks back at a time when a little might have saved the whole, and made *them* happy. I love the man that can smile in trouble, that can gather strength from distress, and grow brave by reflection. 'Tis the business of little minds to shrink; but he whose heart is firm, and whose conscience approves his conduct, will pursue his principles unto death. My own line of reasoning is to myself as straight and clear as a ray of light. Not all the treasures of the world, so far as I believe, could have induced me to suport an offensive war, for I think it murder; but if a thief breaks into my house, burns and destroys my property, and kills or threatens to kill me, or those that are in it, and to *"bind me in all cases whatsoever,"* to his absolute will, am I to suffer it? What signifies it to me, whether he who does it is a king or a common man; my country-man or not my countryman: whether it be done by an individual vil-lain, or an army of them? If we reason to the root of things we shall find no difference: neither can any just cause be assigned why we should punish in the one case and pardon in the other. Let them call me rebel, and welcome, I feel no concern from it; but I should suffer the misery of devils, were I to make a whore of my soul by swearing allegiance to one whose character is that of a sottish, stupid, stubborn, worthless, brutish man. I conceive likewise a horrid idea in receiving mercy from a being, who at the last day shall be shrieking to the rocks and mountains to cover him, and fleeing with terror from the orphan, the widow, and the slain of America.

There are cases which cannot be overdone by language, and this is one. There are persons too who see not the full extent of the evil which threatens them, they solace themselves with hopes that the enemy, if they succeed, will be merciful. It is the madness of folly, to expect mercy from those who have refused to do justice; and even mercy, where conquest is the object, is only a trick of war; the cunning of the fox is as murderous as the violence of the wolf; and we ought to guard equally against both. . . .

I thank God that I fear not. I see no real cause for fear. I know our   5 situation well, and can see the way out of it. . . . By perseverance and fortitude we have the prospect of a glorious issue: by cowardice and submission, the sad choice of a variety of evils—a ravaged country—a depopulated city—habitations without safety, and slavery without hope—our homes turned into barracks and bawdy-houses for Hes-sians, and a future race to provide for, whose fathers we shall doubt of. Look on this picture and weep over it! and if there yet remains one thoughtless wretch who believes it not, let him suffer it unla-mented. . . .

For Journals

Have you heard someone use the expression in the title of this selec-tion? What did it mean to you? If you haven't heard it before, freewrite about your initial reactions to it.

For Discussion

1.   A number of the phrases in this essay became well-known expres-sions over time. Which ones have you heard before? Did you know

they came from the Revolutionary War era? What did they mean to you when you first heard them? What emotions did they inspire in you?

2.   How does Paine characterize the kind of Americans who will answer the call? In what ways does he appeal to his audience so that they will want to support the cause of independence?

3.   How does Paine characterize the enemy? What evidence does he offer to support his characterization? Cite examples of vivid language and concrete images.

4.   Paine develops his argument with parallelism, or grammatically similar phrases; and antithesis, or the setting up of a statement that begins with what is *not* true and then states what *is* true; for example, "I call not upon a few, but upon all." Identify specific examples of these and other stylistic strategies that you believe are particularly effective, and analyze what they contribute to the argument.

5.   Compare this selection with the Franklin woodcut *Join or Die* (Chapter 3) and other Franklin readings included in this book. What common themes and appeals do you find?

For Writing

1.   Using question 2 above as a starting point, develop an essay on Paine's ideal heroic American.

2.   Look up some of Paine's other pamphlets from *The American Crisis*. Study several selections, and write an essay analyzing the most common strategies of language in his writings.

THE GETTYSBURG ADDRESS
1863

Abraham Lincoln

   The son of a pioneer, Abraham Lincoln was born in Hodgesville, Kentucky, in 1809 and moved to Illinois in 1831. After brief experiences as a clerk, postmaster, and county surveyor, he studied law and was elected to the state legislature in 1834. A prominent member of the newly organized Republican party, Lincoln became president on the eve of the Civil War. In 1862, after Union victory at Antietam, Lincoln issued the Emancipation

Proclamation freeing the slaves—the crowning achievement of an illustrious presidency. He delivered "The Gettysburg Address," one of his greatest speeches, at the dedication of the Gettysburg National Cemetery in 1863. Lincoln was assassinated by John Wilkes Booth in 1865, shortly after Robert E. Lee's surrender and the end of the Civil War.

Four score and seven years ago our fathers brought forth on this continent, a new nation, conceived in Liberty, and dedicated to the proposition that all men are created equal.

Now we are engaged in a great civil war, testing whether that nation, or any nation so conceived and so dedicated, can long endure. We are met on a great battlefield of that war. We have come to dedicate a portion of that field as a final resting-place for those who here gave their lives that that nation might live. It is altogether fitting and proper that we should do this.

But, in a larger sense, we cannot dedicate—we cannot consecrate—we cannot hallow—this ground. The brave men, living and dead, who struggled here have consecrated it, far above our poor power to add or detract. The world will little note, nor long remember, what we say here, but it can never forget what they did here. It is for us the living, rather, to be dedicated here to the unfinished work which they who fought here have thus far so nobly advanced. It is rather for us to be here dedicated to the great task remaining before us—that from these honored dead we take increased devotion to that cause for which they gave the last full measure of devotion; that we here highly resolve that these dead shall not have died in vain; this nation, under God, shall have a new birth of freedom; and that government of the people, by the people, for the people, shall not perish from the earth.

For Journals

What phrases from "The Gettysburg Address" have you heard before? What did they mean to you when you first heard them?

For Discussion

1.   After your first reading, do a slow, line-by-line reading out loud. Do you find that the address engages your intellect, or your emotions, or both? Discuss your answer.

2.   Analyze what Lincoln leaves out of the speech as well as what he includes; for example, the address does not mention slavery, or the an-

imosity between North and South. What is the effect of his careful selection of themes and words?

3.   What key ideas does Lincoln evoke in the address? What images?
How do they work together to support Lincoln's persuasive purpose?

4.   In what ways does Lincoln weave the themes of birth and death?
How does the style—the sentence structure, or syntax; the diction, or
word choice—convey those themes?

5.   The address is full of expressions we have heard in other contexts:
for example, Martin Luther King Jr.'s "I Have a Dream" (Chapter 4)
echoes its opening, and countless military funerals have repeated the
phrase "last full measure of devotion." Author Garry Wills wrote,
"Hemingway claimed that all modern American novels are the offspring of *Huckleberry Finn.* It is no greater exaggeration to say that all
modern political prose descends from 'The Gettysburg Address'." Discuss this assertion in view of the examples and other prose you have
heard or read that have sought to invoke "The Gettysburg Address."

For Writing

1.   Do a close textual analysis of the address, considering sentence-
level strategies as they relate to the larger theme or paradox of the address and to Lincoln's persuasive purpose in speaking. Consider the
rhythm of the language, parallelism, pauses, and diction in your analysis.

2.   Research the context of the Battle of Gettysburg or of the address
itself, writing a documented essay that gives the reader an understanding of the significance of the battle and the context of the speech.

THE WAR PRAYER
1904–1905

Mark Twain

    *Mark Twain (1835–1910) is the pen name of Samuel Clemens. He was
born in Florida, Missouri, and explored a variety of jobs—printer, riverboat
pilot, gold prospector—before discovering success as a writer with the publication of* The Celebrated Jumping Frog of Calavaras County and Other

Sketches *(1867), and* The Innocents Abroad *(1869). Twain established his reputation as a humorist through his classic novels* The Adventures of Tom Sawyer *(1876) and* The Adventures of Huckleberry Finn *(1885). Twain was always a critic of American society*—Huckleberry Finn *attacks racism, for example—but in later years he grew especially somber, even pessimistic. "The War Prayer" exemplifies the darker side of his satire.*

It was a time of great and exalting excitement. The country was up in arms, the war was on, in every breast burned the holy fire of patriotism; the drums were beating, the bands playing, the toy pistols popping, the bunched firecrackers hissing and spluttering; on every hand and far down the receding and fading spread of roofs and balconies a fluttering wilderness of flags flashed in the sun; daily the young volunteers marched down the wide avenue gay and fine in their new uniforms, the proud fathers and mothers and sisters and sweethearts cheering them with voices choked with happy emotion as they swung by; nightly the packed mass meetings listened, panting, to patriot oratory which stirred the deepest deeps of their hearts, and which they interrupted at briefest intervals with cyclones of applause, the tears running down their cheeks the while; in the churches the pastors preached devotion to flag and country, and invoked the God of Battles, beseeching His aid in our good cause in outpouring of fervid eloquence which moved every listener. It was indeed a glad and gracious time, and the half dozen rash spirits that ventured to disapprove of the war and cast a doubt upon its righteousness straightway got such a stern and angry warning that for their personal safety's sake they quickly shrank out of sight and offended no more in that way.

Sunday morning came—next day the battalions would leave for the front; the church was filled; the volunteers were there, their young faces alight with martial dreams—visions of the stern advance, the gathering momentum, the rushing charge, the flashing sabers, the flight of the foe, the tumult, the enveloping smoke, the fierce pursuit, the surrender!—them home from the war, bronzed heroes, welcomed, adored, submerged in golden seas of glory! With the volunteers sat their dear ones, proud, happy, and envied by the neighbors and friends who had no sons and brothers to send forth to the field of honor, there to win for the flag, or, failing, die the noblest of noble deaths. The service proceeded; a war chapter from the Old Testament was read; the first prayer was said; it was followed by an organ burst that shook the building, and with one impulse the house rose, with glowing eyes and beating hearts, and poured out that tremendous invocation—

> "God the all-terrible!   Thou who ordainest,
> Thunder thy clarion and lightning thy sword!"

Then came the "long" prayer. None could remember the like of it for passionate pleading and moving and beautiful language. The burden of its supplication was, that an ever-merciful and benignant Father of us all would watch over our noble young soldiers, and aid, comfort, and encourage them in their patriotic work; bless them, shield them in the day of battle and the hour of peril, bear them in His mighty hand, make them strong and confident, invincible in the bloody onset; help them to crush the foe, grant to them and to their flag and country imperishable honor and glory—

An aged stranger entered and moved with slow and noiseless step up the main aisle, his eyes fixed upon the minister, his long body clothed in a robe that reached to his feet, his head bare, his white hair descending in a frothy cataract to his shoulders, his seamy face unnaturally pale, pale even to ghastliness. With all eyes following him and wondering, he made his silent way; without pausing, he ascended to the preacher's side and stood there, waiting. With shut lids the preacher, unconscious of his presence, continued his moving prayer, and at last finished it with the words, uttered in fervent appeal, "Bless our arms, grant us the victory, O Lord our God, Father and Protector of our land and flag!"

The stranger touched his arm, motioned him to step aside—which the startled minister did—and took his place. During some moments he surveyed the spellbound audience with solemn eyes, in which burned an uncanny light; then in a deep voice he said:

5   "I come from the Throne—bearing a message from Almighty God!" The words smote the house with a shock; if the stranger perceived it he gave no attention. "He has heard the prayer of His servant your shepherd, and will grant it if such shall be your desire after I, His messenger, shall have explained to you its import—that is to say, its full import. For it is like unto many of the prayers of men, in that it asks for more than he who utters it is aware of—except he pause and think.

"God's servant and yours has prayed his prayer. Has he paused and taken thought? Is it one prayer? No, it is two—one uttered, the other not. Both have reached the ear of Him Who heareth all supplications, the spoken and the unspoken. Ponder this—keep it in mind. If you would beseech a blessing upon yourself, beware! lest without intent you invoke a curse upon a neighbor at the same time. If you pray for the blessing of rain upon your crop which needs it, by that act you are possibly praying for a curse upon some neighbor's crop which may not need rain and can be injured by it.

"You have heard your servant's prayer—the uttered part of it. I am commissioned of God to put into words the other part of it—that part which the pastor—and also you in your hearts—fervently prayed silently. And ignorantly and unthinkingly? God grant that it was so! You heard these words: 'Grant us the victory, O Lord our God!' That is sufficient. The *whole* of the uttered prayer is compact into those pregnant words. Elaborations were not necessary. When you have prayed for victory you have prayed for many unmentioned results which follow victory—*must* follow it, cannot help but follow it. Upon the listening spirit of God the Father fell also the unspoken part of the prayer. He commandeth me to put it into words. Listen!

"O Lord our Father, our young patriots, idols of our hearts, go forth to battle—be Thou near them! With them—in spirit—we also go forth from the sweet peace of our beloved firesides to smite the foe. O Lord our God, help us to tear their soldiers to bloody shreds with our shells; help us to cover their smiling fields with the pale forms of their patriot dead; help us to drown the thunder of the guns with the shrieks of their wounded, writhing in pain; help us to lay waste their humble homes with a hurricane of fire; help us to wring the hearts of their unoffending widows with unavailing grief; help us to turn them out roofless with their little children to wander unfriended the wastes of their desolated land in rags and hunger and thirst, sports of the sun flames of summer and the icy winds of winter, broken in spirit, worn with travail, imploring Thee for the refuge of the grave and denied it— for our sakes who adore Thee, Lord, blast their hopes, blight their lives, protract their bitter pilgrimage, make heavy their steps, water their way with their tears, stain the white snow with the blood of their wounded feet! We ask it, in the spirit of love, of Him Who is the Source of Love, and Who is the ever-faithful refuge and friend of all that are sore beset and seek His aid with humble and contrite hearts. Amen."

(*After a pause*) "Ye have prayed it: if ye still desire it, speak! The messenger of the Most High waits."

It was believed afterward that the man was a lunatic, because there   10
was no sense in what he said.

For Journals

Do you think of Mark Twain as a humorous writer? As a writer of satire or social commentary? Write about your expectations of this selection based on the title.

For Discussion

1.   Examine the diction in the first two paragraphs. What tone and stance are established? Through which particular words and expressions?

2.   What is your understanding of what the worshippers are praying for? Do you envision people on the other side of the conflict doing the same?

3.   What does the messenger want the people in church to understand? How does he help them to do so? How does Twain convey to us the people's response to the message?

4.   How does Twain show the irony of their prayer and their "spirit of love"? Examine the language, and cite specific examples that support your point.

5.   How do you interpret the ending of the selection, particularly the last two sentences? How do you think the people hearing the stranger would respond? Would the other side respond any differently?

6.   What is Twain's persuasive purpose in writing this selection? Why do you think he selected this genre and format for his purpose?

For Writing

1.   Using question 2 above as a starting point, develop an analytical essay examining the style of this selection and the strategies Twain uses to convey irony.

2.   Write a contemporary war prayer that pertains to a geopolitical situation in the mid- to late twentieth century. Irony is not an easy technique for writing, so aim for a subtle effect; get feedback from peers and revise your language carefully.

"WE SMASH 'EM HARD"
1918

The advertisement that follows, which appeared in popular magazines in 1918, links a product—cigars—with the war effort of World War I. Although the battles were being fought in Europe, Americans at home were called upon to do their part to support the war, whether in military service or through conserving resources. Advertisements and posters for war bonds were abundant; this ad draws on an association with the war as a marketing ploy.

"We smash 'em HARD"

One of the Yank Veterans

WHITE OWL
▼
Invincible Shape
7c

OWL
▼
Square-end
6c

"Did I bayonet my first Hun? Sure! How did it feel? It *doesn't* feel! There *he* is. There *you* are. One of you has got to go. I preferred to stay.

"So when sergeant says, 'Smash 'em, boys'—we do. And we go them one better like good old Yankee Doodle Yanks. For bullets and bayonets are the only kind of lingo that a Hun can *understand!*"

* * * *

The *dependable* Yank, whose photograph appears above, first met the *dependable* Owl Cigar while boosting that *dependable* investment—the Liberty Loan.

We didn't tell him about the $2,000,000 stock of leaf that is always aging for Owl and White Owl. Nor the over 100,000,000 Owls and White Owls sold last year. We just swapped him a White Owl for a smile. And it doesn't look like the smile came hard, does it?

Why don't you, too, try an Owl or White Owl—*today?*

DEALERS:
If your distributor does not sell these dependable cigars, write us.
GENERAL CIGAR CO., INC., 119 West 40th Street, New York City

TWO DEPENDABLE CIGARS

OWL 6¢ whiteOWL 7¢

Branded for your protection
Banded protection

For Journals

What do you think are the most common types of appeals in advertisements? What causes you to want to buy something that you see or hear advertised?

For Discussion

1. What is your emotional response to the ad? What feelings does it evoke in you? How might the response of people in 1918 be similar to, or different from, your own?

2.   Analyze the advertisement carefully, examining placement of pictures and text. What element in the advertisement gets the most emphasis? How does the emphasis contribute to persuasion?

3.   What appeals to pathos, ethos, and logos do you find in the advertisement? Which are most prominent? Give examples. Why do you think the artist chose such appeals? How does the ad's depiction of the enemy, the "Hun," contribute to the persuasive message?

For Writing

1.   The advertisement is an argument. Summarize the argument, and then write an analysis of its logic.

2.   Look through copies of popular magazines from World War I or II. Most college or large public libraries have collections of bound copies of such magazines as *Life, Look,* and *The New Yorker.* Do any advertisers in them use the war to sell their products? Write an essay analyzing the strategies for a particular type of product or a particular theme of war that is evident in advertising for a wide range of products.

DELIVER US FROM EVIL

C A . 1 9 4 0

 This poster reveals a number of typical strategies used by poster artists to invoke American desire to support the war effort in Europe during both world wars—in this case, World War II. As you examine this selection and other visual materials in the chapter, consider what types of appeals are being made and which audiences are being targeted.

For Journals

What could convince you to work toward a war effort, whether by joining the military or contributing money? What are the most compelling ways in which a writer or artist could appeal to you?

For Discussion

1.   What is your immediate emotional response to the image?

2.   What draws your eye? What do the shades and shapes emphasize?

3.   What ethnicity does the child seem to be? How does that affect the viewer's reaction to the image?

4.   The headline is from a Christian prayer. What is the significance of using this allusion?

For Writing

1.   Examine this image in view of Fussell's essay "Type-casting," especially considering the points he makes about portrayals of ethnicity and class in advertising.

2.   Using your journal entry as a starting point if that would be helpful, write an essay on the different types of strategies that poster artists could use to elicit different kinds of support (monetary, military) from different segments of American society in a time of war. Pay special attention to the kinds of images you think would be most persuasive.

PEARL HARBOR ADDRESS
1941

Franklin Delano Roosevelt

> *Franklin Delano Roosevelt (1882–1945) was the thirty-second president of the United States and the only president ever elected to four consecutive terms in office. His innovative New Deal economic recovery plan guided America through the difficult years of the Great Depression, and his cooperation with Winston Churchill helped secure an Allied victory in World War II. He died in Warm Springs, Georgia, in 1945, ironically, three weeks before the Nazi surrender. Roosevelt's address to the House of Representatives after the Japanese attack on Pearl Harbor in 1941, with such ringing phrases as "a date which will live in infamy," remains a classic call to action.*

To the Congress of the United States: Yesterday, December 7, 1941—a date which will live in infamy—the United States of America was suddenly and deliberately attacked by naval and air forces of the Empire of Japan.

The United States was at peace with that nation and, at the solicitation of Japan, was still in conversation with its government and its emperor looking toward the maintenance of peace in the Pacific. Indeed, one hour after Japanese air squadrons had commenced bombing in Oahu, the Japanese ambassador to the United States and his colleague delivered to the secretary of state a formal reply to a recent American message. While this reply stated that it seemed useless to continue the existing diplomatic negotiations, it contained no threat or hint of war or armed attack.

It will be recorded that the distance of Hawaii from Japan makes it obvious that the attack was deliberately planned many days or even weeks ago. During the intervening time the Japanese government had deliberately sought to deceive the United States by false statements and expressions of hope for continued peace.

The attack yesterday on the Hawaiian Islands has caused severe damage to American naval and military forces. I regret to tell you that very many American lives have been lost. In addition American ships have been reported torpedoed on the high seas between San Francisco and Honolulu.

Yesterday the Japanese government also launched an attack   5
against Malaya.

Last night Japanese forces attacked Hong Kong.

Last night Japanese forces attacked Guam.

Last night Japanese forces attacked the Philippine Islands.

Last night the Japanese attacked Wake Island.

This morning the Japanese attacked Midway Island.   10

Japan has, therefore, undertaken a surprise offensive extending throughout the Pacific area. The facts of yesterday speak for themselves. The people of the United States have already formed their opinions and well understand the implications to the very life and safety of our nation.

As commander in chief of the army and navy I have directed that all measures be taken for our defense.

Always will we remember the character of the onslaught against us.

No matter how long it may take us to overcome this premeditated invasion, the American people in their righteous might will win through to absolute victory.

I believe I interpret the will of the Congress and of the people   15
when I assert that we will not only defend ourselves to the uttermost but will make very certain that this form of treachery shall never endanger us again.

Hostilities exist. There is no blinking at the fact that our people, our territory, and our interests are in grave danger.

With confidence in our armed forces—with the unbounded determination of our people—we will gain the inevitable triumph—so help us God.

I ask that the Congress declare that since the unprovoked and dastardly attack by Japan on Sunday, December 7, 1941, a state of war has existed between the United States and the Japanese Empire.

For Journal Writing

Have your parents or grandparents ever talked about World War II or what they did in the war? Write for a few minutes on what you know about the war.

For Discussion

1.   Have you previously heard excerpts from this speech on television or radio? What was your reaction then? If you haven't heard the speech before, talk with people who heard the speech in 1941, and ask them about their reactions; share your findings with your peers and compare accounts.

2.   How does Roosevelt seek to unite Americans? What sense of identity does he evoke? What themes does he dwell upon? What ethos appeals does he make? What pathos appeals?

3.   How does Roosevelt establish a sense of the enemy in his audience? What kinds of logos or other appeals does he use? How do syntax and diction reinforce the appeals? Look, for example, at his use of repetition in the series that opens "last night," at midspeech (paragraph 6).

4.   Examine the second-to-last sentence: "With confidence . . ." What effect does opening with a dependent phrase have on the emphasis in this sentence?

5.   Compare and contrast the rhetorical demands of a presidential address calling for war with an inaugural address or other presidential speech. Which type of speech do you believe would be the more difficult to write? Why?

For Writing

1.   Through library research or through taking oral histories, investigate reactions to this speech at the time it was given. You could examine newspaper commentaries and magazine articles and interview older people about their memories of the occasion. In what ways were they affected, practically and emotionally, by the address? How did the journalistic accounts of the times view the speech? Write an essay summarizing your findings.

2.   Write an essay discussing the ways in which Roosevelt seeks to unite the American people and how he develops an image of the enemy in the speech. Pay special attention to Roosevelt's use of language, syntax, and repetition.

TYPE-CASTING
1989

Paul Fussell

A native of Pasadena, California, Paul Fussell (1924–   ) earned his Ph.D. in education from Harvard University in 1952. In 1976 he won the National Book Award and National Book Critics Circle Award for The Great War and Modern Memory. *In addition to being a Fulbright lecturer and Guggenheim fellow, Fussell was a member of the U.S. Army during World War II and the recipient of two Purple Hearts. More recently, he edited* The Norton Book of Modern War *(1991). His work reflects profoundly on the effect that war has on the individual and society. The selection that follows is from* Wartime *(1989).*

"The Chinese are fine fighting men," declares one of Horatio Stubbs's fellow soldiers. "Your Chink is brought up to fight on a handful of rice a day. A Chink'll go for days on just a handful of rice."[1] [Endnotes appear at the end of this selection—*Ed.*] That's an example, if a rather low one, of the kind of cliché classifications indispensable in wartime. If war is a political, social, and psychological disaster, it is also a perceptual and rhetorical scandal from which total recovery is unlikely. Looking out upon the wartime world, soldiers and civilians alike reduce it to a simplified sketch featuring a limited series of classifications into which people, in the process dehumanized and deprived of individuality or eccentricity, are fitted. In the Second World War many more things than conscripts underwent classifications from 1-A to 4-F. The British working girl Louie, in Elizabeth Bowen's *The Heat of the Day* (1948), receives the classifications determining her vision in 1942 from the newspapers she follows devotedly:

> Was she not a worker, a soldier's lonely wife, a war orphan, a pedestrian, a Londoner, a home and animal-lover, a thinking democrat, a movie-goer, a woman of Britain, a letter-writer, a fuel-saver and a housewife?[2]

Within the soldier's world, the classifications are clearly indicated by insignia of rank and branch of service. The result is that with people, you always know what to expect. A captain of artillery will be a certain type, and so will a major in the Judge Advocate General's department, a first lieutenant of Ordnance, and an infantry staff-sergeant. You can count on it. And gazing outward toward the civilian scene, the soldierly imagination rudely consigns people to four categories:

1. The female, consisting of mother, grandmother, and sister, on the one hand, and, on the other, agents of sexual solace.
2. Elderly men, who are running the draft boards, as well as the rationing, transportation, and propaganda apparatus.
3. The infantine, who will be in the war if it lasts long enough.
4. And the most despised of categories, the 4-F or physically unfit and thus defective, the more despicable the more invisible the defect, like a heart murmur, punctured ear-drum, or flat feet.

One might think the most vigorous soldierly contempt might be directed at conscientious objectors, but no: since most of them were set to hard labor in camps, they were regarded as virtually members, if a bit disgraced, of the armed services, and their circumstances were conceived to be little more degrading than those of the troops in, say, the non-combatant quartermaster corps. That the COs endured lots of chickenshit made them like brothers. Civilians were different, more like "foreigners," indeed rather like the enemy.

For the war to be prosecuted at all, the enemy of course had to be severely dehumanized and demeaned, and in different ways, depending on different presumed national characteristics. One way of classifying the Axis enemy was to arrange it by nationalities along a scale running from courage down to cowardice. The Japanese were at the brave end, the Italians at the pusillanimous, and the Germans were in the middle. This symmetrical arrangement also implied a scale of animalism, with the Japanese accorded the most feral qualities and the Italians the most human, including a love of music, ice-cream, and ostentatious dress.

Americans detested the Japanese the most, for only they had had the effrontery to attack the United States directly, sinking ships, killing sailors, and embarrassing American pretenses to alertness and combat adequacy. They must be animals to behave thus, and cruel ones at that. "Bestial apes"—that is what Admiral William F. Halsey termed them and added the good news that "we are drowning and burning [them] all over the Pacific, and it is just as much pleasure to burn them as to drown them."[3] A marine on Guadalcanal could perceive the Japanese only as beasts of various species. He told John Hersey, "They hide up in the trees like wildcats. Sometimes when they attack, they scream like a bunch of terrified cattle in a slaughter house." Another said, "I wish we were fighting against Germans. They are human beings, like us. . . . But the Japs are like animals. . . .They take to the jungle as if they had been bred there, and like some beasts you never see them until they are dead."[4] What harm, then, in cleaning, polishing, and sending home their animal skulls as souvenirs, so that a standard snapshot depicts a soldier or marine proudly exhibiting a cleansed Japanese skull, while a poem of the period, by Winfield Townley Scott, meditates without moral comment on "The U.S. Sailor with the Japanese Skull":

> our
> Bluejacket, I mean, aged 20, in August strolled
> Among the little bodies on the sand and hunted
> Souvenirs: teeth, tags, diaries, boots; but bolder still
> Hacked off this head and under a Ginkgo tree skinned it.[5]

Then dragged it behind his ship for many days and finally scrubbed it thoroughly with lye and had a perfect souvenir. Dealing that way with the skull of a German or Italian, that is, "a white man," would be clearly inappropriate, perhaps sacrilegious. This treatment of Japanese corpses as if they were animal became so flagrant as early as September, 1942, that the Commander in Chief of the Pacific Fleet ordered that "No part of the enemy's body may be used as a souvenir. Unit Commanders will take stern disciplinary action. . . ."[6]

The civil, unbloodthirsty American sailor James J. Fahey, a Roman 5 Catholic from Waltham, Massachusetts, and a respecter of all the decencies, after a *kamikaze* attack on his ship wrote home that "one of the men on our [gun] mount got a Jap rib and cleaned it up" because "his sister wants part of a Jap body."[7] No censorious reaction whatever from Fahey, for that rib is like one you can buy in a meat market. "Oh, the inhuman brutes!" exclaimed Mrs. John Milburn, as news of Japanese behavior reached the United Kingdom.[8] Among the Allies the Japanese were also known as "jackals" or "monkey-men" or "subhumans," the term of course used by the Germans for Russians, Poles, and assorted Slavs, amply justifying their vivisection. Personnel of the United States Marine Corps sought to popularize the term *Japes* (*Japs* + *apes*), but the word never caught on, and the Japanese remained *Japs*, or, slightly less contemptuously, *Nips*. Like the *Huns* of the Great War, *Japs*—"the yellow Huns of the East," Australian General Gordon Bennett called them[9]—was a brisk monosyllable handy for slogans like "Rap the Jap" or "Let's Blast the Jap Clean Off the Map," the last a virtual prophecy of Hiroshima. It is a truism of military propaganda that monosyllabic enemies are easier to despise than others. A *kraut* or *wop* is instantly disposable in a way a German or Italian isn't quite, just as in the Great War a *boche* or a *hun* betrayed by their very names their vileness and worthlessness. Like the later *gook*. In July, 1943, a large sign on the damaged bow of the U.S. Cruiser *Honolulu* quoted Admiral Halsey urging everyone to

> Kill Japs.   Kill Japs.
> Kill More Japs.[10]

Because they were animals, Japanese troops had certain advantages over Americans. They could see in the dark, it was believed, and survive on a diet of roots and grubs. The very tiny-ness of the Japanese was another reason for contempt. They were little the way insects and rodents are little—little but nasty. In 1942, in the pamphlet *Individual Battle Doctrine*, the United States Marine Corps assured its members of Japanese combat inferiority by pointing out that "the Jap is much too short to enter the Marine Corps." One result of this puniness is that "he is really a poor bayonet fighter." Americans held in Japanese prison camps noticed the way their captors liked to get up onto something, a box, podium, platform, or stand, when haranguing the prisoners. "They loved to elevate themselves," one prisoner said.[11] Americans of standard height could understand the Japanese problem immediately as the "Runt's Complex," familiar from high school, the need of the short to "get back at" people of normal height and their customary use of guile or fraud to do so. The "sneak attack" on Pearl Harbor thus explains itself.

A rumor popular during the war told of a mother receiving a letter from her soldier son in a Japanese POW camp. He tells her that he is well and surviving OK and not to worry, and he adds that she might like to soak off the stamp on the envelope to give a friend who's a collector. When she does so, she finds written under the stamp, "THEY HAVE CUT OUT MY TONGUE." Given the notorious cruelty of the Japanese, in wartime that story could be received as entirely credible, making everyone forget that letters from captured soldiers bear no postage stamps. Typecasting assured that the Pacific War would be particularly cruel, and the cruelty was on both sides. The Japanese, as former marine E. B. Sledge says, "killed solely for the sake of killing, without hope and without higher purpose," and so did the Americans. The Japanese fired programmatically on stretcher-bearers and tortured to death Americans who fell into their hands. Sledge once encountered a group of dead marines whose bodies had been defiled, one man's penis having been sliced off and inserted in his mouth, another man's head and hands having been chopped off.[12] Similarly, the marines loved to use the few Japs who came forward to surrender as amusing rifle targets, just as they felt intense satisfaction watching them twist and writhe when set afire by the napalm of the flame-thrower. Japanese skulls were not the only desirable trophies: treasured also were Japanese gold teeth, knocked out, sometimes from the mouths of the still-living, by a USMC Ka-bar knife-hilt. During wartime it was impossible to complicate "the Japanese character" in any way, to recognize that the same auspices were behind the Bataan Death March and the Noh drama. It was not to be widely publicized that the same "types" who had bayoneted hospital patients in Hong Kong also flew out over the sea where they had sunk HMS *Repulse* and *Prince of Wales* and dropped a memorial wreath on the water. Once the war was over and the Americans were installed on the home islands as occupiers, the Japanese capacity for subtlety and delicacy could again be recognized. Then, Admiral Nimitz, doubtless with Halsey and such in mind, reminded his subordinates that "the use of insulting epithets in connection with the Japanese as a race or individuals does not now become the officers of the United States Navy."[13]

If the Japanese were type-cast as animals of an especially dwarfish but vicious species, the Germans were recognized to be human beings, but of a perverse type, cold, diagrammatic, pedantic, unimaginative, and thoroughly sinister. We had submarines, but they had U-boats. Their instinct for discipline made them especially dangerous, and their admitted distinction in technology made their cruelty uniquely effective. That it was the same people who were shooting hostages and hanging Poles and gassing Jews, on the one hand, and enjoying Beethoven and Schubert, on the other, was a complication too difficult to be faced during wartime. In March, 1942, John Steinbeck found that he had seriously misjudged the popular necessity of type-casting German troops as simply wicked. In his novella (later a play) *The Moon Is Down*, he depicted the Germans occupying a Norwegian town as human, subject like other people to emotions of love, pride, envy, and jealousy. None was characterized as an anti-Semitic monster. To his astonishment, a cascade of intellectual and moral abuse fell upon him. Artistically he may have deserved it: *The Moon Is Down* is a sort of narrative *Our Town* relocated to a wartime Continent. The story overflows with folksiness and jocosity, and the small-town scene is peopled with sentimental would-be lovable characters. But the badness of the book lies rather in its aesthetic clumsiness than in any ideological defect. As a writer dependent on popular suffrage, Steinbeck had simply not noticed that the days of light duty were past and henceforth Germans, all Germans—Wehrmacht, SS, sailors, housewives, hikers, the lot—had to be cast as confirmed enemies of human decency.

In normal times, the characteristic most often imputed to the Germans, thoroughness, would have constituted a compliment. But in wartime it was a moral defect, implying an inhuman mechanism, monotony, and rigidity. Heartless classification and analysis were considered a German specialty, and German soldiers were said to have a passion for straight lines and rigid postures. In one British theater showing a newsreel scene of German soldiers standing at exaggerated attention, someone was heard to shout, "Take t'coat hanger out then."[14] RAF bomber crews were not often deceived by decoy burning cities located five to ten miles from the actual ones because the fake fires were disposed in lines that were too straight. One photograph in Len Deighton's *Fighter* (1977) carries this legend:

> *Junkers JU 88 Bomber Crews Go to Work.* Most of the photographs . . . of the airmen, German and British . . . are strikingly alike—as the fliers pat their dogs, play chess, or relax near their aircraft—but it would be difficult to imagine RAF crews marching to their aircraft in the long rays of the early-morning sun singing as these men do.[15]

The German aircrewmen depicted there are marching in three precise files, an officer at their head, past a line-up of planes. And of course the group singing of such troops was more objectionably disciplined than that of the British or Americans could ever be. British General Sir John Hackett heard a lot of German army singing during his months as a prisoner of war, and he found himself offended by the communal abrupt "shortening of the final note of any line, as though according to a drill."[16] As a German characteristic, "thoroughness" was recognized even by the Germans. Visiting a Luftwaffe establishment in France in 1940, Josef Goebbels notes with satisfaction that it's operated with "German thoroughness," although it is "a very complex organizational machine."[17] Popular historiography especially preserves the German reputation for being foolishly "methodical." Thus Seymour Reit's *Masquerade: The Amazing Camouflage Deceptions of World War II* (1978) speaks critically of "the very methodical and systematic way" the Germans went about their visual deceptions. "Teutonic thoroughness" is the term for their technique,[18] and there is clearly something reprehensible about it.

10   While the Japanese were calumniated for being animals, the Germans were simply "sick," the very embodiment of disease. Hearing that the Germans have been manacling British prisoners of war (actually, in retaliation for the British order to handcuff prisoners taken at Dieppe), Mrs. Milburn explodes: "One can't think of anything bad enough for these diseased Germans. Their minds are all wrong."[19] Indeed, "They are like a loathsome disease spreading and spreading over Europe."[20] And a disease is what they were held to resemble in a whimsical "receipt" by which General Troy Middleton took over the town of Bastogne from the 101st Airborne Division in January, 1945.

The condition of the town was said to be "Used but Serviceable," and it was held to be "Kraut Disinfected."[21] Sick or not, the Germans were different in every way. Even their planes sounded different. Flying over England, their motors seemed to throb, sounding like "grunt-a-grunt-a-grunt-a-grunt-a." Some heard in the throbbing sound the message, "It's for you, It's for you, It's for you." One report printed in a newspaper ("ROUGED GERMAN AIRMEN") could never have been fastened on the bestial Japanese, namely, that some captured German fliers were found to have rouged cheeks, together with waved hair, lipstick, and painted finger- and toenails.[22]

Social envy and social snobbery, respectively, seem to lie behind Hitler's view of Churchill as "a superannuated drunkard supported by Jewish gold" and Churchill's view of Hitler as a "bloodthirsty guttersnipe."[23] Down below, where the troops were, the Germans had some respect for British soldiers but none for Americans. The Americans were spoiled, lazy, ignorant, unpolitical loud-mouths, and, as Goebbels put it, they seemed afflicted with "a spiritual emptiness that really makes you shake your head."[24] Few in Germany had any idea why the Americans had invaded Europe. One German officer could conclude only, as he told his interrogator, that they had attacked the Reich "in order to save Churchill and the Yews."[25] It was only their superiority in numbers, ordnance, and equipment that brought any victories to the Americans—and the British as well. High British officers privately admitted as much. Max Hastings observes of the state of Allied sensibility just before the invasion of Normandy:

> Four years of war against the Wehrmacht had convinced Britain's commanders that Allied troops should engage and could defeat their principal enemy only on the most absolutely favorable terms. Throughout the Second World War, whenever British or American troops met the Germans in anything like equal strength, the Germans prevailed.[26]

It was only wealth that tipped the scales in favor of the Allies.

A sensitive German woman, Christabel Bielenberg, accidentally came upon an American flier hidden in a room in her small town. She instantly perceived that the war was lost when she observed "the general air of health and well being, of affluence, about him." What struck her was

> the quality of the stuff his overalls were made of, his boots and the silk scarf which he had tied into his belt, and a soft leather wallet he held in one hand. Suddenly I felt shabby, old, dilapidated, and defeated. Everything he had on was so real: real wool, real leather, real silk—so real and he looked so young.[27]

German troops could often tell when the "Amis" were nearby. Their positions seemed to give off a sweet smell, probably because they smoked Virginia, rather than "Turkish" and ersatz, tobacco.

Those fighting on the same side type-cast each other just as enemies did. One reason the Italians were held in such contempt by the Germans is that they seemed to resemble the Americans, with their unmilitary concern with comfort and their lack of the sacrificial impulse. But the Italians were patronized even by the Americans. One American officer in the North African desert was outraged to hear a German prisoner, asked what he thought of the American troops he'd encountered, assert: "The Americans are to us what the Italians are to you."[28] If the Germans were sadists and bullies, the Italians were dandies motivated by both vainglory and cowardice. Popular culture had them surrendering not just en masse but pomaded and scented, accompanied by framed pictures, birdcages, and similar domestic amenities, their elegant spare uniforms neatly folded in extra suitcases and trunks. One British prisoner of the Italians who was often moved from camp to camp was astonished at the Italian understanding of the comforts appropriate to commissioned rank, even when held by an enemy. He was allowed two suitcases, a pack, a blanket roll, and a case of books. "It never seemed to worry the Italians how much kit we took," he says, "since they regarded it as quite normal for officers. Their own took thirty large trunks, mostly full of different uniforms, wherever they moved, even on active service."[29]

Since it was not until late in the war that the Allies entered France, and since by that time there was little food there, Italy, even afflicted as it was by widespread starvation, became a place where the troops' food fantasies could sometimes be realized. In Taranto in June, 1944, one British soldier had an experience he set down in his diary this way: "Wonderful meal in T. Steak—eggs—cherries—white wine—macaroni—and Marsala." He added: "We should never have fought these people."[30] The Italian reputation as the surviving custodians of the cuisine depended in part on their fame in London as waiters and chefs and restaurant owners. Many were interned in the United Kingdom to be shipped to Canada out of harm's way. When a ship carrying them, the *Arandora Star,* was torpedoed and sunk, "a number of London's most famous *restaurateurs,*" says Vera Brittain, "perished in the Atlantic."[31] Because the Italians were also associated with ice cream—making it, selling it, and eating it—British soldiers seldom let the idea of "Italians" pass through their understandings without some half-melancholy, half-contemptuous allusion to ice cream, a commodity rare in the British army. In one battalion magazine for February, 1941, a comic story, "Wops in Action," introduces its characters thus: "Alphonse and Toni were two soldiers in a crack Wop infantry regiment. On their right arms they wore three enamel ice cream cones, awarded by their C.O. for the smartest pair of heels."[32]

If the Germans were held to sing with conspicuous group disci-   15 pline, "shortening . . . the final note of any line, as though according to a drill," the Italians were likely to burst into song out of the sheer "Latin" joy of being alive, a feeling intensified beyond measure by the hazards of wartime. When Farley Mowat's unit invaded the Italian mainland near Messina, there were no Germans about, and "since the Italian troops manning the coast defenses already knew that Mussolini had fallen, they were in no mood to die heroically in a lost cause." Thus,

> as the Allied column labored upward like an attenuated khaki-colored snake, another descended parallel to it, this one bluish-green in hue. The Italian soldiers came down from the hills, not like members of a defeated army but in a mood of fiesta, marching raggedly along with their personal possessions slung about them, filling the air with laughter and song.[33]

"A lot of opera singers" was Roosevelt's characterization of resident Italian aliens as he decided not to intern them in 1942.[34] And speaking of the association between wartime and cliché, *"O Sole Mio"* was the song actually being sung when Edward Blishen saw a group of Italian prisoners in England for the first time,[35] while some of the British in North Africa maintained that it was "to the strains of *Aida*" that the Italians planned to march triumphantly into Egypt. Says Tanker H. L. Sykes, "We actually found the music, the instruments, and the ceremonial dress they intended to use."[36]

When in the earlier war Frederic Henry, in Hemingway's *A Farewell to Arms* (1929), feels some guilt about deserting, Catherine Barkley comforts him by reminding him that "It's only the Italian army."[37] This myth of Italian military haplessness served a useful psychological function in the Second World War, helping secretly to define what Allied soldiers wanted the "enemy" universally to be—pacifists, dandies, sensitive and civilized non-ideologues, even clowns. The antithesis of committed, fanatic National Socialists. At the same time the Italians could serve as the definition of incompetence, fraudulence, and cowardice: no one really wanted to be like them to be sure, but how everyone wished it were possible! The world was laughing at Italy, and yet the Italians were sensibly declining to be murdered. The Allied soldier couldn't help wondering that if contempt and ridicule are the price of staying alive, perhaps the price is worth paying. While constituting one of the war's most simple-minded clichés, the Italians thus posed a challenge to cliché, shaking up and complicating the standard uncomplex attitude toward "the enemy." It was their presence in the war that kept a degree of ambiguity and paradox alive in a wartime world of stark and easily dealt-with oppositions. Were the Italians properly sized up by ridicule, as in the popular London dance-step The Tuscana ("based on the Italians' way of fighting, . . . one step forward, two steps back")?[38] Was A. P. Herbert right to refer to Mussolini on the BBC as "the Top Wop"? Or were they a serious enemy, more correctly treated respectfully? One who fought them, Peter Cochrane, in his book *Charlie Company* (1977), praises their courage, flair, and discipline, and goes out of his way to celebrate Italian skill in road engineering and artillery ranging and to note Italian compassion toward wounded prisoners. Is that the correct view? Or did General Montgomery have the right attitude when he told the troops preparing to invade Sicily,

> "Someone said to me a few days ago that the Italians are really decent people and that if we treat them properly they will come over to us. I disagree with him. Our job is to kill them. That is what we have to do. Once we have killed them we can see if they are good fellows or not. But they must be killed first."[39]

Whatever the Italians actually were, the myth that they were the sweetest people in the war survives. The cover illustration of the American magazine *Men Today* for July, 1963, depicts a scene from one of the sadoerotic narratives within. Two girls are busy torturing an American soldier of the Second World War. He is tied to a chair. One girl, dressed in tight blouse and short shorts, is playing a blowtorch over his chest. The other looks on, coiled whip at the ready. The first girl is shouting, "Scream for my kisses, Amerikaner Soldat!" She wears a swastika armband. The other girl wears a German officer's jacket and cap.[40] The Italian wartime image becomes doubly clear if one tries to imagine the insignia and trappings of Italian fascism used with significations like these. They would produce not a frisson or even an erection but a laugh.

The force and to a degree the validity of wartime type-casting can be appreciated by trying to imagine German troops crawling on their stomachs through the malarial jungles of the South Pacific. Just as hard to conceive as Japanese soldiers defending the Apennines from behind mountain barricades built up from stones or determined Italian youths resisting to the death the American assault on the Rhine or the Russian assault on Berlin. Each enemy has taken on the characteristics of his primary geography, both literal and otherwise, and it is impossible to imagine them any other way. Similarly it is impossible to believe about one enemy what it is easy to believe about another. For example: according to Captain M. J. Brown, British troops once came upon a highly desirable billet abandoned by the Germans whose front door was invitingly half-open. Entering cautiously through a window to avoid the likely booby-trap, they approached the front door from inside and found attached to it the expected explosive charge set to go off when the door was moved. They left the house carefully and tied a string to the outside knob of the front door, taking cover in a slit-trench across the road. When they were all in the slit-trench, they pulled the string and the slit-trench exploded, killing them all. "The layer of the trap had anticipated their process of reasoning," notes Captain Brown, "step by step."[41] The Japanese would probably not think such a caper funny enough to be worthwhile. The Italians would, but would be too "unmethodical" to set it up efficiently. The Americans and British would like the idea but would be too lazy to waste time on it. But assigned to the Germans, the story, apocryphal as it may be, rings true.

And although a whole book could be devoted to the sort of stereotyping necessary for Americans (and British) to see themselves as attractive, moral, and exemplary, some of the conventions can be noted briefly. A good way to get a feel for the subject would be to go through any number of *Life* magazine, or *Look,* or *Collier's,* or *The Saturday Evening Post* issued from 1942 to 1945. Attending to the display advertisements, mostly in color, one would immediately understand the wartime thrill Americans achieved by imagining themselves good-looking Aryans, blond and tall, beloved by slim blonde women and surrounded by much-desired consumer goods. If the illustrations are to be believed, all young men are in the Air Corps, where they are officers almost by definition (or, in 1942, cadets destined soon to be officers). If by some misfortune they are in any other part of the army, they are almost never privates or NCOs but young officers beaming on their fiancée's assiduity in accumulating flatware of International Sterling. Notable is the absence of any features which might be interpreted as Jewish, or Central European, or in any remote way "Colored." The people on whose behalf the war is being fought are Anglo-Saxons, "nice people"—that is, upper-middle class. Readers of these advertisements could not help inferring that the war was designed primarily to defend and advance the interests of such tall, clean blonds, as well as the suppliers of the cars, tires, and refrigerators the blonds will own and exhibit once the war is won. If the Jews, like those in New York, liked to think the war was in some way about them, it's clear that most people didn't want to be like them in any way or even reminded of them. You could spend your life studying the magazine ads of wartime without once coming upon a yarmulkah or prayer shawl, or even features suggestive of Jewishness. Philip Roth's Alexander Portnoy, too young for the war but not too young to associate himself with the thrill of being on the winning and the righteous side, conceives of it as entirely an upper-middle-class Anglophile-American victory, less about the right to wear phylacteries than argyle socks and loafers.

The advertising artists sometimes had to face facts and recognize that many of those fighting the Axis were, regrettably, quite unromantic enlisted men, but such are generally depicted without women and usually alone, unwrapping a gift watch sent by the folks, celebrating the possession of a candy bar ("Boy! I'm strong for Milky Ways"), enjoying being included at a strange family's dinner table at Thanksgiving, waiting to board a train which, it is to be hoped, is not already full of idle civilians, or delighting in the Chelsea cigarettes included in a K-ration. The man shown in bed enjoying the luxury of Pacific Sheets is a Pfc., not an officer, because he is alone. Yawning and stretching in an ad in *Life* in February, 1945, he thinks, "'Hallelujah, what a day is coming! A day when a fellow can drop his gear in his tracks, climb into a real bed as soft as a marshmallow, and s-t-r-e-t-c-h every last muscle! A day when he can feel again the caress of sleek, soft, white Pacific Sheets against his tired body.'" But when women enter, the male models get promoted instantly to officer rank, and their looks improve, too. Thus the woman enjoying a Honeymoon in Mexico on behalf of DuBarry Beauty Preparations is attended by her young naval-officer husband in whites. A young woman fortunate enough to have found a lover who appreciates the benefits of an extremely smooth Barbasol Shave is doubly blessed, for he is also an officer (branch of service not revealed). One young woman appearing on behalf of a brand of woolen goods is being met at her front door at a snowy Christmastime by a young man in a sleigh bearing a Christmas tree. At first glance he seems to be wearing an enlisted soldier's rough overcoat, but the ad-man has saved the day by remembering to affix a gold bar to his shoulder. Another young woman, lonely, has been left behind as a result of Rough Hands, but in the background wiser women who have learned to use Campana Balm swarm past in crowds, each with her date: only two are servicemen, but one is a naval ensign, the other a commissioned Air Corps pilot. If an enlisted man must be depicted in close proximity to a desirable woman, as in one ad for Chesterfield cigarettes, the situation can be salvaged by displaying on his shoulder the insignia ("patch") not, surely, of the 3rd Armored Division but of the United States Army Air Corps. In fiction or film, the GI might be Jewish or Italian, Polish or Hispanic or "Colored," but never in advertising, a medium where only ideal imagery can be allowed to enter. In advertising, the Allied war is fought by white Anglo-Saxons, officers or aviators, with neat, short hair, clear eyes, gleaming teeth, and well-defined jawlines. That is the wartime "we," fighting against the beast-like yellow-skinned Japanese, the "sick" Germans, and the preposterous Italians. Naturally we won. As Admiral

Halsey said in his victory message to his fleet when the Japanese surrendered, "The forces of righteousness and decency have triumphed."[42]

Endnotes

1. *A Soldier Erect, or Further Adventures of the Hand-Reared Boy* (London, 1971).
2. (New York, 1948 [1979]), 134.
3. Dwight Macdonald, *Memoirs of a Revolutionist: Essays in Political Criticism* (New York, 1957), 93.
4. *Into the Valley* (New York, 1943), 20, 56.
5. *Collected Poems: 1937–1962* (New York, 1962), 121.
6. Samuel Cosman Papers, U.S. Marine Corps Historical Center, Washington, D.C.
7. James Fahey, *Pacific War Diary* (New York, 1963), 231.
8. Peter Donnelly, ed., *Mrs. Milburn's Diaries: An Englishwoman's Day-to-Day Reflections, 1939–1945* (London, 1979 [1980]), 248.
9. *Why Singapore Fell* (Bombay, 1945), 58.
10. John W. Dower, *War Without Mercy: Race and Power in the Pacific War* (New York, 1986), 36.
11. Donald Knox, *Death March* (New York, 1981), 364.
12. *With the Old Breed* (Novato, Calif., 1981), 142, 148.
13. John Costello, *The Pacific War* (New York, 1981), 616.
14. Norman Longmate, *How We Lived Then* (London, 1971), 404.
15. No. 51, between pp. 248–49.
16. *I Was a Stranger* (London, 1977 [1979]), 74–75.
17. Fred Taylor, ed., *The Goebbels Diaries, 1939–1941* (New York, 1983), 148.
18. (1980), 5, 148.
19. Donnelly, *Mrs. Milburn's Diaries*, 216.
20. *Ibid.*, 185.
21. Napier Crookenden, *The Battle of the Bulge* (New York, 1980), 124.
22. Arthur Marshall, "Odd Man In," *New Statesman*, Nov. 21, 1980, p. 15.
23. John Strawson, *Hitler's Battles for Europe* (New York, 1971), 113.
24. Louis Lochner, ed., *The Goebbels Diaries, 1942–1943* (Garden City, N.Y., 1948), 317.
25. Franklyn Johnson, *One More Hill* (New York, 1949), 157.
26. Hastings, *Overlord* (New York, 1984), 24.
27. *The Past Is Myself* (London, 1970), 148.
28. M. J. Brown, Diary, IWM.
29. Anthony Deane-Drummond, *Return Ticket* (London, 1953 [1967]), 82.
30. Oliver Carpenter, Diary, IWM.
31. *Testament of Experience*, 258.
32. C. C. Rand, *The Ordinary Fellow* (Magazine of the 1st Bn., London Irish Rifles), I, #5, 54–55.
33. *And No Birds Sang* (Boston, 1979), 143.
34. James MacGregor Burns, *Roosevelt: The Soldier of Freedom* (New York, 1970), 214.
35. Edward Blishen, *A Cackhanded War* (London, 1972), 119.
36. Memoir, IWM.
37. (New York, 1929), 260.
38. Longmate, *How We Lived Then*, 422.
39. Neil McCallum, *Journey with a Pistol* (London, 1959), 145.
40. Gillian Freeman, *The Undergrowth of Literature* (London, 1967), facing p. 86.
41. Diary, IWM.
42. E. B. Potter, *Bull Halsey* (Annapolis, Md., 1985), 348.

For Journals

Write about some common stereotypes that you are aware of and the ways in which they are depicted in film, paintings, advertisements, posters, or other media.

For Discussion

1. In view of Fussell's essay, discuss some kinds of typecasting or stereotyping that are familiar to you.

2. In what ways is constructing an "other," especially an enemy, similar to or different from the process of establishing a national identity? Review the readings in Chapter 3 as needed.

3. Fussell's preface to the book *Wartime,* from which this excerpt is taken, notes that the book is about "the rationalizations and euphemisms people needed to deal with an unacceptable actuality from 1939 to 1945." Does Fussell achieve his purpose of exposing such rationalizations and euphemism?

4. In what ways, according to Fussell, are people "dehumanized and deprived of individuality" in wartime? Examine this claim, citing specific examples you find especially convincing.

5. Identify and analyze some of the metaphors used to stereotype different nationalities during World War II. From your own observation and experience, are any of these stereotypes still in popular use?

6. Contrast other nation's impressions of American soldiers in World War II with impressions you may have already gained from American popular culture—films, photographs, books and the like, or from family narratives.

For Writing

1. Follow Fussell's suggestion and research American popular magazines published during World War II—*Life* or *Time,* for example. You will find collections in your college library or in a public library, and you may need to work with microfilm or microfiche. A local historian may have information to share. Browse through a number of magazines, taking notes on what you see, particularly in the advertisements, but also reading editorials and letters to the editor as they seem relevant. Develop an essay based on your findings, focusing on some theme or aspect of your findings and supporting your core assertion with examples from your research.

2. Interview people who lived during World War II about their perceptions of the enemy during the war.

SAIGON EXECUTION

1969

Edward T. Adams

This photograph (on the next page) became one of the most famous im-ages of the Vietnam War. Colonel Nguyen Ngoc Loan, South Vietnam's po-lice chief, executes a Vietcong suspect in Saigon. The filmed version of this execution was shown on television all over the world. Adams's photograph won the Pulitzer Prize for News Photography in 1969.

For Journal Writing

Describe the visual images that come to mind when you think of the Vietnam War.

For Discussion

1. Analyze the photograph. What is emphasized? Whose face is more visible, and how does that visibility affect how you react to the photo-graph? How are the respective figures dressed? Where are their hands? What do these details tell you about the relative power of each man? How do such elements of the photograph contribute to your logical, ethical, and emotional reactions to the image?

2. In what ways is this sort of event expected in wartime? In what ways is it surprising?

3. What effects would this photograph have on Americans' percep-tions of their "friends" and "enemies" during the war?

For Writing

1. What impact do you think that this photograph, and others like it, may have had on the American public and their perception of the Viet-nam War?

2. Research the Vietnam War in pictures and photographs, and see if you can discern changes over time in the ways in which the war was covered in the popular print media.

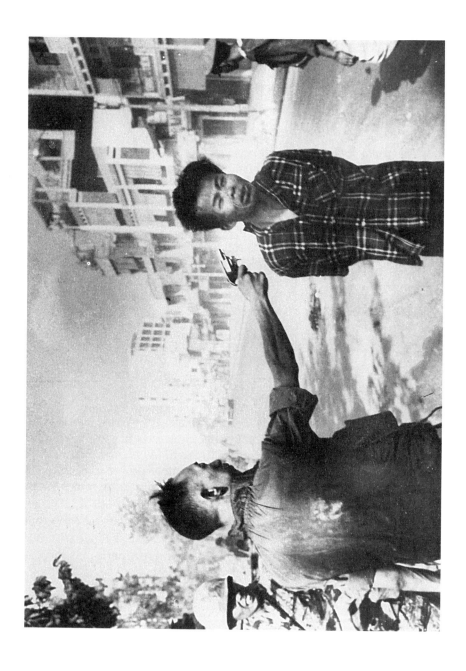

THE TERROR OF WAR
1973

Huynh Cong "Nick" Ut

This photograph (on the next page), taken by Associated Press photographer Huynh Cong "Nick" Ut, brought with it the horrifying realization of the many civilian participants in, and victims of, the war in Vietnam. Napalm, a gel developed in World War II, was used widely in Vietnam in flame throwers and incendiary bombs; it burns hotly and rather slowly and sticks to its target. The children pictured were apparently the victims of napalm bombs dropped by the South Vietnamese air force. This photograph won the Pulitzer Prize for News Photography in 1973.

For Journals

Think about the truism that a picture is worth a thousand words. Do you agree?

For Discussion

1.   What are your immediate reactions to the photograph? Do you respond primarily on an emotional or intellectual level? What does your response tell you about the power of an image?

2.   Examine the composition and content of the photograph. What is being conveyed? Do you find it more reportorial or persuasive? Of what might a viewer of this photograph be persuaded?

3.   Who are the primary victims of war? To what extent do you think they are represented in war images? Do you think the image in the next photograph is more, or less, persuasive than images of young American men on the battlefield? Explain.

For Writing

1.   Write a report describing the event portrayed in this essay, using precise, concrete language. Then, in view of your journal entry, analyze the relative power of visual images and language.

2.   Talk with people who remember the Vietnam War, and ask them about whom they perceived as America's friends and enemies during that war. Analyze the ways in which this photograph confirms or contradicts what you learned from your interviewees.

NURSES IN VIETNAM
1987

Jacqueline Navarra Rhoads

Jacqueline Navarra Rhoads was born in 1948 in Albion, New York, resided for some time in San Antonio, and now lives in Albuquerque, New Mexico, where she is on the nursing faculty of the University of New Mexico. She served as an army nurse in Vietnam in 1970–1971 and spent most of her tour with the 18th Surgical Hospital in Quang Tri. Her personal account of her tour focuses the politically charged conflict on a personal level, dealing with both the pain and exhilaration of her work and the long-term effects it has had on her life.

We arrived in Vietnam on April 26, 1970, right in the middle of a rocket attack. We were ordered off the plane and everyone was supposed to lay down on the ground. So here I am with my dress uniform, stockings, shoes, and skirt, and suddenly I'm lying down on a cement pavement at Tan Son Nhut wondering, "My God, what did I get myself into?" The noise was so deafening. The heat—I remember how hot it was. We eventually got inside this terminal building where there were all these guys waiting to get on the plane to go home. They were whooping it up, running around with signs saying things like: "Only one hour and thirty-five minutes left!" They saw us coming and one of them said, "Cheer up, the worst is yet to come." We stayed there sixteen hours before we could get out. When we got on the bus, all the windows were screened. I learned from the bus driver that this was to prevent the Vietnamese from throwing grenades in through the windows. I said, "But I thought the enemy was up north somewhere." He told me, "No, the enemy is all around you here. You never know who you're fighting."

My first assignment was in Phu Bai. I was there for thirty days because they needed some emergency room nurses there. Then I was transferred to the 18th Surgical Hospital in Quang Tri, just a few miles from the DMZ. They had just put a MUST (Medical Unit Self-Transportable) unit in there from Camp Evans and they needed operating and emergency room nurses right away. I was there the remainder of my tour.

I was a very young twenty-one. At St. Mary's School of Nursing in Rochester (New York), I kept these Army recruiting posters all over my room. There was a big push at that time for nurses, and we had recruiters coming to the school constantly from the time I started in 1966. I don't know what it was, I loved nursing so much. I always thought—I know it sounds crazy—but I wanted to do something for my country. I just had a feeling that being a nurse in the Army was what I wanted to do. And of course my uncles were all in the Army in World War II. There were nine brothers in my mother's family, and they all went into the Army within six months of each other.

Everyone thought I was crazy. I remember my mother saying, "Jacque, do you know what you're getting yourself into?" Of course, when you're young you have no fear.

5   I did basic training at Fort Sam Houston in San Antonio. My main memory of that time is the parties, big parties. I never took basic training very seriously. It was only later I realized that I should have. What to do in case of a nuclear attack, what to do for chemical warfare, how to handle a weapon—these were things we laughed at. We went out to Camp Bullis and shot weapons, but as nurses we never thought that shooting a weapon was something we needed to know. True, we never had to fire weapons, but we had wounded who came in with weapons as splints, and they were loaded weapons. When that happened, I thought, "Why didn't I listen when they taught us how to take this weapon apart?" You know, an M-16 with a full magazine. We had a young guy come in, he had a grenade with the pin pulled wrapped in a handkerchief and stuffed into his fatigue pocket, a live grenade! I thought, "Gosh, if only I had listened."

I think the practice village out where we trained at Camp Bullis is still in existence. The bamboo sticks smeared with excrement, they were authentic. There was an instructor in black pajamas, camouflage makeup on his face. Well, we kind of laughed. We didn't take it seriously until we started seeing these kinds of injuries in Vietnam.

My first real exposure to the war came five days after I landed. It was at Phu Bai. We received twenty-five body bags in on this giant Chinook helicopter. You know, the Chinook is this great big helicopter, this two-blade deal that can carry one hundred to one hundred and fifty people. And this Chinook came in with twenty-five body bags aboard. One of the nurses' responsibilities was to look inside these body bags to determine cause of death. Of course, they couldn't release the doctors for such trivial work. What you had to do was open the bag, look inside and see what possibly could have killed this person, and then write down on the tag what you felt the cause of death was. It was so obvious most of the time. That's something I still have flashbacks about—unzipping those bags. It was my first exposure to maggots, something I had never seen before in my life.

One was a young guy who had had his face blown away, with

hundreds of maggots eating away where his face used to be. Another one, he had his eyes wide open. He was staring up at me. I remember he had a large hole in his chest and I knew it was a gunshot wound or a grenade injury. It had blown his heart, his lungs, everything to shreds. He had nothing left but a rib cage. Evidently, they had lain out on the ground awhile before someone could get to them. The corps-men were told to take care of the wounded first, instead of spending time getting the dead in the bags. There were GIs exposed to flame throwers or gas explosions. We used to call them "crispy critters" to keep from getting depressed. They'd come in and there would be nothing more than this shell of a person. That was a little easier to take, they didn't have a face. It could have been an animal's carcass for all you knew. But to have to go looking for the dog tags, to find the dog tags on a person, that bothered me. I remember the first time I looked in a body bag I shook so badly. One of the doctors was kind enough to help me through it, saying, "Come on, it's your duty and you're going to have to do this. It's just something that I'm going to help you through. It's just a dead person." It was such a close-knit group. We were considered the most beautiful women in the world. The guys treated us special. You could have been the ugliest woman in the world, but still you were treated special.

The mass-cal, that's mass-casualty situation, traditionally was anything more than ten or fifteen wounded. It was mass chaos, bordering on panic. There'd be a corpsman walking around saying, "Dust off just called and they're bringing in twenty-five wounded. Everybody get going." So we'd pull out all our supplies. The nurses would put extra tourniquets around their necks to get ready to clamp off blood vessels. The stretchers were all prepared, and we'd go down each row hanging IVs all plugged and ready to go. It was mass production. You'd start the IVs on those people where the doctor was able to say, "This one is saved, this one is saved." We put them in triage categories. The expectant ones were the ones who required too much care. We'd make them comfortable and allow them to die. I guess it was making us comfortable too.

I remember this guy named Cliff, a triple amputee we once had. 10 He came in with mast-trousers on. Mast-trousers is an apparatus you inflate that puts pressure on the lower half of your body to allow adequate blood flow to your heart and brain. When Cliff came in, he was conscious, which was amazing. He looked like a stage dummy who'd been thrown haphazardly in a pile. One of his legs was up underneath his chin so that he was able to look down at the underside of his foot. His left arm was twisted behind his head in a horrible way. We couldn't even locate his second leg. He had stepped on a land mine. With his legs that bad, we knew there probably wasn't much backbone left. He was alive because of these trousers. The corpsman must have been right there when he got wounded. He had put him in this bag and inflated it. Cliff should have been dead.

It was really funny because he looked at two of us nurses there and said, "God, I think I've died and gone to heaven . . . a round-eye, an American, you look so beautiful." He was so concerned about the way he looked because of us standing there, "Gee, I must look a mess." But he was alert, he knew where he was. "Doc, take good care of me. I know my leg is pretty bad because I can see it, but take good care of me, doc." The docs couldn't put him in the expectant category and give him morphine to make him comfortable, because he was too alert. The docs had trouble letting go. So one of them finally said, "Well, let's get him into the operating room, deflate the bag, and let's get in there and see if we can't do something."

Well, we knew just by looking at him in that condition that he wasn't going to last, that as soon as we deflated the bag he'd bleed to death in a matter of seconds. Somehow, he knew it too. I remember I was getting blood prepared for him. He called me from across the room, "Jacque, come here quick." I went over to him and said, "What's the matter Cliff, what's wrong?" He said, "Just hold my hand and don't leave me." I said, "Why, Cliff? Are you in pain?" We always worried about pain, alleviating pain. We'd do anything to alleviate pain. He said, "I think I'm going to die and I don't want to be alone." So I stood there crying, with him holding my hand. And when we deflated the trousers, we lost him in seconds. We found no backbone, no lower part of his body. Really, he had been cut in half.

The leg that was folded underneath his neck was completely severed from his body. It was just there. The corpsmen had evidently bundled him together into the bag hoping maybe something would be there that was salvageable. And he just died. I remember he had blond hair, blue eyes—cute as a button. I had to take his body myself to graves registration. I just couldn't let him go alone. I just couldn't do that. I had to pry my hand away from his hand, because he had held on to my hand so tightly. I had to follow him to graves registration and put him in the bag myself. I couldn't let go of him. It was something I had to do.

Usually the expectants had massive head injuries. They were practically gone, they couldn't communicate with you. You were supposed to clean them up, call the chaplain. You did all that stuff, I guess, to make you feel as though you were helping them. To preserve their lives, you would've had to put them on a respirator and evac them to a neuro facility, which in our case would have been all the way to Da Nang, which was hours, miles away. I was an operating room nurse, but when there was a mass-cal, since there were only twelve of us, we'd be called into triage to work there. After that, I'd follow them into the operating room and help do the surgery. A lot of the shrapnel extractions we'd do ourselves, and a lot of the closures too. The docs would say, "Why don't you close? I got this next case in the next room." You didn't have to worry about it too much, if you got into trouble he'd be right there next door.

We wanted to save everyone. We had a lot of ARVNs (Army of the   15 Republic of Vietnam), we called them "Marvin the ARVN." We tried to take care of the Americans first, but we also had to take care of who-ever needed care—period, whether he was a Vietnamese, a POW, or whatever. In fact, when we tried to save Cliff, they brought in the Viet-namese who had laid the mine. He had an amputation. He was bleed-ing badly and had to be treated right away. And we saved him. I guess in my heart I felt angry about what happened.

We were short on anesthesia and supplies. And we were giving anesthesia to this POW, which made me angry because I thought, "What if—what happens if someone comes in like Cliff and we don't have any anesthesia left because we gave it all to this POW?" Again, because I was very strongly Catholic, as soon as I heard myself think-ing this, I thought, "God, how can you think that? The tables could be turned, and what if it was Cliff in the POW's place, and how would I feel if he received no anesthesia simply because he was an enemy?" First of all, it shocked me and embarrassed me. It made me think, "Gosh, I'm losing my values, what's happened to me?" I had been taught in nursing school to save everybody regardless of race, creed, color, ethnic background, whatever. Life is life. But suddenly I wasn't thinking that anymore. I was thinking, "I'm American, and they're the enemy. Kill the enemy and save the American."

Before I went to Vietnam, I was kind of bubbly, excited about life. I haven't changed that much really, I'm still that way. But back then, suddenly, I began questioning things, wondering about what we were doing there. I remember talking with the chaplain, saying, "What are we doing? For what purpose are we here?" We were training Viet-namese helicopter pilots to go out and pick up their wounded and take them to their hospitals. And we treated plenty of them at our hospitals, too. Yet when we'd call up and say, "We got a wounded soldier in Timbuktu," they'd say, "It's five o'clock and we don't fly at night." We had soldiers in the hospital shot by ten-year-old boys and girls. We had women who'd invite GIs to dinner—nice women—and they'd have someone come out from behind a curtain and shoot them all down dead. I mean, what kind of war was this?

The chaplain told me, "Hey Jacque, you can't condemn the Ameri-can government. We can't say the American government is wrong to put us in this position here. We can't say, because there is so much we don't know." It was good advice at the time, it really helped me. I was thinking, "Here I am judging, and I'm saying what the heck are we doing here, look at all these lives lost, all these young boys and for what? And who am I to judge that? There has to be a reason." I guess I'm still trying to hold on to that belief, even though people laugh at me when I say it. They think I'm living in a dream world because I'm hoping there was a good reason.

I didn't really have much time to worry about right and wrong back then, because during these mass-cals we'd be up for thirty-six hours at a stretch. Nobody wanted to quit until the last surgery case was stabilized. By that time, we were emotionally and physically numb. You couldn't see clearly, you couldn't react. Sounds were distant. We kind of policed each other. When we saw each other reacting strangely or slowly, we'd say, "Hey, Jacque, get some sleep, someone will cover, go get some sleep." That's how close we were. That's how we coped with stress.

20   You didn't have time to think about how unhappy you were. It was afterwards, when you couldn't go to sleep . . . here you were without sleep for thirty-six hours, lying in your bed expecting sleep to overwhelm you, but you couldn't fall asleep because you were so tensed and stressed from what you saw. I knew I had a problem the day I was with a nurse I was training who was going to replace someone else. I remember I had completed this amputation and I had the soldier's leg under my arm. I was holding the leg because I had to dress it up and give it to graves registration. They'd handle all the severed limbs in a respectful manner. They wouldn't just throw them in the garbage pile and burn them. They were specially labeled and handled the good old government way.

I remember this nurse came in and she was scheduled to take the place of another nurse. When she saw me, I went to greet her and I had this leg under my arm. She collapsed on the ground in a dead faint. I thought, "What could possibly be wrong with her?" There I was trying to figure out what's wrong with her, not realizing that here I had this leg with a combat boot still on and half this man's combat fatigue still on, blood dripping over the exposed end. And I had no idea this might bother her.

We had a lot of big parties, too. The Army had all these rules about fraternization, how officers couldn't fraternize with enlisted. In Quang Tri, we were just one big family. You didn't worry about who had an E-2 stripe or who had the colonel's insignia. I'm not saying we didn't have problems with officers and enlisted people or things like insubordination. But everybody partied together.

I never had a sexual relationship over there. You have to remember how Catholic I was. Dating, well, you'd walk around bunkers and talk about home. Every hooch had a bunker, so you'd bring a bottle of wine and he'd bring glasses and—this sounds gross, I guess—you'd sit and watch the B-52s bomb across the DMZ. It produced this northern lights effect. The sky would light up in different colors and you'd sit and watch the fireworks. I know it sounds strange, watching somebody's village get blown up. We didn't want to think about the lives being lost.

The grunts always knew where the female nurses were. They all knew that at the hospital there was a good chance of seeing a "round-eye." Once, during monsoon season, we received a dust off call saying there'd been a truck convoy ambush involving forty or fifty guys. They were in bad shape but not far from the hospital, maybe seven or eight miles. We could stand on the tops of our bunkers and see flashes of light from where they were fighting the VC. One of these deuce-and-a-half trucks with a load of wounded came barreling up right into our triage area. Like I said, they all knew where the hospital was. The truck's canvas and wood back part were all on fire. Evidently they had just thrown the wounded in back and driven straight for us.

We were concerned about the truck, about getting it out of the way, but we were also trying to get to the wounded. There were two guys in the back, standing up. There was a third guy we couldn't see, and the first two were carrying him and shrieking at the top of their lungs. One was holding the upper part of his torso, under the arms, and the other held the legs. Their eyes were wild and they were screaming. I couldn't see what was wrong with the guy they were carrying. Everyone else on the truck was jumping off. We were shouting to these guys to get off too, that the truck was about to explode. We were screaming, "You're OK, you're at the hospital."

Two of the corpsmen got up in the truck, grabbing them to let go and get moving. The corpsmen literally had to pick them up and throw them off the truck. Once they were off, they sat down in a heap, still shrieking. It wasn't until then that I got a look at the wounded one. He didn't have a head. He must have been a buddy of theirs. The buddy system was very strong, and these two evidently weren't going to leave without their friend. We brought them to the docs and had them sedated. We didn't have any psychiatric facilities, so we got them evac'd to Da Nang. We never heard what happened to them.

After awhile in Vietnam, I guess I wasn't so young anymore. I was seeing things, doing things that I never imagined could happen to anyone. I had to do a lot of things on my own, making snap decisions that could end up saving someone or costing him his life. Like once, when

I'd been there about seven months, they brought in this guy who'd been shot square in the face. It was the middle of the night and I was on duty with a medical corpsmen, no doctors around at all. They were sleeping, saving their strength. We got the call from dust off that this guy was coming in. Apparently he'd been shot by a sniper. Amazingly enough, he was conscious when they brought him in. As a matter of fact, he was sitting up on the stretcher. It was incredible.

His face was a huge hole, covered with blood. You couldn't see his eyes, his nose, or his mouth. There was no support for his jaw and his tongue was just hanging. You could hear the sound of blood gurgling as he took a breath, which meant he was taking blood into his lungs. We were afraid he'd aspirate. The corpsman was this older guy, over 40 anyway, an experienced sergeant. I took a look at this guy and knew we'd have to do a trach on him pretty fast. He couldn't hear us and we couldn't get him to lie down.

I told the sergeant, "We gotta call the doc in." He told me we didn't have time for that. We had to stabilize him with a trach and ship him out to Da Nang. I told the corpsman that the only time I'd ever done a trach was on a goat back in basic training at Fort Sam Houston. The corpsman said, "If you don't do it, he'll die." So he put my gloves on for me, and handed me the scalpel. I was shaking so badly I thought I'd cut his throat. I remember making the incision, and hearing him cough. The blood came out of the hole, he was coughing out everything he was breathing in. The drops flew into my eyes, spotting my contact lenses. After the blood finished spurting out, we slid the tube in. He laid back and I worried, "What's going on?"

30   But he was breathing. He didn't have to fight or struggle for breath anymore. I could see the air was escaping from the trach, just like it was supposed to. It was a beautiful feeling, believe me. We packed his face with four-by-fours and roller gauze to stop the bleeding. We told him what we were doing and he nodded his head. When they finally loaded him up for the trip to Da Nang, I was shaking pretty badly. The whole thing had taken less than forty-five minutes, from the time dust off landed to the time we packed him off. We never did get his name.

But three months later, I was sitting in the mess hall in Da Nang, waiting to take a C-130 to Hong Kong for R&R. I'd been in country ten months by then, and I was in the mess hall alone, drinking coffee and eating lunch, still in my fatigues. Somebody tapped me on the shoulder. I remember turning around. You have to remember, I was used to guys being friendly. I saw this guy standing there in hospital pajamas, the green-gray kind with the medical corps insignia on it. He had blond hair on the sides, bald on top. His face was a mass of scars, and you could see the outline of a jaw and chin. He had lips and a mouth, but no teeth. He looked like he had been badly burned, with a lot of scar tissue. You couldn't really tell where his lips began and the scar tissue ended.

The rest of his body was fine, and he could talk. "Do you remember me?" I was used to that, too, people coming up to me and saying, "Hey, I drove that tank by you the other day. . . ." Then he pointed to his trach scar and I said, "You can't be the same guy." He said something like, "I'll never forget you." I asked him how he knew who I was, because, I mean, there had been nothing left of his face. Apparently, the shot had flipped this skin flap up over his eyes so he could still see through the corners. I couldn't believe it. They called my flight right then, so I started saying a hasty goodbye. He mumbled something about how they had taken his ribs from his ribcage and artificially made a jawbone, and reconstructed portions of his face, taking skin from the lower legs, the buttocks.

Well, they began calling my name over the loud speaker. I remember giving him a big hug, saying I wished I had more time to talk to him. I wanted to learn his name, but I don't think he ever said it. I wanted to go back to the hospital and tell the others, "Hey, you remember what's-his-name? He's from Arkansas and he's doing fine." We always wanted to put names to faces, but we rarely got a chance to do it. You kept believing that everyone who left the hospital actually lived. When you found out someone actually had survived, it helped staff morale.

I came back home on a Friday, on a Pan American flight that landed in Seattle. I remember how we were told not to wear our uniforms, not to go out into the streets with our uniforms on. That made us feel worthless. There was no welcome home, not even from the Army people who processed your papers to terminate your time in the service. That was something. I felt like I had just lost my best friend. I decided to fly home to upstate New York in my uniform anyway. Nobody said anything. There were no dirty looks or comments. I was kind of excited. I wanted to say to people, "I just got back from Vietnam." Nobody cared. When I got home, my parents had a big banner strung up across the garage, "Welcome Home, Jacque." But that was about it. My parents were proud of me, of course. But other civilians? "Oh, you were in Vietnam? That's right, I remember reading something in the newspaper about you going there. That's nice." And then they'd go on talking about something else.

You were hungry to talk about it. You wanted so badly to say, "Gee, don't you want to hear about what's going on there, and what we did, and how proud you should be of your soldiers and your nurses and your doctors?" I expected them to be waiting there, waving the flag. I remember all those films of World War II, with the tape that flew from the buildings in New York City, the motorcades. Of course, I had my mother. My mom was always willing to listen, but of course she couldn't understand it when I started talking about "frag wounds" or "claymore mines." There was no way she could.

The first six months at home, I just wanted to go back to Vietnam. I wanted to go back to where I was needed, where I felt important. The first job I took was in San Francisco. It was awful. Nobody cared who I was. I remember the trouble I got into because I was doing more than a nurse was supposed to do. I got in trouble because I was a "mini-doctor." They kept saying, "You're acting like you're a doctor! You're doing all these things a doctor is supposed to do. What's the big idea? You're a nurse, not a doctor." And I thought, how can I forget all the stuff I learned—putting in chest tubes, doing trachs. True, doctors only do that, but how do you prevent yourself from doing things that came automatically to you for eighteen months? How do you stop the wheels, and become the kind of nurse you were before you left?

I was completely different. Even my parents didn't recognize me as the immature little girl who left Albion, New York, just out of nursing school. San Francisco was a bomb, and there wasn't an Army post for miles around Albion. So that's why I came back to San Antonio. All my friends were back in and around Fort Sam Houston, so I just naturally gravitated back toward my network. I came to San Antonio in 1974 to get my B.S. in nursing from Incarnate Word College. The best thing I did was to get into the reserve unit there. That's where I met my husband. It gave me a chance to share my feelings with other Vietnam veterans. It kept me in touch with Army life, the good things and the bad. It was like a family.

On weekends at North Fort Hood, we really do sit around the campfire and talk about 'Nam, about what we as reservists can do to be better prepared than we were back there. If there is another Vietnam-type war, God forbid, I just know I'd want to be part of it. I couldn't sit on the sidelines. We usually just talk about these things among ourselves. I think the reason a lot of people are hesitant to talk about it is that they don't know anyone who wants to listen. A lot of people don't want to hear those kinds of stories. A lof of people just want to forget that time altogether. I don't know why. I guess I'm just not like that.

I'm not saying you don't pay a price for your memories. Last year, I had an intense flashback while flying on a Huey (helicopter) around North Fort Hood. It was the last day of this reserve unit exercise and I was invited on this tour of the area. We were flying a dust off, a medevac helicopter, just like the ones we had back then. It was my first time up in a helicopter since. I thought "Gee, this is going to be great." One of the other nurses said to me, "Are you sure you want to do this? You're pretty tired." I brushed her aside, "No problem." We sat in back in seats strapped in next to where they held the litters. I was sitting in the seat, the helicopter was reving up . . . I don't know how to describe it. It was like a slide show, one of the old-fashioned kind where you go through this quick sequence . . . flick, flick, flick . . . now I know where they got the term flashback.

At first, it was as though I was daydreaming. What scared me to death was that I couldn't turn it off. I couldn't control my mind. The cow grazing in the field became a water buffalo. Fields marked off and cross-sectioned became cemeteries. We flew over this tent, it was the 114th (reserve hospital unit) and suddenly it became the 18th surg. I was scared. All I could do was grasp the hand of this friend of mine. We couldn't talk above the helicopter roar. I just started to cry, I couldn't control myself. I saw blood coming down onto the win shield and the wiper blades swishing over it. There was blood on the floor, all over the passenger area where we were sitting. The stretchers clicked into place had bodies on top of them. I was crying. The nurse next to me kept shouting about whether I was all right. My contacts were swimming around, I wanted the ride to end. I could see why GIs felt scared . . . I couldn't just turn around and open up to the nurse sitting next to me. How could you explain something like that?

I had had a flashback or two before, but the difference was I could control them. Even when the nurse started shaking me, I couldn't turn it off. I just looked past her toward the racks in the helicopter, with bodies on stretchers, body bags on the floor, blood everywhere. When we landed, everyone saw I was visibly upset. The pilot came over to see if I was OK. The only thing I could say was, "It brought back a lot of memories." How could I explain my feelings to these people at North Fort Hood. A lot of them were too young to remember Vietnam as anything more than some dim kind of image on the nightly news. I was scared to death, because all these feelings were brought back that I never knew I had.

I still try to think of the good memories from Vietnam, the people we were able to save. A flashback has certain negative connotations. It's a flashback when they can't think of another way of explaining it. I guess I'm lucky it took fourteen years for it to hit me like that. The one positive thing I can say about it is that it felt awfully good to come back and hover down to that red cross on the top of the tent. It felt good to come home.

For Journals

Do you know anyone who served in Vietnam? Do you know anyone who is a nurse or a nursing student? In what ways do they talk about their work?

For Discussion

1.   What is your personal response to the story Rhoads tells and the ways in which she relates it? In what ways does her story confirm, or dispute, what you have heard about the Vietnam War?

2.   Rhoads is a woman telling about an experience more often associated with men. In what ways do you think her perspective differs from or is similar to that of the men who served in Vietnam, leaving aside for the moment considerations of age and rank?

3.   Doctors and nurses who serve in the military have in some ways a fundamentally different mission from the soldiers whose job, in the words of an army colonel, is to "kill people and break things." What kinds of personal conflicts do you imagine existed for the military health care workers in Vietnam? In what ways do you think they might have resolved this conflict?

4.   The personal narrative can bring geopolitical conflict to a human scale. Examine the ways in which Rhoads clarifies your understanding of both the human cost of war and the painful homecoming of returning Vietnam veterans.

5.   In what ways does Rhoads seem transformed by her experience? Do you sense a shift in her perspective, in her approach or attitudes, as she tells the story of her tour of duty?

For Writing

1.   Interview someone who served in Vietnam or in some other war, using the oral history technique (see Studs Terkel's oral history of Frank Chin in Chapter 3 as one possible model). Write up the oral history, and then compose a brief analysis that responds to the following questions: In what ways is the individual's story similar to, or different from, Rhoads's story? In what ways does your interviewee's language compare to Rhoads's style?

2.   Research newspaper and magazine articles from the late sixties and early seventies, selecting articles and opinion pieces that covered the Vietnam War. Examine the language in which stories about Vietnam are conveyed, and write an essay analyzing the attitudes about the war, and about the Vietnam service personnel, in the press coverage.

METAPHOR AND THE GULF WAR
1990

George Lakoff

George Lakoff is a professor of linguistics at the University of California at Berkeley. He distributed this essay over the Internet network shortly before the war in the Persian Gulf was to begin. In his introductory note, Lakoff explains why he used the medium of electronic mail for his message. As you read his introductory letter and the text that follows, try to evaluate the ways in which his medium may have affected his message, and vice versa.

December 31, 1990

To Friends and Colleagues on the Net:

From George Lakoff,
Professor of Linguistics,
University of California at Berkeley
lakoff@cogsci.berkeley.edu

January 15 is getting very close. As things now stand, President Bush seems to have convinced most of the country that war in the gulf is morally justified, and that it makes sense to think of "winning" such a war.

I have just completed a study of the way the war has been justified. I have found that the justification is based very largely on a metaphorical system of thought in general use for understanding foreign policy. I have analyzed the system, checked it to see what the metaphors hide, and have checked to the best of my ability to see whether the metaphors fit the situation in the gulf, even if one accepts them. So far as I can see, the justification for war, point by point, is anything but clear.

The paper I have written is relatively short—7,000 words. Yet it is far too long for the op-ed pages, and January 15 is too close for journal or magazine publication. The only alternative I have for getting these ideas out is via the various computer networks.

While there is still time, it is vital that debate over the justification for war be seriously revived. I am therefore asking your help. Please look over the enclosed paper. If you find it of value, please send it on to members of your newsgroup, to friends, and to other newsgroups. Feel free to distribute it to anyone interested.

More importantly, if you feel strongly about this issue, start talking and writing about it yourself.

Computer networks have never before played an important role in a matter of vital public importance. The time has come. The media

5

have failed to question what should be questioned. It is up to us to do so. There are a lot of us connected by these networks, and together we have enormous influence. Just imagine the media value of a major computerized debate over the impending war!

We have a chance to participate in the greatest experiment ever conducted in vital, widespread, instantaneous democratic communication. Tens of thousands of lives are at stake. During the next two weeks there is nothing more important that we can send over these networks than a fully open and informed exchange of views about the war.

Here is the first contribution. Pass it on!

Metaphor and War:
The Metaphor System Used to Justify War in the Gulf

Metaphors can kill. The discourse over whether we should go to war in the gulf is a panorama of metaphor. Secretary of State Baker sees Saddam as "sitting on our economic lifeline." President Bush sees him as having a "stranglehold" on our economy. General Schwartzkopf characterizes the occupation of Kuwait as a "rape" that is ongoing. The President says that the U.S. is in the gulf to "protect freedom, protect our future, and protect the innocent," and that we must "push Saddam Hussein back." Saddam is seen as Hitler. It is vital, literally vital, to understand just what role metaphorical thought is playing in bringing us to the brink of war.

10   Metaphorical thought, in itself, is neither good nor bad; it is simply commonplace and inescapable. Abstractions and enormously complex situations are routinely understood via metaphor. Indeed, there is an extensive, and mostly unconscious, system of metaphor that we use automatically and unreflectively to understand complexities and abstractions. Part of this system is devoted to understanding international relations and war. We now know enough about this system to have an idea of how it functions.

The metaphorical understanding of a situation functions in two parts. First, there is a widespread, relatively fixed set of metaphors that structure how we think. For example, a decision to go to war might be seen as a form of cost-benefit analysis, where war is justified when the costs of going to war are less than the costs of not going to war. Second, there is a set of metaphorical definitions that allow one to apply such a metaphor to a particular situation. In this case, there must be a definition of "cost," including a means of comparing relative "costs." The use of a metaphor with a set of definitions becomes pernicious when it hides realities in a harmful way.

It is important to distinguish what is metaphorical from what is not. Pain, dismemberment, death, starvation, and the death and injury of loved ones are not metaphorical. They are real and in a war, they could afflict tens, perhaps hundreds of thousands, of real human beings, whether Iraqi, Kuwaiti, or American.

War as Politics; Politics as Business

Military and international relations strategists do use a cost-benefit analysis metaphor. It comes about through a metaphor that is taken as definitional by most strategic thinkers in the area of international politics.

CLAUSEWITZ'S METAPHOR:
WAR IS POLITICS PURSUED BY OTHER MEANS

Karl von Clausewitz was a Prussian general who perceived war in terms of political cost-benefit analysis. Each nation-state has political objectives, and war may best serve those objectives. The political "gains" are to be weighed against acceptable "costs." When the costs of war exceed the political gains, the war should cease.

There is another metaphor implicit here: 15

POLITICS IS BUSINESS

where efficient political management is seen as akin to efficient business management. As in a well-run business, a well-run government should keep a careful tally of costs and gains. This metaphor for characterizing politics, together with Clausewitz's metaphor, makes war a matter of cost-benefit analysis: defining beneficial "objectives", tallying the "costs", and deciding whether achieving the objectives is "worth" the costs.

The *New York Times*, on November 12, 1990, ran a front-page story announcing that "a national debate has begun as to whether the United States should go to war in the Persian Gulf." The *Times* described the debate as defined by what I have called Clausewitz's metaphor (though it described the metaphor as literal), and then raised the question, "What then is the nation's political object in the gulf and what level of sacrifice is it worth?" The "debate" was not over whether Clausewitz's metaphor was appropriate, but only over how various analysts calculated the relative gains and losses. The same has been true of the hearings of the Senate Foreign Relations Committee, where Clausewitz's metaphor provides the framework within which most discussion has taken place.

The broad acceptance of Clausewitz's metaphor raises vital questions: What, exactly, makes it a metaphor rather than a literal truth? Why does it seem so natural to foreign policy experts? How does it fit into the overall metaphor system for understanding foreign relations and war? And, most importantly, what realities does it hide?

To answer these questions, let us turn to the system of metaphorical thought most commonly used by the general public in comprehending international politics.

What follows is a two-part discussion of the role of metaphorical reasoning about the gulf crisis. The first part lays out the central metaphor systems used in reasoning about the crisis: both the system used by foreign policy experts and the system used by the public at large. The second part discusses how the system has been applied to the crisis in the gulf.

Part 1: The Systems

The State-as-Person System

20   A state is conceptualized as a person, engaging in social relations within a world community. Its land-mass is its home. It lives in a neighborhood, and has neighbors, friends and enemies. States are seen as having inherent dispositions: they can be peaceful or aggressive, responsible or irresponsible, industrious or lazy.

Well-being is wealth. The general well-being of a state is understood in economic terms: its economic health. A serious threat to economic health can thus be seen as a death threat. To the extent that a nation's economy depends on foreign oil, that oil supply becomes a "lifeline" (reinforced by the image of an oil pipeline).

Strength for a state is military strength.

Maturity for the person-state is industrialization. Unindustrialized nations are "underdeveloped," with industrialization as a natural state to be reached. Third-world nations are thus immature children, to be taught how to develop properly or disciplined if they get out of line. Nations that fail to industrialize at a rate considered normal are seen as akin to retarded children and judged as "backward" nations.

Rationality is the maximization of self-interest.

25   There is an implicit logic to the use of these metaphors:

Since it is in the interest of every person to be as strong and healthy as possible, a rational state seeks to maximize wealth and military might.

Violence can further self-interest. It can be stopped in three ways: Either a balance of power, so that no one in a neighborhood is strong enough to threaten anyone else. Or the use of collective persuasion by the community to make violence counter to self-interest. Or a cop strong enough to deter violence or punish it. The cop should act morally, in the community's interest, and with the sanction of the community as a whole.

Morality is a matter of accounting, of keeping the moral books balanced. A wrongdoer incurs a debt, and he must be made to pay. The moral books can be balanced by a return to the situation prior to the wrongdoing, by giving back what has been taken, by recompense, or by punishment. Justice is the balancing of the moral books.

War in this metaphor is a fight between two people, a form of hand-to-hand combat. Thus, the U.S. might seek to "push Iraq back out of Kuwait" or "deal the enemy a heavy blow," or "deliver a knockout punch." A just war is thus a form of combat for the purpose of settling moral accounts.

The most common discourse form in the West where there is combat to settle moral accounts is the classic fairy tale. When people are replaced by states in such a fairy tale, what results is a scenario for a just war.   30

The Fairy Tale of the Just War

Cast of characters: A villain, a victim, and a hero. The victim and the hero may be the same person.

The scenario: A crime is committed by the villain against an innocent victim (typically an assault, theft, or kidnapping). The offense occurs due to an imbalance of power and creates a moral imbalance. The hero either gathers helpers or decides to go it alone. The hero makes sacrifices; he undergoes difficulties, typically making an arduous heroic journey, sometimes across the sea to a treacherous terrain. The villain is inherently evil, perhaps even a monster, and thus reasoning with him is out of the question. The hero is left with no choice but to engage the villain in battle. The hero defeats the villain and rescues the victim. The moral balance is restored. Victory is achieved. The hero, who always acts honorably, has proved his manhood and achieved glory. The sacrifice was worthwhile. The hero receives acclaim, along with the gratitude of the victim and the community.

The fairy tale has an asymmetry built into it. The hero is moral and courageous, while the villain is amoral and vicious. The hero is rational, but though the villain may be cunning and calculating, he cannot be reasoned with. Heroes thus cannot negotiate with villains; they must defeat them. The enemy-as-demon metaphor arises as a consequence of the fact that we understand what a just war is in terms of this fairy tale.

The most natural way to justify a war on moral grounds is to fit this fairy tale structure to a given situation. This is done by metaphorical definition, that is, by answering the questions: Who is the victim? Who is the villain? Who is the hero? What is the crime? What counts as victory? Each set of answers provides a different filled-out scenario.

35   As the gulf crisis developed, President Bush tried to justify going
to war by the use of such a scenario. At first, he couldn't get his story
straight. What happened was that he was using two different sets of
metaphorical definitions, which resulted in two different scenarios:

> The Rescue Scenario: Iraq is villain, the U.S. is hero, Kuwait is vic-
> tim, the crime is kidnap and rape.
>
> The Self-Defense Scenario: Iraq is villain, the U.S. is hero, the U.S.
> and other industrialized nations are victims, the crime is a death
> threat, that is, a threat to economic health.

The American people could not accept the second scenario, since it
amounted to trading lives for oil. The administration has settled on the
first, and that seems to have been accepted by the public, the media,
and Congress as providing moral justification for going to war.

The Ruler-for-State Metonymy

There is a metonymy that goes hand-in-hand with the State-as-Person
metaphor:

THE RULER STANDS FOR THE STATE

Thus, we can refer to Iraq by referring to Saddam Hussein, and so
have a single person, not just an amorphous state, to play the villain in
the just war scenario. It is this metonymy that is invoked when the
President says "We have to get Saddam out of Kuwait."
    Incidentally, the metonymy only applies to those leaders perceived
as rulers. Thus, it would be strange for us, but not for the Iraqis, to describe an American invasion of Kuwait by saying, "George Bush
marched into Kuwait."

The Experts' Metaphors

40   Experts in international relations have an additional system of
metaphors that are taken as defining a "rational" approach. The principal ones are the Rational Actor metaphor and Clausewitz's metaphor,
which are commonly taught as truths in courses on international relations. We are now in a position to show precisely what is metaphorical about Clausewitz's metaphor. To do so, we need to look at a system
of metaphors that is presupposed by Clausewitz's metaphor. We will
begin with an everyday system of metaphors for understanding
causation:

The Causal Commerce System

The Causal Commerce system is a way to comprehend actions intended to achieve positive effects, but which may also have negative effects. The system is composed of three metaphors:

> Causal Transfer: An effect is an object transferred from a cause to an affected party. For example, sanctions are seen as "giving" Iraq economic difficulties. Correspondingly, economic difficulties for Iraq are seen as "coming from" the sanctions. This metaphor turns purposeful actions into transfers of objects.

> The Exchange Metaphor for Value: The value of something is what you are willing to exchange for it. Whenever we ask whether it is "worth" going to war to get Iraq out of Kuwait, we are using the Exchange Metaphor for Value plus the Causal Transfer metaphor.

> Well-being is Wealth: Things of value constitute wealth. Increases in well-being are "gains"; decreases in well-being are "costs." The metaphor of Well-being-as-Wealth has the effect of making qualitative effects quantitative. It not only makes qualitatively different things comparable, it even provides a kind of arithmetic calculus for adding up costs and gains.

Taken together, these three metaphors portray actions as commercial transactions with costs and gains. Seeing actions as transactions is crucial to applying ideas from economics to actions in general.

Risks

A risk is an action taken to achieve a positive effect, where the outcome is uncertain and where there is also a significant probability of a negative effect. Since Causal Commerce allows one to see positive effects of actions as "gains" and negative effects as "costs," it becomes natural to see a risky action metaphorically as a financial risk of a certain type, namely, a gamble.

Risks Are Gambles

In gambling to achieve certain "gains," there are "stakes" that one can "lose." When one asks what is "at stake" in going to war, one is using the metaphors of Causal Commerce and Risks-as-Gambles. These are also the metaphors that President Bush uses when he refers to strategic moves in the gulf as a "poker game" where it would be foolish for him to "show his cards," that is, to make strategic knowledge public.

The Mathematicization of Metaphor

45   The Causal Commerce and Risks-as-Gambles metaphors lie behind our everyday way of understanding risky actions as gambles. At
this point, mathematics enters the picture, since there is mathematics
of gambling, namely, probability theory, decision theory, and game
theory. Since the metaphors of Causal Commerce and Risks-as-Gambles are so common in our everyday thought, their metaphorical nature often goes unnoticed. As a result, it is not uncommon for social
scientists to think that the mathematics of gambling literally applies to
all forms of risky action, and that it can provide a general basis for the
scientific study of risky action, so that risk can be minimized.

Rational Action

Within the social sciences, especially in economics, it is common to
see a rational person as someone who acts in his own self-interest, that
is, to maximize his own well-being. Hard-core advocates of this view
may even see altruistic action as being one's self-interest if there is a
value in feeling righteous about altruism and in deriving gratitude
from others.

In the Causal Commerce system, where well-being is wealth, this
view of Rational Action translates metaphorically into maximizing
gains and minimizing losses. In other words:

Rationality Is Profit Maximization

This metaphor presupposes Causal Commerce plus Risks-as-Gambles, and brings with it the mathematics of gambling as applied to
risky action. It has the effect of turning specialists in mathematical economics into "scientific" specialists in acting rationally so as to minimize risk and cost while maximizing gains.

Suppose we now add the State-as-Person metaphor to the Ratio-
nality-as-Profit-Maximization metaphor. The result is:

International Politics Is Business

50   Here the state is a Rational Actor, whose actions are transactions
and who is engaged in maximizing gains and minimizing costs. This
metaphor brings with it the mathematics of cost-benefit calculation
and game theory, which is commonly taught in graduate programs in
international relations.

Clausewitz's metaphor, the major metaphor preferred by international relations strategists, presupposes this system.

Clausewitz's Metaphor: War is Politics, pursued by other means.

Since politics is business, war becomes a matter of maximizing political gains and minimizing losses. In Clausewitzian terms, war is justified when there is more to be gained by going to war than by not going to war. Morality is absent from the Clausewitzian equation, except when there is a political cost to acting immorally or a political gain from acting morally.

Clausewitz's metaphor only allows war to be justified on pragmatic, not moral, grounds. To justify war on both moral and pragmatic grounds, the Fairy Tale of the Just War and Clausewitz's metaphor must mesh: The "worthwhile sacrifices" of the fairy tale must equal the Clausewitzian "costs" and the "victory" in the fairy tale must equal the Clausewitzian "gains."

Clausewitz's metaphor is the perfect expert's metaphor, since it requires specialists in political cost-benefit calculation. It sanctions the use of the mathematics of economics, probability theory, decision theory, and game theory in the name of making foreign policy rational and scientific.

Clausewitz's metaphor is commonly seen as literally true. We are now in a position to see exactly what makes it metaphorical. First, it uses the State-as-Person metaphor. Second, it turns qualitative effects on human beings into quantifiable costs and gains, thus seeing political action as economics. Third, it sees rationality as profit-making. Fourth, it sees war in terms of only one dimension of war, that of political expediency, which is in turn conceptualized as business. 55

War as Violent Crime

To bear in mind what is hidden by Clausewitz's metaphor, we should consider an alternative metaphor that is not used by professional strategists nor by the general public to understand war as we engage in it.

WAR IS VIOLENT CRIME:
MURDER, ASSAULT, KIDNAPPING, ARSON, RAPE, AND THEFT

Here, war is understood only in terms of its moral dimension, and not, say, its political or economic dimension. The metaphor highlights those aspects of war that would otherwise be seen as major crimes.

There is an Us–Them asymmetry between the public use of Clausewitz's metaphor and the War-as-Crime metaphor. The Iraqi invasion of Kuwait is reported on in terms of murder, theft and rape. The planned American invasion is never discussed in terms of murder, assault, and arson. Moreover, the U.S. plans for war are seen, in Clausewitzian terms, as rational calculation. But the Iraqi invasion is discussed not as a rational move by Saddam, but as the work of a madman. We see U.S. as rational, moral, and courageous and Them as criminal and insane.

War as a Competitive Game

It has long been noted that we understand war as a competitive game like chess, or as a sport, like football or boxing. It is a metaphor in which there is a clear winner and loser, and a clear end to the game. The metaphor highlights strategic thinking, team work, preparedness, the spectators in the world arena, the glory of winning and the shame of defeat.

60   This metaphor is taken very seriously. There is a long tradition in the West of training military officers in team sports and chess. The military is trained to win. This can lead to a metaphor conflict, as it did in Vietnam, since Clausewitz's metaphor seeks to maximize geopolitical gains, which may or may not be consistent with absolute military victory.

The situation at present is that the public has accepted the rescue scenario of the just war fairy tale as providing moral justification. The president, for internal political reasons, has accepted the competitive game metaphor as taking precedence over Clausewitz's metaphor: If he must choose, he will go for the military win over maximizing geopolitical gains. The testimony of the experts before Congress falls largely within Clausewitz's metaphor. Much of it is testimony about what will maximize gains and minimize losses.

For all that been questioned in the Congressional hearings, these metaphors have not. It important to see what they hide.

Is Saddam Irrational?

The villain in the Fairy Tale of the Just War may be cunning, but he cannot be rational. You just do not reason with a demon, nor do you enter into negotiations with him. The logic of the metaphor demands that Saddam be irrational. But is he?

Administration policy is confused on the issue. Clausewitz's metaphor, as used by strategists, assumes that the enemy is rational: He too is maximizing gains and minimizing costs. Our strategy from the outset has been to "increase the cost" to Saddam. That assumes he is rational and is maximizing his self-interest.

65   At the same time, he is being called irrational. The nuclear weapons argument depends on it. If he is rational, he should follow the logic of deterrence. We have thousands of hydrogen bombs in warheads. Israel is estimated to have between 100 and 200 deliverable atomic bombs. It would take Saddam at least eight months and possi-

bly five years before he had a crude, untested atomic bomb on a truck. The most popular estimate for even a few deliverable nuclear warheads is ten years. The argument that he would not be deterred by our nuclear arsenal and by Israel's assumes irrationality.

The Hitler analogy also assumes that Saddam is a villainous madman. The analogy presupposes a Hitler myth, in which Hitler too was an irrational demon, rather than a rational self-serving brutal politician. In the myth, Munich was a mistake and Hitler could have been stopped early on had England entered the war then. Military historians disagree as to whether the myth is true. Be that as it may, the analogy does not hold. Whether or not Saddam is Hitler, Iraq isn't Germany. It has 17 million people, not 70 million. It is economically weak, not strong. It simply is not a threat to the world.

Saddam is certainly immoral, ruthless, and brutal, but there is no evidence that he is anything but rational. Everything he has done, from assassinating political opponents, to using poison gas against his political enemies, the Kurds, to invading Kuwait can be seen as furthering his own self-interest.

Kuwait as Victim

The classical victim is innocent. To the Iraqis, Kuwait was anything but an innocent ingenue. The war with Iran virtually bankrupted Iraq. Iraq saw itself as having fought that war partly for the benefit of Kuwait and Saudi Arabia, where Shiite citizens supported Khomeini's Islamic Revolution. Kuwait had agreed to help finance the war, but after the war, the Kuwaitis insisted on repayment of the "loan." Kuwaitis had invested hundreds of billions in Europe, America and Japan, but would not invest in Iraq after the war to help it rebuild. On the contrary, it began what amounted to economic warfare against Iraq by overproducing its oil quota to hold oil prices down.

In addition, Kuwait had drilled laterally into Iraqi territory in the Rumailah oil field and had extracted oil from Iraqi territory. Kuwait further took advantage of Iraq by buying its currency, but only at extremely low exchange rates. Subsequently, wealthy Kuwaitis used that Iraqi currency on trips to Iraq, where they bought Iraqi goods at bargain rates. Among the things they bought most flamboyantly were liquor and prostitutes (widows and orphans of men killed in the war, who, because of the state of the economy, had no other means of support). All this did not endear Kuwaitis to Iraqis, who were suffering from over 70% inflation.

Moreover, Kuwaitis had long been resented for good reason by Iraqis and Moslems from other nations. Capital rich, but labor poor, Kuwait imported cheap labor from other Moslem countries to do its   70 least pleasant work. At the time of the invasion, there were 400,000 Kuwaiti citizens and 2.2 million foreign laborers who were denied rights of citizenry and treated by the Kuwaitis as lesser beings. In short, to the Iraqis and to labor-exporting Arab countries, Kuwait is badly miscast as a purely innocent victim.

This does not in any way justify the horrors perpetrated on the Kuwaitis by the Iraqi army. But it is part of what is hidden when Kuwait is cast as an innocent victim. The "legitimate government" that we seek to reinstall is an oppressive monarchy.

What Is Victory?

In a fairy tale or a game, victory is well-defined. Once it is achieved, the story or game is over. Neither is the case in the gulf crisis. History continues, and "victory" makes sense only in terms of continuing history.

The president's stated objectives are total Iraqi withdrawal and restoration of the Kuwaiti monarchy. But no one believes the matter will end there, since Saddam would still be in power with all of his forces intact. General Powell said in his Senate testimony that if Saddam withdrew, the U.S. would have to "strengthen the indigenous countries of the region" to achieve a balance of power. Presumably that means arming Assad, who is every bit as dangerous as Saddam. Would arming another villain count as victory?

If we go to war, what will constitute "victory"? Suppose we conquer Iraq, wiping out its military capability. How would Iraq be governed? No puppet government that we set up could govern effectively since it would be hated by the entire populace. Since Saddam has wiped out all opposition, the only remaining effective government for the country would be his Ba'ath party. Would it count as a victory if Saddam's friends wound up in power? If not, what other choice is there? And if Iraq has no remaining military force, how could it defend itself against Syria and Iran? It would certainly not be a "victory" for us if either of them took over Iraq. If Syria did, then Assad's Arab nationalism would become a threat. If Iran did, then Islamic fundamentalism would become even more powerful and threatening.

75   It would seem that the closest thing to a "victory" for the U.S. in case of war would be to drive the Iraqis out of Kuwait; destroy just enough of Iraq's military to leave it capable of defending itself against Syria and Iran; somehow get Saddam out of power, but let his Ba'ath party remain in control of a country just strong enough to defend itself, but not strong enough to be a threat; and keep the price of oil at a reasonably low level.

The problems: It is not obvious that we could get Saddam out of power without wiping out most of Iraq's military capability. We would have invaded an Arab country, which would create vast hatred for us throughout the Arab world, and would no doubt result in decades of increased terrorism and lack of cooperation by Arab states. We would, by defeating an Arab nationalist state, strengthen Islamic fundamentalism. Iraq would remain a cruel dictatorship run by cronies of Saddam. By reinstating the government of Kuwait, we would inflame the hatred of the poor toward the rich throughout the Arab world, and thus increase instability. And the price of oil would go through the roof. Even the closest thing to a victory doesn't look very victorious.

In the debate over whether to go to war, very little time has been spent clarifying what a victory would be. And if "victory" cannot be defined, neither can "worthwhile sacrifice."

The Arab Viewpoint

The metaphors used to conceptualize the gulf crisis hide the most powerful political ideas in the Arab world: Arab nationalism and Islamic fundamentalism. The first seeks to form a racially-based all-Arab nation, the second, a theocratic all-Islamic state. Though bitterly opposed to one another, they share a great deal. Both are conceptualized in family terms, an Arab brotherhood and an Islamic brotherhood. Both see brotherhoods as more legitimate than existing states. Both are at odds with the state-as-person metaphor, which sees currently existing states as distinct entities with a right to exist in perpetuity.

Also hidden by our metaphors is perhaps the most important daily concern throughout the Arab world: Arab dignity. Both political movements are seen as ways to achieve dignity through unity. The current national boundaries are widely perceived as working against Arab dignity in two ways: one internal and one external.

The internal issue is the division between rich and poor in the 80 Arab world. Poor Arabs see rich Arabs as rich by accident, by where the British happened to draw the lines that created the contemporary nations of the Middle East. To see Arabs metaphorically as one big family is to suggest that oil wealth should belong to all Arabs. To many Arabs, the national boundaries drawn by colonial powers are illegitimate, violating the conception of Arabs as a single "brotherhood" and impoverishing millions.

To those impoverished millions, the positive side of Saddam's invasion of Kuwait was that it challenged national borders and brought to the fore the divisions between rich and poor that result from those lines in the sand. If there is to be peace in the region, these divisions must be addressed, say, by having rich Arab countries make extensive investments in development that will help poor Arabs. As long as the huge gulf between rich and poor exists in the Arab world, a large number of poor Arabs will continue to see one of the superstate solutions, either Arab nationalism or Islamic fundamentalism, as being in their self-interest, and the region will continue to be unstable.

The external issue is the weakness. The current national boundaries keep Arab nations squabbling among themselves and therefore weak relative to Western nations. To unity advocates, what we call "stability" means continued weakness.

Weakness is a major theme in the Arab world, and is often conceptualized in sexual terms, even more than in the West. American officials, in speaking of the "rape" of Kuwait, are conceptualizing a weak, defenseless country as female and a strong militarily powerful country as male. Similarly, it is common for Arabs to conceptualize the colonization and subsequent domination of the Arab world by the West, especially the U.S., as emasculation.

An Arab proverb that is reported to be popular in Iraq these days is that "It is better to be a cock for a day then a chicken for a year." The message is clear: It is better to be male, that is, strong and dominant for a short period of time than to be female, that is, weak and defenseless for a long time. Much of the support for Saddam among Arabs is due to the fact that he is seen as standing up to the U.S., even if only for a while, and that there is a dignity in this. If upholding dignity is an essential part of what defines Saddam's "rational self-interest," it is vitally important for our government to know this, since he may be willing to go to war to "be a cock for a day."

85   The U.S. does not have anything like a proper understanding of the issue of Arab dignity. Take the question of whether Iraq will come out of this with part of the Rumailah oil fields and two islands giving it a port on the gulf. From Iraq's point of view these are seen as economic necessities if Iraq is to rebuild. President Bush has spoken of this as "rewarding aggression," using the Third-World-Countries-As-Children metaphor, where the great powers are grown-ups who have the obligation to reward or punish children so as to make them behave properly. This is exactly the attitude that grates on Arabs who want to be treated with dignity. Instead of seeing Iraq as a sovereign nation that has taken military action for economic purposes, the president treats Iraq as if it were a child gone bad, who has become the neighborhood bully and should be properly disciplined by the grown-ups.

The issue of the Rumailah oil fields and the two islands has alternatively been discussed in the media in terms of "saving face." Saving face is a very different concept than upholding Arab dignity and insisting on being treated as an equal, not an inferior.

What Is Hidden By Seeing the State as a Person?

The State-as-Person metaphor highlights the ways in which states act as units, and hides the internal structure of the state. Class structure is hidden by this metaphor, as is ethnic composition, religious rivalry, political parties, the ecology, the influence of the military and of corporations (especially multi-national corporations).

Consider "national interest." It is in a person's interest to be healthy and strong. The State-as-Person metaphor translates this into a "national interest" of economic health and military strength. But what is in the "national interest" may or may not be in the interest of many ordinary citizens, groups, or institutions, who may become poorer as the GNP rises and weaker as the military gets stronger.

The "national interest" is a metaphorical concept, and it is defined in America by politicians and policy makers. For the most part, they are influenced more by the rich than by the poor, more by large corporations than by small business, and more by developers than ecological activists.

When President Bush argues that going to war would "serve our vital national interests," he is using a metaphor that hides exactly whose interests would be served and whose would not. For example, poor people, especially blacks and Hispanics, are represented in the military in disproportionately large numbers, and in a war the lower classes and those ethnic groups will suffer proportionally more casualties. Thus war is less in the interest of ethnic minorities and the lower classes than the white upper classes. 90

Also hidden are the interests of the military itself, which are served when war is justified. Hopes that, after the cold war, the military might play a smaller role have been dashed by the president's decision to prepare for war. He was advised, as he should be, by the national security council, which consists primarily of military men. War is so awful a prospect that one would not like to think that military self-interest itself could help tilt the balance to a decision for war. But in a democratic society, the question must be asked, since the justifications for war also justify continued military funding and an undiminished national political role for the military.

Energy Policy

The State-as-Person metaphor defines health for the state in economic terms, with our current understanding of economic health taken as a given, including our dependence on foreign oil. Many commentators have argued that a change in energy policy to make us less dependent on foreign oil would be more rational than going to war to preserve our supply of cheap oil from the gulf. This argument may have a real force, but it has no metaphorical force when the definition of economic health is taken as fixed. After all, you don't deal with an attack on your health by changing the definition of health. Metaphorical logic pushes a change in energy policy out of the spotlight in the current crisis.

I do not want to give the impression that all that is involved here is metaphor. Obviously there are powerful corporate interests lined up against a fundamental restructuring of our national energy policy. What is sad is that they have a very compelling system of metaphorical thought on their side. If the debate is framed in terms of an attack on our economic health, one cannot argue for redefining what economic health is without changing the grounds for the debate. And if the debate is framed in terms of rescuing a victim, then changes in energy policy seem utterly beside the point.

The "Costs" of War

Clausewitz's metaphor requires a calculation of the "costs" and the "gains" of going to war. What, exactly, goes into that calculation and what does not? Certainly American casualties, loss of equipment, and dollars spent on the operation count as costs. But Vietnam taught us that there are social costs: trauma to families and communities, disruption of lives, psychological effects on veterans, long-term health problems, in addition to the cost of spending our money on war instead of on vital social needs at home.

95   Also hidden are political costs: the enmity of Arabs for many years, and the cost of increased terrorism. And barely discussed is the moral cost that comes from killing and maiming as a way to settle disputes. And there is the moral cost of using a "cost" metaphor at all. When we do so, we quantify the effects of war and thus hide from ourselves the qualitative reality of pain and death.

But those are costs to us. What is most ghoulish about the cost-benefit calculation is that "costs" to the other side count as "gains" for us. In Vietnam, the body counts of killed Viet Cong were taken as evidence of what was being "gained" in the war. Dead human beings went on the profit side of our ledger.

There is a lot of talk of American deaths as "costs", but Iraqi deaths aren't mentioned. The metaphors of cost-benefit accounting and the fairy tale villain lead us to devalue the lives of Iraqis, even when

most of those actually killed will not be villains at all, but simply innocent draftees or reservists or civilians.

America as Hero

The classic fairy tale defines what constitutes a hero: it is a person
who rescues an innocent victim and who defeats and punishes a guilty
and inherently evil villain, and who does so for moral rather than
venal reasons. If America starts a war, will it be functioning as a hero?

It will certainly not fit the profile very well. First, one of its main
goals will be to reinstate "the legitimate government of Kuwait." That
means reinstating an absolute monarchy, where women are not accorded anything resembling reasonable rights, and where 80% of the
people living in the country are foreign workers who do the dirtiest
jobs and are not accorded the opportunity to become citizens. This is
not an innocent victim whose rescue makes us heroic.

Second, the actual human beings who will suffer from an all-out   100
attack will, for the most part, be innocent people who did not take part
in the atrocities in Kuwait. Killing and maiming a lot of innocent bystanders in the process of nabbing a much smaller number of villains
does not make one much of a hero.

Third, in the self-defense scenario, where oil is at issue, America is
acting in its self-interest. But, in order to qualify as a legitimate hero in
the rescue scenario, it must be acting selflessly. Thus, there is a contradiction between the self-interested hero of the self-defense scenario
and the purely selfless hero of the rescue scenario.

Fourth, America may be a hero to the royal families of Kuwait and
Saudi Arabia, but it will not be a hero to most Arabs. Most Arabs do
not think in terms of our metaphors. A great many Arabs will see us as
a kind of colonial power using illegitimate force against an Arab
brother. To them, we will be villains, not heroes.

America appears as classic hero only if you don't look carefully at
how the metaphor is applied to the situation. It is here that the State-
as-Person metaphor functions in a way that hides vital truths. The
State-as-Person metaphor hides the internal structure of states and allows us to think of Kuwait as a unitary entity, the defenseless maiden
to be rescued in the fairy tale. The metaphor hides the monarchical
character of Kuwait, and the way Kuwaitis treat women and the vast
majority of the people who live in their country. The State-as-Person
metaphor also hides the internal structures of Iraq, and thus hides the
actual people who will mostly be killed, maimed, or otherwise harmed
in a war. The same metaphor also hides the internal structure of the
U.S., and therefore hides the fact that is the poor and minorities who

will make the most sacrifices while not getting any significant benefit. And it hides the main ideas that drive Middle Eastern politics.

Things to Do

War would create much more suffering than it would alleviate, and should be renounced in this case on humanitarian grounds. There is no shortage of alternatives to war. Troops can be rotated out and brought to the minimum level to deter an invasion of Saudi Arabia. Economic sanctions can be continued. A serious system of international inspections can be instituted to prevent the development of Iraq's nuclear capacity. A certain amount of "face-saving" for Saddam is better than war: As part of a compromise, the Kuwaiti monarchy can be sacrificed and elections held in Kuwait. The problems of rich and poor Arabs must be addressed, with pressures placed on the Kuwaitis and others to invest significantly in development to help poor Arabs. Balance of power solutions within the region should always be seen as moves toward reducing, not increasing armaments; positive economic incentives can be used, together with the threat of refusal by us and the Soviets to supply spare parts needed to keep hi-tech military weaponry functional.

105   If there is a moral to . . . the Congressional hearings, it is that there are a lot of very knowledgeable people in this country who have thought about alternatives to war. They should be taken seriously.

For Journal Writing

What do you know about electronic mail as a device for communication? How important do you think its role is or will be in the future in maintaining free speech?

For Discussion

1. Lakoff declares his agenda for writing in his introductory note. To what degree does knowing that agenda, or purpose, bias your reading of the essay? Are you more or less likely to accept his arguments, or do you believe you are unaffected by knowing his views?
2. Metaphors are frequently used to explain something unknown in terms of the known. Do the metaphors Lakoff discusses help you to understand the political maneuvering that war entails?
3. Lakoff focuses on metaphor as a means by which wars are waged. How powerful is metaphor in invoking support for a war?

4. Select one of Lakoff's metaphors, such as that of the fairy tale, and analyze both the metaphor and Lakoff's interpretation of it. Do you agree, or disagree, with his assertions about the metaphor as it applies to the Gulf War?

5. Analyze the structure and style of the essay. To what degree is it affected by the medium of electronic communication, or e-mail?

6. Examine Lakoff's language about language. To what degree does he maintain a scholarly stance? Do you think the language he uses is intended to bias readers' interpretations?

For Writing

1. Select a metaphor used by modern politicians or commentators and analyze its persuasiveness—for example, Camelot, a metaphor for the Kennedy era; the space race; or the Great Society or War on Poverty of the Johnson administration.

2. Examine the "fairy tale of the just war." Are there other fairy tales that you could apply to the subject of war? Write an essay developing a metaphor of or an analogy between some other tale and the process of justifying war.

RHETORICAL DIVISIVENESS IN NATION-BUILDING AND WAR: AN ANALYSIS OF FDR'S "PEARL HARBOR ADDRESS"
1994

Jeremy Kassis

Jeremy Kassis is a college student who is interested in the emerging science of nanotechnology, among other topics. He wrote the essay that follows in response to chapter assignment #5 for his first-year writing course on the art of persuasion. As you read it, consider the ways in which he evaluated language as a vehicle for persuasion.

Franklin Delano Roosevelt's "Pearl Harbor Address" survives as a reflection of the national horror and outrage elicited by the Japanese bombing of Pearl Harbor. To what extent did his address actually create that outrage? Think of his words as a photograph of national sentiment, not innocently packed away in a photo album, but enlarged to propagandistic proportions. The national tide had shifted against Japan upon news of the bombing, but FDR's speech wove a subtle tapestry of logic and emotion with threads of American justice and history to whip public fervor against the Empire of Japan, to name it "enemy."

December 7, 1941, has been "a date that will live in infamy," as FDR predicted. But the date does not live alone. It lives inextricably joined to the phrase our thirty-second president coined to characterize it. Destiny, it would seem, formed an iron fist that day, holding the furiously scrawling pen that forced us to recognize that our national history, and future, was being determined before our eyes. It is FDR's clever use of double-appositional structure in these lines, emphasized by the certainty and timeliness of the response, that sends chills up our spines, preparing us for the incensed speech to follow.

In fact, analysis of FDR's first paragraph reveals careful integration and overview of all his subsequent themes. He continues, "The United States of America was suddenly and deliberately attacked by naval and air forces of the Empire of Japan." Drawing upon American notions of justice, FDR characterizes the United States as victim and Japan as aggressor, but not so simply. The Japanese are unsportsmanlike, as "suddenly" might suggest, and "deliberate" aggressors, which is to say that they are "premeditative murderers of the first degree" as per the American legal distinction in trials of homicide. Not only do they deserve punishment in this interpretation; they deserve death. We are inclined to perceive them as we perceive our criminals, as subhuman. The Japanese have already been reduced in the speech to barbarians or even animals, preying upon the vulnerable.

But mere barbarism is not descriptive enough. They are an organized people, intensifying the threat to Americans. They constitute an "Empire," a political system that would make any red-blooded, democratic, American patriot cringe with the notions of conquest and domination that the term evokes. This is not political convention; FDR might have referred to the Japanese nation merely as "Japan," as he does throughout the remainder of the speech. It is political manipulation, not of the kind that would be condemned, but manipulation nonetheless.

5   The balance of the address concretizes the themes already introduced, and the second paragraph begins by explaining the scenario of deception. Roosevelt's reference to Japan as "that nation" effectively excommunicates it. Japan has become an unmentionable. "Indeed" of

the next paragraph extends the scenario, as though to exclaim of the audacity of the trick.

FDR then asserts himself through the construction "It will be recorded," which bolsters the president's ethos by placing him in a position of command. His word shall be done, history shall be created, in an almost biblical sense. The paragraph concludes the scenario of deceit with an "awful truth" clincher line. "Makes it obvious that the attack was deliberately planned many days or even weeks ago" is an appeal to logos, calling for the audience to assimilate the information just received to determine for themselves the obviousness of the conclusion.

As a student of rhetoric, FDR knows that the appeal to logos does not complete the argument. He brings his personal ethos to bear by asserting an encapsulated conclusion, validating the one he has just asked his audience to produce, which improves his pathos. It is easy to follow a leader who makes you feel intelligent. "During the intervening time, the Japanese government has deliberately sought to deceive the United States by false statements and expressions of hope for continuing peace," he says. This shocking statement is followed by a list of consequences. Material casualty is followed by human casualty, delicately demonstrating his human sensitivity. But FDR ends the story of destruction again on a material note to provoke resolution and action, not the bitter sorrow that human death brings. He ends by turning anguish into anger and the Japanese into marauders, pirates "on the high seas."

He then pursues the point with relentless parallelism. Malaya, Hong Kong, Guam, the Philippines, Wake Island, and, finally, Midway. The last frightens us with its immediacy. Attacked the very morning of the speech, Midway reminds us that the violence continues and that every moment wasted in deliberation is a moment in which the Japanese advance.

Later, the speech evolves into a proclamation of manifest destiny: "American people in their righteous might will win through to absolute victory." In this case, "right" makes "might," and the Americans are, of course, right. The shift to use of the pronoun "we" emphasizes the collectivity of the action, and the invocation of the deity is the culmination of this statement of national purpose. God and our determination shall save us.

Finally, FDR makes a humble shift in tense. Persuasion is turned to 10 request, one of burning intensity, sealing the fate of U.S. involvement in World War II. "I ask that the Congress declare that since the unprovoked and dastardly attack by Japan on Sunday, December 7, 1941, a State of War has existed between the United States and the Japanese Empire."

For Journals

Do you remember a memorable speech given in a time of crisis—by a public figure or by someone in your community or school? What do you think made it memorable?

For Discussion

1.   What is Kassis's thesis? What does he assert about FDR's speech? Does his introduction lead into his assertion effectively? How well does his evidence support his thesis?
2.   Examine Kassis's language. What tone, stance, and approach toward the topic are suggested? To what degree might he be creating a reaction in the way he asserts that Roosevelt does? Cite examples of specific words and phrases that support your assessment.
3.   Identify the organizing principle Kassis uses to develop his essay. Is it appropriate for an analytical essay? What other methods of organization might have been suitable?

For Writing

1.   Find and listen to a recording of Roosevelt's "Pearl Harbor Address." Are you more, or less, persuaded of Kassis's thesis after listening to the president?
2.   In what ways does Kassis himself use appeals to ethos, pathos, and logos to support his view? Write an analysis of his analytical essay.

FILMS ON WAR AND THE ENEMY

Images of war have pervaded American film, from *The World at War* to *Apocalypse Now*. View one or more of the films or television programs suggested below, or another of your choosing, and examine the ways in which films can serve to unite a society in a common purpose, to create or vilify an enemy, to justify national and personal sacrifice, or to explore the ambiguities of warfare.

The Red Badge of Courage
All Quiet on the Western Front

Watch on the Rhine
From Here to Eternity
Apocalypse Now
Platoon
Full Metal Jacket
Bridge on the River Kwai
The Civil War series
Faces of the Enemy
Gettysburg
Glory
Casablanca
Dr. Strangelove
China Beach
*M*A*S*H*

THE LANGUAGE OF PERSUASION

Reading and writing arguments entails an understanding of the role of language in persuasion. The words we read or write, the ways in which we, or the writers we read, put those words into phrases, clauses, and sentences, contribute to the persuasive power of an argument in ways both apparent and hidden. Through language, the writer conveys voice, tone, and stance. Logical structures, clear connections between points, parallelism, balance, coordination and subordination, active verbs, and concrete nouns all work to produce persuasive arguments. Through language, appeals to ethos engage beliefs and values and invoke credibility and authority; through language appeals to logos engage the mind, and appeals to pathos engage the heart and emotions.

Analyzing Persuasive Language in Arguments

To understand how we persuade through language—for example, in this chapter, the ways we create an "other," or enemy—we need to understand the ways in which language can evoke associations and emotional responses, the ways in which language unites the rhetor, or communicator, and audience to make meaning. Studying the persuasive texts of this chapter and other readings in this book can help you to sharpen your ability to analyze persuasive language.

Style, or language and structure, reflects a rhetor's purpose in communicating and the rhetor's relationship with the audience. Through their language and the structure of their persuasive messages, combined with careful attention to the targeted audience, the authors in this chapter argue about war and develop images of us versus them, the good versus the evil. Thomas Paine wanted to sound an alarm and move people to action, and his lively, barn-burning style supported this end. Abraham Lincoln, in "The Gettysburg Address," strove not to divide a people or to evoke feelings of animosity, but to unify North and South, and "take increased devotion to that cause." Lincoln linked the themes of life and death, of endings and beginnings. His language is somber and appropriate to the event, and his syntax utilizes balance and antithesis to reflect the division and unity of his rhetorical situation.

Twain's "The War Prayer" relies on an ironic stance, in which the words convey meaning other than their ostensible, literal meaning, while the advertisement *We Smash 'em HARD"* is obvious on some levels—in attacking the evil "Huns"—and subtle on others—in its suggestions about manliness and virility. Roosevelt's "Pearl Harbor Address" relies on forceful, clear, but highly connotative diction ("dastardly," "treachery") that is reinforced by the repetition and parallelism of the sentence structure.

Three analytical essays in this chapter confront the issue of language in wartime. Paul Fussell's essay, itself written in straightforward, general English, notes the reductive and at times overly simplistic quality of language, especially in creating stereotypes of enemies, and George Lakoff's essay directly confronts the use of imagery, particularly metaphor, to create a justification for one country to wage war on another; Lakoff employs a style that may reflect the new medium in which he distributed his essay, electronic mail. The third analytical essay, by student writer Jeremy Kassis, combines an analysis of Roosevelt's language in the Pearl Harbor Address with the author's own lively use of language.

Included in this chapter is a different kind of persuasive "language": that of visual images. That "language" offers students the opportunity to examine the truism "a picture is worth a thousand words," and to compare the currencies of words and images in analyzing effective strategies of persuasion. Images for this exercise include posters, advertising, and photographs as well as argumentative texts and the narrative of Vietnam nurse Jacqueline Navarra Rhoads. In contemporary cultures, words and images frequently keep company in persuasive texts; examining both types of persuasion, singly and in tandem, can sharpen skills in looking critically at persuasion in print, video, and audio media.

Using Persuasive Language in Arguments

First, let us look at the basic unit of language: words. Words can be connotative as well as denotative. *Denotation* refers to the explicit, "dictionary" meaning of a word. *Connotation* refers to the associations or evocations of a word or expression. Compare *house* and *home*, for example. Which word would you select if you were a real estate agent? Which word conveys more positive associations to a reader/potential buyer? In the sentences below, what connotations do the different versions of the same event convey?

> The besieged governor, looking exhausted yet thoughtful, rode away in a government vehicle.
>
> The indicted politician, unshaven and frowning, sped away in his taxpayer-supported limousine.

As a writer, you need to pay attention to your word choice and to your readers' associations with and reactions to words. Not only adjectives and adverbs but also the nouns and verbs you choose will convey your stance, position, and biases toward the subject. In the above sentences, for example, *politician, sped,* and *limousine* are a noun, a verb, and a noun, respectively, but they convey quite different associations from the words they replaced.

Another element of style that serves argumentative goals is syntax, or sentence structure. The syntax used can reinforce and underscore the themes and associations you are trying to convey. When you use parallel structure, or grammatically equivalent elements in a sentence, you are drawing parallels between the ideas represented in that parallel form, as Lincoln does in his parallel prepositional phrases: "government *of* the people, *by* the people, *for* the people." When you set up an antithesis, or state what something is not and then what it is, you are drawing a sharp contrast, as Paine does when he writes, "I call not upon a few but upon all." When you craft coordinate phrases or clauses (A *or* B, C *and* D, E *yet* F, *neither* G *nor* H), you suggest equivalence; when you use subordinate or dependent phrases and clauses, you also suggest a relationship between parts in the sentence.

Political speeches often rely heavily on parallelism because speech, except on recorded media such as video, cannot be reread, reviewed, underlined, or annotated, the way written texts can. Parallelism and coordination, combined with transitional words and phrases such as *first, second, next,* and the like, help the audiences keep track of points and help the speaker keep the audience tuned into his or her argument. Such strategies also underscore and stress points that the speaker wants to drive home. Roosevelt, for example, uses a repeated parallel structure—or series—to outline the extent of the Japanese attack on Pearl Harbor and to reinforce the premeditated nature of the attack—a significant point in Roosevelt's argument:

> Last night, Japanese forces attacked Hong Kong. Last night, Japanese forces attacked Guam. Last night, Japanese forces attacked the Philippine Islands. Last night, Japanese forces attacked Wake Island.

Subordinate, or dependent clauses, can deemphasize certain points which must be included but which the speaker wants to move to the background. For example, Roosevelt says,

> No matter how long it may take us to overcome this premeditated invasion, the American people in their righteous might will win through to absolute victory.

Subordinating "No matter how long it may take" effectively sets up the statement as an assumption or foregone conclusion. A rallying cry such as this one must acknowledge the effort war will involve, but the smart rhetor will, as does Roosevelt, emphasize the positive—"American people," "righteous might," "absolute victory."

In persuasion, language is an important means of inducing cooperation, identification, and agreement. But where is the line between reader awareness and audience manipulation? How do you persuade your reader to see things from your point of view, to identify with your concerns and interests? Does presenting your own evidence in a positive light constitute unethical conduct? Does delaying the bad news in a letter until the second paragraph indicate a lack of fairness? How do we determine when something is argument and when it is propaganda?

As you review your writing, consider some of the following questions: Are you using emotionally charged words to evoke a sentiment you don't want to elicit outright? Are you appealing to hatred, bigotry, or stereotypes? Are you substituting loaded terms for evidence and logical reasoning? Are you being deliberately ambiguous or euphemistic to hide your true purposes? Are you dishonestly selecting the material you include as evidence and misrepresenting the evidence or the position of someone you are quoting? Are you arguing to pursue truth or to obscure it? Your own ethics, your values and beliefs, will need to guide you as you develop your ability to persuade with evidence, with sound reasoning, and with language that fairly represents both your position and that of opposing views.

Your academic essays will need to attend to language as well. You may, in certain disciplines, need to use language that deemphasizes the writer and reports results or events in as neutral a language and tone as possible. But in striving for passive voice, writing that emphasizes the action and not the actor, take care that you don't end up with convoluted prose that links up series of prepositional phrases and abstract nouns. The efficient, precise use of language in a comprehensible style is appreciated by nearly any audience, but certainly by your instructors. Much of your college writing, though, and certainly argumentative writing, not only allows for, but calls for a point of view, a sense of a real person behind the prose with beliefs, values, opinions, intellect. You will generally be expected to convey a point of view, whether it is your interpretation of a literary text or your assessment of recent elections in Nicaragua and the economic ramifications for the United States.

WRITING ASSIGNMENTS

1.   Observe a simple or brief event at school, in class, at home—someone coming to class late, for example, or an argument at mealtime, or perhaps a traffic mishap. Write up the event in three ways: (1) positively biased toward the subject or main character, (2) negatively biased, and (3) as neutral as possible. Indicate an ostensible purpose for writing the report in each situation (i.e., for your friend who was driving the car; for the other driver, for a no-fault insurance report). Exchange assignments with a peer, and assess the differences in the 3 accounts. Did you change the passages by selecting different details to include or exclude? By changing nouns and verbs? By changing modifiers? Analyze the differences, and discuss in class or in an analytical essay.

2.   Select a political event or issue of current national interest. Then select three or four magazines, such as *National Review, U.S. News and World Report,* the *New Republic,* or the *Nation,* and read their coverage of the event or issue. Do a close textual analysis of the selections, and write an essay comparing and contrasting their styles.

3.   Write a rallying cry to get fellow students or neighbors involved in an issue or plan of action. Revise the argument for a special interest

magazine, an academic publication, or a broader audience in the greater community. Submit both with an explanation for the change you made in style for the different writing situations.

4.   Write an argument on an issue you care about. Use every trick in the book, every bit of persuasive, connotative language you can think of, every stylistic strategy you have learned. Then exchange essays with a peer, and write out your immediate, and then studied, responses to each other's essays. How effective was the language? How convincing the argument? Were you persuaded or put off by the language of the argument?

5.   Analyze a persuasive speech or text from a war era, whether historical material from the world wars or Vietnam or more recent material. As do Lakoff and Kassis in this chapter, watch for patterns of imagery or other tactics for creating an "us" and "them" system. How does the imagery help to unite? How does it divide?

CHAPTER

FRONTIERS

*A*t the beginning of the nineteenth century, New York state was on the frontier, and most people thought it would take a hundred years to get to the Pacific, if in fact they ever thought in those terms at all. They certainly would have been surprised to learn that by 1849 Americans had moved across the entire continent, all the way to California, thanks to the political and economic charms of expansion and the incentive of the Gold Rush. What they would have found even more unlikely is that a hundred years after the frontier had ceased to exist as a geographic marker, Americans would still be so attached to it, or to what it represents, that the search for new frontiers—even technological ones—continues to occupy the American vocabulary and the American psyche.

The American idea of frontier is of an invisible border between settled and unsettled, civilized and uncivilized areas. It is recognized more by what it is not than by what it is: it's not civilization as you know it, it's not domesticated, it's not safe. Of course, the idea of the frontier was a reality only to the European settlers who saw themselves as the bearers of culture and developers of empty country, not to American Indians who had their own indigenous cultures and knew the country wasn't empty because they were already there.

Whether or not everyone accepted the idea of a frontier—receding before the development of towns and farms but always out there somewhere, leading to newer undiscovered places—it became so embedded in our culture that it is what Americans think they know best about their own country, and it is the way we are identified by the rest of the world. In Germany, for example, there are vacation places complete with wigwams so tourists can play cowboys and Indians. Blue jeans, invented by young merchant Levi Strauss during the Gold Rush so prospectors could put ore in their pockets without tearing them, are an American national uniform and a status symbol in Eastern Europe and Russia. American theme parks have frontier towns; movie studios have mock shoot-outs between good guys and bad guys; and Americans have been watching western movies as long as there have been movies to watch.

How much all of this re-creation has to do with what the frontier was actually like seems to matter much less than what most people prefer to think it was like. Wherever Americans live, they infuse some sense of the centrality of the frontier into their image of the United States. Whatever changes are wrought in that image are the cause of pitched emotional and intellectual battles between groups with an interest in preserving the idea of the frontier. In the last forty or fifty years, many scholars have explored the difference between the actual American frontier and the frontier of the American imagination, and many American Indians have campaigned successfully for reevaluations of the image of Indians in American history.

Frontiers through History

Most Americans never saw the frontier, wherever it happened to be at the time. In the eighteenth and most of the nineteenth centuries, whether they lived in towns, on farms and in rural areas, or in the bigger eastern cities, they got their information about the frontier from newspaper reports, narratives—accurate or exaggerated—paintings by artists who had accompanied expeditions, and eventually from photographs.

The people who know from firsthand experience what the West felt like were Indians, trappers, hunters, and the pioneer families who crossed the plains, particularly after the start of the 1849 Gold Rush. These families were in search of land, not gold, and even then California was the destination of choice. To get there they had to cross about two thousand miles of frequently inhospitable country, and very few of them made it without illness or death intervening. Jane Gould Tortillott, whose family went from Ohio to California in 1862, was one of many pioneer women who kept a diary of her journey, and it provides a rare and immediate look at frontier life, a life far more interesting and complicated than it usually is portrayed, in the movies.

For a lucky few, the idea of the frontier was an adventure of absolutely glorious proportions, and no one left a record of a better time than the young Samuel Clemens, otherwise known as Mark Twain.

Accompanying his brother, who had been appointed secretary to the governor of the Nevada Territory, Clemens saw the continent as few other people but the Indians had ever been privileged to see it—stagecoaches, the Pony Express, the Southwest, clear lakes full of fish, early San Francisco, silver mining in Nevada, even Hawaii. His early book, *Roughing It*, is ironic from title to finish, but Twain's irrepressible humor communicates the reality of the frontier at the same time that it embroiders and sustains the mythology.

Twain could find amusement in almost anything, but as Jane Gould Tortillott could testify, the trip was extremely difficult, and relations between settlers and Indians deteriorated in proportion to the number of settlers who arrived and the realization that they were not going to stop coming. Tortillott both feared and pitied the Indians, but for Americans back east the picture was less complicated. People who went through their entire lives without ever seeing an Indian believed in the popular image of crazed savages bent on destroying civilization.

There were real instances of brutality as competition for diminishing natural resources raised the stakes on both sides. But the tabloid newspapers such as the *Police Gazette* knew their audience and catered to its prejudices against Indians. In a typical example, the *Gazette* gives its version of a clash between U.S. Cavalry and Indians in South Dakota, complete with headline (Indian Treachery and Bloodshed) and violent illustration.

Even in the midst of the final struggles between the white settlers and the Indians, the commercialization of the frontier idea had begun. And, as Richard Slotkin later describes in "Staging Reality: The Creation of Buffalo Bill, 1869–1883," no one did better or was transformed more in the process than the man known as Buffalo Bill. Beginning in 1869, Buffalo Bill Cody, so nicknamed for having killed thousands of plains buffalo, became the subject of dime novels by Ned Buntline; eventually he authored books about himself and parlayed his fame into Buffalo Bill's Wild West, a show that featured stylized scenes starring such famous western figures as sharpshooter Annie Oakley. The reality of the West had turned into an act—and a highly successful one at that.

By 1893, the frontier was essentially closed; Oklahoma would not become a state until 1912, but the Indians were no longer a factor, the railroad had long since become transcontinental, industrialization had transformed American cities and multiplied their populations, and people who wanted to see Indians could buy a ticket to Buffalo Bill's show; he had the great Indian chief Sitting Bull as one of his acts.

Chicago, the youngest of America's great cities, celebrated its status by holding a World's Fair in 1893. A brilliant young professor, Frederick Jackson Turner, took the opportunity to speak about the impact the closing of the frontier had on the American consciousness. The result, his essay "The Significance of the Frontier in American History," is the first and still the most famous analysis of the frontier. Turner's address had profound effects on the development of economics as a discipline, as well as on the study of American history, and the argument he started about the significance of the frontier to the development of American character and democracy has continued ever since. Richard Hofstadter's response that follows is the most famous, but it is only one of many.

Among the many tangible effects of the closing of the frontier was the confinement of Indians to reservations and, not coincidentally, the beginnings of what was to become the national parks system. As the actual frontier disappeared, and with it the real conflict between whites and Indians, the need to preserve some portion of a pristine landscape grew, with the West and Far West as the primary beneficiaries. A conservationist movement led by naturalist and writer John Muir successfully campaigned for Yosemite and the Sequoias in California, which were declared national parks in 1890.

The size of the parks system has gradually increased over the years, but not without debate about the need for development versus the need for open space. One western writer who dedicated much of his work to the significance of the wilderness in an industrialized America was the novelist and conservationist Wallace Stegner. In his famous "Coda: Wilderness Letter," Stegner argues not just for the wilderness but for the *idea* of the wilderness, even for Americans who have never seen it and don't really want to, except in the movies.

For most American Indians, the closing of the frontier inaugurated a period of severe economic hardship and deprivation. Where they tended to be most visible was in movie westerns, usually in the act of being shot off their horses by cowboy heroes in general and John Wayne in particular. In her poem "Dear John Wayne," American Indian writer Louise Erdrich captures the ironic experience of American Indians who go to the drive-in to watch Hollywood versions of what happened to their ancestors.

It is typical of Americans that, when one kind of frontier disappears, we look for another one. In the 1950s, when the Soviet Union shocked Americans by being the first country to put a man in space, we embarked on a wildly ambitious program to put a man on the moon by 1970; the venture was described as venturing into the frontiers of space. That program succeeded, and the idea of the frontiersman entering uncharted territory found a new incarnation in science fiction films about space exploration, in *Life* magazine's continuing articles about the seven original astronauts, in Tom Wolfe's best seller, *The Right Stuff*, in the *Star Wars* movie trilogy, and especially in the cult status of the television series *Star Trek*. An article by John S. Davis in *Star Trek* magazine puts the series squarely in the tradition of the American frontier.

Recently, with the space program in some disfavor, the frontier has changed yet again: from physical to technological journeys. This time it's down the new information highway and the undiscovered country of computer connections and interactions. As Americans start off again, on yet another Oregon Trail of infinite possibilities, Peggy Orenstein examines one of the inescapable dangers of promoting the possibilities of any new American frontier—the possibility of confusing reality with a manipulation of reality.

Finally, the continued search for frontiers means a revision and reworking of old myths in new and satisfying ways. There is a line of descent from one icon of American individualism to another—from the frontier heroes of James Fenimore Cooper, to the cowboys of dime novels and western movies, to the cynical private detectives of this century, all loners who come into a situation disordered by violence, set things right, and then go off, still independent and still alone. These keepers of law and order have always been portrayed as men; but Anne Woolley addresses the most recent development in this genre—women private detectives. While sexually at odds with the presentation of heroic male figures, they take over in a previously macho landscape, preserving some elements of the frontier personality and transforming others.

Exploring American Frontiers through Revision

The selections in this chapter express familiar American themes and often refer to familiar American images: the West, the frontier, the New World, the American character. You will notice how often one writer revises the opinion of another. Sometimes the revision is factual—different versions of related experiences, like Twain and Tortillott going west at almost the same time but definitely not with the same results. At other times the revision is explicitly thematic—Frederick Jackson Turner found a defining connection between the frontier and American democracy, but Richard Hofstadter found it in different places and saw in it different lines of development. And sometimes the revision is both factual and thematic—Buffalo Bill revised his own role in American history, and Richard Slotkin revised Buffalo Bill.

Revision is such a powerful force here because these authors are taking the long view of their country's past and future. They know that an earlier version of history is not necessarily wrong and that the most recent view is not necessarily right. And they understand that however Americans have come to see themselves, in some combination of fact, legend, self-delusion, and blind optimism, that compound has long since taken on a life of its own.

As you read these selections, think about your own experiences of and ideas about frontiers as you were growing up. Do you still believe in the Wild West, or romantic cowboys, or fearless sharpshooters, or the crew of the *Enterprise*? If not, how has your vision been revised, and what have you gained and lost in the revision? How do you feel about future frontiers? Can you predict how they may affect our national self-image?

WESTWARD JOURNEY FROM IOWA TO CALIFORNIA
1862

Jane Gould Tortillott

Jane Gould Tortillott was born in 1833, grew up in Ohio, and crossed the plains to California with her family in 1862. Her husband, who was ill during most of the trip, died in 1863. She went to work as a cook in a lumber camp and later married a man she met there, and her many descendants still live in California. Her diary—one of many kept by women who wanted to make a record for their families of their overland trip to the West—was not published until 1982, when historian Lillian Schlissel selected it for her book, Women's Diaries of the Western Journey. *It reflects the uniqueness of female experience in one of the great American adventures.*

Sunday, April 27 Left home this morning, traveled through sloughy prairie, found some hay in an old stack, nooned, and went on to camp four miles from Chickesaw. Camped in a grove near a house where we got grain and hay for our teams. The lady of the house offered us some milk but we had that, came sixteen miles. . . .

Tuesday, April 29 When we got up this morning found a white frost on everything. The weather is rather cool for camping yet. Having no stove it is rather unpleasant cooking. Our road is very good today.

Wednesday, April 30 It was raining this morning when we awoke. Had to get breakfast in the rain, having no tent. . . .

Thursday, May 1 Took nearly an hour to build a fire this morning, the ground was very wet and the wind blew cold from the Northwest. Started late. Bought some hay during the forenoon, carried it in bundles. Nooned in a grove, camped for night near an old house which served as a wind breaker. . . .

Friday, May 16 We are to stay some time to recruit our teams at this place. Most of the women of our company are washing. I am baking. I made some yeast bread for the first time for three weeks, which tasted very good after eating hot biscuits for so long.

Saturday, May 17 Awoke this morning, found it raining hard as it could pour down. The men went out of the wagon, made some coffee and warmed some beans and brought the breakfast to the wagon, which we all crowded into. Used a trunk for a table and made out a very comfortable meal. After eating they put the dishes under the wagon where they remained till four o'clock, when the rain ceased and I left the shelter of the wagon for the first time today. It had grown very cold through the day, most of the men were wet through.

Sunday, May 18 The air was pure this morning but very cold. We were all shivering till about nine, when the sun shone out clear and made the air much warmer. I went out with the children to take a walk and gather flowers. We went in a path through the hazel bushes, saw some hazelnuts laying on the ground. We picked up some and cracked [them] and finding them good, gathered two quarts, which were quite a luxury this time of the year. Some of the women are washing, Sunday though it be. Two gents and ladies of our company went out horseback riding for their health.

Tuesday, May 20 The weather was fair this morning but towards noon it clouded up. Our company all left us to go on. We were detained waiting for a part of our company. While we were preparing our supper it began to rain so that by the time supper was ready we were slightly dampened and what was worse, we had to eat in the rain. . . .

Friday, May 30 . . . Lou and I shot at a mark with a revolver. The boys said we did first rate for new beginners. . . .

Saturday, May 31 . . . Gus was fiddling in the evening and two ladies and one gent came over. Albert played some. They wished us to come up to the house and have a little dance but Albert, feeling rather indisposed, we decline the invitation. . . .

Monday, June 2 . . . Albert went fishing and caught two fish about as long as one's finger. I cooked one for him. His appetite is rather capricious, he not being well.

Tuesday, June 3 . . . In the afternoon we passed a lonely nameless grave on the prairie. It had a headboard. It called up a sad train of thoughts, to my mind, it seems so sad to think of being buried and left alone in so wild a country with no one to plant a flower or shed a tear o'er one's grave. . . .

Wednesday, June 4 Had an early start this morning. A beautiful morning it was too. Clear, bright and warm. We traveled nearly ten miles. I should think, nooned on the Platte banks. The boys waded across on to an island and brought some chips in a sack which were sufficient to get our supper with. . . .

Wednesday, June 11 . . . Lou and I went calling on a new neighbor who has a sick child. . . .

15   *Friday, June 13* . . . A lady on our train was thrown from her horse and injured quite severely. They sent on ahead a mile for Doctor, who was in the next train. . . .

Monday, June 23 'Twas somewhat cloudy this morning when we arose. Had a rough road this forenoon. Stopped for noon near the Platte. It is filled with small islands. The boys have gone bathing. There is a grave of a woman near here. The tire of a wagon is bent up and put for a head and foot stone, her name and age is filed upon it. . . .

Tuesday, June 24 Were up rather late this morning, but had a choice breakfast of antelope meat, which was brought us by Mr. Bullwinkle, some that he bought of the Indians. He brought it for us to cook on shares. It was really delicious. We passed through a small Indian village (a temporary one) this forenoon. We saw that they had over a hundred ponies. There were sixteen wigwams. The road has been better today. Nooned on the Platte banks. While we were eating our lunch there was an Indian Chief rode up on a nice mule, his bridle was covered with silver plates, he had the Masonic emblems on it (he the Indian) was dressed in grand style. He had a looking glass and comb suspended by a string, had a fan and silver ornaments made of half dollars made into fancy shapes. I can't describe half the ornaments that he wore. He was real good looking for an Indian. He wore earrings as much as eight inches long. . . .

Wednesday, June 25 . . . The Indians came around, so many that we hardly had a chance to get our dinners. They were very anxious to "swap" moccasins and lariats for money, powder and whiskey, but we had none to trade. Charley traded a little iron teakettle for a lariat. Two of them shot at a mark with Albert's gun. He beat them. . . .

Saturday, June 28 Did not travel today. Stayed over to let the cattle have a chance to rest. Albert set the tire of his wagon wheels and set some shoes on the horses, which made a pretty hard days work for him. He also shortened the reach for his wagon. The smith here only charges ten dollars for shoeing a yoke of oxen. I did a large washing and Lucy did a large quantity of cooking. Made herself nearly sick working so hard. Gus and I took my clothes to the river to rinse them. Was a little island covered with wild bushes nearby. Gus tried to wade

over to it—to hang the clothes but it was too deep so we were obliged
to hang them on some low bushes close to the river. . . .

Tuesday, July 1 . . . In the night I heard Mrs. Wilson's baby crying   20
very hard indeed, it had fallen from the wagon. It cried for nearly an
hour, he struck his head. . . .

Friday, July 4 Today is the Fourth of July and here we are away off
in the wilderness and can't even stay over a day to do any extra cooking. The men fired their guns. We wonder what the folks at home are
doing and oh, how we wish we were there. Albert is not well today, so
I drive. I have been in the habit of sleeping a while every forenoon, so
naturally I was very sleepy driving. Went to sleep a multitude of times,
to awaken with a start fancying we were running into gullies. After
going a short distance we came in sight of a mail station, on the other
side of the river there were several buildings. They are of adobe, I suppose. Nearly opposite on this side of the river we passed a little log hut
which is used for a store. It was really a welcome sight after going four
hundred miles without seeing a house of any kind. . . .

Wednesday, July 9 . . . We hear many stories of Indians depredations, but do not feel frightened yet. . . .

Friday, July 11 . . . There was a little child run over by a wagon in
Walker's train, who are just ahead of us. The child was injured quite
seriously. . . . They sent for a German physician that belongs to our
train, to see the child that was injured. He said he thought it would get
better. . . .

Sunday, July 20 . . . The men had a ball-play towards night. Seemed
to enjoy themselves very much, it seemed like old times.

Monday, July 21 . . . Our men went to work this morning to build-   25
ing a raft. Worked hard all day. Half of the men in the water, too. . . .

Tuesday, July 22 . . . Went to work this morning as early as possible
to ferrying the wagons over. Had to take them apart and float the box
and cover behind. The two boxes were fastened together by the rods,
one before to tow in and the other to load. Worked till dark. We were
the last but one to cross tonight. Got some of our groceries wet, some
coffee, sugar dissolved. . . .

Saturday, July 26 . . . Annie McMillen had lagged behind, walking,
when we stopped. The whole train had crossed the creek before they
thought of her. The creek was so deep that it ran into the wagon boxes,
so she could not wade. A man on horseback went over for her, and another man on a mule went to help her on. The mules refused to go
clear across, went where the water was very deep, threw the man off
and almost trampled him, but he finally got out safe, only well wet
and with the loss of a good hat, which is no trifling loss here. . . .

Monday, July 28 . . . Came past a camp of thirty six wagons who
have been camped for some time here in the mountains. They have

had their cattle stampeded four or five times. There was a woman died in this train yesterday. She left six children, one of them only two days old. Poor little thing, it had better have died with its mother. They made a good picket fence around the grave. . . .

Sunday, August 3 . . . We passed by the train I have just spoken of. They had just buried the babe of the woman who died days ago, and were just digging a grave for another woman that was run over by the cattle and wagons when they stampeded yesterday. She lived twenty-four hours, she gave birth to a child a short time before she died. The child was buried with her. She leaves a little two year old girl and a husband. They say he is nearly crazy with sorrow. . . .

30   *Tuesday, August 5* . . . Did not start very early. Waited for a train to pass. It seems today as if I *must* go home to fathers to see them all. I can't wait another minute. If I could only *hear* from them it would do some good, but I suppose I shall have to wait whether I am patient or not. . . .

Sunday, August 10 Traveled five or six miles when we came to Snake River. We stayed till two o'clock then traveled till about four or five, when *we* from the back end of the train saw those on ahead all get out their guns. In a short time the word came back that a train six miles on had been attacked by the Indians, and some killed and that was cause enough for the arming. In a short time were met by two men. They wanted us to go a short distance from the road and bring two dead men to their camp, five miles ahead.

Albert unloaded his little wagon and sent Gus back with them and about forty armed men from both trains, to get them. We learned that a train of eleven wagons had been plundered of all that was in them and the teams taken and the men killed. One was Mr. Bullwinkle who left us the 25th of last month, at the crossing of Green River. He went on with this Adams train. Was intending to wait for us but we had not overtaken him yet. He was shot eight times. His dog was shot four times before he would let them get to the wagon. They took all that he had in his wagon, except his trunks and books and papers. They broke open his trunks and took all that they contained. (He had six.) It is supposed that they took six thousand dollars from him, tore the cover from his wagon, it was oilcloth. He had four choice horses. They ran away when he was shot, the harnesses were found on the trail where it was cut from them when they went. It was a nice silver one. The Captain had a daughter shot and wounded severely. This happened yesterday. This morning a part of their train and a part of the Kennedy train went in pursuit of the stock. They were surrounded by Indians on ponies, two killed, several wounded and two supposed to be killed. They were never found. One of those killed was Capt. Adams' son, the other was a young man in the Kennedy train. Those that we carried to camp were those killed this morning. Mr. Bullwinkle and the two others were buried before we got to the camp. There were one hundred and fifty wagons there and thirty four of ours. Capt. Kennedy was severely wounded. Capt. Hunter of Iowa City train was killed likewise by an Indian. We camped near Snake River. We could not get George to ride after the news, he *would* walk and carry his loaded pistol to help.

Monday, August 11 . . . The two men we brought up were buried early this morning with the other three, so they laid five men side by side in this vast wilderness, killed by guns and arrows of the red demons. The chief appeared yesterday in a suit of Mr. Bullwinkle's on the battlefield. . . .

Tuesday, August 12 Capt. Adams' daughter died this morning from the effects of her wound. Was buried in a box made of a wagon box. Poor father and mother lost one son and one daughter, all of his teams, clothing and four thousand dollars. Is left dependent on the bounty of strangers. . . . In the evening we took in Mrs. Ellen Ives, one of the ladies of the plundered train. Her husband goes in the wagon just ahead of us. She was married the morning she started for California. Not a very pleasant wedding tour. . . .

Thursday, August 13 . . . After going up the canyon about four miles, we came to a wagon that had been stopped. There was a new harness, or parts of one, some collars and close by we saw the bodies of three dead men, top of the ground. They had been dead two or three weeks. Some one had been along and thrown a little earth over them, but they were mostly uncovered again. One had his head and face out, another his legs, a third, his hands and arms. Oh! it is a horrid thing. I wish all of the Indians in Christendom were exterminated. . . .

Friday, August 15 We were aroused this morning at one o'clock by the firing of guns and yelling of Indians, answered by our men. The Capt. calling, "come on you red devils." It did not take us long to dress, for once. I hurried for the children and had them dress and get into our wagon, put up a mattress and some beds and quilts on the exposed side of the wagon to protect us. The firing was from the willows and from the mouth of the corrall. There were two other trains with us. There are one hundred and eleven wagons of all and two hundred or more men. The firing did not continue long nor do any harm. Our men shot a good many balls into the willows but I presume they were not effectual. We sat and watched and waited till morning. Yoked the cattle and turned them out with a heavy guard and several scouts to clear the bushes. Cooked our breakfast and started. There were ball holes through two or three wagon covers. . . . We nooned in a little valley but kept our eyes open to all that might be hidden in the bushes and behind the rocks. . . . In the night we were all startled by the bark of the kiota [coyote], which sounded very much like the Indians when they attacked us last night. The alarm gun was fired, which awakened us all. After a while we concluded it was the wolves and went to bed. Most of the train slept under the wagons, dug a trench and blockaded on the outside of the wagon. Set up flour sacks and all manner of stuff. We hung up a cotton mattress and some quilts, and slept in the wagon. . . . It is not an enviable situation to be placed in, not to know at night when you go to bed, whether you will be alive in the morning or not.

August 16–20: [Each night the emigrants dug trenches and kept anxious watch for Indians.]

Thursday, August 21 The road was rough some of the way. Some steep hills to pass over. We saw several Indians today for the first time. They were Snakes. One of them said that he was chief. Three of the men in the Newburn train burned their wigwams in their absence. They came on at noon, were very indignant about it and wanted us to pay for it. Capt. Walker told them who it was that burned them. They got quite a good deal of bread and bacon from different ones from our camp. After being in trouble with them for so long, we are glad to let them be friendly if they will. Albert, Lucy and I went a short way from the road and got our arms full of currant bushes laden with fruit, both red and white. We ate what we wished and had nearly two quarts to eat with sugar for supper. They were real refreshing.

Saturday, August 23 . . . Oh dear, I do so want to get there. It is now almost four months since we have slept in a house. If I could only be set down at home with all the folks I think there would be some talking as well as resting. Albert is so very miserable too, that I don't enjoy myself as well as I would if he was well. There have been Indians around today begging. We are glad to see them do so now, for all we are disgusted with the wretched creatures. . . .

40   *Wednesday, August 27* The first thing I heard this morning was that Mr. McMillen was dead. Died at ten last night. He died quite suddenly. Was buried early this morning. They could not get boards to make a coffin. They dug his grave vault fashion made it just the right size for him, high enough for him to lay in, then wider to lay short boards over him. He was in his clothes with a sheet around him. It seems hard to have to bury ones friends in such a way. I do feel so sorry for the poor wife and daughter, strangers in a strange land. All of her relatives are in Ohio. . . . [Gus, the friend and hired man of the Goulds, took over the driving of Mrs. McMillen's team.] . . .

Friday, August 29 . . . We came to where there have been Indian depredations committed. There were feathers strewn around, a broken wagon, and a large grave with stones over it, a bloody piece of a shirt on it. It had probably two or more persons in it. There was a hat and a nightcap found near, also some small pieces of money. It had been done only a few days. We camped after dark on the Humboldt river for which we were very thankful. . . .

Friday, September 5 . . . Here we are obliged to separate some of the train go the Honey Lake Route and some the Carson River Route. We and 24 others go the latter one. The Capt. goes with the former. We seem like a family of children without a father. *We* think he is the best Capt. on the road. Some could hardly refrain from shedding tears at parting. Tears came into the Capt.'s eyes as he bade them good-bye. . . .

Sunday, September 7 . . . We hear such discouraging account of our road to Carson River, that the female portion of our little train are almost discouraged. We sat by moonlight and discussed matters till near eleven o'clock. Had quite a number of gentlemen visitors during the evening. They say there is no grass between here and Carson River. If not, I don't know what we can do.

Monday, September 8 . . . Some of the train had a dance, but we did not join them.

Tuesday, September 9 When we arose the men told us that if we   45
were in a hurry with our work we might have time to walk up to see [Humboldt] City. So we hurried. Lucy and I. Mrs. McMillen and Annie went to see. Found it a long walk, I should think all of the way up hill. There are some twenty-five buildings. Some of them rough stone and some adobe, some plastered and some not (on the outside) mostly covered with cotton cloth. We called to see a woman who has a sick husband. They are emigrants. Have only been here a week, are waiting for him to recover. He has the typhoid fever. They wished to cross the Nevada range this fall. Provisions are very high here. Flour is thirteen dollars per cwt., coffee 45 cts. per pound, sugar three pound for a dollar, bacon 35 cts per pound. Mrs. McMillen and Annie went into a house and stayed for a few minutes. When she came out she said she intended to stay there, and in the face of all the opposition we raised, she stayed. There were none of us that had any more than provisions enough to last through and some I fear, *not* enough, so Gus was obliged to stay too. I was sorry to leave him this side of Cal. as long as he started with us, and is an old acquaintance. I was sorry to leave Mrs. McMillen, it does not seem like a good place for a woman to stay, there are only four families here, the rest are single men. We came on six or eight miles and stopped without much grass for noon (I am just as homesick as I can be). I chanced to make this remark and Albert has written it down. . . .

Sunday, September 14 . . . Ellen and Will Jones got a chance to go to Virginia City free of charge for which we were very glad, on account of our heavy load. We are nearly out of provisions too. We have to pay five cts. per lb. for hay. Albert sold his wiffletree* and neck yoke for five and a half dollars. We had ten miles to go to get to the desert. . . . Lou and I walked a great deal. The roads are literally lined with wagon irons and keg hoops and piles of bones every five rods. . . .

Monday, September 15 . . . The road is the worst I ever saw. Lou and I walked the whole ten miles, till we came to within a mile of Ragtown. We saw the trees on Carson River and thought we were almost there but we kept going and going and it seemed as if I never could get there.

September 16–18. [They were now passing through the California mining camps.]

Friday, September 19 . . . Were quite surprised to find Ellen here. She had hired out for a month for twenty dollars. Her husband is at Virginia City working for fifty dollars per month. After coming five miles farther we come to another well and a tent for a station. Found Mrs. McMillen here, just ready to go. Went on together a mile and a half. Lou and I and she and Annie walked so as to visit. [Mrs. McMillen decided not to remain in Humboldt City, but came with Gus all the way to the coast, where the Goulds met her.] . . .

50   *Sunday, September 21* . . . There are houses and public wells all along on the road to Empire City, which is ten miles from Dayton. We stayed at Empire all night. This town is not as large as Dayton, but the streets are full of freight wagons. We see a great many fruit wagons here from Cal. There is a quartz mill here also. Money seems to be plenty. Buildings going up fast. Here is the place to make money, especially for a man without a family can get fifty dollars per month, and board, for most any kind of work and mechanics get more.

September 22–30 . . . [The party came through the Great Redwood Forest, where Jane found the Big Tree Hotel already a prosperous inn. She and Lou danced a "schottische" on the surface of a polished giant redwood.]

Wednesday, October 1 Our roads are rather rough. I walked on before the teams two miles or more, called at a farm for a drink and to rest. Had the pleasure of sitting in a large rocking chair, the first time in five months. They have plenty of fruit trees. Albert called for me and bought some fine grapes, and a pail of tomatoes. The lady of the house gave me some roses and verbenas, they were beautiful and fragrant too. . . .

Friday, October 3 . . . Arrived at the first house in the settlement in the San Joaquin Valley on this road at ten o'clock. The moon shone brightly, we pitched our tent and got supper. In this part of the country all of the water is pumped by power of windmills. The orchards are

---

*The wiffletree (or whiffletree) is the pivoted swinging bar to which the traces of a harness are fastened and by which the wagon is drawn.

not as they are in the States, they are so small and the trees so near together. Every garden and orchard has its windmill to irrigate it. . . .

Monday, October 6 Lou washed today. The men went to town to
see what was to be seen and done. Albert came home sick, went to bed
and did not sit up but a few minutes, the rest of the day. . . .

Tuesday, October 7 Are still staying here. Albert seems to be no bet-   55
ter. I have almost have the "blues" having to camp out and Albert sick
too. . . . This day seems long, I can't set myself to sewing although I
have so much to do.

Wednesday, October 8 Arose this morning with the intention of
going to town. Lou and I went over a few minutes to call on Mrs. Bur-
kett, she had a visitor from town, she regaled us with some very fine
peaches. Went to town and pitched our tent. A lady called by the fence
and told us of a house to rent, also gave us some green corn, the first
we have had this year. Charlie went with her to the house, made a bargain, provided it pleased all around, which it did, we picked up and
went right over. Slept in a house the first time for over five months.
The house is one block east of the Lunatic Asylum. The block which intervenes is vacant. We are to board the owner of the house, Mr. Bray.
The house is very convenient. We pay ten dollars per month rent. The
house is over half a mile from the business part of town.

Farewell to the old Journal.
(Signed) *Jane A. Gould*

For Journals

Before you read this diary, how aware were you of the role of
women in the frontier? Did your image include women at all?

For Discussion

1.   In what ways does the experience of Jane Gould Tortillott's on the
journey west support or revise your own image of what settlers experienced? Of the way movies portray the westward movement?

2.   How would you describe Jane Gould Tortillott's view of the frontier? You may want to compare and contrast it with Mark Twain's in
the next selection. What might account for some of the differences?

3.   At one point the author says that she wishes all the Indians would
be exterminated; at another point she describes the Indians who beg
for food as wretched creatures. What do you think her feelings were
toward Indians? What evidence does she provide both for and against
them?

4. How much does the picture of Indians you see in this diary corre-spond to your ideas of Indians on the plains? Did any of it cause you to revise images you have seen of Indians in the movies or on television?

5. It has been said that history is written by the victors. How do you imagine these encounters with the whites would have been described if the Indians were the ones writing about them?

6. What was your reaction to the rather casual way Tortillott refers to deaths of children and adults and the loss of friends on the frontier? Why do you think she doesn't write more emotionally about these tragedies?

For Writing

1. Tortillott's diary excerpt comes from the book *Women's Diaries of the Westward Journey*, by Lillian Schlissel. Read the diaries of any other two women in it (or in another collection of woman pioneers' writ-ings). Then write a paper comparing their views with regard to In-dians, food, weather, work, and loss. Schlissel's book gives a bibliography for background research you can use to find explanations for the differences in the experiences of these women.

2. Keep a diary or journal for all or part of the school semester; try to write something every day. When you're finished, write an essay ex-plaining how much and why you would revise what you wrote de-pending on who you would be willing to show the results to—peers, teachers, or someone else. Discuss what you learned about yourself and the appropriateness of material for a particular audience.

FROM *ROUGHING IT*
1872

Mark Twain

    Mark Twain (pseudonym of Samuel Clemens, 1835–1910), humorist, novelist, satirist, and lecturer, is one of the foremost writers in American lit-erature, and probably the most beloved. He grew up in Missouri before the Civil War and worked as a printer and a Mississippi riverboat pilot before ac-companying his brother Orion to Nevada in 1862. Roughing It, *with its ad-ventures, tall tales, and absolutely American voice, came out in 1872.*

By eight o'clock everything was ready, and we were on the other side of the river. We jumped into the stage, the driver cracked his whip, and we bowled away and left "the States" behind us. It was a superb summer morning, and all the landscape was brilliant with sunshine. There was a freshness and breeziness, too, and an exhilarating sense of emancipation from all sorts of cares and responsibilities, that almost made us feel that the years we had spent in the close, hot city, toiling and slaving, had been wasted and thrown away. We were spinning along through Kansas, and in the course of an hour and a half we were fairly abroad on the great Plains. Just here the land was rolling— a grand sweep of regular elevations and depressions as far as the eye could reach—like the stately heave and swell of the ocean's bosom after a storm. And everywhere were cornfields, accenting with squares of deeper green, this limitless expanse of grassy land. But presently this sea upon dry ground was to lose its "rolling" character and stretch away for seven hundred miles as level as a floor!

Our coach was a great swinging and swaying stage, of the most sumptuous description—an imposing cradle on wheels. It was drawn by six handsome horses, and by the side of the driver sat the "conductor," the legitimate captain of the craft; for it was his business to take charge and care of the mails, baggage, express matter, and passengers. We three were the only passengers, this trip. We sat on the back seat, inside. About all the rest of the coach was full of mail-bags—for we had three days' delayed mails with us. Almost touching our knees, a perpendicular wall of mail matter rose up to the roof. There was a great pile of it strapped on top of the stage, and both the fore and hind boots were full. We had twenty-seven hundred pounds of it aboard, the driver said—"a little for Brigham, and Carson, and 'Frisco, but the heft of it for the Injuns, which is powerful troublesome 'thout they get plenty of truck to read." But as he just then got up a fearful convulsion of his countenance which was suggestive of a wink being swallowed by an earthquake, we guessed that his remark was intended to be facetious, and to mean that we would unload the most of our mail matter somewhere on the Plains and leave it to the Indians, or whosoever wanted it.

We changed horses every ten miles, all day long, and fairly flew over the hard, level road. We jumped out and stretched our legs every time the coach stopped, and so the night found us still vivacious and unfatigued.

It was now just dawn; and as we stretched our cramped legs full length on the mail-sacks, and gazed out through the windows across the wide wastes of greensward clad in cool, powdery mist, to where there was an expectant look in the eastern horizon, our perfect enjoyment took the form of a tranquil and contented ecstasy. The stage

whirled along at a spanking gait, the breeze flapping curtains and suspended coats in a most exhilarating way; the cradle swayed and
swung luxuriously, the pattering of the horses' hoofs, the cracking of
the driver's whip, and his "Hi-yi! g'lang!" were music; the spinning
ground and the waltzing trees appeared to give us a mute hurrah as
we went by, and then slack up and look after us with interest, or envy,
or something; and as we lay and smoked the pipe of peace and compared all this luxury with the years of tiresome city life that had gone
before it, we felt that there was only one complete and satisfying happiness in the world, and we had found it. . . .

5   Really and truly, two thirds of the talk of drivers and conductors
had been about this man Slade, ever since the day before we reached
Julesburg. In order that the Eastern reader may have a clear conception
of what a Rocky Mountain desperado is, in his highest state of development, I will reduce all this mass of Overland gossip to one straightforward narrative, and present it in the following shape:

Slade was born in Illinois, of good parentage. At about twenty-six
years of age he killed a man in a quarrel and fled the country. At St.
Joseph, Missouri, he joined one of the early California-bound emigrant
trains, and was given the post of trainmaster. One day on the Plains he
had an angry dispute with one of his wagon-drivers, and both drew
their revolvers. But the driver was the quicker artist, and had his
weapon cocked first. So Slade said it was a pity to waste life on so
small a matter, and proposed that the pistols be thrown on the ground
and the quarrel settled by a fist-fight. The unsuspecting driver agreed,
and threw down his pistol—whereupon Slade laughed at his simplicity, and shot him dead!

He made his escape, and lived a wild life for a while, dividing his
time between fighting Indians and avoiding an Illinois sheriff, who
had been sent to arrest him for his first murder. It is said that in one Indian battle he killed three savages with his own hand, and afterward
cut their ears off and sent them, with his compliments, to the chief of
the tribe.

Slade soon gained a name for fearless resolution, and this was sufficient merit to procure for him the important post of Overland divi-
sion-agent at Julesburg, in place of Mr. Jules, removed. For some time
previously, the company's horses had been frequently stolen, and the
coaches delayed, by gangs of outlaws, who were wont to laugh at the
idea of any man's having the temerity to resent such outrages. Slade
resented them promptly. The outlaws soon found that the new agent
was a man who did not fear anything that breathed the breath of life.
He made short work of all offenders. The result was that delays
ceased, the company's property was let alone, and no matter what
happened or who suffered, Slade's coaches went through, every time!

True, in order to bring about this wholesome change, Slade had to kill several men—some say three, others say four, and others six—but the world was the richer for their loss. The first prominent difficulty he had was with the ex-agent Jules, who bore the reputation of being a reckless and desperate man himself. Jules hated Slade for supplanting him, and a good fair occasion for a fight was all he was waiting for. By and by Slade dared to employ a man whom Jules had once discharged. Next, Slade seized a team of stage-horses which he accused Jules of having driven off and hidden somewhere for his own use. War was declared, and for a day or two the two men walked warily about the streets, seeking each other, Jules armed with a double-barreled shot-gun, and Slade with his history-creating revolver. Finally, as Slade stepped into a store, Jules poured the contents of his gun into him from behind the door. Slade was pluck, and Jules got several bad pistol wounds in return. Then both men fell, and were carried to their respective lodgings, both swearing that better aim should do deadlier work next time. Both were bedridden a long time, but Jules got on his feet first, and gathering his possessions together, packed them on a couple of mules, and fled to the Rocky Mountains to gather strength in safety against the day of reckoning. For many months he was not seen or heard of, and was gradually dropped out of the remembrance of all save Slade himself. But Slade was not the man to forget him. On the contrary, common report said that Slade kept a reward standing for his capture, dead or alive!

After a while, seeing that Slade's energetic administration had restored peace and order to one of the worst divisions of the road, the Overland Stage Company transferred him to the Rocky Ridge division in the Rocky Mountains, to see if he could perform a like miracle there. It was the very paradise of outlaws and desperadoes. There was absolutely no semblance of law there. Violence was the rule. Force was the only recognized authority. The commonest misunderstandings were settled on the spot with the revolver or the knife. Murders were done in open day, and with sparkling frequency, and nobody thought of inquiring into them. It was considered that the parties who did the killing had their private reasons for it; for other people to meddle would have been looked upon as indelicate. After a murder, all that Rocky Mountain etiquette required of a spectator was, that he should help the gentleman bury his game—otherwise his churlishness would surely be remembered against him the first time he killed a man himself and needed a neighborly turn in interring him.

Slade took up his residence sweetly and peacefully in the midst of   10 this hive of horse-thieves and assassins, and the very first time one of them aired his insolent swaggerings in his presence he shot him dead! He began a raid on the outlaws, and in a singularly short space of time he had completely stopped their depredations on the stage stock, re-covered a large number of stolen horses, killed several of the worst desperadoes of the district, and gained such a dread ascendancy over the rest that they respected him, admired him, feared him, obeyed him! He wrought the same marvelous change in the ways of the com-munity that had marked his administration at Overland City. He cap-tured two men who had stolen Overland stock, and with his own hands he hanged them. He was supreme judge in his district, and he was jury and executioner likewise—and not only in the case of of-fences against his employers, but against passing emigrants as well. On one occasion some emigrants had their stock lost or stolen, and told Slade, who chanced to visit their camp. With a single companion he rode to a ranch, the owners of which he suspected, and opening the door, commenced firing, killing three, and wounding the fourth.

From a bloodthirstily interesting little Montana book* I take this paragraph:

> While on the road, Slade held absolute sway. He would ride down to a station, get into a quarrel, turn the house out of windows, and maltreat the occupants most cruelly. The unfortunates had no means of redress, and were compelled to recuperate as best they could. On one of these occasions, it is said, he killed the father of the fine little half-breed boy, Jemmy, whom he adopted, and who lived with his widow after his execution. Stories of Slade's hanging men, and of innumerable assaults, shootings, stabbings and beatings, in which he was a principal actor, form part of the legends of the stage line. As for minor quarrels and shootings, it is absolutely certain that a minute history of Slade's life would be one long record of such practices.

Slade was a matchless marksman with a navy revolver. The leg-ends say that one morning at Rocky Ridge, when he was feeling com-fortable, he saw a man approaching who had offended him some days before—observe the fine memory he had for matters like that—and, "Gentlemen," said Slade, drawing, "it is a good twenty-yard shot—I'll clip the third button on his coat!" Which he did. The bystanders all ad-mired it. And they all attended the funeral, too.

On one occasion a man who kept a little whiskey-shelf at the sta-tion did something which angered Slade—and went and made his will. A day or two afterward Slade came in and called for some brandy. The man reached under the counter (ostensibly to get a bot-tle—possibly to get something else), but Slade smiled upon him that peculiarly bland and satisfied smile of his which the neighbors had long ago learned to recognize as a death-warrant in disguise, and told

---

*The Vigilantes of Montana, by Prof. Thos. J. Dimsdale. [Au.]

him to "none of that!—pass out the high-priced article." So the poor bar-keeper had to turn his back and get the high-priced brandy from the shelf; and when he faced around again he was looking into the muzzle of Slade's pistol. "And the next instant," added my informant, impressively, "he was one of the deadest men that ever lived."

The stage-drivers and conductors told us that sometimes Slade would leave a hated enemy wholly unmolested, unnoticed and unmentioned, for weeks together—had done it once or twice at any rate. And some said they believed he did it in order to lull the victims into unwatchfulness, so that he could get the advantage of them, and others said they believed he saved up an enemy that way, just as a schoolboy saves up a cake, and made the pleasure go as far as it would by gloating over the anticipation. One of these cases was that of a Frenchman who had offended Slade. To the surprise of everybody Slade did not kill him on the spot, but let him alone for a considerable time. Finally, however, he went to the Frenchman's house very late one night, knocked, and when his enemy opened the door, shot him dead—pushed the corpse inside the door with his foot, set the house on fire and burned up the dead man, his widow and three children! I heard this story from several different people, and they evidently believed what they were saying. It may be true, and it may not. "Give a dog a bad name," etc.

Slade was captured, once, by a party of men who intended to   15 lynch him. They disarmed him, and shut him up in a strong log-house, and placed a guard over him. He prevailed on his captors to send for his wife, so that he might have a last interview with her. She was a brave, loving, spirited woman. She jumped on a horse and rode for life and death. When she arrived they let her in without searching her, and before the door could be closed she whipped out a couple of revolvers, and she and her lord marched forth defying the party. And then, under a brisk fire, they mounted double and galloped away unharmed!

In the fulness of time Slade's myrmidons captured his ancient enemy Jules, whom they found in a well-chosen hiding-place in the remote fastnesses of the mountains, gaining a precarious livelihood with his rifle. They brought him to Rocky Ridge, bound hand and foot, and deposited him in the middle of the cattle-yard with his back against a post. It is said that the pleasure that lit Slade's face when he heard of it was something fearful to contemplate. He examined his enemy to see that he was securely tied, and then went to bed, content to wait till morning before enjoying the luxury of killing him. Jules spent the night in the cattle-yard, and it is a region where warm nights are never known. In the morning Slade practised on him with his revolver, nipping the flesh here and there, and occasionally clipping off a finger, while Jules begged him to kill him outright and put him out of his misery. Finally Slade reloaded, and walking up close to his victim, made some characteristic remarks and then dispatched him. The body lay there half a day, nobody venturing to touch it without orders, and then Slade detailed a party and assisted at the burial himself. But he first cut off the dead man's ears and put them in his vest pocket, where he carried them for some time with great satisfaction. That is the story as I have frequently heard it told and seen it in print in California newspapers. It is doubtless correct in all essential particulars.

In due time we rattled up to a stage station, and sat down to breakfast with a half-savage, half-civilized company of armed and bearded mountaineers, ranchmen and station employ[ees]. The most gentlemanly-appearing, quiet and affable officer we had yet found along the road in the Overland Company's service was the person who sat at the head of the table, at my elbow. Never youth stared and shivered as I did when I heard them call him SLADE!

Here was romance, and I sitting face to face with it!—looking upon it—touching it—hobnobbing with it, as it were! Here, right by my side, was the actual ogre who, in fights and brawls and various ways, *had taken the lives of twenty-six human beings*, or all men lied about him! I suppose I was the proudest stripling that ever traveled to see strange lands and wonderful people.

He was so friendly and so gentle-spoken that I warmed to him in spite of his awful history. It was hardly possible to realize that this pleasant person was the pitiless scourge of the outlaws, the rawhead-and-bloody-bones the nursing mothers of the mountains terrified their children with. And to this day I can remember nothing remarkable about Slade except that his face was rather broad across the cheek bones, and that the cheek bones were low and the lips peculiarly thin and straight. But that was enough to leave something of an effect upon me, for since then I seldom see a face possessing those characteristics without fancying that the owner of it is a dangerous man.

20   The coffee ran out. At least it was reduced to one tin-cupful, and Slade was about to take it when he saw that my cup was empty. He politely offered to fill it, but although I wanted it, I politely declined. I was afraid he had not killed anybody that morning, and might be needing diversion. But still with firm politeness he insisted on filling my cup, and said I had traveled all night and better deserved it than he—and while he talked he placidly poured the fluid, to the last drop. I thanked him and drank it, but it gave me no comfort, for I could not feel sure that he would not be sorry, presently, that he had given it away, and proceed to kill me to distract his thoughts from the loss. But

nothing of the kind occurred. We left him with only twenty-six dead people to account for, and I felt a tranquil satisfaction in the thought that in so judiciously taking care of No. 1 at that breakfast-table I had pleasantly escaped being No. 27. Slade came out to the coach and saw us off, first ordering certain reärrangements of the mail-bags for our comfort, and then we took leave of him.

For Journals

What had you read of Twain's before? What did you know about him or his work?

For Discussion

1. Twain's journey across the plains sounds so different from Jane Gould Tortillott's that they might almost be looking at two different countries. What might account for the difference in experience?
2. Tall tales are very characteristic of Twain and of western humor. Why do you think the frontier lent itself to such wildly exaggerated stories about people and places?
3. How do you respond to the idea that giving a biography to Slade or any other western character gives a history to a frontier that doesn't have any history of its own?
4. How does Twain's encounter with the real Slade make us revise our expectations of what he would be like?
5. What image of the frontier do you think Twain's eastern readers had? Does Twain's way of writing reinforce or revise that image?
6. How does Twain's humor contribute to his portrait of himself as a man who knows absolutely nothing about the frontier? Why do you think he chose that way of presenting himself?

For Writing

1. Read a couple of other chapters from *Roughing It*—for example, on Mono Lake, on an earthquake in San Francisco, on Hawaii, on the desert, on striking it rich for ten days in a silver mine—and write a paper on how these episodes support or contradict your own expectations of what the frontier was like, what frontier heroes were like, and what American values these heroes lived by.
2. Write an essay about a trip you took when you were younger to a place—a national park or a city, for example—that made a big impression on you at the time. Write a paragraph about it as you experienced

it in childhood and a paragraph on the same experience as you recall it now. Analyze both paragraphs, and write an essay examining the ways you revised your understanding of your own experience.

GIANT REDWOOD TREES OF CALIFORNIA
1874

Albert Bierstadt

    Albert Bierstadt (1830–1902), was born in Germany but became famous in America as a painter of Western scenery. After travelling and sketching the mountains of Europe, he went on a trail-making expedition to the West in 1859. He painted huge grand canvasses, whose subjects included a Shoshone village, the last of the buffalo, the Rocky Mountains, and Yosemite, and his work was extremely popular.

For Journals

    Whom do you think was the original audience for this painting? What was your own first reaction to it?

For Discussion

1.   Why do you think Bierstadt includes human beings in the painting? How would the overall impression given by the sequoias be changed if there were no figures of people at all?

2.   How would the dramatic impact of the picture be changed if the figures in it were white rather than Indian? Why do you think Bierstadt made the choice he did?

3.   How would you describe the mood conveyed by this painting? How do its features—the angle from which you view it, the vertical placement of the trees, the subject matter—contribute to that mood?

4.   Today Americans take the sequoias for granted, but in the nineteenth century many Easterners, faced with the spectacular Western scenery of paintings like Bierstadt's, couldn't believe their eyes until they saw photographs of the same places. What would be the advantages and disadvantages of a photograph of a scene like this versus a painting of the same scene?

For Writing

1.   Compare this painting with the *California Cornucopia* poster in Chapter 4, and write an analysis of their respective persuasive strategies: who their intended audiences might have been; what they told their audiences about California; what details conveyed that information; which one you find most effective, and why.

2.   John Muir was the founder of the modern conservationist movement; his campaigns on behalf of Yosemite led to its establishment as a national park. Read John Muir's descriptions of Yosemite and the sequoias. Write an essay in which you include your analysis of his appreciation of the landscape, the relevance of his concerns as conservation issues today, the attempt in his writing to revise the idea of land development as an unquestioned good.

INDIAN TREACHERY AND BLOODSHED
1891

Police Gazette

The Police Gazette *was a popular and lurid newspaper that was begun in 1846 but was at its height—or depth— in the 1880s and 1890s. It specialized in stories about crime, prostitution, and sports, was copiously illustrated, never had a story without a melodramatic title, and freely expressed the biases of its publisher, James Fox, who entertained lifelong prejudices against Chinese, African Americans, Jews, American Indians, ministers, and college students, among others.*

The Indian war in South Dakota, so long anticipated, has at last become a reality, and with it has come the death of a number of brave troops of the United States Cavalry. The leader of the warriors was Big Foot and he and his braves tricked the troops into ambush. Then a wholesale slaughter began, the Indians being nearly annihilated, those who were not killed seeking refuge in the Bad Lands, where they will be frozen or starved out. As soon as the troops had cornered the Indians they fell upon them with Hotchkiss guns. The Indians fell in heaps

but, determined to the last, they fought to the death even after being sorely wounded.

The saddest scene of the carnage was the killing of Captain George D. Wallace of the Seventh Cavalry, who was brutally tomahawked. Captain Wallace was appointed to the Military Academy from South Carolina in 1868 and upon being graduated in 1872 was commissioned a second lieutenant in the Seventh. He received his promotion to first lieutenant in 1876 and was commissioned captain in September 1885.

It is said that General Sheridan first remarked that "a dead Indian is the best Indian" and the action of the soldiers appears to coincide with Little Phil's views. The action teaches the lesson that if the Sioux are of any use at all they should be fairly dealt with, and if not, that they should at once be given free passes to the happy hunting grounds. As they speak highly of the happy hunting grounds, it might be as well to start them on the journey in any case, and then, if the decision be found unjust, to write them an apology.

For Journals

How does the news style of the *Police Gazette* compare to that of contemporary tabloid newspapers?

For Discussion

1. How would you describe the author's attitude toward the Indians? What values do you think the writer places on the lives of both Indians and soldiers?

2. How closely do you think the contents of the article and the illustration are related? What would you describe as the theme of the article? Of the illustration?

3. Look at the headline of the article and then at the first paragraph. How does the article support or revise the sentiments in the headline? Given the headline, what would you have expected?

4. Look at the illustration starting at the top and working down to the bottom. How successfully does each grouping convey violent action? If there were no headline for the picture and text, what headline would you supply?

5. Whom do you think read the *Police Gazette*? What would its audience have to do with the kinds of articles it published?

6. Suppose that Indians were writing the article and drawing the illustrations. In what specific ways do you think they would have revised the results?

For Writing

1.   At the library, look at a book with copies of George Catlin's paintings of American Indians—*North American Indians* or *Catlin's Indians*, for example—and write a paper in which you discuss and compare any two of the portraits. Among the points for you to consider: What is your impression of the character and personality of the Indians in the pictures? Exactly what in the paintings conveyed that impression to you—color, body posture, expression, background? What words would you use to describe the mood of the paintings? Your college library would be a good source of material on the history of the tribes and on Catlin's artistry.

2.   Research the development of the idea of the reservation: how it was developed, what treaties surrounded the setting up of reservations, or what conditions prevail on reservations today. If you write about reservations today, focus on one area of the country or one or two reservations.

THE SIGNIFICANCE OF THE FRONTIER IN AMERICAN HISTORY
1893

Frederick Jackson Turner

Frederick Jackson Turner (1862–1932) was born in Wisconsin and taught at the University of Wisconsin and Harvard. He presented this paper during the Chicago World's Fair of 1893 before the American Historical Association. Although Jackson did not publish a great deal, this essay alone made him one of the most famous historians in American studies.

In a recent bulletin of the Superintendent of the Census for 1890 appear these significant words: "Up to and including 1880 the country had a frontier of settlement, but at present the unsettled area has been so broken into by isolated bodies of settlement that there can hardly be said to be a frontier line. In the discussion of its extent, its westward movement, etc., it can not therefore, any longer have a place in the census reports." This brief official statement marks the closing of a great historic movement. Up to our own day American history has been in a large degree the history of the colonization of the Great West. The existence of an area of free land, its continuous recession, and the advance of American settlement westward, explain American development.

Behind institutions, behind constitutional forms and modifications, lie the vital forces that call these organs into life and shape them to meet changing conditions. The peculiarity of American institutions is, the fact that they have been compelled to adapt themselves to the changes of an expanding people—to the changes involved in crossing a continent, in winning a wilderness, and in developing at each area of this progress out of the primitive economic and political conditions of the frontier into the complexity of city life. Said Calhoun in 1817, "We are great, and rapidly—I was about to say fearfully—growing!" So saying, he touched the distinguishing feature of American life. All peoples show development; the germ theory of politics has been sufficiently emphasized. In the case of most nations, however, the development has occurred in a limited area; and if the nation has expanded, it has met other growing peoples whom it has conquered. But in the case of the United States we have a different phenomenon. Limiting our attention to the Atlantic coast, we have the familiar phenomenon of the evolution of institutions in a limited area, such as the rise of representative government; the differentiation of simple colonial governments into complex organs; the progress from primitive industrial society, without division of labor, up to manufacturing civilization. But we have in addition to this a recurrence of the process of evolution in each western area reached in the process of expansion. Thus American development has exhibited not merely advance along a single line, but a return to primitive conditions on a continually advancing frontier line, and a new development for that area. American social development has been continually beginning over again on the frontier. This perennial rebirth, this fluidity of American life, this expansion westward with its new opportunities, its continuous touch with the simplicity of primitive society, furnish the forces dominating American character. The true point of view in the history of this nation is not the Atlantic coast, it is the great West. Even the slavery struggle, which is made so exclusive an object of attention by writers like Professor von Holst, occupies its important place in American history because of its relation to westward expansion.

In this advance, the frontier is the outer edge of the wave—the meeting point between savagery and civilization. Much has been written about the frontier from the point of view of border warfare and the chase, but as a field for the serious study of the economist and the historian it has been neglected.

The American frontier is sharply distinguished from the European frontier—a fortified boundary line running through dense populations. The most significant thing about the American frontier is, that it lies at the hither edge of free land. In the census reports it is treated as the margin of that settlement which has a density of two or more to the square mile. The term is an elastic one, and for our purposes does not need sharp definition. We shall consider the whole frontier belt, including the Indian country and the outer margin of the "settled area" of the census reports. This paper will make no attempt to treat the subject exhaustively; its aim is simply to call attention to the frontier as a fertile field for investigation, and to suggest some of the problems which arise in connection with it.   5

In the settlement of America we have to observe how European life entered the continent, and how America modified and developed that life and reacted on Europe. Our early history is the study of European germs developing in an American environment. Too exclusive attention has been paid by institutional students to the Germanic origins, too little to the American factors. The frontier is the line of most rapid and effective Americanization. The wilderness masters the colonist. It finds him a European in dress, industries, tools, modes of travel, and thought. It takes him from the railroad car and puts him in the birch canoe. It strips off the garments of civilization and arrays him in the hunting shirt and the moccasin. It puts him in the log cabin of the Cherokee and Iroquois and runs an Indian palisade around him. Before long he has gone to planting Indian corn and plowing with a sharp stick; he shouts the war cry and takes the scalp in orthodox Indian fashion. In short, at the frontier the environment is at first too strong for the man. He must accept the conditions which it furnishes, or perish, and so he fits himself into the Indian clearings and follows the Indian trails. Little by little he transforms the wilderness, but the outcome is not the old Europe, not simply the development of Germanic germs, any more than the first phenomenon was a case of reversion to the Germanic mark. The fact is, that here is a new product that is American. At first, the frontier was the Atlantic coast. It was the frontier of Europe in a very real sense. Moving westward, the frontier became more and more American. As successive terminal moraines result from successive glaciations, so each frontier leaves its traces behind it, and when it becomes a settled area the region still partakes of the frontier characteristics. Thus the advance of the frontier has meant a steady movement away from the influence of Europe, a steady growth of independence on American lines. And to study this advance, the men who grew up under these conditions, and the political, economic, and social results of it, is to study the really American part of our history. . . .

The Frontier Furnishes a Field for Comparative Study of Social Development

At the Atlantic frontier one can study the germs of processes repeated at each successive frontier. We have the complex European life sharply precipitated by the wilderness into the simplicity of primitive conditions. The first frontier had to meet its Indian question, its question of the disposition of the public domain, of the means of intercourse with older settlements, of the extension of political organization, of religious and educational activity. And the settlement of these and similar questions for one frontier served as a guide for the next. The American student needs not to go to the "prim little townships of Sleswick" for illustrations of the law of continuity and development. For example, he may study the origin of our land policies in the colonial land policy; he may see how the system grew by adapting the statutes to the customs of the successive frontiers. He may see how the mining experience in the lead regions of Wisconsin, Illinois, and Iowa was applied to the mining laws of the Rockies, and how our Indian policy has been a series of experimentations on successive frontiers. Each tier of new States has found in the older ones material for its constitutions. Each frontier has made similar contributions to American character, as will be discussed farther on.

But with all these similarities there are essential differences, due to the place element and the time element. It is evident that the farming frontier of the Mississippi Valley presents different conditions from the mining frontier of the Rocky Mountains. The frontier reached by the Pacific Railroad, surveyed into rectangles, guarded by the United States Army, and recruited by the daily immigrant ship, moves forward at a swifter pace and in a different way than the frontier reached by the birch canoe or the pack horse. The geologist traces patiently the shores of ancient seas, maps their areas, and compares the older and the newer. It would be a work worth the historian's labors to mark these various frontiers and in detail compare one with another. Not only would there result a more adequate conception of American development and characteristics, but invaluable additions would be made to the history of society.

Loria, the Italian economist, has urged the study of colonial life as an aid in understanding the stages of European development, affirming that colonial settlement is for economic science what the mountain is for geology, bringing to light primitive stratifications. "America," he says, "has the key to the historical enigma which Europe has sought for centuries in vain, and the land which has no history reveals luminously the course of universal history." There is much truth in this. The United States lies like a huge page in the history of society. Line by line as we read this continental page from west to east we find the record of social evolution. It begins with the Indian and the hunter; it goes on to tell of the disintegration of savagery by the entrance of the trader, the pathfinder of civilization; we read the annals of the pastoral stage in ranch life; the exploitation of the soil by the raising of unrotated crops of corn and wheat in sparsely settled farming communities; the intensive culture of the denser farm settlement; and finally the manufacturing organization with city and factory system. This page is familiar to the student of census statistics, but how little of it has been used by our historians. Particularly in eastern States this page is a palimpsest. What is now a manufacturing State was in an earlier decade an area of intensive farming. Earlier yet it had been a wheat area, and still earlier the "range" had attracted the cattle herder. Thus Wisconsin, now developing manufacture, is a State with varied agricultural interests. But earlier it was given over to almost exclusive grain-raising, like North Dakota at the present time.

Each of these areas has had an influence in our economic and political history; the evolution of each into a higher stage has worked political transformations. But what constitutional historian has made any adequate attempt to interpret political facts by the light of these social areas and changes?

The Atlantic frontier was compounded of fisherman, fur-trader,   10
miner, cattle-raiser, and farmer. Excepting the fisherman, each type of industry was on the march toward the West, impelled by an irresistible attraction. Each passed in successive waves across the continent. Stand at Cumberland Gap and watch the procession of civilization, marching single file—the buffalo following the trail to the salt springs, the Indian, the fur-trader and hunter, the cattle-raiser, the pioneer farmer— and the frontier has passed by. Stand at South Pass in the Rockies a century later and see the same procession with wider intervals between. The unequal rate of advance compels us to distinguish the frontier into the trader's frontier, the rancher's frontier, or the miner's frontier, and the farmer's frontier. When the mines and the cow pens were still near the fall line the traders' pack trains were tinkling across the Alleghanies, and the French on the Great Lakes were fortifying their posts, alarmed by the British trader's birch canoe. When the trappers scaled the Rockies, the farmer was still near the mouth of the Missouri. . . .

Land

The exploitation of the beasts took hunter and trader to the west, the exploitation of the grasses took the rancher west, and the exploitation of the virgin soil of the river valleys and prairies attracted the farmer. Good soils have been the most continuous attraction to the farmer's frontier. The land hunger of the Virginians drew them down the rivers into Carolina, in early colonial days; the search for soils took the Massachusetts men to Pennsylvania and to New York. As the eastern lands were taken up migration flowed across them to the west. Daniel Boone, the great backwoodsman, who combined the occupations of hunter, trader, cattle raiser, farmer, and surveyor—learning, probably from the traders, of the fertility of the lands on the upper Yadkin, where the traders were wont to rest as they took their way to the Indians, left his Pennsylvania home with his father, and passed down the Great Valley road to that stream. Learning from a trader whose posts were on the Red River in Kentucky of its game and rich pastures, he pioneered the way for the farmers to that region. Thence he passed to the frontier of Missouri, where his settlement was long a landmark on the frontier. Here again he helped to open the way for civilization, finding salt licks, and trails, and land. His son was among the earliest trappers in the passes of the Rocky Mountains, and his party are said to have been the first to camp on the present site of Denver. His grandson, Col. A. J. Boone, of Colorado, was a power among the Indians of the Rocky Mountains, and was appointed an agent by the Government. Kit Carson's mother was a Boone. Thus this family epitomizes the backwoodsman's advance across the continent. . . .

Composite Nationality

First, we note that the frontier promoted the formation of a composite nationality for the American people. The coast was preponderantly English, but the later tides of continental immigration flowed across to the free lands. This was the case from the early colonial days. The Scotch-Irish and the Palatine Germans, or "Pennsylvania Dutch," furnished the dominant element in the stock of the colonial frontier. With these peoples were also the freed indentured servants, or redemptioners, who at the expiration of their time of service passed to the frontier. Governor Spottswood of Virginia writes in 1717, "The inhabitants of our frontiers are composed generally of such as have been transported hither as servants, and, being out of their time, settle themselves where land is to be taken up and that will produce the necessarys of life with little labour." Very generally these redemptioners were of non-English stock. In the crucible of the frontier the immigrants were Americanized, liberated, and fused into a mixed race, English in neither nationality nor characteristics. The process has gone on from the early days to our own. Burke and other writers in the middle of the eighteenth century believed that Pennsylvania was "threatened with the danger of being wholly foreign in language, manners, and perhaps even inclinations." The German and Scotch-Irish elements in the frontier of the South were only less great. In the middle of the present century the German element in Wisconsin was already so considerable that leading publicists looked to the creation of a German state out of the commonwealth by concentrating their colonization. Such examples teach us to beware of misinterpreting the fact that there is a common English speech in America into a belief that the stock is also English.

Industrial Independence

In another way the advance of the frontier decreased our dependence on England. The coast, particularly of the South, lacked diversified industries, and was dependent on England for the bulk of its supplies. In the South there was even a dependence on the Northern colonies for articles of food. Governor Glenn, of South Carolina, writes in the middle of the eighteenth century: "Our trade with New York and Philadelphia was of this sort, draining us of all the little money and bills we could gather from other places for their bread, flour, beer, hams, bacon, and other things of their produce, all which, except beer, our new townships begin to supply us with, which are settled with very industrious and thriving Germans. This no doubt diminishes the number of shipping and the appearance of our trade, but it is far from being a detriment to us." Before long the frontier created a demand for merchants. As it retreated from the coast it became less and less possible for England to bring her supplies directly to the consumer's wharfs, and carry away staple crops, and staple crops began to give way to diversified agriculture for a time. The effect of this phase of the frontier action upon the northern section is perceived when we realize how the advance of the frontier aroused seaboard cities like Boston, New York, and Baltimore, to engage in rivalry for what Washington called "the extensive and valuable trade of a rising empire." . . .

Growth of Democracy

But the most important effect of the frontier has been in the promotion of democracy here and in Europe. As has been indicated, the frontier is productive of individualism. Complex society is precipitated by the wilderness into a kind of primitive orgaization based on the family. The tendency is anti-social. It produces antipathy to control, and particularly to any direct control. The tax gatherer is viewed as a representative of oppression. Professor Osgood, in an able article, has pointed out that the frontier conditions prevalent in the colonies are important factors in the explanation of the American Revolution, where individual liberty was sometimes confused with absence of all effective government. The same conditions aid in explaining the difficulty of instituting a strong government in the period of the confederacy. The frontier individualism has from the beginning promoted democracy.

15   The frontier States that came into the Union in the first quarter of a century of its existence came in with democratic suffrage provisions, and had reactive effects of the highest importance upon the older States whose peoples were being attracted there. An extension of the franchise became essential. It was *western* New York that forced an extension of suffrage in the constitutional convention of that State in 1821; and it was *western* Virginia that compelled the tide-water region to put a more liberal suffrage provision in the constitution framed in 1830, and to give to the frontier region a more nearly proportionate representation with the tide-water aristocracy. The rise of democracy as an effective force in the nation came in with western preponderance under Jackson and William Henry Harrison, and it meant the triumph of the frontier—with all of its good and with all of its evil elements. . . .

So long as free land exists, the opportunity for a competency exists, and economic power secures political power. But the democracy born of free land, strong in selfishness and individualism, intolerant of administrative experience and education, and pressing individual liberty beyond its proper bounds, has its dangers as well as its benefits. Individualism in America has allowed a laxity in regard to governmental affairs which has rendered possible the spoils system and all the manifest evils that follow from the lack of a highly developed civic spirit. In this connection may be noted also the influence of frontier conditions in permitting lax business honor, inflated paper currency and wild-cat banking. The colonial and revolutionary frontier was the region whence emanated many of the worst forms of an evil currency. The West in the War of 1812 repeated the phenomenon on the frontier of that day, while the speculation and the wild-cat banking of the period of the crisis of 1837 occurred on the new frontier belt of the next tier of States. Thus each one of the periods of lax financial integrity coincides with periods when a new set of frontier communities had arisen, and coincides in area with these successive frontiers, for the most part. The recent Populist agitation is a case in point. Many a State that now declines any connection with the tenets of the Populists, itself adhered to such ideas in an earlier stage of the development of the State. A primitive society can hardly be expected to show the intelligent appreciation of the complexity of business interests in a developed society. The continual recurrence of these areas of paper-money agitation is another evidence that the frontier can be isolated and studied as a factor in American history of the highest importance. . . .

Intellectual Traits

From the conditions of frontier life came intellectual traits of profound importance. The works of travelers along each frontier from colonial days onward describe certain common traits, and these traits have, while softening down, still persisted as survivals in the place of their origin, even when a higher social organization succeeded. The result is that to the frontier the American intellect owes its striking characteristics. That coarseness and strength combined with acuteness and inquisitiveness; that practical, inventive turn of mind, quick to find expedients; that masterful grasp of material things, lacking in the artistic but powerful to effect great ends; that restless, nervous energy; that dominant individualism, working for good and for evil, and withal that buoyancy and exuberance which comes with freedom—these are traits of the frontier. Since the days when the fleet of Columbus sailed into the waters of the New World, America has been another name for opportunity, and the people of the United States have taken their tone from the incessant expansion which has not only been open but has even been forced upon them. He would be a rash prophet who should assert that the expansive character of American life has now entirely ceased. Movement has been its dominant fact, and, unless this training has no effect upon a people, the American energy will continually demand a wider field for its exercise. But never again will such gifts of free land offer themselves. For a moment, at the frontier, the bonds of custom are broken and unrestraint is triumphant. There is not *tabula rasa*. The stubborn American environment is there with its imperious summons to accept its conditions; the inherited ways of doing things are also there; and yet, in spite of environment, and in spite of custom, each frontier did indeed furnish a new field of opportunity, a gate of escape from the bondage of the past; and freshness, and confidence, and scorn of older society, impatience of its restraints and its ideas, and indifference to its lessons, have accompanied the frontier. What the Mediterranean Sea was to the Greeks, breaking the bond of custom, offering new experiences, calling out new institutions and activities, that, and more, the ever retreating frontier has been to the United States directly, and to the nations of Europe more remotely. And now, four centuries from the discovery of America, at the end of a hundred years of life under the Constitution, the frontier has gone, and with its going has closed the first period of American history.

For Journals

What is your own idea of what the American frontier represents? Cowboys and Indians? The Gold Rush? The space program? Movie westerns?

For Discussion

1. Turner saw the existence of a frontier as crucial to the formation of the American character and American democracy. What are his premises in this argument? What evidence does he provide to support them?

2. How do you respond to Turner's assertion that the frontier was the meeting point between civilization and savagery "the outer edge of the wave—"? How positively do you regard the idea of settlers moving through the frontier in order to create a different and distinctly American civilization?

3. Why does Turner see the life of Daniel Boone as a prototype of the frontiersman? What combination of elements makes Boone, in Turner's thesis, so suitable an example of the positive side of westward expansion?

4. How do you think Turner defines the idea of progress in American civilization? Progress from what to what? What do you think of as an example of progress in America?

5. One writer has said that Turner's essay is not *an* explanation of American history but rather *the* explanation of American history. Why would an analysis of the frontier be an analysis of American history altogether?

6. Turner said that the frontier had made the American character expansive, and that once the free land disappeared, Americans would have to find other ways of stretching their horizons. Where do you think Americans have turned to find psychological substitutions for the western frontier?

For Writing

1. Watch a video of one of the following movies: *High Noon; Shane; A Fistful of Dollars; Little Big Man; She Wore a Yellow Ribbon; Unforgiven.* Then write an essay in which you address the following issues: What picture does the movie give of life in the West? How closely does that picture coincide with your own idea of that life? What are the primary ethical and social values expressed in the movie, and who in the film embodies them?

2. Since it was written, there have been many revisions of Turner's thesis. Read one of them, such as David Potter's *People of Plenty* and then write your own evaluation of whether the revision refutes all of Turner's claims effectively. Then write your own response to Turner's ideas.

THE THESIS DISPUTED

1949

Richard Hofstadter

> *Richard Hofstadter (1916–1970) was a highly original American histo-*
> *rian who spent his career at Columbia University. His amazingly diverse*
> *body of work paid particular attention to the importance of ideas in American*
> *history and to the development of political institutions. He won the Pulitzer*
> *Prize twice. When he wrote this essay, the most famous analysis of Frederick*
> *Jackson Turner's thesis on the role of the frontier in American history, the*
> *thesis had just undergone a period of attack by other historians. Hofstadter*
> *was able to appreciate the significance as well as the faults of Turner's*
> *theory.*

American historical writing in the past century has produced two major theories or models of understanding, the economic interpretation of politics associated with Charles A. Beard, and the frontier interpretation of American development identified with Frederick Jackson Turner. Both views have had a pervasive influence upon American thinking, but Beard himself felt that Turner's original essay on the frontier had "a more profound influence on thought about American history than any other essay or volume ever written on the subject." It is the frontier thesis that has embodied the predominant American view of the American past. . . .

American evolution, Turner believed, had been a repeated return to primitive conditions on a continually receding frontier line, a constant repetition of development from simple conditions to a complex society. From this perennial rebirth and fluidity of American life, and from its continual re-exposure to the simplicity of primitive society, had come the forces dominant in the American character. And as the frontier advanced, society moved steadily away from European influences, grew steadily on distinctive American lines. To study this advance and the men who had been fashioned by it was "to study the really American part of our history."

Of all the effects of the frontier, the most important was that it promoted democracy and individualism. So long as free land existed, there was always opportunity for a man to acquire a competency, and economic power secured political power. Each succeeding frontier furnished "a new field of opportunity, a gate of escape from the bondage of the past." The lack of binding tradition and organized restraints promoted a distinctively American passion for individual freedom, antipathy to direct control from outside, aggressive self-interest, and intolerance of education and administrative experience. But by the year 1890, this process had come to an end; the frontier, the hither edge of unsettled land, no longer existed, and with its passing the first epoch of American history had closed. . . .

The initial plausibility of the Turner thesis lies in the patent fact that no nation could spend more than a century developing an immense continental empire without being deeply affected by it. Few critics question the great importance of the inland empire, or that Turner originally performed a service for historical writing by directing attention to it. Many accept Turner's emphasis on the frontier as one of several valid but limited perspectives on American history. But it has been forcefully denied that the frontier deserves any special preeminence among several major factors in "explaining" American development. The question has also been raised (and frequently answered in the negative) whether Turner analyzed the frontier process itself clearly or correctly.

5   It became plain, as new thought and research was brought to bear upon the problem, that the frontier theory, as an analytic device, was a blunt instrument. The terms with which the Turnerians dealt—the frontier, the West, individualism, the American character—were vague at the outset, and as the Turnerian exposition developed, they did not receive increasingly sharp definition. Precisely because Turner defined the frontier so loosely ("the term," he said, "is an elastic one"), he could claim so much for it. At times he referred to the frontier literally as the edge of the settled territory having a population density of two to the square mile. But frequently he identified "the frontier" and "the West," so that areas actually long settled could be referred to as frontier. At times he spoke of both the "frontier" and the "West" not as places or areas, but as a social process: "The West, at bottom, is a form of society rather than an area." When this definition is followed to its logical conclusion, the development of American society is "explained" by "a form of society"—certainly a barren tautology. Again, at times Turner assimilated such natural resources as coal, oil, timber, to the idea of "the West"; in this way the truism that natural wealth has an important bearing upon a nation's development and characteristics was subtly absorbed into the mystique of the frontier and took on the guise of a major insight.

However, the central weakness of Turner's thesis was in its intellectual isolationism. Having committed himself to an initial overemphasis on the uniqueness of the historical development of the United States, Turner compounded the error by overemphasizing the frontier as a factor in this development. The obsession with uniqueness, the subtly demagogic stress on "the truly American part of our history," diverted the attention of historical scholarship from the possibilities of comparative social history; it offered no opportunity to explain why so many features of American development—for example, the rise of democracy in the nineteenth century—were parallel to changes in countries that did not have a contiguous frontier. Historians were encouraged to omit a host of basic influences common to both American and Western European development—the influence of Protestantism and the Protestant ethic, the inheritance from English republicanism, the growth of industrialism and urbanism. More than this, factors outside the frontier process that contributed to the singularity of American history were skipped over: the peculiar American federal structure, the slave system and the Southern caste complex, immigration and ethnic heterogeneity, the unusually capitalistic and speculative character of American agriculture, the American inheritance of *laissez faire*. The interpretation seems particularly weak for the corporate-industrial phase of American history that followed the Civil War. Indeed, if the historian's range of vision had to be limited to one explanatory idea, as it fortunately does not, one could easily argue that the business corporation was the dominant dynamic factor in American development during this period.

As a form of geographical determinism, the frontier interpretation is vulnerable on still another ground. If the frontier alone was a self-sufficient source of democracy and individualism, whatever the institutions and ideas the frontiersmen brought with them, frontiers elsewhere ought to have had a similar effect. The early frontier of seignorial French Canada, the South American frontier, and the Siberian frontier should have fostered democracy and individualism. The frontier should have forged the same kind of democracy when planters came to Mississippi as when yeomen farmers came to Illinois. Turner's dictum, "American democracy came out of the American forest," proved to be a questionable improvement upon the notion of his predecessors that it came out of the German forest. Plainly the whole complex of institutions, habits and ideas that men brought to the frontier was left out of his formula, and it was these things, not bare geography, that had been decisive. Turner's analysis, as George Warren Pierson aptly put it, hung too much on real estate, not enough on a state of mind. . . .

One of the most criticized aspects of Turner's conception of American history, the so-called safety-valve thesis, maintains that the availability of free land as a refuge for the oppressed and discontented has alleviated American social conflicts, minimized industrial strife, and contributed to the backwardness of the American labor movement. As

Turner expressed it, the American worker was never compelled to accept inferior wages because he could "with a slight effort" reach free country and set up in farming. "Whenever social conditions tended to crystallize in the East, whenever capital tended to impede the freedom of the mass, there was this gate of escape to the free conditions of the frontier," where "free lands promoted individualism, economic equality, freedom to rise, democracy."

The expression "free land" is itself misleading. Land was relatively cheap in the United States during the nineteenth century, but the difference between free land and cheap land was crucial. Up to 1820 the basic price of land was $2.00 an acre, and for years afterward it was $1.25. Slight as it may seem, this represented a large sum to the Eastern worker, whose wage was generally about $1.00 a day. Economic historians have estimated that during the 1850s, $1,000 represented a fairly typical cost for setting up a farm on virgin prairie land, or buying an established one; and the cost of transporting a worker's family from, say, Massachusetts or New York to Illinois or Iowa was a serious additional burden. Farming, moreover, is no enterprise for an amateur, nor one at which he has a good chance of success. The value of "free land" in alleviating distress has been challenged by several writers who have pointed out that periods of depression were the very periods when it was most difficult for the Eastern worker to move. Scattered instances of working-class migration to the West can be pointed to, but detailed studies of the origins of migrants have failed to substantiate the Turner thesis. . . .

10   Finally, Turner acknowledged but failed to see the full importance for his thesis of the fact that the United States not only had a frontier but was a frontier—a major outlet for the countries of Western Europe during the nineteenth century. From 1820 to 1929, the total European emigration to the United States was more than 37,500,000—a number only a million short of the entire population of the United States in 1870. In one decade alone, 1901–1910, 8,795,000 people came from Europe. If Europe shared to such a major extent in this safety-valve economy, its uniqueness for American development must be considerably modified. The mingling of peoples that took place in the United States must be placed alongside the presence of "free land" in explaining American development; the closure of the American gates after the First World War becomes an historical event of broader significance than the disappearance of the frontier line in 1890. And the facts of immigration probably provide a better key to the character of the American labor movement than any speculation about the effects of "free land" upon workers who could not reach it.

It should be added, in justice to Turner, that his historical writing was better than his frontier thesis, and not least because he regularly made use in practice of historical factors which were not accounted for in his theory. Although he often stated his ideas with the vigor of a propagandist, his was not a doctrinaire mind, and he was willing, as time went on, to add new concepts to his analysis. In 1925 he went so far as to admit the need of "an urban reinterpretation of our history." "I hope," he frequently said, "to propagate inquiry, not to produce disciples." In fact he did both, but he propagated less inquiry among his disciples than among his critics.

For Journals

Hofstadter says he is revising Turner, but in effect he comes up with a thesis of his own. How would you state Hofstadter's central idea?

For Discussion

1. What do you think Hofstadter means when he states that, as an analytic device, Turner's frontier theory is a blunt instrument (paragraph 5)? What kinds of problems in Turner's approach does that phrase suggest?

2. Hofstadter accuses Turner of intellectual isolationism. In revising Turner's thesis, what kinds of evidence does he include that he says Turner failed to consider in developing his ideas?

3. Hofstadter revises Turner but does not reject him. Where do you find points of agreement or overlap in their theories?

4. Hofstadter thought that Turner overstated the significance of rural life in American history at the expense of the city. Which do you think—rural life or urban life—was more significant as a source of values? Of power?

5. Based on your other readings in this book, what do you think of Hofstadter's assertion that emigration to America of millions of people from Europe is a better key to the American character than the idea of available free land in the West?

6. Look back over Turner's thesis and Hofstadter's revision. Which one is more satisfying to you? Intellectually, are they equally interesting? Which one coincides more with your own ideas about why America developed as it did?

For Writing

1. In your college library, look for primary and secondary materials, including books, periodicals, or photographs, for a research paper on one of the following topics: African American cowboys and the West;

the great Mexican ranches of California; the Indian cultures of the Southwest; or any other group that is not a part of Turner's thesis. You could focus on an aspect of this group's life in frontier days (for example, influential individuals, significant events, or contributions to American culture). How does being aware of the group cause you to revise your image of a frontier without them?

2.   Turner and Hostadter are both interested in the idea of American progress. Write an essay about a change in American life that has come about in your own lifetime that you think represents real progress. Is it a result of technology, or of social and political change? Why do you think this change is important? For contrast, you might ask someone in your parents' generation what they think of as a major contribution to progress in America.

CODA: WILDERNESS LETTER
1960

Wallace Stegner

Wallace Stegner (1909–1993) grew up in Canada and the American West, and much of his writing, including his novels and essays, reflects his love for the wilderness. Stegner was active in the conservationist movement, often working with photographer Ansel Adams to promote national parks and a balance between development and the preservation of open space. The recipient of both the National Book Award and the Pulitzer Prize, Stegner founded the Creative Writing Program at Stanford University.

Los Altos, Calif.
Dec. 3, 1960

David E. Pesonen
Wildland Research Center
Agricultural Experiment Station
243 Mulford Hall
University of California
Berkeley 4, Calif.

Dear Mr. Pesonen:

I believe that you are working on the wilderness portion of the Outdoor Recreation Resources Review Commission's report. If I may, I should like to urge some arguments for wilderness preservation that involve recreation, as it is ordinarily conceived, hardly at all. Hunting, fishing, hiking, mountain-climbing, camping, photography, and the enjoyment of natural scenery will all, surely, figure in your report. So will the wilderness as a genetic reserve, a scientific yardstick by which we may measure the world in its natural balance against the world in its man-made imbalance. What I want to speak for is not so much the wilderness uses, valuable as those are, but the wilderness *idea*, which is a resource in itself. Being an intangible and spiritual resource, it will seem mystical to the practical-minded—but then anything that cannot be moved by a bulldozer is likely to seem mystical to them.

I want to speak for the wilderness idea as something that has helped form our character and that has certainly shaped our history as a people. It has no more to do with recreation than churches have to do with recreation, or than the strenuousness and optimism and ex- pansiveness of what historians call the "American Dream" have to do with recreation. Nevertheless, since it is only in this recreation survey that the values of wilderness are being compiled, I hope you will per- mit me to insert this idea between the leaves, as it were, of the recre- ation report.

Something will have gone out of us as a people if we ever let the remaining wilderness be destroyed; if we permit the last virgin forests to be turned into comic books and plastic cigarette cases; if we drive the few remaining members of the wild species into zoos or to extinc- tion; if we pollute the last clear air and dirty the last clean streams and push our paved roads through the last of the silence, so that never again will Americans be free in their own country from the noise, the exhausts, the stinks of human and automotive waste. And so that never again can we have the chance to see ourselves single, separate, vertical and individual in the world, part of the environment of trees and rocks and soil, brother to the other animals, part of the natural world and competent to belong in it. Without any remaining wilder- ness we are committed wholly, without chance for even momentary reflection and rest, to a headlong drive into our technological termite- life, the Brave New World of a completely man-controlled environ- ment. We need wilderness preserved—as much of it as is still left, and as many kinds—because it was the challenge against which our char- acter as a people was formed. The reminder and the reassurance that it is still there is good for our spiritual health even if we never once in ten years set foot in it. It is good for us when we are young, because of the incomparable sanity it can bring briefly, as vacation and rest, into our insane lives. It is important to us when we are old simply because it is there—important, that is, simply as idea.

We are a wild species, as Darwin pointed out. Nobody ever tamed or domesticated or scientifically bred us. But for at least three millennia we have been engaged in a cumulative and ambitious race to modify and gain control of our environment, and in the process we have come close to domesticating ourselves. Not many people are likely, any more, to look upon what we call "progress" as an unmixed blessing. Just as surely as it has brought us increased comfort and more material goods, it has brought us spiritual losses, and it threatens now to become the Frankenstein that will destroy us. One means of sanity is to retain a hold on the natural world, to remain, insofar as we can, good animals. Americans still have that chance, more than many peoples; for while we were demonstrating ourselves the most efficient and ruthless environment-busters in history, and slashing and burning and cutting our way through a wilderness continent, the wilderness was working on us. It remains in us as surely as Indian names remain on the land. If the abstract dream of human liberty and human dignity became, in America, something more than an abstract dream, mark it down at least partially to the fact that we were in subtle ways subdued by what we conquered.

5   The Connecticut Yankee, sending likely candidates from King Arthur's unjust kingdom to his Man Factory for rehabilitation, was over-optimistic, as he later admitted. These things cannot be forced, they have to grow. To make such a man, such a democrat, such a believer in human individual dignity, as Mark Twain himself, the frontier was necessary, Hannibal and the Mississippi and Virginia City, and reaching out from those the wilderness; the wilderness as opportunity and as idea, the thing that has helped to make an American different from and, until we forget it in the roar of our industrial cities, more fortunate than other men. For an American, insofar as he is new and different at all, is a civilized man who has renewed himself in the wild. The American experience has been the confrontation by old peoples and cultures of a world as new as if it had just risen from the sea. That gave us our hope and our excitement, and the hope and excitement can be passed on to newer Americans, Americans who never saw any phase of the frontier. But only so long as we keep the remainder of our wild as a reserve and a promise—a sort of wilderness bank.

As a novelist, I may perhaps be forgiven for taking literature as a reflection, indirect but profoundly true, of our national consciousness. And our literature, as perhaps you are aware, is sick, embittered, losing its mind, losing its faith. Our novelists are the declared enemies of their society. There has hardly been a serious or important novel in this century that did not repudiate in part or in whole American technological culture for its commercialism, its vulgarity, and the way in which it has dirtied a clean continent and a clean dream. I do not expect that the preservation of our remaining wilderness is going to cure this condition. But the mere example that we can as a nation apply some other criteria than commercial and exploitative considerations would be heartening to many Americans, novelists or otherwise. We need to demonstrate our acceptance of the natural world, including ourselves; we need the spiritual refreshment that being natural can produce. And one of the best places for us to get that is in the wilderness where the fun houses, the bulldozers, and the pavements of our civilization are shut out.

Sherwood Anderson, in a letter to Waldo Frank in the 1920s, said it better than I can. "Is it not likely that when the country was new and men were often alone in the fields and the forest they got a sense of bigness outside themselves that has now in some way been lost. . . . Mystery whispered in the grass, played in the branches of trees overhead, was caught up and blown across the American line in clouds of dust at evening on the prairies. . . . I am old enough to remember tales that strengthen my belief in a deep semi-religious influence that was formerly at work among our people. The flavor of it hangs over the best work of Mark Twain. . . . I can remember old fellows in my home town speaking feelingly of an evening spent on the big empty plains. It had taken the shrillness out of them. They had learned the trick of quiet. . . ."

We could learn it too, even yet; even our children and grandchildren could learn it. But only if we save, for just such absolutely non-recreational, impractical, and mystical uses as this, all the wild that still remains to us.

It seems to me significant that the distinct downturn in our literature from hope to bitterness took place almost at the precise time when the frontier officially came to an end, in 1890, and when the American way of life had begun to turn strongly urban and industrial. The more urban it has become, and the more frantic with technological change, the sicker and more embittered our literature, and I believe our people, have become. For myself, I grew up on the empty plains of Saskatchewan and Montana and in the mountains of Utah, and I put a very high valuation on what those places gave me. And if I had not been able periodically to renew myself in the mountains and deserts of western America I would be very nearly bughouse. Even when I can't get to the back country, the thought of the colored deserts of southern Utah, or the reassurance that there are still stretches of prairie where the world can be instantaneously perceived as disk and bowl, and where the little but intensely important human being is exposed to the five directions and the thirty-six winds, is a positive consolation. The idea alone can sustain me. But as the wilderness areas are progressively exploited or "improved," as the jeeps and bulldozers of uranium prospectors scar up the deserts and the roads are cut into the alpine timberlands, and as the remnants of the unspoiled and natural world are progressively eroded, every such loss is a little death in me. In us.

10   I am not moved by the argument that those wilderness areas which have already been exposed to grazing or mining are already deflowered, and so might as well be "harvested." For mining I cannot say much good except that its operations are generally short-lived. The extractable wealth is taken and the shafts, the tailings, and the ruins left, and in a dry country such as the American West the wounds men make in the earth do not quickly heal. Still, they are only wounds; they aren't absolutely mortal. Better a wounded wilderness than none at all. And as for grazing, if it is strictly controlled so that it does not destroy the ground cover, damage the ecology, or compete with the wildlife it is in itself nothing that need conflict with the wilderness feeling or the validity of the wilderness experience. I have known enough range cattle to recognize them as wild animals; and the people who herd them have, in the wilderness context, the dignity of rareness; they belong on the frontier, moreover, and have a look of rightness. The invasion they make on the virgin country is a sort of invasion that is as old as Neolithic man, and they can, in moderation, even emphasize a man's feeling of belonging to the natural world. Under surveillance, they can belong; under control, they need not deface or mar. I do not believe that in wilderness areas where grazing has never been permitted, it should be permitted; but I do not believe either that an otherwise untouched wilderness should be eliminated from the preservation plan because of limited existing uses such as grazing which are in consonance with the frontier condition and image.

Let me say something on the subject of the kinds of wilderness worth preserving. Most of those areas contemplated are in the national forests and in high mountain country. For all the usual recreational purposes, the alpine and forest wildernesses are obviously the most important, both as genetic banks and as beauty spots. But for the spiritual renewal, the recognition of identity, the birth of awe, other kinds will serve every bit as well. Perhaps, because they are less friendly to life, more abstractly nonhuman, they will serve even better. On our Saskatchewan prairie, the nearest neighbor was four miles away, and at night we saw only two lights on all the dark rounding earth. The earth was full of animals—field mice, ground squirrels, weasels, ferrets, badgers, coyotes, burrowing owls, snakes. I knew them as my little brothers, as fellow creatures, and I have never been able to look upon animals in any other way since. The sky in that country came clear down to the ground on every side, and it was full of great weathers, and clouds, and winds, and hawks. I hope I learned something from knowing intimately the creatures of the earth; I hope I learned something from looking a long way, from looking up, from being much alone. A prairie like that, one big enough to carry the eye clear to the sinking, rounding horizon, can be as lonely and grand and simple in its forms as the sea. It is as good a place as any for the wilderness experience to happen; the vanishing prairie is as worth preserving for the wilderness idea as the alpine forests.

So are great reaches of our western deserts, scarred somewhat by prospectors but otherwise open, beautiful, waiting, close to whatever God you want to see in them. Just as a sample, let me suggest the Robbers' Roost country in Wayne County, Utah, near the Capitol Reef National Monument. In that desert climate the dozer and jeep tracks will not soon melt back into the earth, but the country has a way of making the scars insignificant. It is a lovely and terrible wilderness, such a wilderness as Christ and the prophets went out into; harshly and beautifully colored, broken and worn until its bones are exposed, its great sky without a smudge or taint from Technocracy, and in hidden corners and pockets under its cliffs the sudden poetry of springs. Save a piece of country like that intact, and it does not matter in the slightest that only a few people every year will go into it. That is precisely its value. Roads would be a desecration, crowds would ruin it. But those who haven't the strength or youth to go into it and live can simply sit and look. They can look two hundred miles, clear into Colorado; and looking down over the cliffs and canyons of the San Rafael Swell and the Robbers' Roost they can also look as deeply into themselves as anywhere I know. And if they can't even get to the places on the Aquarius Plateau where the present roads will carry them, they can simply contemplate the *idea,* take pleasure in the fact that such a timeless and uncontrolled part of earth is still there.

These are some of the things wilderness can do for us. That is the reason we need to put into effect, for its preservation, some other principle than the principles of exploitation or "usefulness" or even recreation. We simply need that wild country available to us, even if we never do more than drive to its edge and look in. For it can be a means of reassuring ourselves of our sanity as creatures, a part of the geography of hope.

Very sincerely yours,
Wallace Stegner

For Journals

Do you go hiking or camping in national parks or other wilderness areas? If not, do you nevertheless support the idea of saving wilderness?

For Discussion

1. Stegner says that he wants to argue not for the wilderness but for the idea of the wilderness (paragraph 1). What do you think he means by the idea as opposed to the reality of the wilderness? Why should the idea be protected?

2. How did you respond to Stegner's assertion that Americans—even Americans who have never set foot in the wilderness—will lose the wilderness if it is destroyed?

3. How does Stegner think the development of technology and urban life have affected Americans? What advantage does he feel Americans who were exposed to the frontier gained?

4. Why does Stegner think that the relatively undramatic prairies and the deserts are as worthy of preservation as the more spectacular forest and alpine areas? How does emphasizing them help or harm his thesis?

5. Stegner was always interested in conflicting attitudes toward nature and development. Where do his sympathies lie? Yours?

For Writing

1. Write an essay about an urban place you know—an open space, a part of an old neighborhood, a small city park, a favorite store, a place that a parent used to take you to or that you shared with a childhood friend—and you want to see preserved. Explain its emotional and spiritual value to you and why you would like it to stay the way it is. Your research may include firsthand observation, interviews with other people familiar with the place, and library research. For example, if you are interested in an old movie theater, look for source materials on historic preservation and old movie palaces.

2. Write a paper in which you compare Stegner's and Turner's ideas of the wilderness. How does each man think the idea of the wilderness has shaped Americans? What represents progress to each author? In which instances does Stegner sound like Turner? Revise Turner? How did reading Stegner revise your reading of Turner?

DEAR JOHN WAYNE
1 9 8 4

Louise Erdrich

    Louise Erdrich (1954–) is an American Indian novelist, poet, and essayist who teaches at Dartmouth College. She was born in Minnesota and grew up near a reservation in North Dakota, where her American Indian mother and German father worked for the Bureau of Indian Affairs. She is the author of two novels, Love Medicine *(1984) and* The Beet Queen *(1986), as well as short stories and poems. She and her husband, Michael Dorris, coauthored a novel,* The Crown of Columbus *(1991). "Dear John Wayne" is a wonderful example of Erdrich's ability to explore how differently white Americans and American Indians experience the mythology of the frontier.*

August and the drive-in picture is packed.
We lounge on the hood of the Pontiac
surrounded by the slow-burning spirals they sell
at the window, to vanquish the hordes of mosquitoes.
Nothing works. They break through the smoke-screen   5
    for blood.

Always the look-out spots the Indians first,
spread north to south, barring progress.
The Sioux, or Cheyenne, or some bunch
in spectacular columns, arranged like SAC missiles,
their feathers bristling in the meaningful sunset.   10

The drum breaks. There will be no parlance.
Only the arrows whining, a death-cloud of nerves
swarming down on the settlers
who die beautifully, tumbling like dust weeds
into the history that brought us all here   15
together: this wide screen beneath the sign of the bear.

The sky fills, acres of blue squint and eye
that the crowd cheers. His face moves over us,
a thick cloud of vengeance, pitted
like the land that was once flesh. Each rut,
each scar makes a promise: *It is*   20
not over, this fight, not as long as you resist.

Everything we see belongs to us.
A few laughing Indians fall over the hood
25   slipping in the hot spilled butter.
The eye sees a lot, John, but the heart is so blind.
How will you know what you own?
He smiles, a horizon of teeth
the credits reel over, and then the white fields
30   again blowing in the true-to-life dark.
The dark films over everything.
We get into the car
scratching our mosquito bites, speechless and small
as people are when the movie is done.
35   We are back in ourselves.

How can we help but keep hearing his voice,
the flip side of the sound-track, still playing:
Come on, boys, we've got them
where we want them, drunk, running.
40   *They will give us what we want, what we need:*
The heart is a strange wood inside of everything
we see, burning, doubling, splitting out of its skin.

For Journals

Where do your own ideas of the West come from? Movies? If so, which ones? What other sources? Where else could you find information about the West?

For Discussion

1.   Read the poem out loud, all the way through. Then go back to the beginning, and in each stanza find three or four words that are either unexpected or particularly effective. What do they contribute to the theme of each stanza? How?

2.   Compare this poem with the article and illustration from the *Police Gazette.* How does the view of Indians in the *Gazette* compare with the portrayal of them in the John Wayne movie? With the Indians watching the movie at the drive-in?

3.   What values does the image of John Wayne usually represent? How does Erdrich's attitude toward him revise that image?

4.   How do you think Erdrich would see the settling of the West compared to the way Turner sees it? Whose evidence do you find more persuasive? Why?

5. If the Indians had written the film script, how do you think they would write the battle scene? What kind of movie do you think they could make about whites and Indians on the frontier?

6. How does Erdrich use ironic details like the drive-in movie and the fact that the American Indians have a car named for an Indian chief to suggest Indians' ambivalence toward American culture and their place in it? What other examples of this irony can you find in the poem?

For Writing

1. Write an essay comparing Erdrich's story in Chapter 5, "American Horse," and this poem, focusing on how she treats cultural perspectives and differences between whites and Indians. How does Erdrich's work revise your understanding of contemporary American Indian culture?

2. Investigate books and scholarly articles for material on the Battle of Little Big Horn. Write a documented paper in which you compare an earlier version of the story—from newspaper stories at the time of the battle, or older books about it—with recent versions, like Evan Connell's *Son of the Morning Star*. How have evaluations of Custer, his strategy, and the battle been revised?

STAGING REALITY: THE CREATION OF BUFFALO BILL, 1869–1883

1992

Richard Slotkin

Richard Slotkin, born in 1942, is the John M. Olin professor of English and director of American Studies at Wesleyan University. This selection is from his book Gunfighter Nation, *which is the last of a three-volume series; the other volumes are* Regeneration through Violence *(1973) and* The Fatal Environment *(1985). Slotkin sees the frontier not as an experience of the distant past but as a powerful influence on contemporary political and cultural life.*

Until 1869 William F. Cody had been a minor actor on the stage of western history, a frontier jack of all trades who had been a farmer, teamster, drover, trapper, Civil War soldier in a Jayhawk regiment, Pony Express rider, stagecoach driver, posse-man, meat hunter for the Kansas Pacific Railroad, and army scout. The upsurge of interest in the Plains that accompanied construction of the transcontinental railroads brought numerous tourists to the region, along with journalists, gentlemen-hunters in search of big game, and dime novelists looking for material. There was money to be made guiding such folk on hunting trips, and fame (and more hunting clients) to be garnered when the trips were written up back east. Wild Bill Hickok and Cody both achieved early fame in this way—Hickok as the subject of an article written for *Harper's Weekly* by G. W. Nichols, Cody in a Ned Buntline dime novel published in 1869 and a stage melodrama that premiered in 1871. Cody had already acquired a word-of-mouth reputation as an excellent scout and hunting guide, but after 1869 his newly acquired dime-novel celebrity made his name familiar to a national audience while linking it with spectacular and utterly fictitious adventures.

In 1871 James Gordon Bennett, Jr., editor and publisher of the New York *Herald,* hired Cody as a guide on one of the more elaborate celebrity hunting trips of the era (covered of course by a *Herald* reporter). The next year General Philip Sheridan named Cody to guide the hunting party of the Russian Grand Duke Alexis, who was in the country on a state visit. General Custer was among the American notables who accompanied the expedition, and Cody again figured prominently in the elaborate press coverage of the event. When Bennett, hoping to capitalize on this journalistic coup, urged Cody to visit him in New York, Cody, encouraged by his army superiors and friends, seized the opportunity to cash in on his celebrity. The visit was a turning point in Cody's career. In New York he took control of the commodity of his fame by forming a partnership with Ned Buntline for the production of Buffalo Bill dime novels and stage melodramas.

Between 1872 and 1876 Cody alternated between his career as scout for the U.S. Cavalry and his business as star of a series of melodramas in the East. His theatrical enterprises prospered, so that by 1873 he was able to form his own "Buffalo Bill Combination" with Wild Bill Hickok and "Texas Jack" Omohundro. The plays themselves were trivial and the acting amateurish, but the success of the "Combination" was evidence of the public's deep and uncritical enthusiasm for "the West," which could best be addressed through a combination of dime-novel plots and characters with "authentic" costumes and personages identified with "the real thing." A poster for the 1877 edition of the "Combination" advertises the main feature of the entertainment as a performance of *May Cody or, Lost and Won,* a melodramatic variation on the capitivity narrative featuring both Indians and Mormons as villains. An actor impersonates Brigham Young, but two genuine Sioux chiefs appear in the play and in the dance performances "incidental" to the drama which "introduc[e] . . . THE RED MEN OF THE FAR WEST." The play featured a series of "THRILLING TABLEAUX" in "Panoramic Order" depicting the famous "Mountain Meadows Massacre" (in which Mormon fanatics abet Indians in wiping out a wagon train) and recreations of "Brigham Young's Temple" and his residence, the "Lion House." In addition, there was a display of marksmanship by the "Austin Brothers." The mixture of elements anticipates the program of the Wild West, although these performances did not approach the scale of ambition of the Wild West.

Combinations of this kind were not unprecedented. In 1766 Major Robert Rogers, the famous commander of "Rogers' Rangers," wrote and staged in London a tragedy titled *Ponteach* based on the recently concluded Indian war and featuring authentic Indian dances, costumes, and performers. In the 1830s and '40s George Catlin's touring "Indian Gallery" combined displays of Indian dances with exhibitions of paintings. Similar authenticating devices were used by the various panoramas and cycloramas—aggregations of painted scenes with a narrative program of one sort or another—which toured the country between 1850 and 1890. Cody's creative achievement was his organization of these various conventions and media around a coherent set of plot formulas drawn from a literary mythology whose structure and language were (by 1870) well developed and widely recognized.

Cody's continuing engagement with the Plains wars strengthened his claims of authenticity and in 1876 provided him with a windfall of public celebrity. The outbreak of war with the Sioux and Northern Cheyenne had been expected since the failure in 1875 of government attempts to compel the sale of the Black Hills, and preparations for three major expeditions into "hostile" territory began in the winter of 1875–76. Cody was then performing in the East, but his services as Chief of Scouts had been solicited for the column led by General Crook out of Fort Fetterman. His theatrical engagements prevented his joining Crook, whose command moved out in May, but General Carr had also been trying to recruit him for the 5th Cavalry. On the 11th of June Cody announced from the stage in Wilmington, Delaware, that he was abandoning "play acting" for "the real thing" and within the week had joined the 5th (now commanded by Merritt) in southern Wyoming. While the three main columns under Terry (with Custer), Gibbon, and Crook attempted to encircle and engage the main body of "hostiles," Merritt's command moved toward the Black Hills to prevent additional warriors from leaving the reservation to join Sitting Bull and Crazy Horse. On July 7 the command learned of Custer's disastrous defeat at the Little Big Horn (June 25). Ten days later a battalion of the 5th under Captain Charles King—a professional soldier with literary ambitions—caught up with a band of off-reservation Cheyenne which it had been tracking. In a rapid sequence of ambush and counter-ambush, Cody and his scouts engaged a small party of Cheyenne out-riders. Merritt and his officers, watching from a low hill, saw Cody and one of the Cheyenne meet—seemingly in mutual surprise—and spon-taneously fire. They saw Cody's horse stumble and fall (the horse had stepped in a prairie-dog hole). But Cody extricated himself from the saddle, took a kneeling position and deliberate aim, and shot the charging Indian from his horse. Then, as King's advancing troopers swept by him, he walked over to the corpse, scalped it, and waved his trophy in the air.

This scene became the core of the Buffalo Bill legend and the basis of his national celebrity. Before the year was over he would be hailed as the man who took "The First Scalp for Custer." It would be claimed that the Indian he slew was a leading chief, one of the leaders at the Little Big Horn, and even that Cody had announced his intention to avenge Custer from the stage in Wilmington—an absurdity, since the Last Stand did not occur until three weeks later. Although the fight it-self had elements of exciting drama, it was in fact a small skirmish in a dusty, empty place. The Signal Corps observer who had the best sight of the action said only that he saw "just a plain Indian riding a calico or a paint pony." but the dusty details were immediately transformed into melodrama by Captain King, whose literary ambitions reveal themselves in the sensational prose with which he described Cody's fight in his official report (and later in a book). King's report was given to a correspondent of Bennett's New York *Herald*, who added his own touches.

But the chief mythologizer of the event was Cody himself. That winter he would star in *The Red Right Hand; or, The First Scalp for Custer,* a melodrama in which the "duel" with Yellow Hand becomes the climax of a captivity-rescue scenario. (The story also appeared as a dime novel.) Moreover, it seems that Cody approached the event itself with just such a performance in mind. On the morning of July 17, knowing that the proximity of the Indians made battle probable, Cody abandoned his usual buckskin clothing for one of his stage costumes, "a brilliant Mexican *vaquero* outfit of black velvet slashed with scarlet and trimmed with silver buttons and lace"—the sort of costume that dime-novel illustrations had led the public to suppose was the proper dress of the wild Westerner. He was preparing for that moment when he would stand before his audience, wearing the figurative laurels of the day's battle and the *vaquero* suit, able to declare with truth that he stood before them in a plainsman's authentic garb, indeed the very clothes he had worn when he took "The First Scalp for Custer." In that one gesture he would make "history" and fictive convention serve as mutually authenticating devices: the truth of his deeds "historicizes" the costume, while the costume's conventionality allows the audience—which knows the West only through such images—to recognize it as genuine.

Cody also displayed the relics of Yellow Hand—a warbonnet, shield, gun, and scabbard, and the dried human scalp itself—outside theaters in which the "Combination" performed, as indisputable evidence of his claims as a historical actor. Their impact was augmented when the display was condemned as obscene and barbaric by the self-appointed keepers of public morality. Even the anti-Indian and sensation-loving *Herald* criticized Cody; and in Boston, where Friends of the Indian were numerous and influential, the "Combination" was banned. The effect of this action was roughly the same as the banning of *Huckleberry Finn* by the Boston Library Committee—or better, the advertisements in that novel of "The Royal Nonesuch" as a show to which women and children would not be admitted. It brought sensation-seekers to the show in droves.

Here the Buffalo Bill signature appears clearly, in its characteristic confusion of the theatrical and the historical or political. The deed itself is unquestionably real—blood was shed, a battle won—but the event is framed by fiction from start to finish, and its ultimate meaning is determined by its re-enactment in the theater. It soon ceased to matter that the skirmish itself was unimportant, that Yellow Hand was not a war chief; that his was not "the first scalp for Custer," and that the "revenge" symbolized by Cody's deed had no counterpart in reality (since the Indians he fought had not been at the Little Big Horn). Cody and Custer had been associated very briefly (and distantly) in the Southern Plains war of 1867–70 and the Grand Duke's buffalo hunt; but beginning in 1876 Cody (and his associates) exploited his connection with the Last Stand and Custer by every means available. In addition to *The Red Right Hand*, Cody appeared as Custer's trusty scout in a series of dime novels, figuring (in terms of the Cooper formula) as a kind of Hawkeye to Custer's Duncan Heyward, or Kit Carson to Custer's Fremont. The Yellow Hand fight was transformed from a lucky accident to the climax of a program of deliberate revenge. The "duel" itself became even more sensational in Cody's 1879 autobiography, where it culminated in a hand-to-hand knife fight. The image of Cody waving the scalp in the air was reduced to a crude woodcut, which became a permanent feature of Buffalo Bill iconography. It appeared in most of the Wild West Programs, as a dime-novel cover, a poster, and—elaborated in oils—as the centerpiece of several heroic paintings.

After 1876, the Buffalo Bill mythology developed in two forms, the   10 dime novel and (after 1882) the Wild West. Buffalo Bill was the protagonist of more dime novels than any other character, real or fictional, with the possible exception of Jesse James. But after 1883, the Wild West was the basis of his fame and of his increasingly legendary status. The early Buffalo Bill dime novels (written by Cody himself, as well as by Buntline and Prentiss Ingraham) were based (loosely) on his frontier exploits; they placed Buffalo Bill in the traditional pantheon of frontier heroes derived from Boone, Hawkeye, Carson, and Crockett. But the Wild West framed Cody in a mythic spectacle that enlarged and transformed this legend; eventually even his dime novels celebrated him as the proprietor of the Wild West rather than as an old-time plainsman.

For Journals

What did you know about Buffalo Bill before you read this selection? Do you approve or disapprove of how he became famous? Why?

For Discussion

1.   Slotkin says that violence is a crucial part of the American idea of the frontier. Do you agree with him? Can you imagine the frontier without violence? Why or why not? What do you think Slotkin is assuming here about the American character?

2.   What strikes you as unexpected or unusual about the development of Cody's show? Why do you think he called it "Buffalo Bill's Wild West" instead of "Buffalo Bill's Wild West Show"?

3.   How did the sensational official report of Captain King on the Cheyenne wars and Cody's version of scalping an Indian revise history at the time? How does Slotkin's recovery of the actual story revise your own idea of frontier heroism?

4.   What is the portrait of America that emerges from the different scenes in the Wild West show? Why do you think the show was such a success?

5.   Slotkin says that Cody framed history in fiction and mixed reality with theater. Is the idea of the frontier better or worse for this kind of revision? How influential do you think this revision has been in shaping modern American ideas about the frontier?

For Writing

1.   Research the career of Buffalo Bill, Daniel Boone, Davy Crockett, Annie Oakley, Sitting Bull, Crazy Horse, or Geronimo. Then write a

paper in which you separate out some of the legends and stories about your subject from what he or she really did. When did the stories about your subject begin to circulate? How did his or her reputation benefit from a revised history? What did this person represent in the American imagination?

2.   Watch a video of the Mel Brooks movie *Blazing Saddles,* and write a paper comparing it with this selection. How does Brooks's movie revise previous traditional stereotypes of the frontier and its heroes? How does its hero compare to the heroic image created by Buffalo Bill?

WHAT IS STAR TREK TODAY?
1992

John S. Davis

> *John S. Davis is vice-president of* Star Trek *Magazine. He wrote the essay as part of an issue in memory of the creator of the series, Gene Roddenberry, who died the year of the show's twenty-fifth anniversary.*

Everything begins with a vision. Whether it's a new mode of transportation, the abolishment of slavery, the discovery of new trade routes, a medical cure, or a television show, the vision is at the heart of it. This past and coming fall both mark the anniversaries of two particular visions. First, it heralded the twenty-fifth year of Gene Roddenberry's vision of the future, *Star Trek,* and second, the upcoming five hundredth anniversary of Christopher Columbus' first voyage to the new world.

Over twenty-five years ago, *Star Trek* began as one man's vision. It was a desire to create a television series which could speak to the day's issues, something that could reflect the shortcomings, hopes, fears and frustrations of humanity, to show us that we can solve our difficulties, thereby creating a better future.

When NBC cancelled *Star Trek* it seemed as though the vision had died. It hadn't, of course, it was just in temporary hibernation. But when it finally bloomed in syndication it began to touch the lives of many people. Some became writers, some doctors and others engineers. It created a desire in some people to be more than what they already were, to help make the world more than what it already was.

Roddenberry didn't foresee the impact that *Star Trek* would have any more than Columbus foresaw the impact of what the discovery of the New World would have on the rest of the world. Columbus thought only of opening new trade routes to the east and enriching Spain and himself. Roddenberry wanted to create something people would enjoy and remember. Each vision became so much more.

5   But what is *Star Trek* today? *Star Trek* is a culmination of one man's vision and many other people's interpretation of that vision. It is twenty-five years of toys, games, books, conventions, seventy-nine original episodes, twenty-two animated episodes, six feature films and over one hundred episodes of *Star Trek: The Next Generation. Star Trek* is more than a fad, it is an institution.

As with all institutions *Star Trek* has over the years developed its own dogma and faith, its own leaders and followers. It has become more than just a money machine for Paramount Pictures. It has become a part of our culture. It has become a legend in its own time.

It's safe to say that we do live in interesting times. In the past fifty years, we have seen the rise of incredible new technologies and the potential of that technology to either benefit or destroy humanity. In the sixties, the underlying paranoia of the fifties finally manifested itself as vocal and sometimes violent protests against the establishment. Even the science fiction films of the era mirrored the anxiety and fear of the time, which was a feeling that those in positions of authority and the proliferation of new technologies were somehow out of control. The depiction was that of an uncertain future. Then out of the doom and gloom came a ray of light: *Star Trek.* It depicted a positive future, and became an anchor of hope for millions of people around the world. That sense of hope has continued to this day.

But now *Star Trek* is at a critical crossroads. How will *Star Trek* be affected by the passing of Gene Roddenberry? Will the vision be lost now that the visionary is no longer with us?

Who knows? Only time will give us an answer to these questions. Perhaps the real question is, "Who is responsible for keeping Gene's vision alive?" Is it Paramount Pictures' responsibility? Well, not exactly. Paramount is in the business of creating various forms of entertainment and hopefully making money with their creations. They are not in the business of perpetuating one man's vision to the exclusion of all else.

10   Keeping Gene's vision alive falls to each and every one of us as individuals. Simply watching *Star Trek* isn't enough. Buying merchandise or going to conventions isn't enough. Memorizing *Star Trek* trivia isn't enough. In fact, these things are just a part of the institution of *Star Trek,* and by no means the most important part. The vision is what matters, and it goes far beyond the tangible institution of goods and

services, it is an intangible feeling of hope that resides in our hearts and minds. And the way that we keep it alive is through our actions each and every day.

In other words, don't sit around waiting for someone else to do something to improve our future. Everyone can do something. You don't have to be a doctor, entrepreneur, research scientist or in a position of power in order to affect the world. All change begins with attitude. If we present a positive attitude to the people around us then that attitude has a tendency to spread. A negative attitude has the same effect. Which environment would you rather be a part of?

This is what *Star Trek* and Gene Roddenberry's vision is all about. Not how many moons the planet Vulcan has or whether Kirk is a better or worse captain than Picard. These things are just threads in the allegorical tapestry which represents *Star Trek*.

So what is *Star Trek* today? An institution? Certainly. It is also a challenge from Gene Roddenberry to all of us to begin building the foundation for a better future today, so that hopefully, someday, the vision will become reality.

For Journals

When did you first see or hear about the *Star Trek* series? Do you watch any of it? If so, what about it do you find most interesting?

For Discussion

1. Look at the pictures of the *Star Trek* "families" and compare them with the family in the Edsel ad in Chapter 6. What do the differences in presentation say about possible revisions in American attitudes towards the appropriate roles for men and women?

2. The *Star Trek* "Prime Directive," its code, is a code of noninterference with other cultures; it also allows for the natural development of other less technologically advanced cultures. Based on other selections you have encountered in this book, how does this frontier ideology compare to American frontier ideas of interaction with other societies?

3. The composition of both crews varies by gender, ethnicity, and heritage. Do you think the popularity of the *Star Trek* series means that Americans are more accepting of diversity in everyday society or only in science fiction? Why or why not?

For Writing

1. Watch an episode or more from each of the older and newer *Star Trek* series, and write an essay in which you compare them and analyze the following: interactions between different cultures; the frontier values expressed in those interactions; what is and what is not human; and the extent to which experience causes the participants to revise or rethink their own frontier ideologies.

2.   Watch a video of a 1950s or 1960s movie about space exploration, like *Forbidden Planet,* and a later movie like *Close Encounters of the Third Kind, Aliens,* or one of the *Star Trek* films. Write an essay in which you compare the following: the inherent evil or benevolence of alien cultures; attitudes toward the hazards or benefits of technology; attitudes toward the roles of women; attitudes toward the development or exploitation of other cultures.

GET A CYBERLIFE
1991

Peggy Orenstein

Peggy Orenstein is a former editor of the progressive magazine Mother Jones. *This essay is the result of her experience at a twenty-four–hour marathon demonstration of virtual reality in northern California in 1991.*

I've never been wed to reality. I've never even been engaged to it. I'll fling myself wholeheartedly into anything that can help me forget, at least momentarily, the thrum of war, toxic waste, ecological disaster, nuclear annihilation, poverty, destitution, or the fact that the tremendous amount of effort I just put into redecorating my apartment may be for naught if the entire city that I live in shakes, rattles, and rolls into the sea. There are times when I've looked at the world's problems and wished that I could just go find another world, one I would populate only with people I like. Sometimes I'm not so sure about them. There are people out there in California's Silicon Valley, at the University of Washington in Seattle, and at the University of North Carolina who are responding to such escapist fantasies. They're using computers to generate three-dimensional alternative environments—of, say, Tahiti to the inside of the human brain or Mars—that, at least some day, will be as photographically "real" as the room you're sitting in right now. This winter I got a preview of that future at Cyberthon, a twenty-four-hour marathon conference and demonstration of Virtual Reality, the newest, fringiest, most talked about technological boom since artificial intelligence went bust.

Standard VR gear consists of heavy, computerized, blacked-out goggles and a Lycra glove. When you move your goggled head, the computer responds by changing your perspective on the scene around you, just like in "real" reality. If you grab an image with your gloved hand, the computer notes that too and moves the image accordingly.

Some architects are using VR (also called "cyberspace," a term coined by writer William Gibson, who dreamed up VR in his novel *Neuromancer*) to show clients what a structure will look like before it's built. Doctors are using it to practice surgery without making a single cut. A cyberpunk counterculture, spearheaded by people like Brian Eno and director George Coates, is creating a whole new technology-driven spectrum of post-postmodern, nihilistic art. And, of course, NASA and the Defense Department (which hopes to replace jet pilots with VR screens) have been following—and funding—VR since its inception.

Cyberthon took place at a soundstage at the edge of San Francisco, in a specially built maze designed with a calculated irreverence toward day, night, right, left, and the entire history of empiricist philosophy. The exhibits within these virtual walls were mostly technological pupae; visual, tactile, and aural bits and bytes, which, their inventors believe, will someday achieve the sum of their parts and blossom into
5   something revolutionary.

In the nethermost reaches of the maze I found Sense8. Among the big three VR companies (the others being VR granddaddy Virtual Programming Languages Research [VPL] and Autodesk, Inc., which caters primarily to architects). Sense8 is the cheap seats, either the lowest tech or the most practical, depending on your perspective. Whereas VPL uses two computers to generate its virtual world, Sense8 and Autodesk use only a single computer. The difference in quality is significant, and so is the difference in price: about $15,000 a pop as opposed to VPL's $250,000. (In fact, VPL declined to haul its more complex, high-wattage gear down to San Francisco for a demo.)

I waited in line impatiently for my turn at the Cyberhood, a long, View-Master-like contraption, which focuses your eyes on a computer-generated 3-D image; you manipulate yourself, or "fly," by gripping a ball to the left of the machine. The ball, Sense8 president Eric Gullichsen kept repeating to the users, is like your head, think of it as your head. The trouble with that notion is that most people don't yank, twist, twirl, and push their heads, so most people were having trouble with the image: flipping it upside down, pulling their "head" back so far that the image became tiny and distant, hitting the floor with their wide-open eyeballs.

The man in front of me, a shortish, plump guy in a blue shirt and jeans, was muttering to himself as he yanked at his "head." Finally he gave in and straightened up. He turned out to be Robin Williams, but no one paid much attention in this crowd—the machines were the celebrities.

I asked him what it was like.

"Try it," he said, then dropped his voice to a Bela Lugosi whisper. "Don't be scared."

Was it fun?

"Yeah," he said, unconvincingly. "In a vertigo kind of way."

In the Cyberhood I saw a room with a purple-and-chartreuse linoleum floor. There was a red chair, a brown desk, preternaturally blue walls, a book, a lamp, a painting on the wall. None of it looked particularly "real." It looked flat and cartoonish—I've heard it compared to Toontown, a sort of two-dimensional three-dimensionality, if you can grok that.

I yanked my "head" and moved in on the chair. Suddenly the purple-and-green floor cracked me in the "face." I pulled back and the whole thing flipped over. I took a deep breath and steadied myself. I'm not very good at Nintendo either. To my right (my real right, not my virtual right) there was a joystick. I hit the button and a red-and-white-checked missile flew down from the ceiling and bounced on the floor. A woman's rude laugh followed. Gullichsen explained that you're supposed to move the joystick to make the missiles hit the target. I tried again; this time a yellow airplane came out and I manipulated it toward the chair. It hit and exploded with a crash of broken glass.

I'd had enough.

Back in the real room, Gullichsen introduced me to Alison Kennedy, aka Queen Mu, the "domineditrix" of the sporadically published cyberpunk rag *Mondo2000* as well as the anthropologist who first explained that licking a certain genus of toad can induce a hallucinogenic experience. Genuinely pleased to initiate a sister-in-publishing into the VR scene, she broke into a wide, ethereal grin and invited me to visit her house in the Berkeley hills once she returned from a Druid festival in Graz. Queen Mu and her stunning smile seem to have many of the VR boys wrapped like the gold bracelet around her upper arm. The new cyberians all publish in *M2*, which is as hot hot hot as Mickey Rourke and Jerry Lewis in France and Japan.

She was chatting with Stephen Beck about his Virtual Light exhibit, which wasn't working (and never did). Virtual Light? I asked. Don't we already have that? Isn't it called the light bulb?

"I guess you could think of it that way," Beck answered thoughtfully. "But no, the light bulb is artificial light. This is Virtual Light. You can see it with your eyes closed."

"I can see electric light with my eyes closed."

At this, Beck launched into a long explanation of Virtual Light, the only word of which I recognized was "photon." And I'm not quite sure what that means.

20   By now I was hungry, so I strolled over to the virtual eating exhibit that a group of local art students had set up. I didn't know what to expect—perhaps it could make me feel virtually full. Perhaps no calories would be involved. There was a reservation book graced with a real red rose outside the closed-off room. I wrote my name down. There was a ten- to fifteen-minute wait for a table. Just like real life, I thought. I wondered where I could get a virtual Stoli while I waited.

I told the man in front of me in line, a guy with a stringy ponytail down to the center of his back, that I had done Virtual Reality. He asked how it was. I told him the most exciting thing about it was that Robin Williams was next to me.

"You mean you were virtually with Robin Williams? That's great!"

No, I tried to explain, he was really next to me.

"You mean virtually really, or really really?"

25   I began to get a headache.

"Robin Williams was actually next to me, in line, waiting for a turn on the machine."

Mr. Ponytail looked crestfallen. "Well, did he say anything funny?" he asked, perking up some.

Virtual eating turned out to be a bunch of 3-D video images of food, projected onto a plate-shaped screen. A well-rounded meal, yes, but inedible.

Since I was already experiencing a taste of the third dimension, I hustled over to something called a Flying Mouse. If you've ever used an Apple computer, you know that you move the cursor with something that does not resemble but is nevertheless called a mouse. You move the mouse up and down to make the cursor move up and down, left and right to move the cursor back and forth. If you're feeling really crazy, you can spin the mouse in a circle, but that's about the most exciting effect you could achieve. Up until now.

30   The Flying Mouse is shaped like a manta ray and operates in 3-D. Simgraphics president Steve Tice called up a double image of Gum-

by's twin sister on screen and handed me a pair of LCD glasses. The lenses blink so rapidly—sixty times a second—that the eye can't perceive it. Suddenly, the two images on the screen merged into one three-dimensional figure. I could move her back and forth and up and down the conventional way, but, by lifting the mouse up off the table, I could also pull her out toward my face, push her back deep into the screen, or make her legs and arms kick and twist in agony. And when I "selected" a body part, I felt a tingly pressure on my index finger—tactile feedback! It didn't reflect notions of hard or soft or round or sharp, but I definitely felt like I'd touched something.

Habitat, an interactive, two-dimensional, animated program originally designed for Commodore computers, touched something in me, too. Like a raw nerve. To its users, Habitat is clearly much more than a computer game: it's truly an alternative universe, a mythical place where cartoon figures representing users throughout the country travel about, talk via typed overhead balloons, earn "money" through entrepreneurial ventures to purchase various luxury items, and observe strict codes of etiquette (if someone talks to you, it's rude not to talk back). Habitat users, programmer Randy Farmer explained to me, can go to a head shop and trade in their heads and bodies for new ones. Farmer himself had a large, blue dragon head. On screen, that is. In real life, he conformed to the stereotype of a hacker: shaggy hair, scruffy clothes, glasses, bad skin, paunchy.

And self-aware: "A lot of these people," he told me, "buy Marilyn Monroe heads, or Robert Redford heads, or some other gorgeous head-body combination. But the truth is, the kind of people who stare into a computer screen for hours and hours a day probably aren't the most beautiful people. On the outside, anyway. They're beautiful on the inside. So sometimes you meet one of these people who've represented themselves with these beautiful faces, and you're disappointed. You think, 'Oh, she doesn't look like Marilyn Monroe at all. I figure, if I have a monster head and someone meets me someday, I come out ahead. The way I really look won't seem so bad."

As he talked, two figures appeared on the screen, a "man" with a nondescript head and body (all the men's bodies are nondescript, all the women's bodies have huge breasts and wasp waists. Guess which gender designed Habitat?) who said he was from Nebraska, and a headless female with major mamambas from North Carolina.

The man reached out and grabbed the woman's breasts. "Nice boobs," he said.

Randy told me the gesture was bad form, but then again, so was 35 walking around without a head. In the meantime, the woman had begun to talk.

"I'm a man, you idiot," she said.

"What's with the boobs, then?" typed man number one, in consternation.

"They're muscles. Now get off 'em."

Let's talk about the birds and the cyberbees. Everyone I told about Cyberthon (including the editors of *Mother Jones*) asked if virtual sex was possible. At first I thought maybe that was just the kind of lowlife I hang around with, but during a question-and-answer session later that night, Jaron Lanier—the thirty-one-year-old founder of VPL, who is renowned for his spherical belly and the light-brown, lichen-like dreadlocks that sprout from his visionary skull—rolled his eyes when he was asked what he calls "the sex question."

40   But "the sex question" is really a misnomer. These guys, the bedrock of this new technology, didn't, and don't, really ask "the sex question"; they ask "the porn question": they don't want to know how to enhance intimacy with a partner; they want to know if they can make that Habitat babe 3-D and then spend all day feeling her virtual breasts.

There's even a word for VR sex: "dildonics." Note the emphasis here. It's not ovanics, or clitonics, or even cybersex. Dildonics. And Lanier, who has struggled to keep his Virtual Reality squeaky-clean, denied that people will want to use his machine for dildonic ends. "VR won't be used successfully as a porn media," he insisted. "Porn is cinema and photography that leaves something to the imagination. Completely knowing makes you deal with what's really on your plate. The reality here, the virtual reality, is that you'd have a girl made of polygons. And no one wants to have sex with a bunch of polygons."

Lanier went on to tout VR as a great equalizer. "Virtual Reality is the ultimate lack of class or race distinctions or any other form of pretense, since all form is variable," he said. In VR, said Lanier, gender, race, age—all become invention. You can be who or even what you want. If you can choose your form, you don't have to make it a human one: you can appear as a cat, a table, a piano. He told the crowd that, because VR is interactive, it can be community-enhancing, like the telephone or the light bulb, rather than reinforcing the numbing alienation of the television. "We live in this very weird time in history where we're passive recipients of a very immature, noninteractive broadcast media," he said. "Mission number one is to kill TV."

Someone commented that Nintendo is interactive, but it doesn't seem like a stride toward establishing an authentic electronic community.

"Nintendo is a little interactive," Lanier corrected. "You're being guided down a narrow set of predetermined possibilities, like a rat in a maze. VR is an endless range. If we're going to call Nintendo interactive, then I want a different word for VR."

Throughout Cyberthon, William Gibson played Darth Vader to   45
Lanier's Luke Skywalker. His vision of Virtual Reality, as articulated
in *Neuromancer,* was a bleak one, in which those unfortunate enough to
be mired in the physical world were called "meat" by those who
roamed the cyberrange. When someone subsequently asked *him*
whether he believed VR could be an electronic utopia, he shot back, "I
think it could be lethal, like freebasing American TV." Disheveled,
hunched over, looking like he'd rather be out back smoking, Gibson
leaned into the microphone. "I don't think that anyone who read my
book seems to have understood it," he said in his adenoidal twang. "It
was supposed to be ironic. The book was really a metaphor about how
I felt about the media. I didn't expect anyone to actually go out and
build one of these things."

You want VR? Try staying among black-walled mazes for eighteen
hours straight. Try making a Jif peanut butter and generic white bread
sandwich in "Mom's Kitchen," assuming Mom was just thawed after
being cryonically frozen in 1932 (and, given this crowd, that's a pretty
fair assumption). Walk into a big room at 3 A.M. and have Timothy
Leary tell you all reality is virtual. Believe him.

At six in the morning, Kit Galloway, the ponytailed artist whose
"Electronic Cafe" provides communal video-telephone hookups in
public places, free of charge, got up to speak. He suggested that cyber-
elitism could be avoided by using the technology we already have. "To
get into computer-shared electronic space, you need to be rich," he
said to a bleary-eyed but attentive audience. "The telephone has all
kinds of potential. There are gridlocks in the cities, and people can't
run around the country in jet planes, punching holes in the ozone, for
an ecology conference in Chicago—it doesn't make sense. Why not
telecommute or teleconference by videophone? Telephones are the
only thing that will get cheaper—they're our magic, our epitaph."
Galloway said that the new technology we need to achieve VR's
grand claims could be found in the least likely places, and, just before
breakfast, I discovered he was right. Chris Hardman, whose Antenna
Theater produces taped tours that re-create the pivotal events of historical sites like Dallas's School Book Depository, was exhibiting his virtual jump off the Golden Gate Bridge.
I strapped on a Walkman and stood by a waist-high cadmium-
red–painted wooden fence overlooking a blue plastic ocean. Voices
came from all sides—a soft, seductive man's voice telling me "Tense
your shoulders, clench your fists. Relax your shoulders. Don't look
down. Don't look down . . . look down. Put one foot on the rail. Feel
the rail. . . ." A nasal, Brooklyn-accented woman's voice relating

the story of her averted suicide: "So he said: 'You're gonna jump? So jump. I haven't got all day.' And I said: 'You shit! I'm going to kill myself, and you're not going to stay here and talk to me?'" A young, angry woman, out for a walk on the bridge to get some air. . . . "Don't look down. Look down." The voices rising like so many waves, swirling together, repeating themselves, urging me up and over the rail. . . .

50   ". . . Everyone jumps off the east side. Why? They face the city. You jump off the west side, you face nothing as you go down. . . ."

". . . Don't look down. Look down."

". . . If you don't do it, it's okay. Because after that, everything is a gift. Everything in life that comes after is a gift . . ."

As I listened, the fog rolled out of machines; the plastic ocean covering a soft mattress beckoned.

Some of the people around me climbed the wooden railing.

55   Some people jumped.

I did not, although I'm not sure why. Shyness, perhaps. Or maybe the spell was broken by the sound of bodies crunching on plastic instead of being swallowed silently by waves. Or maybe the whole thing was, finally, just too real.

I came to Cyberthon curious, but terribly smug (indeed superior) in my neoluddism. By daybreak, though, I was convinced that people who care about media, art, and education shouldn't just pass this off as the latest trend among techno-weenies with weird hair. This time, we have the chance to enter the debate about the direction of a revolutionary technology, before that debate has been decided for us.

How to do that is, of course, hard to say, if you're the kind of person who still hasn't mastered all ten function keys on your PC. During a panel on the social implications of VR, a woman who identified herself as an artist and educator stepped up to the microphone and announced. "Who gets to use this should be part of the design."

It was a nice idea, and everyone agreed, but the discussion went no further. How could it? You can't prevent technology from being abused. There will be those who use VR rudely, stupidly, dangerously—just as they do the telephone or the computer. Like the telephone and the modem, its popular rise will also eliminate the need for certain fundamental kinds of human contact, even as it enhances our ability to communicate. That's not comforting, but it is inevitable, and worth noting. At the very least, Cyberthon, where nontechnicians—teachers, artists, and writers—were included in the discourse, gave me hope that if we all are plugged into VR someday, there's a possibility that more than just one hand will control the switch.

Before I left Cyberthon, I watched the crowd around Atari's Hard   60
Drivin' computer game. Drivers were surrounded on three sides by
screens, which projected various racecourse scenes. They drove as fast
as they could around curves (watch those cows!), through loops (accel-
erate . . . now!), along straightaways (gun it, man, gun it!). When they
crashed, the computer showed an instant replay from the third-person
perspective. As it turns out, it's a lot more fun (not to mention boffo
yucks) to watch devastation from the outside. I watched the game for
half an hour, then walked into the bright light of what I still perceive
as the real world and hopped into my car.

As I rode down the freeway, I found myself going a little faster
than usual, edging my curves a little sharper, coming a little closer
than was really comfortable to the truck merging in the lane ahead of
me. Maybe I was just tired. It had been a long night. But maybe it just
doesn't take the mind that long to grab onto the new and make it real.
Even when you don't want it to.

For Journals

Given the opportunity, would you like to try virtual reality? Why
or why not?

For Discussion

1. What tone is established by the title at the outset, and is it consistent in the rest of the essay? What does the title tell you about Orenstein's audience and purpose in writing?

2. Based on this article, how would you define virtual reality (VR) for
someone who has never heard of it before? Why do you think Orenstein choose the title she did?

3. One expert says that VR could be an electronic utopia; another
says it could be lethal, like freebasing TV. Based on Orenstein's evidence, which view seems more realistic to you? Why?

4. What was your response to the form of VR known as Habitat, in
which cartoon characters can trade in their heads and bodies for ones
the players of the game like better?

5. Do you see VR on the frontier of American technology or as just a
variant of computer games? Does Orenstein's article cause you to revise your views?

6. At the conference, Orenstein participates in a virtual reality jump
from the Golden Gate Bridge but resists the impulse to "jump" in VR.
On the way home she drives more dangerously than usual and says,

"Maybe it just doesn't take the mind that long to grab onto the new and make it real" (paragraph 62). What connections do you think she is trying to draw between the experience of virtual reality and experience of the real world? Do you agree?

For Writing

1. One believer in VR described it as a peculiarly democratic invention because gender, race, and age all become invention, and you can become whomever you want. Write an essay in which you argue that this opportunity is either American technological progress or American social horror, or something else altogether.

2. Since 1991, when this essay was written, virtual reality has been developed further. Read some recent articles on it, and write a documented paper detailing new developments. What is the frontier of VR today? How does this new information revise what Orenstein wrote, as well as your own sense of the power and perils of the computer age?

HARD-BOILED HEROINES
1994

Anne Woolley

Anne Woolley is a college student who grew up in Los Angeles; her academic interests include art history and premedical studies. She wrote this essay in a first year writing class as a response to a question comparing the code and behavior of the private detective with that of the frontier hero.

Until quite recently, the hard-boiled detective in American mystery novels was a strong male figure. One of the best-known authors of this genre, Raymond Chandler, holds that the detective

> must be a complete man and a common man and yet an unusual man. . . . He is a common man or he could not go among the common people. . . . He is a lonely man. . . . The story is his adventure in search of a hidden truth, and it would be no adventure if it did not happen to a man fit for adventure. (Paul 129)

Women were secondary characters, usually sex objects. The few female detectives were always confined to a sanitary form of detection where horror was isolated. None of them is comparable to the traditional hard-boiled private investigator. With the introduction of three unique, female characters, this image has become antiquated. Private investigators Sharon McCone, Kinsey Millhone, and V. I. Warshawski are intelligent, liberated detectives, as capable in all aspects as the men who preceded them. By incorporating their own femininity in their work, they are forming a new breed of detective fiction. Their books are highly popular with women for they address issues and relate to situations as we can envision ourselves doing. As a result of the feminine influence, the mystery genre is changing, shedding some of the hard-boiled detective facade.

The mystery story has had a long and illustrious history in America. Edgar Allan Poe, writing in the early nineteenth century, started the trend with suspenseful short stories such as *The Purloined Letter*. During the early part of this century, the "hard-boiled" detective became popular. The private investigator was aloof, self-controlled, and fully independent. In between bouts of drinking and womanizing, sleuths would find and destroy the "bad guy." "Detective stories became a kind of battleground for the feminist-antifeminist debate, which concentrated almost totally on the competence or treachery of women" (Lawrence 39). The hard-boiled genre clearly defined women as unfaithful, unreliable, utterly dispensable sex objects. In *The Big Sleep*, regarded by many as the pinnacle of hard-nosed detective stories, Philip Marlowe utters the famous line, "I hate women" (*The Big Sleep* 159). Battle lines were clearly drawn. The traditional hard-core detective story had no place for a woman who might test such a sentiment.

Even at this time, however, women were not unknown in the mystery world. In 1878, Anna Katharine Green introduced the first American detective series. The female investigator, Rita Van Arsdale, was an inquisitive young woman. To negate the possibility of an antifeminist backlash, the "heroine's feminist statements or tendencies must have been sufficiently understated to avoid offending or stirring up antagonism among readers or other writers" (Lawrence 39). Also popular in this country were two British authors, Agatha Christie and Patricia Wentworth. Both authors featured elderly female sleuths, Miss Marple and Miss Silver, respectively, in their 1920s series. These women solved their crimes with cerebral *and* physical activity. Their cores were of steel, but their facades were those of gentle grandmothers. The younger women in the books were always naive. Intelligence came only with age. More recently, authors such as Amanda Cross have popularized younger detectives. Cross's heroine, Kate Fansler, however, could never be classified as a hard-boiled private investigator for she is too upper class to identify with the common people. Not until the advent of Sharon McCone did a woman fulfill Chandler's definition of a detective. This original character was soon followed by others, most notably Kinsey Millhone and V. I. Warshawski.

Published in 1976, *Edwin of the Iron Shoes* was the first Marcia Muller novel starring Sharon McCone. The heroine was not like any previous female detective. A graduate of the University of California, Berkeley with a degree in sociology, Sharon McCone became a security agent when jobs in her field proved impossible to find. She trained with a large detective agency before affiliating herself with All Souls Legal Cooperative.

5   In the V. I. Warshawski novels, written by Sara Paretsky, the lead character is a divorced, independent private investigator. Half Italian and half Polish Jew, she was raised by a cop father and an opera-enthused mother. V. I. was briefly a district attorney in Chicago but quit when the justice system failed to provide justice:

> [As public defenders] either we had to defend maniacs who ought to have been behind bars for the good of the world at large, or we had poor chumps who were caught in the system and couldn't buy their way out. You'd leave court every day feeling as though you'd just helped worsen the situation. (Reddy 117)

The idealism that led Warshawski to the investigative field turned into cynicism. The conscientious spirit, however, never left her. The first V. I. Warshawski msytery was published in 1982. Since then, Sara Paretsky has written seven more novels starring this detective.

Sue Grafton also writes about an independent private investigator, Kinsey Millhone, who managed to estrange two husbands before we meet her. She was raised by a feminist aunt after the death of her parents when she was quite young. She served as a police officer in Santa Barbara. However, the strict regulations of the force were unbearable to her. Like V. I., Kinsey turned to the detective business out of frustration with the legal system. Now she is loosely affiliated with the California Fidelity Insurance Company, in Santa Teresa. The first of this "alphabet" series was published in 1982.

These three characters have been modeled after hard-boiled personalities rather than the traditional woman. This relationship is implied from the beginning of Sue Grafton's *"A" Is for Alibi.* The opening paragraph, where Kinsey Millhone tells us, "I am thirty-two years old, twice divorced, no kids" (1), is an echo of the great detective, Philip Marlowe when he describes himself: "I'm thirty-three years old. . . . I'm unmarried because I don't like policemen's wives" (Paul 136).

Clearly, the author is establishing her place in the community of writers. This comparison is emphasized by the straightforward, first-person narrative used by all three authors as well as Raymond Chandler in the Philip Marlowe series.

In attitude and action, the new detectives imitate the old. Each of the authors continuously refers to the "details of her [detective's] bathing, dressing and interest in food—for some obscure reason, all fictional male private eyes have those traits" (Lawrence 45). Clothing preferences are related constantly, helping to establish the personalities of the characters. Just as Chandler relates the details of Marlowe's navy suit, we are told of the one black dress owned by the casual Kinsey Millhone, and of the more extensive wardrobe of V. I. Warshawski, as well as the latter's penchance for Magali shoes. Such descriptions are effective in creating a specific setting. The reader is not left in doubt.

The women imitate the men in various other ways as well. "V. I. drinks a lot, as do Sharon McCone and Kinsey Millhone, talks tough, and carries a gun (as do the others), all characteristics also of the male private eyes" (Reddy 95). Their extensive knowledge of their cities far surpasses any reasonable expectations, as Marlowe's did in Los Angeles. These women are attempting to take the place of men in a predominantly male world. By adopting these stereotypically tough actions, they are better accepted by readers who might otherwise be prejudiced against them. Were they not to exhibit such a dominating exterior, the quality of their work could not be so high. 10

All three detectives satisfy Chandler's criteria for a private eye. All come from working- or middle-class backgrounds and associate equally well with the wealthy as with the poor, but fitting into neither class too well. V. I. was originally on the track of yuppiedom, married to an aspiring young lawyer while practicing law herself. She later chooses to associate with people whose values do "not" revolve around traditional ideas of "success." This is a decision about which most of her readers can only imagine, for they are too attached to the security of their own lives. The importance of their backgrounds is raised by Muller when Sharon McCone is presented with a more prestigious desk job. She wonders:

> Maybe, I thought now, I'd forgotten where I'd come from. Lost sight of who and what I really was. Maybe because I've achieved more than I'd expected to—a certain professional reputation, a newly remodeled home of my own, a comfortable life-style—maybe I'd lost my ability to relate to people ... who deserved far more credit for their accomplishments than I for mine. (Wolf in the Shadows 28)

McCone's ability to relate to people, all people, is her living. Had she been raised in a different class, higher or lower, this ability to communicate would not have been a part of her personality.

Like the detectives of old, these private eyes are all loners, at least in the beginning. None works or lives closely with other people, preferring to do everything solo. They build their relationships on their own terms. As the characters grow, they gradually pull away from the guides set by Chandler. Circles of friends begin to develop and families form. We can see a crucial family structure grow. The detectives become women, dependent on others emotionally. Men are allowed to become attached and still retain their macho image. For women private eyes, this is remarkable in the extreme. When a woman in the same situation shows her vulnerability, she is regarded as a weaker human. Thus, these detectives must prove their strength before showing their attachment.

Kinsey Millhone began her series living in a modified garage: "The room itself is fifteen feet square, outfitted as living room, bedroom, kitchen, bathroom, closet and laundry facility" ('A' is for Alibi 14). There is no room for another occupant, and that is exactly as she desires. She has casual friends who are introduced in passing. Henry Pits, a retired baker, is her landlord; Rosie, a Hungarian restaurateur, feeds her. While few new characters are introduced, this couple becomes increasingly close to the younger woman. When Kinsey's abode is blown up, Henry builds an economy apartment in its place. This signals the major change in Millhone's emotional status. By admitting her attachment to her landlord and not just the residence, Kinsey is exposing her vulnerability. Once the first step is taken, Kinsey builds a family of friends necessary for psychological survival.

V. I. Warshawski has continuously received this support from one friend, Lotty. Lotty is V. I.'s protective mother figure. On the other hand, Lieutenant Bobby Mallory is V. I.'s catalyst. Mallory had been a friend of V. I.'s father and feels protective of her. He firmly believes that "if Tony had turned [her] over his knee more often instead of spoiling [her] rotten, [she'd] be a happy housewife now, instead of playing at detective" (Indemnity 28). However, it is V. I.'s ex-husband, Dick, who affects her most strongly; his presence is felt every time V. I. meets an attractive man. Not until a direct confrontation with him does V. I. truly allow others to matter to her. At the end of the novel, not only is she still involved with someone, but she also admits her fears: "It's Lotty. I'm so scared—scared that she's going to leave me the way my mother did. . . . I don't think I can bear it if Lotty abandons me too" (416). This vulnerability indicates a crack in the strong facade that Warshawski presents to the world.

Sharon McCone is the most fully evolved of the characters. She has always had a close group of confidantes, both male and female, through her work. She has had several long relationships with men that reflect her emotional state, as well as that of the era in which they occur. In her first novel, *Edwin of the Iron Shoes* (1976), McCone meets Gregory Marcus, a homicide lieutenant. He affectionately calls her "papoose," a nickname she abhors. When working on cases together in *The Cheshire Cat's Eye,* Gregory's overprotectiveness increased Sharon's competitive drive. During the eighties, two men came into her life: Dan, a feminist disk jockey who could not clean his own apartment, and George, a professor at Stanford University who filed everyone away in categories based on personality traits. Unable to be filed, Sharon leaves. Finally, she meets Hy Ripinsky, a man able to work with a woman detective on an equal basis. In *Where Echoes Live* and *Wolf in the Shadows,* Hy proves his respect by giving McCone freedom to do her job. When they work together, neither worries unduly about the other, for both are capable adults. It would have been impossible for McCone to have begun her series eighteen years ago with such a relationship for her strength as an investigator would have been undermined had she had a partner. Now that she has proved herself, and society is becoming more comfortable with women as equals rather than replacements, she is able to shed some of her extreme independence.

These women have all proved themselves capable of acting independently. But because of their gender, certain protective devices are necessary. The drinking, tough talking, and gun toting that allow the women to fit in are examples. More subtly, their names are all carefully chosen to create a facade behind which the women hide. Victoria Iphigenia Warshawski openly uses her initials as a way of preventing condescension. When one of her clients patronizingly asks her what the "V" stood for, she answers "My first name" (*Indemnity* 19). As she says, it is harder to be supercilious to a woman if you do not know her given name. V. I. takes for granted that her clients will assume that she is a man (*Indemnity* 34). Even her preferred nickname, Vic, can be male or female. Only by adopting this disguise can she hope to make a living in an occupation thought by many to be unsuitable for a woman. The name of Sue Grafton's detective, Kinsey Millhone, is unusual, denoting no particular ethnicity. Since it can be androgynous, Kinsey too can hide her sex and, thus, her identity. For Sharon McCone, the disguise is more subtle. The eighth of her blood that is Native American dominates her features, but her decidedly American name throws people off enough to give her an edge, advantageous in an occupation ruled by wits.

15

Other protective devices include forethought and instinct. Fear is acknowledged and "woman's intuition" given its due. The gun becomes secondary to their wits in extracting them from touchy situations. In fact, violence in all of its forms, while definitely existing, is best to be avoided. To a contemporary woman who has been educated in self-defense, this makes sense. As women, we know that we can defend ourselves if we must. But the physical and emotional pain that accompanies this self-reliance is not pleasurable. Rather than making us respect the heroine, unnecessary injury seems wasteful. And the violence that does occur is all the more powerful for its relative rarity. When the women are required to defend themselves, they do so with aplomb, disproving the stereotype of the wilting female sidekick.

V. I. views the gun as an extension of the male psyche. In *Indemnity Only* she asks: "Why do you think the boy carries a gun? He can't get it up, never could, so he has a big old penis he carries around in his hand" (Reddy 98). Warshawski does realize that only by having her own firearm will she be on an equal basis with the men, and so she purchases a gun. However, she hesitates to use it as it is assumed a man would. In *Killing Orders,* she traps her would-be killer by shooting him in the leg. She must "force down the desire to kill [him] where he lay" (Reddy 113). Just the fact that she aimed for his limbs rather than his torso gives lie to her murderous instinct. She is not able to commit murder.

Sharon McCone uses her gun twice. The first time, she kills a man in self-defense. Emotionally, neither she nor her friends come to terms with her actions over the next several books in this series. She knows she is more than justified, for the dead man would have killed a friend had she not acted. Her assistant, Rae, witnesses the incident and is unable to assimilate this new image of Sharon with the caring friend she has always been in the past. Muller has us realize that the woman detective is not a one-dimensional being. Facets of McCone's personality can and do exist simultaneously. Years later, McCone is again forced to kill a man. He is hunting her at the Mexican border. This time, however, Sharon believes she is committing murder. As she aims for the sniper, she rationalizes: "Everything I believed in told me this was wrong. Everything I cared about told me this was right" (*Wolf* 344). The emotional overcomes the rational as Kinsey shoots to kill.

At the beginning of *"A" Is for Alibi,* Kinsey tells us, "The day before yesterday [she] killed someone and the fact weighs heavily on [her] mind" (1). This killing too was clearly in self-defense. Her opponent, a former lover, was attacking her with a butcher's knife. The shooting disturbs her, for "it has moved [her] into the same camp with soldiers and maniacs" (215). The originality in this situation comes from Millhone's fear during the ordeal. She lost the calm for which the hard-boiled detective is so famous. She was almost overcome by tears. But she survived, proving that female sensibilities were not incompatible with danger.

This new detective is a mirror of our society. The growth of all 20 three of these women has paralleled the expanded role of women. In the mid-1970s, the female hard-boiled detective developed to fill a hole in the mystery market. As Marcia Muller explains,

> my puzzle prone friends and I noticed that one figure was missing from the mystery scene. There were scores of male sleuths, both hard- and soft-boiled. There were old ladies with knitting needles and noses for secrets. . . . But nowhere, at that time, could we find a female private eye. ("Creating a Female Sleuth")

Her new character, Sharon McCone, needed to express the values and emotions of the readers to whom she was to appeal. Women were beginning to realize fully their potential in all professions, including that of detecting. They sought books that reinforced this potential. McCone is a traditional hero in the sense that she is an idealized version. But she is a hero of her time, the ideal of her era. In creating her, Muller "conditioned [herself] to think of what [she] would do if [she] were brave, tall, an expert at judo, and so on" ("Creating" 21). Sharon McCone became an extension of her author and in doing so could not help incorporating the emotions of her author.

Sue Grafton started the Kinsey Millhone series after her own bitter divorce. *"A" Is for Alibi* is partly based on a little scheme she came up with to kill her ex-husband. She knew that substituting oleander in allergy capsules would land her in jail, so she poured her aggressions into her novel instead. Kinsey too is a hero in that she reflects the idealized personality of her author. In a world where working mothers outnumber housewives and time seems to slip by, Kinsey is "the person [Sue Grafton] would be had [she] not married young and had children. She'll always be thinner and younger and braver" ("Interview" 10).

Sara Paretsky has created a character who is more of an idiosyncratic feminist icon than an individual representation:

> It can be very difficult to be a professional woman and try to develop a career. You don't know whether you're losing your femininity as you become more aggressive or how you're being judged and what margin for error you have. . . . V. I. came out of that experience. ("Trouble Is Her Business" 263)

In her evolution, V. I. has proved to every doubting reader that it is possible. According to one of Paretsky's critics, Robert Sandels, "Paretsky has borrowed all her symbols of professional authenticity from a male myth, updated to allow for Warshawski's jogging, her reading of the *Wall Street Journal,* and her brand-name consumerism" (390). What this critic condemns, however, is that which separates V. I. Warshawski novels from the old hard-boiled genre and makes her so popular today. The contemporary, mundane activities bring the idealized character to a human level. We, as readers, can relate to the pain of a morning jog, thus relating to the detective herself.

These new detective novels have been vastly popular. According to Kate Miciak, senior editor of Bantam Books, "'Women mystery writers and their books with female protagonists have become the hottest segment of the market.' . . . [She] believes that currently they are writing at least 40% of the books being published." The growing demand is for characters such as Sharon McCone, V. I. Warshawski, and Kinsey Millhone—women who do not "pass their problems on to men; they solve them all by themselves. Often they protect other characters along the way and they certainly don't defer to men." The number of readers, as well as authors, has risen dramatically. One mystery shop in California reports that "'the women can outsell the men in hard-cover by two to one'" (Feldman 37). While other forms of mysteries—softboiled, academic, procedural, and others—continue to be widely read, the hard-boiled genre has its own magic. Paretsky says that she has "heard from women from as far away as Tokyo and from as near as the South Side of Chicago to tell [her] that reading about [her] characters has given them courage to face difficult situations in their lives" ("Interview" 270). This belief in the detectives as role models is possible because of the feminine reality of the characters.

Works Cited

Chandler, Raymond. *The Big Sleep.* New York: First Vintage Crime, 1966.
Feldman, Gayle. "The Sisterhood of Sleuths." *The Armchair Detective* 23 (May-June 1989): 37.
Grafton, Sue. *"A" is for Alibi.* New York: Bantam Books, 1982.
Klein, Kathleen Gregory. *The Woman Detective: Gender and Genre.* Chicago: University of Illinois Press, 1988.
Lawrence, Barbara. "Female Detectives: Feminist—Anti-feminist Debate" 3 (1982): 38–47.
Muller, Marcia. *The Cheshire Cat's Eye.* New York: Mysterious Press, 1983.
Muller, Marcia. *Eye of the Storm.* New York: Mysterious Press, 1988.
Muller, Marcia. *Where Echoes Live.* New York: Mysterious Press, 1991.
Muller, Marcia. *Wolf in the Shadows.* New York: Mysterious Press, 1993.
Nelson, Catherine. "Trouble is her business." *The Armchair Detective* 24 (1991): 260–270.
Nichols, Victoria and Susan Thompson. *Silk Stockings: When Women Write of Murder.* Berkeley: Black Lizard Books, 1988.
Paretsky, Sara. *Guardian Angel.* New York: Dell Publishing, 1992.
Paretsky, Sara. *Indemnity Only.* New York: Dell Publishing, 1982.
Paul, Robert S. *Whatever Happened to Sherlock Holmes.* Carbondale: Southern Illinois University Press. 1991.
Reddy, Maureen. *Sisters in Crime.* New York: Continuum Publishing Company, 1988.
Sandels, Robert. "It Was a Man's World." *The Armchair Detective.* 32 (1989): 388–396.

Bibliography

Grafton, Sue. *"C" is for Corpse*. New York: Bantam Books, 1986.
Grafton, Sue. *"E" is for Evidence*. London: Pan Books Ltd., 1990.
Greenberg, Martin H. and Bill Prozini, eds. *Women Sleuths*. Chicago: Academy Chicago Publishers, 1985.

For Journals

Have your ever read any detective stories? If so, have any of them had women as detectives?

For Discussion

1. Wooley sees the traditional hard-boiled detective, always a man investigating the treachery of women, as the source for the new breed of women detectives. What evidence does she provide to show that women can take over men's roles and make them their own?

2. How would you describe the concept of the hard-boiled detective? What does the term suggest?

3. What ways would you expect a woman who is a detective to behave differently from her male counterpart? What advantages or disadvantages might she have?

4. How do you respond to the idea that the character of the American detective is a descendant of the frontier hero: independent, capable, honest, and alone?

For Writing

1. Write a response to Wooley agreeing or disagreeing with her conclusions; use other writers in this chapter as support for your argument.

2. Write an essay discussing how any of the detectives in Wooley's analysis, or other women detectives you have read, revise the traditional idea of the male private eye. Include your opinion on how successful this transformation is and what is gained or lost in the process.

FILMS ON THE FRONTIER

There are enough movies about the western frontier—and other American frontiers—to fill entire film libraries. Watch one or two of these movies with your peers, and discuss the ways themes in this chapter are raised, what myths they echo, who the heroic or admirable characters are, and whether values remain constant or change. Following is a short suggestion list to use as a starter.

Squaw Man

Shane

High Noon

The Wild Bunch

Blazing Saddles

The Right Stuff

Unforgiven

They Died with Their Boots On

My Darling Clementine

Stagecoach

The Ox-Bow Incident

A Fistful of Dollars

The Star Wars trilogy

Star Trek

Terminator II

Blade Runner

Red River

The Man Who Shot Liberty Valence

REVISION

Using Revision in Arguments

Revision entails work on many levels. It begins by reviewing the thesis—the core claim or idea—in the light of what you have read, discussed, understood, or thought about your initial working thesis or hypothesis. What surprised you? What didn't you expect to find? What challenges your previous views or understanding? And how can or will you incorporate this new information into what you already know?

Keeping an open mind is at the heart of scholarly endeavor. To generate and transmit new knowledge and learning, scholars have to be willing to consider new views, alternative hypotheses, adjusted thesis statements and claims. At the heart of scientific inquiry is *hypothesis testing:* advancing a hypothesis and proving it or not (always being ready to acknowledge that an experiment showed the opposite of what was expected).

Throughout life, you will often be asked to reconsider your views, or you will find that new evidence encourages you to modify your beliefs or position on an issue. Revising conceptually entails a kind of synthesis, or merging of what you knew with what you learn to create new knowledge and understanding. Following are some ideas you can use to revise the texts you write.

1. *Start early.* It's impossible to revise a paper at 3:00 A.M. of the day it's due. If you are writing a research paper, you will have more time to work on it than on a short expository paper, but there is so much material to gather and evaluate that it's still risky to procrastinate on the actual writing.

2. *After you write the first draft, put the paper aside for a day or longer, and then look at again.* You will have left it long enough so that it will have lost its absolute familiarity. When you reread it, you will be seeing it freshly, and the act of revision will begin automatically as you look it over.

3. *Note rough spots as you read.* In the process of looking at it again, you will notice sentences or ideas that aren't synchronized with the rest of the text, or paragraphs that don't lead in to one another. Mark them, or take notes on them, as you are reading; later you won't remember exactly what corrections you wanted to make and will be happy to have made a list.

4. *Look for your topic ideas and thesis statement.* Start by identifying the thesis statement and the most important sentence in every paragraph and underline them. When you have one sentence in each paragraph underlined, read all of them over. They should make sense, and it should be possible to tell where your paper is headed. If not, you will at least be able to tell where the paper started to go off track. You can take your revision another step by trying to rephrase the underlined sentences, and then rebuilding their paragraphs around them.

This strategy serves another purpose as well: If you *cannot* find a topic sentence in every paragraph, you will have identified the precise area in your paper that is most in need of revision. Try to fill in that missing sentence by writing down, even in completely colloquial language, what it is that you wanted to say. You can refine it later. Alternatively, read the paragraph out loud: that will also give you a sense of what is missing.

5. *Show your paper to a peer whose reading and writing skills you trust*—a friend or a tutor, for example. Ask that person to read your paper over, partly to get an overall sense of it and partly to look for the topic sentences you were trying to find yourself. A second reader is invaluable. You are more likely to pay attention to an evaluation when it comes from someone else; another person may notice points you have missed; and he or she will be seeing the paper from another perspective and without preconceived notions.

If the second reader brings up a problem—a lack of clarity, or a fuzzy thesis—that you had suspected yourself, the second opinion is good confirmation that you were on the right track. But the reader will also see where your strengths are: for example, ideas could be expanded or paragraphs could be moved to give your argument greater vitality.

6. *Trade papers with someone else in your class.* To focus your mutual reviews, you might make up a short list of questions for both of you to keep in mind when reading each other's drafts. What is this paper about? Is it interesting? Why or why not? What is the thesis? Is it clearly organized? How could it be improved? What are its strongest points?

Reading someone else's paper is good for the person who wrote it, but it's also useful for the person who does the reading. From reviewing someone else's work, you can get ideas about how to solve problems in your own paper, and that will make you see your own writing more clearly. It is easier to be objective about someone else's work, but that objectivity carries over at least as far as helping you to recognize similar problems to your partner's in your own work.

7. *Look at your title.* Make sure that it fits your paper. If it doesn't—say, if you chose it because you like the way it sounded—it may not have much to do with the point of your paper. On the other hand, if the title is the one part of the paper you have confidence in, then it can act as a pointer when you are checking on how consistently you have made your point. In any case, the title is the first indication of where your paper is headed, and it can be an additional check on your work as well as a guide to the direction in which you really want your writing to go.

Analyzing Revisions in Argument

There is no way to tell from reading any finished piece of writing how many revisions it went through. This is true for the writers in this chapter as well, except in those cases where the author's previous drafts have been preserved by relatives or by scholars or the writer has left letters or diaries that demonstrate the process. Mark Twain, for example, wrote some delightful letters about how glad he was to be hired to write *Roughing It* and how miserable he was later as the deadline grew closer. The original manuscript of Franklin's *Autobiography* in the Huntington Library in Santa Monica California, shows all the marks and corrections that went into producing such a smoothly written book.

The kind of revision that we can see in a finished piece of work, though, is the revision of ideas and beliefs. Sometimes authors revise their own beliefs over many years. Twain was always funny, but the deaths of three of his four daughters toward the end of his life embittered him, and his later writings posess a dark and cynical tone that does not appear in the high spirited adventurousness of *Roughing It.*

Of the selections in this chapter, the most obvious and best-known instance of thoughtful revision is Richard Hofstadter's reevaluation of Turner's frontier thesis. The importance of Turner's work is so clear that subsequent writers interested in American history and personality had to deal with it. Theories go in and out of fashion, however, and some of Turner's previous critics seemed less interested in analyzing his theories than in substituting their own. Turner's ideas touch such a deep nerve in the American psyche that those ideas have survived for over a hundred years. Hofstadter's balanced appraisal—a mixture of admiration and disagreement that appreciates Turner's enormous impact but reviews his conclusions thoughtfully—is a revision that does credit to the original.

A different species of revision is Richard Slotkin's story of Buffalo Bill. Here, a man who is a part of American folklore turns out to be a cheerful participant in the creation of what American folklore–expert Richard Dorson called "fakelore." What is so fascinating about Buffalo Bill is that he really did fight in battles, kill people, demonstrate physical bravery, and so on. But what he became famous for was a wildly glorified version of his experiences, sold through the books he commissioned and shows in which he performed. What Americans came to see as the Wild West was, at least partly, an image that had less to do with the frontier than with Buffalo Bill's grand entrepreneurial talents.

Finally, Peggy Orenstein's article on virtual reality explores a technology that supporters claim can revise reality itself. Orenstein, who describes herself as a neo-Luddite—an opponent of new technologies—recognizes the power of the medium to override previous experience when she participates in a virtual reality (VR) marathon. In one VR simulation of jumping off the Golden Gate Bridge, she finds that some of her fellow participants are so taken with with the medium that they try to climb over the tiny fence in the demonstration room, which

VR has transformed into the bridge railing. She comes away with considerably changed ideas about new technologies. She is not necessarily a convert to VR, but she will keep an open mind. This is the key to revision.

Writing Assignments

1. Write an essay on an issue you feel strongly about, but take a stand absolutely against your usual position. Analyze a poem, take a side of a debate, or examine an advertisement from the perspective of someone with a different background, or gender from yours. Your paper can be research oriented or expository, or narrative. Then write a reflective essay on how the change in perspective affected your writing process and your conclusions, and whether or how it caused you to revise your previous certainties on the topic.

2. Go through copies of old magazines—*Century* or *McClure's* from the early twentieth century, or *Colliers, Harpers, Saturday Evening Post* through the 1950s and 1960s—and look for images of American Indians in advertisements. Write a paper in which you include your reflections on the following questions. What are the Indians being used to sell? If there are any whites in the ads, what is the relationship between them and the Indians? What stereotypes or clichés do you find in these ads? If you were writing any of these advertisements, how would you revise the pictures or the text, or both?

3. Try to locate any of the following: the old television series on Daniel Boone and Davy Crockett (starring, incidentally, the same actor, Fess Parker, as though these historical figures were interchangeable) or the musical based on the life of Annie Oakley, *Annie Get Your Gun.* How does the image of these figures put forth by articles and books revise or coincide with the image of them in television and theater? What do you think is lost or gained when the revised versions of their lives become more important than the reality?

4. In one of his essays, Richard Slotkin, the author of the Buffalo Bill selection, says that the real descendant of frontier heroes is the American private eye of popular detective fiction—alone, independent, honorable. If you are interested in detective stories, read one or two by an American author, and write a paper in which you analyze the code and behavior of the detective in relation to the image of the frontier hero. Do you think the private eye is directly related to the frontier hero? A revised version of a frontier hero? You can turn this essay into a documented research paper by consulting some of the many critical articles and books that have been written recently about the American fascination with police and private investigators.

5. Write an essay in which you discuss the negative stereotyping of any group to which you belong: your gender, racial heritage, the region of the country you come from, your religious affiliation, your love of computers. Consider the following questions: How do you think your group is perceived by others? What stereotyping, negative and positive, do you have to contend with? How would your revise the stereotype to make it a more accurate reflection?

6. Research any American hero or heroine in sports, movies, politics, or some other area who has become the subject of a mythology. Some of the most obvious are Elvis Presley, Marilyn Monroe, F. Scott Fitzgerald, and JFK, but anyone who can persistently fascinate the American public and is the subject of endless restructuring and remaking would be a good subject. Concentrate on separating some of the reality from the subsequent revision; or on the way your subject's standing is revised positively or negatively in people's estimation. What would you argue is the cultural significance of your subject to America?

ACKNOWLEDGMENTS

"Home, Mom, and Apple Pie" from *Redesigning the American Dream: The Future of Housing, Work, and Family Life* by Dolores Hayden, with the permission of W.W. Norton & Company. Copyright © 1984 by Dolores Hayden.

"The Thesis Disputed," by Richard Hofstadter from *The Frontier Thesis* by Ray Billington. Copyright © 1949; copyright renewed 1977. Used by permission of Robert Krieger Publishing Co., Inc.

"Let America be America Again" from *A New Song* by Langston Hughes. Copyright © 1938 by Langston Hughes; copyright renewed 1965 by Langston Hughes. Reprinted by permission of Harold Ober Associates, Incorporated.

"I Have A Dream" by Martin Luther King, Jr. Reprinted by arrangement with The Heirs to the Estate of Martin Luther King, Jr., c/o Joan Daves Agency as agent for the proprietor. Copyright © 1963 by Martin Luther King., Jr., copyright renewed 1991 by Coretta Scott King.

"Letter from Birmingham City Jail" from *Why We Can't Wait* by Martin Luther King., Jr., c/o Joan Daves Agency as agent for the proprietor. Copyright © 1963 by Martin Luther King., Jr., copyright renewed 1991 by Coretta Scott King.

"Metaphor and the Gulf War," by George Lakoff. Copyright © 1993 by George Lakoff. Used by permission of the Author.

"Bricklayer's Boy" by Alfred Lubrano. Copyright © 1989 by Alfred Lubrano, who is a reporter for *New York Newsday* and an essayist for National Public Radio. Used by permission of the author.

"How Marriages Are Arranged," "The Feminist Attire," and "Male Beauty," from *In Defense of Women* by H. L. Mencken. Copyright © 1922 by Alfred A. Knopf, Inc. and renewed 1950 by H. L. Mencken. Reprinted by permission of the publisher.

"Get a Cyberlife" by Peggy Ornstein from *Mother Jones Magazine*. Copyright © 1991 by the Foundation for National Progress. Used with permission.

"When 'Family' Is Not a Household Word," by Keenan Peck. Copyright © 1988 by Keenan Peck. Reprinted by permission form *The Progressive*, 409 East Main Street, Madison, WI 53703.

"Split at the Root: An Essay on Jewish Identity," abridged, is reprinted from *Blood, Bread, and Poetry*, Selected Prose 1979-1985, by Adrienne Rich, by permission of the author and W.W. Norton & Company, Inc. Copyright © 1986 by Adrienne Rich.

"On Shopping" [Shopping and Other Spiritual Adventures], by Phyllis Rose from *Never Say Goodbye*. Copyright © 1984, 1985, 1986, 1987, 1988, 1989, 1990 by Phyllis Rose. Reprinted by permission of Georges Borchardt, Inc., for the author.

"Touring from Mitchell, Iowa to California," from *Women's Diaries of the Westward Journey* by Lillian Schussel. Copyright © 1983 by Schocken Books, Inc. Reprinted by permission of Schocken Books, published by Pantheon Books, Inc.

"Staging Reality: The Creation of Buffalo Bill, 1869-1883." Reprinted with permission of Atheneum Publishers, an imprint of Macmillian Publishing Company from *Gunfighter Nation: The Myth of the Frontier in Twentieth-Century America* by Richard Slotkin. Copyright © 1992 by Richard Slotkin.

"Divide We Stand: The Immigration Backlash". Copyright © 1994 *San Francisco Chronicle*. Reprinted by permission of *San Francisco Chronicle*.

"The American Mosaic " from *Ethnic America* by Thomas Sowell. Copyright © 1981 by Basic Books, Inc. Reprinted by permission of Basic Books, a division of Harper Collins Publishers, Inc.

"Coda: Wilderness Letter" from *The Sound of Mountain Water* by Wallace Stegner. Copyright © 1969 by Wallace Stegner. Used by permission of Doubleday, a division of Bantam Doubleday Dell Publishing Group, Inc.

"The Importance of Work" from *Outrageous Acts and Everyday Rebellions* by Gloria Steinem. Copyright © 1983 by Gloria Steinem. Copyright © 1984 by East Toledo Productions, Inc. Reprinted by permission of Henry Holt and Company, Inc.

"Marriage Is A Fundamental Right," by Thomas Stoddard. Copyright © 1984/89 by The New York Times Company, Reprinted by permission.

"Frank Chin" from *Race* by Studs Terkel. Copyright © 1992 by Studs Terkel. Reprinted by permission of the New Press.

Art

INDEX OF AUTHORS
AND TITLES

INDEX OF RHETORICAL TERMS

Essays (*cont.*)
  thesis statement, 9
Ethos, 14
Examples
  analyzing the use of, 204
  arguments, using in, 203–4, 206
  chapter theme and, 135
  evidence, used as, 203, 204
  from field research, 207
  form of persuasion, 24, 202
  functions of, 202–3
  identification, 203, 205
  from library research, 207–8
  and personal experience, 205, 206
Expository. *See* Essays, argumentative

False-dilemma argument, 19

Generalization, 18

Induction
  defined, 15
  problems of, 16, 18–19
  to structure arguments, 42

Logos, 15. *See also* Induction; Deduction

Non sequitur, 19

Parallelism, 21, 519
Paraphrasing (sources), 58
  and plagiarism, 59
Pathos, 14–15
Persuasion
  and American culture, 11
  as argument, 10–11
  errors in logic of, 18–19
  faulty types of, 18–19
  genres of, 28–33, 35–36
  historically, 13
  in homogeneous cultures, 13
  and structure, 20, 21
  and style, 21–22
  understanding, 20–23
  See also Argument
Persuasive language, 25–26, 517, 520–21
  analyzing the use of, 517–18
  arguments, using in, 519
  chapter theme and, 448–49
  connotative, 519

denotative, 519
imagery, 25–26, 518
manipulation and, 520
parallelism, and, 519
style, 518
syntax and, 519
visual images as, 518
Plagiarism, 59–60
Post hoc, ergo propter hoc, 19
Premises, 366

Quoting (sources), 58
  and plagiarism, 59

Refutation
  analyzing the use of, 440–41
  arguments, using in, 441
  chapter theme and, 378–79
  form of persuasion, 25, 439–40
  of opposing views, 378
  strategies of 442–43
Repetition, in arguments, 22–23
Research, 44, 48, 49
  examples, using for, 207–8
  essays, 45–47
  libraries, using in, 49
  process of, 47–48, 56–57
  questions, 47
  schedule, 47
  sources for, 51–56, 57
Revisions
  analyzing the use of, 606–8
  arguments, using in, 604–5
  chapter theme and, 527–28
  form of persuasion, 26, 604
  process of, 605–6
Rhetor, 10–11
  audience and, 12
  deductive arguments, use of, 16–17
  ethos, use of, 14
  inductive argument, use of, 15–16
  logos, use of, 16
  pathos, use of, 14–15

Samples, inadequate or biased, 18
Slippery slope argument, 19
Straw-man argument, 18
Summarizing (sources), 58
  and plagiarism, 59
Syllogism, 16

Thesis statement, 39–42, 366